"The limits of my language means the limits of my world."
—Ludwig Wittgenstein

" 'Meow' means 'woof' in cat."
—George Carlin

*"Because without our language, we have lost ourselves.
Who are we without our words?"*
—Melina Marchetta

"Language is the only homeland."
—Czesław Miłosz

PREFACE

Since its first edition *Language Awareness* has had a twofold purpose: to foster an appreciation of the richness, flexibility, and vitality of the English language; and to help students use their language more responsibly and effectively in speech and particularly in writing. Because of these purposes, *Language Awareness* has been used successfully in a variety of courses over the years. Its primary use, however, has been and continues to be in college composition courses. Clearly, many instructors believe as we do—that the study of language and the study of writing go hand in hand.

Because the study of language is so multifaceted, we cover a broad spectrum of topics, including language acquisition, regional dialects of American English, the relationship between language and culture, the language of new technologies, the language of prejudice, and the power of language in influencing advertising, politics, the media, and gender roles. Opening students' eyes to the power of language—its ability to shape and influence perceptions and cultural attitudes—is, we believe, one of the worthiest goals a writing class can pursue.

NEW TO THE THIRTEENTH EDITION

As in previous editions of *Language Awareness*, the selections in the thirteenth edition are written primarily in nontechnical language on topics of current interest. Our questions and introductory material help students by providing clearly defined opportunities for thoughtful writing. Guided by comments and advice from hundreds of colleagues and students across the country who have used the previous editions, we have made some dramatic improvements in this thirteenth edition.

New Selections

Twenty-eight of the sixty-three professional selections in *Language Awareness* are new to this edition. We have retained many of the classic, informative, and well-written essays from earlier editions, such as Gordon Allport's "The Language of Prejudice," Helen Keller's "The Day

Language Came into My Life," Andrew Sullivan's "What's So Bad about Hate?", and Chimamanda Ngozi Adichie's "Happy Feminist."

The twenty-eight new selections, chosen for their insight and clear, thought-provoking writing, also reflect the language issues of an increasingly complex, multicultural America. Representing a wide variety of voices, the readings address a range of language concerns on issues from deaf culture to gender roles and the #MeToo movement.

- Sara Nović's "Sign of the Times" and Julie Sedivy's "The Strange Persistence of First Languages" bring fresh perspectives to the chapter on speech communities.
- John McWhorter's "Language on the Move" and Yesenia Padilla's "What Does 'Latinx' Mean?" explore recent trends in our evolving language.
- Rebecca Solnit's "The Case of the Missing Perpetrator" and Benjamin Horne's "Fake News Starts with the Title" examine deceptive and misleading language—and teach us how we can avoid being fooled by such language tricks.
- Laurie Penny's "We're All Mad Here: Weinstein, Women, and the Language of Lunacy" looks at how language has historically been used to silence women and dismiss their experiences—and how the #MeToo movement has changed our language.
- Stephanie Golden's "We Need the Singular *They*" investigates the growing popularity of the gender-neutral, singular *they*.

We believe that the new selections will spark student interest and bring currency to the class-proven essays retained from earlier editions.

A New Two-Part Organization

With this edition, the book has been organized into two parts.

- **Part 1** contains reading and writing guidance, with instructional chapters on reading critically, academic writing, writing with sources, and writing a research paper. Part 1 also contains the reimagined chapter "Writers on Reading and Writing," with five readings—including two new readings—in which professional authors offer their insights on the writing process and on critical reading.
- **Part 2** contains the bulk of the thematic readings, including the new thematic chapters (see below).

This two-part organization allows instructors and students to more easily find the support and the reading selections that they need.

New Thematic Chapters

Students and teachers, pleased with the relevancy of the thematic chapters in past editions of *Language Awareness*, asked us to provide fresh new themes to prompt lively discussion. In response to their feedback, we have added three new thematic chapters.

- **Chapter 8, "Language Evolution: How and Why Does Language Change?,"** contains six new readings that explore how language is changing today. By understanding the ways language is changing in response to new cultural and technological developments, we can better understand our own language and use it more effectively. Each author in this chapter looks at a different aspect of language evolution. John McWhorter opens the chapter and provides context on language change in an excerpt from his book *Words on the Move*. Next, Andy Bodle, in "How New Words Are Born," describes thirteen specific processes by which words enter the lexicon. Yesenia Padilla takes a close look at one particular gender-neutral term and the conversation surrounding it in "What Does 'Latinx' Mean?" In the second half of the chapter, we turn to the impact of technology on language, with new readings by Lauren Collister, Adam Sternbergh, and Deborah Tannen examining the language of textspeak, emojis, and metamessages, respectively. Overall, this new chapter will help students understand that language is always changing, and that English itself is a language on the move.
- The previous edition's chapter on "Language and Conflict" has been reimagined as **Chapter 13, "The Language of Conflict Resolution: Dignity, Apology, De-escalation,"** featuring three new readings. This chapter aims to help students understand the central role of language in both instigating and de-escalating conflict, and provides practical readings that may help them resolve conflicts in their own lives.
- The unit on the language of lying—which was a casebook in Chapter 13 in the previous edition—has been expanded as a full thematic chapter: **Chapter 12, "The Language of Lying: Ethics, White Lies, and Fraud."** The chapter includes two new readings for a total of six readings, each with a different perspective on lying, its consequences, and its potential utility. These readings challenge students to think about how and why we use language to lie—and whether lying can ever be beneficial.

Arguing about Language

In the thirteenth edition, we have brought back the chapter on argument. Chapter 14, "Arguing about Language: Two Contemporary Debates," includes two argument casebooks, each containing three new readings that offer different perspectives on a language-related topic:

- **"The Campus Free Speech Controversy"** examines the conversation surrounding freedom of speech on college campuses. The three authors in this unit take stances on related topics such as safe spaces and trigger warnings.
- **"The Great Gender-Neutral Pronoun Debate"** explores the growing popularity of gender-neutral pronouns like the singular *they*, with three authors who take different perspectives on this issue.

In each casebook, the end-of-selection questions and activities invite students to bring the language concepts and ideas they have learned in the earlier core chapters of *Language Awareness* to bear on the topics of the language debates. At the end of each casebook, Writing Suggestions offer students opportunities to join the debate themselves by extending their analyses of the readings in the unit and making connections among the various arguments of the writers.

KEY FEATURES OF *LANGUAGE AWARENESS*

Class-Tested Topics

Instructors have told us that the chapters on "Understanding the Power of Language," "Language Communities," "Language that Manipulates," "The Language of Discrimination," and "Language and Gender" are indispensable in the courses they teach. Not only do the readings in these chapters represent essential areas of language study, but they also teach students useful ways to look at and write about the world around them. Each of these chapters has been updated with new essays that reflect recent trends, but they retain the spirit and purpose of their predecessors.

Introductory Chapters on Reading and Writing

To supplement the study of language with instruction in reading and writing, we have reorganized our coverage of the twin tasks of reading and writing. Based on years of classroom experience, the five chapters in Part 1 provide students with the essentials of college reading and writing, as well as writing with sources and writing the research paper. The first chapter, "Reading Critically," provides students with guidelines for critical reading, demonstrates how they can get the most out of their reading by taking advantage of the apparatus accompanying each selection, and shows how they can generate their own writing from the reading they do. The second chapter, "Writing in College and Beyond," explores the world of academic writing. Here students learn how to master the core elements that all instructors expect in academic essays, starting with an understanding of the writing assignment itself, establishing a thesis, determining an organization, using evidence, and culminating with documenting sources and avoiding plagiarism. Each step in the process is illustrated with a student essay in progress. Chapter 3, "Writers on Reading and Writing," contains five readings from professional authors with insights that complement the guidelines in Chapters 1 and 2. Chapters 4 and 5 turn to writing with sources and researched writing. Chapter 4, "Writing with Sources," offers guidelines for integrating and synthesizing sources while avoiding plagiarism. Chapter 5, "A Brief Guide to Writing a Research Paper," provides in-depth documentation models and citation guidelines for writing in MLA and APA styles.

Chapter Introductions

Brief, one- to two-page chapter introductions discuss the key elements of each chapter's topic and why the topic is important to study. In addition, the introductions briefly discuss individual readings, explaining how they connect to larger language issues and how they relate to each other.

Student-Tested Headnotes, Journal Prompts, Questions, Activities, and Writing Suggestions

INFORMATIVE HEADNOTES. Headnotes preceding each selection discuss the content of the essay and provide pertinent information about the author and where and when the selection was first published.

"WRITING TO DISCOVER" JOURNAL PROMPTS. Each selection begins with a journal prompt designed to get students writing—before they start reading—about their own experiences with the language issues discussed in the selection. Students are then more likely to approach the selection with a critical eye. From time to time, class activities or writing assignments ask students to return to these journal writings and to reflect on them before proceeding with more formal writing tasks.

END-OF-SELECTION QUESTIONS. The "Thinking Critically about the Reading" questions at the end of each selection emphasize content and writing strategies. Content questions challenge students to develop a deeper understanding of ideas contained in the essay, in some cases by drawing connections to other readings or analyzing their own experiences. Other questions ask students to explore and analyze the writer's strategies in developing the selection to determine how effective writing achieves its aims.

LANGUAGE IN ACTION ACTIVITIES. The "Language in Action" activities that follow every selection give students a chance to analyze real-world examples of the language issues discussed by the essayists, with poems, cartoons, parodies, advertisements, photographs, letters to the editor, syndicated columns, and more. Designed to be completed either in class or at home in about twenty minutes, these activities ask students to take a hands-on approach to what they are learning from the essays as well as give them a chance to demonstrate their growing language aptitude.

END-OF-SELECTION WRITING ASSIGNMENTS. Several Writing Suggestions at the end of every selection give students more opportunities to practice thinking and writing. Each assignment is designed to elicit a three- to five-page paper. Some assignments ask students to use their "Writing to Discover" journal entries as springboards for an extended essay; others encourage students to use their analytical skills to make critical connections among articles on the same topic.

Glossary of Rhetorical and Linguistic Terms

The Glossary of Rhetorical and Linguistic Terms includes definitions of key language terms and concepts as well as the standard terminology of rhetoric. References to glossary entries appear where needed in the questions that accompany each selection, which allows students to look up unfamiliar terms as they read.

Rhetorical Contents

Conveniently placed after the main table of contents, an alternate table of contents classifies the selections in *Language Awareness* according to the rhetorical strategies they exemplify (e.g., Analogy, Argument and Persuasion, Comparison and Contrast, Definition, Illustration, Cause and Effect Analysis), making it easier for instructors to assign readings that parallel the types of writing their students are doing.

BEDFORD/ST. MARTIN'S PUTS YOU FIRST

From day one, our goal has been simple: to provide inspiring resources that are grounded in best practices for teaching reading and writing. For more than 35 years, Bedford/St. Martin's has partnered with the field, listening to teachers, scholars, and students about the support writers need. We are committed to helping every writing instructor make the most of our resources.

How Can We Help You?

- Our editors can align our resources to your outcomes through correlation and transition guides for your syllabus. Just ask us.
- Our sales representatives specialize in helping you find the right materials to support your course goals.
- Our *Bits* blog on the Bedford/St. Martin's English Community (**community.macmillan.com**) publishes fresh teaching ideas weekly. You'll also find easily downloadable professional resources and links to author webinars on our community site.

Contact your Bedford/St. Martin's sales representative or visit **macmillanlearning.com** to learn more.

Print and Digital Options for *Language Awareness*

Choose the format that works best for your course, and ask about our packaging options that offer savings for students.

PRINT

- *Paperback*. To order the paperback edition, use ISBN 978-1-319-05630-8.

DIGITAL

- *Innovative digital learning space*. Bedford/St. Martin's suite of digital tools makes it easy to get everyone on the same page by putting student writers at the center. For details, visit **macmillanlearning.com/englishdigital**.
- *Popular e-book formats*. For details about our e-book partners, visit **macmillanlearning.com/ebooks**.
- *Inclusive Access*. Enable every student to receive their course materials through your LMS on the first day of class. Macmillan Learning's Inclusive Access program is the easiest, most affordable way to ensure all students have access to quality educational resources. Find out more at **macmillanlearning.com/inclusiveaccess**.

Your Course, Your Way

No two writing programs or classrooms are exactly alike. Our Curriculum Solutions team works with you to design custom options that provide the resources your students need. (Options below require enrollment minimums.)

- *ForeWords for English*. Customize any print resource to fit the focus of your course or program by choosing from a range of prepared topics, such as Sentence Guides for Academic Writers.
- *Macmillan Author Program (MAP)*. Add excerpts or package acclaimed works from Macmillan's trade imprints to connect students with prominent authors and public conversations. A list of popular examples or academic themes is available upon request.
- *Bedford Select*. Build your own print handbook or anthology from a database of more than 900 selections, and add your own materials to create your ideal text. Package with any Bedford/St. Martin's text for additional savings. Visit **macmillanlearning.com/bedfordselect**.

Instructor Resources

You have a lot to do in your course. We want to make it easy for you to find the support you need—and to get it quickly.

The Instructor's Manual for *Language Awareness,* Thirteenth Edition is available as a PDF that can be downloaded from the book's online catalog page at **macmillanlearning.com**. In addition to chapter overviews and teaching tips, the instructor's manual includes sample student answers to all Thinking Critically about the Reading questions in the book, as well as guidance for getting the most out of each Language in Action activity.

ACKNOWLEDGMENTS

We are grateful to the following reviewers, whose comments helped us shape this edition: Katherine Booth, Moorpark College; Angelo Costanzo, Bloomburg University of Pennsylvania; Joshua Dickinson, Jefferson Community College; Kristin di Gennaro, Pace University; Janice Fioravante, College of Staten Island; Elizabeth Gadbois, Minnesota State University, Mankato; Lisa Johnson, Casper College; Tom Laughlin, Middlesex Community College; Robert Milde, Eastern Kentucky University; Jodi Pugliese, College of Staten Island; Guy Shebat, Youngstown State University; Yu-Li Shen, University of Southern Indiana; Kathryn Swanson, Augsburg College; and Karolyn Walz, Eastern Kentucky University.

We would like to express our appreciation to the staff at Bedford/St. Martin's, especially Development Editor Will Stonefield for supporting us in our efforts to find innovative and engaging new readings and to update and energize our Language in Action activities so they provide strong links between language study and real-world issues. Assistant Editor William Hwang coordinated the pre-revision review, facilitated manuscript flow, and helped greatly with updating the Instructor's Manual. Thanks go to John Sullivan, Senior Program Manager; to Pamela Lawson, Content Project Manager; to Gunjan Chandola Bhatt, Program Manager at Lumina Datamatics Inc.; to Ann Warren, our superlative copyeditor; and to our permissions team, including Hilary Newman, Director of Rights and Permissions; Kalina Ingham, Permissions Manager; Angela Boehler, Photo Permissions Editor; and permissions researchers Arthur Johnson and Mark Schaefer.

Our thanks also to all those who helped find new readings and contributed to the reading apparatus for this edition, including Samantha Looker-Koenigs, University of Wisconsin Oshkosh; Courtney Novosat, Duquesne University; and Jeff Ousborne. Thanks also to Courtney Novosat and Jeff Ousborne for preparing the new material in the Instructor's Manual for this edition.

Without our students at the University of Vermont over the years, a book such as *Language Awareness* would not have been possible. Their enthusiasm for language study and writing, and their responses to materials included in this book have proved invaluable.

We thank our wives, Betsy and Maggie. Without their assistance finding meaningful essays and reading proofs, and their unflagging support, none of this would have been possible. Finally, we thank each other. Since 1971 we have collaborated on many textbooks in language and writing, all of which have gone into multiple editions. With this thirteenth edition of *Language Awareness*, we enter the forty-eighth year of working together. Ours must be one of the longest-running and most mutually satisfying writing partnerships in college textbook publishing. The journey has been invigorating and challenging as we have come to understand the complexities and joys of good writing and sought out new ways to help students become better writers.

PAUL ESCHHOLZ
ALFRED ROSA

Brief Contents

CONTENTS

Part 2

6. UNDERSTANDING THE POWER OF LANGUAGE: HOW WE FIND OUR VOICES   131

"Each word steamed with the hot lava juices of my primordial making, and I crawled out of stanzas dripping with birth-blood, reborn and freed from the chaos of my life."

"Everything had a name, and each name gave birth to a new thought."

"We share a commitment to language and to the power of language, and to the reclaiming of that language which has been made to work against us."

"Language for me has always been inseparable from what I am, from what and who people are."

"I want to draw thick that perforated line to my past. I want to claim the voices belonging to my people."

> "Our strong free speech views should not distract attention away from a wide range of activities that campuses can (and must) do to protect student well-being and promote an inclusive environment."

The Great Gender-Neutral Pronoun Debate

> "A language that collapses the spectrum of gender identities into male and female reflects a society that refuses to acknowledge the identity and very existence of a significant segment of its population."

> "Ideas are merely the concatenations of words; if you can compel the use of certain words, you control thought and force those who differ into silence."

> "I'm deeply skeptical of claims that humans or speakers of a given language will inevitably think about gender in a certain way—or what languages are intrinsically built to do."

Rhetorical Contents

COMPARISON AND CONTRAST

DEFINITION

DESCRIPTION

DIVISION AND CLASSIFICATION

ILLUSTRATION

NARRATION

PROCESS ANALYSIS

PART **I**

1

READING CRITICALLY

The readings in *Language Awareness* emphasize the crucial role language plays in virtually every aspect of our lives, and they reveal the essential elements of the writer's craft. As you read and study the selections in this text, you will discover the power of language in our world: You will become more aware of your own language usage and how it affects others, and, at the same time, you will become more sensitive to how the language of others affects you. An additional benefit of close, critical reading is that you will become more familiar with different types of writing and learn how good writers make decisions about writing strategies and techniques. All of these insights will help you become a more thoughtful, discerning reader and, equally important, a better writer.

As the word *critical* suggests, reading critically means questioning what you read in a thoughtful, organized way and with an alert, inquiring mind. Critical reading is a skill you need if you are truly to engage and understand the content of a piece of writing as well as the craft that shapes the writer's ideas into an effective, efficient, and presentable form. Never accept what you read simply because it's in print. Instead, scrutinize it, challenge it, and think about its meaning and significance.

Critical reading is also a skill that takes time and practice to acquire. While most of us learned before we got to college how to read for content and summarize what a writer said, not all of us learned how to analyze what we were reading. Reading critically is like engaging a writer in a conversation — asking for the meaning of a particular statement, questioning the definition of a crucial term, or demanding more evidence to support a generalization. In addition, critical reading requires asking ourselves why we like one piece of writing and not another, or why one argument is more believable or convincing than another.

As you learn more about reading thoughtfully and purposefully, you will come to a better understanding of both the content and the craft of any piece of writing. As an added bonus, learning to read critically will help you read your own work with more insight and, as a result, write more persuasively.

GETTING THE MOST OUT OF YOUR READING

Critical reading requires, first of all, that you commit time and effort. Second, it requires that you apply goodwill and energy to understanding and appreciating what you are reading, even if the subject matter does not immediately appeal to you. Remember, your mission is twofold: You must analyze and comprehend the content of what you are reading; and then you must understand the writer's methods to see firsthand the kinds of choices a writer makes.

To help you grow as a critical reader and to get the most out of what you read, use the following classroom-proven steps:

1. Prepare yourself to read the selection.
2. Read the selection to get an overview of it.
3. Annotate the selection with marginal notes.
4. Summarize the selection in your own words.
5. Analyze the selection to come to an understanding of it.
6. Complete the "Language in Action" activity to discover the far-reaching connections between the selection and language in the real world.

To demonstrate how these steps can work for you, we've applied them to an essay by the popular nonfiction writer Natalie Goldberg. Like the other selections in *Language Awareness,* Goldberg's essay "Be Specific" is accessible and speaks to an important contemporary language issue. She points to the importance of using specific names in speaking and writing, and she demonstrates how we give things their proper dignity and integrity when we name them.

1. Prepare Yourself to Read the Selection

Instead of diving into any given selection in *Language Awareness* or any other book, there are a few things that you can do that will prepare you to get the most out of what you will read. It's helpful, for example, to get a context for what you'll read. What's the essay about? What do you know about the writer's background and reputation? Where was the essay first published? Who was the intended audience for the essay? And, finally, how much do you already know about the subject of the reading selection? We encourage you to consider carefully the materials that precede each selection in this book. Each selection begins with a title, headnote, and journal prompt. From the **title** you often discover the writer's position on an issue or attitude toward the topic. On occasion, the title can give clues about the intended audience and the writer's purpose in writing the piece. The **headnote** contains a biographical note about the author followed by publication information and rhetorical highlights about the selection. In addition to information on the person's life and work, you'll read about his or her reputation and authority to write on the subject of the piece. The **publication information** indicates when the essay was published and in what book or magazine it first appeared. This information, in turn, gives you insight about the intended audience. The **rhetorical highlights** direct your attention to one or more aspects of how the selection was written. Finally, the Writing to Discover **journal prompt** encourages you to collect your thoughts and opinions about the topic or related issues before you commence reading. The journal prompt makes it easy to keep a record of your own knowledge or thinking on a topic before you see what the writer has to offer.

To understand how these context-building materials can work for you, carefully review the following informational materials that accompany Natalie Goldberg's essay "Be Specific."

Be Specific
Title

N<small>ATALIE</small> G<small>OLDBERG</small>

Born in 1948, author Natalie Goldberg is a teacher of writing who has conducted writing workshops across the country. In addition to her classes and workshops, Goldberg shares her love of writing in her books; she has made writing about writing her speciality. Her first and best-known work, *Writing Down the Bones: Freeing the Writer Within,* was published in 1986. Goldberg's advice to would-be writers is practical and pithy, on the one hand, and mystical or spiritual, on the other, in its call to writers to know and become more connected to the environment. In short, as one reviewer observed, "Goldberg teaches us not only how to write better, but how to live better." *Writing Down the Bones* was followed by five more books about writing: *Wild Mind: Living the Writer's Life* (1990), *Thunder and Lightning: Cracking Open the Writer's Craft* (2000), *Old Friend from Far Away: The Practice of Writing Memoir* (2002), and *The True Secret of Writing: Connecting Life with Language* (2014). Altogether, more than a million copies of these books are now in print. Goldberg has also written the novel *Banana Rose* (1995), the memoirs *Long Quiet Highway: Waking Up in America* (1993), *The Great Failure: A Bartender, a Monk, and My Unlikely Path to Truth* (2004), and *Let the Whole Thundering World Come Home: A Memoir* (2018).

Headnote

Biographical information

"Be Specific" is taken from Goldberg's *Writing Down the Bones* and is representative of the book as a whole. Notice the ways in which Goldberg demonstrates her advice to be specific, to use names and concrete diction whenever possible. Which of her many examples resonates best with you?

Publication information

Rhetorical highlight

WRITING TO DISCOVER: *Suppose someone says to you,*   Journal
"I walked in the woods today." What do you envision? Write down   prompt
what you see in your mind's eye. Now suppose someone says,
"I walked in the redwood forest today." Again, write what you see.
What's different about your two descriptions, and why?

From reading these preliminary materials, what expectations do
you have for the selection itself? How does this knowledge equip you
to engage the selection before you actually read it? From the *title* you
probably inferred that Goldberg will explain what she means by the command "be specific" and what is to be gained by following this advice. Her
purpose clearly is to give advice to writers. The *biographical note* reveals
that Goldberg has written a number of books detailing her own experiences with writing as well as giving advice to aspiring writers of all ages,
and that she has taught writing courses and conducted writing workshops
for many years. This experience gives her the knowledge and authority to
write on this topic. The *publication information* indicates that the subject of Goldberg's essay is an argument in favor of being specific in writing. Because the selection was first published as part of her book *Writing
Down the Bones: Freeing the Writer Within*, Goldberg can anticipate that
readers, who we can assume are looking for writing advice, will be open
to her argument. The *rhetorical highlight* alerts you to be mindful of how
Goldberg practices what she's preaching in her own writing and prompts
you to consider her examples. Finally, the *journal prompt*—a hands-on
exercise in specificity—asks you to describe in writing the visuals con-
jured up in your mind by two statements and to draw conclusions about
any differences you note in your responses.

It's always a good practice to take several minutes before reading a selection to reflect on what you already know about a particular
issue, where you stand on it, and why. After reading Goldberg's essay,
you can compare your own experiences with being specific—or being
unspecific—in writing with those of Goldberg.

2. Read the Selection to Get an Overview of It

Always read the selection at least twice, no matter how long it is. The
first reading gives you a chance to get acquainted with the essay and to
form first impressions. With the first reading you want to get an overall
sense of what the writer is saying, keeping in mind the essay's title and
what you learned about the writer in the headnote. The essay will offer
you information, ideas, and arguments—some you may have expected;
some you may not have. As you read, you may find yourself questioning
or modifying your sense of what the writer is saying. Resist the urge to
annotate at this point; instead, concentrate on the content, on the main
points of what's being said. Now read Natalie Goldberg's essay.

Be Specific

N<small>ATALIE</small> G<small>OLDBERG</small>

Be specific. Don't say "fruit." Tell what kind of fruit—"It is a pomegran-ate." Give things the dignity of their names. Just as with human beings, it is rude to say, "Hey, girl, get in line." That "girl" has a name. (As a matter of fact, if she's at least twenty years old, she's a woman, not a "girl" at all.) Things, too, have names. It is much better to say "the geranium in the window" than "the flower in the window." "Geranium"—that one word gives us a much more specific picture. It penetrates more deeply into the beingness of that flower. It immediately gives us the scene by the window—red petals, green circular leaves, all straining toward sunlight. 1

About ten years ago I decided I had to learn the names of plants and flowers in my environment. I bought a book on them and walked down the tree-lined streets of Boulder, examining leaf, bark, and seed, trying to match them up with their descriptions and names in the book. Maple, elm, oak, locust. I usually tried to cheat by asking people working in their yards the names of the flowers and trees growing there. I was amazed how few people had any idea of the names of the live beings inhabiting their little plot of land. 2

When we know the name of something, it brings us closer to the ground. It takes the blur out of our mind; it connects us to the earth. If I walk down the street and see "dogwood," "forsythia," I feel more friendly toward the environment. I am noticing what is around me and can name it. It makes me more awake. 3

If you read the poems of William Carlos Williams, you will see how specific he is about plants, trees, flowers—chicory, daisy, locust, poplar, quince, primrose, black-eyed Susan, lilacs—each has its own integrity. Williams says, "Write what's in front of your nose." It's good for us to know what is in front of our noses. Not just "daisy," but how the flower is in the season we are looking at it—"The dayseye hugging the earth/in August . . . brownedged,/green and pointed scales/armor his yellow."* Continue to hone your awareness: to the name, to the month, to the day, and finally to the moment. 4

Williams also says: "No idea, but in things." Study what is "in front of your nose." By saying "geranium" instead of "flower," you are penetrat-ing more deeply into the present and being there. The closer we can get to what's in front of our nose, the more it can teach us everything. "To see the World in a Grain of Sand, and a heaven in a Wild Flower . . ."** 5

In writing groups and classes too, it is good to quickly learn the names of all the other group members. It helps to ground you in the group and make you more attentive to each other's work. 6

---

* William Carlos Williams, "Daisy," in *The Collected Earlier Poems* (New York: New Directions, 1938). [Goldberg's note.]

** William Blake, "The Auguries of Innocence." [Goldberg's note.]

Learn the names of everything: birds, cheese, tractors, cars, build-   7
ings. A writer is all at once everything—an architect, French cook,
farmer—and at the same time, a writer is none of these things.

3. Annotate the Selection with Marginal Notes

Some students find it valuable to capture their first impressions,
thoughts, or reactions immediately after they've finished reading a selection. If you keep a reading journal, record your ideas in a paragraph or
two. You are now ready for the second reading of the essay, this time with
pencil or pen in hand to annotate the text.

As you read the essay a second time, engage it—highlight key passages and make marginal annotations. Your second reading will be quite
different from your first, because you already know what the essay is
about, where it is going, and how it gets there. Now you can relate the
parts of the essay more accurately to the whole. Use the second reading
to test your first impressions against the words on the page, developing
and deepening your sense of the writer's argument. Because you already
have a general understanding of the essay's content and structure, you
can focus on the writer's purpose and means of achieving it. You can look
for features of organization and style that you can learn from and adapt to
your own work.

One question that students frequently ask us is "What should I annotate?" When you annotate a text, you should do more than simply underline or highlight what you think are the important points to remember.
Instead, as you read, write down your thoughts, reactions, and questions
in the margins or on a separate piece of paper. Think of your annotations
as an opportunity to have a conversation with the writer of the essay.

Mark what you believe to be the selection's main point when you
find it stated directly. Look for the pattern or patterns of development the
author uses to explore and support that point, and record the information. If you disagree with a statement or conclusion, object in the margin:
"No!" If you're not convinced by the writer's claims or evidence, indicate
that response: "Why?" or "Who says?" or "Explain." If you are impressed
by an argument or turn of phrase, compliment the writer: "Good point."
If there are any words that you do not recognize or that seem to you to
be used in a questionable way, circle them so that you can look them up
in a dictionary.

Jot down whatever marginal notes come naturally to you. Most readers combine brief responses written in the margins with their own system
of underlining, circling, highlighting, stars, vertical lines, and question
marks.

Remember that there are no hard-and-fast rules for which elements
you annotate. Choose a method of annotation that works best for you and
that will make sense to you when you go back to recollect your thoughts

---

How to Annotate a Text

Here are some suggestions of elements you may want to mark to help you keep a record of your responses as you read:

- Memorable statements of important points
- Key terms or concepts
- Central issues or themes
- Examples that support a main point
- Unfamiliar words
- Questions you have about a point or passage
- Your responses to a specific point or passage

---

and responses to the essay. When annotating a text, don't be timid. Mark up your book as much as you like, or jot down as many responses in your notebook as you think will be helpful. Don't let annotating become burdensome. A word or phrase is usually as good as a sentence. Notice how one of our students, Libby, used marginal annotations to record her responses to Goldberg's text.

Be specific. Don't say "fruit." Tell what kind of fruit — "It is a pomegranate." Give things the dignity of their names. Just as with human beings, it is rude to say, "Hey, girl, get in line." That "girl" has a name. (As a matter of fact, if she's at least twenty years old, she's a woman, not a "girl" at all.) Things, too, have names. It is much better to say "the geranium in the window" than "the flower in the window." "Geranium" — that one word gives us a much more specific picture. It penetrates more deeply into the beingness of that flower. It immediately gives us the scene by the window — red petals, green circular leaves, all straining toward sunlight.

About ten years ago I decided I had to learn the names of plants and flowers in my environment. I bought a book on them and walked down the tree-lined streets of Boulder, examining leaf, bark, and seed, trying to match them up with their descriptions and names in the book. Maple, elm, oak, locust. I usually tried to cheat

Marginal annotations:

I agree — tho my grandma calls her friends "the girls" — ?

I think I do pay more attn. when people call me by name.

She's practicing what she preaches — but that's a LOT of work....

I doubt I could tell the difference between a maple and an elm.

by asking people working in their yards the names of
the flowers and trees growing there. I was amazed how
few people had any idea of the names of the live beings
inhabiting their little plot of land.

When we know the name of something, it brings us
closer to the ground. It takes the blur out of our mind; it
connects us to the earth. If I walk down the street and see
"dogwood," "forsythia," I feel more friendly toward the
environment. I am noticing what is around me and can
name it. It makes me more awake.

THESIS

*Interesting —
wonder if it's true.
(How could you
test it?)*

If you read the poems of William Carlos Williams,
you will see how specific he is about plants, trees,
flowers—chicory, daisy, locust, poplar, quince, primrose,
black-eyed Susan, lilacs—each has its own integrity.
Williams says, "Write what's in front of your nose." It's
good for us to know what is in front of our noses. Not
just "daisy," but how the flower is in the season we are
looking at it—"The dayseye hugging the earth/in August
. . . brownedged,/green and pointed scales/armor his
yellow." Continue to hone your awareness: to the name,
to the month, to the day, and finally to the moment.

*Is Williams a
really famous
poet? LOOK THIS
UP. Why does she
keep quoting him?*

Williams also says: "No idea, but in things." Study
what is "in front of your nose." By saying "geranium"
instead of "flower," you are penetrating more deeply
into the present and being there. The closer we can get
to what's in front of our nose, the more it can teach us
everything. "To see the World in a Grain of Sand, and a
heaven in a Wild Flower . . . "

*I know I couldn't
name all the
people in my
writing class.
(Wonder if it
would make a
difference.)*

In writing groups and classes too, it is good to
quickly learn the names of all the other group members.
It helps to ground you in the group and make you more
attentive to each other's work.

Learn the names of everything: birds, cheese,
tractors, cars, buildings. A writer is all at once
everything—an architect, French cook, farmer—and at
the same time, a writer is none of these things.

*Not sure what
she means
here. How can
a writer be "all"
and "none"
of these things??*

After she annotated the Goldberg selection, we asked Libby, "How do you know what things you annotate?" She replied, "It's a skill that has kind of grown over time. I haven't always been comfortable with it. The first time my instructor asked me to annotate a reading back in September, I panicked. I ended up underlining way too much, and I was self-conscious about what I was writing in the margins. When I read and annotated 'Be Specific' about four weeks into the semester I was more relaxed because I knew that my marginal notes were for *my* eyes—to help me remember and understand the essay. I had a sense of what to look for. From my first reading of 'Be Specific,' I learned that Goldberg was giving me some writing instruction or advice—she wanted me to know why it's important to be specific and how I can be specific in my own writing. Once I understood her message and purpose, I annotated the essay. In my annotations, I tried to 1) engage with ideas that resonated with me, 2) circle or underline key phrases or sentences, and 3) write questions to myself that I thought were worth considering."

4. Summarize the Selection in Your Own Words

After carefully annotating the selection, you will find it worthwhile to summarize what the writer has said, to see how the main points work together to give support to the writer's thesis. An efficient way to do this is to make a simple paragraph-by-paragraph outline of what you've read. Try to capture the essence of each paragraph in a single sentence. Such an outline enables you to understand how the essay works, to see what the writer's position is and how he or she has structured the essay and organized the main ideas.

Consider the following paragraph-by-paragraph outline Luis, one of our students, made after reading Goldberg's essay:

Paragraph 1: Goldberg announces her topic and demonstrates the power of names with the example of the geranium.

Paragraph 2: She recounts how she went about learning the names of plants and trees in her Colorado neighborhood.

Paragraph 3: She explains how knowing the names of things makes her feel connected to the world around her.

Paragraph 4: She uses the example of poet William Carlos Williams to support her point about the power of names.

Paragraph 5: She continues with the example of Williams to broaden the discussion of what it means to "penetrate more deeply" into the world that is "in front of your nose."

Paragraph 6: She says that knowing the names of people in your writing group or class creates community.

Paragraph 7: She advises writers to "learn the names of everything" as a way of being "at once everything" and "at the same time . . . none of these things."

When asked if he found doing the paragraph-by-paragraph out-line helpful, Luis said, "I did. I liked the way it made me focus on what Goldberg was saying in each paragraph. Once I could summarize what she was saying as a single sentence for each paragraph, I think I got a better understanding of what she meant."

With your paragraph-by-paragraph outline in hand, you are now ready to analyze the reading.

5. Analyze the Selection to Come to an Understanding of It

After reading the essay a second time and annotating it, you are ready to analyze it, to probe for a deeper understanding of and appreciation for what the writer has done. In analyzing an essay, you will examine its basic parts methodically to see the significance of each part and under-stand how they relate to one another. One of the best ways to analyze an essay is to answer a basic set of questions—questions that require you to do some critical thinking about the essay's content and form (see the box on p. 13).

Each essay in *Language Awareness* is followed by a set of "Think-ing Critically about the Reading" questions similar to the ones suggested here but more specific to the essay. These questions help you analyze both the content of an essay and the writer's craft. In answering each of these questions, always look for details from the selection itself to support your position.

Having read and reread Goldberg's essay and studied the student annotations to the text, consider the following set of answers that a stu-dent, Angela, gave to the key questions listed above. Are there places where you would have answered the questions differently? Explain.

1. *What is the writer's main point or thesis?*

   Goldberg wants to tell her readers why it's important for people, especially writers, to be specific and to learn the names of everything in their part of the world. She states her main point in paragraph 3: "When we know the name of something, it brings us closer to the ground. It takes the blur out of our mind; it connects us to the earth." In short, being specific in what we call things makes us see, think, and write more clearly.

2. *To whom is the essay addressed? To a general audience with little or no background knowledge of the subject? To a specialized group familiar with the topic? To those who are likely to agree or disagree with the argument?*

   Goldberg's intended audience seems to be writers who are looking for advice. In para-graph 4, she quotes William Carlos Williams: "Write what's in front of your nose." In paragraph 6, Goldberg stresses the importance of knowing classmates' or group mem-bers' names and how this knowledge "helps to ground you in the group and make you

Questions to Help You Analyze What You Read

1. What is the writer's main point or thesis?

2. To whom is the essay addressed? To a general audience with little or no background knowledge of the subject? To a specialized group familiar with the topic? To those who are likely to agree or disagree with the argument?

3. What is the writer's purpose in addressing this audience?

4. What is the writer's attitude toward the subject of the essay — positive, critical, objective, ironic, hostile?

5. What assumptions, if any, does the writer make about the subject and/or the audience? Are these assumptions explicit (stated) or implicit (unstated)?

6. What kinds of evidence does the writer use to support his or her thesis — personal experience, expert opinions, statistics? Does the writer supply enough evidence to support his or her position? Is the evidence reliable, specific, and up-to-date?

7. Does the writer address opposing views on the issue?

8. How is the essay organized and developed? Does the writer's strategy of development suit his or her subject and purpose?

9. How effective is the essay? Is the writer convincing about his or her position?

more attentive to each other's work." In her final paragraph Goldberg acknowledges her audience of writers by emphasizing the writer's duty to learn the names of everything.

3. What is the writer's purpose in addressing this audience?

Goldberg's purpose is to give her readers some direct advice about writing and life: "Be specific." More specifically, she advises her readers to give people and things names and to create a specific time context (month, day, moment, etc.) for what they're describing ("Not just 'daisy,' but how the flower is in the season we are looking at it . . .").

4. What is the writer's attitude toward the subject of the essay—positive, critical, objective, ironic, hostile?

Goldberg is enthusiastic and extremely positive about the importance of naming things. She believes that "[w]hen we know the name of something, it brings us closer to the ground. It takes the blur out of our mind; it connects us to the earth" and makes us more "awake" to the environment; it allows us to "[penetrate] more deeply" into what is in front of us and to learn from it; and it grounds us and makes us more attentive in a group. She's excited to share her own experiences with learning the names of things.

5. *What assumptions, if any, does the writer make about the subject and/or the audience? Are these assumptions explicit (stated) or implicit (unstated)?*

Goldberg makes several key assumptions in this essay:
- The title assumes that readers will be comfortable with commands.
- The examples of "pomegranate," "geranium," "maple," "elm," "oak," "locust," "dogwood," and "forsythia" assume that readers have a basic knowledge of fruits, flowers, and trees — or that they'll be motivated enough to look them up.
- The reference to the poet William Carlos Williams assumes that the audience will know who he is and perhaps be familiar with his poetry — or, again, that they will be motivated enough to look him up. Goldberg's footnotes, however, show that she does not assume readers will recognize the poem "Daisy" (4) or "The Auguries of Innocence," quoted in paragraph 5.
- Goldberg assumes that readers, after learning the names of the plants, flowers, trees, and people in their environment, will have experiences similar to the ones she has had: "I feel more friendly toward the environment. I am noticing what is around me and can name it. It makes me more awake" (3).

6. *What kinds of evidence does the writer use to support his or her thesis — personal experience, expert opinions, statistics? Does the writer supply enough evidence to support his or her position? Is the evidence reliable, specific, and up-to-date?*

To support her claim that writers need to be specific, Goldberg uses the examples of "fruit/pomegranate," "girl/[name]," and "flower/geranium" in her opening paragraph — hoping that her readers will agree that the specific terms are better than the general ones. She follows these examples with personal experience: She explains how she went about learning the names of plants and flowers in Boulder, Colorado, and shares what she felt as a result. In paragraphs 4 and 5, Goldberg cites the poetry of William Carlos Williams as evidence that specific language creates great poems.

It is difficult to say whether this evidence is enough. Assuming her readers are beginning writers eager to learn, as she seems to have intended, it is probably safe to say that her evidence will be convincing. If a less receptive audience or an audience of nonwriters were reading the essay, though, more evidence or a different kind (maybe examples of how being specific helps in everyday life) might be needed.

7. *Does the writer address opposing views on the issue?*

While Goldberg does not directly address opposing views, she does discuss what happens when writers or speakers are not specific. For example, in paragraph 1 she says that calling someone "girl" instead of calling her by name can be rude, which is another way of saying that it denies that person her dignity — a pretty serious charge. In addition, when she tells us how knowing the names of things brings us closer to our environment, she implies that not knowing these names actually makes us feel disconnected from the world around us — something no one wants to feel.

8. *How is the essay organized and developed? Does the writer's strategy of development suit his or her subject and purpose?*

Goldberg organizes her essay in a straightforward and logical manner. She introduces her topic with her central directive, "Be specific," and then immediately shows through three examples what happens when a writer is specific. She organizes the examples in the body of her essay — paragraphs 2 through 6 — by telling how she learned to be more specific, quoting William Carlos Williams's advice to "Write what's in front of your nose," and advising us that we should learn the names of people in the groups and classes we belong to. Goldberg concludes her essay where she began, by directing us to "Learn the names of everything." In learning the names of every-thing, she reminds us that "A writer is all at once everything — an architect, French cook, farmer — and at the same time, a writer is none of these things." Although it seems paradoxical at first, this statement, when you stop to think about it, is very empowering — you're not really an architect or a French cook or a farmer, but, when you write, you get to experience the world the way they do.

9. *How effective is the essay? Is the writer convincing about his or her position?*

Goldberg's essay is effective because it serves her purpose very well. She raises her readers' awareness of the value of names and demonstrates why it is so important to give things their names in order to understand our world and to write effectively about it. Her argument about being specific is convincing — after reading the essay, it's difficult to look at a flower and not wonder, at least, whether it's a tulip, poppy, daffodil, rose, or something else. Goldberg offers practical advice on how each of us can get started learning the names of things, be they the names of the other people in our class or the names of the plants, trees, and flowers on our campus.

Once Angela finished writing out answers to the Goldberg study questions she said, "At first, I thought that the study questions after each article were a waste of time, and my answers usually showed it — they were brief, and I didn't put much effort into them. But the more we talked in class about the study questions, the more I started to see how they could help me with my own writing. I read Goldberg's essay several times and then answered the study questions. As I wrote my answers, I realized that Goldberg's essay was no accident. It's a solid piece of writing because she knew her subject and had a purpose. Her varied examples hammer home her main point: be specific! Over time I realized that the study questions also helped me to become a better annotator of what I read, and that good annotations in turn helped me give better answers to the study questions. I ended up participating more actively in class discussions, and I became a better reader, too."

6. Complete the "Language in Action" Activity to Discover the Far-Reaching Connections between the Selection and Language in the Real World

The "Language in Action" activities that accompany each selection in *Language Awareness* give you an opportunity to work with real world examples of language issues or concepts discussed in the selections, with exercises, cartoons, advertisements, photographs, poems, movie reviews, parodies, essay excerpts, syndicated columns, letters to the editor and more. Designed to be completed either in class or at home in about fifteen to twenty minutes, these activities invite you to take a hands-on approach to what you're learning from the essays and give you a chance to demonstrate your growing language aptitude. Consider the following activity that accompanied the Goldberg essay:

LANGUAGE IN ACTION

A useful exercise in learning to be more specific in our writing is to see the words we use for people, places, things, and ideas as being positioned somewhere on what might be called a "ladder of abstraction." In the following chart, notice how the words progress from more general to more specific.

More General	General	Specific	More Specific
Organism	Plant	Flower	Iris
Vehicle	Car	Chevrolet	1958 Chevrolet Impala

Using the examples above as models, fill in the missing part for each of the following ladders of abstraction:

More General	General	Specific	More Specific
Writing instrument	_____	Fountain pen	Waterman fountain pen
_____	Sandwich	Corned beef sandwich	Reuben
Fruit	Dessert	Pie	_____
American	_____	Pueblo	Laguna Pueblo
_____	Reference book	Dictionary	_____
School	_____	Technical high school	_____
Medicine	Oral medicine	Gel capsule	_____

After filling in the blanks yourself, compare your answers with those of your classmates. Now compare them to those provided by one of our students and discuss the variety of possible answers:

Line 1: Pen

Line 2: Lunch food

Line 3: Blueberry pie

Line 4: Native American

Line 5: Book, *American Heritage Dictionary of the English Language*

Line 6: High school, Essex Junction Technical Education Center

Line 7: Tylenol Gel Caps

PRACTICE READING, ANNOTATING, AND ANALYZING

Before you read the following essay, think about its title, the biographical and rhetorical information in the headnote, and the journal prompt. Make some marginal notes of your expectations for the essay, and write out a response to the journal prompt. Then, as you read the essay itself for the first time, try not to stop; take it all in as if in one breath. The second time, however, pause to annotate key points in the text, using the marginal rules we have provided alongside each paragraph. As you read, remember the nine basic questions we listed earlier on page 13.

What's in a Name?

HENRY LOUIS GATES JR.

Title: _____

The preeminent African American scholar of our time, Henry Louis Gates Jr. is the Alphonse Fletcher University Professor and director of the W. E. B. Du Bois Institute for African and African American Research at Harvard University. Among his impressive list of publications are *Figures in Black: Words, Signs, and the "Racial" Self* (1987), *The Signifying Monkey: A Theory of African-American Literary Criticism* (1988), *Loose Canons: Notes on Culture Wars* (1992), *The Future of the Race* (1997), and *Thirteen Ways of Looking at a Black Man* (1999). His most recent books are *Mr. Jefferson and Miss Wheatley* (2003), *Finding Oprah's Roots: Finding Your Own* (2007), *Life Upon These Shores: Looking at African American History, 1513–2008* (2011),

Biographical note: _____

Publication information: _____

and *100 Amazing Facts about the Negro* (2017). His *Colored People: A Memoir* (1994) recollects in a wonderful prose style his youth growing up in Piedmont, West Virginia, and his emerging sexual and racial awareness. Gates first enrolled at Potomac State College and later transferred to Yale, where he studied history. With the assistance of an Andrew W. Mellon Foundation Fellowship and a Ford Foundation Fellowship, he pursued advanced degrees in English at Clare College at the University of Cambridge. He has been honored with a MacArthur Foundation Fellowship, inclusion on *Time* magazine's "25 Most Influential Americans" list, a National Humanities Medal, and election to the American Academy of Arts and Letters.

In "What's in a Name?," excerpted from a longer article published in the fall 1989 issue of *Dissent* magazine, Gates tells the story of an early encounter with the language of prejudice. In learning how one of the "bynames" used by white people to define African Americans robs them of their identity, he feels the sting of racism firsthand. Notice how Gates's use of dialogue gives immediacy and poignancy to his narration.

Rhetorical highlight: _____

WRITING TO DISCOVER: *Reflect on racially charged language you have heard. For example, has anyone ever used a racial or ethnic epithet to refer to you? When did you first become aware that such terms existed? How do you feel about being characterized or defined by your race or ethnicity? If you yourself have ever used such terms, what was your intent in using them? What was the response of others?*

Journal prompt: _____

The question of color takes up much space in these pages, but the question of color, especially in this country, operates to hide the graver questions of the self.
— JAMES BALDWIN, 1961

Epigraphs: _____

...blood, darky, Tar Baby, Kaffir, shine...moor, blackamoor, Jim Crow, spooks....quadroon, meriney, red bone, high yellow...Mammy, porch monkey, home, homeboy, George...spearchucker, schwarze, Leroy, Smokey...mouli, buck, Ethiopian, brother, sistah...
— TREY ELLIS, 1989

I had forgotten the incident completely, until I read Trey Ellis's essay, "Remember My Name," in a recent issue of the *Village Voice*[1] (June 13, 1989). But there, in the middle of an extended italicized list of the bynames of "the race" ("the race" or "our people" being the terms my parents used in polite or reverential discourse, "jigaboo" or "nigger" more commonly used in anger, jest, or pure disgust), it was: "George." Now the events of that very brief exchange return to mind so vividly that I wonder why I had forgotten it.

Para. 1. _____

My father and I were walking home at dusk from his second job. He "moonlighted" as a janitor in the evenings for the telephone company. Every day but Saturday, he would come home at 3:30 from his regular job at the paper mill, wash up, eat supper, then at 4:30 head downtown to his second job. He used to make jokes frequently about a union official who moonlighted. I never got the joke, but he and his friends thought it was hilarious. All I knew was that my family always ate well, that my brother and I had new clothes to wear, and that all of the white people in Piedmont, West Virginia, treated my parents with an odd mixture of resentment and respect that even we understood at the time had something directly to do with a small but certain measure of financial security.

Para. 2. _____

He had left a little early that evening because I was with him and I had to be in bed early. I could not have been more than five or six, and we had stopped off at the Cut-Rate Drug Store (where no black person in town but my father could sit down to eat, and eat off real plates with real silverware) so that I could buy some caramel ice cream, two scoops in a wafer cone, please, which I was busy licking when Mr. Wilson walked by.

Para. 3. _____

Mr. Wilson was a very quiet man, whose stony, brooding, silent manner seemed designed to scare off any overtures of friendship, even from white people. He was Irish, as was one-third of our village (another third being Italian), the more affluent among whom sent their children to "Catholic School" across the bridge in Maryland. He had white straight hair, like my Uncle Joe, whom he uncannily resembled, and he carried a black worn metal lunch pail, the kind that Riley[2] carried on the television show. My father always spoke to him, and for reasons that we never did understand, he always spoke to my father.

Para. 4. _____

---

1. *Village Voice:* a nationally distributed weekly newspaper published in New York City.
2. A character on the U.S. television show *The Life of Riley*, a blue-collar, ethnic sitcom popular in the 1950s.

"Hello, Mr. Wilson," I heard my father say.   Para. 5–8.

"Hello, George."   _____

I stopped licking my ice cream cone, and asked my Dad   _____
in a loud voice why Mr. Wilson had called him "George."   _____

"Doesn't he know your name, Daddy? Why don't you   _____
tell him your name? Your name isn't George."   _____

For a moment I tried to think of who Mr. Wilson
was mixing Pop up with. But we didn't have any Georges
among the colored people in Piedmont; nor were there colored Georges living in the neighboring towns and working
at the mill.

"Tell him your name, Daddy."   Para. 10–14.

"He knows my name, boy," my father said after a long   _____
pause. "He calls all colored people George."   _____

A long silence ensued. It was "one of those things," as   _____
my Mom would put it. Even then, that early, I knew when   _____
I was in the presence of "one of those things," one of those _____
things that provided a glimpse, through a rent[3] curtain, at _____
another world that we could not affect but that affected   _____
us. There would be a painful moment of silence, and you   _____
would wait for it to give way to a discussion of a black   _____
superstar such as Sugar Ray[4] or Jackie Robinson.[5]

"Nobody hits better in a clutch than Jackie Robinson."

"That's right. Nobody."

I never again looked Mr. Wilson in the eye.   Para. 15. __

                                                         _____

                                                         _____

Once you have read and reread Gates's essay and annotated the text,
write out answers to the six Thinking Critically about the Reading questions as well as the Language in Action activity found below. Then compare your answers with those of the other students in class.

THINKING CRITICALLY ABOUT THE READING

1. In the epigraph to this essay, Gates presents two quotations, one by James
    Baldwin. What do you think Baldwin meant when he wrote, "The question of
    color, especially in this country [America], operates to hide the graver ques-
    tions of self"? How does this statement relate to the theme of Gates's essay?

---

3. Torn.

4. Walker Smith Jr. (1921–1989), American professional boxer and six-time world
champion.

5. (1919–1972): the first black baseball player in the National League.

2. In his opening paragraph, Gates refers to the other quotation in the epigraph—a list of bynames used to refer to African Americans that appeared in an article by Trey Ellis—and states that his reading of this article triggered a childhood memory for him. How did you first feel after reading Ellis's list of bynames for African Americans? What did you find offensive about these racial slurs? Explain.

3. Later in his opening paragraph Gates reveals that "'the race' or 'our people' [were] the terms my parents used in polite or reverential discourse, 'jigaboo' or 'nigger' more commonly used in anger, jest, or pure disgust." Why does Gates make so much of Mr. Wilson's use of "George" when his own parents used words so much more obviously offensive? What do you see as the essential difference between white people using Trey Ellis's list of terms to refer to people of color and African Americans using the same terms to refer to themselves? Explain.

4. Gates describes Mr. Wilson and provides some background information about him in paragraph 4. What do you think is Gates's purpose in providing this information? (Glossary: *Description*)

5. Explain what happens in paragraph 12. What is "one of those things," as Gates's mother put it? In what ways is "one of those things" really Gates's purpose in telling his story? Why does Gates say, "I never again looked Mr. Wilson in the eye" (15)?

6. In paragraphs 5 and 6, Gates uses dialogue to capture the key exchange between his father and Mr. Wilson. What does this dialogue add to his narration? (Glossary: *Narration*) What would have been lost if Gates had simply described the conversation between the two men?

LANGUAGE IN ACTION

Comment on the importance of one's name as revealed in the following Ann Landers column. Ann Landers is the pen name created for advice columnist Ruth Crowley in 1943 and later used by Eppie Lederer for her "Ask Ann Landers" syndicated lifestyle advice column that was featured in newspapers across the country from 1955 to 2002. Though fictional, Ann Landers became an institution and cultural icon for the era.

Refusal to Use Name Is the Ultimate Insult

DEAR ANN LANDERS: Boy, when you're wrong, you're really wrong. Apparently, you have never been the victim of a hostile, nasty, passive-aggressive person who refuses to address you by name. Well, I have.

My husband's mother has never called me by my name in the 21 years I've been married to her son. Nor has she ever said "please" or "thank you," unless someone else is within hearing distance. My husband's children by his first wife are the same way. The people they care about are always referred to by name, but the rest of us are not called anything.

If you still think this is a "psychological glitch," as you said in a recent column, try speaking to someone across the room without

> addressing that person by name. To be nameless and talked at is the ultimate put-down, and I wish you had said so. — "Hey You" in Florida
>
> **DEAR FLORIDA:** Sorry I let you down. Your mother-in-law's refusal to call you by name is, I am sure, rooted in hostility. Many years ago, Dr. Will Menninger said, "The sweetest sound in any language is the sound of your own name." It can also be a valuable sales tool. My former husband, one of the world's best salesmen, said if you want to make a sale, get the customer's name, use it when you make your pitch, and he will be half sold. His own record as a salesman proved him right.

What is the meaning of Dr. Will Menninger's statement: "The sweetest sound in any language is the sound of your own name"?

READING AS A WRITER

Reading and writing are the two sides of the same coin: Active critical reading is a means to help you become a better writer. By reading we can begin to see how other writers have communicated their experiences, ideas, thoughts, and feelings in their writing. We can study how they have used the various elements of the essay — thesis, unity, organization, beginnings and endings, paragraphs, transitions, effective sentences, word choice, tone, and figurative language — to say what they wanted to say. By studying the style, technique, and rhetorical strategies of other writers, we learn how we might effectively do the same. The more we read and write, the more we begin to read as writers and, in turn, to write knowing what readers expect.

What does it mean to read as a writer? Most of us have not been taught to read with a writer's eye, to ask why we like one piece of writing and not another. Likewise, most of us do not ask ourselves why one piece of writing is more believable or convincing than another. When you learn to read with a writer's eye, you begin to answer these important questions and, in the process, come to appreciate what is involved in selecting and focusing a subject as well as the craftsmanship involved in writing — how a writer selects descriptive details, uses an unobtrusive organizational pattern, opts for fresh and lively language, chooses representative and persuasive examples, and emphasizes important points with sentence variety.

On one level, reading stimulates your thinking by providing you with subjects to write about. After reading Amy Tan's essay "Mother Tongue," Helen Keller's "The Day Language Came into My Life," or Jimmy Santiago Baca's "Coming into Language," you might, for example, be inspired to write about a powerful language experience you have had and how that experience, in retrospect, was a "turning point" in your life.

On a second level, reading provides you with information, ideas, and perspectives for developing your own paper. In this way, you respond to what you read, using material from what you've read in an essay. For example, after reading Richard Lederer's essay on regional language differences in America, you might want to elaborate on what he has written, drawing on your own experiences and either agreeing with his examples or generating better ones for the area of the country in which you were raised. You could also qualify his argument for the preservation of these language differences or take issue with it. The two casebooks in Chapter 14, "Arguing about Language: Two Contemporary Debates," offer you an opportunity to read extensively about focused topics — "The Campus Free Speech Controversy" and "The Great Gender-Neutral Pronoun Debate" — and to use the information and opinions expressed in these essays as resources for your own thesis-driven paper.

On a third level, active reading can increase your awareness of how others' writing affects you, thus making you more sensitive to how your own writing will affect your readers. For example, if you have been impressed by an author who uses convincing evidence to support each claim, you might be more likely to back up your own claims carefully. If you have been impressed by an apt turn of phrase or absorbed by a writer's new idea, you may be less inclined to feed your readers dull, worn out, and trite phrases. More to the point, however, the active reading that you will be encouraged to do in *Language Awareness* will help you to recognize and analyze the essential elements of the essay. When you see, for example, how a writer like Roxane Gay uses a strong thesis statement, about how "careless language" fails to capture the horror of sexual assault, to control and direct the parts of her essay, you can better appreciate the importance of having a clear thesis statement in your writing. When you see the way Bharati Mukherjee uses transitions to link key phrases with important ideas so that readers can recognize clearly how the parts of her essay are meant to flow together, you have a better idea of how to achieve such coherence in your own writing. And when you see the way Donna Woolfolk Cross uses a division and classification organizational plan to differentiate clearly the various categories of propaganda, you see a powerful way in which you too can organize an essay using this method of development.

Finally, another important reason to master the skills of critical reading is that you will be your own first reader and critic for everything you write. How well you are able to scrutinize your own drafts will powerfully affect how well you revise them, and revising well is crucial to writing well. Reading others' writing with a critical eye is a useful and important practice; the more you read, the more practice you will have in sharpening your skills. The more sensitive you become to the content and style decisions made by the writers in *Language Awareness,* the more skilled you will be at making similar decisions in your own writing.

2

WRITING IN COLLEGE AND BEYOND

Nothing is more important to your success in school and in the workplace than learning to write well. You've heard it so often you've probably become numb to the advice. Let's ask the big question, however. Why is writing well so important? The simple answer is that no activity develops your ability to think better than writing does. Writing allows you to develop your thoughts and to "see" and reflect critically on what you think: In that sense, writing also involves its twin sister, reading. Writing well often means organizing your thoughts into a compelling argument and engaging readers by using concise, specific language. Small wonder, then, that academic programs and employers in all fields are constantly looking for people who can read and write well. Simply put, the ability to read and write well is a strong indication of a good mind.

College is a practical training ground for learning to write and think well. Whenever you write in college, you are writing as a member of a community of scholars, teachers, and students. By questioning, researching, and writing in company with other members of the college community, you come both to understand college material and to demonstrate your knowledge of it. In college, with the help of instructors, you will write essays, analyses, term papers, reports, reviews of research, critiques, and summaries. What you learn now will be fundamental, not only to your education, but also to your later success, no matter what career you intend to pursue.

DEVELOPING AN EFFECTIVE WRITING PROCESS

Writers cannot rely on inspiration alone to produce effective writing. Good writers follow a writing *process*: They analyze their assignment, gather ideas, draft, revise, edit, and proofread. It is worth remembering, however, that the writing process is rarely as simple and straightforward as it might appear to be. Often the process is recursive, moving back and forth among different stages. Moreover, writing is personal—no two people go about it exactly the same way. Still, it is possible to describe basic guidelines for developing a writing process, thereby allowing you to devise your own reliable method for undertaking a writing task.

1. Understand Your Assignment

Much of your college writing will be done in response to specific assignments from your instructors or research questions that you develop in consultation with your teachers. Your environmental studies professor, for example, may ask you to write a report on significant new research on carbon dioxide emissions and global warming; your American history professor may ask you to write an analysis of the long-term effects of Japanese Americans' internment during World War II. From the outset you need to understand precisely what your instructor is asking you to do. The keys to understanding assignments such as these are *subject* words (words that focus on content) and *direction* words (words that indicate your purpose for and method of development in writing). For example, consider what you are being asked to do in each of the following language-related assignments:

> Tell about an experience you have had that dramatically revealed to you the importance of being accurate and precise in your use of language.

> Many languages are lost over time because speakers of those languages die. When a language is lost, the particular culture embodied in the language is also lost. Using an extinct language and culture as an example, explain how the language embodies a culture and exactly what is lost when a language becomes extinct.

> Advocates of the English-only movement want to see English adopted as our country's official language. Argue for or against the philosophy behind this movement.

In the first example above, the subject words are *experience* and *importance of being accurate and precise in your use of language*. The direction word is *tell*, which means that you must share the details of the experience so that your readers can appreciate them as if they were there, sharing the experience. The content words in the second example are *languages, culture,* and *extinct language and culture*. The direction word is *explain*. In the third example, the content words are *English-only movement* and *our country's official language*. The direction word is *argue*. In each case the subject words limit and focus the content, and the direction words dictate how you will approach this content in writing.

The words *tell, explain,* and *argue* are only a few of the direction words that are commonly found in academic writing assignments. The following list of additional direction words and their meanings will help you better understand your writing assignments and what is expected of you.

Direction Words

Analyze: take apart and examine closely

Categorize: place into meaningful groups

Compare: look for differences, stress similarities

Contrast: look for similarities, stress differences

Critique: point out positive and negative features

Define: provide the meaning for a term or concept

Describe: give detailed sensory perceptions for a person, a place, or an event

Evaluate: judge according to some established standard

Identify: recognize or single out

Illustrate: show through examples

Interpret: explain the meaning of a document, an action, an event, or a behavior

Prove: demonstrate truth by logic, fact, or example

Synthesize: bring together or make meaningful connections among elements

---

After reading an assignment several times, check with your instructor if you are still unsure about what is being asked of you. He or she will be glad to clear up any possible confusion before you start writing. Be sure, as well, that you understand any additional requirements of the assignment, such as length or format.

2. Find a Subject and Topic

Although your instructor will sometimes give you specific writing assignments, you will often be asked to choose your own subject and topic. In a course in which you are using *Language Awareness,* you would in this case first select a broad subject within the area of language studies that you think you may enjoy writing about, such as professional jargon, dialects, political speeches, advertising language, or propaganda. A language issue that you have experienced firsthand (discrimination, for example) or something you've read may bring other subjects to mind. In the student essay that concludes this chapter (pp. 43–46), Rebekah Sandlin revisits her own racial prejudices as an elementary school

student and what she has learned from them. You might also consider
a language-related issue that involves your career ambitions, such as the
areas of business (avoiding exaggerated advertising claims), law (eliminating obscure legal language), nursing (communicating effectively with
patients), or journalism (reporting the news objectively). Another option
is to list some subjects you enjoy discussing with friends and that you can
approach from a language perspective: music (gender bias in rap lyrics),
work (decoding insurance policies and medical benefits), and college life
(speech codes on campus).

Next, try to narrow your general subject until you arrive at a topic
that you think will be both interesting to your readers and appropriate
for the length of your paper (and the time you have to write it). The
following chart shows how the general areas of jargon, journalism, and
television commercials might be narrowed to a specific essay topic.
(If you're having trouble coming up with general subjects or specific
topics, try some of the discovery techniques discussed in Step 3 on
pp. 31–35.)

General Subject Area	Narrowed Topic	Specific Essay Topic
Jargon	Medical jargon	Medical jargon used between doctors and terminally ill patients
Journalism	Slanted language in newswriting	Slanted language in newspapers' coverage of international events
Television commercials	Hidden messages in television commercials	Hidden messages in television commercials on children's Saturday morning programs

USE THE WRITING SUGGESTIONS IN *LANGUAGE AWARENESS*. As far as
writing about the subjects and topics discussed in *Language Awareness* is
concerned, there is no shortage of ideas and approaches at your disposal.
There are two Writing Suggestions at the end of every selection in the
book. If you have the freedom to choose your own subject and topic,
and the approach you take, you may want to use one of the suggestions
as a springboard for your own creativity. If, on the other hand, you are
assigned a Writing Suggestion, be sure you understand what is being asked
of you. If you are unclear about the assignment or you want to widen or
narrow its focus or change its intent in any way, be sure to do so in consultation with your instructor. You can and should be creative in using even
an assigned suggestion, maybe even using it as a starting point for your
own research and thesis, but again, get your instructor's approval before
starting your paper so no misunderstandings result.

DETERMINE YOUR PURPOSE.   All effective writing springs from a clear purpose. Most good writing seeks specifically to accomplish any one of the following three purposes:

- To express thoughts and feelings about life experiences
- To inform readers by explaining something about the world around them
- To persuade readers to adopt some belief or take some action

In *expressive writing,* or writing from experience, you put your thoughts and feelings before all other concerns. When Jimmy Santiago Baca explains how he finds refuge and freedom in his writing (Chapter 6) and when Amy Tan describes how her mother's use of English shaped her own approach to writing (Chapter 7), each one is writing from experience. In each case, the writer has clarified an important life experience and has conveyed what he or she learned from it.

Informative writing focuses on telling the reader something about the outside world. In informative writing, you report, explain, analyze, define, classify, compare, describe a process, or examine causes and effects. When Paul Roberts explains the formation of speech communities (Chapter 6), he is writing to inform.

Argumentative writing seeks to influence readers' thinking and attitudes toward a subject and, in some cases, to move them to a particular course of action. Such persuasive writing uses logical reasoning, authoritative evidence, and testimony, and it sometimes includes emotionally charged language and examples. For instance, John Palfrey (Chapter 14) uses logical reasoning, evidence, and examples to make the case that restrictions on freedom of speech are sometimes necessary and justified. And Stephanie Golden (Chapter 14), in "Why We Need the Singular 'They'," uses everyday examples to support her argument for this ever more popular change in pronoun usage.

KNOW YOUR AUDIENCE.   The best writers always keep their audience in mind. Once they have decided on a topic and a purpose, writers present their material in a way that empathizes with their readers, addresses their difficulties and concerns, and appeals to their rational and emotional faculties. Based on knowledge of their audience, writers make conscious decisions on content, sentence structure, and word choice.

Writing for an Academic Audience   Academic writing most often employs the conventions of formal standard English, or the language of educated professionals. Rather than being heavy or stuffy, good academic writing is lively and engaging and holds the reader's attention by presenting interesting ideas supported with relevant facts, statistics, and detailed information. Informal writing, usually freer and simpler in form, is typically used in notes, journal entries, email, text messages, instant messaging, and the like.

In order not to lessen the importance of your ideas and your credibility, be sure that informal writing does not carry over into your academic writing. Always keeping your audience and purpose in mind will help you achieve an appropriate style.

When you write, your audience might be an individual (your instructor), a group (the students in your class), a specialized group (art history majors), or a general readership (readers of your student newspaper). To help identify your audience, ask yourself the questions posed on page 31.

Using Discipline-Specific Language   The point of discipline-specific language, sometimes referred to as professional language or even jargon, is not to make a speaker or writer sound like a scientist, or a humanities scholar, or a geologist. Rather, discipline-specific language provides a kind of "shorthand" means of expressing complex concepts. Its proper use will grow from your knowledge of the discipline, from the reading you have done in the field, and from the hours you have spent in the company of your teachers and peers.

While the meaning of some disciplinary language will become clear to you from context as you read and discuss course material, some of it, left undefined, will present a stumbling block to your understanding of the material. Glossaries of disciplinary terms exist for most disciplines: Make use of them. Also, never be shy about asking your instructor or more experienced classmates for help when you're unsure of the meaning of a term.

Considering Opposing Arguments   You will likely not have trouble convincing those who agree with your argument from the outset, but what about those who are skeptical or think differently from you? You need to discover who these people are by talking with them or by reading what they have written. Do your research, be reasonable, and find common ground where possible, but take issue where you must. To refute an opposing argument, you can present evidence showing that the opposition's data or evidence is incomplete or distorted, that its reasoning is faulty, or that its conclusions do not fit the evidence.

Formal versus Informal Writing

Formal Writing	*Informal Writing*
Uses standard English, the language of public discourse typical of newspapers, magazines, books, and speeches	Uses nonstandard English, slang, colloquial expressions (*anyways, dude, freaked out*), and shorthand (*OMG, IMHO*)
Uses mostly third person	Uses first and second person most often

Avoids most abbreviations (*Professor, brothers, miles per gallon, digital video recorder*)	Uses abbreviations and acronyms (*Prof., bros., mpg, DVR*)
Uses an impersonal tone (*The speaker took questions from the audience at the end of her lecture.*)	Uses an informal tone (*It was great the way she answered questions at the end of her talk.*)
Uses longer, more complex sentences	Uses shorter, simpler sentences
Adheres to the rules and conventions of proper grammar	Takes a casual approach to the rules and conventions of proper grammar

Questions about Audience

- Who are my readers? Are they a specialized or a general group?
- What do I know about my audience's age, gender, education, religious affiliation, economic status, and political views?
- What does my audience know about my subject? Are they experts or novices?
- What does my audience need to know about my topic in order to understand my discussion of it?
- Will my audience be interested, open-minded, resistant, or hostile to what I have to say?
- Do I need to explain any specialized language so that my audience can understand my subject? Is there any language that I should avoid?
- What do I want my audience to do as a result of reading my essay?

3. Gather Ideas

Ideas and information (facts and details) lie at the heart of good prose. Ideas grow out of information; information supports ideas. Before you begin to draft, gather as many ideas as possible and as much information as you can about your topic in order to inform and stimulate your readers intellectually.

Most writers use one or more discovery techniques to help them gather information, zero-in on a specific topic, or find connections among ideas. In addition to your reading and discussing writing ideas with your classmates and friends, you may want to experiment with some of the discovery techniques explained below.

KEEPING A JOURNAL. Many writers use a journal to record thoughts and observations that might be mined for future writing projects. They have learned not to rely on their memories to retain ideas, facts, and statistics they have heard or read about. Writers also use journals to keep all kinds of lists: lists of questions they would like answers to; lists of issues that concern them; lists of topics they would like to write about someday.

To aid your journal writing as you use this text, each reading selection in *Language Awareness* begins with a journal prompt called "Writing to Discover." The purpose of each prompt is to get you thinking and writing about your own experiences with the language issues discussed in the selection before you start reading. You thus have the opportunity to discover what you already know about a particular topic and to explore your observations, feelings, and opinions about it. The writing you do at this point is something you can always return to after reading each piece.

FREEWRITING. Journals are also useful if you want to freewrite. *Freewriting* is simply writing for a brief uninterrupted period of time—say, ten or fifteen minutes—on anything that comes to your mind. It is a way to get your mind working and to ease into a writing task. Start with a blank sheet of paper or computer screen and write about the general subject you are considering. Write as quickly as you can, don't stop for any reason, and don't worry about punctuation, grammar, or spelling. Write as though you were talking to your best friend, and let your writing take you in any direction. If you run out of ideas, don't stop; just repeat the last few things you wrote over and over again, and you'll be surprised—more ideas will begin to emerge. Just as regular exercise gets you in shape, regular freewriting will help you feel more natural and comfortable when writing.

OPEN-ENDED WRITING. A useful extension of freewriting is a discovery strategy called open-ended writing. Follow the same directions for freewriting but also stop every ten minutes or so to evaluate what you have written. Analyze your freewriting and identify ideas, issues, expressions, phrases, and terms that show relationships and themes, and that may also engender questions about your material. Copy only those related elements onto a new sheet of paper and begin freewriting again. By repeating the process several times, following your freewrites with analysis each time, you will inevitably deepen your thinking about your topic and get closer to being able to write your first draft.

BRAINSTORMING. Another good way to generate ideas and infor-mation about a topic is to *brainstorm*—to list everything you know about a topic, freely associating one idea with another. Don't worry about order or level of importance. Try to capture everything that comes to mind because you never know what might prove valuable later on. Write quickly, but if you get stalled, reread what you have written; doing so will help you move in new directions. Keep your list handy so that you can add to it over the course of several days. Here, for example, is a student's brainstorming list on why Martin Luther King Jr.'s speech, "I Have a Dream," has endured:

> *Why "I Have a Dream" Is Memorable*
>
> *civil rights demonstration in Washington, D.C., delivered on steps of Lincoln Memorial*
>
> *repetition of "I have a dream"*
>
> *references to the Bible, spirituals*
>
> *"bad check" metaphor*
>
> *other memorable figures of speech*
>
> *200,000 people*
>
> *reminds me of other great American documents and*
> *speeches — Declaration of Independence and Gettysburg Address*
>
> *refers to various parts of the country*
>
> *embraces all races and religions*
>
> *sermon format*
>
> *displays energy and passion*

ASKING QUESTIONS. *Asking questions* about a particular topic or experience may help you generate information before you start to write. If you are writing about a personal experience, for example, asking ques-tions may refresh your memory about the details and circumstances of the incident or help you discover why the experience is still so memorable. The newspaper reporter's five Ws and an H—Who? What? Where? When? Why? and How?—are excellent questions to start with. One student, for example, developed the following questions to help her explore an expe-rience of verbal abuse:

1. *Who was involved in the abusive situation?*

2. *What specific language was used?*

3. *Where did the abuse most often take place?*

4. *When did the verbal abuse first occur?*

5. *Why did the abusive situation get started? Why did it continue?*

6. *How did I feel about the abuse as it was happening? How do I feel about it now?*

As the student jotted down answers to these questions, other questions came to mind, such as, *What did I try to do after the verbal abuse occurred? Did I seek help from anyone else? How can I help others who are being verbally abused?* Before long, the student had recalled enough information for a rough draft about her experience.

CLUSTERING. Another strategy for generating ideas and gathering information is *clustering*. Put your topic, or a key word or phrase about your topic, in the center of a sheet of paper and draw a circle around it. (The student example below shows the topic "Hospital jargon at summer job" in the center.) Draw three or more lines out from this circle, and jot down main ideas about your topic, drawing a circle around each one. Repeat the process by drawing lines from the main-idea circles and adding examples, details, or questions you have. You may wind up pursuing one line of thought through many add-on circles before beginning a new cluster.

One advantage of clustering is that it allows you to sort your ideas and information into meaningful groups right from the start. As you carefully sort your ideas and information, you may begin to see an organizational plan for your writing. In the following example, the student's clustering is based on the experiences he had while working one summer

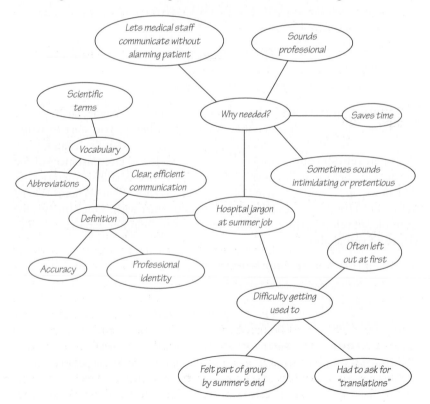

in a hospital emergency room. Does the clustering provide any clues to how he might organize his essay?

4. Formulate a Thesis

The thesis of an essay is its main idea, the major point the writer is trying to make. A thesis should be

- the most important point you make about your topic
- more general than the ideas and facts used to support it
- focused enough to be covered in the space allotted for the essay

The thesis is often expressed in one or two sentences called a *thesis statement*. Here's an example of a thesis statement about television news programs:

> The so-called serious news programs are becoming too like tabloid news shows in both their content and their presentation.

A thesis statement should be an assertion, not a question. If you find yourself writing a question for a thesis statement, answer the question first—this answer will be your thesis statement.

An effective strategy for developing a thesis statement is to begin by writing, "What I want to say is that . . ."

> *What I want to say is that* unless language barriers between patients and health care providers are bridged, many patients' lives in our most culturally diverse cities will be endangered.

Later you can delete the formulaic opening, and you will be left with a thesis statement.

To determine whether your thesis is too general or too specific, think hard about how easy it will be to present data—that is, facts, statistics, names, examples or illustrations, and opinions of authorities—to support it. If you stray too far in either direction, your task will become much more difficult. A thesis statement that is too general will leave you overwhelmed by the number of issues you must address. For example, the statement "Political attack speeches damage the American political system" would lead to the question "How?" To answer it, you would probably have to include information about national politics, free speech, libel, character assassination, abusive language, the fallacy of ad hominem arguments, and so on. To cover all of this in the time and space you have for a typical college paper would mean taking shortcuts, and your paper would be ineffective. On the other hand, too specific a thesis statement would leave you with too little information to present. "Governor Wright's speech implies that Senator Smith's personal life is a disgrace" does not leave you with any opportunity to develop an argument. An appropriate thesis statement like "Political attack speeches have harmed politicians' images and turned off voters in Big City's mayoral elections over the past decade" leaves room for argument but can still be proven by examining poll responses, voter turnout records, and other evidence.

The thesis statement is usually presented near the beginning of the essay. One common practice in shorter college papers is to position the thesis statement as the final sentence of the first paragraph.

Is Your Thesis Solid?

Once you have a possible thesis statement in mind, ask yourself the following questions:

- Does my thesis statement take a clear position on an issue? (Could I imagine someone agreeing or disagreeing with it? If not, it might be a statement of fact, instead of an arguable thesis.)
- Will I be able to find evidence that supports my position? Where? What kinds? (If you're unsure, it wouldn't hurt to take a look at a few secondary sources at this point.)
- Will I be able to make my claim and present sufficient evidence to support it in a paper of the assigned length, and by the due date? (If not, you might need to scale back your claim to something more manageable.)

---

5. Support Your Thesis with Evidence

The types of evidence you use in your academic writing will be determined to some extent by the discipline in which you are working. For example, for a research project in psychology on the prejudice shown toward people with unusual names, you will almost certainly rely heavily on published studies from peer-reviewed journals. Depending on the assignment, however, you might also devise an experiment of your own or interview people with unusual names to gather firsthand accounts of their experiences. For an argument essay on the same topic in a composition course, as in many courses in the humanities, languages, and literatures, you would cite a wide range of sources, perhaps including — but not limited to — peer-reviewed journals. Depending on the assignment, you might also include your own experience and informal observations.

To support her argument on book banning, one student derives most of her evidence from an array of experts, as in the following example, where she cites scholar Henry Reichman:

> Henry Reichman writes that in 1990, Frank Mosca's *All-American Boys* (1983) and Nancy Garden's *Annie on My Mind* (1982), two books with gay themes, were donated to high schools in Contra Costa, California; at three of these high schools, the books were seized by administrators and then "lost" (53).

PRIMARY AND SECONDARY SOURCES. In general, researchers and writers work with two types of evidence: primary sources and secondary sources.

Primary sources in the humanities and languages/literatures are works that grow out of and are close to a time, place, or culture under study. These can include documents such as letters, speeches, interviews, manuscripts, diaries, treaties, and maps; creative written works such as novels, plays, poems, songs, and autobiographies; and three-dimensional artifacts such as paintings, sculptures, pottery, weaving, buildings, tools, and furniture. Primary sources in the social, natural, and applied sciences are the factual reports and descriptions of discoveries, experiments, surveys, and clinical trials.

Secondary sources in the humanities and languages/literatures restate, analyze, and interpret primary sources. Common secondary sources include analyses, critiques, histories, and commentaries in the form of books, articles, encyclopedia entries, and documentaries. Secondary sources in the sciences analyze and interpret discoveries and experiments and often comment on the validity of the research models and methods and the value of those discoveries and experiments.

Writing in a specific discipline requires that you use the most authoritative and reliable source materials available for that discipline. Your instructors can help you in this regard by either providing you with a list of resources commonly used in their fields or directing you to such a list in your library or on the internet. Many academic libraries include helpful subject study guides on their home pages as well.

For a brief guide to finding, evaluating, and documenting sources in print and online, see Chapter 5.

FACTS, STATISTICS, EXAMPLES, AND EXPERT TESTIMONY. The evidence you use in your academic writing should place a high value on facts and statistics, examples and illustrations, and the testimony of experts. You must be accurate in your use of facts and statistics, and you must check and double-check that you have cited them correctly. Be sure that you carefully consider the examples and illustrations you use to support your thesis: Use those that work best with your subject and the audience you have in mind. Finally, be selective in citing the works and comments of experts in your discipline. If you choose wisely, the works of respected scholars and experts will be immediately recognizable to others familiar with the subject area, and your argument will have a much better chance of succeeding.

The following passage illustrates how student Jake Jamieson uses examples in his paper on the Official English movement:

> Ed Morales, the author of *Living in Spanglish*, reports that the mayor of Bogota, New Jersey, called for a boycott of McDonald's restaurants after the "company displayed a billboard advertising a new iced coffee drink in Spanish," calling "the ad . . . 'offensive' and 'divisive' because it sends a message that Hispanic immigrants do not need to learn English" (par. 2–3).

6. Determine Your Organization

There are several organizational patterns you might follow in drafting an essay. Most of you are already familiar with the most common one — *chronological order*. In this pattern, which is often used to narrate a story, explain a process, or relate a series of events, you start with the earliest event or step and move forward in time.

In a comparison-and-contrast essay, you might follow a *block* pattern or a *point-by-point* organization. In a block pattern, a writer provides all the information about one subject, followed by a block of comparable information about the other subject. In a point-by-point comparison, on the other hand, the writer starts by comparing both subjects in terms of a particular point, then compares both on a second point, and so on. In an essay comparing two dialects of American English, for example, you could follow the block pattern, covering all the characteristics of one dialect and then all the characteristics of the other. Alternatively, you could organize your material in terms of defining characteristics (for example, geographical range; characteristics of speakers; linguistic traits), filling in the details for each dialect in turn.

Other patterns of organization include moving from *the general to the specific*, from *smallest to largest*, from *least important to most important*, or from *the usual to the unusual*. In an essay about medical jargon, for instance, you might cover its general characteristics first and then move to specifics, or you might begin with what is most usual (or commonly known) about doctors' language and then discuss what is unusual about it. Whatever order you choose, keep in mind that what you present first and last will probably stay in the reader's mind the longest.

After you choose an organizational pattern, jot down the main ideas in your essay. In other words, make a scratch outline. As you add more information and ideas to your scratch outline, you may want to develop a formal, more detailed outline of your paper. In writing a formal outline, follow these rules:

1. Include the title of your essay, a statement of purpose, and the thesis statement.
2. Write in complete sentences unless your meaning is immediately clear from a phrase.

3. If you divide any category, make sure there are at least two subcategories. The reason for this is simple: You cannot divide something into fewer than two parts.
4. Observe the traditional conventions of formal outlining. Notice how each new level of specificity is given a new letter or number designation.

Title:
Purpose:
Thesis:
   I.
      A.
      B.
         1.
         2.
            a.
            b.
            c.
  II.

7. Write Your First Draft

Sometimes we are so eager to get on with the writing of a first draft that we begin before we are ready, and the results are disappointing. Before beginning to write, therefore, ask yourself, "Have I done enough prewriting? Is there a point to what I want to say?" If you have done a thorough job of gathering ideas and information, if you think you can accomplish the purpose of your paper, and if you are comfortable with your organizational plan, your answers will be "yes."

If, however, you feel uneasy, review the various prewriting steps to try to resolve the problem. Do you need to gather more information? Sharpen your thesis? Rethink your purpose? Refine your organization? Now is the time to think about these issues, to evaluate and clarify your writing plan. Time spent at this juncture is time well spent because it will not only improve your paper but will save you time and effort later on.

As you write, don't be discouraged if you do not find the most appropriate language for your ideas or if your ideas do not flow easily. Push ahead with the writing, realizing that you will be able to revise the material later, adding information and clarifications wherever necessary. Be sure to keep your audience in mind as you write so that your diction and coverage stay at the appropriate level. Remember also to bridge all the logical and emotional leaps for your audience. Rereading what you have already written as you go along will help you to further develop your ideas and tie them together. Once completed, a first draft will give you a sense of accomplishment. You will see that you have something to work with, something to build on and improve during the revision process.

8. Revise

After you complete your first draft, you will need to revise it. During the revision stage of the writing process, you will focus on the large issues of thesis, purpose, evidence, organization, and paragraph structure to make sure that your writing says what you want it to say. First, though, it is crucial that you set your draft aside for a while. Then you can come back to it with a fresh eye and some objectivity. When you do, resist the temptation to plunge immediately into a second draft: Scattered changes will not necessarily improve the piece. Instead, try to look at your writing as a whole and to tackle your writing problems systematically. Use the following guidelines:

- Make revisions on a hard copy of your paper. (Triple-space your draft so that you can make changes more easily.)
- Read your paper aloud, listening for parts that do not make sense.
- Ask a fellow student to read your essay and critique it.

A Brief Guide to Peer Critiquing

When critiquing someone else's paper:

- Read the essay carefully. Read it to yourself first, and then, if possible, have the writer read it to you at the beginning of the session. Some flaws become obvious when read aloud.
- Ask the writer to state his or her purpose for writing and to identify the thesis statement within the paper itself.
- Be positive, but be honest. Never denigrate the paper's content or the writer's effort, but do your best to identify how the writer can improve the paper through revision.
- Try to address the most important issues first. Think about the thesis and the organization of the paper before moving on to more specific topics like word choice.
- Do not be dismissive, and do not dictate changes. Ask questions that encourage the writer to reconsider parts of the paper that you find confusing or ineffective.

When someone critiques your work:

- Give your reviewer a copy of your paper before your meeting.
- Listen carefully to your reviewer, and try not to discuss or argue each issue. Record comments and evaluate them later.

- Do not get defensive or explain what you wanted to say if the reviewer misunderstands what you meant. Try to understand the reviewer's point of view, and learn what you need to revise in order to clear up the misunderstanding.
- Consider every suggestion, but only use those that make sense to you in your revision.
- Be sure to thank your reviewer for his or her effort on your behalf.

One way to begin the revision process is to compare the earlier outline of your first draft to an outline of how it actually came out. This will help you see, in abbreviated form, the organization and flow of the essential components of your essay and perhaps detect flaws in reasoning.

Another method you can use in revising is to start with large-scale issues, such as your overall structure, and then concentrate on finer and finer points. As you examine your essay, ask yourself about what you have written and address the large elements of your essay: thesis, purpose, organization, paragraphs, and evidence.

Revising the Large Elements of an Essay

- Is my topic specific enough?
- Does my thesis statement identify my topic and make an assertion about it?
- Is my essay organized the best way, given my purpose?
- Are my paragraphs adequately developed, and does each support my thesis?
- Have I accomplished my purpose?
- How effective is my beginning? My ending?
- Is my title effective?

Once you have addressed the major problems in your essay by writing a second draft, you should be ready to turn your attention to the finer elements of sentence structure, word choice, and usage.

Revising Sentence-Level Elements

- Do my sentences convey my thoughts clearly, and do they emphasize the most important parts of my thinking?
- Are my sentences stylistically varied?
- Is my choice of words fresh and forceful, or is my writing weighed down by clichés and unnecessary wordiness?
- Have I made any errors of usage?

Finally, if you find yourself dissatisfied with specific elements of your draft, look at several essays in *Language Awareness* to see how other writers have dealt with the particular situation you are confronting. For example, if you don't like the way the essay starts, find some beginnings you think are particularly effective; if your paragraphs don't seem to flow into one another, examine how various writers use transitions; if an example seems unconvincing, examine the way other writers include details, anecdotes, facts, and statistics to strengthen their illustrations. Remember that the readings in the text are there as a resource for you as you write.

9. Edit and Proofread

Now that you have revised in order to make your essay "right," it is time to think about making it "correct." During the editing stage of the writing process, check your writing for errors in grammar, punctuation, capitalization, spelling, and manuscript format. Both your dictionary and your college handbook will help you answer specific editing questions about your paper.

Addressing Common Editing Problems and Errors

- Do my verbs agree in number with their subjects?
- Do my pronouns have clear antecedents — that is, do they clearly refer to specific nouns earlier in my sentences?
- Do I have any sentence fragments, comma splices, or run-on sentences?
- Have I made any unnecessary shifts in person, tense, or number?
- Have I used the comma properly in all instances?
- Have I checked for misspellings, mistakes in capitalization, and typos?

- Have I inadvertently confused words like *their, they're,* and *there* or *it's* and *its?*
- Have I followed the prescribed guidelines for formatting my manuscript?

Having revised and edited your essay, you are ready to print your final copy. Be sure to proofread your work before submitting it to your instructor. Even though you may have used your computer's spell checker, you might find that you have typed *worm* instead of *word,* or *form* instead of *from.* Also, be mindful that grammar check and auto-correct—normally very helpful utilities—can insert errors into your text that may go unnoticed without careful proofreading. Finally, check to see that your essay is properly line spaced and that the text is legible.

10. Sample Student Essay Using Writing Process

The following essay was written by Rebekah Sandlin while she was a student at Miami University in Oxford, Ohio. After Rebekah read the essays in the chapter on prejudice, stereotypes, and language, her instructor, Linda Parks, asked her to write about a personal experience with biased language and how that language affected her. Rebekah vividly remembered an experience she had in the third grade, when she used the phrase "just like a nigger" to mock a classmate. Using that experience as the starting point of her essay, she then traces a series of subsequent encounters she had with the word *nigger* and recounts her resulting personal growth. By the end of her essay, Rebekah makes it clear to her readers why she felt compelled to tell her story.

Sandlin 1

Rebekah Sandlin

English 111 sec. BD

October 23, 2018

Paper #3

The "Negro Revolt" in Me

She said "seven" when the answer was clearly "ten." We were in the third grade and had been studying multiplication for a few weeks. Our teacher, Mrs. Jones, reminded Monica that "we are multiplying now, not adding. Five times two will always be ten" I laughed at Monica. How

> Brief introductory anecdote captures readers' attention.

Sandlin 2

did she not know the answer to five times two? We had been over it and practiced it so many times. My laughter encouraged the other kids in the class to join in with me. Within seconds the laughing had escalated into pointing fingers and calling her stupid. That's when "it" happened. That's when I said what I will always regret for the rest of my life. I said, "Just like a nigger."

Playing on her weaknesses in math, laughing at her, encouraging the rest of the class to point at her, and calling her the most degrading word in history still eats at my insides. The class stopped laughing. Monica cried. Mrs. Jones gasped and yanked me into the hallway where she scolded me for a good half an hour. That is how I learned that language could be used as a dangerous tool. That's when I learned about prejudice and its effects on people. That's how it happened. This is how it has affected my life.

> Writer introduces the main point (thesis) of the story (narrative) she's about to write.

Mrs. Jones sent me home with a note explaining my "behavior" in class. I remember being terribly afraid to give that note to my mom. I felt guilty, confused, and embarrassed, but I wasn't sure why I felt that way. No one had taken the time to explain to me why the word had such a negative connotation. No one told me that blacks were once treated terribly wrong or that they were used as slaves. No one told me about the interracial rapes that occurred on plantations or about the children being taken and sold to rich white landowners. No one told me about them being denied an education and proper shelter. No one told me. I was just a small white girl living in a predominately white city and going to a predominately white school. I knew nothing about diversity and equal rights for everyone. I knew nothing.

> Writer uses chronological organization.

My mom sat me down at the kitchen table and asked me how I could have said such a terrible thing. "Where did you learn that word?" she asked. She sounded furious and embarrassed. She kept asking me

Sandlin 3

where I had heard the word and who taught it to me. Before I had a

chance to respond she knew the answer. My dad was on the phone in

the next room talking to his father. He was laughing and he said, "just

like a nigger." My mom lowered her head and whispered, "go to your

room." I quietly got up and obeyed her command. I'm not sure what she

said to him, but I could hear their mumbled fighting through the vents.

I pressed my ear to the vent on the floor to try and make sense of my

mother's cries. It was no use. Two hours later they came upstairs to give

me one of their "you did something wrong" speeches. Except this speech

was different from most. It began with an apology and an attempt to

justify my father's words.

> Powerful use of dialogue, especially her father speaking on the phone—show, don't tell.

    It started with a story. My dad grew up on a tobacco farm in

southern Georgia. His family hired blacks to work out in the fields.

"No," he reassured, "they weren't slaves. We paid them." His family

was prejudiced toward blacks. Their language and actions rubbed off

onto my dad. The only difference was that my dad learned that what

he said and how he treated blacks was wrong. Through growing up

and living in integrated working environments, he learned how "not to

act" in the presence of a black person. However, when he talked to his

father he still acted and talked like he was prejudiced. He said that he

didn't understand why he did it other than he desperately wanted to be

accepted by his own father. He admitted that he was wrong and told me

that I was lucky because I was going to learn the "real way" to treat

people. He promised to never use the word again as long as I promised to

do the same thing. I agreed.

> Writer introduces her father's story within her own story.

    I was in the fifth grade the next time I heard the word used.

Ironically, I was in a math class again. Except this time I didn't say it,

someone else did. Unlike Monica, this girl didn't cry. Instead, she gave an

evil glare. I was the one that stood up to say something in her defense.

> "I was in the fifth grade" signals the passage of time and orients readers to new incident.

Sandlin 4

I yelled at Dan and told him that what he had said was rude and degrading. "How would you like it if someone called you honky?" I screamed. He hauled off and hit me right in the arm! He called me a "nigger-lover."

The teacher broke it up, and we were sent to the principal's office. I was suspended for using vulgar language. I had used the word "honky." Dan was given a warning and sent back to class. I had plenty of time to think about what I had done wrong while I waited in the office for my mom to come and pick me up. No matter how hard I tried, I couldn't see what I had done wrong. That girl did not want to be called a nigger. I was just trying to show him what it would feel like if someone had said something like that to him. My mom did not agree with me. I learned an important lesson that day. Using bad words to stop other bad words is like using violence to stop violence — it doesn't work. My mom was supportive and said that she respected what I was trying to do but next time I should use better sense. I didn't want there to be a next time.

> Writer gives her narrative purpose by sharing what she learned about language and prejudice from her experiences.

THINKING CRITICALLY ABOUT THE STUDENT ESSAY

1. What is Sandlin's thesis? Why do you think she stated her thesis where she did?
2. How does Sandlin use stories to structure her essay? How does she balance narrative with analysis and reflection of the events she experienced?
3. Do you agree with Sandlin's assessment of the times when she used derogatory language? If not, why not?
4. How would you have ended this essay, if you were the one writing it?

3

WRITERS ON READING
AND WRITING

Learning to write well is a demanding and difficult pursuit, but the ability to express exactly what you mean is one of the most enjoyable and rewarding skills you can possess. And, as with any sought-after goal, there is plenty of help available for the aspiring writer. In this chapter, we have gathered some of the best of that advice, offered by professional writers and respected teachers of writing.

The essays included in this chapter are based on current research and thinking on how writers go about their work. We begin with best-selling author Stephen King's "Reading to Write," wherein he argues that anyone who wishes to become an effective writer needs to be an active and critical reader, much as we have done in Chapter 1. The rest of the essays in this section look more deeply into the writer's tool bag. Popular novelist and teacher of writing Anne Lamott recognizes that even though writers may start out with firm purpose and clear thinking, rough drafts are inevitably messy affairs. In "The First Sentence," Lebanese novelist Iman Humaydan reflects on the way she writes, how the process she follows reflects both her character and the organic nature of composition. For her, writing is a journey of self-discovery, "like being born over and over again." Next, in "The Maker's Eye: Revising Your Own Manuscripts," the late Donald M. Murray recognizes the need to produce a first draft, no matter how messy, in order to move to the real job of writing. For him, as for almost all practicing writers, writing is revising. Finally, in "How to Mark a Book," Mortimer Adler advises us to write in our books—to give our responses, to argue, to ask questions, to affirm. Then and only then, he believes, do we really own a book. All these experts are worth reading not just once but again and again as you develop your own skills, confidence, and authority as a writer.

Reading to Write

STEPHEN KING

Born in 1947, Stephen King is a 1970 graduate of the University of Maine. He worked as a janitor in a knitting mill, a laundry worker, and a high school English teacher before he struck it big with his writing. Today, many people consider King's name synonymous with the macabre; he is, beyond dispute, the most successful writer of horror fiction today. He has written dozens of novels and hundreds of short stories, novellas, and screenplays, among other works. His books have sold well over 300 million copies worldwide, and many of his novels have been made into popular motion pictures, including *Stand by Me, Misery, The Green Mile, Dreamcatcher*, and *The Dark Tower*. His fiction, starting with *Carrie* in 1974, includes *Salem's Lot* (1975), *The Shining* (1977), *The Dead Zone* (1979), *Christine* (1983), *Pet Sematary* (1983), *The Dark Half* (1989), *The Girl Who Loved Tom Gordon* (1999), *From a Buick 8* (2002), *Everything's Eventual: Five Dark Tales* (2002), *The Colorado Kid* (2005), *Cell* (2006), *Lisey's Story* (2006), *Duma Key* (2008), *Under the Dome* (2009), *11/22/63* (2011), *Mile 81* (2011), *The Bazaar of Bad Dreams* (2015), *End of Watch* (2016), *The Outsider* (2018), and *Elevation* (2018). Other works include *Danse Macabre* (1981), a nonfiction look at horror in the media, and *On Writing: A Memoir of the Craft* (2000).

In the following passage taken from *On Writing*, King discusses the importance of reading in learning to write. Reading, in his words, "offers you a constantly growing knowledge of what has been done and what hasn't, what is trite and what is fresh, what works and what just lies there dying (or dead) on the page."

WRITING TO DISCOVER: *In your opinion, are reading and writing connected in some way? If the two activities are related, what is the nature of that relationship? Do you have to be a reader to be a good writer, or is writing an activity that can be learned quite apart from reading?*

If you want to be a writer, you must do two things above all others: Read a lot and write a lot. There's no way around these two things that I'm aware of, no shortcut.

I'm a slow reader, but I usually get through seventy or eighty books a year, mostly fiction. I don't read in order to study the craft; I read because

I like to read. It's what I do at night, kicked back in my blue chair. Similarly, I don't read fiction to study the art of fiction, but simply because I like stories. Yet there is a learning process going on. Every book you pick up has its own lesson or lessons, and quite often the bad books have more to teach than the good ones.

When I was in the eighth grade, I happened upon a paperback novel by Murray Leinster, a science fiction pulp writer who did most of his work during the forties and fifties, when magazines like *Amazing Stories* paid a penny a word. I had read other books by Mr. Leinster, enough to know that the quality of his writing was uneven. This particular tale, which was about mining in the asteroid belt, was one of his less successful efforts. Only that's too kind. It was terrible, actually, a story populated by paper-thin characters and driven by outlandish plot developments. Worst of all (or so it seemed to me at the time), Leinster had fallen in love with the word *zestful*. Characters watched the approach of ore-bearing asteroids with *zestful smiles*. Characters sat down to supper aboard their mining ship with *zestful anticipation*. Near the end of the book, the hero swept the large-breasted, blonde heroine into a *zestful embrace*. For me, it was the literary equivalent of a smallpox vaccination: I have never, so far as I know, used the word *zestful* in a novel or a story. God willing, I never will.

Asteroid Miners (which wasn't the title, but that's close enough) was an important book in my life as a reader. Almost everyone can remember losing his or her virginity, and most writers can remember the first book he/she put down thinking: *I can do better than this, Hell, I* am *doing better than this!* What could be more encouraging to the struggling writer than to realize his/her work is unquestionably better than that of someone who actually got paid for his/her stuff?

If you want to be a writer, you must do two things above all others: Read a lot and write a lot.

One learns most clearly what not to do by reading bad prose—one novel like *Asteroid Miners* (or *Valley of the Dolls, Flowers in the Attic,* and *The Bridges of Madison County,* to name just a few) is worth a semester at a good writing school, even with the superstar guest lecturers thrown in.

Good writing, on the other hand, teaches the learning writer about style, graceful narration, plot development, the creation of believable characters, and truth-telling. A novel like *The Grapes of Wrath* may fill a new writer with feelings of despair and good old-fashioned jealousy—"I'll never be able to write anything that good, not if I live to be a thousand"—but such feelings can also serve as a spur, goading the writer to work harder and aim higher. Being swept away by a combination of great story and great writing—of being flattened, in fact—is part of every writer's necessary formation. You cannot hope to sweep someone else away by the force of your writing until it has been done to you.

So we read to experience the mediocre and the outright rotten; such experience helps us to recognize those things when they begin to creep into our own work, and to steer clear of them. We also read in order to measure ourselves against the good and the great, to get a sense of all that can be done. And we read in order to experience different styles.

You may find yourself adopting a style you find particularly exciting, and there's nothing wrong with that. When I read Ray Bradbury as a kid, I wrote like Ray Bradbury—everything green and wondrous and seen through a lens smeared with the grease of nostalgia. When I read James M. Cain, everything I wrote came out clipped and stripped and hard-boiled. When I read Lovecraft, my prose became luxurious and Byzantine. I wrote stories in my teenage years where all these styles merged, creating a kind of hilarious stew. This sort of stylistic blending is a necessary part of developing one's own style, but it doesn't occur in a vacuum. You have to read widely, constantly refining (and redefining) your own work as you do so. It's hard for me to believe that people who read very little (or not at all in some cases) should presume to write and expect people to like what they have written, but I know it's true. If I had a nickel for every person who ever told me he/she wanted to become a writer but "didn't have time to read," I could buy myself a pretty good steak dinner. Can I be blunt on this subject? If you don't have time to read, you don't have the time (or the tools) to write. Simple as that.

Reading is the creative center of a writer's life. I take a book with me everywhere I go, and find there are all sorts of opportunities to dip in. The trick is to teach yourself to read in small sips as well as in long swallows. Waiting rooms were made for books—of course! But so are theater lobbies before the show, long and boring checkout lines, and everyone's favorite, the john. You can even read while you're driving, thanks to the audiobook revolution. Of the books I read each year, anywhere from six to a dozen are on tape. As for all the wonderful radio you will be missing, come on—how many times can you listen to Deep Purple sing "Highway Star"?

Reading at meals is considered rude in polite society, but if you expect   10
to succeed as a writer, rudeness should be the second-to-least of your concerns. The least of all should be polite society and what it expects. If you intend to write as truthfully as you can, your days as a member of polite society are numbered, anyway.

Where else can you read? There's always the treadmill, or whatever you use down at the local health club to get aerobic. I try to spend an hour doing that every day, and I think I'd go mad without a good novel to keep me company. Most exercise facilities (at home as well as outside it) are now equipped with TVs, but TV—while working out or anywhere else—really is about the last thing an aspiring writer needs. If you feel you must have the news analyst blowhards on CNN while you exercise, or the stock market blowhards on MSNBC, or the sports blowhards on ESPN, it's time for you to question how serious you really are about becoming a writer. You must be prepared to do some serious turning inward toward the life of the imagination, and that means, I'm afraid, that Geraldo, Keith Olbermann, and Jay Leno must go. Reading takes time, and the glass teat takes too much of it.

Once weaned from the ephemeral craving for TV, most people will find they enjoy the time they spend reading. I'd like to suggest that turning off that endlessly quacking box is apt to improve the quality of your life as well as the quality of your writing. And how much of a sacrifice are we talking about here? How many *Frasier* and *ER* reruns does it take to make one American life complete? How many Richard Simmons infomercials? How many whiteboy/fatboy Beltway insiders on CNN? Oh man, don't get me started. Jerry-Springer-Dr.-Dre-Judge-Judy-Jerry-Falwell-Donny-and-Marie, I rest my case.

When my son Owen was seven or so, he fell in love with Bruce Springsteen's E Street Band, particularly with Clarence Clemons, the band's burly sax player. Owen decided he wanted to learn to play like Clarence. My wife and I were amused and delighted by this ambition. We were also hopeful, as any parent would be, that our kid would turn out to be talented, perhaps even some sort of prodigy. We got Owen a tenor saxophone for Christmas and lessons with Gordon Bowie, one of the local music men. Then we crossed our fingers and hoped for the best.

Seven months later I suggested to my wife that it was time to discontinue the sax lessons, if Owen concurred. Owen did, and with palpable relief—he hadn't wanted to say it himself, especially not after asking for the sax in the first place, but seven months had been long enough for him to realize that, while he might love Clarence Clemons's big sound, the saxophone was simply not for him—God had not given him that particular talent.

I knew, not because Owen stopped practicing, but because he was practicing only during the periods Mr. Bowie had set for him: half an hour after school four days a week, plus an hour on the weekends. Owen mastered the scales and the notes—nothing wrong with his memory, his lungs, or his eye-hand coordination—but we never heard him taking off, surprising himself with something new, blissing himself out. And as soon as his practice time was over, it was back into the case with the horn, and there it stayed until the next lesson or practice time. What this suggested to me was that when it came to the sax and my son, there was never going to be any real playtime; it was all going to be rehearsal. That's no good. If there's no joy in it, it's just no good. It's best to go on to some other area, where the deposits of talent may be richer and the fun quotient higher.

Talent renders the whole idea of rehearsal meaningless; when you find something at which you are talented, you do it (whatever *it* is) until your fingers bleed or your eyes are ready to fall out of your head. Even when no one is listening (or reading, or watching), every outing is a bravura performance, because you as the creator are happy. Perhaps even

15

ecstatic. That goes for reading and writing as well as for playing a musical instrument, hitting a baseball, or running the four-forty. The sort of strenuous reading and writing program I advocate—four to six hours a day, every day—will not seem strenuous if you really enjoy doing these things and have an aptitude for them; in fact, you may be following such a program already. If you feel you need permission to do all the reading and writing your little heart desires, however, consider it hereby granted by yours truly.

The real importance of reading is that it creates an ease and intimacy with the process of writing; one comes to the country of the writer with one's papers and identification pretty much in order. Constant reading will pull you into a place (a mind-set, if you like the phrase) where you can write eagerly and without self-consciousness. It also offers you a constantly growing knowledge of what has been done and what hasn't, what is trite and what is fresh, what works and what just lies there dying (or dead) on the page. The more you read, the less apt you are to make a fool of yourself with your pen or word processor.

THINKING CRITICALLY ABOUT THE READING

1. What does King mean when he writes that reading a bad novel is "worth a semester at a good writing school, even with the superstar guest lecturers thrown in" (5)? Do you take his observation seriously? Why or why not?

2. In paragraph 3, King berates the author Murray Leinster for his repeated use of the word *zestful*. He says he himself has, as far as he knows, never used the word. Why do you suppose he doesn't like the word? Have you ever used it in your own writing? Explain. (Glossary: *Diction*)

3. In paragraph 7 King says that "we read in order to experience different styles." What examples does he use to support this statement? If you have learned from someone else's style, what exactly was it that you learned? (Glossary: *Evidence*)

4. Authors, especially those as famous as King, are very much sought after as guests on television shows, at writing conferences, and at celebrity and charity events. Why does King believe that it is incompatible for one to be both a member of polite society and an author? Do you agree with him? Why or why not?

5. King does not like TV. What does he find wrong with it, especially for writers?

6. Admittedly, not everyone who wants to write well also aspires to be a great novelist. What value, if any, does King's advice about reading and writing have for you as a college student? Explain.

LANGUAGE IN ACTION

King closes paragraph 11 with the observation that "Reading takes time, and the glass teat takes too much of it." Identify your own "glass teat." Perhaps you're less inclined to turn to television and more attached to your smartphone. Try detaching from it in a substantial way for twenty-four hours.

While you're disconnected, do what King describes and fill your spare moments with reading—a good book, a lousy book, whatever sort of book will hold your interest. Carry that book with you, turning to it when you might otherwise distract yourself, and observe how your thinking changes. Does increasing the amount of time you spend reading actually do what King suggests it does? Do you find you have more access to language, and more inclination and ability to write? After twenty-four hours steeped in a book and disconnected from other media, try writing something inspired by the style of that writer. Can you identify specific ways your impulses with language have changed?

WRITING SUGGESTIONS

1. King shares with his readers both his reading and writing experiences and the way they have influenced and shaped his development as a writer. Each of us has also been influenced by the reading and writing we have done. Some of us have done a lot of reading and writing in and out of school while others have not done as much as we would have liked. Write an essay explaining what your experiences have been with reading and writing, especially how your reading has influenced your writing, and vice versa. Here are some of the many questions you might want to address in your essay: What writers have you envied and wanted to imitate? What subjects have interested you? What style of writing do you favor? What style annoys you? Have your tastes changed? What particular texts have had a great influence on your thinking and outlook?

2. King seems to be especially averse to watching television. Is it the medium, the types of programs aired, or a combination that annoys him? After all, consider that movies and miniseries made from his novels have appeared on television. Why do you suppose he finds pleasure in reading and not television? Does the same relationship between reading and writing take place between watching television and writing? Write an essay in which you argue against his rejection of television or in which you, like King, take issue with it and with those programs you find a waste of time.

Shitty First Drafts

ANNE LAMOTT

Born in San Francisco in 1954, Anne Lamott attended Goucher College in Baltimore and is the author of six novels, including *Rosie* (1983), *Crooked Little Heart* (1997), *All New People* (1989), *Blue Shoe* (2002), and *Imperfect Birds* (2010). She has also been the food reviewer for *California* magazine, a book reviewer for *Mademoiselle*, and a regular contributor to *Salon's* "Mothers Who Think." Her nonfiction books include *Operating Instructions: A Journal of My Son's First Year* (1993), in which she describes her adventures as a single parent; *Traveling Mercies: Some Thoughts on Faith* (1999), in which she charts her journey toward faith in God; *Plan B: Further Thoughts on Faith* (2005); *Grace (Eventually): Thoughts on Faith* (2007); with her son Sam, *Some Assembly Required: A Journal of My Son's First Son* (2012); and *Small Victories: Spotting Improbable Moments of Grace* (2014).

In the following selection, taken from Lamott's popular book about writing, *Bird by Bird* (1994), she argues for the need to let go and write those "shitty first drafts" that lead to clarity and sometimes brilliance in our second and third drafts.

WRITING TO DISCOVER: *Many professional writers view first drafts as something they have to do before they can begin the real work of writing — revision. How do you view the writing of your first drafts? What patterns, if any, do you see in your writing behavior when working on first drafts? Is the work liberating? Restricting? Pleasant? Unpleasant? Explain in a paragraph or two.*

Now, practically even better news than that of short assignments is the idea of shitty first drafts. All good writers write them. This is how they end up with good second drafts and terrific third drafts. People tend to look at successful writers, writers who are getting their books published and maybe even doing well financially, and think that they sit down at their desks every morning feeling like a million dollars, feeling great about who they are and how much talent they have and what a great story they have to tell; that they take in a few deep breaths, push back their sleeves, roll their necks a few times to get all the cricks out, and dive in, typing fully formed passages as fast as a court reporter. But this is just the fantasy of the uninitiated. I know some very great writers, writers you love who write beautifully and have made a great deal of money, and not one of them sits down routinely feeling wildly enthusiastic and confident. Not one of them writes elegant first drafts. All right, one of them does, but we do not like her very much. We do not think that she has a rich inner life or that God likes her or can even stand her. (Although when I mentioned this to my priest friend Tom, he said you can safely assume you've created God in your own image when it turns out that God hates all the same people you do.)

Very few writers really know what they are doing until they've done it. Nor do they go about their business feeling dewy and thrilled. They do not type a few stiff warm-up sentences and then find themselves bounding along like huskies across the snow. One writer I know tells me that he sits down every morning and says to himself nicely, "It's not like you don't have a choice, because you do—you can either type or kill yourself." We all often feel like we are pulling teeth, even those writers whose prose ends up being the most natural and fluid. The right words and sentences just do not come pouring out like ticker tape most of the time. Now, Muriel Spark is said to have felt that she was taking dictation from God every morning—sitting there, one supposes, plugged into a Dictaphone, typing away, humming. But this is a very hostile and aggressive position. One might hope for bad things to rain down on a person like this.

For me and most of the other writers I know, writing is not rapturous. In fact, the only way I can get anything written at all is to write really, really shitty first drafts.

The first draft is the child's draft, where you let it all pour out and then let it romp all over the place, knowing that no one is going to see it and that you can shape it later. You just let this childlike part of you channel whatever voices and visions come through and onto the page. If one of the characters wants to say, "Well, so what, Mr. Poopy Pants?," you let her.

> **Very few writers really know what they are doing until they've done it.**

No one is going to see it. If the kid wants to get into really sentimental, weepy, emotional territory, you let him. Just get it all down on paper, because there may be something great in those six crazy pages that you would never have gotten to by more rational, grown-up means. There may be something in the very last line of the very last paragraph on page six that you just love, that is so beautiful or wild that you now know what you're supposed to be writing about, more or less, or in what direction you might go—but there was no way to get to this without first getting through the first five and a half pages.

I used to write food reviews for *California* magazine before it folded. 5 (My writing food reviews had nothing to do with the magazine folding, although every single review did cause a couple of canceled subscriptions.

Some readers took umbrage at my comparing mounds of vegetable puree with various ex-presidents' brains.) These reviews always took two days to write. First I'd go to a restaurant several times with a few opinionated, articulate friends in tow. I'd sit there writing down everything anyone said that was at all interesting or funny. Then on the following Monday I'd sit down at my desk with my notes, and try to write the review. Even after I'd been doing this for years, panic would set in. I'd try to write a lead, but instead I'd write a couple of dreadful sentences, XX them out, try again, XX everything out, and then feel despair and worry settle on my chest like an x-ray apron. It's over, I'd think, calmly. I'm not going to be able to get the magic to work this time. I'm ruined. I'm through. I'm toast. Maybe, I'd think, I can get my old job back as a clerk-typist. But probably not. I'd get up and study my teeth in the mirror for a while. Then I'd stop, remember to breathe, make a few phone calls, hit the kitchen and chow down. Eventually I'd go back and sit down at my desk, and *sigh* for the next ten minutes. Finally I would pick up my one-inch picture frame, stare into it as if for the answer, and every time the answer would come: all I had to do was to write a really shitty first draft of, say, the opening paragraph. And no one was going to see it.

So I'd start writing without reining myself in. It was almost just typing, just making my fingers move. And the writing would be terrible. I'd write a lead paragraph that was a whole page, even though the entire review could only be three pages long, and then I'd start writing up descriptions of the food, one dish at a time, bird by bird, and the critics would be sitting on my shoulders, commenting like cartoon characters. They'd be pretending to snore, or rolling their eyes at my overwrought descriptions, no matter how hard I tried to tone those descriptions down, no matter how conscious I was of what a friend said to me gently in my early days of restaurant reviewing. "Annie," she said, "it is just a piece of *chicken*. It is just a bit of *cake*."

But because by then I had been writing for so long, I would eventually let myself trust the process—sort of, more or less. I'd write a first draft that was maybe twice as long as it should be, with a self-indulgent and boring beginning, stupefying descriptions of the meal, lots of quotes from my black-humored friends that made them sound more like the Manson girls than food lovers, and no ending to speak of. The whole thing would be so long and incoherent and hideous that for the rest of the day I'd obsess about getting creamed by a car before I could write a decent second draft. I'd worry that people would read what I'd written and believe that the accident had really been a suicide, that I had panicked because my talent was waning and my mind was shot.

The next day, though, I'd sit down, go through it all with a colored pen, take out everything I possibly could, find a new lead somewhere on the second page, figure out a kicky place to end it, and then write a second draft. It always turned out fine, sometimes even funny and weird and helpful. I'd go over it one more time and mail it in.

Then, a month later, when it was time for another review, the whole process would start again, complete with the fears that people would find my first draft before I could rewrite it.

THINKING CRITICALLY ABOUT THE READING

1. What is Lamott's thesis, and where is her statement of the thesis? (Glossary: *Thesis*)

2. Lamott says that the perceptions most people have of how writers work is different from the reality of the work itself. She refers to this in paragraph 1 as "the fantasy of the uninitiated." What does she mean?

3. In paragraph 7 Lamott refers to a time when, through experience, she "eventually let [herself] trust the process—sort of, more or less." She is referring to the writing process, of course, but why "more or less"? Do you think her wariness is personal, or is she speaking for all writers in this regard? Explain.

4. From what Lamott has to say, is writing a first draft more about content or psychology? Do you agree in regard to your own first drafts? Explain.

5. Lamott adds humor to her argument for "shitty first drafts." Give some examples. Do her attempts at humor add or detract from the points she makes? Explain.

6. In paragraph 5, Lamott offers a narrative of her experiences writing a food review in which she refers to an almost ritualistic set of behaviors. What is her purpose in telling her readers this story and the difficulties she has? (Glossary: *Narration*) Is it helpful for us to know this information? Explain.

7. What do you think of Lamott's use of the word *shitty* in her title and in the essay itself? Is it in keeping with the tone of her essay? (Glossary: *Tone*) Are you offended by her use of the word? Why or why not? What would be lost or gained if she used a different word?

LANGUAGE IN ACTION

In his 1990 book *The Play of Words*, Richard Lederer presents the following activity called "Verbs with Verve." What do you learn about the power of verbs from this exercise? Explain.

> Verbs create specific images in the mind's eye. Because verbs are the words in a sentence that express action and movement, they are the spark plugs of effective style. The more specific the verbs you choose in your speaking and writing, the more sparky will be the images you flash on the minds of your listeners and readers.

Suppose you write, "'No,' she said and left the room." Grammatically there is nothing wrong with this sentence. But because the verbs *say* and *leave* are among the most general and colorless in the English language, you have missed the chance to create a vivid word picture. Consider the alternatives:

Said		*Left*	
apologized	jabbered	backed	sauntered
asserted	minced	bolted	skipped
blubbered	mumbled	bounced	staggered
blurted	murmured	crawled	stamped
boasted	shrieked	darted	stole
cackled	sighed	flew	strode
commanded	slurred	hobbled	strutted
drawled	snapped	lurched	stumbled
giggled	sobbed	marched	tiptoed
groaned	whispered	plodded	wandered
gurgled	whooped	pranced	whirled

If you had chosen from among these vivid verbs and had crafted the sentence "'No,' she sobbed, and stumbled out of the room," you would have created a powerful picture of someone quite distraught.

Here are brief descriptions of ten different people. Choosing from the two lists of synonyms for *said* and *left*, fill in the blanks of the sentence "'No,' he/she _____, and _____ out of the room." Select the pair of verbs that best create the most vivid picture of each person described. Throughout your answers try to use as many different verbs as you can:

1. an angry person
2. a baby
3. a braggart
4. a child
5. a clown
6. a confused person
7. a cowboy/cowgirl
8. someone crying
9. a drunkard
10. an embarrassed person

WRITING SUGGESTIONS

1. In order to become a better writer, it is essential to be conscious of what you do as a writer. In other words, you need to reflect on what you are thinking and feeling at each stage of the writing process. Lamott has done just this

in writing her essay. Think about what you do at other stages of the writing process—prewriting (gathering information, selecting evidence, checking on the reliability of sources, separating facts from opinions), revising, editing, and proofreading, for example. Write an essay modeled on Lamott's in which you narrate an experience you have had with a particular type of writing or assignment.

2. Lamott's essay is about appearances versus reality. Write an essay in which you set the record straight by exposing the myths or misperceptions people have about a particular job, place, thing, or situation. Naturally, you need to ask yourself how much of an "inside story" you can reveal based on actual experiences you have had. In other words, you know that being a lifeguard is not as romantic as most people think because you have been one. Try to create the same informative but lighthearted tone that Lamott does in her essay by paying particular attention to the language you use.

The First Sentence

IMAN HUMAYDAN

Born in Lebanon in 1956, Iman Humaydan is the author of four novels as well as numerous short stories and essays. Her work has been published in Arabic, French, German, English, Italian, and Dutch. She is also the co-founder of PEN Lebanon, an international association of writers promoting friendship and intellectual freedom, and has been its president since 2015. A trained anthropologist and researcher, Humaydan studied sociology at the American University in Beirut and is also the founder of ARRAWI, a non-profit organization that promotes freedom of expression among marginalized youth in Lebanon.

Given the tumultuous political landscape in which Humaydan has lived and worked, both regional and familial history inform her writing. For example, her novel *Wild Mulberries* (2008) draws inspiration from the tale of her grandfather's second wife, who fled to escape "the violence and power hunger of this patriarch." The following brief essay on writing was first published in Arabic in the collection *Kitabat alkitabah (Writers on Writing)* (2010); Humaydan later translated the essay into English. Here she describes an approach that is markedly different from the traditional, chronological writing process—an approach that reflects her more fragmented experience of the world.

WRITING TO DISCOVER: *What stories from your family history inspire you? Why do you find those stories inspirational? How do they inform your understanding of your home culture and ideas about the world?*

When I started rereading what I had written in the early 1980s, I was slow to recognize my writing—no doubt an indication that writing is, like a living organism, prone to growth and change. And just as we change, so does our writing, and what or how I write now may well be quite different tomorrow.

The import of the above statement is that creative writing does not have one defining characteristic. Creative writing can be done in so many different ways, with the approaches, ideas and rituals involved subject to constant change, even for the same writer.

It is not easy to talk about writing and its rituals.

Sitting with a pencil in hand (for those still using writing implements) or in front of a computer screen is one of these rituals, and only the first.

Every writer writes in his or her own way according to his or her per-   5
sonality, and there is no absolute pre-requisite to the act of sitting down and
writing. From my vantage-point, the common thread in all creative writing
is that it constitutes the only moment of certainty in the life of writers.

What truly exercises me, however, is the first sentence: how shall I
begin?

That first sentence is the torment of most writers. The Turkish Nobel
Prize laureate Orhan Pamuk claims to rewrite his first sentence 50 to 100
times. Canadian writer Margaret Atwood says that if you place your left
arm on the table and raise your right hand in the air for long enough
you will stumble on a story. When she was asked if she followed her own
advice, her answer was "No, I don't need to."

I find that what other writers counsel or suggest does not generally
hold true for me. For my part, I write on whatever is available: papers
lying in my car, paper napkins or even menus in cafes and restaurants,
the margins of newspapers, or the back of electricity bills and purchase
receipts. Going over all the ideas I jotted down earlier, I have often found
my way out of an impasse I may have reached with one of my story's
characters or plotlines.

Sometimes I begin with an idea that I've been mulling over; or a
snatch of overheard conversation; or a news item from the paper; or a
scene I have witnessed. Sometimes, just an advertising slogan glimpsed
on a billboard while driving will set off a train of thought or images in my
mind.

I go back and forth between writing by hand and using a computer.   10
Every so often, I gather everything I have jotted down—on stray pieces
of paper, in my office planner or the little writing journal I keep, as well as
on supermarket receipts and the backs of faxes that land in my office, or
on conference papers where my notations have nothing to do with what I
am listening to; even on the tickets that I get after parking my car in No
Parking spaces—something I do habitually. I recognize that this way of
proceeding exposes me to some writing "loss"—thus, for example, when
I found a fairly long piece of narration that was supposed to go into my
first novel, *B as in Beirut*, after the book had appeared.

Is this perhaps because my writing resembles my life? I wrote my first
novel during the Lebanese civil war when I went back and forth between
the two Beiruts (East and West), or between Beirut and the mountains—
hence the fragmented and unsettled nature of the writing in that story
which mirrored my life at the time.

I proceed by writing scene fragments, which I rework into a narrative structure using elements of collage and free expression, as well as
poetry. I then type into my computer all the handwritten fragments. This
fragment-gathering sometimes takes longer than I anticipate: there are
papers everywhere as I type up the various fragments separately, and only
incorporate them into the main body of the story after I have rewritten

them. The fragments thus become kernels from which an entire chapter will emerge, or I attach them to a chapter I have already written.

For me, a novel is a continuous act of construction: it takes shape incrementally, not in a linear fashion, but in a sequence of alternating and differing forms as the writing progresses. Scene fragments form the core of my characters, and these characters grow as I pursue the process of writing scenes and dialogues, in a manner reminiscent of film.

I don't write in a chronological fashion but rather in a circular one. Sometimes I go back to where I had started, and sometimes not. As I write, the question of chronology is irrelevant. I may start at the end and then go back to the beginning because there is an inner logic that I submit to when writing which has nothing to do with the sequence of events. Sequencing is a secondary consideration which I craft later. It is what I see in my mind's eye as well as the characters' situations that drive the narrative, not the unfolding of a time-line.

> **But writing about reality is quintessentially a journey and on this writing journey, we write about what we know.**

After I have incorporated the new fragments into the body of the story, I print fresh copies—it is something that I find upsetting, I mean all that paper. When I reread and edit, I do so using a hard copy of what I wrote, making corrections or revisions with a pencil. I always use a pencil, not a pen, because I am unsure that the changes I am making are final. Sometimes the manuscript will lie unfinished without my going back to it—usually a sign that there is some kind of problem with the characters or that I have led them into a situation from which I am unsure how to proceed. And so at times, I end up throwing away a lot of paper into the waste-basket, forgetting all that I have written, save for a few sentences here and there which stay with me and become the starting-point of a new piece of writing or text.

The advent of computers has of course revolutionized the writer's work. In the advanced stages of writing *B as in Beirut* I wasn't yet comfortable with computers. I wrote by hand, and then rearranged and reordered the paragraphs and their contents either physically, with a pair of scissors, or by crossing out entire chunks and rewriting. Now, I just press a key and the sequence of paragraphs is rearranged: whether that alters a writer's relationship to the text remains a question for me.

That question notwithstanding, writing is first and foremost a journey of discovery. There is of course a huge difference between reality and writing about it. But writing about reality is quintessentially a journey and on this writing journey, we write about what we know. Understanding what we know, or rather explaining it, is not as important as writing it as *we* understand it or experience it. In my new novel, currently being finished, there is a grandmother figure called Naheel to whom everyone attributes a legendary and mysterious power to influence the lives and destinies of others. I recount all of this without intervening, without trying to explain this extraordinary power of hers, or to analyze the connection between the things she says and what happens to people. I do not think it is my task to explain. That I understand what is going on in no way means that I insert myself as a narrator and explain this almost blinding force that Naheel possesses, but that I accept her and tell her as she is.

The process usually starts as a sea of ideas swirling in my head, which I know neither how to organize or set out on the page. As I said earlier, writing that first elusive sentence formally marks the beginning. I aspire to write what I know, things that are exquisitely simple. They seem obvious, and I know all about them, and yet, before a blank sheet of paper or computer screen they are hard to capture. Thus in that moment of committing to writing what I know for sure I have the feeling that I have lost all my moorings.

All of them . . . in spite of my unwavering faith in the nature of creative writing as the only instant of certainty, everything feels adrift.

This feeling of total uncertainty is the portal to both heaven and hell, 20 as the drift carries the writer in so many different directions, far exceeding the four cardinal ones, with memory, imagination, the recreating of meaning and the manipulation of word order offering an infinite number of possibilities.

When I started *B as in Beirut*, I did not know that it would turn into a novel. I just needed to unearth my own words, to give them utterance. The characters were born as the narrative developed because we cannot put all the words one has in the mouth of only one character. Making up a character is also an opportunity to say what we want and to create the dynamic interplay between people, place and time that develops with the story-line and the unfolding of events.

That much is autobiographical in the characters we create is indisputable. It is a given. We create characters as vehicles for our own utterances and no one character can possibly express everything we have to say. Sometimes, we need to express our utter lack of faith in any certainty or certitude whatsoever. In so doing, we create a fully fledged character without impeding the development of its own inner logic.

What I have just said appears contradictory.

Sometimes, we intervene in a character's place in the development of the story, and we decide whether to give it voice, or not, or whether the character is necessary to the plotline. In *B as in Beirut*, I could have bestowed speech on Josepha, one of the main protagonists. Instead I chose to disperse statements associated with her throughout the text. Perhaps this was due to the fact that she is stronger than me, and I was afraid that I would lose control of her or be unable to contain her; maybe it was because there was no way to stop talking about her and I couldn't close the door behind her, like I did with Warda, the other character who went to her death in a drowning accident or suicide in the ocean.

In my second novel, *Wild Mulberries*, the narrator, Sara, recounts her 25
story and that of her family as it unfolds in the interval between the two
world wars, which wrought major social and economic changes in Lebanon. In order to recount the history of a family, a village, and a society, I
had to come up with an all-encompassing character. Despite the fact that
Sara is nothing but an invention and does not actually exist in "real life,"
it is not impossible to conceive that she might exist.

Thus, we are able to create a character to recount reality as we see it.

In writing, we learn to be ourselves on a daily basis. With every word
that we write, we doubt the truth of its authenticity. Is it really mine? In
that sense, writing is like being born over and over again. It is as if we had
no cognitive memory, or any received knowledge. In searching for that
knowledge, we fashion our own language. While undoubtedly difficult,
that is what creative writing is about.

THINKING CRITICALLY ABOUT THE READING

1. Why do you think Humaydan titles her essay "The First Sentence"? What
   do you think of this title? Would you have chosen a different title? Why or
   why not?

2. How does Humaydan describe the relationship between her writing and her
   life? Make a list of the terms and phrases she uses to describe this relationship.

3. Humaydan has an unconventional approach to writing. Re-read the text and
   try to characterize the steps in her writing process. How does your own writing process compare?

4. According to Humaydan, how and why does a writer "recount reality as
   [they] see it" (26) through the creation of characters?

5. List a few examples of figurative language that Humaydan uses to describe
   the act of writing. How does such figurative language help her express her
   ideas about the act of writing? How does her figurative language affect you as
   a reader? How does such language shape her tone?

LANGUAGE IN ACTION

As Humaydan puts it, "that first sentence is the torment of most writers" (6). Below, you will find the opening sentences of ten well-known
novels. What do these lines convey to you? Which do you like best and
why? If you've read any of these novels, how does the first line prepare
you for the story to come? As a whole, do you notice any structural similarities or patterns when you compare these first sentences? After you
read and reflect on the lines, work with a group of three to four classmates to see if you can agree on a successful "first sentence formula."
Can your group identify any consistent characteristics among all of these
first sentences?

"Call me Ishmael."
— HERMAN MELVILLE, *Moby-Dick* (1851)

"You better not never tell nobody but God."
— ALICE WALKER, *The Color Purple* (1982)

"It was a queer, sultry summer, the summer they electrocuted the Rosenbergs, and I didn't know what I was doing in New York."
— SYLVIA PLATH, *The Bell Jar* (1963)

"We started dying before the snow, and like the snow, we continued to fall."
— LOUISE ERDRICH, *Tracks* (1988)

"He was an old man who fished alone in a skiff in the Gulf Stream and he had gone eighty-four days now without taking a fish."
— ERNEST HEMINGWAY,
The Old Man and the Sea (1952)

"It was the best of times, it was the worst of times, it was the age of wisdom, it was the age of foolishness, it was the epoch of belief, it was the epoch of incredulity, it was the season of Light, it was the season of Darkness, it was the spring of hope, it was the winter of despair."
— CHARLES DICKENS, *A Tale of Two Cities* (1859)

"All this happened, more or less."
— KURT VONNEGUT, *Slaughterhouse-Five* (1969)

"Through the fence, between the curling flower spaces, I could see them hitting."
— WILLIAM FAULKNER,
The Sound and the Fury (1929)

"It was a bright cold day in April, and the clocks were striking thirteen."
— GEORGE ORWELL, *1984* (1949)

"It is a truth universally acknowledged, that a single man in possession of a good fortune, must be in want of a wife."
— JANE AUSTEN, *Pride and Prejudice* (1813)

WRITING SUGGESTIONS

1. Choose a family story that inspires you. What central characteristic or trait does this story help to define within your family? Why is the story important to you personally? Write a brief essay that begins with your re-telling of that

family story in your own words. Then explain the story's importance to you and how it relates to your family today.

2. Throughout this essay, Humaydan comments on the nature of writing and the writing process. She describes an episodic process characterized by fragments. Unlike most Western writers—including those in this book, like Stephen King (pp. 48–52) and Anne Lamott (pp. 54–57)—Humaydan's writing process is not linear. Reflect on the writing process or processes that you've been taught through your own formal education and the process that you typically use in your own writing. How do these processes differ from Humaydan's process? Are there any similarities between your writing process and Humaydan's? If so, what are they? Write a brief essay answering these questions.

The Maker's Eye: Revising Your Own Manuscripts

Donald M. Murray

Born in Boston, Massachusetts, Donald M. Murray (1924–2006) taught writing for many years at the University of New Hampshire, his alma mater. He served as an editor at *Time* magazine, and he won the Pulitzer Prize in 1954 for editorials that appeared in the *Boston Herald*. Murray's published works include novels, short stories, poetry, and sourcebooks for teachers of writing, like *A Writer Teaches Writing: A Complete Revision* (1985), *The Craft of Revision* (1991), and *Learning by Teaching* (1982), in which he explores aspects of the writing process. *Write to Learn* (8th ed., 2004), a textbook for college composition courses, is based on Murray's belief that writers learn to write by writing, by taking a piece of writing through the whole process, from invention to revision. In the last decades of his life, Murray produced a weekly column entitled "Now and Then" for the *Boston Globe*.

In the following essay, first published in *The Writer* magazine in October 1973 and later revised for this text, Murray discusses the importance of revision to the work of the writer. Most professional writers live by the maxim that "writing is rewriting." And to rewrite or revise effectively, we need to become better readers of our own work, open to discovering new meanings, and sensitive to our use of language. Murray draws on the experiences of many writers to make a compelling argument for careful revising and editing.

WRITING TO DISCOVER: *Thinking back on your education to date, what did you think you had to do when teachers asked you to revise a piece of your writing? How did the request to revise make you feel? Write about your earliest memories of revising some of your writing. What kinds of changes do you remember making?*

When students complete a first draft, they consider the job of writing done—and their teachers too often agree. When professional writers complete a first draft, they usually feel that they are at the start of the writing process. When a draft is completed, the job of writing can begin.

That difference in attitude is the difference between amateur and professional, inexperience and experience, journeyman and craftsman. Peter F. Drucker, the prolific business writer, calls his first draft "the zero draft" — after that he can start counting. Most writers share the feeling that the first draft, and all of those which follow, are opportunities to discover what they have to say and how best they can say it.

To produce a progression of drafts, each of which says more and says it more clearly, the writer has to develop a special kind of reading skill. In school we are taught to decode what appears on the page as finished writing. Writers, however, face a different category of possibility and responsibility when they read their own drafts. To them the words on the page are never finished. Each can be changed and rearranged, can set off a chain reaction of confusion or clarified meaning. This is a different kind of reading which is possibly more difficult and certainly more exciting.

When a draft is completed, the job of writing can begin.

Writers must learn to be their own best enemy. They must accept the criticism of others and be suspicious of it; they must accept the praise of others and be even more suspicious of it. Writers cannot depend on others. They must detach themselves from their own pages so that they can apply both their caring and their craft to their own work.

Such detachment is not easy. Science-fiction writer Ray Bradbury supposedly puts each manuscript away for a year to the day and then rereads it as a stranger. Not many writers have the discipline or the time to do this. We must read when our judgment may be at its worst, when we are close to the euphoric moment of creation.

Then the writer, counsels novelist Nancy Hale, "should be critical of everything that seems to him most delightful in his style. He should excise what he most admires, because he wouldn't thus admire it if he weren't . . . in a sense protecting it from criticism." John Ciardi, the poet, adds, "The last act of the writing must be to become one's own reader. It is, I suppose, a schizophrenic process, to begin passionately and to end critically, to begin hot and to end cold; and, more important, to be passion-hot and critic-cold at the same time."

Most people think that the principal problem is that writers are too proud of what they have written. Actually, a greater problem for most professional writers is one shared by the majority of students. They are overly critical, think everything is dreadful, tear up page after page, never complete a draft, see the task as hopeless.

The writer must learn to read critically but constructively, to cut what is bad, to reveal what is good. Eleanor Estes, the children's book author, explains: "The writer must survey his work critically, coolly, as though he were a stranger to it. He must be willing to prune, expertly and hard-heartedly. At the end of each revision, a manuscript may look . . . worked over, torn apart, pinned together, added to, deleted from, words changed and words changed back. Yet the book must maintain its original freshness and spontaneity."

Most readers underestimate the amount of rewriting it usually takes to produce spontaneous reading. This is a great disadvantage to the student writer, who sees only a finished product and never watches the craftsman who takes the necessary step back, studies the work carefully, returns to the task, steps back, returns, steps back, again and again. Anthony Burgess, one of the most prolific writers in the English-speaking world, admits, "I might revise a page twenty times." Roald Dahl, the popular children's writer, states, "By the time I'm nearing the end of a story, the first part will have been reread and altered and corrected at least 150 times. . . . Good writing is essentially rewriting. I am positive of this."

Rewriting isn't virtuous. It isn't something that ought to be done. 10 It is simply something that most writers find they have to do to discover what they have to say and how to say it. It is a condition of the writer's life.

There are, however, a few writers who do little formal rewriting, primarily because they have the capacity and experience to create and review a large number of invisible drafts in their minds before they approach the page. And some writers slowly produce finished pages, performing all the tasks of revision simultaneously, page by page, rather than draft by draft. But it is still possible to see the sequence followed by most writers most of the time in rereading their own work.

Most writers scan their drafts first, reading as quickly as possible to catch the larger problems of subject and form, and then move in closer and closer as they read and write, reread and rewrite.

The first thing writers look for in their drafts is *information*. They know that a good piece of writing is built from specific, accurate, and interesting information. The writer must have an abundance of information from which to construct a readable piece of writing.

Next writers look for *meaning* in the information. The specifics must build to a pattern of significance. Each piece of specific information must carry the reader toward meaning.

Writers reading their own drafts are aware of *audience*. They put 15 themselves in the reader's situation and make sure that they deliver information which a reader wants to know or needs to know in a manner which is easily digested. Writers try to be sure that they anticipate and answer the questions a critical reader will ask when reading the piece of writing.

Writers make sure that the *form* is appropriate to the subject and the audience. Form, or genre, is the vehicle which carries meaning to the reader, but form cannot be selected until the writer has adequate information to discover its significance and an audience which needs or wants that meaning.

Once writers are sure the form is appropriate, they must then look at the *structure*, the order of what they have written. Good writing is built on a solid framework of logic, argument, narrative, or motivation which runs through the entire piece of writing and holds it together. This is the time when many writers find it most effective to outline as a way of visualizing the hidden spine by which the piece of writing is supported.

The element on which writers may spend a majority of their time is *development*. Each section of a piece of writing must be adequately developed. It must give readers enough information so that they are satisfied. How much information is enough? That's as difficult as asking how much garlic belongs in a salad. It must be done to taste, but most beginning writers underdevelop, underestimating the reader's hunger for information.

As writers solve development problems, they often have to consider questions of *dimension*. There must be a pleasing and effective proportion among all the parts of the piece of writing. There is a continual process of subtracting and adding to keep the piece of writing in balance.

Finally, writers have to listen to their own voices. *Voice* is the force 20 which drives a piece of writing forward. It is an expression of the writer's authority and concern. It is what is between the words on the page, what glues the piece of writing together. A good piece of writing is always marked by a consistent, individual voice.

As writers read and reread, write and rewrite, they move closer and closer to the page until they are doing line-by-line editing. Writers read their own pages with infinite care. Each sentence, each line, each clause, each phrase, each word, each mark of punctuation, each section of white space between the type has to contribute to the clarification of meaning.

Slowly the writer moves from word to word, looking through language to see the subject. As a word is changed, cut, or added, as a construction is rearranged, all the words used before that moment and all those that follow that moment must be considered and reconsidered.

Writers often read aloud at this stage of the editing process, muttering or whispering to themselves, calling on the ear's experience with language. Does this sound right—or that? Writers edit, shifting back and forth from eye to page to ear to page. I find I must do this careful editing in short runs, no more than fifteen or twenty minutes at a stretch, or I become too kind with myself. I begin to see what I hope is on the page, not what actually is on the page.

This sounds tedious if you haven't done it, but actually it is fun. Making something right is immensely satisfying, for writers begin to learn what they are writing about by writing. Language leads them to meaning, and there is the joy of discovery, of understanding, of making meaning clear as the writer employs the technical skills of language.

Words have double meanings, even triple and quadruple meanings. 25 Each word has its own potential of connotation and denotation. And when writers rub one word against the other, they are often rewarded with a sudden insight, an unexpected clarification.

The maker's eye moves back and forth from word to phrase to sentence to paragraph to sentence to phrase to word. The maker's eye sees the need for variety and balance, for a firmer structure, for a more appropriate form. It peers into the interior of the paragraph, looking for coherence, unity, and emphasis, which make meaning clear.

I learned something about this process when my first bifocals were prescribed. I had ordered a larger section of the reading portion of the glass because of my work, but even so, I could not contain my eyes within this new limit of vision. And I still find myself taking off my glasses and bending my nose toward the page, for my eyes unconsciously flick back and forth across the page, back to another page, forward to still another, as I try to see each evolving line in relation to every other line.

When does this process end? Most writers agree with the great Russian writer Tolstoy, who said, "I scarcely ever reread my published writings, if by chance I come across a page, it always strikes me: all this must be rewritten; this is how I should have written it."

The maker's eye is never satisfied, for each word has the potential to ignite new meaning. This article has been twice written all the way through the writing process. . . . Now it is to be republished in a book. The editors made a few small suggestions, and then I read it with my maker's eye. Now it has been re-edited, re-revised, re-read, and re-re-edited, for each piece of writing to the writer is full of potential and alternatives.

A piece of writing is never finished. It is delivered to a deadline, torn   30 out of the typewriter on demand, sent off with a sense of accomplishment and shame and pride and frustration. If only there were a couple more days, time for just another run at it, perhaps then. . . .

THINKING CRITICALLY ABOUT THE READING

1. What are the essential differences between revising and editing? What types of language concerns are dealt with at each stage? Why is it important to revise before editing?

2. According to Murray, at what point(s) in the writing process do writers become concerned about the individual words they are using? What do you think Murray means when he says in paragraph 24 that "language leads [writers] to meaning"?

3. How does Murray define *information* and *meaning* (13–14)? Why is the distinction between the two terms important?

4. The phrase "the maker's eye" appears in Murray's title and in several places throughout the essay. What do you suppose he means by this? Consider how the maker's eye could be different from the reader's eye.

5. According to Murray, when is a piece of writing finished? What, for him, is the function of deadlines?

6. What does Murray see as the connection between reading and writing? How does reading help the writer? What should writers be looking for in their reading? What kinds of writing techniques or strategies does Murray use in

his essay? Why should we read a novel or magazine article differently than we would a draft of one of our own essays?

7. According to Murray, writers look for information, meaning, audience, form, structure, development, dimension, and voice in their drafts. What rationale or logic do you see, if any, in the way Murray has ordered these items? Are these the kinds of concerns you have when reading your drafts? Explain.

8. Murray notes that writers often reach a stage in their editing where they read aloud, "muttering or whispering to themselves, calling on the ear's experience with language" (23). What exactly do you think writers are listening for when they read aloud? Try reading several paragraphs of Murray's essay aloud. Explain what you learned about his writing. Have you ever read your own writing aloud? If so, what did you discover?

LANGUAGE IN ACTION

Carefully read the opening four paragraphs of Annie Dillard's "Living Like Weasels," which is taken from *Teaching a Stone to Talk* (1982). Using two different color pens, first circle the subject and underline the verb in each main clause in one color, and then circle the subject and underline the verb in each subordinate clause with the other. What does this exercise reveal about Dillard's diction (nouns and verbs) and sentence structure? (Glossary: *Diction*)

A weasel is wild. Who knows what he thinks? He sleeps in his underground den, his tail draped over his nose. Sometimes he lives in his den for two days without leaving. Outside, he stalks rabbits, mice, muskrats, and birds, killing more bodies than he can eat warm, and often dragging the carcasses home. Obedient to instinct, he bites his prey at the neck, either splitting the jugular vein at the throat or crunching the brain at the base of the skull, and he does not let go. One naturalist refused to kill a weasel who was socketed into his hand deeply as a rattlesnake. The man could in no way pry the tiny weasel off, and he had to walk half a mile to water, the weasel dangling from his palm, and soak him off like a stubborn label.

And once, says Ernest Thompson Seton—once, a man shot an eagle out of the sky. He examined the eagle and found the dry skull of a weasel fixed by the jaws to his throat. The supposition is that the eagle had pounced on the weasel and the weasel swiveled and bit as instinct taught him, tooth to neck, and nearly won. I would like to have seen that eagle from the air a few weeks or months before he was shot: was the whole weasel still attached to his feathered throat, a fur pendant? Or did the eagle eat what he could reach, gutting the living weasel with his talons before his breast, bending his beak, cleaning the beautiful airborne bones?

I have been reading about weasels because I saw one last week. I startled a weasel who startled me, and we exchanged a long glance.

WRITING SUGGESTIONS

1. Why do you suppose teachers report that revision is the most difficult stage in the writing process for their students? What is it about revision that makes it difficult, or at least makes people perceive it as being difficult? Write an essay in which you explore your own experiences with revision. You may find it helpful to review what you wrote for the Writing to Discover prompt at the beginning of this essay.

2. Writing about pressing social issues usually requires a clear statement of a particular problem and the precise definition of critical terms. For example, if you were writing about the increasing number of people being kept alive by machines, you would need to examine the debate surrounding the legal and medical definitions of the word *death*. Debates continue about the meanings of other controversial terms, such as *morality, minority* (ethnic), *alcoholism, racism, sexual harassment, life* (as in the abortion issue), *pornography, liberal, gay, censorship, conservative, remedial, insanity, literacy, political correctness, assisted suicide, lying, high crimes and misdemeanors, kidnapping* (as in custody disputes), and *immigrant*. Select one of these words or one of your own. After carefully researching some of the controversial people, situations, and events surrounding your word, write an essay in which you discuss the problems associated with the term and its definition.

How to Mark a Book

MORTIMER ADLER

Writer, editor, and educator Mortimer Adler (1902–2001) was born in New York City. A high school dropout, Adler completed the undergraduate program at Columbia University in three years, but he did not graduate because he refused to take the mandatory swimming test. Adler is recognized for his editorial work on the *Encyclopaedia Britannica* and for his leadership of the Great Books Program at the University of Chicago, where adults from all walks of life gathered twice a month to read and discuss the classics.

However, Adler's definition of "great" is no stranger to controversy. In a 1990 interview, he justified the exclusion of African American novels from the list by asserting that "I think probably in the next century there will be some Black that writes a great book, but there hasn't been so far." Leading African American literary scholars like Henry Louis Gates Jr. and Leon Forrest challenged Adler's exclusion of prominent works by black Americans, expressing incredulity about any definition of "greatness" that would exclude works by Fredrick Douglass, W. E. B. Du Bois, Francis Harper, Zora Neal Hurston, and Ralph Ellison, to name a few. In other words, Adler's interpretation of a single word sparked a debate not only about the practice of reading, but about the power of language — a theme explored later in this text.

In the following essay, which first appeared in the *Saturday Review of Literature* in 1940, Adler offers a timeless lesson: He explains how to take full ownership of a book by marking it up, by making it "a part of yourself."

WRITING TO DISCOVER: *Before you read, look up Adler's "Great Books" reading list, which was originally published with this essay. Have you read any of the works on the list? If so, did that work or those works strike you as great? If not, what books have spoken to you and why? How do you define a great book?*

You know you have to read "between the lines" to get the most out of anything. I want to persuade you to do something equally important in the course of your reading. I want to persuade you to "write between the lines." Unless you do, you are not likely to do the most efficient kind of reading.

I contend, quite bluntly, that marking up a book is not an act of mutilation but of love.

You shouldn't mark up a book which isn't yours. Librarians (or your friends) who lend you books expect you to keep them clean, and you should. If you decide that I am right about the usefulness of marking books, you will have to buy them. Most of the world's great books are available today in reprint editions.

There are two ways in which one can own a book. The first is the property right you establish by paying for it, just as you pay for clothes and furniture. But this act of purchase is only the prelude to possession. Full ownership comes only when you have made it a part of yourself, and the best way to make yourself a part of it is by writing in it. An illustration may make the point clear. You buy a beefsteak and transfer it from the butcher's icebox to your own. But you do not own the beefsteak in the most important sense until you consume it and get it into your bloodstream. I am arguing that books, too, must be absorbed in your bloodstream to do you any good.

Confusion about what it means to *own* a book leads people to a false reverence for paper, binding, and type—a respect for the physical thing—the craft of the printer rather than the genius of the author. They forget that it is possible for a man to acquire the idea, to possess the beauty, which a great book contains, without staking

I contend, quite bluntly, that marking up a book is not an act of mutilation but of love.

his claim by pasting his bookplate inside the cover. Having a fine library doesn't prove that its owner has a mind enriched by books; it proves nothing more than that he, his father, or his wife, was rich enough to buy them.

There are three kinds of book owners. The first has all the standard sets and best-sellers—unread, untouched. (This deluded individual owns woodpulp and ink, not books.) The second has a great many books—a few of them read through, most of them dipped into, but all of them as clean and shiny as the day they were bought. (This person would probably like to make books his own, but is restrained by a false respect for their physical appearance.) The third has a few books or many—every one of them dog-eared and dilapidated, shaken and loosened by continual use, marked and scribbled in from front to back. (This man owns books.)

Is it false respect, you may ask, to preserve intact and unblemished a beautifully printed book, an elegantly bound edition? Of course not. I'd no more scribble all over a first edition of *Paradise Lost* than I'd give my baby a set of crayons and an original Rembrandt! I wouldn't mark up a painting or a statue. Its soul, so to speak, is inseparable from its body. And the beauty of a rare edition or of a richly manufactured volume is like that of a painting or a statue.

But the soul of a book *can* be separated from its body. A book is more like the score of a piece of music than it is like a painting. No great musician confuses a symphony with the printed sheets of music. Arturo Toscanini reveres Brahms, but Toscanini's score of the C-minor Symphony is so thoroughly marked up that no one but the maestro himself can read it. The reason why a great conductor makes notations on his musical scores — marks them up again and again each time he returns to study them — is the reason why you should mark your books. If your respect for magnificent binding or typography gets in the way, buy yourself a cheap edition and pay your respects to the author.

Why is marking up a book indispensable to reading? First, it keeps you awake. (And I don't mean merely conscious; I mean wide awake.) In the second place, reading, if it is active, is thinking, and thinking tends to express itself in words, spoken or written. The marked book is usually the thought-through book. Finally, writing helps you remember the thoughts you had, or the thoughts the author expressed. Let me develop these three points.

If reading is to accomplish anything more than passing time, it must   10 be active. You can't let your eyes glide across the lines of a book and come up with an understanding of what you have read. Now an ordinary piece of light fiction, like say, *Gone with the Wind*, doesn't require the most active kind of reading. The books you read for pleasure can be read in a state of relaxation, and nothing is lost. But a great book, rich in ideas and beauty, a book that raises and tries to answer great fundamental questions, demands the most active reading of which you are capable. You don't absorb the ideas of John Dewey[1] the way you absorb the crooning of Mr. Vallee.[2] You have to reach for them. That you cannot do while you're asleep.

If, when you've finished reading a book, the pages are filled with your notes, you know that you read actively. The most famous active reader of great books I know is President Hutchins, of the University of Chicago. He also has the hardest schedule of business activities of any man I know. He invariably reads with a pencil, and sometimes, when he picks up a book and pencil in the evening, he finds himself, instead of making intelligent notes, drawing what he calls "caviar factories" on the margins. When that happens, he puts the book down. He knows he's too tired to read, and he's just wasting time.

But, you may ask, why is writing necessary? Well, the physical act of writing, with your own hand, brings words and sentences more sharply before your mind and preserves them better in your memory. To set down your reaction to important words and sentences you have read, and the questions they have raised in your mind, is to preserve those reactions and sharpen those questions.

---

[1] John Dewey (1859–1952) was an educational philosopher who had a profound influence on learning through experimentation. — Eds.

[2] Rudy Vallee (1901–1986) was a popular singer of the 1920s and '30s, famous for his crooning high notes. — Eds.

Even if you wrote on a scratch pad, and threw the paper away when you had finished writing, your grasp of the book would be surer. But you don't have to throw the paper away. The margins (top and bottom, as well as side), the end-papers, the very space between the lines, are all available. They aren't sacred. And, best of all, your marks and notes become an integral part of the book and stay there forever. You can pick up the book the following week or year, and there are all your points of agreement, disagreement, doubt, and inquiry. It's like resuming an interrupted conversation with the advantage of being able to pick up where you left off.

And that is exactly what reading a book should be: a conversation between you and the author. Presumably he knows more about the subject than you do; naturally, you'll have the proper humility as you approach him. But don't let anybody tell you that a reader is supposed to be solely on the receiving end. Understanding is a two-way operation; learning doesn't consist in being an empty receptacle. The learner has to question himself and question the teacher. He even has to argue with the teacher, once he understands what the teacher is saying. And marking a book is literally an expression of your differences, or agreements of opinion, with the author.

There are all kinds of devices for marking a book intelligently and   15
fruitfully. Here's the way I do it:

1. *Underlining:* of major points, of important or forceful statements.
2. *Vertical lines at the margin:* to emphasize a statement already underlined.
3. *Star, asterisk, or other doo-dad at the margin:* to be used sparingly, to emphasize the ten or twenty most important statements in the book. (You may want to fold the bottom corner of each page on which you use such marks. It won't hurt the sturdy paper on which most modern books are printed, and you will be able to take the book off the shelf at any time and, by opening it at the folded-corner page, refresh your recollection of the book.)
4. *Numbers in the margin:* to indicate the sequence of points the author makes in developing a single argument.
5. *Numbers of other pages in the margin:* to indicate where else in the   20
book the author made points relevant to the point marked; to tie up the ideas in a book, which, though they may be separated by many pages, belong together.
6. *Circling:* of key words or phrases.
7. *Writing in the margin, or at the top or bottom of the page, for the sake of:* recording questions (and perhaps answers) which a passage raised in your mind; reducing a complicated discussion to a simple statement; recording the sequence of major points right through the book. I use the end-papers at the back of the book to make a personal index of the author's points in the order of their appearance.

The front end-papers are, to me, the most important. Some people reserve them for a fancy bookplate. I reserve them for fancy thinking. After I have finished reading the book and making my personal index on the back end-papers, I turn to the front and try to outline the book, not page by page, or point by point (I've already done that at the back), but as an integrated structure, with a basic unity and an order of parts. This outline is, to me, the measure of my understanding of the work.

If you're a die-hard anti-book-marker, you may object that the margins, the space between the lines, and the end-papers don't give you room enough. All right. How about using a scratch pad slightly smaller than the page-size of the book—so that the edges of the sheets won't protrude? Make your index, outlines, and even your notes on the pad, and then insert these sheets permanently inside the front and back covers of the book.

Or, you may say that this business of marking books is going to slow   25
up your reading. It probably will. That's one of the reasons for doing it. Most of us have been taken in by the notion that speed of reading is a measure of our intelligence. There is no such thing as the right speed for intelligent reading. Some things should be read quickly and effortlessly, and some should be read slowly and even laboriously. The sign of intelligence in reading is the ability to read different things differently according to their worth. In the case of good books, the point is not to see how many of them you can get through, but rather how many can get through you—how many you can make your own. A few friends are better than a thousand acquaintances. If this be your aim, as it should be, you will not be impatient if it takes more time and effort to read a great book than it does a newspaper.

You may have one final objection to marking books. You can't lend them to your friends because nobody else can read them without being distracted by your notes. Furthermore, you won't want to lend them because a marked copy is a kind of intellectual diary, and lending it is almost like giving your mind away.

If your friend wishes to read your *Plutarch's Lives, Shakespeare,* or *The Federalist Papers,* tell him gently but firmly to buy a copy. You will lend him your car or your coat—but your books are as much a part of you as your head or your heart.

THINKING CRITICALLY ABOUT THE READING

1. According to Adler, what is the benefit of "marking" a book? How does marking a book create a "conversation"?
2. In paragraph 6, Adler says there are "three kinds of book owners." How does he characterize these three kinds? Do you agree with his characterization?

3. What kinds of devices do you use for "marking a book intelligently and fruit-fully" (15)? How useful do you find these devices?

4. What does Adler mean in paragraph 8 when he writes: "the soul of a book can be separated from its body"? What type of figurative language is he using here? What other figurative language does he use to describe the act of reading? Why do you think he chooses such language?

5. Adler makes an analogy that links reading books with the statement "A few friends are better than a thousand acquaintances" (25). Explain how this analogy works. Why is this analogy important to Adler's overall argument? (Glossary: *Analogy*)

6. What does Adler mean by the phrase "read actively" (11)?

LANGUAGE IN ACTION

Occasionally, literature that is considered great by some is considered offensive by others. Each year, a number of books are banned or challenged for a variety of reasons centered on their use of language. Visit the American Library Association (ALA) website page on banned and challenged books (http://www.ala.org/advocacy/bbooks) and explore the lists of books that have been banned or challenged. Have you read any of these books? If you have, can you figure out why that book was or those books were banned or challenged?

After you've considered your own experiences with banned or challenged books, compare them to Adler's reading list of "Great Books," which was originally published alongside the essay above and which you can now view online on Goodreads: see https://www.goodreads.com/list/show/120742.Mortimer_J_Adler_s_reading_list. Are any of the books on Adler's reading list also books that have been banned or challenged? Why do you think this is?

WRITING SUGGESTIONS

1. Adler devotes a large portion of his essay to persuading his audience that marking books is a worthwhile task. Drawing on some of Adler's techniques (simile, analogy, personification), write a persuasive essay in which you instruct your audience about how to do something they do not necessarily wish to do or they do not think they need to do. For instance, before explaining how to buy the best robot vacuum, you may need to convince readers that they *should* buy a robot vacuum.

2. Revisit your response to the "Writing to Discover" assignment above and spend more time thinking about a book, poem, or short story that has affected you. Would you characterize this literary work as "great"? Are there other words that you would use to characterize the work instead? Write an essay in which you explain why the work of your choosing is either "great" or another word that you prefer to use to characterize it. Be sure to use specific passages from the work to support your argument and to explain why this work is significant to you.

4

WRITING WITH SOURCES

WHAT DOES IT MEAN TO WRITE WITH SOURCES?

Some of the writing you do in college will be experiential—that is, based on your personal experiences—but many of your college assignments will call upon you to do some research, to write with sources. While most of us have had some experience with basic research practices—locating and evaluating print and online sources, taking notes from those sources, and documenting those sources—we have not learned how to integrate these sources effectively and purposefully into our papers. (For more information on basic research and documentation practices, see Chapter 5, "A Brief Guide to Writing a Research Paper.") Your purpose in writing with sources is not to present a collection of quotations that show you can report what others have said about your topic. Your goal is to analyze, evaluate, and synthesize the materials you have researched so that you can take ownership of your topic. You learn how to view the results of research from your own perspective and arrive at an informed opinion of your topic. In short, you become a participant in a conversation with your sources about your topic.

To help you on your way, this chapter provides advice on (1) summarizing, paraphrasing, and quoting sources, (2) integrating summaries, paraphrases, and quotations into the text of your paper using signal phrases, and (3) avoiding plagiarism when writing with sources. In addition, one student paper models different ways of engaging meaningfully with outside sources and of reflecting that engagement in writing.

WRITE WITH SOURCES

Each time that you introduce an outside source into your paper, be sure that you are using that source in a purposeful way. Outside sources can be used to

- support your thesis and main points with statements from noted authorities,
- offer memorable wording of key terms or ideas,

- extend your ideas by introducing new information, and
- articulate opposing positions for you to argue against.

Consider the following passage from "Why the U.S. Needs an Official Language," in which Mauro E. Mujica uses outside sources to present the position that he will ultimately argue against.

> Historically, the need to speak and understand English has served as an important incentive for immigrants to learn the language and assimilate into the mainstream of American society. For the last 30 years, this idea has been turned on its head. Expecting immigrants to learn English has been called "racist." Marta Jimenez, an attorney for the Mexican American Legal Defense and Educational Fund, speaks of "the historical use of English in the United States as a tool of oppression."
>
> Groups such as the National Association for Bilingual Education complain about the "restrictive goal" of having immigrant children learn in English. The former mayor of Miami, Maurice Ferre, dismissed the idea of even a bilingual future for the city. "We're talking about Spanish as a main form of communication, as an official language," he averred. "Not on the way to English."
>
> Perhaps this change is best illustrated in the evolving views of the League of United Latin American Citizens (LULAC). Started in 1929, the group was originally pro-English and pro-assimilation. One of the founding aims and purposes of LULAC was "to foster the acquisition and facile use of the Official Language of our country that we may hereby equip ourselves and our families for the fullest enjoyment of our rights and privileges and the efficient discharge of our duties and obligations to this, our country." By the 1980s the executive director of LULAC Arnoldo Torres, could proudly proclaim, "We cannot assimilate and we won't!"

By letting the opposition articulate their position themselves, Mujica reduces the possibility of being criticized for misrepresenting his opponents while at the same time sets himself up to give strong voice to his belief that the United States should declare English its official language.

Sometimes source material is too long and detailed to be quoted directly in its entirety. In such cases, a writer will choose to summarize or paraphrase the material in his or her own words before introducing it in an essay. For example, notice how Janet Holmes summarizes two lengthy reports about male-female discourse in the workplace for use in her essay "Women Talk Too Much" that appeared in *Language Myths* in 1999.

> Despite the widespread belief that women talk more than men, most of the available evidence suggests just the opposite. When women and men are together, it is the men who talk most. Two Canadian researchers, Deborah James and Janice Drakich, reviewed sixty-three studies which examined the amount of talk used by American women and men in different contexts. Women talked more than men in only two studies.

In New Zealand, too, research suggests that men generally dominate the talking time. Margaret Franken compared the amount of talk used by female and male "experts" assisting a female TV host to interview well-known public figures. In a situation where each of three interviewers was entitled to a third of the interviewers' talking time, the men took more than half on every occasion.

Here Holmes introduces each summary with a signal phrase — "Two Canadian researchers, Deborah James and Janice Drakich, reviewed" and "Margaret Franken compared." Holmes concludes each summary with a pointed statement of the researchers' conclusion.

LEARN TO SUMMARIZE, PARAPHRASE, AND QUOTE FROM YOUR SOURCES

When taking notes from your sources, you must decide whether to summarize, paraphrase, or quote directly. The approach you take is largely determined by the content of the source passage and the way you envision using it in your paper. Each of these techniques — summarizing, paraphrasing, and quoting — will help you better incorporate source material into your essays. Making use of all three of these techniques, rather than relying on only one or two, will keep your text varied and interesting. In most cases it is better to summarize or paraphrase material from sources — which by definition means using your own words — instead of quoting verbatim (word for word). Capturing an idea in your own words ensures that you have thought about and understood what your source is saying.

Summary

When you *summarize* material from one of your sources, you capture in condensed form the essential idea of a passage, an article, or an entire chapter. Summaries are particularly useful when you are working with lengthy, detailed arguments or long passages of narrative or descriptive background information in which the details are not germane to the overall thrust of your paper. You simply want to capture the essence of the passage because you are confident that your readers will readily understand the point being made or do not need to be convinced about its validity. Because you are distilling information, a summary is always shorter than the original; often a chapter or more can be reduced to a paragraph, or several paragraphs to a sentence or two. Remember in writing a summary you should use your own wording.

Consider the following paragraphs from Gordon Allport's "The Language of Prejudice" which appears on pages 350–359 of this text.

Some labels such as "blind man," are exceedingly salient and powerful. They tend to prevent alternative classification, or even cross-classification. Ethnic labels are often of this type, particularly if they refer to some highly visible feature, e.g., Negro, Oriental. They resemble the labels that point to some outstanding incapacity—*feeble-minded, cripple, blind man*. Let us call such symbols "labels of primary potency." These symbols act like shrieking sirens, deafening us to all finer discriminations that we might otherwise perceive. Even though the blindness of one man and the darkness of pigmentation of another may be defining attributes for some purposes, they are irrelevant and "noisy" for others.

Most people are unaware of this basic law of language—that every label applied to a given person refers properly only to one aspect of his nature. You may correctly say that a certain man is *human, a philanthropist, a Chinese, a physician, an athlete.* A given person may be all of these; but the chances are that *Chinese* stands out in your mind as the symbol of primary potency. Yet neither this nor any other classificatory label can refer to the whole of a man's nature. (Only his proper name can do so.)

A student wishing to capture the gist of Allport's point without repeating his detailed explanation wrote the following summary.

Allport warns about the dangers of using labels—especially ethnic labels—because of their power to distort our perceptions of other human beings.

Paraphrase

When you *paraphrase* material from a source, you restate the information in your own words instead of quoting directly. Unlike a summary, which gives a brief overview of the essential information in the original, a paraphrase seeks to maintain the same level of detail as the original to aid readers in understanding or believing the information presented. A paraphrase presents the original information in approximately the same number of words but with different wording. To put it another way, your paraphrase should accurately present ideas in the original, but it should not use the same words or sentence structure as the original. Even though you are using your own words in a paraphrase, it's important to remember that you are borrowing ideas and therefore must acknowledge the source of these ideas with a citation.

How would you paraphrase the following passage from "Selection, Slanting, and Charged Language" by Newman P. and Genevieve B. Birk, which appears on pages 285–293 of this text?

When we put our knowledge into words, a second process of selection, the process of slanting, takes place. Just as there is something, a rather mysterious principle of selection, which chooses for us what we will notice, and what will then become our knowledge, there is also a principle which operates, with or without our awareness, to select certain facts and feelings from our store of knowledge, and to choose the words and the emphasis that we shall use to communicate our meaning.

Note how one student paraphrased this passage:

Every time we communicate information and ideas, we engage in a secondary process known as slanting. An even earlier selection process, that of acquiring knowledge, remains something of a mystery because who can say why we notice what we do and why it becomes a part of what we know. Slanting, a conscious or subconscious process, further selects the facts and emotions we convey; it finds not only the words we use but also the way we emphasize them when we communicate.

Notice how carefully the student captures the essence of the Birks' ideas in her own words as well as her own sentence structures. Capturing an idea in your own words demonstrates that you have thought about and understood what your source is saying.

Direct Quotation

When you *quote* a source directly, you copy the words of your source exactly, putting all quoted material in quotation marks. When you take a note that is a direct quotation, check the passage carefully for accuracy, including punctuation and capitalization. Be selective about what you choose to quote. Reserve direct quotation for important ideas stated memorably, for especially clear explanations by authorities, and for arguments by proponents of a particular position in their own words.

Consider, for example, the following passage quoted directly from William Zinsser's essay "Simplicity," emphasizing the importance—and current rarity—of clear, concise writing.

"Clutter is the disease of American writing. We are a society strangling in unnecessary words, circular constructions, pompous frills, and meaningless jargon."

On occasion you'll find a useful passage with some memorable wording in it. Avoid the temptation to quote the whole passage; instead, try combining summary or paraphrase with direct quotation.

Consider, for example, the following excerpt from a student paper about Martin Luther King Jr.'s "Letter from Birmingham Jail." Notice that the student carefully added quotation marks around all the words that she borrowed directly from the original source.

King is quick to answer his fellow clergy who question his "willingness to break laws." He addresses their concerns by explaining that there are "just and unjust" laws. King strongly believes that we all have a "legal" and "moral responsibility to obey just laws" as well as "a moral responsibility to disobey unjust laws."

INTEGRATE BORROWED MATERIAL INTO YOUR TEXT

Being familiar with the material in your notes will help you decide how to integrate your sources into your drafts. Though it is not necessary to use all of your notes, nor to use them all at once in your first draft, you do need to know which ones support your thesis, extend your ideas, offer better wording of your ideas, and reveal the opinions of noted authorities. Occasionally you will want to use notes that include ideas contrary to your own so that you can rebut them in your own argument. Once you have analyzed your notes, you may even alter your thesis slightly in light of the information and ideas you have discovered.

Whenever you want to use borrowed material, be it a quotation, a paraphrase, or summary, your goal always is to integrate these sources smoothly and logically so as not to disrupt the flow of your paper or confuse your readers. It is best to introduce borrowed material with a *signal phrase*, which alerts readers that borrowed information is about to be presented.

SELECTING APPROPRIATE SIGNAL PHRASES. A signal phrase minimally consists of the author's name and a verb (e.g., *Michael Pollan contends*). Signal phrases help readers better follow your train of thought. When you integrate a quote, paraphrase, or summary into your paper, vary your signal phrases and choose verbs for the signal phrases that accurately convey the tone and intent of the writer you are citing. If a writer is arguing, use the verb *argues* (or *asserts, claims,* or *contends*); if a writer is contesting a particular position or fact, use the verb *contests* (or *denies, disputes, refutes,* or *rejects*). Verbs that are specific to the situation in your paper will bring your readers into the intellectual debate (and avoid the monotony of all-purpose verbs like *says* or *writes*). The following examples illustrate how you can vary signal phrases to add precision and interest to your writing:

> Jimmy Santiago Baca confesses that "at seventeen I still didn't know how to read" (p. 134).

> Using a series of vivid examples, Deborah Tannen reminds us that "metamessages—intended or not—can reside in just about any aspect of digital communication" (p. 266).

> Anne Lamott encourages aspiring writers to give up their fears of first drafts because "few writers really know what they are doing until they've done it" (p. 55).

> "Hate, like much of human feeling, is not rational," argues Andrew Sullivan, "but it usually has its reasons. And it cannot be understood, let alone condemned, without knowing them" (p. 339).

> Bharati Mukherjee asserts that "the price that the immigrant willingly pays, and that the exile avoids, is the trauma of self-transformation" (p. 206).

Sara Nović argues that "unless we actively work to restore value to culture over convenience, Deaf people and American Sign Language will be but two of many casualties in the wake of an all-powerful monoculture" (p. 201).

Other verbs that you should keep in mind when constructing signal phrases include the following:

acknowledges	compares	grants	reasons
adds	confirms	implies	reports
admits	declares	insists	responds
believes	endorses	points out	suggests

Well-chosen signal phrases help you integrate quotations, paraphrases, and summaries into the flow of your paper. Besides, signal phrases let your reader know who is speaking and, in the case of summaries and paraphrases, exactly where your ideas end and someone else's begin. Never confuse your reader with a quotation that appears suddenly without introduction. Unannounced quotations leave your reader wondering how the quoted material relates to the point you are trying to make. Look at the following example from the first draft of a student's paper on the pros and cons of social networking on Facebook. The quotation is from Daniel Lyons's article "The High Price of Facebook," which appeared May 15, 2010, on *Newsweek.com.*

Unannounced Quotation

Many Facebook users worry that the privacy settings are not clear enough to protect people. "I also suspect that whatever Facebook has done so far to invade our privacy, it's only the beginning. Which is why I'm considering deactivating my account. Facebook is a handy site, but I'm freaked out by the idea that my information is in the hands of people I don't trust" (Lyons). But we should remember that every time a privacy setting is changed, websites like Gizmodo.com and Slate.com alert users to the changes. Viral copy-and-paste status updates start circulating on Facebook notifying users of the privacy changes and the need to make updates to your profile if necessary. All of the criticisms Facebook is subjected to due to its rapid growth and evolution are overblown because users who are not satisfied with their level of privacy can simply delete personal information from their profiles, or routinely check their privacy settings.

In the following revision, the student integrates the quotation into the text by means of a signal phrase and in a number of other ways as well. By giving the name of the writer being quoted, referring to his authority on the subject, and noting that the writer is speaking from experience, the student provides more context so that the reader can better understand how this quotation fits into the discussion.

Integrated Quotation

Many Facebook users worry that the privacy settings are not clear enough to protect people. Tech-savvy commentator Daniel Lyons, a senior editor at *Forbes* magazine, has joined the chorus of critics. He warns, "I also suspect that whatever Facebook has done so far to invade our privacy, it's only the beginning. Which is why I'm considering deactivating my account. Facebook is a handy site, but I'm freaked out by the idea that my information is in the hands of people I don't trust" (Lyons). But we should remember that every time a privacy setting is changed, websites like Gizmodo.com and Slate.com alert users to the changes. Viral copy-and-paste status updates start circulating on Facebook notifying users of the privacy changes and the need to make updates to your profile if necessary. All of the criticisms Facebook is subjected to due to its rapid growth and evolution are overblown because users who are not satisfied with their level of privacy can simply delete personal information from their profiles or routinely check their privacy settings.

AVOID PLAGIARISM

The importance of honesty and accuracy in working with outside sources—whether print, digital, or personal interview or correspondence—cannot be stressed enough. In working closely with the ideas and words of others, intellectual honesty demands that we distinguish between what we borrow—acknowledging it with a citation—and what is our own. Any material borrowed word for word must be placed within quotation marks and be properly cited. Any idea, explanation, or argument you have paraphrased or summarized must be properly cited, and it must be clear where the paraphrase or summary begins and ends. In short, to use someone else's ideas, whether in their original form or in an altered form, without proper acknowledgment is to be guilty of **plagiarism**.

You must acknowledge and document the source of your information whenever you do any of the following:

- quote a source exactly, word for word
- paraphrase or summarize information and ideas from a source
- cite statistics, tables, charts, graphs, or other visuals

You do *not* need to document the following types of information:

- your own observations, experiences, ideas, and opinions
- factual information available in a number of reference works (information known as "common knowledge")
- proverbs, sayings, or familiar quotations

For a discussion of MLA style for in-text documentation practices, see pages 110–112.

The Council of Writing Program Administrators offers the following helpful definition of *plagiarism* in academic settings for administrators, faculty, and students: "In an instructional setting, plagiarism occurs when a writer deliberately uses someone else's language, ideas, or other (not common knowledge) material without acknowledging its source."

Accusations of plagiarism can be upheld even if plagiarism is unintentional. A little attention and effort can help to eliminate this possibility. While taking notes, check and recheck all direct quotations against the wording of the original, and be sure you've labeled them clearly as quotations. Double-check your paraphrases to be sure that you have not used the writer's wording or sentence structure.

While writing your paper, make sure that you put quotation marks around material taken verbatim, and double-check the text against the original to make sure that the quotation is accurate. When using paraphrases or summaries, be sure to cite the source.

The sections that follow provide examples of appropriate use of quotation, paraphrase, and summary.

USING QUOTATION MARKS FOR LANGUAGE BORROWED DIRECTLY.
Again, when you use another person's exact words or sentences, you must enclose the borrowed language in quotation marks. Even if you cite the source, you are guilty of plagiarism if you fail to use quotation marks. The following example demonstrates both plagiarism and a correct citation for a direct quotation.

Original Source

Public language matters. Words are free, and every politician and journalist and citizen can draw on an unlimited supply of them. But there are days when the right words are all that count, and it is the speaker who can find them who determines what happens next. Over time, leaders and commentators and activists with empathy and eloquence can use words not just to exploit the public mood but to shape it. And the result? Peace, prosperity, progress, inequality, prejudice, persecution, war. Public language matters.

> —Mark Thompson, *Enough Said: What's Gone Wrong with the Language of Politics,* New York: St. Martin's, 2016, page 1.

Plagiarism

Mark Thompson, president and CEO of The New York Times Company, points out that public language matters. Words are free, and every politician and journalist and citizen can draw on an unlimited supply of them. But there are days when the right words are all that count, and it is the speaker who can find them who determines what happens next. Over time, leaders and commentators and activists with empathy and eloquence can use words not just to exploit the public mood but to shape it. And the result? Peace, prosperity, progress, inequality, prejudice, persecution, war. Public language matters (1).

Correct Citation of Borrowed Words in Quotation Marks

"Public language matters," insists Mark Thompson, president and CEO of The New York Times Company. "Words are free, and every politician and journalist and citizen can draw on an unlimited supply of them. But there are days when the right words are all that count, and it is the speaker who can find them who determines what happens next. Over time, leaders and commentators and activists with empathy and eloquence can use words not just to exploit the public mood but to shape it. And the result? Peace, prosperity, progress, inequality, prejudice, persecution, war. Public language matters" (1).

USING YOUR OWN WORDS IN PARAPHRASE AND SUMMARY. When summarizing or paraphrasing a source, you must use your own language. It is not enough simply to change a word here or there; you must restate the idea(s) from the original *in your own words,* using your own style and sentence structure. In the following example, notice how plagiarism can occur when care is not taken in the wording or sentence structure of a paraphrase.

Original Source

Stereotypes are a kind of gossip about the world, a gossip that makes us prejudge people before we ever lay eyes on them. Hence it is not surprising that stereotypes have something to do with the dark world of prejudice. Explore most prejudices (note that the word means prejudgment) and you will find a cruel stereotype at the core of each one.
> — Robert L. Heilbroner, "Don't Let Stereotypes Warp Your
> Judgment," *Reader's Digest* Jan. 1962, page 254.

Unacceptably Close Wording

According to Heilbroner, we prejudge other people even before we have seen them when we think in stereotypes. That stereotypes are related to the ugly world of prejudice should not surprise anyone. If you explore the heart of most prejudices — beliefs that literally prejudge — you will discover a mean stereotype lurking (254).

Unacceptably Close Sentence Structure

Heilbroner believes that stereotypes are images of people, images that enable people to prejudge other people before they have seen them. Therefore, no one should find it surprising that stereotypes are somehow related to the ugly world of prejudice. Examine most prejudices (the word literally means prejudgment) and you will uncover a vicious stereotype at the center of each (254).

Acceptable Paraphrase

Heilbroner believes that there is a link between stereotypes and the hurtful practice of prejudice. Stereotypes make for easy conversation, a kind of shorthand that enables people to find fault with others before ever meeting them. Most human prejudices, according to Heilbroner, have an ugly stereotype lurking somewhere inside them (254).

Finally, as you proofread your final draft, check your citations one last time. If at any time while you are taking notes or writing your paper you have a question about plagiarism, consult your instructor for clarification and guidance before proceeding.

Preventing Plagiarism

Questions to Ask about Direct Quotations

- Do quotation marks clearly indicate the language that I borrowed verbatim (word for word)?
- Is the language of the quotation accurate, with no missing or misquoted words or phrases?
- Do the brackets or ellipsis marks clearly indicate any changes or omissions I have introduced?
- Does a signal phrase naming the author introduce each quotation? If not, is the author's name in the parenthetical citation?
- Does a parenthetical page citation follow each quotation?

Questions to Ask about Summaries and Paraphrases

- Is each summary and paraphrase written in my own words and style?
- Does each summary and paraphrase accurately represent the opinion, position, or reasoning of the original writer?
- Does each summary and paraphrase start with a signal phrase so that readers know where my borrowed material begins?
- Does each summary and paraphrase conclude with a parenthetical page citation?

Questions to Ask about Facts and Statistics

- Do I use a signal phrase or some other marker to introduce each fact or statistic that is not common knowledge so that readers know where the borrowed material begins?
- Is each fact or statistic that is not common knowledge clearly documented with a parenthetical page citation?

A SAMPLE STUDENT ESSAY USING LIBRARY AND INTERNET SOURCES

Jake Jamieson wrote the following essay while he was a student at the University of Vermont and has updated it for inclusion in this book. His assignment was to write an argument, and he was free to choose his own topic from among the language issues covered in class. After considering a number of possible topics and doing some preliminary searches on several of them, Jamieson decided to tackle the issue of legislating English as the official language for the United States. As one who believes in the old axiom "if it isn't broken, don't fix it," Jamieson was intrigued by the supporters of the Official English movement, who feel the need to fix a system that seems to be working just fine. As you read, notice how he uses outside sources to set out the various pieces of the Official English position and then uses his own thinking and examples as well as experts who support him to undercut that position. Throughout his essay Jamieson uses MLA-style in-text citations together with a list of works cited.

Jamieson 1

Jake Jamieson

Professor A. Rosa

Written Expression 001

12 April 2015

The "Official English" Movement:

Can America Proscribe Language with a Clear Conscience?

Many people think of the United States as a giant cultural "melting

pot" where people from other countries come together and bathe in the

warm waters of assimilation. In this scenario the newly arrived immigrants

readily adopt American cultural ways and learn to speak English. For

others, however, this serene picture of the melting pot analogy does not

ring true. These people see the melting pot as a giant cauldron into which

immigrants are tossed; here their cultures, values, and backgrounds are

boiled away in the scalding waters of discrimination. At the center of

the discussion about immigrants and assimilation is language: Should

immigrants be required to learn English or should accommodations be

made so they can continue to use their native languages?

Those who argue that the melting pot analogy is valid believe

that immigrants who come to America do so willingly and should be

expected to become a part of its culture instead of hanging on to their

past. For them, the expectation that immigrants will celebrate this

country's holidays, dress as Americans dress, embrace American values,

and, most importantly, speak English is not unreasonable. They believe

that assimilation offers the only way for everyone in this country to live

together in harmony and the only way to dissipate the tensions that

inevitably arise when cultures clash. President Theodore Roosevelt first

gave voice to this belief in 1907. He said, "We have room for but one

language in this country, and that is the English language, for we intend

to see that the crucible turns our people out as Americans, of American

Title: Writer
introduces
subject and
provides focus.

**Writer sets
context for
discussion,
identifies central
problem of the
"Official English"
language debate.**

Thesis question:
Writer states
the key question
to be addressed
in paper.

**Writer
introduces a
major problem
with assimilation
model.**

Jamieson 2

nationality, and not as dwellers in a polyglot boarding house" (qtd. in Blumenfeld, par. 3). One major problem with this argument, however, is that there is no agreement on what exactly constitutes the "American way" of doing things.

Not everyone in America is of the same religious persuasion or has the same set of values, and different people affect vastly different styles of dress. There are so many sets of variables that it would be hard to defend the argument that there is only one culture in the United States. Currently, the one common denominator in America is that the overwhelming majority of us speak English, and because of this a major movement is being staged in favor of making English the country's "official" language while it is still the country's national and common language. Making English America's "official" language would change the ground rules and expectations surrounding immigrant assimilation. According to columnist and social commentator Charles Krauthammer, making English the "official" language has important implications:

> "Official" means the language of the government and its insti-
> tutions. "Official" makes clear our expectations of acculturation.
> "Official" means that every citizen, upon entering America's most
> sacred political space, the voting booth, should minimally be able
> to identify the words President and Vice President and county
> commissioner and judge. The immigrant, of course, has the right
> to speak whatever he wants. But he must understand that when
> he comes to the U.S., swears allegiance and accepts its bounty, he
> undertakes to join its civic culture. In English. (112)

Many reasons are given to support the notion that making English the official language of the land is a good idea and that it is exactly what this country needs, especially in the face of the growing diversity of languages in metropolitan areas. Economics is a major reason. As Mauro

Opposition argument: English as the common denominator in America—time to act.

Quotation: Writer quotes Krauthammer to present the "Official English" perspective.

Writer indents long quotation according to MLA style.

Jamieson 3

E. Mujica, chairman and CEO of U.S. English, reports, "Los Angeles County spent $3.3 million, 15 percent of the entire election budget, to print election ballots in seven languages and hire multilingual poll workers for the March 2002 primary. The county also spends $265 per day for each of the 420 full-time court interpreters" (par. 16).

Supporters of Official English contend that all government communication must be in English. Because communication is absolutely necessary for democracy to survive, they believe that the only way to ensure the existence of our nation is to make sure a common language exists. Making English official would ensure that all government business, from ballots to official forms to judicial hearings, would have to be conducted in English. From this vantage point championing English as our national language is not hostile at all because as Mujica asserts, "Parents around the world know that English is the global language and that their children need to learn it to succeed. English is the language of business, higher education, diplomacy, aviation, the internet, science, popular music, entertainment, and international travel" (par. 3). Political and cultural commentator Greg Lewis echoes Mujica's sentiments when he boldly states, "to succeed in America . . . it's important to speak, read, and understand English as most Americans speak it. There's nothing cruel or unfair in that; it's just the way it is" (par. 5).

For those who do not subscribe to this way of thinking, however, this type of legislation is anything but a welcoming act or invitation to participate. Many of them, like Myriam Marquez, readily acknowledge the importance of English but fear that "talking in Spanish — or any other language, for that matter — is some sort of litmus test used to gauge American patriotism" (497). Others suggest that anyone attempting to regulate language is treading dangerously close to the First Amendment and must have a hidden agenda of some type. Why, it is asked, make a

Writer uses MLA in-text citation format which includes introductory signal phrase and parenthetical paragraph number to integrate a quotation about the economic impact of not having English as the nation's official language.

Writer presents the opposition argument favoring Official English.

Writer introduces the anti-Official English position.

language official when it is already firmly entrenched and widely used in
this country without legislation to mandate it? For many, the answer is
plain and simple — discrimination.

   This tendency of Official English proponents to put down other
languages is one that shows up again and again, even though they
maintain that they have nothing against other languages or the people
who speak them. If there is no malice intended toward other languages,
why is the use of any language other than English tantamount to lunacy
according to an almost constant barrage of literature and editorial
opinion? Ed Morales, the author of *Living in Spanglish,* reports that
the mayor of Bogota, New Jersey, called for a boycott of McDonald's
restaurants after the "company displayed a billboard advertising a
new iced coffee drink in Spanish," calling "the ad . . . 'offensive' and
'divisive' because it sends a message that Hispanic immigrants do not
need to learn English" (par. 2–3). Now, according to this mindset, not
only is speaking any language other than English offensive, but it is also
irrational and bewildering. What is this world coming to when businesses
want to attract new customers using Spanish or people just want to
speak and make transactions in their native language? Why do they
refuse to change and become more like us? Why can't immigrants see that
speaking English is quite simply the right way to go? These and many
other questions like them are implied by Official English proponents when
they discuss the issue.

   The scariest prospect of all is that this opinion is quickly gaining
popularity all around the country. It appears to be most prevalent in
areas with high concentrations of Spanish-speaking residents. To date the
English Language Unity Act and one amendment to the Constitution have
been proposed in the House and Senate. There are more than twenty-
eight states — including Arizona, Missouri, North Dakota, Florida,

Quotation:
Writer cites
author Morales
to support
claim about
official English
proponents.

Writer asks
a series of
rhetorical
questions.

Writer updates
readers on
the status of
Official English
legislation.

Jamieson 5

California, Virginia, and New Hampshire—that have made English

their official language, and more are debating the issue at this time

(Crawford). An especially disturbing fact about this debate—and it

was front and center in 2010 during the discussions and protests about

what to do with America's over 12.5 million illegal immigrants—is

that Official English laws always seem to be linked to anti-immigration

legislation, such as proposals to limit immigration or to restrict

government benefits to immigrants.

    Although Official English proponents maintain that their bid for

language legislation is in the best interest of immigrants, the facts

tend to show otherwise. University of Texas professor Robert D. King

strongly believes that "language does not threaten American unity." He

recommends that "we relax and luxuriate in our linguistic richness and

our traditional tolerance of language differences" (64). University of

Massachusetts professor Warren J. Blumenthal echoes these sentiments,

believing that "rather than resisting the concept of multilingualism and

multiculturalism, viewing it as a challenge to our country's unity and very

existence, we need to embrace our rich diversity" (par. 9).

    A decision has to be made in this country about what kind of

message we will send to the rest of the world. Do we plan to allow

everyone in this country the freedom of speech that we profess to

cherish, or will we decide to reserve it only for those who speak English?

Will we hold firm to our belief that everyone is deserving of life, liberty,

and the pursuit of happiness in this country? Or will we show the world

that we believe in these things only when they pertain to ourselves

and people like us? "The irony," as Hispanic columnist Myriam Marquez

observes, "is that English-only laws directed at government have done

little to change the inevitable multi-cultural flavor of America" ("English-

Only Laws" A10).

Writer cites University of Texas professor to assure readers that the United States does not need to make English the nation's official language.

Writer concludes with an observation by a Hispanic journalist about the impact of English-only legislation to date.

Jamieson 6

Works Cited

Blumenfeld, Warren J. "'English Only' Laws Divide and Demean."

Huffington Post, 16 Jan. 2013, www.huffingtonpost.com/warren-j-

blumenfeld/English-only-laws-divide-_b_2141330.html.

Crawford, James. "Language Legislation in the U.S.A." Issues in U.S.

Language Policy, Feb. 2012, www.languagepolicy.net/archives

/langleg.htm.

King, Robert D. "Should English Be the Law?" Atlantic Monthly, Apr. 1997,

pp. 55–64.

Krauthammer, Charles. "In Plain English: Let's Make It Official." Time, 12

June 2006, p. 112.

Lewis, Greg. "An Open Letter to Diversity's Victims." GregLewis.org, 12

Aug. 2003, www.greglewis.org/CulturalCommentary/081203.htm.

Marquez, Myriam. "English-Only Laws Serve to Appease Those Who Fear

the Inevitable." Orlando Sentinel, 10 July 2000, p. A10.

---. "Why and When We Speak Spanish Among Ourselves in Public."

Orlando Sentinel, 28 June 1999, www.articles.orlandosentinel

.com/1999-06-28/news/9906250566_1_speaking-spanish-english-

native-tongue.

Morales, Ed. "English-only Debate Turns Absurd." Progressive.org, 19 July

2006.

Mujica, Mauro E. "Why the U.S. Needs an Official Language." WorldandI

.com, Dec. 2003, www.highbeam.com/doc/1G1-112178399.html.

The heading
Works Cited is
centered at the
top on page.

Writer uses
MLA style for
his list of works
cited. The list
begins on a new
page. Entries
are presented
in alphabetical
order by
authors' last
names. The first
line of each
entry begins at
the left margin;
subsequent lines
are indented
five spaces.
Double space
within entries as
well as between
entries.

The correct
MLA forms
for various
other kinds of
publications
are given on
pages 112–116.

5

A BRIEF GUIDE TO WRITING A RESEARCH PAPER

The research paper is an important part of a college education for good reason. In writing such a paper, you acquire a number of indispensable research skills that you can adapt to other college assignments and, after graduation, to important life tasks.

The real value of writing a research paper, however, goes beyond acquiring basic skills; it is a unique hands-on learning experience. The purpose of a research paper is not to present a collection of quotations that show you can report what others have said about your topic. Rather, your goal is to analyze, evaluate, and synthesize the materials you research—and thereby learn how to do so with any topic. You learn how to view the results of research from your own perspective and arrive at an informed opinion of a topic.

Writing a researched essay is not very different from the other writing you will be doing in your college writing course. You will find yourself drawing heavily on what you have learned in "Writing in College and Beyond" (pp. 25–46). First you determine what you want to write about. Then you decide on a purpose, consider your audience, develop a thesis, collect your evidence, write a first draft, revise and edit, and prepare a final copy. What differentiates the researched paper from other kinds of papers is your use of outside sources and how you acknowledge them.

Your library research will involve working with print and electronic sources. Your aim is to select the most appropriate sources for your research from the many that are available on your topic. (See also Chapter 4, "Writing with Sources.")

In this chapter, you will learn some valuable research techniques:

- How to establish a realistic schedule for your research project
- How to conduct research on the internet using keyword searches
- How to evaluate sources
- How to analyze sources

- How to develop a working bibliography
- How to take useful notes
- How to acknowledge your sources using Modern Language Association (MLA) and American Psychological Association (APA) style in-text citations and a list of works cited
- How to present your research paper using MLA and APA manuscript format

ESTABLISH A REALISTIC SCHEDULE

A research project easily spans several weeks. So as not to lose track of time and find yourself facing an impossible deadline at the last moment, establish a realistic schedule for completing key tasks. By thinking of the research paper as a multi-staged process, you avoid becoming overwhelmed by the size of the whole undertaking.

Your schedule should allow at least a few days to accommodate unforeseen needs and delays. Use the following template, which lists the essential steps in writing a research paper to plan your own research schedule:

Research Paper Schedule

Task	Completion Date
1. Choose a research topic and pose a worthwhile question.	/ /
2. Locate print and electronic sources.	/ /
3. Develop a working bibliography.	/ /
4. Evaluate your sources.	/ /
5. Read your sources, taking complete and accurate notes.	/ /
6. Develop a preliminary thesis and make a working outline.	/ /
7. Write a draft of your paper, integrating sources you have summarized, paraphrased, and quoted.	/ /
8. Visit your college writing center for help with your revision.	/ /
9. Decide on a final thesis and modify your outline.	/ /

10. Revise your paper and properly cite   //
    all borrowed materials.

11. Prepare a list of works cited.   //

12. Prepare the final manuscript and   //
    proofread.

13. Submit research paper.   //

LOCATE AND USE PRINT AND ONLINE SOURCES

The distinction between print sources and electronic sources is fast disappearing. Many sources that used to appear only in print are now available in electronic format as well; some, in fact, are moving entirely to electronic format, as a more efficient and in many cases less expensive means of distribution.

There are, however, still important distinctions between print sources (or their electronic equivalent) and internet sources. Many of the sources you will find through an internet search will not be as reliable as those that traditionally appeared in print. For this reason, in most cases you should use print sources or their electronic versions (books, newspapers, journals, periodicals, encyclopedias, pamphlets, brochures, and government publications) as your primary tools for research. These sources, unlike many internet sources, are often reviewed by experts in the field before they are published, are generally overseen by a reputable publishing company or organization, and are examined by editors and fact checkers for accuracy and reliability. Unless you are instructed otherwise, you should try to use these sources in your research.

The best place to start any search for sources is your college library's home page. Here you will find links to the computerized catalog of book holdings, online reference works, periodical databases, electronic journals, and a list of full-text databases. You'll also find links for subject study guides and for help conducting your research.

To get started, decide on some likely search terms and try them out. (For tips on conducting and refining keyword searches, see pages 102–103.) Search through your library's reference works, electronic catalog, periodical indexes, and other databases to generate a preliminary listing of books, magazine and newspaper articles, public documents and reports, and other sources that may be helpful in exploring your topic. At this early stage, it is better to err on the side of listing too many sources. Then, later on, you will not have to backtrack to find sources you discarded too hastily.

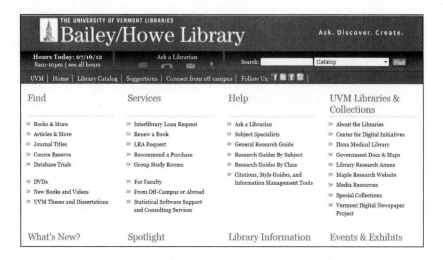

Sources that you find through an internet search can also be informative and valuable additions to your research. The internet is especially useful in providing recent data, stories, and reports. For example, you might find a just-published article from a university laboratory, or a news story in your local newspaper's online archives. Generally, however, internet sources should be used alongside sources you access through your college library and not as a replacement for them. Practically anyone with access to a computer and an internet connection can put text and pictures on the internet; there is often no governing body that checks for content or accuracy. Therefore, while the internet offers a vast number of useful and carefully maintained resources, it also contains much unreliable information. It is your responsibility to determine whether a given internet source should be trusted. (For advice on evaluating sources, see pages 104–106.)

If you need more instruction on conducting internet searches, go to your on-campus learning center or library for more information, or consult one of the many books written for internet research beginners.

Conduct Keyword Searches

When searching for sources about your topic in an electronic database, in the library's computerized catalog, or on the internet, you should start with a keyword search. To make the most efficient use of your time, you will want to know how to conduct a keyword search that is likely to yield solid sources and leads for your research project. As obvious or simple as it may sound, the key to a successful keyword search is the quality of the keywords you generate about your topic. You might find it helpful to start a list of potential keywords as you begin your research and add to it as your work proceeds. Often you will discover combinations of keywords that will lead you right to the sources you need.

Databases and library catalogs index sources by author, title, and year of publication, as well as by subject headings assigned by a cataloger who has previewed the source. The key here is to find a keyword that matches one of the subject headings. Once you begin to locate sources that are on your topic, be sure to note the subject headings listed for each source. You can use these subject headings as keywords to lead you to additional book sources or to articles in periodicals, using full-text databases like *InfoTrac, LexisNexis, Expanded Academic ASAP,* or *JSTOR* to which your library subscribes.

The keyword search process is somewhat different — more wide open — when you are searching on the web. It is always a good idea to look for search tips on the help screens or advanced search instructions for the search engine you are using before initiating a keyword search.

When you type a keyword in the "Search" box on a search engine's home page, the search engine goes looking for websites that match your term. One problem with keyword searches is that they can produce tens of thousands of matches, making it difficult to locate sites of immediate value. For that reason, make your keywords as specific as you can, and make sure that you have the correct spelling. Once you start a search, you may want to narrow or broaden it depending on the number of hits, or matches, you get.

Refining Keyword Searches on the Web

While some variation in command terms and characters exists among electronic databases and popular search engines on the internet, the following functions are almost universally accepted. If you have a particular question about refining your keyword search, seek assistance by clicking on "Help" or "Advanced Search."

- Use quotation marks or parentheses to indicate that you are searching for words in exact sequence — e.g., "bilingual education"; (college slang).
- Use AND or a plus sign (+) between words to narrow your search by specifying that all words need to appear in a document — e.g., prejudice AND Asians; doublespeak + advertisements.
- Use NOT or a minus sign (–) between words to narrow your search by eliminating unwanted words — e.g., advertisements NOT public service; natural–organic.
- Use an asterisk (*) to indicate that you will accept variations of a term — e.g., euphemism*.

EVALUATE YOUR SOURCES

You will not have to spend much time in the library to realize that you do not have time to read every print and online source that appears relevant. Given the abundance of print and internet sources, the key to successful research is identifying those books, articles, websites, and other online sources that will help you most. You must evaluate your potential sources to determine which materials you will read, which you will skim, and which you will simply eliminate. Here are some evaluation strategies and questions to assist you in identifying your most promising sources.

Strategies for Evaluating Print and Online Sources

EVALUATING A BOOK

- Read the book jacket or cover copy for insights into the book's coverage and currency as well as the author's expertise.
- Scan the table of contents and identify any promising chapters.
- Read the author's preface, looking for his or her thesis and purpose.
- Check the index for key words or key phrases related to your research topic.
- Read the opening and concluding paragraphs of any promising chapter; if you are unsure about its usefulness, skim the whole chapter.
- Ask yourself: Does the author have a discernable bias? If so, you must be aware that this bias will color any claims and evidence.

EVALUATING AN ARTICLE

- Ask yourself what you know about the journal or magazine publishing the article:
  - Is the publication scholarly or popular? Scholarly journals (*American Economic Review, Journal of Marriage and the Family, The Wilson Quarterly*) publish articles about original research written by authorities in the field. Research essays always cite their sources in footnotes or bibliographies. Popular news and general interest magazines (*National Geographic, Smithsonian, Time, Ebony*), on the other hand, publish informative, entertaining, and easy-to-read articles written by editorial staff or freelance writers. Popular essays sometimes cite sources but often do not.
  - What is the reputation of the journal or magazine? Determine the publisher or sponsor. Is it an academic institution

---

or a commercial enterprise or individual? Does the publisher or publication have a reputation for accuracy and objectivity?

- Who are the readers of this journal or magazine?

- What are the author's credentials?
- Consider the title or headline of the article as well as the opening paragraph or two and the conclusion. Does the source appear to be too general or too technical for your needs and audience?
- For articles in journals, read the abstract (a summary of the main points) if there is one.
- Examine any photographs, charts, graphs, or other illustrations that accompany the article. Determine how useful they might be for your research purposes.

EVALUATING A WEBSITE

- Consider the type of website. Is this site a personal blog or a professional publication? Often the URL, especially the top-level domain name, can give you a clue about the kinds of information provided and the type of organization behind the site. Common suffixes include:

  .com — business/commercial/personal

  .edu — educational institution

  .gov — government sponsored

  .net — various types of networks

  .org — nonprofit organization, but also some commercial/personal

- Be advised that *.org* is not regulated like *.edu* and *.gov*, for example. Most nonprofits use *.org*, but many commercial and personal sites do as well.
- Examine the home page of the site.

  - Does the content appear to be related to your research topic?
  - Is the home page well maintained and professional in appearance?
  - Is there an *About* link on the home page that takes you to background information on the site's sponsor? Is there a mission statement, history, or statement of philosophy? Can you verify whether the site is official — actually sanctioned by the organization or company?

- Identify the author of the site. What are the author's qualifications for writing on this subject?
- Determine whether a print equivalent is available. Is the web version more or less extensive than the print version?
- Determine when the site was last updated. Is the content current enough for your purposes?

On the basis of your evaluation, select the most promising books, articles, and websites to pursue in depth for your research project.

ANALYZE YOUR SOURCES FOR POSITION AND BIAS

Before beginning to take notes, it is essential that you carefully analyze your sources for their thesis, overall argument, amount and credibility of evidence, bias, and reliability in helping you explore your research topic. Look for the writers' main ideas, key examples, strongest arguments, and conclusions. Read critically. While it is easy to become absorbed in sources that support your own beliefs, always seek out several sources with opposing viewpoints, if only to test your own position. Look for information about the authors themselves—information that will help you determine their authority and where they position themselves in the broader conversation on the issue. You should also know the reputation and special interests of book publishers and magazines, because you are likely to get different views—conservative, liberal, international, feminist—on the same topic depending on the publication you read. Use the following checklist to assist you in analyzing your print and online sources.

Checklist for Analyzing Print and Online Sources for Position and Bias

- What is the writer's thesis or claim?
- How does the writer support this thesis? Does the evidence seem reasonable and ample, or is it mainly anecdotal?
- Does the writer consider opposing viewpoints?
- Does the writer have any obvious political or religious biases? Is the writer associated with any special-interest groups such as Planned Parenthood, Greenpeace, Amnesty International, or the National Rifle Association?

- Is the writer an expert on the subject? Do other writers mention this author in their work?
- Does the publisher or publication have a reputation for accuracy and objectivity?
- Is important information documented through footnotes or links so that it can be verified or corroborated in other sources?
- What is the author's purpose—to inform or to argue for a particular position or action?
- Do the writer's thesis and purpose clearly relate to your research topic?
- Does the source appear to be too general or too technical for your needs and audience?
- Does the source reflect current thinking and research in the field?

DEVELOP A WORKING BIBLIOGRAPHY OF YOUR SOURCES

As you discover book, journal and magazine articles, newspaper stories, and other online sources that you think might be helpful, you need to manage these sources by keeping an accurate record of the materials you look at. Perhaps the best way to keep track of your sources is to make a copy of each one that you think will help you to answer your research question.

For each source that you copy, be sure that you have the requisite bibliographic information. With the computerization of most library sources, you now have the opportunity to copy bibliographic information from the library's computer catalog and periodical indexes or from the internet into a document you create on your computer. This document, for all practical purposes, is your working bibliography. Because the information for each source has been saved electronically, you can be assured of its accuracy. And that's important when punctuation, spelling, and capitalization are so essential in accessing websites.

As your collection of sources grows, alphabetize them by the authors' last names. You can continue to edit your working bibliography, dropping sources that do not prove helpful for one reason or another and adding new ones. In all likelihood your working bibliography will contain more sources than you actually consult and include in your list of works cited. Your working bibliography together with the copies of the sources you made will facilitate your research writing and make it easy to assemble your list of works cited or final bibliography at project's end (for MLA Works Cited list, see pp. 112–116; for APA References list, see pp. 122–126).

Checklist for a Working Bibliography

FOR BOOKS

- Library call number
- Names of all authors, editors, and translators
- Title and subtitle
- Publication data:

> Place of publication (city and state)
> Publisher's name
> Date of publication

- Edition (if not first) and volume number (if applicable)
- Date you accessed the source (online sources only)

FOR PERIODICAL ARTICLES

- Names of all authors
- Title and subtitle of article
- Title of journal, magazine, or newspaper
- Publication data:

> Volume number and issue number
> Date of issue
> Page numbers

- Date you accessed the source (online sources only)

FOR INTERNET SOURCES

- Names of all authors, editors, compilers, or sponsoring agents
- Title and subtitle of the document
- Title of the longer work to which the document belongs (if applicable)
- Title of the site or discussion list
- Author, editor, or compiler of the website or online database
- Name of company or organization that owns the website
- Date of release, online posting, or latest revision
- Name and vendor of database or name of online service or network
- Format of online source (web page, .pdf, podcast)
- Date you accessed the site
- Digital object identifier (DOI), if available
- URL of the source's home page, if DOI is not available
- Date you accessed the source

FOR OTHER SOURCES

- Name of author, government agency, organization, company, recording artist, personality, etc.

- Title of the work
- Format (pamphlet, unpublished diary, interview, television broadcast, etc.)
- Publication or production data:

  Name of publisher or producer
  Date of publication, production, or release
  Identifying codes or numbers (if applicable)

- Date you accessed the source (online sources only)

TAKE NOTES

As you read, take notes. You're looking for ideas, facts, opinions, statistics, examples, and other evidence that you think will be useful as you write your paper. As you read through books and articles, look for recurring themes, and notice where writers are in agreement and where they differ. Try to remember that the effectiveness of your paper is largely determined by the quality—not necessarily the quantity—of your notes. Your purpose is not to present a collection of quotes to show that you've read all the material and know what others have said about your topic. Your goal is to analyze, evaluate, and synthesize the information you collect—in other words, to enter into the discussion of the issues and thereby take ownership of your topic. You want to view the results of your research from your own perspective and arrive at an informed opinion of your topic. (For more information on writing with sources, see Chapter 4.)

Now for some practical advice on taking notes. First, be systematic in your note-taking. Consider creating a separate file for each topic or source. By keeping your notes organized you will be able to sequence them according to the plan you have envisioned for your paper when you get to the planning and writing stage. Furthermore, should you decide to alter your organizational plan, you can easily reorder your notes to reflect those revisions.

Second, try not to take too many notes. One good way to control your note-taking is to ask yourself, "How exactly does this material help prove or disprove my thesis?" Try to envision where in your paper you will use the information. If it does not seem relevant to your thesis, don't bother to take a note.

Once you decide to take a note, you must decide whether to summarize, paraphrase, or quote directly. The approach you take should be determined by the content of the passage and the way you plan to use it in your paper. For detailed advice on summaries, paraphrases, and quotations, see Chapter 4, pages 83–85.

DOCUMENT YOUR SOURCES

Whenever you summarize, paraphrase, or quote a person's thoughts and ideas, and whenever you use facts or statistics that are not commonly known or believed, you must properly acknowledge the source of your information. If you do not properly acknowledge ideas and information created by someone else, you are guilty of *plagiarism*, or using someone else's material but making it look as if it were your own. (For more information on plagiarism and how to avoid it, see pages 88–91.) You must document the source of your information whenever you:

- Quote a source word for word
- Refer to information and ideas from another source that you present in your own words as either a paraphrase or a summary
- Cite statistics, table, charts, graphs, or other visuals

You do not need to document:

- Your own observations, experiences, and ideas
- Factual information available in a number of reference works (information known as "common knowledge")
- Proverbs, sayings, and familiar quotations

A reference to the source of your borrowed information is called a *citation*. There are many systems for making citations, and your citations must consistently follow one of these systems. The documentation style recommended by the Modern Language Association (MLA) is commonly used in English and the humanities. Another common system is the American Psychological Association (APA) style, which is generally used in the social sciences. Your instructor will probably tell you which style to use. For more information on documentation styles, consult the appropriate manual or handbook.

There are two components of documentation. *In-text citations* are placed in the body of your paper, and the *list of works cited* provides complete publication data for your in-text citations and is placed on a separate page at the end of your paper. Both of these components are necessary for complete documentation.

MLA IN-TEXT CITATIONS

In-text citations, also known as *parenthetical citations,* give the reader citation information immediately, at the point at which it is most meaningful. Rather than having to find a footnote or an endnote, the reader sees the citation as a part of the writer's text.

Most in-text citations consist of only the author's last name and a page reference. Usually the author's name is given in an introductory signal phrase at the beginning of the borrowed material, and the page reference is given in parentheses at the end. If the author's name is not given at the beginning, put it in parentheses along with the page reference. When you borrow material from two or more works by the same author, you must include the title of the work in the signal phrase or parenthetically at the end. (For examples of signal phrases and in-text citations, see pages 86–88.) The parenthetical reference signals the end of the borrowed material and directs your readers to the list of works cited should they want to pursue a particular source. Treat electronic sources as you do print sources, keeping in mind that some electronic sources use paragraph numbers instead of page numbers. Consider the following examples of in-text citations, taken from student Richard Carbeau's paper on the debate over whether or not to make English America's official language.

Many people are surprised to discover that English is not the official language of the United States. Today, even as English literacy becomes a necessity for people in many parts of the world, some people in the United States believe its primacy is being threatened right at home. Much of the current controversy focuses on Hispanic communities with large Spanish-speaking populations who may feel little or no pressure to learn English. Columnist and cultural critic Charles Krauthammer believes English should be America's official language. He notes that this country has been "blessed . . . with a linguistic unity that brings a critically needed cohesion to a nation as diverse, multiracial and multiethnic as America" and that communities such as these threaten the bond created by a common language (112). There are others, however, who think that "Language does not threaten American unity. Benign neglect is a good policy for any country when it comes to language, and it's a good policy for America" (King 64).

Citation with author's name in the signal phrase

Citation with author's name in parentheses

Works Cited

King, Robert D. "Should English Be the Law?" *Atlantic Monthly,* Apr. 1997,
  pp. 55-64.

Krauthammer, Charles. "In Plain English: Let's Make It Official." *Time,*
  12 June 2006, p. 112.

In the preceding example, the student followed MLA style guidelines for his Works Cited list. When constructing the works cited page for your paper, consult the following MLA guidelines, based on the *MLA Handbook*, eighth edition (2016), where you will find model entries for periodical print publications, nonperiodical print publications, web publications, and other common sources.

MLA LIST OF WORKS CITED

In this section, you will find general MLA guidelines for creating a works cited list followed by sample entries that cover the citation situations you are most likely to encounter. Make sure that you follow the formats as they appear on the following pages.

GUIDELINES FOR CONSTRUCTING YOUR WORKS CITED PAGE

1. Begin the list on a fresh page following the last page of text.
2. Center the title *Works Cited* at the top of the page.
3. Double-space both within and between entries on your list.
4. Alphabetize your sources by the authors' last names. If you have two or more authors with the same last name, alphabetize first by last names and then by first names.
5. If you have two or more works by the same author, alphabetize by the first word of the titles, not counting *A, An,* or *The.* Use the author's name in the first entry and three unspaced hyphens followed by a period in subsequent entries:

Twitchell, James B. *Branded Nation: The Marketing of Megachurch, College Inc., and Museumworld.* Simon & Schuster, 2004.

---. "The Branding of Higher Ed." *Forbes,* 25 Nov. 2002: 50.

---. *Living It Up: America's Love Affair with Luxury.* Columbia UP, 2002.

6. For two authors, reverse only the name of the first author. For three or more authors, provide the first author's last name and first name, followed by a comma and *et al.* ("and others").
7. If no author is known, alphabetize by title.
8. Begin each entry at the left margin. If the entry is longer than one line, indent the second and subsequent lines five spaces or one-half inch.
9. Italicize the titles of books, journals, magazines, and newspapers. Use quotation marks with titles of periodical articles, chapters and essays within books, short stories, and poems.
10. Provide the names of other contributors, such as editors, translators, or illustrators, with explanations such as *translated by.*

11. Include edition or version numbers, if the source has them.

12. If the source is part of a sequence, include volume or issue number.

13. If the source has a publisher whose name differs significantly from the work it embodies or is contained by, include this publisher's name; otherwise, omit it.

14. If your source was accessed through a database, application, streaming service, or other larger "container," include information about the larger container after information about the original source. For a database, for example, include its name and the DOI or URL, separated by a comma.

15. Provide the location where the source was accessed. For print sources, this means page numbers, preceded by the prefix *p.* or *pp.* For online sources, this means a DOI or URL.

Periodical Print Publications: Journals, Magazines, and Newspapers

ARTICLE IN A SCHOLARLY JOURNAL

For all scholarly journals — whether they paginate continuously throughout a given year or not — provide the volume and issue numbers (if both are given) separated by a period, the year, the page numbers, and the medium.

> Gazzaniga, Michael S. "Right Hemisphere Language Following Brain Bisection: A Twenty-Year Perspective." *American Psychologist,* vol. 38, no. 5, 1983, pp. 528-49.

If the journal does not use volume numbers, cite the issue number alone.

> Harpham, Geoffrey Galt. "Roots, Races, and the Return to Philology." *Representations,* no. 106, 2009, pp. 34-62.

ARTICLE IN A MAGAZINE

When citing a weekly or biweekly magazine, give the complete date (day, month, year).

> Begley, Sharon. "What's in a Word?" *Newsweek,* 20 July 2009, p. 31.

When citing a magazine published every month or every two months, provide the month or months and year.

> Bernstein, Charles. "Sounding the Word." *Harper's Magazine,* Mar. 2011, pp. 15-18.

If an article in a magazine is not printed on consecutive pages — for example, an article might begin on page 45, then skip to 48 — include only the first page followed by a plus sign.

ARTICLE IN DAILY OR WEEKLY NEWSPAPER

Carney, Heather. "Unlocking English." *Naples Daily News,* 18 Dec. 2011, final ed.,
    pp. A1+.

Evelyn, Jamilah. "The 'Silent Killer' of Minority Enrollments." *Chronicle of Higher
    Education,* 20 June 2003, pp. A17-18.

REVIEW (OF A BOOK OR FILM)

Morozov, Evgeny. "Sharing It All." Review of *I Know Who You Are and I Saw What You
    Did: Social Networks and the Death of Privacy,* by Lori Andrews. *New York Times
    Book Review,* 29 Jan. 2012, p. 18.

Dargis, Manohla. "The King's English, Albeit with Twisted Tongue." Review of *The
    King's Speech,* directed by Mike Leigh. *The New York Times,* national ed., 25 Nov.
    2010, p. AR18.

If the review has no title, simply begin with *Review* after the author's
name. If there is neither title nor author, begin with *Review* and alphabetize by the title of the book or film being reviewed.

ANONYMOUS ARTICLE

When no author's name is given, begin the entry with the title.

"Pompeii: Will the City Go from Dust to Dust?" *Newsweek,* 1 Sept. 1997, p. 8.

EDITORIAL (SIGNED/UNSIGNED)

Jackson, Derrick Z. "The Winner: Hypocrisy." *Boston Globe,* 6 Feb. 2004,
    p. A19. Editorial.

"Beginning of the End." *The New York Times,* national ed., 19 Feb. 2012, p. SR10.
    Editorial.

LETTER TO THE EDITOR

Lakind, Alexandra. "Constructive Criticism." *New Yorker,* 13 & 20 Feb. 2012, p. 8.
    Letter.

Nonperiodical Print Publications: Books, Brochures, and Pamphlets

BOOK BY A SINGLE AUTHOR

Thompson, Mark. *Enough Said: What's Gone Wrong with the Language of Politics?*
    St. Martin's, 2016.

You may use a shortened version of the publisher's name — for example, *Houghton* for Houghton Mifflin, or *Cambridge UP* for Cambridge University Press.

ANTHOLOGY

Heti, Sheila, editor. *The Best American Nonrequired Reading, 2018.* Mariner, 2018.

BOOK BY TWO OR MORE AUTHORS

For a book by two authors, list the authors in the order in which they appear on the title page.

Perry, Theresa, and Lisa Delpit. *The Real Ebonics Debate.* Beacon, 1998.

For a book by three or more authors, list the first author in the same way as for a single-author book, followed by a comma and the abbreviation *et al.* ("and others").

Chomsky, Noam, et al. *Acts of Aggression.* Seven Stories, 1999.

BOOK BY A CORPORATE AUTHOR

Carnegie Foundation for the Advancement of Teaching. *Campus Life: In Search of Community.* Jossey-Bass, 1990.

WORK IN AN ANTHOLOGY

Smith, Seaton. "'Jiving' with Your Teen." *The Best American Nonrequired Reading, 2002,* edited by Dave Eggers. Houghton, 2002, pp. 217-20.

INTRODUCTION, PREFACE, FOREWORD, OR AFTERWORD TO A BOOK

McCourt, Frank. Foreword. *Eats, Shoots & Leaves: The Zero Tolerance Approach to Punctuation,* by Lynne Truss, Gotham, 2004, pp. xi-xiv.

TRANSLATION

Chaucer, Geoffrey. *The Canterbury Tales: A Complete Translation into Modern English.* Translated by Ronald L. Ecker and Eugene J. Crook. Hodge & Braddock, 1993.

CHAPTER OR SECTION IN A BOOK

Lamott, Anne. "Shitty First Drafts." *Bird by Bird: Some Instructions on Writing and Life.* Pantheon, 1994, pp. 21-27.

BOOK PUBLISHED IN A SECOND OR SUBSEQUENT EDITION

Aitchison, Jean. *Language Change: Process or Decay?* 2nd ed., Cambridge UP, 1991.

Modern Language Association of America. *MLA Handbook.* 8th ed., MLA, 2016.

BROCHURE/PAMPHLET

Harry S. Truman Library and Museum. *Museum Guide.* Truman Library, 2008.

GOVERNMENT PUBLICATION

United States, Department of Justice. *Hate Crime Victimization, 2003-2011: Special Report.* Government Printing Office, 2013.

Give the government, the agency, and the title with a period and a space after each. The publisher is the Government Printing Office.

Online Publications

The following guidelines and models for citing information retrieved from the internet have been adapted from the most recent advice of the MLA, as detailed in the *MLA Handbook,* eighth edition (2016), and from the MLA's website (mla.org).

For sources located or accessed online or through an online database, MLA style requires you to include either DOIs or direct URLs in your works cited list. The following example illustrates a works cited entry with a URL included:

Butler, Janine. "Where Access Meets Multimodality: The Case of ASL Music Videos." *Kairos,* vol. 21, no. 1, Fall 2016, kairos.technorhetoric.net/21.1/topoi/butler/index.html.

To format the URL, omit the *http://* prefix, but include the rest of the URL in full, including *www.* when applicable. Precede a DOI with *doi:* (no space). End both with a period. MLA style requires that you break URLs extending over more than one line only after a punctuation mark, ideally a slash, but not a hyphen or period. Do *not* add spaces, hyphens, or any other punctuation to indicate the break.

Periodical Articles Published or Accessed Online

To cite an article, a review, an editorial, or a letter to the editor in a periodical (journal, magazine, or newspaper) accessed online, provide the author, the title of the article, the title of the publication, the volume and issue (for scholarly journals), and the date of issue, followed by the page numbers (if available), the publisher (if distinct from the publication), and the article's DOI or direct URL. Because the nature of online news can be fluid and content can change over time, include the time the story was posted, if available.

ARTICLE IN AN ONLINE SCHOLARLY JOURNAL

Domahidi, Emese. "The Associations Between Online Media Use and Users' Perceived Social Resources: A Meta-Analysis." *Journal of Computer-Mediated Communication,* vol. 23, no. 4, 2018, doi.org/10.1093/jcmc/zmy007.

ARTICLE IN AN ONLINE MAGAZINE

Baron, Naomi. "Do Students Lose Depth in Digital Reading?" *Salon,* 13 Aug. 2018, www.salon.com/2018/08/12/do-students-lose-depth-in- digital-reading_partner/.

ARTICLE IN AN ONLINE NEWSPAPER

Baker, Geoff. "What's in a Name? For Seattle's Future NHL Team, More Than Meets the Sock-eye." *The Seattle Times,* 13 Aug. 2018, www.seattletimes.com/sports/hockey/ whats-in-a-name-for-seattles-future-nhl-team-more-than-meets-the-sock-eye/.

STORY FROM AN ONLINE NEWS SERVICE

"Iran Police Clash with Protesters." *CNN,* 7 Dec. 2009, www.cnn.com/2009/WORLD/ meast/12/7/iran.protest.warnings/index.html/?iref=topnews.

Periodical Publications Accessed In Online Databases

JOURNAL ARTICLE WITH A DOI

Diaz, Robert. "Transnational Queer Theory and Unfolding Terrorisms." *Criticism,* vol. 50, no. 3, 2009, pp. 533-41. *Project Muse,* doi:l0.1353/crt.0.0072.

JOURNAL ARTICLE WITHOUT A DOI (USE URL)

Bachi, Salim, and Alison Rice. "The Place of Islam in Literature, Geography, Memory, and Exile." *Religion and Literature,* vol. 43, no. 1, 2011, pp. 162-66. *JSTOR,* www.jstor.org.proxy.wexler.hunter.cuny.edu/stable/23049365.

MAGAZINE ARTICLE

Keizer, Garret. "Sound and Fury: The Politics of Noise in a Loud Society." *Harper's Magazine,* Mar. 2001, pp. 39-48. *Academic Search Complete,* ebscohost.com.

NEWSPAPER ARTICLE

Porter, Eduardo. "Racial Identity Returns to American Politics." *The New York Times,* 6 Jan. 2016, p. Bl. *LexisNexis Academic,* www.nytimes.com/2016/01/06/business/ econmy/racial-identity-and-its-hostilities-return-to-american-politics.html.

Other Web Publications

BOOK OR PART OF A BOOK ACCESSED ONLINE

For a book available online, provide the author, the title, the editor (if any), original publication date, the name of the database or website where it was accessed.

Sapir, Edward. *Language: An Introduction to the Study of Speech.* Harcourt, 1921. *Bartleby,* www.bartleby.com/186/.

If you are citing only part of an online book, include the title or name of the part directly after the author's name.

Johnson, Samuel. "Of Irregular Verbs." *A Grammar of the English Tongue,* 1812. *Project Gutenberg,* 2005, www.gutenberg.org/files/15097/15097-h/ 15097-h.htm.

SPEECH, ESSAY, POEM, OR SHORT STORY FROM AN ONLINE SITE

Faulkner, William. "On Accepting the Nobel Prize." 10 Dec. 1950. *The History Place: Great Speeches Collection,* www.historyplace.com/speeches/faulkner.htm.

ONLINE GOVERNMENT PUBLICATION

United States, Department of Justice, Federal Bureau of Investigation. *Hate Crimes,* 2016, www.fbi.gov/investigate/civil-rights/hate-crimes.

WIKI ENTRY

"Sign Language." *Wikipedia: The Free Encyclopedia,* Wikimedia Foundation, Inc., 6 Aug. 2018, en.wikipedia.org/w/index.php?title=Sign_ language&oldid=853670161.

Wiki entries do not have authors because the content is written collaboratively. Be sure to list the date of the exact version you are citing, and to provide a stable URL.

Find the stable URL by selecting the "View history" link at the top right corner of the page.

VIDEO RECORDING POSTED ONLINE

Marron, Dylan. "Why Should We Speak with People Who Hate Us?" *TED Radio Hour,* NPR, 13 July 2018, www.npr.org/2018/07/13/628617942/Dylan-marron-why-should-we-speak-with-people-who-hate-us.

SOUND RECORDING

Muri, John T., and Ravin I. McDavid Jr. *Americans Speaking.* NCTE, 1967.

FILM

The Gods Must Be Crazy. Directed by Jamie Uys, performances by Nixau, Marius Weyers, Sandra Prinsloo, Twentieth Century Fox, 1980.

CARTOON

Ramirez, Michael. "Erdogan's Turkey." *Michael P. Ramirez,* 19 Aug. 2018, www.michaelpramirez.com/erdogans-tyranny-takes-a-bite.htm.

LETTER, MEMO, OR EMAIL MESSAGE

Britto, Marah. Letter to the author. 28 Sept. 2017.

Stonefield, Will. "New Online Language Articles." Received by Alfred Rosa.
20 Aug. 2018.

MLA MANUSCRIPT FORMAT

The following guidelines for formatting manuscripts have been adapted from Modern Language Association recommendations.

Paper and Type

For academic papers use 8½-by-11-inch, twenty-pound white paper, and print in black on one side of each sheet. Use a standard type style such as Times New Roman or Courier. Use a paper clip (do not staple) to secure the pages unless instructed otherwise. Finally, be sure you keep both a paper copy and an electronic copy of your paper.

Title, Name, and Course Information

Beginning at the left margin one inch from the top of the first page, type your name, your instructor's name, the name and number of the course, and the date on separate lines, double-spaced. Double-space again, and center your title. Double-space between your title and the first sentence of your paper. For example, see page 43.

Margins, Line Spacing, and Paragraph Indentation

Leave a one-inch margin on all sides of the page. Double-space the text of the paper including long, set-off quotations, information notes, and the entries on the Works Cited page. Do not justify (make even) the right-hand margin. Indent the first line of each paragraph one-half inch (or five spaces).

Page Numbers

Place your last name and the page number (e.g., DeAngelus 1) in the upper right corner of each page, approximately one-half inch from the top and one inch from the right edge of the page. Do not use the word *page* or its abbreviation *p.*; do not use a period or any other mark of punctuation with your name and page number. Number all pages of your paper, including the first and last. For example, see pages 39–42.

Long Quotations

Set off prose quotations that are longer than four lines to help your reader more clearly see the quotation as a whole. Poetry quotations are set off when longer than three lines. Set-off quotations are indented one-half inch from the left margin and are double-spaced; no quotation marks are necessary because the format itself indicates that the passage is a quotation. When you are quoting two or more paragraphs from the same source, indent the first line of each paragraph three additional spaces. Note that, unlike an integrated quotation in which the parenthetical citation is inside the end punctuation, with a long, set-off quotation the parenthetical citation is placed outside the final punctuation. For example, see page 94.

Spacing for Punctuation

Leave one space after a comma, colon, or semicolon and between the three periods in an ellipsis. MLA recommends one space after a period, question mark, or exclamation point at the end of a sentence. Form dashes by using two hyphens with no space between them. Do not leave a space before or after a dash. Most word processors will convert your two hyphens into a dash, as seen in the sample student paper on pages 93–97.

URLs

Should you have occasion to divide a URL at the end of a line in the text of your paper or in your list of Works Cited, break it before a period or hyphen or after any other mark of punctuation. Never insert a hyphen to mark the break.

Works Cited Page

The list of Works Cited is placed on a separate page at the end of your paper and titled *Works Cited*. Place your last name and page number in the upper right-hand corner, one-half-inch from the top and one inch from the right edge of the page. Double-space and then center the words *Works Cited*. For a model Works Cited page from a student paper, see page 98. For the specific requirements of the format of each entry in the list of Works Cited, refer to the model entries on pages 112–119.

APA-STYLE DOCUMENTATION

The American Psychological Association (APA) recommends a simple, two-part system for documenting sources. The system consists of a brief *in-text citation* at the point where words or ideas have been borrowed from a source, and a *list of references* at the end of the paper, which includes complete bibliographical information for all sources cited in the text. The following recommendations are based on the *Publication Manual of the American Psychological Association,* sixth edition (2010), as well as the APA's website.

APA IN-TEXT CITATIONS

In-text citations in the American Psychological Association (APA) style generally consist of the author's last name, the year of publication, and a page reference. Usually the author's name and year of publication are given in an introductory signal phrase at the beginning of the borrowed material, and the page reference is given in parentheses at the end. If the author's name and publication year are not given at the beginning, put them in parentheses along with the page reference. When you borrow material from two or more works by the same author, you must include the title of the work in the signal phrase or parenthetically at the end. (For examples of signal phrases and in-text citations, see pages 86–88.) The parenthetical reference signals the end of the borrowed material and directs your readers to the list of References should they want to pursue a particular source. Treat electronic sources as you do print sources, keeping in mind that some electronic sources use paragraph numbers instead of page numbers. Consider the following examples of in-text citations, taken from student Richard Carbeau's paper on the debate over whether or not to make English America's official language.

Many people are surprised to discover that English is not the official language of the United States. Today, even as English literacy becomes a necessity for people in many parts of the world, some people in the United States believe its primacy is being threatened right at home. Much of the current controversy focuses on Hispanic communities with large Spanish-speaking populations who may feel little or no pressure to learn English. Columnist and cultural critic Charles Krauthammer believes English should be America's official language. Krauthammer (2006) noted that this country has been "blessed . . . with a linguistic unity that brings a critically needed cohesion to a nation as diverse, multiracial and multiethnic as America" and that communities

Citation with author's name and publication year in the signal phrase such as these threaten the bond created by a common language (p. 112).

There are others, however, who think that "Language does not threaten

American unity. Benign neglect is a good policy for any country when it

comes to language, and it's a good policy for America"

(King, 1997, p. 64).

Citation with author's name, publication year, and page number in parentheses

References

King, R. D. (1997, April). Should English be the law? *The Atlantic*

   Monthly, 55-64.

Krauthammer, C. (2006, June 12). In plain English: Let's make it official.

   Time, 112.

In the preceding example, the student followed APA style guidelines for his References list. When constructing the References list page for your paper, consult the following APA guidelines, where you will find model entries for common types of print and online sources.

APA LIST OF REFERENCES

In this section, you will find general APA guidelines for creating a list of References followed by sample entries that cover the citation situations you are most likely to encounter. Make sure that you follow the formats as they appear on the following pages.

GUIDELINES FOR CONSTRUCTING YOUR REFERENCE PAGE

1. Begin your list of references on a fresh page following the last page of text.
2. Center the title *References* at the top of the page.
3. Double-space both within and between entries on your list.
4. Arrange your sources alphabetically by the authors' or editors' last names. If you have two or more authors with the same last name, alphabetize by the initials of the first name.
5. If you have two or more works by the same author, arrange them chronologically by year of publication, starting with the one published earliest. Arrange works published in the same year alphabetically by title, and use lowercase letters to differentiate them (2017a), (2017b), (2017c). Include the author's name, together with any initials, with all entries.
6. Reverse *all* authors' names within each entry, and use initials, not first or middle names (Burns, E. A.). Name up to seven authors, separating names and parts of names with commas. Use an ampersand (&) instead of *and*

before the last author's name. If there are more than seven authors, use an ellipsis (...) after the sixth author, followed by the last author's name.

7. If no author or editor is known, alphabetize by the first word of the title, not counting *A, An,* or *The.*

8. Begin each entry at the left margin, and indent subsequent lines five spaces or one-half inch.

9. Give the date of publication in parentheses after the last author's name. For some journal, magazine, and newspaper articles, you will need to include the month and sometimes the day as well as the year (2018, December 2).

10. For book and article titles, capitalize the first word of the title, the first word of the subtitle if there is one, and any proper names. Begin all other words with lowercase letters. With titles of journals, capitalize all significant words (*Social Work with Groups: A Journal of Community and Clinical Practice*).

11. Italicize the titles of books, journals, magazines, and newspapers. Do not italicize or put quotation marks around article titles.

12. For book publications, provide the city of publication followed by the two-letter postal abbreviation of the state (Davenport, IA). Follow the city and state with a colon.

13. For books, provide the publisher's name after the place of publication. For many commercial publishers, you may use shortened names, such as *Houghton* for Houghton Mifflin Harcourt. Provide the full name of university presses, corporations, and professional associations. Omit such terms as *Publishers, Co.,* and *Inc.* Retain the term *Books* and, for academic publishers, *Press.*

14. Use the abbreviations *p.* and *pp.* for page numbers of all newspaper articles and for chapters or articles in edited books. Do not use these abbreviations for articles in journals or magazines. When citing inclusive page numbers, give complete figures: 217–233.

15. For an online source, include the same elements, in the same order, as you would for a reference to a print source, and add as much electronic retrieval information as is needed for others to locate the same source. APA also recommends using a DOI (digital object identifier), when available, in place of a URL in references to electronic texts. The DOI is more permanent and consistent than a URL. No retrieval date is necessary if the content is not likely to be updated or changed.

16. When dividing a URL at the end of a line, never insert a hyphen to mark the break. Break the address immediately *before* most marks of punctuation (an exception is http:// , which should never break). Do not italicize, underline, or use angle brackets with URLs, and do not add a period at the end of a URL.

Periodicals

JOURNAL ARTICLE WITH A DOI

Ziegler, N. A. (2014). Fostering self-regulated learning through the European language portfolio: An embedded mixed methods study. *The Modern Language Journal, 98,* 921-936. doi:10.1111/modl.1214

If the journal is paginated by volume, the issue number is not needed. When a journal is paginated by issue, APA requires that the issue number be given parenthetically after the volume number.

> Harpham, G. G. (2009). Roots, race, and the return to philology. *Representations, 106*(1), 34-62. doi:10.1525/rep.2009.106.1.34

JOURNAL ARTICLE WITH A DOI AND MULTIPLE AUTHORS

> Ruppel, E. K. & Burke, T. J. (2014). Complementary channel use and the role of social competence. *Journal of Computer-Mediated Communication, 20,* 37-51. doi:10.1111/jcc4.12090

JOURNAL ARTICLE WITHOUT A DOI

> Stephens, R. (2012). What if? Preparing schools and communities for the unthinkable. *Law Enforcement Executive Forum, 12*(4), 1-7.

If there is no DOI assigned and the article is retrieved online, provide the URL of the home page of the journal.

> Winter, Y. On the grammar of a Senegalese drum language. *Language, 90,* 644-668. Retrieved from http://muse.jhu.edu/login?auth=0&type=summary&url=/journals/language/90.3.winter.html

PRINT MAGAZINE ARTICLE (MONTHLY OR WEEKLY)

> Crawford, A. (2018, June). The defiant ones. *Smithsonian, 49,* 42-51.

> Abend, L. (2013, December 16). Boys won't be boys. *Time, 182,* 40-44.

ONLINE MAGAZINE ARTICLE

> DeAngelis, T. (2013, December). When the conflict comes home. *Monitor on Psychology, 44*(11). Retrieved from http://www.apa.org/monitor/

PRINT NEWSPAPER ARTICLE (DAILY OR WEEKLY)

> Carney, H. (2011, December 18). Unlocking English. *Naples Daily News,* p. A1.

> Evelyn, J. (2003, June 20). The "silent killer" of minority enrollments. *Chronicle of Higher Education,* pp. A17-18.

ONLINE NEWSPAPER ARTICLE

> Nakamura, D. (2018, August 18). On Twitter, Trump accuses "social media" of limiting free speech of conservatives. *The Washington Post.* Retrieved from http://www.washingtonpost.com

BOOK REVIEW

Morozov, E. (2012, January 29). Sharing it all. [Review of the book *I know who you are and I saw what you did: Social networks and the death of privacy,* by L. Andrews]. *The New York Times Book Review,* p. 18.

Other Sources

BOOK WITH ONE AUTHOR

Mundy, L. (2017). Code girls: The untold story of the American women code breakers of World War II. New York, NY: Hachette Books.

Use the publisher's full name, but do not include words like *Inc.* or *Co.*

BOOK WITH TWO TO SEVEN AUTHORS

Beck, E., Britto, S., & Andrews, A. (2007). *In the shadow of death: Restorative justice and death row families.* New York, NY: Oxford University Press.

ELECTRONIC VERSION OF A PRINT BOOK

Webster, N. (1789). *Dissertations on the English language: with notes, historical and critical.* Retrieved from http://www.gutenberg.org/files/45738/45738-h /45738-h.htm

BOOK WITH A GROUP OR AN INSTITUTIONAL AUTHOR

World Health Organization. (2015). *Handbook for the assessment of capacities at the human-animal interface.* Geneva, Switzerland: WHO Press.

EDITED BOOK

Clark, V., Eschholz, P., Rosa, A., & Simon, B. L. (Eds.). (2008). *Language: Introductory readings* (7th ed.). Boston, MA: Bedford/St. Martin's.

EDITION OTHER THAN FIRST

Zinsser, W. (2006). *On writing well: The classic guide to writing nonfiction* (30th anniversary ed.). New York, NY: Harper Perennial.

ARTICLE OR CHAPTER IN AN EDITED BOOK OR ANTHOLOGY

O'Gorman, A. (2011). Defense through disarmament. In M. Andreas (Ed.), *Sweet fruit from the bitter tree: 61 stories of creative and compassionate ways out of conflict* (pp. 27-28). Boulder, CO: Real People Press.

ARTICLE IN A REFERENCE BOOK

Anagnost, G. T. (2005). Sandra Day O'Connor. In *The Oxford Companion to the Supreme Court* (2nd ed., pp. 701-704). New York, NY: Oxford University Press.

ENTRY IN AN ONLINE REFERENCE BOOK

Van Mill, D. (2017). Freedom of speech. In E. N. Zalta (Ed.), *The Stanford encyclopedia of philosophy* (Summer 2018 ed.). Retrieved from http://plato .stanford.edu/entries/freedom-speech/

GOVERNMENT PUBLICATION, PRINT AND ONLINE

U.S. Department of Justice, Federal Bureau of Investigation. (2017). *The FBI story 2017*. Washington, DC: Government Printing Office.

U.S. Department of Justice. (2016). *Combating religious discrimination today: Final report*. Retrieved from http://www.justice.gov/crt/file/884181/download

ADVERTISEMENT, PRINT AND ONLINE

Consumer Cellular. (2018, June). [Advertisement]. *Smithsonian, 49,* 75.

Rosetta Stone. (2018). The only language software with TruAccent. [Advertisement]. Retrieved from http://www.rosettastone.com/

WIKI ENTRY

Bilingual Education Act. (n.d.). In *Wikipedia*. Retrieved November 26, 2018 from http://en.wikipedia.org/wiki/Bilingual_Education_Act

VIDEO RECORDING POSTED ONLINE

AlyssaTalkingBack. (2012, January 30). Alyssa talking backwards [Video file]. Retrieved from http://www.youtube.com/watch?v=CRse-IePpbE

APA MANUSCRIPT FORMAT

The following guidelines for formatting manuscripts have been adapted from American Psychological Association recommendations.

Paper and Type

For academic papers use 8½-by-11-inch paper, and use a standard type style such as Times New Roman in 12-point font. On each page be sure to include a running head, which consists of the title of your paper abbreviated to fifty characters, in all capital letters on the left side of the upper margin; also include a page number on the right side of the upper margin. Finally, be sure you keep both a paper copy and an electronic copy of your paper.

Title Page

The title page should include a special running head in the upper left margin of the page:

Running head: TITLE OF PAPER

In the center of the page, in double-spaced type, include the full paper title, your name, and the name of your institution.

Margins, Line Spacing, and Paragraph Indentation

Leave a one-inch margin on all sides of the page. Double-space the text of the paper including long, set-off quotations, information notes, and the entries in the list of References. Do not justify (make even) the right-hand margin. Indent the first line of each paragraph one-half inch (or five spaces).

Page Numbers

Place the page number (e.g., 1) in the upper right corner of each page, approximately one inch from the top and one inch from the right edge of the page. Do not use the word *page* or its abbreviation *p.*; do not use a period or any other mark of punctuation with the page number. Number all pages of your paper, including the first and last.

Spacing for Punctuation

Leave one space after a comma, colon, or semicolon, and between the three periods in an ellipsis. APA recommends one space after a period, question mark, or exclamation point at the end of a sentence. Form dashes by using two hyphens with no space between them. Do not leave a space before or after a dash. Most word processors will convert your two hyphens into a dash.

Web Addresses

Should you have occasion to divide a web address at the end of a line in the text of your paper, break only after a double slash or before any other mark of punctuation. Never insert a hyphen to mark the break.

References Page

The list of References is placed on a separate page at the end of your paper and titled *References*. Continue the running head and page numbering on this page. Double-space and then center the words *References*. For the specific requirements of the format of each entry in the list of References, refer to the model entries on pages 123–126.

PART **2**

6

Understanding the Power of Language: How We Find Our Voices

Most of us accept language as we accept the air we breathe; we cannot get along without it, and we take it for granted almost all of the time. Many days we find ourselves on language overload, bombarded by a steady stream of verbal and written messages—some invited, others not—but how much do we really know about language? How well do we understand how language works? Few of us are aware of the extent to which language is used to mislead and manipulate. Still fewer of us are fully conscious of the ways, subtle and not, in which our use of language may affect others. And even fewer of us recognize that our very perceptions of the world are influenced, and our thoughts at least partially shaped, by language. However, we are also the beneficiaries of language far more than we are its victims. Language is one of humankind's greatest achievements and most important resources, and it is a subject endlessly fascinating in itself.

If it is true that we are all in some sense prisoners of language, it is equally true that liberation begins with an awareness of that fact. This chapter presents six essays in which individuals share their struggles with language and their discoveries about the power and centrality of language in their lives. In "Coming into Language," Jimmy Santiago Baca relates how he first came to understand the power of words while listening to other inmates read aloud in a county jail in Albuquerque, New Mexico. Baca remembers his frustration and feelings of shame and inadequacy once he acknowledges his illiteracy. Later, while serving time in Florence, Arizona, he dares to put pencil to paper and experiment with words, a decision that empowered and liberated his mind. Next, we read the inspiring story of Helen Keller, a woman who broke the chains of blindness and deafness and connected to the world around her. In "The Day Language Came into My Life," Keller recounts the day she, with the help of her teacher Anne Mansfield Sullivan, discovered "everything had a name, and each name gave birth to a new thought." In the third essay, "The Transformation of Silence into Language and Action," Audre Lorde recounts how she used a breast cancer diagnosis to help her gain perspective on her fears. Now that death was a real possibility, she discovered that her fears had rendered her silent over the years. Only when she learned to wage war against the tyrannies of silence was she able to speak her truth. Here she helps other women turn their silences into words that need to be spoken and actions that need to be taken.

In the fourth essay, "Stupid Rich Bastards," Laurel Johnson Black explores the relationship between class and language as she shares her experience growing up in a poor, working-class, white family in Massachusetts. As the family member selected by her parents to go to college, Black struggles in school, trying to bridge the gap between the working-class language she grew up with and the "well phrased" language of the "stupid rich bastards" who control their lives. Next, in "On and On: Appalachian Accent and Academic Power," Meredith McCarroll tells what it was like growing up and going to college in Appalachia, moving to Boston, and later attending graduate school. Her essay reveals how the language that we are born into influences who we are, how we see ourselves, and how others see us. In the end McCarroll comes to a solid understanding of what it means to be an Appalachian. And in the final selection, Malala Yousafzai speaks at the Youth Takeover of the United Nations in 2013, less than a year after she was shot by the Taliban because of her education advocacy work. In this speech, she positions herself as an advocate for children the world over who have no voice, calling for all governments to provide children access to education as well as protection from terrorism and violence. She uses strong, inclusive language to counter the extreme rhetoric of the Taliban and to show the power of education to affect change.

Coming into Language

JIMMY SANTIAGO BACA

"Through language I was free," writes essayist, poet, and screenwriter Jimmy Santiago Baca in the selection below. "I could respond, escape, indulge; embrace or reject earth or the cosmos." The word "free" carries special meaning in the context of his life. Born in 1952 in Santa Fe, New Mexico, and abandoned by his parents, he dropped out of school and spent several years in prison in the 1970s after being convicted on drug charges. During his incarceration, he learned how to read and began to write, a process that he describes in "Coming into Language." He published his first poems in *Mother Jones* magazine while he was still in prison. In 1979 he was released and published his first book of poetry, *Immigrants in Our Own Land & Selected Early Poetry.*

Although he identifies as a Chicano writer, Baca's influences and enthusiasms are various, including William Wordsworth, Walt Whitman, Pablo Neruda, Malcolm X, and Beat poets such as Allen Ginsberg. He also works in a variety of forms and genres, from *Martin and Meditations on the South Valley* (1987), a long autobiographical novel-in-verse that won the American Book Award, to the screenplay *Bound by Honor,* which became the 1993 crime film *Blood In, Blood Out.* His other works include *Spring Poems Along the Rio Grande* (2007) and the novel *A Glass of Water* (2009). The following literacy narrative was originally published in *Working in the Dark: Reflections of a Poet of the Barrio* (1992). Here, Baca not only discovers the redemptive power of language and literature but also finds a "deep faith in the voice of my heart."

WRITING TO DISCOVER: *Do you think words have the power to take you different places and even change you in fundamental ways? What texts or readings have transported you? What texts have transformed you, or made you a different person in some way?*

On weekend graveyard shifts at St. Joseph's Hospital I worked the emergency room, mopping up pools of blood and carting plastic bags stuffed with arms, legs and hands to the outdoor incinerator. I enjoyed the quiet, away from the screams of shotgunned, knifed, and mangled kids writhing on gurneys outside the operating rooms. Ambulance sirens shrieked and squad car lights reddened the cool nights, flashing against the hospital walls: gray—red, gray—red. On slow nights I would lock the door of the administration office, search the reference library for a book on female anatomy and, with my feet propped on the desk, leaf through the illustrations, smoking my cigarette. I was seventeen.

One night my eye was caught by a familiar-looking word on the spine of a book. The title was *450 Years of Chicano History in Pictures.* On the cover were black-and-white photos: Padre Hidalgo exhorting Mexican peasants to revolt against the Spanish dictators; Anglo vigilantes hanging two Mexicans from a tree; a young Mexican woman with rifle and ammunition belts crisscrossing her breast; César Chávez and field workers marching for fair wages; Chicano railroad workers laying creosote ties; Chicanas laboring at machines in textile factories; Chicanas picketing and hoisting boycott signs.

From the time I was seven, teachers had been punishing me for not knowing my lessons by making me stick my nose in a circle chalked on the blackboard. Ashamed of not understanding and fearful of asking questions, I dropped out of school in the ninth grade. At seventeen I still didn't know how to read, but those pictures confirmed my identity. I stole the book that night, stashing it for safety under the slop sink until I got off work. Back at my boardinghouse, I showed the book to friends. All of us were amazed; this book told us we were alive. We, too, had defended ourselves with our fists against hostile Anglos, gasping for breath in fights with the policemen who outnumbered us. The book reflected back to us our struggle in a way that made us proud.

Most of my life I felt like a target in the crosshairs of a hunter's rifle. When strangers and outsiders questioned me I felt the hang-rope tighten around my neck and the trapdoor creak beneath my feet. There was nothing so humiliating as being unable to express myself, and my inarticulateness increased my sense of jeopardy. Behind a mask of humility, I seethed with mute rebellion.

Before I was eighteen, I was arrested on suspicion of murder after 5 refusing to explain a deep cut on my forearm. With shocking speed I found myself handcuffed to a chain gang of inmates and bused to a holding facility to await trial. There I met men, prisoners, who read aloud to each other the works of Neruda, Paz, Sabines, Nemerov, and Hemingway. Never had I felt such freedom as in that dormitory. Listening to the words of these writers, I felt that invisible threat from without lessen — my sense of teetering on a rotting plank over swamp water where famished alligators clapped their horny snouts for my blood. While I listened to the words of the poets, the alligators slumbered powerless in their lairs. The language of poetry was the magic that could liberate me from myself, transform me into another person, transport me to places far away.

And when they closed the books, these Chicanos, and went into their own Chicano language, they made barrio life come alive for me in the fullness of its vitality. I began to learn my own language, the bilingual words and phrases explaining to me my place in the universe. Months later I was released, as I had suspected I would be. I had been guilty of nothing but shattering the windshield of my girlfriend's car in a fit of rage.

Two years passed. I was twenty now, and behind bars again. The federal marshals had failed to provide convincing evidence to extradite me to

Arizona on a drug charge, but still I was being held. They had ninety days
to prove I was guilty. The only evidence against me was that my girlfriend
had been at the scene of the crime with my driver's license in her purse.
They had to come up with something else. But there was nothing else.
Eventually they negotiated a deal with the actual drug dealer, who took
the stand against me. When the judge hit me with a million-dollar bail, I
emptied my pockets on his booking desk: twenty-six cents.

One night in my third month in the county jail, I was mopping the
floor in front of the booking desk. Some detectives had kneed an old
drunk and handcuffed him to the booking bars. His shrill screams raked
my nerves like a hacksaw on bone, the desperate protest of his dignity
against their inhumanity. But the detectives just laughed as he tried to
rise and kicked him to his knees. When they went to the bathroom to pee
and the desk attendant walked to the file cabinet to pull the arrest record,
I shot my arm through the bars, grabbed one of the attendant's university textbooks, and tucked it in my overalls. It was the only way I had of
protesting.

It was late when I returned to my cell. Under my blanket I switched
on a pen flashlight and opened the thick book at random, scanning the
pages. I could hear the jailer making his rounds on the other tiers. The
jangle of his keys and the sharp click of his boot heels intensified my solitude. Slowly I enunciated the words . . . p-o-n-d, ri-pple. It scared me
that I had been reduced to this to find comfort. I always had thought
reading a waste of time, that nothing could be gained by it. Only by
action, by moving out into the world and confronting and challenging
the obstacles, could one learn anything worth knowing.

Even as I tried to convince myself that I was merely curious, I became   10
so absorbed in how the sounds created music in me and happiness, I forgot
where I was. Memories began to quiver in me, glowing with a strange but
familiar intimacy in which I found refuge. For a while, a deep sadness over-
came me, as if I had chanced on a long-lost friend and mourned the years
of separation. But soon the heartache of having missed so much of life, that
had numbed me since I was a child, gave way, as if a grave illness lifted itself
from me and I was cured, innocently believing in the beauty of life again.
I stumblingly repeated the author's name as I fell asleep, saying it over and
over in the dark: Words-worth, Words-worth.

Before long my sister came to visit me, and I joked about taking her
to a place called Xanadu and getting her a blind date with this *vato*[1] named
Coleridge who lived on the seacoast and was *malias*[2] on morphine. When
I asked her to make a trip into enemy territory to buy me a grammar
book, she said she couldn't. Bookstores intimidated her, because she, too,
could neither read nor write.

---

1. In Chicano dialect: dude.
2. In Chicano dialect: strung out.

Days later, with a stub pencil I whittled sharp with my teeth, I propped a Red Chief notebook on my knees and wrote my first words. From that moment, a hunger for poetry possessed me.

Until then, I had felt as if I had been born into a raging ocean where I swam relentlessly, flailing my arms in hope of rescue, of reaching a shoreline I never sighted. Never solid ground beneath me, never a resting place. I had lived with only the desperate hope to stay afloat; that and nothing more.

I crawled out of stanzas dripping with birth-blood, reborn and freed from the chaos of my life.

But when at last I wrote my first words on the page, I felt an island rising beneath my feet like the back of a whale. As more and more words emerged, I could finally rest: I had a place to stand for the first time in my life. The island grew, with each page, into a continent inhabited by people I knew and mapped with the life I lived.

I wrote about it all—about people I had loved or hated, about the brutalities and ecstasies of my life. And, for the first time, the child in me who had witnessed and endured unspeakable terrors cried out not just in impotent despair, but with the power of language. Suddenly, through language, through writing, my grief and my joy could be shared with anyone who would listen. And I could do this all alone; I could do it anywhere. I was no longer a captive of demons eating away at me, no longer a victim of other people's mockery and loathing, that had made me clench my fist white with rage and grit my teeth to silence. Words now pleaded back with the bleak lucidity of hurt. They were wrong, those others, and now I could say it.

Through language I was free. I could respond, escape, indulge, embrace or reject earth or the cosmos. I was launched on an endless journey without boundaries or rules, in which I could salvage the floating fragments of my past, or be born anew in the spontaneous ignition of understanding some heretofore concealed aspect of myself. Each word steamed with the hot lava juices of my primordial making, and I crawled out of stanzas dripping with birth-blood, reborn and freed from the chaos of my life. The child in the dark room of my heart, who had never been able to find or reach the light switch, flicked it on now; and I found in the room a stranger, myself, who had waited so many years to speak again. My words struck in me lightning crackles of elation and thunderhead storms of grief.

When I had been in the county jail longer than anyone else, I was made a trustee. One morning, after a fistfight, I went to the unlocked and unoccupied office used for lawyer–client meetings, to think. The bare white room with its fluorescent tube lighting seemed to expose and illuminate my dark and worthless life. When I had fought before, I never gave it a thought. Now, for the first time, I had something to lose—my chance to read, to write; a way to live with dignity and meaning, that had opened for me when I stole that scuffed, second-hand book about the Romantic poets.

"I will never do any work in this prison system as long as I am not allowed to get my G.E.D." That's what I told the reclassification panel. The captain flicked off the tape recorder. He looked at me hard and said, "You'll never walk outta here alive. Oh, you'll work, put a copper penny on that, you'll work."

After that interview I was confined to deadlock maximum security in a subterranean dungeon, with ground-level chicken-wired windows painted gray. Twenty-three hours a day I was in that cell. Then, just before Christmas, I received a letter from Harry, a charity house Samaritan who doled out hot soup to the homeless in Phoenix. He had picked my name from a list of cons who had no one write to them. I wrote back asking for a grammar book, and a week later received one of Mary Baker Eddy's treatises on salvation and redemption, with Spanish and English on opposing pages. Pacing my cell all day and most of each night, I grappled with grammar until I was able to write a long true-romance confession for a con to send to his pen pal. He paid me with a pack of smokes. Soon I had a thriving barter business, exchanging my poems and letters for novels, commissary pencils, and writing tablets.

One day I tore two flaps from the cardboard box that held all my belongings and punctured holes along the edge of each flap and along the border of a ream of state-issue paper. After I had aligned them to form a spine, I threaded the holes with a shoestring, and sketched on the cover a hummingbird fluttering above a rose. This was my first journal.   20

Whole afternoons I wrote, unconscious of passing time or whether it was day or night. Sunbursts exploded from the lead tip of my pencil, words that grafted me into awareness of who I was; peeled back to a burning core of bleak terror, an embryo floating in the image of water, I cracked out of the shell wide-eyed and insane. Trees grew out of the palms of my hands, the threatening otherness of life dissolved, and I became one with the air and sky, the dirt and the iron and concrete. There was no longer any distinction between the other and I. Language made bridges of fire between me and everything I saw. I entered into the blade of grass, the basketball, the con's eye and child's soul.

At night I flew. I conversed with floating heads in my cell, and visited strange houses where lonely women brewed tea and rocked in wicker rocking chairs listening to sad Joni Mitchell songs.

Before long I was frayed like rope carrying too much weight, that suddenly snaps. I quit talking. Bars, walls, steel bunk and floor bristled with millions of poem-making sparks. My face was no longer familiar to me. The only reality was the swirling cornucopia of images in my mind, the voices in the air. Midair a cactus blossom would appear, a snake-flame in blinding dance around it, stunning me like a guard's fist striking my neck from behind.

The prison administrators tried several tactics to get me to work. For six months, after the next monthly prison board review, they sent cons to my cell to hassle me. When the guard would open my cell door to let one of them in, I'd leap out and fight him—and get sent to thirty-day isolation. I did a lot of isolation time. But I honed my image-making talents in that sensory-deprived solitude. Finally they moved me to death row, and after that to "nut-run," the tier that housed the mentally disturbed.

As the months passed, I became more and more sluggish. My eyelids were heavy, I could no longer write or read. I slept all the time.   25

One day a guard took me out to the exercise field. For the first time in years I felt grass and earth under my feet. It was spring. The sun warmed my face as I sat on the bleachers watching the cons box and run, hit the handball, lift weights. Some of them stopped to ask how I was, but I found it impossible to utter a syllable. My tongue would not move, saliva drooled from the corners of my mouth. I had been so heavily medicated I could not summon the slightest gestures. Yet inside me a small voice cried out, I am fine! I am hurt now but I will come back! I'm fine!

Back in my cell, for weeks I refused to eat. Styrofoam cups of urine and hot water were hurled at me. Other things happened. There were beatings, shock therapy, intimidation.

Later, I regained some clarity of mind. But there was a place in my heart where I had died. My life had compressed itself into an unbearable dread of being. The strain had been too much. I had stepped over that line where a human being has lost more than he can bear, where the pain is too intense, and he knows he is changed forever. I was now capable of killing, coldly and without feeling. I was empty, as I have never, before or since, known emptiness. I had no connection to this life.

But then, the encroaching darkness that began to envelop me forced me to re-form and give birth to myself again in the chaos. I withdrew even deeper into the world of language, cleaving the diamonds of verbs and nouns, plunging into the brilliant light of poetry's regenerative mystery. Words gave off rings of white energy, radar signals from powers beyond me that infused me with truth. I believed what I wrote, because I wrote what was true. My words did not come from books or textual formulas, but from a deep faith in the voice of my heart. I had been steeped in self-loathing and rejected by everyone and everything—society, family, cons, God and demons. But now I had become as the burning ember floating in darkness that descends on a dry leaf and sets flame to forests. The word was the ember and the forest was my life. . .

Writing bridged my divided life of prisoner and free man. I wrote   30 of the emotional butchery of prisons, and my acute gratitude for poetry. Where my blind doubt and spontaneous trust in life met, I discovered empathy and compassion. The power to express myself was a welcome storm rasping at tendril roots, flooding my soul's cracked dirt. Writing was water that cleansed the wound and fed the parched root of my heart.

I wrote to sublimate my rage, from a place where all hope is gone, from a madness of having been damaged too much, from a silence of killing rage. I wrote to avenge the betrayals of a lifetime, to purge the bitterness of injustice. I wrote with a deep groan of doom in my blood, bewildered and dumbstruck; from an indestructible love of life, to affirm breath and laughter and the abiding innocence of things. I wrote the way I wept, and danced, and made love.

THINKING CRITICALLY ABOUT THE READING

1. In his younger years, what did Baca find to be the most humiliating experience? How was it related to language?

2. As a form of protest against police brutality, Baca steals something from a desk attendant at the county jail. What does he steal? How does this stolen object become important to his story?

3. Why did Baca refuse to work while in prison? What were the consequences of his refusal?

4. Baca is a poet, and his language is highly figurative. How do you respond to his frequent use of metaphor and simile? Do you find that it helps reinforce his points and support his purpose? Do you find his figures of speech confusing, or even distracting? Using specific examples from his text, explain your answer. (Glossary: *Figurative Language*)

5. While Baca relies on figurative language extensively throughout the essay, he does not use a simile or a metaphor in paragraph 28. Why do you think he made that choice?

LANGUAGE IN ACTION

Baca experiences language not merely in abstract or intellectual terms, but as a physical, emotional, visceral, and sensuous *thing*. For example, in paragraph 12, he claims, "I became so absorbed in how the sounds created music in me and happiness, I forgot where I was." Later, in paragraph 17, he writes, "Each word steamed with the hot lava juices of my primordial making, and I crawled out of stanzas dripping with birth-blood, reborn and freed from the chaos of my life."

Consider your own experience with language—in poems, novels, song lyrics, speeches, or even lines from movies. Do any passages make you happy in the way they *sound*? Are there any sentences, paragraphs, lines of poems, or other texts that seem to have a physical or concrete quality to you: words that "steam with . . . hot lava juices"? Bring a brief text that affects you viscerally or sensuously to class. Explain its effects on you. What is it about the words (their sound, for example) that give them this powerful, physical quality?

WRITING SUGGESTIONS

1. In this essay, Baca writes about his formative experiences with the English language. These memories not only include specific books, but also specific words, as when he "enunciated the words . . . p-o-n-d, ri-pple" (11). Reflect on your own early experiences with language, and write a personal narrative about the process, using any specific memory or example that you recall. For instance, what is a specific word that you remember being able to say, spell, or read? What is a specific book, poem, rhyme, or other piece of language that you can recall seeing, saying, reading, and enjoying (or even disliking)? Why does this example stand out?

2. Baca recalls finding the book *450 Years of Chicano History in Pictures* in the library of a hospital where he worked. He is fascinated by the book because it reflects and confirms his identity. He even shares it with some friends, claiming: "All of us were amazed; this book told us we were alive" (3). Essentially, Baca is writing about the importance and power of media representation. Why do we feel the need to see people like ourselves in books, movies, television shows, and other forms? In what ways do these images tell us that we are "alive"? How do you respond to current debates about racial, ethnic, religious, and gender representation in movies and television? Do you think such representation is important? Why or why not? You could also respond to this writing prompt by writing about a personal experience of representation in a book, movie, or other media form—an experience that confirmed an aspect of your identity or told you that you were alive.

The Day Language Came into My Life

HELEN KELLER

Helen Keller (1880–1968) became blind and deaf at the age of eighteen months as a result of a disease. As a child, then, Keller became accustomed to her limited world, for it was all that she knew. She experienced only certain fundamental sensations, such as the warmth of the sun on her face, and few emotions, such as anger and bitterness. It wasn't until she was almost seven years old that her family hired Anne Sullivan, a young woman who would turn out to be an extraordinary teacher, to help her. As Keller learned to communicate and think, the world opened up to her. She recorded her experiences in an autobiography, *The Story of My Life* (1903), from which the following selection is taken.

Helen Keller is in a unique position to remind us of what it is like to pass from the "fog" of prethought into the world where "everything had a name, and each name gave birth to a new thought." Her experiences as a deaf and blind child also raise a number of questions about the relationship between language and thought, emotions, ideas, and memory. Over time, Keller's acquisition of language allowed her to assume all the advantages of her birthright. Her rapid intellectual and emotional growth as a result of language suggests that we, too, have the potential to achieve a greater measure of our humanity by further refining our language abilities.

WRITING TO DISCOVER: *Consider what your life would be like today if you had been born without the ability to understand language or to speak, or if you had suddenly lost the ability to use language later in life. Write about those aspects of your life that you think would be affected most severely.*

The most important day I remember in all my life is the one on which my teacher, Anne Mansfield Sullivan, came to me. I am filled with wonder when I consider the immeasurable contrast between the two lives which it connects. It was the third of March 1887, three months before I was seven years old.

On the afternoon of that eventful day, I stood on the porch, dumb, expectant. I guessed vaguely from my mother's signs and from the hurrying to and fro in the house that something unusual was about to happen, so I went to the door and waited on the steps. The afternoon sun penetrated the mass of honeysuckle that covered the porch and fell on my upturned face. My fingers lingered almost unconsciously on the familiar leaves and blossoms which had just come forth to greet the sweet southern spring. I did not know what the future held of marvel or surprise for me. Anger and bitterness had preyed upon me continually for weeks and a deep languor had succeeded this passionate struggle.

Have you ever been at sea in a dense fog, when it seemed as if a tangible white darkness shut you in, and the great ship, tense and anxious, groped her way toward the shore with plummet and sounding-line, and you waited with beating heart for something to happen? I was like that ship before my education began, only I was without compass or sounding-line and had no way of knowing how near the harbor was. "Light! give me light!" was the wordless cry of my soul, and the light of love shone on me in that very hour.

I felt approaching footsteps. I stretched out my hand as I supposed to my mother. Someone took it, and I was caught up and held close in the arms of her who had come to reveal all things to me, and, more than all things else, to love me.

The morning after my teacher came she led me into her room and gave me a doll. The little blind children at the Perkins Institution had sent it and Laura Bridgman had dressed it; but I did not know this until afterward. When I had played with it a little while, Miss Sullivan slowly spelled into my hand the word "d-o-l-l." I was at once interested in this finger play and tried to imitate it. When I finally succeeded in making the letters correctly I was flushed with childhood pleasure and pride. Running downstairs to my mother I held up my hand and made the letters for doll. I did not know that I was spelling a word or even that words existed; I was simply making my fingers go in monkeylike imitation. In the days that followed I learned to spell in this uncomprehending way a great many words, among them *pin, hat, cup* and a few verbs like *sit, stand* and *walk*. But my teacher had been with me several weeks before I understood that everything has a name.

One day, while I was playing with my new doll, Miss Sullivan put my big rag doll into my lap also, spelled "d-o-l-l" and tried to make me understand that "d-o-l-l" applied to both. Earlier in the day we had had a tussle over the words "m-u-g" and "w-a-t-e-r." Miss Sullivan had tried to impress it upon me that "m-u-g" is *mug* and that "w-a-t-e-r" is *water,* but I persisted in confounding the two. In despair she had dropped the subject for the time, only to renew it at the first opportunity. I became impatient at her repeated attempts and, seizing the new doll, I dashed it upon the floor. I was keenly delighted when I felt the fragments of the broken doll at my feet. Neither sorrow nor regret followed my passionate outburst. I had not loved the doll. In the still, dark world in which I lived there was no strong sentiment or tenderness. I felt my teacher sweep the fragments to one side of the hearth, and I had a sense of satisfaction that the cause of my discomfort was removed. She brought me my hat, and I knew I was going out into the warm sunshine. This thought, if a wordless sensation may be called a thought, made me hop and skip with pleasure.

5

We walked down the path to the well-house, attracted by the fragrance of the honeysuckle with which it was covered. Some one was drawing water and my teacher placed my hand under the spout. As the cool stream gushed over one hand she spelled into the other the word *water,* first slowly, then rapidly. I stood still, my whole attention fixed upon the motions of her fingers. Suddenly I felt a misty consciousness as of something forgotten — a thrill of returning thought; and somehow the mystery of language was revealed to me. I knew then that "w-a-t-e-r" meant the wonderful cool something that was flowing over my hand. The living word awakened my soul, gave it light, hope, joy, set it free! There were barriers still, it is true, but barriers that could in time be swept away.

> **I knew then that "w-a-t-e-r" meant the wonderful cool something that was flowing over my hand.**

I left the well-house eager to learn. Everything had a name, and each name gave birth to a new thought. As we returned to the house every object which I touched seemed to quiver with life. That was because I saw everything with the strange, new sight that had come to me. On entering the door I remembered the doll I had broken. I felt my way to the hearth and picked up the pieces. I tried vainly to put them together. Then my eyes filled with tears; for I realized what I had done, and for the first time I felt repentance and sorrow.

I learned a great many new words that day. I do not remember what they all were; but I do know that *mother, father, sister, teacher* were among them — words that were to make the world blossom for me, "like Aaron's rod, with flowers." It would have been difficult to find a happier child than I was as I lay in my crib at the close of that eventful day and lived over the joys it had brought me, and for the first time longed for a new day to come.

THINKING CRITICALLY ABOUT THE READING

1. In paragraph 6, Keller writes, "One day, while I was playing with my new doll, Miss Sullivan put my big rag doll into my lap also, spelled 'd-o-l-l' and tried to make me understand that 'd-o-l-l' applied to both." Why do you think Miss Sullivan placed a different doll in her lap? What essential fact about language did the action demonstrate to Keller?

2. In paragraph 6, Keller also tells us that in trying to learn the difference between "m-u-g" and "w-a-t-e-r" she "persisted in confounding the two" terms. In a letter to her home institution, Sullivan elaborated on this confusion, revealing that it was caused by Keller thinking that both words meant "drink." How in paragraph 7 does Keller finally come to understand these words? What does she come to understand about the relationship between them?

3. In paragraph 8, after the experience at the well, Keller comes to believe that "everything had a name, and each name gave birth to a new thought." Reflect on that statement. Does she mean that the process of naming leads to thinking?

4. Keller realized that over time words would make her world open up for her. Identify the parts of speech of her first words. In what ways do these parts of speech open up one's world? Explain how these words or parts of speech provide insights into the nature of writing. How does Keller's early language use compare with her use of English in her essay?

5. While it is fairly easy to see how Keller could learn the names of concrete items, it may be more difficult for us to understand how she learned about her emotions. What does her difficulty in coming to terms with abstractions—such as love, bitterness, frustration, repentance, sorrow—tell us as writers about the strategies we need to use to effectively convey emotions and feelings to our readers? In considering your answer, examine the diction Keller uses in her essay. (Glossary: *Diction*)

LANGUAGE IN ACTION

In paragraph 3, Keller uses figurative language—the metaphor of being lost in a fog—to explain her feeling of helplessness and her frustration at not being able to communicate. (Glossary: *Figures of Speech*) Metaphors and similes—brief, imaginative comparisons that highlight the similarities between things that are basically dissimilar—can be extremely helpful when trying to communicate a new concept or a strange or difficult feeling. Create a metaphor (implied comparison) or a simile (implicit comparison introduced by *like* or *as*) that would be helpful in describing each item in the following list. The first one has been completed for you to illustrate the process.

1. Skyscraper: The skyscraper sparkled in the sunlight like a huge glass needle. (Simile)

   The skyscraper, a huge glass needle, sparkled in the sunlight. (Metaphor)
2. Sound of an explosion
3. Happy person
4. Greasy French fries
5. Disagreeable roommate
6. Cold wind
7. Crowded elevator
8. Loneliness
9. Slow-moving car
10. Rainy day

Compare your metaphors and similes with those written by other members of your class. Which metaphors and similes for each item on the list seem to work best? Why? Do any seem tired or clichéd?

WRITING SUGGESTIONS

1. It could be said that we process our world in terms of our language. Using a variety of examples from your own experience, write an essay illustrating the validity of this observation. For example, aside from the photographs you took on your last vacation, your trip exists only in the words you use to describe it, whether in conversations or in writing.

2. Helen Keller explains that she felt no remorse when she shattered her doll. "In the still, dark world in which I lived there was no strong sentiment or tenderness" (6) she recalls. However, once she understood that things had names, Keller was able to feel repentance and sorrow. In your own words, try to describe why you think her feelings changed. Before you begin to write, you may want to reread your Writing to Discover entry for the Keller article. You may also want to discuss this issue with classmates or your instructor and do some research of your own into the ways language alters perception among people who are blind or deaf.

The Transformation of Silence into Language and Action

Audre Lorde

The fierce and prolific Audre Lorde (1934–1992) was a poet, novelist, essayist, and activist whose work and life often embodied a line from her 1973 poem "New Year's Day": "I am deliberate/and afraid/of nothing." Born in New York City to Caribbean immigrants, she graduated from Hunter College and earned her MLA from Columbia University. Lorde then worked as a public librarian before publishing her first book of poetry, *First Cities*, in 1968. In the years that followed, she taught at Tougaloo College in Mississippi, as well as John Jay College and Hunter College in New York City.

Lordes's poetry, along with all her other writing, manages to be deeply personal while addressing broader issues of racism, gender, sexuality, civil rights, and social justice. As she once said in an interview, "[M]y poetry comes from the intersection of me and my worlds." Her more well-known collections of poems include *Cables to Rage* (1970), *Coal* (1976), and *The Black Unicorn* (1978). She also wrote one novel, *Zami: A New Spelling of My Name* (1982). The following selection is a speech that Lorde delivered at the Modern Language Association's "Lesbian and Literature Panel" in Chicago on December 28, 1977. Here, she reflects on the necessity of speaking our truths in the face of fear and committing to the "transformation of silence into language and action."

WRITING TO DISCOVER: *What true or important aspects of yourself are you afraid to express in words? Are there things you would sincerely like to say, but are afraid to? Have you ever regretted your silence or unwillingness to speak up or speak out? Have you ever regretted speaking out?*

I have come to believe over and over again that what is most important to me must be spoken, made verbal and shared, even at the risk of having it bruised or misunderstood. That the speaking profits me, beyond any other effect. I am standing here as a Black lesbian poet, and the meaning of all that waits upon the fact that I am still alive, and might not have been. Less than two months ago I was told by two doctors, one female and one male, that I would have to have breast surgery, and that there was a 60 to 80 percent chance that the tumor was malignant. Between that telling and the actual surgery, there was a three-week period of the agony of an involuntary reorganization of my entire life. The surgery was completed, and the growth was benign.

But within those three weeks, I was forced to look upon myself and my living with a harsh and urgent clarity that has left me still shaken but much stronger. This is a situation faced by many women, by some of you here today. Some of what I experienced during that time has helped elucidate for me much of what I feel concerning the transformation of silence into language and action.

In becoming forcibly and essentially aware of my mortality, and of what I wished and wanted for my life, however short it might be, priorities and omissions became strongly etched in a merciless light, and what I most regretted were my silences. Of what had I *ever* been afraid? To question or to speak as I believed could have meant pain, or death. But we all hurt in so many different ways, all the time, and pain will either change or end. Death, on the other hand, is the final silence. And that might be coming quickly, now, without regard for whether I had ever spoken what needed to be said, or had only betrayed myself into small silences, while I planned someday to speak, or waited for someone else's words. And I began to recognize a source of power within myself that comes from the knowledge that while it is most desirable not to be afraid, learning to put fear into a perspective gave me great strength.

I was going to die, if not sooner then later, whether or not I had ever spoken myself. My silences had not protected me. Your silence will not protect you. But for every real word spoken, for every attempt I had ever made to speak those truths for which I am still seeking, I had made contact with other women while we examined the words to fit a world in which we all believed, bridging our differences. And it was the concern and caring of all those women which gave me strength and enabled me to scrutinize the essentials of my living.

The women who sustained me through that period were Black and   5 white, old and young, lesbian, bisexual, and heterosexual, and we all shared a war against the tyrannies of silence. They all gave me a strength and concern without which I could not have survived intact. Within those weeks of acute fear came the knowledge—within the war we are all waging with the forces of death, subtle and otherwise, conscious or not—I am not only a casualty, I am also a warrior.

What are the words you do not yet have? What do you need to say? What are the tyrannies you swallow day by day and attempt to make your own, until you will sicken and die of them, still in silence? Perhaps for some of you here today, I am the face of one of your fears. Because I am woman, because I am Black, because I am lesbian, because I am myself—a Black woman warrior poet doing my work—come to ask you, are you doing yours?

And of course I am afraid, because the transformation of silence into language and action is an act of self-revelation, and that always seems fraught with danger. But my daughter, when I told her of our topic and my difficulty with it, said, "Tell them about how you're never really a whole person if you remain silent, because there's always that one little piece inside you that wants to be spoken out, and if you keep ignoring it, it gets madder and madder and hotter and hotter, and if you don't speak it out one day it will just up and punch you in the mouth from the inside."

In the cause of silence, each of us draws the face of her own fear—fear of contempt, of censure, or some judgment, or recognition, of challenge, of annihilation. But most of all, I think, we fear the visibility without which we cannot truly live. Within this country where racial difference creates a constant, if unspoken, distortion of vision, Black women have on one hand always been highly visible, and so, on the other hand, have been rendered invisible through the depersonalization of racism. Even within the women's movement, we have had to fight, and still do, for that very visibility which also renders us most vulnerable, our Blackness. For to survive in the mouth of this dragon we call America, we have had to learn this first and most vital lesson—that we were never meant to survive. Not as human beings. And neither were most of you here today, Black or not. And that visibility which makes us most vulnerable is that which also is the source of our greatest strength. Because the machine will try to grind you into dust anyway, whether or not we speak. We can sit in our corners mute forever while our sisters and our selves are wasted, while our children are distorted and destroyed, while our earth is poisoned; we can sit in our safe corners mute as bottles, and we will still be no less afraid.

Each of us is here now because in one way or another we share a commitment to language and to the power of language ...

In my house this year we are celebrating the feast of Kwanza, the African-American festival of harvest which begins the day after Christmas and lasts for seven days. There are seven principles of Kwanza, one for each day. The first principle is Umoja, which means unity, the decision to strive for and maintain unity in self and community. The principle for yesterday, the second day, was Kujichagulia—self-determination—the decision to define ourselves, name ourselves, and speak for ourselves, instead of being defined and spoken for by others. Today is the third day of Kwanza, and the principle for today is Ujima—collective work and responsibility—the decision to build and maintain ourselves and our communities together and to recognize and solve our problems together.

Each of us is here now because in one way or another we share a commitment to language and to the power of language, and to the reclaiming of that language which has been made to work against us. In the transformation of silence into language and action, it is vitally necessary for each one of us to establish or examine her function in that transformation and to recognize her role as vital within that transformation.   10

For those of us who write, it is necessary to scrutinize not only the truth of what we speak, but the truth of that language by which we speak it. For others, it is to share and spread also those words that are meaningful to us. But primarily for us all, it is necessary to teach by living and speaking those truths which we believe and know beyond understanding. Because in this way alone we can survive, by taking part in a process of life that is creative and continuing, that is growth.

And it is never without fear—of visibility, of the harsh light of scrutiny and perhaps judgment, of pain, of death. But we have lived through all of those already, in silence, except death. And I remind myself all the time now that if I were to have been born mute, or had maintained an oath of silence my whole life long for safety, I would still have suffered, and I would still die. It is very good for establishing perspective.

And where the words of women are crying to be heard, we must each of us recognize our responsibility to seek those words out, to read them and share them and examine them in their pertinence to our lives. That we not hide behind the mockeries of separations that have been imposed upon us and which so often we accept as our own. For instance, "I can't possibly teach Black women's writing—their experience is so different from mine." Yet how many years have you spent teaching Plato and Shakespeare and Proust? Or another, "She's a white woman and what could she possibly have to say to me?" Or, "She's a lesbian, what would my husband say, or my chairman?" Or again, "This woman writes of her sons and I have no children." And all the other endless ways in which we rob ourselves of ourselves and each other.

We can learn to work and speak when we are afraid in the same way we have learned to work and speak when we are tired. For we have been socialized to respect fear more than our own needs for language and definition, and while we wait in silence for that final luxury of fearlessness, the weight of that silence will choke us.

The fact that we are here and that I speak these words is an attempt to break that silence and bridge some of those differences between us, for it is not difference which immobilizes us, but silence. And there are so many silences to be broken.

15

THINKING CRITICALLY ABOUT THE READING

1. After fearing for her life because of a cancer scare, what did Lorde discover that she most regretted about her life?

2. What advice did Lorde's daughter give her about writing her talk?

3. In the opening sentence of this speech, Lorde says, "I have come to believe over and over again that what is most important to me must be spoken, made verbal and shared, even at the risk of having it bruised or misunderstood." Do you think she is referring specifically to speech and *oral* communication, or do you think she means to include writing, as well? Explain.

4. In paragraph 6, Lorde writes, "Perhaps for some of you here today, I am the face of one of your fears." What is she referring to here? How is it related to her purpose—and her argument about language?

5. In paragraphs 4 and 15, Lorde suggests that language can "bridg[e] our differences." What does she mean by this? Do you agree with this idea? Why or why not?

6. The occasion for "The Transformation of Silence into Language and Action" was a "Lesbian and Literature" panel at the Modern Language Association: an organization of literary scholars who, like Lorde, write and teach professionally. That is to say, her audience was a relatively specialized group of listeners. Is the meaning or power of her claims and arguments limited by that audience? Does her writing carry an important message for a more general group of readers and listeners? Explain.

LANGUAGE IN ACTION

Lorde argues for the necessity of turning silence into language and action, even though doing so is dangerous: "And of course I am afraid, because the transformation of silence into language and action is an act of self-revelation, and that always seems fraught with danger." Read the following quotations on the virtues of silence and the virtues of speaking out, respectively:

On silence:

Wise men say nothing in dangerous times.
— AESOP

Silence is a true friend who never betrays.
— CONFUCIUS

Silence is more eloquent than words.
— THOMAS CARLYLE

On speaking out:

The ultimate tragedy is not the oppression and cruelty by the bad people but the silence over that by the good people.
— MARTIN LUTHER KING JR.

We must take sides. Neutrality helps the oppressor, never the victim.
— ELIE WIESEL

Truth is not only violated by falsehood; it may be equally outraged by silence.

— HENRI-FRÉDÉRIC AMIEL

Discuss the following questions as a class: What are the dangers of speaking out? What are the dangers of silence? What examples of the respective dangers can you think of? When is speaking out necessary, regardless of our fears? When is it best to remain silent? Are there times when silence itself is a form of speech or even action?

WRITING SUGGESTIONS

1. Lorde argues that language can bridge differences between people. In paragraph 13, she implies that this is especially true in the context of literature, where readers encounter authors and characters who are fundamentally different than themselves:

   > For instance, "I can't possibly teach Black women's writing — their experience is so different from mine." Yet how many years have you spent teaching Plato and Shakespeare and Proust? Or another, "She's a white woman and what could she possibly have to say to me?" . . . Or again, "This woman writes of her sons and I have no children." And all the other endless ways in which we rob ourselves of ourselves and each other.

   What is your own experience reading, identifying with, and learning from writers and characters who are profoundly different from you? Write an essay that addresses this question. You may expand your scope to include other media forms, including movies and music. How do artists (writers, filmmakers, musicians) make connections with — and between — people with different backgrounds, genders, races, nationalities, religions, cultures, and perspectives? How do they reach across different eras (as in the case of a writer from the past, such as Shakespeare)?

2. Lorde writes extensively about the risks and dangers associated with speaking out. According to her, we might not speak out of "fear of contempt, of censure, or some judgment, or recognition, of challenge, of annihilation" (8). Write a personal narrative about a time when you spoke out, despite your reluctance or fear of doing so. What caused you to break your silence? What were the consequences? What did you learn from the experience? Alternatively, you may also write about a time when you wanted to speak up, but did not. What stopped you? Were you inhibited by fear, or was there some other reason? Did you regret your choice? Why or why not?

Stupid Rich Bastards

LAUREL JOHNSON BLACK

Laurel Johnson Black is an associate professor of English and the former director of the Center for Teaching Excellence at Indiana University of Pennsylvania. She has also served as a co-director of the Reflective Practice Project and teaches courses in composition, creative writing, the paranormal, language and gender, and law and literature. In her book *Between Talk and Teaching: Reconsidering the Writing Conference* (1998), Black discusses theoretical and practical approaches to conferencing effectively with students, work that prioritizes the mentorship that was critical to her own education, as she describes in "Stupid Rich Bastards." In this essay, which first appeared in the collection *This Fine Place So Far from Home: Voices of Academics from the Working Class* (1995), Black explores the relationship between words and power through her experience as a working-class outsider in academia.

WRITING TO DISCOVER: *Think about a time when you had a conference with a teacher about your writing. Was the conference helpful to you? If so, why? If not, why not? Did you find you needed to alter your way of speaking, or were you anxious about what you would say?*

Language for me has always been inseparable from what I am, from what and who people are. My house was filled with the language I associate with the working class and the poor, people who haven't the means to physically keep all the "dirty" parts of life at bay and who see no reason to do so with words. Shouting to each other across the yards in the old mill town where I grew up, my mother and her friends Pat and Barbara kept up their friendship and shared gossip and complaints about their lives. They wove their voices into the fabric of words and life I knew. As we played after school in the stand of woods along the river down behind the factory, we heard our names called for supper. The more time we took to get home to the table, the sharper the tone became and the longer the wonderful string of curses stretched out, echoing off the brick walls.

We talked about whatever touched us as we sat down to eat—who had stopped up the upstairs toilet, who had fought in the hallway at school, the girl who was stabbed in the head with a fork in the lunchroom, name calling on the bus, whether the home economics teacher was having an affair with the phys. ed. teacher, what my father saw in the house he'd just put a tub in, who we knew who'd been arrested. Bodily functions, secretions, garbage, crimes and delinquency, who got away with what were as much a part of our language as they were of our lives. They were part of the humor that filled my home. My father rising up from his chair to fart, shouting out in mock seriousness, "'Repoaht from the reah!' the sahgent replied," set us off in hysterics, imitations, and stories of passed gas and the contexts that made them so funny. Swearing was also a part of our lives—among adults, among kids away from their parents, and in the bad kids' homes, everyone swore fluently before they were eighteen or out of school. "Damn" and "shit" were every other word and so became like "and" and "well" to us as we talked with each other.

I lived in a web of narrative, something I've missed in graduate school. My father was a storyteller and a traveler, a man who would go away for a week or two at a time on "business" of an undetermined nature. When he came back, he didn't bring presents but stories. Only a few years ago did I realize why the tale of Odysseus had seemed so familiar to me in the eighth grade and again as an undergraduate. He was a relative, or a friend, not just a character in an old story. In the tales told by my father and the men he bartered with, the "stupid rich bastards" almost always "got it" in the end, outwitted by the poor little guy. I learned that the stupid rich bastards always underestimated us, always thought we were as dumb as we were poor, always mistook our silence for ignorance, our shabby clothes and rusted cars for lack of ambition or enterprise. And so they got taken, and sharing stories about winning these small battles made us feel better about losing the war.

My father knew all the regular merchants at the flea markets. As we wandered along the aisles he'd yell over to Tony, a heavy man with thinning black hair patted into an ugly, oily arc across his head, "Hey! Ya fat Guinea! Ya still sellin' the same old junk? Huh? I've seen stuff move fasta in the toilets I unplug!" Tony would wave him off, turning a little away from him and throwing back over his shoulder, "What would you know about merchandise, ya stupid Swede? Huh? Shit for brains!" He'd touch his forehead with his middle finger, grin maliciously, and so would my father. As we worked our way closer to Tony, past the booth with old tools, past the book booth, Dad would ask, "So why haven't the cops bustid ya yet for alla this, Tony? What, you got a captain on ya payroll? This stuff is hot enough to burn ya hands off!" He'd blow on his fingers and wave them in the air, grinning. Tony grinned back at the compliment. "Naah, I buy this legit." He'd widen his eyes and look cherubic. "Really." They'd both laugh.

During the week, during my life, my father was a sometimes plumber, sometimes car salesman, sometimes junkman, sometimes something. My mother worked as a cook, a school crossing guard, at a McDonald's counter for a while. It was never enough. I remember one Saturday afternoon in August, my father was melting down old lead pipes. All afternoon he cut the soft pipes into small pieces and fed them into the heat of the kettle, then poured the liquid metal out into the little cupcake-shaped molds he'd

5

set in the dirt of the driveway. Late in the afternoon, the heavy clouds broke and rain began spattering down on his back and shoulders. While I watched from the kitchen he kept working, the rain hissing and turning into steam as it struck the melting lead. Over and over, he reached forward to drop chunks of pipe in to melt, and his arms, then shoulders, then head disappeared in the fog of metal and mist. He became that man to me, the half-man in steam. He was the back I saw sometimes wearily climbing the stairs to sleep for a few hours. He was the chains rattling in the truck as it bounced down the pitted driveway and whined back up late at night as he came home. It wasn't enough. There was a stack of dunnings and notices that covered the end of the old stereo.

I remember when the man from the bank came to repossess our car. I had just broken my foot, and I hung onto the car door handle while my mother stood next to me talking to the man who wanted to take the car. Her voice was high, and with one hand she opened and closed the metal clasp on her purse. Finally she opened the car door, pushing me in and sliding in next to me. The man from the bank stepped back as she started the engine, and she rolled up the window as he leaned over to say something to us. She gunned it, careening wildly backward across the yard out into the street, crying. "So this is what we've got," she said. "This is it."

We were working poor and so we were alternately afraid and ashamed and bold and angry. We prayed to nothing in particular that no one would notice our clothes or that the police wouldn't notice the car didn't have a valid inspection sticker. My mother had to decide between a tank of gas and an insurance payment. She had to decide whether or not we really needed a doctor. We shopped as a group so that if my new dress for the year cost two dollars less than we had thought it would, my sister could get one that cost two dollars more. We didn't say such things out loud, though we thought them all the time. Words are ideas, ways of believing, connected to desire and fear. If I ate seconds, maybe I was eating my sister's dress. If Susan was really sick, then maybe I couldn't get new shoes. But if anyone ever said those things, it would all come crashing in. All of it—the idea that working hard would get you some place better, that we were just as good as anyone else—would crash to the floor like some heirloom dish that would never be the same again, even if we could find all the shards.

At some point in my life, when I was very young, it had been decided that I would be the one who went on to college, who earned a lot of money, who pulled my family away from the edge of the pit, and who gave the stupid rich bastards what they had coming to them. I would speak like them but wouldn't be one of them. I would move among them, would spy on them, learn their ways, and explain them to my own people—a guerrilla fighter for the poor. My father had visions of litigation dancing in his head, his daughter in a suit, verbally slapping the hell out of some rich asshole in a courtroom.

As I was growing up, the most important people I knew, the ones I most respected, were my teachers. I wanted to be like them. They had made the supreme sacrifice, had gone away and succeeded, but had chosen to come back to help us. They drove cars I could imagine appearing occasionally in my father's lot. They wore scuffed shoes and shopped at K-Mart. They didn't belong to a country club, didn't refuse to teach us because we were poor, didn't treat us with pity or condescension. They often worked year round, teaching summer school or even, as with my history teacher, driving a beer truck from June through August.

They were the only people I knew and trusted who might be able   10
to teach me to speak like and understand the stupid rich bastards who held our lives in their hands and squeezed us until we couldn't breathe: doctors who refused to treat us without money up front; lawyers who wrote short, thick, nasty letters for credit companies who, in turn, spoke for someone else; insurance agents who talked in circles and held up payment; loan officers who disappeared into the backs of banks and didn't look at us when they told us we were too much of a risk; police and town selectmen who told us to get rid of our cars and clean up our disgraceful yards and lives—all the people who seemed always to be angry that they had to deal with us in any way. My teachers moved, I thought, with ease between my world and this other world. I hoped they would help me do the same.

My teachers tried to bridge the gap with speech. "In other words," they said, looking from the text to us, "what they're saying is . . ." They tried to bridge the gap with their bodies, one hand pointing to the board, the other hand stretched out palm up, fingers trying to tug words from mouths contorted with the effort to find the right speech. We were their college-bound students, the ones who might leave, might be them again, might even do better. They were like our parents in their desire to have us succeed, but they had skills and knowledge that counted to the white-shirted men who sat behind the glass windows at the savings and loan, to the woman who handled forms for free butter, cheese, and rice.

I wanted to be like my teachers, but I was afraid of standing up before a classroom filled with students like the ones who laughed in the back of the classroom. The only writing these students did was carving names and sexual slurs or boasts on their desks, and their dreams, I imagined, were of lives like they already knew. I was afraid, too, that when I had become like these teachers I admired so much, I would still drive down the main street of a rotting industrial town and go into the 7-Eleven and somehow I would be no different than I was now. The very ones I admired most I also most suspected: if my teachers were such successes, why were they back here? Why did they make so little money? Drive those cars? I was afraid I would have nothing to say or show to the students who sat in the back, afraid that if they actually asked what I only thought—"So what?"—I would have no answer.

I worked summers at a resort in Maine, making beds and scrubbing toilets, earning tips and room and board. During the school year, I worked as a cook in a nursing home and as a maid for rich women who made me change sheets, crawl out on window ledges to clean glass, and scrub their kitchen floors on my knees. I had saved about five hundred dollars. I sent in cards to request material from any college that would send it to me. Every day, stacks of brochures and catalogues and letters awaited me when I came home from school. One or two that looked good—smiling students on the cover—I brought with me to work at the nursing home, and I read the captions while I ate my supper. The others I looked through at night for the cost to attend and the amount of aid usually awarded. When I filled out the financial aid forms, my father told me to put a zero on every line. I told him that no one would believe it. "Yah? So what? Think they'd believe thirteen dollahs eitha? Put it down." I did.

I decided on three colleges, all small, private ones because I was afraid of the throngs of students in the brochures for the state schools. Some of the schools had said they were "teaching institutions"; I avoided those too, believing that I would have to become a teacher if I went there. I was going to be a lawyer, was going to fulfill my father's vision. I was going to go where the kids of lawyers went. I filled out forms largely on my own, knowing that my parents didn't understand the questions and would be embarrassed at not being able to help me. I took all the standardized tests and did only okay, confused by analogies of bulls and bears (I thought they referred to constellations, not the stock market) and questions about kinds of sailing boats.

When my first-choice college sent me a letter telling me I was on their waiting list, my mother hugged me and told me how proud she was. My father asked me how long I'd have to wait and if I'd work in the meantime. My mother thought that merely making the waiting list was an achievement, something she could brag about to Pat and Barbara and the mailman, while my father thought that there was only a limited number of spaces in colleges all over the country and each student waited in turn to get in. I went upstairs and cried for hours. When I came back down for supper, my mother had fixed a cake in celebration.   15

I was in my first English class at my second-choice school, never having made it off the waiting list at my first-choice school. I'd never visited this college and knew little about it. I hadn't gone to orientation, begging off because of work. That was only partially true. Actually, I had begun to look at those smiling catalogue faces and bodies and then to look at myself. I had crooked teeth. I wore makeup. I wasn't tanned and lithe from summers of tennis and sailing. I wore old jeans patched at the thighs and ragged around the cuffs. I wore T-shirts and work boots, not clothing from L. L. Bean's. I read statements from the happy students, moving my lips and trying to make the words sound like they could be mine, but I realized that it was wrong, that I was wrong. What could I

say to all these people? What could they say to me? And what people did
I belong to?

My mother had also seen the pictures. She tried to buy me some
clothes that matched theirs, and she watched as I packed, anxious that I
not be made fun of. My grandfather, who had completed grade school,
told me gruffly, "Now that youah goin' to college, you'll be too good
t' talk to us anymoah." I protested but he shook his head; it was the
last thing he ever said to me. I felt like my family wanted me so badly to
be something other than what I was. And suddenly, all I wanted to be
was "Lau-doop," as my father had called me when I was younger. It was
enough to have been accepted at a college, to have been a high school
valedictorian. That was bragging rights forever for my mother. Why did I
need more? What was wrong with what I had and was?

Now I was here, dropped off by my sister and brother, who had
turned the car around and headed for home after dumping off my
box and bag. My roommate was crying because she couldn't fit all her
Pendleton wools in her closet and drawers and had taken over some of
mine. Her father, a successful lawyer, sized up the situation, watching me
sit in silence in my flannel shirt and unfashionable jeans. "What should
we call you?" he asked politely. I thought for a moment. "Johnson."
He laughed delightedly. "Johnson? That's great! Sue, this'll be good for
you," he chortled as he led his sniffling daughter and perfectly coiffed
wife out to get lunch.

Now I was being asked to write editorials, but I didn't know what
one was. My family had always bought the newspaper with the big photos
in it, and the little local weekly had columns about who'd been arrested
and what stores had gone out of business. I didn't understand the articles
I had to read in order to write my editorials. I summarized what I'd read
in two major paragraphs and turned it in, over and over, week after week.
I got a B each time, no comments.

In French government class, students talked excitedly about their   20
travels abroad. I felt the chip on my shoulder getting heavier and heavier.
I'd been through all of New England; they'd been to France. Big fucking
deal. Lions, Lee-ons, Lyons, it's all the same. Unless someone laughs at
you for not knowing how to say what everyone else can not only say but
describe from personal experience.

Poetry class. I describe in a long narrative poem what things I see
around my neighborhood. The teacher gushes over it. It reminds him of
T. S. Eliot, he says, and when I say, "Who's that?" he is astounded. He
decides he has a diamond in the rough; he calls me a lump of coal with
lots of potential. (Later, he asks me if I want to sleep with him.)

I understand my students where I now teach. I understand their fear
of poverty, of sliding backwards, of not being as successful as their very
successful parents. They recoil in disgust and loathing from the poor,
from the working class, and that, too, is familiar to me. They insist that

if we all just try hard enough, everyone can succeed. But until then, they don't want to live with those who haven't really made it, who haven't tried. I understand how deep and visceral that fear of failure is. It keeps them in college and it keeps them from thinking about possibilities. They are in love with the status quo and terrified of idealism, of a vision and words charged with change.

I was terrified of success. By Thanksgiving of my first year in college, I wanted to go home and stay there. What was I doing at this place for rich kids? What was I accomplishing? How was I helping my family? I was a mute, a heavy drinker, a class skipper. My sister was in a nursing program and was paying rent to my mother; another sister was also working and helping out. What was I doing? I was going to college on grants and loans, and while I was not sucking money from my family, I wasn't contributing to it either. I knew I could go home and each day I had stayed in college would count as part of my success. I could have failed by my fellow students' standards and still not have failed by my own. I would have been part of that story where the system beats down the good ones who try to make it out, where you try and try and try and still the stupid rich bastards squish you just when you might succeed. I could have come home and said, "Hey, they were a bunch of rich assholes. What do you want?" No further explanation would have been demanded or necessary.

In the dormitories at night the girls gathered into groups in the lounges or the hallway floors and told stories about their lives. I was silent, stricken dumb with fear. What would I tell them when my turn came? The truth? A lie? But I needn't have worried. My turn never came. I don't know whether it was out of compassion or snobbishness, but no one ever asked me about my family, my home, my friends, even my major or my hoped-for career. And as much as I hated myself for being ashamed of my life, I hated the girls more for knowing it.

In my conferences with teachers I sat mute, nodding weakly when it seemed called for, when their voices rose as if in a question. Whatever they suggested was right. In lectures, I took notes furiously, narrative notes, full sentences, trying to get the exact words spoken by the teacher. I knew if I took down just a word here and there I would have to fill in the gaps with my own words, and those words were horribly wrong. I was horribly wrong.

Maybe my mother knew. She's dead now and I never asked her. But she wrote me letters every now and then, and not once did she say she'd like me back. Not once did she explicitly give me the option of returning. After one letter in which I came close to admitting my despair, she wrote back, "We love you and we're proud of you. Don't show your face in the door until you're supposed to."

I had gotten an F+ on an English paper. On the bottom of the last page, Dr. B. had written, "Come and see me about this." I was now a second-semester sophomore and still had not gotten an A in my major,

English; in fact, I had barely survived the drinking and class cutting of my first year. My parents had never seen my grade report, only knew that I was allowed to come back a second year, more reason for pride. I had learned to buy my classmates' thrown-away clothes at the local thrift store, and if I kept my mouth shut I could pass as one of them in most of my classes. I stopped wearing makeup, even stopped sitting in the groups in the dorms. Instead, I worked in the library on Friday nights and Saturday mornings, which gave me an excuse (I imagined one day I would need one) for never going out and spending money with anyone on weekends. Now, though, I had to hide from teachers, the people I had once wanted so much to be like.

> **And he reread my idea in words that sounded like all my professors. Words that could have kept a stupid rich bastard listening.**

I went to Dr. B.'s office about one minute before his office hours were over. I made sure the secretary saw me and that I had a piece of paper to write a note like: "Stopped by to talk about my paper. I'll catch you some other time." I inched my way down the hall toward his door, reading the numbers so I could pretend I had missed him because I had gotten lost.

Dr. B was still in his office. He welcomed me in, appearing surprised. He pulled his chair over next to mine, took my paper, and began to go over it, line by line, word by word. He peered over his little glasses, sometimes giving his head a violent nod so they would drop down on his chest and he could sit back and watch my reactions to his statements. I couldn't breathe. My chest felt like it was full, but I had no air. I didn't dare blink because my eyes were full of tears. I kept my head bent, my chin in my hand, and stared at my paper.

He sighed. Finally, he said something like, "Look. See this paragraph? 30 This is a good one. There's a good idea in here. That's your idea. But it's not phrased well. Listen to it phrased this way." And he reread my idea in words that sounded like all my professors. Words that could have kept a stupid rich bastard listening. My idea. His words. But they were connected then. For the first time, I felt like I might make it through. I choked out a thank you, and he looked up, surprised. The conference wasn't over, but I was standing up. I thanked him again, stuffing the paper into my bookbag, and left before the tears came pouring down my face. I didn't know why I was crying, whether it was because I was so stupid that I got an F+ and had to sit there and make a nice man frustrated or because I felt that I could take that one paragraph and begin again, begin learning how to speak about what I thought and felt to people who weren't like me. Stupidity and relief. They've dogged me ever since.

The phone rang at two in the morning. It was my little sister, sobbing and nearly hysterical. Her boyfriend, drunk or high on something, had leaped from a closet and attacked her. She had beaten him off, clubbing him with a brass statue that my mother had given her. Now, while two friends tried to stop her bleeding—she had a broken nose, broken ribs, a broken foot—she choked out why she had called.

"He said the apahtment was in his name an' I gotta be outta heyah tomorrow mohnin' or he's takin' all the stuff heyah an' sellin' it an' he'll keep the dog too! An' I own this stuff, I paid fuh it an' *I* pay the rent but I don't got anywayah to go. You know legal stuff, right? Laurel, ya gotta help me!"

I searched my brain for what little I remembered from my pre-law days at college, a decade earlier. Now in a Ph.D. program in composition and rhetoric, far away from the gritty New England town where my sister lived and near which we grew up, I felt useless. Again. I began to ask her about her lease, to tell her about the Legal Aid Society; I even began to think out loud through cases from a textbook I remembered. Suddenly she interrupted me, screaming over the line, "Fuck you! Fuck you! Don't talk to me like college, talk to me like a sista!"

I remember clearly the first time I chose to say to a professor, "Really!" instead of the more natural (to me), and what others might think of as more colorful, "Get outta heyah!" I remember when I began to believe that I might go into English and not law. It was a course on realism and naturalism. I began to tremble when I read *McTeague* (which I've been told many times since is not great literature but is useful as a demonstration of certain ideas in limited courses). Here were people I recognized! Here were characters who spoke like I did, who swore and hoped and dreamed for so damn little, for a place to stay that was clean, for respect, for something of their own that would last. Here were novels that showed that the poor weren't poor because they wanted to be, because they were lazy, but because of sweeping faceless economic forces that smashed them down and kept them down, and here were stupid rich bastards shown as they were in my own life. Here were writers who had words that spoke to me, that invited me not to join in some fantasy world but to confront and describe my own *real* world.

My parents (and in some ways, my whole family) never got over my defection from law. I tried to soften the blow by going into archeology; while it paid little, it was at least exotic and held out the hope of discovering some kind of lost treasure—imagine, money without working! But it was reconstructing lives and words, not ancient cultures but my own culture, that I kept being drawn to. I have come through poetry, sales, admissions, and finally composition, where first-year students begin to learn how their words hurt and heal, probe and hide, reshape, connect, embrace, and gag. It is a field that feels like work, where the texts are of a home and life so close to the world that the arguments mean something. They are like "sista," not "college."

35

Here, on paper, I can be in two worlds and control them both. But on the phone, my father asks me how that "school thing" is going, and what I still need to do, and what kind of salary I expect next year when I finally get a job. And I find it easier to slip into his world than to bring him into mine, to listen to his odysseys and believe in him as my mother did when she first married him. While a brother and sister are now doing well, two others are still living in poverty, and when I speak to my siblings my world slips around until I am dizzy.

I can bring their world into my own only in narratives, only distantly. No one in my family has ever read what I write. No one has visited my office or my classroom, at least not physically. I tell my students about my family, though; I talk to them in my language to show them there are many ways to say things. When we share our writing, I share a letter to home, full of swear words, little jokes, scatological humor, assertions that will be accepted without evidence solely because my sister and I "know" what stupid rich bastards are like and what they will say and do. And then we look at an essay I've written and then a poem, all dealing with my life, with words. They begin to feel their own words working in different ways, different contexts, begin to value the phrases and words that make them one thing and understand that these same words make it hard to be another thing. For most of my students, these exercises are often just an interesting diversion from reading literature. Some of them write in their journals of their relief. They, too, are first-generation college students, working class, afraid and silent. They appear at my door, ready to talk, knowing that I have been there and do not entirely want to leave.

When I work with my colleagues, with "real" faculty, I say little. I rehearse what I will say if I can predict the course of a meeting, and I miss some of what is going on while I hold my speech in my head, waiting for the opening in which I will speak like them long enough to fool them into thinking I *am* one of them. I am and I am not. My father's dream of how I would live and move between two worlds, two ways of speaking and knowing, haunts me.

I used to sit on the school bus on the way home from high school and look around at my classmates and wonder who would still be in my town in twenty years, who would go on, get out, succeed in ways that no one dreamed of. I used to think I would be one of those. Now I sometimes sit in meetings and classrooms and wonder who else would like to cut the shit and say what they feel. I feel suspended, dangling. If I put my toe down at any point, I might root there. I cannot move among the rich, the condescending, the ones who can turn me into an object of study with a glance or word, cannot speak like them, live in a house like them, learn their ways, and share them with my family without being disloyal to someone. I thought learning would make it easier for me to protect and defend my family, myself, but the more I learn the harder it is to passionately defend anything.

I am seeking a way to keep the language of the working class in aca-   40
demia, not just in my office with my working-class office mate, to nurture its own kind of vitality and rawness and directness, its tendency to ask "Why?" even as it says "Ah, what the fuck." I would like my colleagues to listen for the narratives embedded in their own writing, to feel the power of that movement forward just as they feel the power of the turning

concept, the academic idea. And I would like my colleagues to turn my language over in their mouths with the same respect that my father and I turned over the items on those flea market tables.

THINKING CRITICALLY ABOUT THE READING

1. How would you characterize Black's writing style? Point to her diction and phrasing to support your contention. Why do you think she uses this style to capture the "'dirty' parts" of life among the working-class people she describes (1)?

2. Who are the "stupid rich bastards"? Thinking about the relationship between language and power, why do you think Black's father chooses this term?

3. In paragraph 7, which begins "We were working poor," how does Black describe the experience of poverty? What specific words help you determine the author's feelings about the experience?

4. Why does Black admire the teachers she had in her community while growing up? How does her experience of teachers in her home community differ from her experience of professors at college? What role does language play in each interaction?

5. On several occasions, Black points to words ("waitlist," "teaching institution," "Lyons," "editorials") that she or her family misunderstood. How do these misunderstandings of both connotative and denotative meaning cause conflict or distress? Why do you think Black and her family misinterpret these words? How does the misinterpretation reinforce the relationship between language and power?

LANGUAGE IN ACTION

As Black illustrates, her working-class family members—especially her father—swear a lot. She contrasts their profanity against her professors and fellow students at college, who do not swear as frequently. Recently, researchers from the University of Cambridge, Maastricht University, Hong Kong University, and Stanford found that people who swear *more* frequently are actually more likely to be honest. After studying 276 individuals in a lab as well as the interactions of 73,789 people on Facebook, the researchers concluded that the use of "profanity was associated with less lying and deception at the individual level and higher integrity at the social level."

Swear words have power—unexpectedly, perhaps even the power to convince another of your integrity. Work in small groups to discuss the power of and pitfalls of swearing. Why do you think swearing might be correlated with honesty? What other associations do you make with swearing? In what contexts do you think swearing is acceptable? Regardless of the study's findings, in what contexts do you think swearing may have detrimental effects? Do you or your classmates harbor any biases about people who swear? If so, where might such biases come from?

WRITING SUGGESTIONS

1. In the first sentence of her essay, Black writes: "Language for me has always been inseparable from what I am, from what and who people are." Think about the language that defines your home community. Do those words or phrases help to shape your identity, too? Do you think that your language helps to define you? Why or why not? Write an essay that responds to Black's idea that language is inseparable from what and who people are.

2. Black uses visual imagery throughout her essay. Choose a few examples of such imagery and rewrite the lines with this language removed. How does the writing change? As a reader, do you think each passage is more effective with or without the imagery? Why? What does this reading experience suggest about the power of sensory language? Explain your answers in a brief essay.

On and On: Appalachian Language and Academic Power

MEREDITH MCCARROLL

Meredith McCarroll is the Director of Writing and Rhetoric and Director of the First-Year Seminar Program at Bowdoin College in Brunswick, Maine, but she was born and raised in Haywood County, North Carolina in Southern Appalachia, a region that defines her identity and much of her work. Her book *Unwhite: Appalachia, Race, and Film* (2018) argues that typical literary and filmic representations of ostensibly "white" Appalachian people are used to highlight the "whiteness" of non-Appalachian southerners, pointing to how gradations of whiteness in the south lie at the intersection of language, region, and social class.

In the following essay, originally published in the online journal *Southern Cultures,* McCarroll explores the relationship between words and power through her own experience in academia. Feeling as though she needed to reshape her language in order to "pass" in academia, she recounts shifting her word choice and forcing her "vowels into shape," but finds that in the process she "lost her voice" despite her success.

WRITING TO DISCOVER: *In McCarroll's experience, our language — diction, phrasing, dialect, accent — defines our identity and, perhaps, our success or failure. Have you noticed peculiarities about your home dialect in comparison to the language you hear at college? How do you think your accent, diction, or phrasing affects how others perceive you?*

"Let's go around the room and say where we're from." It was my first day in a class called "Experiencing Appalachia" during my first year of college.

"Raleigh," someone said.

"Just outside of Charlotte," said another.

"High Point."

The professor continually nodded as the circle made its way to me.   5

"Haywood County," I said.

Her eyebrows raised in respect.

My home was only about a hundred winding miles from the classroom in which I was sitting, but "Haywood County" suddenly became more than a place to me. It was a marker of identity.

On day one of class, I learned that the region's boundaries have been constantly contested. I was told that migratory patterns explain some of the dialects of the mountains. And I came to understand that I was Appalachian.

I knew that I was a mountain girl. My family had been in Haywood   10
County for generations and one branch of my family tree started or

stopped—depending on your perspective—when the Cherokee were marched through. But I had to take a class called "Experiencing Appalachia" to even know that I was Appalachian.

To "experience" the region, we studied *Foxfire* magazines like those that had lined the bookshelves in my childhood living room. We practiced churning butter. We read about quilting. Some of this resonated with me because it was familiar. My Granny painstakingly taught me to quilt one summer, which mostly meant that I spent time watching her pull out all of my sloppy handwork. My Granny and Pa, who lived next door, canned homegrown tomatoes and green beans. I knew the difference between half-runners and blue lakes, and know of no sound more satisfying than the *pop* of lids sealing on the kitchen counter in the late afternoon. But there were plenty of Appalachian traditions that I did not know. And there was nothing markedly Appalachian that we did because we *had* to. It is true that I had eaten groundhog on camping trips and could name most of the local peaks by sight, but it is also true that I bought incense and spirulina at a health food store in Asheville. I ate more tempeh than I did fatback, and I loved Ani DiFranco and Doc Watson equally.

After graduation, I moved to Boston and became, for the first time, an outsider. Like so many before me, it took leaving home to understand it. I suddenly saw details in contrast and became proud of my heritage. I grew tomatoes on the fire escape because it connected me to my Granny, whose tomatoes were a month ahead and a foot taller. As distance helped me understand what it meant to be from the mountains, I began to deeply miss them. I felt like Ivy Rowe in Lee Smith's *Fair and Tender Ladies* who says that she's like her daddy because she needs a mountain to "set her eyes against."

Yet while I was proud of my home, I was also learning that powerful stereotypes about Appalachia had arrived in places like Boston well before me and had influenced the way that even the most considerate people thought about me. The banjo lick from *Deliverance* backed many introductory conversations when I said where I was from. Instead of calling people out for their ignorance, I distanced myself from Haywood County. I laughed along. I waited longer and longer to reveal my background. I blended in. During this time, I applied to graduate school. In my visits to prestigious universities in Boston, I actively tried to "talk right" and hide my accent. One lingering linguistic marker caused me the most panic when I slipped. Long after I attached 'G's to my gerunds and bleached out the local color from my language, I stumbled over the word "on." When my mom told me to put my *coat on*, those words rhymed. She told me to call her when I was *on the road*. And those words rhymed. To my Appalachian tongue, "own" and "on" were pronounced exactly the same way. But not for the rest of the world, I learned. This reminder that I was not from around here meant, to me, that I might not belong in a Boston graduate school.

I learned to always use adverbs. I took my groceries from a buggy and put them in a cart. I (nearly) stopped calling my hat a toboggan. I forced my vowels into shape. It worked. I got into graduate school. I got a PhD. I learned to pass. But I lost my voice. With Granny's chiding in my ear — "You're talking uppity now that you live in Baaaaahston" — I developed a new way of speaking. And it wasn't until a decade later that I heard my own repressed voice echoed back to me in West Virginia.

I heard established scholars speak in accents and it did not change the content of what they were saying.

Writer and activist Silas House spoke at a conference addressing the theme of "New Appalachia," urging his audience to bring LGBTQ civil rights issues into our classrooms, our scholarship, and our conversations in order to make Appalachia a safer place. New Appalachia, for House, was tied to Old Appalachian activism. As soon as he began speaking, I began to understand the new in light of the old. Combined with a quiet thoughtfulness, his manner of speaking awakened in me memories that I had long put to rest. In one moment, his voice cracked as he was overcome with emotion remembering the violence enacted upon queer youth in Appalachia. Throats tightened across the room. He paused and then said quietly, "And it will go on and on and on. . ." until we — teachers and writers and students in this room — commit to change. To an outsider, it might have sounded like he was saying "own and own and own," but when I heard Silas House repeat this word in this context, I felt the ground shift beneath me. Because while he talked about justice, I heard the timbre of my Pa. As he read his own poetry, I heard the cadence of my Aunt Betsy. As he addressed his audience, I heard my mom talking. I heard established scholars speak in accents and it did not change the content of what they were saying. It did not change the power of their intellect. Then I stood up to deliver my paper about the politics of representation in Appalachian film. My 'G's were intact. My vowels stood up straight. My "on" was not my "own." And I felt a powerful loss — of my own voice, my own accent.

Television shows, movies, and cartoons rely lazily on the assumption that viewers will associate a southern accent with a lack of intelligence. It is still acceptable in popular discourse to mock "rednecks" and "hillbillies." "Reality" shows exoticize Appalachia as a safer space to show how the other half live, without much interrogation of authenticity. People say to lighten up. It's just a movie. It's just a TV show. It doesn't matter. But it does. It mattered to me as I left home, thinking that the only way to be a legitimate scholar was to attend college in New England and change my voice. I had learned to talk right, but I had gotten it all wrong.

I can't change the fact that my Granny's great-granny was raised as a white girl after her biological parents had to leave her on the Trail of Tears. Passing for white, she had no choice but to assimilate to her surroundings

15

to fit in. I'm unable trace my way back to that culture that was taken from her and connect to a past that was not allowed to happen. But I can claim the past that I have known. Now that I have learned to articulate issues about representation and gender politics, I want to do so in my own voice—to let my vowels relax into to the shape that they wanted to take all along. I want to honor the voices that were the soundtrack to my upbringing and respond to the calls of Uncle Joe, Granny, Aunt Lena, Aunt Betsy, Pa, and Mom. I want to draw thick that perforated line to my past. I want to claim the voices belonging to my people.

Granny mostly made clean, patterned quilts with a recognizable order. But her mother-in-law made crazy quilts, piecing together scraps and favorites, remnants and set-asides. Combined, polka dots, solids, and gingham formed something alluring beyond any pattern. I loved these crazy quilts and as I struggled my way through my first stitching, I thought that perhaps that style would be easier than the log cabin quilt I had settled upon. Knowing this wasn't the case, Granny took one of Ma's quilts down and with few words taught me how to judge it. Flipping it over, she revealed the even, measured hand stitching that held the mismatched pieces together. In it I saw how a thing is made whole, how the intricate gathering together of the unlikely can make sense. I am reminded of it now when I consider the seemingly disparate layers of my own voice and identity—multi-generational Appalachian, first-generation college graduate, economically privileged, queer, feminist, antiracist, mother, writer, teacher. I am reminded of that quilt when I look around and see the multiple ways to be Appalachian and to speak Appalachian. Perhaps with some attention, the voices of the past will not be lost but can find a way to go on and on and on.

THINKING CRITICALLY ABOUT THE READING

1. In paragraph 11, McCarroll puts the term "experience" in quotation marks. Why do you think she does this? What effect do such stylistic choices have on readers?

2. Make a list of the terms and phrases McCarroll uses to define Appalachia and academia. What do these terms and phrases suggest her thoughts and feelings are about each space?

3. Why do you think McCarroll chooses the metaphor of quilting to help explain the relationship among her language, region, and identity?

4. In paragraph 15, how does McCarroll describe Appalachian writer and activist Silas House's diction and manner of speaking? How does her description of House's voice contrast with the typical perceptions of Appalachian voice she describes in paragraph 13?

5. How does McCarroll feel about the change in her own voice since she has become an academic? Point to specific words and phrases in the text to support your response.

LANGUAGE IN ACTION

Toward the end of her essay, McCarroll has a moment of revelation when she hears writer and activist Silas House speaking—in particular, when he says the phrase "on and on," which in his Appalachian accent sounds like "own and own" (15). In this moment, McCarroll comes to recognize the power of Appalachian speech and the strength of a unified Appalachian voice. Is there a specific word or phrase that you strongly associate with your own culture, with your family, or with the town or region where you grew up? If so, what is the word or phrase, and why does it have this association for you? Discuss and compare your responses with two or three classmates.

WRITING SUGGESTIONS

1. McCarroll's essay suggests that there is a hierarchy of speakers, one that places academia near the top and Appalachia near the bottom. Think about a time when you have felt either distinguished or devalued because of the way you speak. What were the reasons that your voice was either distinguished or devalued? What effect did it have on you as a speaker? Drawing from your experiences and McCarroll's, write an essay about the effects that this silencing or amplification had on you as a speaker.

2. After reading both McCarroll's essay and "Stupid Rich Bastards" by Laurel Johnson Black (also in this chapter, pp. 152–162), write a brief essay in which you compare and contrast these two authors. They have several similarities: both are women who grew up in relatively poor, working-class communities, and they both experienced a language transformation when they attended college and were exposed to academic English. Consider both writers' descriptions of their experiences and their attempts at "passing," fitting in, and assimilating in academic culture. What other similarities can you draw between McCarroll and Black? Can you identify any major differences between them? Write an essay in which you answer these questions. As you write, think about each writer's tone, voice, and the specific language that they use.

Address at the Youth Takeover of the United Nations

MALALA YOUSAFZAI

Malala Yousafzai was born on July 12, 1997, in Mingora, Pakistan, which was once a popular tourist destination before the Taliban began to gain control of the region. Yousafzai, whose father is an anti-Taliban activist, educator, and the founder of her school, recognized from an early age the threat the Taliban posed to her education. As early as 2008 she gave a speech entitled "How Dare the Taliban Take Away My Basic Right to Education?" and by 2009, using a pen name to disguise her identity, she began blogging for the BBC about the effects of Taliban rule. Her identity was revealed soon thereafter and her advocacy for women's rights to an education gained a larger platform, earning her Pakistan's National Youth Peace Prize and the International Children's Peace Prize in 2014. But the attention Yousafzai received made her a target, and by the time she was fourteen, the Taliban had issued a death threat against her. Although her family worried for her safety, they did not believe at first that she would be harmed. But on October 9, 2012, when Yousafzai was on her way home from school, the bright and impassioned advocate for girls' education was shot in the head by a member of the Taliban. Incredibly, she survived, becoming not only an international cause célèbre but an even more committed activist for peace and education.

The speech included here was first given at the United Nations in 2013. As a result of the attention the shooting and recovery drew to Yousafzai's activism for women's education, in 2014 Yousafzai was nominated for a Nobel Peace Prize and became the youngest person ever to win the award. She has also written an autobiography entitled *I Am Malala: The Girl Who Stood Up for Education and Was Shot by the Taliban* (2013) and a book for children, *Malala's Magic Pencil* (2017). In the audiobook *We Are Displaced: My Journey and Stories from Refugee Girls Around the World* (2019), Yousafzai starts with her own story of displacement and then shares the stories of other young girls she has met on visits to refugee camps. She is currently a student at the London School of Economics and remains a target of the resurgent Taliban.

WRITING TO DISCOVER: *How has your family influenced how you think? How you speak? The causes you support or any volunteering you've done? Why and how do you think our families affect our convictions?*

Honorable U.N. Secretary-General Mr. Ban Ki-moon, respected president of the General Assembly Vuk Jeremić, honorable U.N. envoy for global education Mr. Gordon Brown, respected elders and my dear brothers and sisters: *A salaam alaikum.*

Today, it is an honor for me to be speaking again after a long time. Being here with such honorable people is a great moment in my life. And it is an honor for me that today I am wearing a shawl of the late Benazir Bhutto Shaheed.

I don't know where to begin my speech. I don't know what people would be expecting me to say, but first of all thank you to God for whom we all are equal, and thank you to every person who has prayed for my fast recovery and a new life. I cannot believe how much love people have shown me. I have received thousands of good-wish cards and gifts from all over the world. Thank you to all of them. Thank you to the children whose innocent words encouraged me. Thank you to my elders whose prayers strengthened me.

> **We call upon all governments to ensure free, compulsory education all over the world for every child. We call upon all the governments to fight against terrorism and violence. To protect children from brutality and harm.**

I would like to thank my nurses, doctors and the staff of the hospitals in Pakistan and the U.K. and the U.A.E. government, who have helped me to get better and recover my strength.

I fully support Mr. Ban Ki-moon, the Secretary-General, in his Global Education First Initiative, and the work of U.N. Special Envoy Gordon Brown and the respected president of the General Assembly Vuk Jeremić. I thank all of them for their leadership, which they continue to give. They continue to inspire all of us to action.   5

Dear brothers and sisters, do remember one thing: Malala Day is not my day. Today is the day of every woman, every boy, and every girl who have raised their voice for their rights. There are hundreds of human rights activists and social workers who are not only speaking for their rights, but who are struggling to achieve their goals of peace, education, and equality. Thousands of people have been killed by the terrorists and millions have been injured. I am just one of them.

So here I stand, one girl among many.

I speak not for myself, but so those without a voice can be heard. Those who have fought for their rights. Their right to live in peace. Their right to be treated with dignity. Their right to equality of opportunity. Their right to be educated.

Dear friends, on 9 October 2012, the Taliban shot me on the left side of my forehead. They shot my friends, too. They thought that the bullets would silence us. But they failed. And out of that silence came thousands of voices. The terrorists thought they would change my aims and stop my ambitions. But nothing changed in my life except this: weakness, fear and hopelessness died. Strength, power and courage was born.

I am the same Malala. My ambitions are the same. My hopes are the   10
same. My dreams are the same.

Dear sisters and brothers, I am not against anyone. Neither am I here
to speak in terms of personal revenge against the Taliban or any other
terrorist group. I am here to speak for the right of education for every
child. I want education for the sons and daughters of the Taliban and all
the terrorists and extremists.

I do not even hate the Talib who shot me. Even if there was a gun in
my hand and he was standing in front of me, I would not shoot him. This
is the compassion I have learned from Muhammad, the prophet of mercy,
and Jesus Christ, and Lord Buddha. This is the legacy of change I have
inherited from Martin Luther King, Nelson Mandela, and Muhammad
Ali Jinnah. This is the philosophy of nonviolence that I have learned from
Gandhiji, Bacha Khan, and Mother Teresa. And this is the forgiveness
that I have learned from my father and from my mother. This is what my
soul is telling me: be peaceful and love everyone.

Dear sisters and brothers, we realize the importance of light when
we see darkness. We realize the importance of our voice when we are
silenced. In the same way, when we were in Swat, the north of Pakistan,
we realized the importance of pens and books when we saw the guns.

The wise saying "the pen is mightier than the sword" is true. The
extremists are afraid of books and pens. The power of education frightens them. They are afraid of women. The power of the voice of women
frightens them. And that is why they killed 14 innocent students in the
recent attack in Quetta. And that is why they killed female teachers and
polio workers in Khyber Pakhtunkhwa. That is why they are blasting
schools every day. Because they were and they are afraid of change, afraid
of the equality that we will bring to our society.

And I remember that there was a boy in our school who was asked by   15
a journalist, "Why are the Taliban against education?" He answered very
simply. By pointing to his book, he said, "A Talib doesn't know what is
written inside this book." They think that God is a tiny little conservative
being who would send girls to hell just for going to school. The terrorists are misusing the name of Islam and Pashtun society for their own
personal benefit. Pakistan is a peace-loving, democratic country. Pashtuns
want education for their daughters and sons. Islam is a religion of peace,
humanity, and brotherhood. Islam says it is not only each child's right to
get an education, rather it is their duty and responsibility to.

Honorable Secretary-General, peace is a necessity for education. In
many parts of the world, especially Pakistan and Afghanistan, terrorism,
war, and conflicts stop children from going to schools. We are really tired
of these wars.

Women and children are suffering in many ways, in many parts of the
world. In India, innocent and poor children are victims of child labor.
Many schools have been destroyed in Nigeria. People in Afghanistan have

been affected by the hurdles of extremism. Young girls have to do domestic child labor and are forced to get married at an early age. Poverty, ignorance, injustice, racism, and the deprivation of basic rights are the main problems faced by both men and women.

Dear fellows, today I am focusing on women's rights and girls' education because they are suffering the most. There was a time when women social activists asked men to stand up for their rights. But this time we will do it by ourselves. I am not telling men to step away from speaking for women's rights, rather I am focusing on women to be independent and fight for themselves.

So dear sisters and brothers, now it is time to speak up. So today, we call upon the world leaders to change their strategic policies in favor of peace and prosperity. We call upon the world leaders that all the peace deals must protect women's and children's rights. A deal that goes against the rights of women is unacceptable.

We call upon all governments to ensure free, compulsory education 20 all over the world for every child. We call upon all the governments to fight against terrorism and violence, to protect children from brutality and harm. We call upon the developed nations to support the expansion of educational opportunities for girls in the developing world. We call upon all communities to be tolerant, to reject prejudice based on caste, creed, sect, color, religion or gender. To ensure freedom and equality for women so they can flourish. We cannot all succeed when half of us are held back. We call upon our sisters around the world to be brave, to embrace the strength within themselves and realize their full potential.

Dear brothers and sisters, we want schools and education for every child's bright future. We will continue our journey to our destination of peace and education. No one can stop us. We will speak up for our rights and we will bring change through our voice. We believe in the power and the strength of our words. Our words can change the whole world, because we are all together, united for the cause of education. And if we want to achieve our goal, then let us empower ourselves with the weapon of knowledge and let us shield ourselves with unity and togetherness.

Dear brothers and sisters, we must not forget that millions of people are suffering from poverty, injustice, and ignorance. We must not forget that millions of children are out of their schools. We must not forget that our sisters and brothers are waiting for a bright, peaceful future.

So let us wage a global struggle against illiteracy, poverty and terrorism. Let us pick up our books and our pens. *They* are our most powerful weapons. One child, one teacher, one book and one pen can change the world.

Education is the only solution. Education first. Thank you.

THINKING CRITICALLY ABOUT THE READING

1. Why do you think Yousafzai uses simple and repeated declarations? What effect does repetition have on listeners and readers? How do simple declarations advance her argument?

2. Why do you think Yousafzai mentions drawing inspiration from a number of different religious and political figures, including many who are not Islamic? Whom does she name, and why might she name these figures in particular? How do you think her initial audience at the United Nations affected her choice?

3. We might characterize Yousafzai's essay as a "call to action," a work meant to stir others to activism. What actions does she call for? Why do you think she makes this type of plea? How does she seem to feel about violence?

4. According to Yousafzai, why are extremists "afraid of books and pens" (14)? Of education? Of women? How does she suggest we address extremists? Must we become extremists?

5. Yousafzai argues that "our words can change the whole world" (21). In what ways does she suggest words can change the world? What words—and whose words—do you think she would have us focus on in addressing extremists and extremisms?

6. Yousafzai makes many grand statements throughout the essay and appeals to her readers for change. What are the most concrete appeals that she makes? What are the most manageable of the grander changes for which she calls? Why might she make such grand statements and appeals, particularly to a young audience? What effect do they have on readers?

LANGUAGE IN ACTION

Malala Yousafzai and her father, Ziauddin, cofounded the Malala Fund to ensure that every girl has access to secondary education. Currently, more than 60 million girls worldwide do not complete their education because of poverty, early marriage, and political crisis and strife. The fund's petition gathered over 1,100,000 signatures, convincing the Global Partnership for Education to expand its focus and support twelve years of safe, quality education for girls around the world. The Malala Fund has invited girls everywhere to stand #withMalala and contribute their creative work—photography, video, drawings, paintings, dance, or spoken word—to an online gallery.

Using your social media outlet of choice, do a search for #withMalala and view some of the stories and artwork that are tagged there. Consider the role of hashtag phrases in contemporary language. How do they operate as tools for human rights advocacy? Does anything you found in your search for #withMalala surprise you?

Discuss in class what you make of the hashtag phrase as a social phenomenon, and the ways you've seen hashtags used. Hashtags lend themselves well to humor and marketing and rallying around a cause, but do they have a dark side, too? If so, where does that come from?

WRITING SUGGESTIONS

1. Yousafzai argues that it is "the power of education" that "frightens" the ultra-conservative Taliban (14). Why is education frightening? What does it offer on a practical level, and what does it represent on an ideological one? Write an essay that explores why education may be "frightening" to some groups. Is frightening the most accurate word? What lies beneath that fear?

2. Yousafzai argues that the Taliban is particularly "afraid of women," that they are "afraid of the equality that we will bring into our society" (14). Can you think of groups in your own nation, region, or community (even your college campus) that could be said to be "afraid of equality"? While few groups act on their fear with the kind of coordinated violence the Taliban uses, there are still repercussions. Choose a group you would argue is "afraid of equality," and write an essay analyzing the effects that group has had on its community. How do people respond to the group? Have any of the changes the group opposes come to be, despite their efforts? What has changed as a result of their stance, and what hasn't?

7

LANGUAGE COMMUNITIES: WHERE DO WE BELONG?

We reveal ourselves—where we come from, who we are, and who we'd like to be—in the language we use every day. At the same time, our use of language shapes us: In writing, speaking, or text messaging, we evolve as individuals in communication with other language users, exchanging signs and meanings and exploring new ways of defining ourselves and our place in the world. In this chapter we offer a collection of seven readings that provide different perspectives on the speech communities to which we belong and how these communities, in turn, shape how we use language.

In the first reading, Paul Roberts explains how speech communities form based on such factors as age, geography, and social class, and how the language patterns we learn in our speech communities affect how the world perceives (and receives) us. In "All-American Dialects," Richard Lederer focuses on the regional varieties or dialects of English that are spoken throughout the United States. Specifically, he explores the current state of these geographical speech communities, which he and others believe are rapidly disappearing because of the pressure from the homogenizing effects of mass media. Next, in an eye-opening article, Sara Nović argues against efforts to erase deaf people and their culture through scientific advancement and technological innovation. She believes that rather than providing a choice for deaf people—some of whom may wish to remain in a deaf culture—researchers may be unwittingly showing disdain for "linguistic multiplicity" and reinforcing our bias against difference in our society. In "Two Ways to Belong in America," Bharati Mukherjee reflects on her experience coming to America from India and how she chose to become an American citizen. In contrast to her expatriate Indian sister, Mukherjee needed "to put roots down, to vote and make the difference that I can." In time she realized that "the price that the immigrant willingly pays, and that the exile avoids, is the trauma of self-transformation."

Next, in "The Strange Persistence of First Languages," linguist Julie Sedivy explores the ways in which first languages, for people who are fluent in more than one language, inform their souls: their intellects, their dreams, their cultural imperatives, their sense of belonging, their devotion to family, their health, and more. Her account is based on both her own story and the latest research into why first languages endure and remain so powerful for those who have them. Meanwhile, the late Filipino American journalist and author Alex Tizon offers a poignant reflection on his search for his Asian self and his family's struggle to belong in the United States. Finally, in "Mother Tongue," Amy Tan recounts her experiences growing up in a bilingual world, with one foot firmly planted in the English-speaking community of school and books and the other in her neighborhood community where she heard Chinese as well as the limited or "broken" English spoken by her immigrant mother.

Speech Communities

PAUL ROBERTS

Paul Roberts (1917–1967) was a linguist, teacher, and writer. Born in California, he received his BA from San Jose State University and his MA and PhD from the University of California at Berkeley. After teaching at San Jose State and then Cornell University, Roberts became director of language at the Center of American Studies in Rome. His books include *Understanding Grammar* (1954), *Patterns of English* (1956), *Understanding English* (1958), *English Sentences* (1962), and *English Syntax* (1964).

In the following selection from *Understanding English*, Roberts writes about the development of speech variations within the United States that are based on what he identifies as "speech communities." These communities—which sometimes have their own dialects, their own jargon, and their own codes, meanings, and pronunciations—are formed by a variety of factors, according to Roberts, including "age, geography, education, occupation, social position."

WRITING TO DISCOVER: *Think about your own way of speaking. What factors do you believe are the most powerful influences on your own use of English—for example, your family, the region you grew up in, your peers? Do you have more than one way of speaking, depending on whom you are with or where you are?*

Imagine a village of a thousand people all speaking the same language and never hearing any language other than their own. As the decades pass and generation succeeds generation, it will not be very apparent to the speakers of the language that any considerable language change is going on. Oldsters may occasionally be conscious of and annoyed by the speech forms of youngsters. They will notice new words, new expressions, "bad" pronunciations, but will ordinarily put these down to the irresponsibility of youth, and decide piously that the language of the younger generation will revert to decency when the generation grows up.

It doesn't revert, though. The new expressions and the new pronunciations persist, and presently there is another younger generation with its own new expressions and its own pronunciations. And thus the language changes. If members of the village could speak to one another across five hundred years, they would probably find themselves unable to communicate.

Now suppose that the village divides itself and half the people move away. They move across the river or over a mountain and form a new village. Suppose the separation is so complete that the people of New Village have no contact with the people of Old Village. The language of both villages will change, drifting away from the language of their common ancestors. But the drift will not be in the same direction. In both villages there will be new expressions and new pronunciations, but not the same ones. In the course of time the languages of Old Village and New Village will be mutually unintelligible with the language they both started with. They will also be mutually unintelligible with one another.

An interesting thing—and one for which there is no perfectly clear explanation—is that the rate of change will not ordinarily be the same for both villages. The language of Old Village changes faster than the language of New Village. One might expect that the opposite would be true—that the emigrants, placed in new surroundings and new conditions, would undergo more rapid language changes. But history reports otherwise. American English, for example, despite the violence and agony and confusion to which the demands of a new continent have subjected it, is probably essentially closer to the language of Shakespeare than London English is.

Suppose one thing more. Suppose Old Village is divided sharply into   5
an upper class and a lower class. The sons and daughters of the upper class go to preparatory school and then to the university; the children of the lower class go to work. The upper-class people learn to read and write and develop a flowering literature; the lower-class people remain illiterate. Dialects develop, and the speech of the two classes steadily diverges. One might suppose that most of the change would go on among the illiterate, that the upper-class people, conscious of their heritage, would tend to preserve the forms and pronunciations of their ancestors. Not so. The opposite is true. In speech, the educated tend to be radical and the uneducated conservative. In England one finds Elizabethan forms and sounds not among Oxford and Cambridge graduates but among the people of backward villages.

A village is a fairly simple kind of speech community—a group of people steadily in communication with one another, steadily hearing one another's speech. But the village is by no means the basic unit. Within the simplest village there are many smaller units—groupings based on age, class, occupation. All these groups play intricately on one another and against one another, and a language that seems at first a coherent whole will turn out on inspection to be composed of many differing parts. Some forces tend to make these parts diverge, other forces hold them together. Thus the language continues in tension.

THE SPEECH COMMUNITIES OF THE CHILD

The child's first speech community is ordinarily his family. The child learns whatever kind of language the family speaks—or, more precisely, whatever kind of language it speaks to him. The child's language learning, now and later, is governed by two obvious motives: the desire to communicate and the desire to be admired. He imitates what he hears. More or less successful imitations usually bring action and reward and tend to be repeated. Unsuccessful ones usually don't bring action and reward and tend to be discarded.

But since language is a complicated business it is sometimes the unsuccessful imitations that bring the reward. The child, making a stab at the word *mother*, comes out with *muzzer*. The family decides that this is just too cute for anything and beams and repeats *muzzer*, and the child, feeling that he's scored a bull's eye, goes on saying *muzzer* long after he has mastered *other* and *brother*. Baby talk is not so much invented by the child as sponsored by the parent.

Eventually the child moves out of the family and into another speech community—other children of his neighborhood. He goes to kindergarten and immediately encounters speech habits that conflict with those he has learned. If he goes to school and talks about his *muzzer*, it will be borne in on him by his colleagues that the word is not well chosen. Even *mother* may not pass muster, and he may discover that he gets better results and is altogether happier if he refers to his female parent as his ma or even his old lady.

Children coming together in a kindergarten class bring with them language that is different because it is learned in different homes. It is all to some degree unsuccessfully learned, consisting of not quite perfect imitations of the original. In school all this speech coalesces, differences tend to be ironed out, and the result differs from the original parental speech and differs in pretty much the same way.

The pressures on the child to conform to the speech of his age group, his speech community, are enormous. He may admire his teacher and love his mother, he may even—and even consciously—wish to speak as they do. But he *has* to speak like the rest of the class. If he does not, life becomes intolerable.

The speech changes that go on when the child goes to school are often most distressing to parents. Your little Bertram, at home, has never heard anything but the most elegant English. You send him to school, and what happens? He comes home saying things like "I done real good in school today, Mom." But Bertram really has no choice in the matter. If Clarence and Elbert and the rest of the fellows customarily say "I done real good," then Bertram might as well go around with three noses as say things like "I did very nicely."

Individuals differ of course, and not all children react to the speech community in the same way. Some tend to imitate and others tend to force imitation. But all to some degree have their speech modified by forces over which neither they nor their parents nor their teachers have any real control.

Individuals differ too in their sensitivity to language. For some, language is always a rather embarrassing problem. They steadily make boners, saying the right thing in the wrong place or the wrong way. They have a hard time fitting in. Others tend to change their language slowly, sticking stoutly to their way of saying things, even though their way differs from that of the majority. Still others adopt new language habits almost automatically, responding quickly to whatever speech environment they encounter.

Indeed some children of five or six have been observed to speak two 15 or more different dialects without much awareness that they are doing so. Most commonly, they will speak in one way at home and in another on the playground. At home they say, "I did very nicely" and "I haven't any"; these become at school, "I done real good" and "I ain't got none."

THE CLASS AS A SPEECH COMMUNITY

Throughout the school years, or at least through the American secondary school, the individual's most important speech community is his age group, his class. Here is where the real power lies. The rule is conformity above all things, and the group uses its power ruthlessly on those who do not conform. Language is one of the chief means by which the school group seeks to establish its entity, and in the high school this is done more or less consciously. The obvious feature is high school slang, picked up from the radio, from other schools, sometimes invented, changing with bewildering speed. Nothing is more satisfactory than to speak today's slang; nothing more futile than to use yesterday's.

There can be few tasks more frustrating than that of the secondary school teacher charged with the responsibility of brushing off and polishing up the speech habits of the younger generation. Efforts to make *real* into *really*, *ain't* into *am not*, *I seen him* into *I saw him*, *he don't* into *he doesn't* meet at best with polite indifference, at worst with mischievous counterattack.

The writer can remember from his own high school days when the class, a crashingly witty bunch, took to pronouncing the word *sure* as *sewer*. "Have you prepared your lesson, Arnold?" Miss Driscoll would ask. "Sewer, Miss Driscoll," Arnold would reply. "I think," said Miss Driscoll, who was pretty quick on her feet too, "that you must mean 'sewerly,' since the construction calls for the adverb not the adjective." We were delighted with the suggestion and went about saying "sewerly" until the very blackboards were nauseated. Miss Driscoll must have wished often that she had let it lay.

CONFRONTING THE ADULT WORLD

When the high school class graduates, the speech community disintegrates as the students fit themselves into new ones. For the first time in the experience of most of the students the speech ways of adult communities begin to exercise real force. For some people the adjustment is a relatively simple one. A boy going to work in a garage may have a good deal of new lingo to pick up, and he may find that the speech that seemed so racy and won such approval in the corridors of Springfield High leaves his more adult associates merely bored. But a normal person will adapt himself without trouble.

For others in other situations settling into new speech communities   20
may be more difficult. The person going into college, into the business world, into scrubbed society may find that he has to think about and work on his speech habits in order not to make a fool of himself too often.

College is a particularly complicated problem. Not only does the freshman confront upperclassmen not particularly disposed to find the speech of Springfield High particularly cute, but the adult world, as represented chiefly by the faculty, becomes increasingly more immediate. The problems of success, of earning a living, of marriage, of attaining a satisfactory adult life loom larger, and they all bring language problems with them. Adaptation is necessary, and the student adapts.

The student adapts, but the adult world adapts too. The thousands of boys and girls coming out of the high schools each spring are affected by the speech of the adult communities into which they move, but they also affect that speech. The new pronunciation habits, developing grammatical features, different vocabulary do by no means all give way before the disapproval of elders. Some of them stay. Elders, sometimes to their dismay, find themselves changing their speech habits under the bombardment of those of their juniors. And then of course the juniors eventually become the elders, and there is no one left to disapprove.

THE SPACE DIMENSION

Speech communities are formed by many features besides that of age. Most obvious is geography. Our country was originally settled by people coming from different parts of England. They spoke different dialects to begin with and as a result regional speech differences existed from the start in the different parts of the country. As speakers of other languages came to America and learned English, they left their mark on the speech of the sections in which they settled. With the westward movement, new pioneers streamed out through the mountain passes and down river valleys, taking the different dialects west and modifying them by new mixtures in new environments.

Today we are all more or less conscious of certain dialect differences in our country. We speak of the "southern accent," the "Brooklyn accent," the "New England accent." Until a few years ago it was often said that American English was divided into three dialects: Southern American (south of the Mason-Dixon line); Eastern American (east of the Connecticut River); and Western American. This description suggests certain gross differences all right, but recent research shows that it is a gross oversimplification.

The starting point of American dialects is the original group of col-   25
onies. We had a New England settlement, centering in Massachusetts; a Middle Atlantic settlement, centering in Pennsylvania; a southern settlement, centering in Virginia and the Carolinas. These colonies were different in speech to begin with, since the settlers came from different parts of England. Their differences were increased as the colonies lived for a century and a half or so with only thin communication with either Mother England or each other. By the time of the Revolution the dialects were well established. Within each group there were of course subgroups. Richmond speech differed markedly from that of Savannah. But Savannah and Richmond were more like each other than they were like Philadelphia or Boston.

> **We speak of America as the melting pot, but the speech communities of this continent are very far from having melted into one.**

The Western movement began shortly after the Revolution, and dialects followed geography. The New Englanders moved mostly into upper New York State and the Great Lakes region. The Middle Atlantic colonists went down the Shenandoah Valley and eventually into the heart of the Midwest. The southerners opened up Kentucky and Tennessee, later the lower Mississippi Valley, later still Texas and much of the Southwest. Thus new speech communities were formed, related to the old ones of the seaboard, but each developing new characteristics as lines of settlement crossed.

New complications were added before and after the Revolution by the great waves of immigration of people from countries other than England: Swedes in Delaware, Dutch in New York, Germans and Scots-Irish in Pennsylvania, Irish in New England, Poles and Greeks and Italians and Portuguese. The bringing in of black slaves had an important effect on the speech of the South and later on the whole country. The Spanish in California and the Southwest added their mark. In [the twentieth and twenty-first centuries], movement of peoples goes on: the trek of southern blacks to northern and western cities, the migration of people from Arkansas, Oklahoma, and Texas to California. All these have shaped and are shaping American speech.

We speak of America as the melting pot, but the speech communities of this continent are very far from having melted into one. Linguists today can trace very clearly the movements of the early settlers in the still-living speech of their descendants. They can follow an eighteenth century speech community west, showing how it crossed this pass and followed that river, threw out an offshoot here, left a pocket there, merged with another group, halted, split, moved on once more. If all other historical evidence were destroyed, the history of the country could still be reconstructed from the speech of modern America.

SOCIAL DIFFERENCES

The third great shaper of speech communities is social class. This has been, and is, more important in England than in America. In England, class differences have often been more prominent than those of age or place. If you were the blacksmith's boy, you might know the son of the local baronet, but you didn't speak his language. You spoke the language of your social group, and he that of his, and over the centuries these social dialects remained widely separated.

England in the twentieth century has been much democratized, but the language differences are far from having disappeared. One can still tell much about a person's family, his school background, his general position in life by the way he speaks. Social lines are hard to cross, and language is perhaps the greatest barrier. You may make a million pounds and own several cars and a place in the country, but your vowels and consonants and nouns and verbs and sentence patterns will still proclaim to the world that you're not a part of the upper crust.

In America, of course, social distinctions have never been so sharp as they are in England. We find it somewhat easier to rise in the world, to move into social environments unknown to our parents. This is possible, partly, because speech differences are slighter; conversely, speech differences are slighter because this is possible. But speech differences do exist. If you've spent all your life driving a cab in Philly and, having inherited a fortune, move to San Francisco's Nob Hill, you will find that your language is different, perhaps embarrassingly so, from that of your new acquaintances.

Language differences on the social plane in America are likely to correlate with education or occupation rather than with birth—simply because education and occupation in America do not depend so much on birth as they do in other countries. A child without family connection can get himself educated at Harvard, Yale, or Princeton. In doing so, he acquires the speech habits of the Ivy League and gives up those of his parents.

Exceptions abound. But in general there is a clear difference between the speech habits of the college graduate and those of the high-school graduate. The cab driver does not talk like the Standard Oil executive, the college professor like the carnival pitch man, or an Illinois merchant like a sailor shipping out of New Orleans. New York's Madison Avenue and Third Avenue are only a few blocks apart, but they are widely separated in language. And both are different from Broadway.

It should be added that the whole trend of modern life is to reduce rather than to accentuate these differences. In a country where college education becomes increasingly everybody's chance, where executives and refrigerator salesmen and farmers play golf together, where a college professor may drive a cab in the summertime to keep his family alive, it becomes harder and harder to guess a person's education, income, and social status by the way he talks. But it would be absurd to say that language gives no clue at all.

GOOD AND BAD

Speech communities, then, are formed by many features: age, geog-   35
raphy, education, occupation, social position. Young people speak differently from old people, Kansans differently from Virginians, Yale graduates
differently from Dannemora graduates. Now let us pose a delicate question: aren't some of these speech communities better than others? That is,
isn't better language heard in some than in others?

Well, yes, of course. One speech community is always better than all
the rest. This is the group in which one happens to find oneself. The
writer would answer unhesitatingly that the noblest, loveliest, purest
English is that heard in the Men's Faculty Club of San Jose State College, San Jose, California. He would admit, of course, that the speech of
some of the younger members leaves something to be desired; that certain recent immigrants from Harvard, Michigan, and other foreign parts
need to work on the laughable oddities lingering in their speech; and that
members of certain departments tend to introduce a lot of queer terms
that can only be described as jargon. But in general the English of the
Faculty Club is ennobling and sweet.

As a practical matter, good English is whatever English is spoken by
the group in which one moves contentedly and at ease. To the bum on
Main Street in Los Angeles, good English is the language of other L.A.
bums. Should he wander onto the campus of UCLA, he would find the
talk there unpleasant, confusing, and comical. He might agree, if pressed,
that the college man speaks "correctly" and he doesn't. But in his heart
he knows better. He wouldn't talk like them college jerks if you paid him.

If you admire the language of other speech communities more than
you do your own, the reasonable hypothesis is that you are dissatisfied
with the community itself. It is not precisely other speech that attracts
you but the people who use this speech. Conversely, if some language
strikes you as unpleasant or foolish or rough, it is presumably because the
speakers themselves seem so.

To many people, the sentence "Where is he at?" sounds bad. It is
bad, they would say, in and of itself. The sounds are bad. But this is very
hard to prove, If "Where is he at?" is bad because it has bad sound combinations, then presumably "Where is the cat?" or "Where is my hat?"
are just as bad, yet no one thinks them so. Well, then, "Where is he at?"
is bad because it uses too many words. One gets the same meaning from
"Where is he?" so why add the *at*? True. Then "He going with us?" is a
better sentence than "Is he going with us?" You don't really need the *is*,
so why put it in?

Certainly there are some features of language to which we can   40
apply the terms *good* and *bad*, *better* and *worse*. Clarity is usually better than obscurity; precision is better than vagueness. But these are not
often what we have in mind when we speak of good and bad English.
If we like the speech of upper-class Englishmen, the presumption is
that we admire upper-class Englishmen—their characters, culture, habits of mind. Their sounds and words simply come to connote the people themselves and become admirable therefore. If we heard the same
sounds and words from people who were distasteful to us, we would
find the speech ugly.

This is not to say that correctness and incorrectness do not exist in
speech. They obviously do, but they are relative to the speech community—
or communities—in which one operates. As a practical matter, correct
speech is that which sounds normal or natural to one's comrades. Incorrect speech is that which evokes in them discomfort or hostility or disdain.

THINKING CRITICALLY ABOUT THE READING

1. Why does Roberts begin with a discussion of "the village"? Is he referring
   literally to villages, or does "the village" stand for something else? What does
   his extended example of "Old Village" and "New Village" (3–5) illustrate?
   (Glossary: *Beginnings and Endings; Examples*)

2. Roberts writes: "Baby talk is not so much invented by the child as sponsored
   by the parent" (8). Explain what he means by this. What are the most basic,
   and motivational, factors in a child's language learning?

3. When children go to school, they move into an entirely new speech community, where, according to Roberts, their speech is modified "by forces over
   which neither they nor their parents nor their teachers have any real control"
   (13). What are these forces? What are some of the ways in which the new
   speech community asserts itself and establishes its own identity?

4. "We speak of America as the melting pot, but the speech communities of this
   continent are very far from having melted into one" (28), writes Roberts.
   What factors have contributed to, and continue to foster, the multiplicity of
   speech communities across the United States?

5. According to Roberts, the impact in England of social class on shaping
   speech communities differs considerably from the impact of class on speech
   communities in the United States. What factors contribute to this difference?
   Do you think these differences are as relevant today as Roberts assumed they
   were when he wrote *Understanding English*?

6. Roberts asks the provocative question: "Aren't some of these speech communities better than others?" (35). What do you think he means by this? Is
   he referring to the language of the community, or the community members
   themselves? What kind of value judgments do you think we make about others based on their particular way of speaking?

LANGUAGE IN ACTION

In his 1995 memoir, *Dreams from My Father: A Story of Race and Inheritance*, then-senator Barack Obama writes:

> I learned to slip back and forth between my black and white worlds, understanding that each possessed its own language and customs and structures of meaning, convinced that with a bit of translation on my part the two worlds would eventually cohere. Still, the feeling that something wasn't quite right stayed with me, a warning that sounded whenever a white girl mentioned in the middle of conversation how much she liked Stevie Wonder or when a woman in the supermarket asked me if I played basketball; or when the school principal told me I was cool. I did like Stevie Wonder, I did love basketball, and I tried my best to be cool at all times. So why did such comments set me on edge?

Why do you think Obama was "set on edge" by the kinds of comments he mentions toward the end of the passage? Can you sympathize with his position? Do you believe that it's possible to make different language communities to which one belongs "eventually cohere"? Why or why not?

WRITING SUGGESTIONS

1. We are often simultaneous members of more than one speech community, especially as we move into young adulthood and are introduced to groups outside of our family. Each of these groups can have its own demands, rules of membership, culture, and identity, to which we must adapt with chameleonlike skill. Write about your own experience moving between or among groups, identifying the most influential groups on your life and what demands were made on you in order to belong. What did you have to do to adapt to each group? How did the groups differ? Were they mutually exclusive, or did they overlap on occasion? Do you consider any one of the groups to be superior to the other, or were they simply equal, but different? If it helps you organize your thinking, make a sketch or a map of your communities. Write an essay in which you discuss what you discover.

2. Roberts writes:

   > If you admire the language of other speech communities more than you do your own, the reasonable hypothesis is that you are dissatisfied with the community itself. It is not precisely the other speech that attracts you but the people who use this speech. Conversely, if some language strikes you as unpleasant or foolish or rough, it is presumably because the speakers themselves seem so (38).

   Write an essay that supports or refutes his argument, providing examples from your own experience as evidence.

All-American Dialects

RICHARD LEDERER

Born in 1938, Richard Lederer has been a lifelong student of language. He holds degrees from Haverford College, Harvard University, and the University of New Hampshire, and for twenty-seven years taught English at St. Paul's School in Concord, New Hampshire. Anyone who has read one of his more than thirty-five books will understand why he has been referred to as "Conan the Grammarian" and "America's wittiest verbalist." Lederer loves language and enjoys writing about its marvelous richness and about how Americans use language. His many published works include *Anguished English* (1987), *Crazy English* (1989), *The Play of Words* (1990), *Adventures of a Verbivore* (1994), *Nothing Risque, Nothing Gained* (1995), *The Bride of Anguished English* (2002), *A Man of My Words: Reflections on the English Language* (2003), *Word Wizard: Super Bloopers, Rich Reflections, and Other Acts of Word Magic* (2006), *Presidential Trivia: The Feats, Fates, Families, Foibles, and Firsts of Our American Presidents* (2007), and *The Joy of Names* (2018). In addition to writing books, Lederer pens a weekly syndicated column called "Looking at Language" for newspapers and magazines throughout the country. He was the "Grammar Grappler" for *Writer's Digest*, the language commentator for National Public Radio, and cohost of *A Way with Words*, a weekly radio program out of San Diego, where he currently lives.

The following essay was first published in *USA Today* magazine in July 2009. Lederer discusses, using multiple examples, regional dialects or speech communities and how they differ one from another in vocabulary, pronunciation, and grammar. Like John Steinbeck before him, Lederer fears that regional speech is rapidly disappearing. He fervently hopes that "American English does not turn into a bland, homogenized, pasteurized, assembly line product."

WRITING TO DISCOVER: *What part of the country did you grow up in? Do you think of yourself as speaking English with a regional "accent"? Are you proud of the way you and your friends and neighbors speak? How do you view speakers from other parts of the United States? Do you readily recognize regional differences in the way English is spoken?*

I have tongue and will travel, so I run around the country speaking to groups of teachers, students, librarians, women's clubbers, guild professionals, and corporate clients. These good people go to all the trouble of putting together meetings and conferences, and I walk in, share my thoughts about language in their lives, and imbibe their collective energy and synergy. I will go anywhere to spread the word about words and, in venturing from California to Manhattan Island, from the redwood forest to the Gulf Stream waters, I hear America singing. We are teeming nations within a nation, a country that is like a world. We talk in melodies of infinite variety; we dance to their sundry measure and lyrics.

Midway through John Steinbeck's epic *The Grapes of Wrath*, young Ivy observes, "Ever'body says words different. Arkansas folks says 'em different, and Oklahomy folks says 'em different, and we seen a lady from Massachusetts, an' she said 'em differentest of all. Couldn't hardly make out what she was sayin'."

One aspect of American rugged individualism is that not all of us say the same word in the same way. Sometimes, we do not even use the same name for the same object. I was born and grew up in Philadelphia a coon's age, a blue moon, a month of Sundays ago—when Hector was a pup. Phillufia, or Philly, which is what we kids called the city, was where the epicurean delight made with cold cuts, cheese, tomatoes, pickles, and onions stuffed into a long, hard-crusted Italian bread loaf was invented. The creation of that sandwich took place in the Italian pushcart section of the city, known as Hog Island. Some linguists contend that it was but a short leap from Hog Island to hoagie, while others claim that the label hoagie arose because only a hog had the appetite or technique to eat one properly.

As a young man, I moved to northern New England (N'Hampsha, to be specific), where the same sandwich designed to be a meal in itself is called a grinder—because you need a good set of grinders to chew it. Yet, my travels around the country have revealed that the hoagie or grinder is called at least a dozen other names—a bomber, Garibaldi (after the Italian liberator), hero, Italian sandwich, rocket, sub, submarine (which is what they call it in California, where I now live), torpedo, wedge, wedgie, and, in the deep South, a poor-boy (usually pronounced poh-boy).

In Philadelphia, we washed down our hoagies with soda. In New England, we did it with tonic and, by that word, I do not mean medicine. Soda and tonic in other parts are known as pop, soda pop, a soft drink, Coke, and quinine.

In northern New England, they take the term milk shake quite literally. To many residing in that corner of the country, a milk shake consists of milk mixed with flavored syrup—and nothing more—shaken up until foamy. If you live in Rhode Island or in southern Massachusetts and you want ice cream in your milk drink, you ask for a cabinet (named after the square wooden cabinet in which the mixer was encased). If you live farther north, you order a velvet or a frappe (from the French *frapper*, "to ice").

Clear—or is it clean or plumb?—across the nation, Americans sure do talk different. What do you call those flat, doughy things you often eat for breakfast—battercakes, flannel cakes, flapjacks, fritters, griddle cakes, or pancakes? Is that simple strip of grass between the street and the sidewalk a berm, boulevard, boulevard strip, city strip, devil strip, green belt, the parking, the parking strip, parkway, sidewalk plot, strip, swale, tree bank, or tree lawn? Is the part of the highway that separates the northbound from the southbound lanes the centerline, center strip, mall, medial strip, median strip, medium strip, or neutral ground? Is it a cock horse, dandle, hicky horse, horse, horse tilt, ridy horse, seesaw, teeter, teeterboard, teetering board, teetering horse, teeter-totter, tilt, tilting board, tinter, tinter board, or tippity bounce? Do fishermen employ an angledog, angleworm, baitworm, earthworm, eaceworm, fishworm, mudworm, rainworm, or redworm? Is a larger worm a dew worm, night crawler, night walker, or town worm? Is it a crabfish, clawfish, craw, crawdab, crawdad, crawdaddy, crawfish, crawler, crayfish, creekcrab, crowfish, freshwater lobster, ghost shrimp, mudbug, spiny lobster, or yabby? Depends where you live and who or whom it is you are talking to.

I figger, figure, guess, imagine, opine, reckon, and suspect that my being bullheaded, contrary, headstrong, muley, mulish, ornery, otsny, pigheaded, set, sot, stubborn, or utsy about this whole matter of dialects makes you sick to, in, or at your stomach. I assure you, though, that when it comes to American dialects, I'm not speaking fahdoodle, flumadiddle, flummydiddle, or flurriddiddle—translation, nonsense. I am no all-thumbs-and-no-fingers, all-knees-and-elbows, all-left-feet, antigoddling, bumfuzzled, discombobulated, flusterated, or foozled bumpkin, clodhopper, country jake, hayseed, hick, hillbilly, hoosier, jackpine savage, mossback, mountain-boomer, pumpkin-husker, rail-splitter, rube, sod-buster, stump farmer, swamp angel, yahoo, or yokel.

The biblical book of Judges tells of how one group of speakers used the word *shibboleth*, Hebrew for "stream," as a military password. The Gileadites had defeated the Ephraimites in battle and were holding some narrow places on the Jordan River that the fleeing Ephraimites had to cross to get home. In those days, it was hard to tell one kind of soldier from another because they did not wear uniforms. The Gileadites knew that the Ephraimites spoke a slightly different dialect of Hebrew and could be recognized by their inability to pronounce an initial "sh" sound. Thus, each time a soldier wanted to cross the river, "the men of Gilead said unto him, Art thou an Ephraimite? If he said, Nay, then they said unto him, Say now Shibboleth, and he said Sibboleth: for he could not frame to pronounce it right. Then they took him and slew him at the passages of Jordan: and there fell at that time of the Ephraimites forty and two thousand."

During World War II, some American officers adapted the strategy   10
of the Old Testament Gileadites. Knowing that many Japanese have difficulty pronouncing the letter "L," these officers instructed their sentries to use only passwords that had L's in them, such as lallapalooza. The closest the Japanese got to the sentries was rarraparooza.

These days, English speakers do not get slaughtered for pronouncing their words differently from other English speakers, but the way those words sound can be labeled "funny" or "quaint" or "out of touch." In the George Bernard Shaw play "Pygmalion," Prof. Henry Higgins rails at Liza Doolittle and her cockney accent: "A woman who utters such depressing and disgusting sounds has no right to be anywhere—no right to live. Remember that you are a human being with a soul and the divine gift of articulate speech:

that your native language is the language of Shakespeare and Milton and the Bible; and don't sit there crooning like a bilious pigeon!"

Most of us are aware that large numbers of people in the U.S. speak very differently than we do. Most of us tend to feel that the way "we" talk is right, and the way "they" talk is weird. "They," of course, refers to anyone who differs from "us." If you ask most adults what a dialect is, they will tell you it is what somebody else in another region passes off as English. These regions tend to be exotic places like Mississippi or Texas — or Brooklyn, where oil is a rank of nobility and earl is a black, slippery substance.

It is reported that many Southerners reacted to the elections of Jimmy Carter (Georgia) and Bill Clinton (Arkansas) by saying, "Well, at last we have a president who talks without an accent." Actually, Southerners, like everyone else, do speak with an accent, as witness these tongue-in-cheek entries in our Dictionary of Southernisms: ah (organ for seeing); are (60 minutes); arn (ferrous metal); ass (frozen water); ast (questioned); bane (small, kidney-shaped vegetable); bar (seek and receive a loan); bold (heated in water); card (one who lacks courage); farst (a lot of trees); fur (distance); har (to employ); hep (to assist); hire yew (a greeting); paw tree (verse); rat (opposite of lef); reckanize (to see); tarred (exhausted); t'mar (the day following t'day); thang (item); thank (to cogitate); and y'all (a bunch of "you's").

When I visited Alexandria, Louisiana, a local pastor offered me proof that y'all has biblical origins, especially in the letters of the apostle Paul: "We give thanks to God always for you all, making mention of you in our prayers" (First Epistle to the Thessalonians, 1:2) and "First, I thank my God through Jesus Christ for you all" (First Epistle to the Romans, 1:8). "Obviously," the good reverend told me, "Saint Paul was a Southerner," before adding, "Thank you, Yankee visitor, for appreciating our beloved Southernspeak. We couldn't talk without it."

An anonymous poem that I came upon in Louisville, Kentucky, 15 clarifies the plural use of the one-syllable pronoun y'all:

> Y'all gather 'round from far and near,
> Both city folk and rural,
> And listen while I tell you this:
> The pronoun y'all is plural.
>
> If I should utter, "Y'all come down,
> Or we-all shall be lonely,"
> I mean at least a couple of folks
> And not one person only.
>
> If I should say to Hiram Jones,
> "I think that y'all are lazy,"
> Or "Will y'all let me use y'all's knife?"
> He'd think that I was crazy.

Don't think I mean to criticize
Or that I'm full of gall,
But when we speak of one alone,
We all say "you," not "y'all."

We all have accents. Many New Englanders drop the r in cart and farm and say "caht" and "fahm." Thus, the Midwesterner's "park the car in Harvard Yard" becomes the New Englander's "pahk the cah in Hahvahd Yahd." Those r's, though, are not lost. A number of upper Northeasterners, including the famous Kennedy family of Massachusetts, add "r" to words, such as "idear" and "Cuber," when those words come before a vowel or at the end of a sentence.

I.D. BY SPEECH PATTERN

When an amnesia victim appeared at a truck stop in Missouri in the fall of 1987, authorities tried in vain to discover her identity. Even after three months, police "ran into a brick wall," according to the *Columbia Daily Tribune.* Then, linguist Donald Lance of the University of Missouri–Columbia was called in to analyze her speech. After only a few sentences, Lance recognized the woman's West Pennsylvania dialect, and, within one month, police in Pittsburgh located her family. Among the clues used to pinpoint the woman's origin was the West Pennsylvanian use of "greezy" instead of "greasy," and "teeter-totter" rather than "seesaw." Dialectologists know that people who pronounce the word as "greezy" usually live south of a line that wiggles across the northern parts of New Jersey, Pennsylvania, Ohio, Indiana, and Illinois.

Linguist Roger Shuy writes about the reactions of Illinois residents in a 1962 survey of regional pronunciations, including the soundings of "greasy": "The northern Illinois informants felt the southern pronunciation was crude and ugly; it made them think of a very messy, dirty, sticky, smelly frying pan. To the southern and midland speakers, however, the northern pronunciation connoted a messy, dirty, sticky, smelly skillet."

Using the tools of his trade, Shuy was able to profile accurately Ted Kaczynski, the elusive Unabomber who terrorized the nation through the 1990s. Culling linguistic evidence from Kaczynski's "Manifesto," published in *The New York Times,* and the notes and letters accompanying the bombs, Shuy deduced the Unabomber's geographical origin, religious background, age, and education level.

Among the clues were the Unabomber's use of "sierras" to mean "mountains," an indication that the writer had spent some time living in Northern California. In his manifesto, Kaczynski used expressions common to a person who was a young adult in the 1960s — "Holy Robots," "working stiff," and "playing footsy." His employment of sociological terms, such as "other directed," and his many references

20

to "individual drives" suggested an acquaintance with the sociology in vogue during that decade, particularly that of David Reisman. The complexity of Kaczynski's sentence structure, including the subjunctive mood, and the learned-ness of his vocabulary, such as the words "surrogate," "sublimate," "overspecialization," and "tautology," pointed to someone highly educated.

All these conclusions were verified when Kaczynski was captured: He was in his early 50s, had grown up in Chicago and lived for a time in Northern California, and was well educated, having once been a university professor.

Face facts; we all speak some sort of dialect. When you learn language, you learn it as a dialect; if you do not speak a dialect, you do not speak. Dialect is not a label for careless, unlettered, nonstandard speech. A dialect is not something to be avoided or cured. Each language is a great pie. Each slice of that pie is a dialect, and no single slice is the language. Do not try to change your language into the kind of English that nobody really speaks. Be proud of your slice of the pie.

In the early 1960s, writer John Steinbeck decided to rediscover America in a camper with his French poodle, Charlie. He reported on his observations in a book called *Travels with Charlie* and included these thoughts on dialects: "One of my purposes was to listen, to hear speech, accent, speech rhythms, overtones, and emphasis. For speech is so much more than words and sentences. I did listen everywhere. It seemed to me that regional speech is in the process of disappearing, not gone but going. Forty years of radio and twenty years of television must have this impact. Communications must destroy localness by a slow, inevitable process."

I can remember a time when I almost could pinpoint a man's place of origin by his speech. That is growing more difficult and, in some foreseeable future, will become impossible. It is a rare house or building that is not rigged with spiky combers of the air. Radio and television speech becomes standardized, perhaps better English than we ever have used. Just as our bread — mixed and baked, packaged, and sold without benefit of accident or human frailty — is uniformly good and uniformly tasteless, so will our speech become one speech.

> **When you learn language, you learn it as a dialect; if you do not speak a dialect, you do not speak.**

Forty years have passed since Steinbeck's trip, and the hum and buzz of electronic voices have since permeated almost every home across our nation. Formerly, the psalmist tells us, "The voice of the turtle was heard in the land"—now, though, it is the voice of the broadcaster, with his or her immaculately groomed diction. Let us hope that American English does not turn into a bland, homogenized, pasteurized, assembly line product. May our bodacious language remain tasty and nourishing—full of flavor, variety, and local ingredients.

THINKING CRITICALLY ABOUT THE READING

1. How does Lederer use the writer John Steinbeck to introduce the subject of his essay? How does he bring the essay full circle by returning to Steinbeck in his conclusion? Did you find this beginning and ending effective? Explain why or why not.

2. What function do paragraphs 3 through 8 serve in the context on Lederer's essay? Why do you suppose that Lederer provides as many examples of vocabulary differences as he does?

3. How does Lederer illustrate the idea that Americans don't all sound the same when they speak, that there are pronunciation differences? Which examples of these pronunciation differences did you find most effective and interesting? Explain why.

4. Lederer explains how linguist Roger Shuy was able to profile the Unabomber Ted Kaczynski. What did you find most interesting about Shuy's contextual analysis of Kaczynski's "Manifesto"? Explain.

5. How effective did you find Lederer's pie analogy to explain a language and its various dialects?

6. According to Lederer, what accounts for the gradual disappearance of regional speech differences? What do we risk losing as American English becomes more uniform and homogenized?

LANGUAGE IN ACTION

In paragraphs 3 through 7, Lederer identifies a number of everyday items—a large sandwich designed to be a meal in itself, a carbonated drink, the part of a highway that separates the northbound from the southbound lanes, a worm used for bait, and a freshwater shellfish with claws, for example—that are called by different names in different parts of the country.

To see what your vocabulary may reveal about your regional or cultural origins, age, sex, and occupation, let's do a mini-dialect vocabulary survey similar to much longer ones used by field investigators preparing the *Linguistic Atlas of New England* and other regional atlases. For each of the following familiar, everyday items, circle the word or words you actually use (don't circle words you've heard used by your parents, grandparents, or friends). If the word you use is not listed, provide it in the space alongside the item. Before beginning, please list the places where you have lived as well as the length of time you lived in each location.

1. Round, flat confection with hole in center, made with baking powder: *crull, cruller, doughnut, fatcake, fried cake, cake doughnut, raised doughnut,* _____

2. Center of a peach: *pit, seed, stone, kernel, heart,* _____

3. Large open plastic container for scrub water: *pail, bucket,* _____

4. Family word for mother: *ma, mama, mammy, maw, mom, mommer, mommy, mother,* _____

5. Over a sink: *faucet, hydrant, spicket, spigot, tap,* _____

6. Policeman: *cop, policeman, copper, fuzz, dick, officer, bull,* _____

7. Place where packaged groceries can be purchased: *grocery store, general store, supermarket, store, delicatessen, grocery, market, food market, food store, supermart,* _____

8. A white lumpy cheese: *clabber cheese, cottage cheese, curd cheese, curd(s), Dutch cheese, homemade cheese, pot cheese, smearcase, cream cheese,* _____

9. Holds small objects together: *rubber band, rubber binder, elastic binder, gum binder, elastic band,* _____

10. Become ill with a cold: *catch a cold, catch cold, get a cold, take cold, take a cold, come down with a cold,* _____

Discuss your answers with your classmates. Did you discover any regional patterns of usage among your classmates? Did other patterns emerge? Were there any items for which you use a different word or words than either your parents or grandparents?

WRITING SUGGESTIONS

1. As Lederer points out, "Most of us are aware that large numbers of people in the U.S. speak very differently than we do. Most of us tend to feel that the way 'we' talk is right, and the way 'they' talk is weird" (12). Do you agree with Lederer? Write an essay in which you discuss how you feel about the way you and your family, friends, and neighbors speak English. How is the way you speak English tied up with your identity, who you are? Before you start writing you may find it helpful to review your response to the journal prompt for this selection.

2. Lederer notes that in the early 1960s author John Steinbeck bemoaned the fact that "regional speech is in the process of disappearing, not gone but going" (23). Lederer himself dreads the day when "our speech [will] become one speech" (24). What do you think would be lost if there were no dialects in the United States? What, if anything, would be gained? If you could wave a wand and make every person in the United States a speaker of Standard American dialect, the uninflected speech of radio and television news anchors that casts an aura of authority and refinement, would you? Write an essay in which you argue for or against Lederer's hope that "American English does not turn into a bland, homogenized, pasteurized, assembly line product. May our bodacious language remain tasty and nourishing—full of flavor, variety, and local ingredients" (25).

Sign of the Times

SARA NOVIĆ

Novelist, translator, and professor Sara Nović, born in 1987, knows three languages especially well: English, Croatian, and American Sign Language. But it is in the latter of these three that she is most "at home," even if it presents a paradox for her as a writer: "The one language in which I am fully comfortable I cannot write, not exactly. But without it I would certainly be a lesser storyteller." Nović grew up dividing her time between Croatia and the United States, where she earned her MFA in fiction and translation at Columbia University. Her first novel, *Girl at War* (2015), won the American Library Association Alex Award. Nović's short fiction and essays have appeared in *The New York Times, The Guardian, Harper's,* and other publications. Currently, she is an assistant professor of creative writing at Stockton University, and the fiction editor for *Blunderbuss Magazine.*

In this challenging selection, first published in the online magazine *Guernica* in March 14, 2016, Nović writes from the perspective of another one of her roles: deaf rights activist. For her, the conventional view that deafness is a disability or a pathology that needs to be cured is not only wrong but also misses the ways in which the richness of deaf culture and sign language are facing marginalization and extinction.

WRITING TO DISCOVER: *What associations do you have with deafness and deaf people? What assumptions do you have about them? Write about your perceptions of the deaf from personal experiences, media images, or any other influence that has shaped your view.*

When I was in college I met a man who was trying to erase me. He was a scientist and a visiting professor at my school, teaching a class called Audiology. I was the co-president of the sign language club and had heard about the course from a few of the other members; many of them were studying to become Speech-Language Pathologists. I signed up, too, wanting to see what the professor might have to say about me.

He spoke mainly of my insides, the broken bits — the cochlea, its basilar membrane and tympanic canal. We learned about the function of each part and every possibility for dysfunction; we memorized terminology down to the cellular level. I tried not to be offended by the way he reduced deafness to a medical defect, how he'd produced a biological vacuum where the trait of deafness was detached from actual Deaf human experience. We never talked about how many Deaf people, myself included, liked being Deaf, liked the close-knit community, the culture and vivid three-dimensional language deafness affords us.

195

Still I tried to give him the benefit of the doubt; it was a science class, after all.

Then he spoke of the cure. His research team across the river at a Harvard lab was working toward the stem cell-based creation of cochlear cells to cure deafness. Far beyond the capacity of aids or implants, a stem cell treatment would be organic, and totally regenerative. If and when it worked, it would be like the person had never been deaf at all.

The professor and the students in the class were intelligent and liberal-minded, some of whom I counted as friends. But my identity was their pathology, and their idea of scientific progress, of a better society, lay in the eradication of people like me. How the removal of Deaf bodies from the human genome would necessarily lead to the extinction of our folk tales, our jokes and word play, our poetry, was another thing the professor never addressed.

I don't know why, but instead of running from the scene I glommed   5
onto this professor. Maybe it was a kind of rubbernecking. Perhaps part of me wanted to keep an eye on him. Whatever it was, I proposed an independent study about his research. I went to his lab and watched them deafen the mice. I stood before the centrifuges where assistants readied samples to grow in petri dishes. The professor did not have to take me on; he was kind and patient with me, a student with little foundation in scientific study. It came out over these sessions that he had Deaf grandparents and knew some sign language.

"But what will happen to Deaf culture if your research works?" I garnered the courage to ask him once.

"Some people would still raise their children Deaf," he replied. "It would still be a choice."

In a vacuum, yes — it's unlikely the US government would legislate mandatory medical treatment of deaf people. But in reality, the choice is more of the Hobson variety; even without my professor's treatment, Deaf culture is already endangered, the result of a centuries-long tradition of stigma and oppression against deafness and sign language.

Today's deaf babies are born into an immediate declaration of their brokenness. Many mothers are informed of their babies' "defects" only hours after giving birth: *your child has failed the universal newborn hearing screening, but don't worry; we can fix it.* Cochlear implants, medical devices inserted into deaf people's skulls, simulate hearing by sending electric impulses to the auditory nerve. Doctors recommend the earliest possible implantation so the brain can learn how to interpret sound. Doctors also recommend aggressive oral-only education to be sure that deaf children are fully dependent on the implant. Bilingualism from the medical viewpoint is a fallback, a distraction from the goal: English speaking. Normalcy. The ability to pass.

It's unsurprising that parents living in a society steeped in this stigma,   10
many of whom have never met an actual Deaf person, take doctors'
recommendations at their word. But cochlear implants fall far short of
replicating natural hearing. Some implants work well, and recipients learn
to speak and communicate the way the hearing world deems correct.
Other implants do not work, or recipients do not succeed at performing
hearingness so seamlessly—here, without a full grasp of English, and having been deprived of American Sign Language (ASL), they are destined
to live a life half-languaged.

America's fear of difference is particularly visible in the current political landscape, but it has long been woven into the
country's cultural values. A deep-seated
disdain for multiculturalism—and multilingualism—is historically evident in the
ruthless genocide of American Indians, in
the whitewashing of immigrants' names
at Ellis Island, and today in the vitriolic demands that immigrants "just
speak English," in the expectation that national languages be bulldozed
such that English be available to us at all times, even abroad.

> **Born on American soil and completely untethered to a spoken language, ASL is a much more "American" language than older forms of English.**

The history of ASL already places it at odds with the way many understand their "Americanness." ASL's primary ancestor is Martha's Vineyard
Sign Language (MVSL), borne out of a high incidence of hereditary deafness on the island in the 18th century. At the deaf population's peak in
1854, one in 155 people were deaf (as opposed to a national average of
one in 5728). Martha's Vineyard is one of a few known communities
of high-rate genetic deafness in which all members knew sign language.
Hearing people were even known to sign to one another without deaf
people present. MVSL, influenced by French Sign Language when Deaf
Frenchman Laurent Clerc co-founded America's first school for the Deaf,
became the standard American Sign Language we use today. No savior
narrative can be extracted; no hearing person gifted language, or schools,
to America's deaf people. Born on American soil and completely unteth-
ered to a spoken language, ASL is a much more "American" language
than older forms of English. And, as America treats all its indigenous cultures, it has been consistently marked for extinction.

Alexander Graham Bell led the charge against Deaf people and *Source incorporated*
sign language at the time, outlining plans for eradication in his speech
"Upon the Formation of a Deaf Variety of the Human Race." A prominent eugenicist, he fought to prevent Deaf people from marrying and
propagating a "defective race of human beings." Though his theory
about the genetic transmission of deafness was wrong—only ten percent of deaf people have deaf children—his understanding of cultural
transmission was better-founded. Disturbed by the socialization among

Deaf people, their creation of clubs and communities, Bell advocated that the deaf should be educated orally, taught to speak and lipread, to ensure successful integration into society. Sign language, he thought, inhibited these goals. For decades after, deaf children's hands were tied to their desks to prevent them from signing. And while tying up students is no longer considered good practice, the Alexander Graham Bell Association remains a prominent American "hearing loss resource center," that continues to advocate for oral-only education, pushing the same outdated notion that bilingualism is in some way harmful to a deaf child's development.

Though Bell's ideas about education don't stand up to actual scientific evidence, they are still upheld by today's system. As decreed by the US Department of Education, the goal for students with disabilities is that they be placed in the "Least Restrictive Environment" (LRE), mainstreamed into regular education classrooms, unless their disability is too "severe" for them to be circulated in gen pop. Deaf schools are framed as places of segregation and failure. This definition of "restrictive" also completely ignores a holistic understanding of a deaf child as a human. What if a deaf school, where children can communicate with their teachers, and perhaps even more importantly, their peers, without assistive technology or an interpreter is the less restrictive of the two? Deaf actor and advocate Tyrone Giordano often speaks about the topic, saying it's a mistake to view Deaf schools as segregated, though they become that way when the educational system uses them as "dumping grounds" for the failures of mainstreaming. Deaf schools, he says, should instead be understood as "bilingual institutions where ASL and English are used every day, in all sorts of contexts." Giordano's involvement in the First Folio project at Gallaudet University exemplifies the success of this model—the exhibition will feature a synthesis of ASL and Shakespearian English.

But Gallaudet, America's only university exclusively for the Deaf, is more the exception in today's educational scene. The question, Giordano says, is "are we trying to build a homogenous society a la the melting pot concept, or are we trying to honor the multiplicity of societies within greater society? The melting pot idea is actually quite harmful, because if you take the analogy a little further, if you stop applying the heat, what happens? There will naturally be separation, and some will rise to the top while others sink to the bottom."

The fact that deafness is not inherently debilitating, that it has no bearing on one's intellect or ability to function in daily life, is evident in communities like the historical Martha's Vineyard, or today among the al-Sayyid Bedouin tribe in Israel. Four percent of al-Sayyid's population is deaf, but everyone knows sign language so everyone has equal access to society. When the majority culture doesn't view deafness as a disability, it isn't.

Almost all the negative impacts of deafness in America, then, are rooted in the cultural misunderstanding that spoken English is dominant due to its intrinsic superiority, rather than the result of the genetic lottery that makes hearing people the majority. Indeed, this mindset broaches more territory than the Deaf world; the concern over English's dominance is a pressing one for language preservationists and language rights activists globally. Japanese novelist Minae Mizumura speaks to the phenomenon in *The Fall of Language in the Age of English,* saying: "the rest of the world would appreciate it if [native English speakers] would at least be aware of their privileged position—and more important, be aware that the privilege is unwarranted." English, she says is an "accidental universal language."

Mizumura concludes her book by imploring Japanese people to read and write Japanese literature, and the Deaf community has responded to its own position similarly, with an explosion of Deaf art and theater. 2015 was a banner year for Deaf-made art. Deaf artist Christine Sun Kim rose to TedTalk prominence presenting on her work in visual and sound art; Deaf West's ASL/English revival of *Spring Awakening* was a Broadway hit, garnering rave reviews from nearly every major media outlet.

These positive responses to displays of Deaf culture at first seem a heartening divergence from America's eugenicist past; however, closer examination reveals that hearing people's move toward ASL is largely an appropriative one. Not unlike Miley's twerk or Urban Outfitters' fake "Navajo collection," sign language is deemed permissible by hearing people in certain contexts—mainly for aesthetic or artistic benefit, and when it's made accessible. Staged musicals and signed music video soundtracks keep listeners abreast of what's being said; ASL classes are designed for hearing consumers.

The evidence for this appropriation lies not in hearing people's 20 praise of Deaf art so much as it does in their co-opting it for their own purposes. Scholarly interest in sign language has skyrocketed over the past decade; a Modern Language Association report has it dethroning German for the slot of third-most studied language for foreign language credit, to say nothing of the recent baby sign language craze. Deaf people have also appeared in recent hearing-made art, notably the Ukrainian Sign Language film *The Tribe*, which took the festival circuit by storm. Even ABC Family has gotten the ASL bandwagon—in its aptly titled drama *Switched at Birth,* one of the birth-switched protagonists is deaf. But the hearing director of *The Tribe* has shown himself to have little understanding of Deaf culture beyond its aesthetic appeal, in some interviews referring to Ukrainian Sign Language as "international sign," and *Switched at Birth* can't resist the high-drama of forbidden, (and schmaltzy) deaf/hearing romances. Instead of reflecting authentic Deaf experiences, hearing people use bits and pieces of Deaf culture to tighten their grip on the cultural narratives of deafness and disability.

To that end, sign language and Deaf people are also welcome in the mainstream as inspiration porn. Videos of deaf children who are cured with implants and "are hearing their mothers' voices for the first time!" or clips in which a hearing person come to the aid of a poor, disenfranchised disabled one, routinely go viral—they serve as a way for hearing people to interact with people with disabilities while simultaneously reinforcing dominant power structures.

Sign language is also appropriate when a gorilla is doing it.[1]

No one seems able to scientifically explain why ASL is detrimental to deaf children, but great for the brain development of hearing babies born to yuppies. This is because the answer lies not in scientific fact but in an insidious feat of cultural control. ASL is held up as artistic spectacle, or literally infantilized as the language of babies and primates, but Deaf schools—the cultural centers for the Deaf community—are closed, and native ASL-users are encouraged to seek treatment and abandon sign for spoken language.

Hearing people continue to enjoy the fruits of Deaf culture while actively eroding the infrastructure that supports the futures of Deaf people. Without Deaf schools, sign language users will continue to dwindle or exist in isolation; in either situation the creation of Deaf art will become increasingly difficult. A language cannot endure without native speakers to engage in language play and evolve it, so despite hearing students' increased study, the future of ASL as a viable, living language remains imperiled.

What can be done to avoid our extinction? Giordano, referring back   25
to the "melting pot" scenario, suggests we aim instead for a "'salad bowl' [...] cultural mosaic, where differences are celebrated parts of the whole." "Salads," he quips, "are healthier for you anyway, and can be damn delicious." But fostering a genuine respect and desire for cultural and linguistic multiplicity is not only a tall order, but a race against the clock.

For my part, I stay up late googling my professor. A YouTube video provides—from what I can tell; it isn't captioned—an overview of his research protocols. Filled with dread, I scan the remaining search results for evidence of a breakthrough, but I don't find anything, not yet.

---

1. This is a reference to Koko, a female gorilla who lived at the Gorilla Foundation in Woodside, California, and learned how to communicate with humans using American Sign Language. Koko died of old age in 2018.

The professor, smart and well-intentioned, is for me the embodiment of cognitive dissonance: I have never before met a person I've both liked and so desperately wished failure upon. I think of his answer, that his research simply provides a choice. But the American people are making the decision already—with their hearts and minds, with their votes and tax dollars.

Will the government pass a law that Deaf people must be treated with stem cells when the time comes? Probably not. But will they cease support to resources until Deaf people are defunded into a corner? They already are. Perhaps the treatment will be pushed through the judiciary system—as early as 2002, a Deaf mother's refusal to give her child a cochlear implant was brought before a Wyoming family court as evidence of child neglect.

More likely, though, it will be quieter. The same misinformation leveled against Deaf people for centuries will continue to be used by educators to close Deaf schools and instill fear in hearing parents, and by scientists to pursue projects with complete detachment from their ethical implications. Unless we actively work to restore value to culture over convenience, Deaf people and American Sign Language will be but two of many casualties in the wake of an all-powerful monoculture. I only hope I won't be around to see this kind of progress achieved.

THINKING CRITICALLY ABOUT THE READING

1. In paragraph 2, Nović writes that she "tried not to be offended" by the visiting professor at her college. What did she find potentially offensive?

2. What has "long been woven into [America's] cultural values," according to Nović (11)?

3. Why is Alexander Graham Bell important to Nović's argument? What is his significance in the story of deafness and deaf people in the United States?

4. In paragraph 6, Nović refers to "Deaf culture." What do you think she means by this? What connotations does the word *culture* have in this context? What things might make up Deaf culture?

5. In paragraph 12, Nović discusses the history of American Sign Language and writes, "No savior narrative can be extracted; no hearing person gifted language, or schools, to America's deaf people." What does the term "savior narrative" mean in this context? What are the problems with these kinds of "savior narratives," from Nović's perspective?

6. Nović states as a "fact" that "deafness is not inherently debilitating, that it has no bearing on one's intellect or ability to function in daily life" (16). Do you agree with this characterization of deafness? Why or why not? Does she provide support for this claim in the essay?

LANGUAGE IN ACTION

At a few points in the essay, Nović uses the word "disability," which is one term commonly applied to people who have physical or mental impairments. Note that even the previous sentence uses a charged term ("impairments") that some people might dispute. Nović, for one, does not see deafness primarily as an impairment. What kind of language should we use when discussing disability? Why is such language important? Consider the following words, and discuss whether you think each word is appropriate or acceptable. How do you make such judgments?

- Able-bodied
- Person with disabilities
- Lame
- Person with a cognitive delay
- Cripple
- Handicapped
- Vision-impaired

- Wheelchair-bound
- Normal
- Deaf
- Nonverbal
- Deaf and dumb
- Invalid

WRITING SUGGESTIONS

1. Nović writes about the growing popularity of—and interest in—American Sign Language, even as it is marginalized in other ways: "Scholarly interest in sign language has skyrocketed over the past decade" (20). Do you think that American Sign Language should be offered along with other languages at the high school level? Why or why not? Do you consider ASL a full-fledged language, with as much practical and cultural importance as, say, French or Spanish? Would you have taken ASL as a high school student, if it had been offered? Would you take it in college? Write an essay that answers these questions.

2. After reading both Nović's essay and Helen Keller's piece "The Day Language Came into My Life" (pp. 141–143), compare and contrast the two essays. Can you identify any common themes in Nović's and Keller's descriptions of deafness? How are these two authors' experiences as members of the deaf community similar or different? Does the fact that Keller is blind, in addition to being deaf, lead her to perceive the world differently than Nović, who is deaf but not blind? Write an essay in which you answer these questions, supporting your claims with specific language from both essays.

Two Ways to Belong in America

BHARATI MUKHERJEE

The prominent Indian American writer and university professor Bharati Mukherjee (1940–2017) was born into an aristocratic family in Calcutta (now Kolkata), India. After India's independence, her family relocated to England because of her father's work. She returned to India in the 1950s where she earned her bachelor's degree at the University of Calcutta in 1959 and a master's degree from the University of Baroda in 1961. Later she pursued her long-held desire to become a writer by earning a master of fine arts degree at the University of Iowa and eventually a doctorate in English and comparative literature. After she married an American, Clark Blaise, the couple moved to Canada, where they lived for fourteen years until legislation there against South Asians led them to move back to the United States. Before joining the faculty at the University of California, Berkeley, Mukherjee taught at McGill University, Skidmore College, Queens College, and City University of New York. Her later work centered on writing and the themes of immigration, particularly concerning women, immigration policy, immigrant communities, and cultural alienation. With her husband, she authored *Days and Nights in Calcutta* (1977) and *The Sorrow and the Terror: The Haunting Legacy of the Air India Tragedy* (1987). In addition, she published seven novels including *The Tiger's Daughter* (1971), *Wife* (1975), *Jasmine* (1989), *The Holder of the World* (1993), and *The Tree Bride* (2004); two collections of short stories, *Darkness* (1985) and *The Middleman and Other Stories* (1988), for which she won the National Book Critics Circle Award; and two works of nonfiction, *Political Culture and Leadership in India* (1991) and *Regionalism in Indian Perspective* (1992).

The following essay was first published in *The New York Times* in 1996 in response to new legislation championed by the then-vice-president, Al Gore, that gave expedited citizenship for legal immigrants living in the United States. As you read Mukherjee's essay, notice the way she has organized her presentation of the contrasting views that she and her sister have toward the various aspects of living as either a legal immigrant or a citizen in the United States.

WRITING TO DISCOVER: *The word immigrant has many connotations. What associations does the word have for you? If you were to move to another country, how do you think it would feel to be considered an immigrant?*

This is a tale of two sisters from Calcutta, Mira and Bharati, who have lived in the United States for some thirty-five years, but who find themselves on different sides in the current debate over the status of immigrants. I am an American citizen and she is not. I am moved that thousands of long-term residents are finally taking the oath of citizenship. She is not.

Mira arrived in Detroit in 1960 to study child psychology and preschool education. I followed her a year later to study creative writing at the University of Iowa. When we left India, we were almost identical in appearance and attitude. We dressed alike, in saris; we expressed identical views on politics, social issues, love and marriage in the same Calcutta convent-school accent. We would endure our two years in America, secure our degrees, then return to India to marry the grooms of our father's choosing.

Instead, Mira married an Indian student in 1962 who was getting his business administration degree at Wayne State University. They soon acquired the labor certifications necessary for the green card of hassle-free residence and employment.

Mira still lives in Detroit, works in the Southfield, Michigan, school system, and has become nationally recognized for her contributions in the fields of preschool education and parent-teacher relationships. After thirty-six years as a legal immigrant in this country, she clings passionately to her Indian citizenship and hopes to go home to India when she retires.

In Iowa City in 1963, I married a fellow student, an American of   5
Canadian parentage. Because of the accident of his North Dakota birth, I bypassed labor-certification requirements and the race-related "quota" system that favored the applicant's country of origin over his or her merit. I was prepared for (and even welcomed) the emotional strain that came with marrying outside my ethnic community. In thirty-three years of marriage, we have lived in every part of North America. By choosing a husband who was not my father's selection, I was opting for fluidity, self-invention, blue jeans and T-shirts, and renouncing three thousand years (at least) of caste-observant, "pure culture" marriage in the Mukherjee family. My books have often been read as unapologetic (and in some quarters overenthusiastic) texts for cultural and psychological "mongrelization." It's a word I celebrate.

Mira and I have stayed sisterly close by phone. In our regular Sunday morning conversations, we are unguardedly affectionate. I am her only blood relative on this continent. We expect to see each other through the looming crises of aging and ill health without being asked. Long before Vice President Gore's "Citizenship USA" drive, we'd had our polite arguments over the ethics of retaining an overseas citizenship while expecting the permanent protection and economic benefits that come with living and working in America.

Like well-raised sisters, we never said what was really on our minds, but we probably pitied one another. She, for the lack of structure in my life, the erasure of Indianness, the absence of an unvarying daily core. I, for the narrowness of her perspective, her uninvolvement with the mythic depths or the superficial pop culture of this society. But, now, with the scapegoating of "aliens" (documented or illegal) on the increase, and the targeting of long-term legal immigrants like Mira for new scrutiny and new self-consciousness, she and I find ourselves unable to maintain the same polite discretion. We were always unacknowledged adversaries, and we are now, more than ever, sisters.

"I feel used," Mira raged on the phone the other night. "I feel manipulated and discarded. This is such an unfair way to treat a person who was invited to stay and work here because of her talent. My employer went to the INS and petitioned for the labor certification. For over thirty years, I've invested my creativity and professional skills into the improvement of *this* country's preschool system. I've obeyed all the rules, I've paid my taxes, I love my work, I love my students, I love the friends I've made. How dare America now change its rules in midstream? If America wants to make new rules curtailing benefits of legal immigrants, they should apply only to immigrants who arrive after those rules are already in place."

> **In one family, from two sisters alike as peas in a pod, there could not be a wider divergence of immigrant experience.**

To my ears, it sounded like the description of a long-enduring, comfortable yet loveless marriage, without risk or recklessness. Have we the right to demand, and to expect, that we be loved? (That, to me, is the subtext of the arguments by immigration advocates.) My sister is an expatriate, professionally generous and creative, socially courteous and gracious, and that's as far as her Americanization can go. She is here to maintain an identity, not to transform it.

I asked her if she would follow the example of others who have decided to become citizens because of the anti-immigration bills in Congress. And here, she surprised me. "If America wants to play the manipulative game, I'll play it too," she snapped. "I'll become a U.S. citizen for now, then change back to Indian when I'm ready to go home. I feel some kind of irrational attachment to India that I don't to America. Until all this hysteria against legal immigrants, I was totally happy. Having my green card meant I could visit any place in the world I wanted to and then come back to a job that's satisfying and that I do very well."

In one family, from two sisters alike as peas in a pod, there could not be a wider divergence of immigrant experience. America spoke to me—I married it—I embraced the demotion from expatriate aristocrat to immigrant nobody, surrendering those thousands of years of "pure culture," the saris, the delightfully accented English. She retained them all. Which of us is the freak?

Mira's voice, I realize, is the voice not just of the immigrant South Asian community but of an immigrant community of the millions who have stayed rooted in one job, one city, one house, one ancestral culture, one cuisine, for the entirety of their productive years. She speaks for

10

greater numbers than I possibly can. Only the fluency of her English and the anger, rather than fear, born of confidence from her education, differentiate her from the seamstresses, the domestics, the technicians, the shop owners, the millions of hardworking but effectively silenced documented immigrants as well as their less fortunate "illegal" brothers and sisters.

Nearly twenty years ago, when I was living in my husband's ancestral homeland of Canada, I was always well-employed but never allowed to feel part of the local Quebec or larger Canadian society. Then, through a Green Paper that invited a national referendum on the unwanted side effects of "nontraditional" immigration, the Government officially turned against its immigrant communities, particularly those from South Asia.

I felt then the same sense of betrayal that Mira feels now. I will never forget the pain of that sudden turning, and the casual racist outbursts the Green Paper elicited. That sense of betrayal had its desired effect and drove me, and thousands like me, from the country.

Mira and I differ, however, in the ways in which we hope to interact   15
with the country that we have chosen to live in. She is happier to live in America as an expatriate Indian than as an immigrant American. I need to feel like a part of the community I have adopted (as I tried to feel in Canada as well). I need to put roots down, to vote and make the difference that I can. The price that the immigrant willingly pays, and that the exile avoids, is the trauma of self-transformation.

THINKING CRITICALLY ABOUT THE READING

1. What is Mukherjee's thesis? (Glossary: *Thesis*) Where does she present it? How has Mukherjee organized her essay? (Glossary: *Comparison and Contrast*)

2. What arguments does Mukherjee make for becoming an American citizen? What arguments does her sister make for retaining her Indian citizenship? Which sister do you think made the "right" decision? Explain.

3. Mukherjee chooses to let her sister Mira speak for herself in this essay. What do you think would have been lost had she spoken for her sister, simply reporting what Mira felt and believed as an immigrant in the United States? Explain. Why do you think Mukherjee's sister feels "used" by attempts to change American laws regarding social security benefits for noncitizens?

4. Mukherjee uses the word *mongrelization* in paragraph 5. What do you think she means by this word, and why does she celebrate it?

5. What do you think Mukherjee's sister means when she says in paragraph 10, "If America wants to play the manipulative game, I'll play it too"? How do you react to her decision and to her possible plans if and when she eventually returns to India? Explain.

6. At the end of paragraph 11 Mukherjee asks a question. How does she answer it? How would you answer it? Do you, like Mukherjee, "need to feel like a

part of the community I have adopted" (15)? What does Mukherjee mean when she says in paragraph 15, "The price that the immigrant willingly pays, and that the exile avoids, is the trauma of self-transformation"?

LANGUAGE IN ACTION

Another Indian American writer, Jhumpa Lahiri, writes about her experience growing up in the United States with dual identities in an essay titled "My Two Lives." In it, she explains the struggle she had in making sense of her combined cultures, especially as a child. She writes:

> According to my parents I was not American, nor would I ever be no matter how hard I tried. I felt doomed by their pronouncement, misunderstood and gradually defiant. In spite of the first lessons of arithmetic, one plus one did not equal two but zero, my conflicting selves always canceling each other out.

Discuss whether or not you see the conclusions Lahiri makes (or is told to make) about her identity in the ways that Bharati Mukherjee and her sister view their immigrant experiences. How might the concept of "conflicting selves canceling each other out" resonate with the Mukherjee sisters? How do they attempt to resolve that conflict? How would you?

WRITING SUGGESTIONS

1. In paragraph 7 Mukherjee writes about the relationship that she had with her sister by saying that "we never said what was really on our minds, but we probably pitied one another." These types of differences are played out on a larger scale when immigrants who have transformed themselves into Americans are confronted by those who have chosen to retain their ethnic identity, and these tensions often lead to name-calling and aggressive prejudice. Such situations exist within the Latino, African American, and Southeast Asian American communities and perhaps among all immigrant groups. Write an essay comparing and contrasting the choices of lifestyle that members of an ethnic or cultural community you are familiar with make as they try to find a comfortable place in American society.

2. Mukherjee presents her sister's reasons for not becoming a citizen and supports them with statements that her sister has made. Imagine that you are Mira Mukherjee. Write a counterargument to the one presented by your sister that gives your reasons for remaining an Indian citizen. Consider that you have already broken with tradition by marrying a man "not of your father's choosing" but also that the "trauma of self-transformation" that your sister raises in the conclusion of her essay is much deeper and more complicated than she has represented it. Can you say that you are holding on to tradition when you are not? Can you engage in a challenging self-transformation if it is not genuinely motivated?

The Strange Persistence of First Languages

JULIE SEDIVY

As she recounts in the following selection, writer, linguist, and cognitive scientist Julie Sedivy was born in Czechoslovakia, but grew up in Austria, Italy, and Canada. She earned her BA at Carleton College, her MA at the University of Ottawa, and her PhD at the University of Rochester. Sedivy then taught at Brown University for twelve years and is currently an adjunct professor at the University of Calgary, where she teaches in the department of Psychology and at the School of Languages, Linguistics, Literatures, and Cultures. She is the author of *Sold on Language: How Advertisers Talk to You and What This Says About You* (2011, written with Greg N. Carlson) and *Language in Mind: An Introduction to Psycholinguistics* (2014). Sedivy is also an associate editor for the journal *Linguistics and Philosophy* and a contributing editor for *Journal of Experimental Psychology: Learning, Memory and Cognition*.

In the following essay, originally published in the online magazine *Nautilus* in November 5, 2015, Sedivy explores the profoundly personal ways in which her native tongue shapes her identity. For her, language is not merely a transparent medium for individual expression, but a kind of cultural and family heirloom to be cherished and savored.

WRITING TO DISCOVER: *The following essay discusses the practice of "code-switching" in the context of bilingual people who need to consciously choose which language to use to express a particular thought or idea, depending on their purpose or audience. But whether we are bilingual or not, all of us practice code-switching to a certain extent: we change our tone, diction, inflection, or conversational style depending on context. How do you understand and practice code-switching in your own life? What circumstances lead you to do code-switch?*

Several years ago, my father died as he had done most things throughout his life: without preparation and without consulting anyone. He simply went to bed one night, yielded his brain to a monstrous blood clot, and was found the next morning lying amidst the sheets like his own stone monument.

It was hard for me not to take my father's abrupt exit as a rebuke. For years, he'd been begging me to visit him in the Czech Republic, where I'd been born and where he'd gone back to live in 1992. Each year, I delayed. I was in that part of my life when the marriage-grad-school-children-career-divorce current was sweeping me along with breath-sucking force, and a leisurely trip to the fatherland seemed as plausible as pausing the flow of time.

Now my dad was shrugging at me from beyond—"You see, you've run out of time."

His death underscored another loss, albeit a far more subtle one: that of my native tongue. Czech was the only language I knew until the age of 2, when my family began a migration westward, from what was then Czechoslovakia through Austria, then Italy, settling eventually in Montreal, Canada. Along the way, a clutter of languages introduced themselves into my life: German in preschool, Italian-speaking friends, the francophone streets of East Montreal. Linguistic experience congealed, though, once my siblings and I started school in English. As with many immigrants, this marked the time when English became, unofficially and over the grumbling of my parents (especially my father), our family language—the time when Czech began its slow retreat from my daily life.

Many would applaud the efficiency with which we settled into   5
English—it's what exemplary immigrants do. But between then and now, research has shown the depth of the relationship all of us have with our native tongues—and how traumatic it can be when that relationship is ruptured. Spurred by my father's death, I returned to the Czech Republic hoping to reconnect to him. In doing so, I also reconnected with my native tongue, and with parts of my identity that I had long ignored.

While my father was still alive, I was, like most young people, more intent on hurtling myself into my future than on tending my ancestral roots—and that included speaking the language of my new country rather than my old one. The incentives for adopting the culturally dominant language are undeniable. Proficiency offers clear financial rewards, resulting in wage increases of 15 percent for immigrants who achieve it relative to those who don't, according to economist Barry Chiswick. A child, who rarely calculates the return on investment for her linguistic efforts, feels the currency of the dominant language in other ways: the approval of teachers and the acceptance of peers. I was mortally offended when my first-grade teacher asked me on the first day of school if I knew "a little English"—"I don't know a little English," was my indignant and heavily accented retort. "I know a *lot* of English." In the schoolyard, I quickly learned that my Czech was seen as having little value by my friends, aside from the possibility of swearing in another language—a value I was unable to deliver, given that my parents were cursing teetotalers.

But embracing the dominant language comes at a price. Like a household that welcomes a new child, a single mind can't admit a new language without some impact on other languages already residing there. Languages can co-exist, but they tussle, as do siblings, over mental resources and attention. When a bilingual person tries to articulate a thought in one language, words and grammatical structures from the other language often clamor in the background, jostling for attention. The subconscious effort of suppressing this competition can slow the retrieval of words—and if the background language elbows its way to the forefront, the speaker may resort to code-switching, plunking down a word from one language into the sentence frame of another.

Meanwhile, the weaker language is more likely to become swamped; when resources are scarce, as they are during mental exhaustion, the disadvantaged language may become nearly impossible to summon. Over time, neglecting an earlier language makes it harder and harder for it to compete for access.

According to a 2004 survey conducted in the Los Angeles metropolitan area, fewer than half of people belonging to Generation 1.5 — immigrants who arrive before their teenage years — claimed to speak the language they were born into "very well." A 2006 study of immigrant languages in Southern California forecast that even among Mexican Americans, the slowest group to assimilate within Southern California, new arrivals would live to hear only 5 out of every 100 of their great-grandchildren speak fluent Spanish.

When a childhood language decays, so does the ability to reach far back into your own private history. Language is memory's receptacle. It has Proustian powers. Just as smells are known to trigger vivid memories of past experiences, language is so entangled with our experiences that inhabiting a specific language helps surface submerged events or interactions that are associated with it.   10

Psychotherapist Jennifer Schwanberg has seen this firsthand. In a 2010 paper, she describes treating a client who'd lived through a brutal childhood in Mexico before immigrating to the United States. The woman showed little emotion when talking about events from her early life, and Schwanberg at first assumed that her client had made her peace with them. But one day, the woman began the session in Spanish. The therapist followed her lead and discovered that "moving to her first language had opened a floodgate. Memories from childhood, both traumatic and non-traumatic, were recounted with depth and vividness . . . It became clear that a door to the past was available to her in her first language."

A first language remains uniquely intertwined with early memories, even for people who fully master another language. In her book *The Bilingual Mind,* linguist Aneta Pavlenko describes how the author Vladimir Nabokov fled the Russian revolution in 1919, arriving in the United Kingdom when he was 20. By the time he wrote his memoir *Conclusive Evidence* in 1951, he'd been writing in English for years, yet he struggled writing this particular text in his adopted language, complaining that his memory was tuned to the "musical key" of Russian. Soon after its publication, he translated the memoir into his native tongue. Working in his first language seems to have prodded his senses awake, leading him to insert new details into the Russian version: A simple anecdote about a stingy old housekeeper becomes perfumed with the scents of coffee and decay, the description of a laundry hamper acquires a creaking sound, the visual details of a celluloid swan and toy boat sprout as he writes about the tub in which he bathed as a child. Some of these details eventually made it into his revised English memoir, which he aptly titled *Speak, Memory*. Evidently, when memory speaks, it sometimes does so in a particular tongue.

Losing your native tongue unmoors you not only from your own early life but from the entire culture that shaped you. You lose access to the books, films, stories, and songs that articulate the values and norms that you've absorbed. You lose the embrace of an entire community or nation for whom your family's odd quirks are not quirks all. You lose your context. This disconnection can be devastating. A 2007 study led by Darcy Hallett found that in British Columbian native communities in which fewer than half of the members could converse in their indigenous language, young people killed themselves six times more often than in communities where the majority spoke the native language. In the Midwestern U.S., psychologist Teresa LaFromboise and her colleagues found that American-Indian adolescents who were heavily involved in activities focused on their traditional language and traditions did better at school and had fewer behavior problems than kids who were less connected to their traditional cultures—in fact, cultural connectedness buffered them against adolescent problems more than having a warm and nurturing mother. Such benefits appear to span continents: In 2011, the Australian Bureau of Statistics reported that aboriginal youth who spoke their traditional language were less likely to binge drink or use illegal drugs.

Why is a heritage language so conducive to well-being? Michael Chandler, one of the authors of the suicide study, emphasizes that a sense of cultural continuity makes people resilient by providing them with a cohesive self-concept. Without that continuity, he warns, aboriginal youth, who have typically experienced plenty of turbulence, are in grave existential danger. They risk losing "the thread that tethers together their past, present, and future."

As my siblings and I distanced ourselves from the Czech language in our youth, a space widened between us and our parents—especially my father, who never wore English with any comfort. Memories of our early family life, along with its small rituals and lessons imparted, receded into a past that drifted ever further out of reach. It was as if my parents' life in their home country, and the values that defined that life, didn't translate credibly into another language; it was much easier to rebel against them in **You lose the embrace of an entire community or nation for whom your family's odd quirks are not quirks at all.** English. Even the English names for our parents encouraged dissent: The Czech words we'd used—*Maminka, Tatinek*—so laden with esteem and affection, impossible to pronounce with contempt, had no corresponding forms. In English, the sweet but childish *Mommy* and *Daddy* are soon abandoned for *Mom* and *Dad*—words that, we discovered, lend themselves perfectly well to adolescent snark.

I watched as my father grew more and more frustrated at his powerlessness to pass on to his children the legacy he most longed to leave: a

15

burning religious piety, the nurturing of family ties, pleasure in the music and traditions of his region, and an abiding respect for ancestors. All of these became diluted by the steady flow of new memories narrated in English, laced with Anglophone aspiration and individualism. As we entered adulthood and dispersed all over North America into our self-reliant lives, my father gave up. He moved back home.

For the next two decades, I lived my adult life, fully absorbed into the English-speaking universe, even adding American citizenship to my Canadian one. My dad was the only person with whom I regularly spoke Czech—if phone calls every few months can be described as "regularly," and if my clumsy sentences patched together with abundant English can be called "speaking Czech." My Czech heritage began to feel more and more like a vestigial organ.

Then my father died. Loss inevitably reveals that which is gone. It was as if the string section of the orchestra had fallen silent—not carrying the melody, it had gone unnoticed, but its absence announced how much depth and texture it had supplied, how its rhythms had lent coherence to the music. In grieving my father, I became aware of how much I also mourned the silencing of Czech in my life. There was a part of me, I realized, that only Czech could speak to, a way of being that was hard to settle into, even with my own siblings and mother when we spoke in English.

After my father's death, my siblings and I inherited a sweet little apartment in a large compound that has been occupied by the Sedivy family since the 1600s, and where my uncle still lives with his sprawling family. This past spring, I finally cleared two months of my schedule and went for a long visit, sleeping on the very same bed where my father and his brothers had been born.

I discovered that, while I may have run out of time to visit my father in his homeland, there was still time for me to reunite with my native tongue. On my first day there, the long drive with my uncle between the airport and our place in the countryside was accompanied by a conversation that lurched along awkwardly, filled with dead ends and misunderstandings. Over the next few days, I had trouble excavating everyday words like *stamp* and *fork*, and I made grammar mistakes that would (and did) cause a 4-year-old to snicker. But within weeks, fluency began to unspool. Words that I'm sure I hadn't used in decades leapt out of my mouth, astounding me. (Often they were correct. Sometimes not: I startled a man who asked about my occupation by claiming to be a savior—*spasitelka*. Sadly, I am a mere writer—*spisovatelka*.) The complicated inflections of Czech, described as "character-building" by an acquaintance who'd learned the language in college, began to assemble into somewhat orderly rows in my mind, and I quickly ventured onto more and more adventurous grammatical terrain. Just a few weeks into my visit, I briefly passed as a real Czech speaker in a conversation with a stranger. Relearning Czech so quickly felt like having linguistic superpowers.

20

Surprised by the speed of my progress, I began to look for studies of heritage speakers relearning childhood languages that had fallen into disuse. A number of scientific papers reported evidence of cognitive remnants of "forgotten" languages, remnants that were visible mostly in the process of relearning. In some cases, even when initial testing hinted at language decay, people who'd been exposed to the language earlier in life showed accelerated relearning of grammar, vocabulary, and most of all, of control over the sounds of the language.

One of the most remarkable examples involved a group of Indian adoptees who'd been raised from a young age (starting between 6 and 60 months) in English-speaking families, having no significant contact with their language of origin. The psychologist Leher Singh tested the children when they were between the ages of 8 and 16. Initially, neither group could hear the difference between dental and retroflex consonants, a distinction that's exploited by many Indian languages. After listening to the contrasting sounds over a period of mere minutes, the adoptees, but not the American-born children, were able to discriminate between the two classes of consonants.

This is revealing because a language's phonology, or sound structure, is one of the greatest challenges for people who start learning a language in adulthood. Long after they've mastered its syntax and vocabulary, a lifelong accent may mark them as latecomers to the language. Arnold Schwarzenegger was the star of many American movies and the governor of the country's biggest state, but his Austrian accent is a constant reminder that he could never run for president. The crucial timing of exposure for native-like speech is evident in my own family: I can pronounce the notoriously difficult "ř" sound in Czech—as in the name of the composer Dvořák—but my brother, born three years after me, in Vienna, cannot.

Phonology's resistance to both attrition and later learning may be due to the fact that the sound structure of a language is fixed in a child's mind very early. Before 6 months of age, infants can distinguish most subtle differences in speech sounds, whether their language makes use of those distinctions or not. But over the second half of their first year, they gradually tune their perception to just the sounds of the language they hear around them. Children who hear only English lose the ability to distinguish between dental and retroflex sounds. Children learning Japanese begin to hear "r" and "l" as variants of the same sound. Linguist Pat Kuhl, who has studied this phenomenon for decades, describes the process as one of perceptual narrowing and increasing neural commitment, eventually excluding native-like perception of other languages.

One of the most striking examples of the brain's attunement to native sounds is apparent in languages such as Mandarin, where varying the tone of an utterance can produce entirely different words. (For instance, the syllable *ma* can mean "mother," "hemp," "horse," or "scold," depending on the pitch contour you lay over it.) When Mandarin speakers hear

25

nonsense syllables that are identical except for their tones, they show heightened activity in the left hemisphere of the brain, where people normally process sounds that signal differences in meaning—like the difference between the syllables "pa" and "ba." But speakers of non-tonal languages like English have more activity in the *right* hemisphere, showing that the brain doesn't treat tone as relevant for distinguishing words. A recent study found that Chinese-born babies adopted into French homes showed brain activity that matched Chinese speakers and was clearly distinct from monolingual French speakers—even after being separated from their birth language for more than 12 years.

The brain's devotion to a childhood language reminds me of a poem by Emily Dickinson:

> The Soul selects her own Society—
> Then—shuts the Door—
> To her divine Majority—
> Present no more—
>
> Unmoved—she notes the Chariots—pausing—
> At her low Gate—
> Unmoved—an Emperor be kneeling
> Upon her Mat—
>
> I've known her—from an ample nation—
> Choose One—
> Then—close the Valves of her attention—
> Like Stone—

Those of us who received more than one language before the valves of our attention closed may find, to our surprise, that our earliest language lingers on in our soul's select society, long after we thought it had faded.

I've become aware of the deep sense in which I belong to the Czech language, as well as the extent to which my formative memories are tinged by its "musical key." For me, the English phrase "pork with cabbage and dumplings" refers to a concept, the national dish of the Czechs. But hearing the Czech phrase *vepřo-knedlo-zelo* evokes the fragrance of roasting meat, pillowy dumpling loaves being pulled steaming out of a tall pot and sliced with sewing thread, and the clink of the nice china as the table is dressed for Sunday dinner, the fulcrum of every week.

Since coming back from the Czech Republic, I've insisted on speaking Czech with my mother. Even though it's more effortful for both of us than speaking in English, our conversation feels softer, more tender this way. English was the language in which I forged my independence, the language of my individuation—but it was in Czech that I was nurtured, comforted, and sung to.

It has also gotten easier to hear the timbre of my father's voice in my mind's ear, especially when working in my garden. It's no accident that many of my conversations with him, and more recently with my uncle, have been on the subject of horticulture. My father's family has lived for centuries in the fertile wine and orchard region of Moravia, and on my recent visit, I saw my relatives gaze out at their land with an expression usually reserved for a beloved spouse or child. Throughout my own life, I've given in to the compulsion to fasten myself to whatever patch of land I happened to be living on by growing things on it, an impulse that has often conflicted with the upwardly and physically mobile trajectory of my life. It's an impulse I submit to once again, living now in the lee of the Rocky Mountains; neither grapes nor apricots will thrive in the brittle mountain air, but I raise sour cherries and saskatoons, small fruits native to western Canada. As I mulch and weed and prune, I sometimes find myself murmuring to my plants in Czech as my father did, and the Moravian homestead doesn't seem very far away.

My newly vocal native tongue, and along with it, the heightened memory of my father's voice, does more than connect me to my past: It is proving to be an unexpected guide in my present work. I've recently left my job as an academic linguist to devote more time to writing, and I often find myself these days conjuring my father's voice by reading a passage in Czech. Like many Czechs I've met, my father treated his language like a lovely object to be turned over, admired, stroked with a fingertip, deserving of deliberate and leisurely attention. He spoke less often than most people, but was more often eloquent. I may never regain enough of my first language to write anything in it worth reading, but when I struggle to write prose that not only informs but transcends, I find myself steering my inner monologue toward Czech. It reminds me of what it feels like to sink into language, to be startled by the aptness of a word or the twist of a phrase, to be delighted by arrangements of its sounds, and lulled by its rhythms. I've discovered that my native language has been sitting quietly in my soul's vault all this time.

30

THINKING CRITICALLY ABOUT THE READING

1. How did Sedivy's parents react when English started to become her family's language?

2. What do "exemplary immigrants" do, according to Sedivy (5)?

3. Sedivy writes that her first-grade teacher asked her whether she knew "a little English" (6). Why was Sedivy offended by this question? How did she respond to her teacher?

4. In paragraph 16, how does Sedivy contrast her father's values with her (and her siblings') values? How would you characterize the difference in your own words?

5. How does Sedivy use academic research in this essay? Does it seem out of place in such a personal piece of writing? Why or why not? What arguments or claims does she use this research to support?

LANGUAGE IN ACTION

Sedivy writes about the idea of a "family language" (4). In her case, English supplants Czech, even though the latter remains in her "soul's vault" (30). What is *your* family language? In some cases, it may literally be a different language than you speak publicly. Or it may be the same language, but with nuances, accents, references, and (to borrow Sedivy's metaphor) a "musical key" (12, 27) specific to your relatives and your home life with them. What are the specific features of your family language? How is it different from the language that you speak when you are away from your family? Does your family language reflect or express different aspects of your personality? Take a few minutes and write down some of the specific elements that identify your home or family language. Then, discuss and share your responses as a class.

WRITING SUGGESTIONS

1. In paragraph 10, Sedivy writes about the power of words to evoke experiences in our pasts: "Just as smells are known to trigger vivid memories of past experiences, language is so entangled with our experiences that inhabiting a specific language helps surface submerged events or interactions that are associated with it." Can you identify with this experience of language and memory? Can you think of a word, a name, a line, a phrase, or any piece of language that triggers memories for you? What is it? Write an essay that identifies, describes, and reflects on a piece of language that has this personal significance to you.

2. For Sedivy's family, who were (in her phrase) "exemplary immigrants," English became a family language "unofficially" (4). But for many years, people have debated whether English should become the *official* national language of the United States. Supporters of this measure argue that it would provide a stronger incentive for new immigrants to learn English and assimilate. Opponents of "Official English," such as Sedivy, point to research that suggests maintaining strong ties to a native language correlates with academic success and good health. What do you think: should English be the official language of the United States? Investigate and research the history of this debate, and then take a position on the issue and support your claims with evidence. As part of your research, you might want to read the student essay "The 'Official English' Movement: Can America Proscribe Language with a Clear Conscience?" by Jake Jamieson (pp. 93–98).

Land of the Giants

ALEX TIZON

Born in the Philippines, Alex Tizon (1959–2017) immigrated to the United States at age four, positioning him as a man between cultures, a theme he would explore in his work. Tizon earned his BA from the University of Oregon and his MA in communication from Stanford University. For two decades he worked as a journalist for *The Seattle Times* and won numerous awards, most notably the Pulitzer Prize for Investigative Reporting in 1997. He also taught journalism at the University of Oregon until his death in 2017.

The following excerpt is drawn from Tizon's memoir, *Big Little Man: In Search of my Asian Self* (2014). As Tizon recounts, he grew up without a clear sense of his own ethnic heritage, a fact that compelled him to "write a book about brown men. . . or indigenous men." As he recounted in an interview, Tizon wanted to address Asian stereotypes alongside what he saw as a "new and emerging presence of Asian men" in American culture, which he ultimately decided to frame within his own life story. As Tizon's essay makes clear, he believed that "his deficit and his exclusion" from his peers "had to do with race," a difference exacerbated by his family's constant focus on measuring up to white Americans in both appearance and speech.

WRITING TO DISCOVER: *Have you ever longed to change something fundamental about yourself, such as your accent, dialect, language, or manner of speaking? If so, why?*

Our early years in America were marked by relentless self-annihilation, though of course we did not see it that way at the time. Everything was done in the name of love, for the cause of fitting in, making friends, making the grade, landing the job, providing for the future, being good citizens of paradise—all so necessary and proper.

First was the abandonment of our native language and our unquestioned embrace of English, even though for my parents that abandonment meant cutting themselves off from a fluency they would never have again. Possessing a language meant possessing the world expressed in its words. Dispossessing it meant nothing less than the loss of a world and the beginning of be-wilderment forever. "Language is the only homeland," said poet Czesław Miłosz. My parents left the world that created them and now would be beginners for the rest of their lives, mumblers searching for the right word, the proper phrase that approximated what they felt inside. I wonder at the eloquence that must have lived inside them that never found a way out. How much was missed on all sides.

We left behind José Rizal and picked up Mark Twain. We gave up Freddie Aguilar for Frank Sinatra and the Beatles, "Bayan Ko" for "The Star-Spangled Banner" and *She loves you yeah, yeah, yeah.*

My parents' adulation of all things white and Western and their open derision of all things brown or native or Asian was the engine of their self-annihilation. Was it purely coincidence that our first car, first house, first dog in America were white? That our culminating moment in America was a white Christmas? White was the apex of humanity, the farthest point on the evolutionary arc and therefore the closest earthly representation of ultimate truth and beauty.

I grew up hearing my parents' offhanded comments about how   5 strong and capable the Americans were, how worthy of admiration, and conversely how weak and incapable and deserving of mockery their own countrymen were: "They can't do it on their own; they need help." I heard it in their breathless admiration for mestizos—persons of mixed European and Asian blood—how elegant and commanding they were, and the more European the better. To be called mestizo was the ultimate flattery. White spouses were prizes; mestizo babies, blessings; they represented an instant elevation, an infusion of royal blood, the promise of a more gifted life.

One late evening at the White House I was playing on the floor of my parents' bedroom closet, behind a row of shirts, when the door opened. It was my father. Instead of revealing myself, I just sat there watching him in silence, cloaked by a wall of sleeves. He changed into his house clothes and then stood at a small mirror appearing to massage his nose, running an index finger and thumb along the bridge, pinching and pulling it as if to make his nose narrower and longer. He stood there doing that for a short time and then left, shutting the door behind him. I thought it curious but did not think about it again until a few months later, when I saw him do it again as he absently watched television. He didn't know I was in the room.

"What are you doing, Papa?"

It startled him. "Nothing, son. Just massaging."

"Does your nose hurt?"

He looked at me, deciding what to say, and then he seemed to relax.   10 "*Halika dito, anak.* Come here, son. You should do this," he said to me gently. He showed me how to use my fingers to pinch the bridge of my nose and then tug on it in a sustained pull, holding it in place for twenty seconds at a time and then repeating. "You should do this every day. If you do, your nose will become more *tangus.* Sharper. Narrower. You'll look more mestizo. Your nose is so round! And so flat! *Talagang Pilipino!* So Filipino!"

"What's wrong with flat?"

"Nothing is wrong with flat. *Pero* sharper is better. People will treat you better. They'll think you come from a better family. They'll think you're smarter and *mas guapo,* more handsome. *Talaga, anak.* This is true. See my nose? The other day a woman, a *puti,* a white, talked to me in Spanish because she thought I was from Spain. That happens to me. I massage every day. Don't you think I look Castilian?" He turned to show his profile. "*Ay anak.* My son. Believe me."

I did believe him. Just as he had believed his father when the lesson was taught to him decades earlier. These were the givens: Aquiline was better than flat. Long better than wide. Light skin better than dark. Round eyes better than *chinky.* Blue eyes better than brown. Thin lips better than full. Blond better than black. Tall better than short. Big better than small. The formula fated us to lose. We had landed on a continent of Big Everything.

One sunny afternoon, my father and I walked to a hardware store a few blocks from our house. As we were about to go inside, three American men in overalls and T-shirts walked out, filling the doorway and inadvertently blocking our path. They were enormous, all of them well over six feet tall, with beards and beefy arms and legs. My father and I stood looking up at this wall of denim and hair. The Americans appeared ready to scoot over. "Excuse us," my father said, and we moved to the side. One of the men said thanks, another snickered as they passed.

My father leaned down and whispered in my ear, *"Land of the* 15 *Giants."* It was the name of a television show my family had started watching, a science-fiction series about a space crew marooned on a planet of gargantuan humans. The crew members were always being picked up by enormous hands and toyed with. The show's tagline: "Mini-people — Playthings in a World of Giant Tormentors," My family was captivated by the show. I think we related to the mini-people who in every episode were confronted by impossibly large humanoids.

Americans did seem to me at times like a different species, one that had evolved over generations into supreme behemoths. Kings in overalls. They were living proof of a basic law of conquest: victors ate better. The first time I sat as a guest at an American dinner table, I could scarcely believe the bounty: a whole huge potato for each of us, a separate plate of vegetables, my own steak. A separate slab of meat just for me! At home, that single slab would have fed my entire family.

> **We had landed on a continent of Big Everything.**

The size of American bodies came to represent American capacities in everything we desired: they were smarter, stronger, richer; they lived in comfort and had the surplus to be generous. They knew the way to beauty and bounty because they were already there, filling the entryway with their meaty limbs and boulder heads and big, toothy grins like searchlights, imploring us with their booming voices to come on in. Have a seat at the table! Americans spoke a few decibels louder than we were used to.

Content

We were small in everything. We were poor. I mean pockets-out immigrant poor. We were undernourished and scrawny, our genetics revealing not-so-distant struggles with famine and disease and war. We were inarticulate, our most deeply felt thoughts expressed in halting, heavily accented English, which might have sounded like grunts to Americans, given how frequently we heard "Excuse me?" or "Come again?" or "What?" The quizzical look on their faces as they tried to decipher the alien sounds.

My father, who was a funny, dynamic conversationalist in his own language, a man about Manila, would never be quite so funny or dynamic or quick-witted or agile or confident again. He would always be a small man in America. My mother was small, too, but it was acceptable, even desirable, for women to be small. American men found my mother attractive. She never lacked attention or employment. My father was the one most demoted in the great new land. He was supposed to be the man of the family, and he did not know which levers to pull or push, and he didn't have the luxury of a lifetime, like his children, to learn them.

I'm convinced it was because of a gnawing awareness of his limitations   20
in the land of the giants that he was a dangerous man to belittle. Gentle and gregarious in the company of friends, he was a different person in the larger world of strangers: wary, opaque, tightly coiled. My father stood all of five feet six inches and 150 pounds, every ounce of which could turn maniacal in an instant. He took offense easily and let his fists fly quickly. He was not deterred by mass. He recognized it, but became blind with fury when it trespassed on him or his family. I once watched him scold a man twice his size, an auto mechanic he thought was taking advantage of him, and threaten to leap over the counter to teach him a lesson. "You kick a man in the balls and he's not so big anymore," he once told me. Actually, he told me more than once.

My mother corroborated the stories of my father challenging other men over perceived slights, losing as many fights as he won and getting downright clobbered on a few occasions, once landing in the hospital for a week. My mother was present at some of those fights; she was the cause of at least one, in which an unfortunate young man ogled her and ended up laid out on the sidewalk.

I got another glimpse of his inner maniac once at a park in New Jersey when I was about twelve. A big red-haired kid on a bike spat on me and rode away laughing and making faces. My father followed him all the way back to where his family was picnicking and confronted the three men in the group, all Americans, one of whom was presumably the kid's father. They all appeared startled. I heard only part of the conversation that followed. "We could take care of it right now, right here," my father told the men in a low, threatening voice, his fists clenched into hard knots. He stood leaning forward, unblinking. The men averted their gaze and kept silent. On the walk back to our spot, my father said, "Tell me if that boy comes near you again." I was speechless. His mettle astonished me. But it was something more than bravery on display that day. His fury was outsized, reckless, as if something larger was at stake, and of course now I know there was.

Unlike my father, I worked hard to get along with strangers. We moved so much in those early years that I got used to strangers as companions as we passed from place to place. I learned American English, trained out whatever accent I had inherited, picked up colloquial mannerisms. I kept a confident front, not in a loudmouthed way but in a reserved, alert manner, and I got more surefooted in my interactions as I got better at English. If I had to guess, I'd say my classmates would have described me as a little shy but smart and likable. I brooded in private. How could someone be ashamed and capable at the same time? I was fated to have a secret life.

So I worked on becoming an American, to be in some ways more American than my American friends. But I learned, eventually, that I could never reach the ideal of the beloved. And when the realization came, it seemed to land all at once, blunt force trauma, and I felt embarrassed to have been a believer.

It's one of the beautiful lies of the American Dream: that you can become anything, do anything, accomplish anything, if you want it badly enough and are willing to work for it. Limits are inventions of the timid mind. You've got to believe. All things are possible through properly channeled effort: work, work, work; harder, faster, more! Unleash your potential! Nothing is beyond your reach! Just do it! I believed it all, drank the elixir to the last drop and licked my lips for residue. I put in the time, learned to read and write and speak more capably than my friends and neighbors, followed the rules, did my homework, memorized the tics and slangs and idiosyncrasies of winners and heroes, but I could never be quite as American as they. The lie is a lie only if you fail, and I most certainly did.

When I ask myself now when this shame inside me began, I see that I inherited the beginnings of it from my father, and he from his father, going back in my imagination as far as the arrival of the Spanish ships almost five hundred years ago. An ancient inherited shame. It accompanied us across the ocean. We carried it into a country that told us: not reaching the summit was no one's fault but your own.

My father continued his pugnacious ways into old age. His last fistfight, which occurred when he was sixty-eight, involved a hugely obese teenager who my father believed had disrespected him. The kid, who weighed over two hundred pounds, ended the fight by lying on my father and crushing the air out of him, almost killing him. Papa had had two heart bypass surgeries and a couple of strokes by then and was by all measures frail. He could not concede weakness. In other ways, he did evolve. His gentleness with us, his children, magnified. His remorse for leaving us haunted him and kept him in a perpetual state of apologizing. *I'm sorry, anak. My son. I'm so, so sorry.* He cried easily.

"Do this every day," he told me.

I followed his advice. As inconspicuously as possible, I hid from the sun. I dangled from tree branches and pull-up bars to stretch my body, praying to gravity, aiming my heels toward the center of the Earth. I tried to eat beyond my appetite, and as a teenager secretly began taking protein supplements to help me grow. I rubbed oils onto my eyelids to keep them supple, to prevent the epicanthic folds from turning my eyes *chinky*. And every night before falling asleep, for at least twenty seconds, I would massage my nose. The shape of your nose determined your fate. It was the symbol of your lineage, the mark that determined which gate you entered. As I got older, I got more obsessive. I began attaching a clothespin to my nose and leaving it there all night. I was already prone to nosebleeds, and sometimes the clothespin was too tight and I'd wake up with blood on my pillow. To make my lips thinner, more mestizo, I would suck them in and place masking tape over my mouth for hours at a time. Anyone who walked into my bedroom on those nights would have thought I was being held hostage. None of it worked. The mirror mocked me. The clay of my face would never change.

THINKING CRITICALLY ABOUT THE READING

1. In paragraph 2, how does Tizon describe his parents' loss of their language? Given this description, how do you think he feels about this loss? What words support your assessment?

2. How does Tizon define the term "white" from his parents' perspective? How does he characterize his parents' feelings about whiteness?

3. Why does Tizon's father try to reshape his nose? Why do you think Tizon renders that passage using both English and Tagalog words?

4. In paragraphs 16 and 17, what types of figurative language does Tizon use to describe Americans? What effect does the description have you as a reader?

5. In several places, Tizon contrasts the word "big" to the word "small." While we know the denotative meaning of each word, what connotative meanings do they take on in the essay and why? How do these meanings differ for Tizon's mother and father?

LANGUAGE IN ACTION

Immigration has long been an embattled concept and term in the United States. As early as 1790, when the Naturalization Act limited citizenship to "any alien, being a free white person," the nation began to limit the notion of belonging. In the last decade, we've seen the term *illegal* come into widespread use as a noun. Why do you think some people have taken to use this word as a noun? To what specific immigrant communities is the term *illegal* most often applied? Do you think an immigrant's race affects the way in which the term is used? If so, why? If not, why not? Discuss in a group with two or three classmates. For additional context on the history of and current debate over the terminology of immigration, you might also want to read "The Fight Over the Words of Immigration" by Jeff Gammage (pp. 372–374).

WRITING SUGGESTIONS

1. For immigrants, Tizon suggests, the American Dream remains a "beautiful lie" (25). In this phrase, Tizon forms a paradox by using two words with opposing connotations. How do you define the American Dream? Do you agree or disagree with Tizon's characterization of it? Do you think that the American Dream can be attained—and, if so, do you think that *anyone* can attain it, or only certain groups or certain individuals? Write an essay that answers these questions. As you write, see if you can coin a paradoxical phrase of your own to describe the American Dream.

2. In paragraph 2, Tizon cites poet Czesław Miłosz, who writes, "language is the only homeland." What do you think Miłosz means by this? Why is language the *only* homeland? How is language a *homeland* at all? After you have spent time thinking about the relationship between home and language, write a letter to a family member in which you discuss your thoughts about how shared language and expression help to define your own personal sense of home.

Mother Tongue

AMY TAN

Amy Tan was born in Oakland, California, in 1952, to Chinese immigrant parents. Growing up in a bilingual world, Tan became interested in languages at an early age. At San Jose State University she earned a BA in English in 1973 and a master's in linguistics the following year. Tan worked as a child language development specialist and a freelance speech writer for corporate executives before she began writing stories for her own personal enjoyment and therapy. These stories resulted in her first book, *The Joy Luck Club* (1989), a tightly woven novel about four Chinese mothers and their American-born daughters. The novel was a finalist for the National Book Award and later adapted into a commercially successful film. Tan has written five other novels including *The Kitchen God's Wife* (1991), *The Hundred Secret Senses* (1995), *The Bonesetter's Daughter* (2001), *Saving Fish from Drowning* (2005), and *The Valley of Amazement* (2013); a collection of nonfiction essays, *The Opposite of Fate: A Book of Musings* (2003); and two children's books, *The Moon Lady* (1992) and *Sagwa, the Chinese Siamese Cat* (1994). Tan currently resides in Sausalito, California.

The following essay was first delivered as a speech and later published in the fall 1990 issue of the *Threepenny Review*. Here Tan explains how she wrote *The Joy Luck Club* and communicated with her mother, using "all the Englishes I grew up with." She explores the limitations of growing up in a household where she heard "broken" English spoken by her immigrant parents.

WRITING TO DISCOVER: *What is your cultural identity? Do you consider yourself an American, or do you identify with another culture? To what extent is your cultural identity tied to language? Explain.*

I am not a scholar of English or literature. I cannot give you much more than personal opinions on the English language and its variations in this country or others.

I am a writer. And by that definition, I am someone who has always loved language. I am fascinated by language in daily life. I spend a great deal of my time thinking about the power of language — the way it can evoke an emotion, a visual image, a complex idea, or a simple truth. Language is the tool of my trade. And I use them all — all the Englishes I grew up with.

Recently, I was made keenly aware of the different Englishes I do use. I was giving a talk to a large group of people, the same talk I had already given to half a dozen other groups. The nature of the talk was about my writing, my life, and my book *The Joy Luck Club*. The talk was going along well enough, until I remembered one major difference that made the whole talk sound wrong. My mother was in the room. And it was perhaps the first time she had heard me give a lengthy speech, using the kind of English I have never used with her. I was saying things like "The intersection of memory upon imagination" and "There is an aspect of my fiction that relates to thus-and-thus"—a speech filled with carefully wrought grammatical phrases, burdened, it suddenly seemed to me, with nominalized forms, past perfect tenses, conditional phrases, all the forms of standard English that I had learned in school and through books, the forms of English I did not use at home with my mother.

Just last week, I was walking down the street with my mother, and I again found myself conscious of the English I was using, the English I do use with her. We were talking about the price of new and used furniture and I heard myself saying this: "Not waste money that way." My husband was with us as well, and he didn't notice any switch in my English. And then I realized why. It's because over **Language is the tool of my trade. And I use them all—all the Englishes I grew up with.** the twenty years we've been together I've often used that same kind of English with him, and sometimes he even uses it with me. It has become our language of intimacy, a different sort of English that relates to family talk, the language I grew up with.

So you'll have some idea of what this family talk I heard sounds like, I'll quote what my mother said during a recent conversation which I videotaped and then transcribed. During this conversation, my mother was talking about a political gangster in Shanghai who had the same last name as her family's, Du, and how the gangster in his early years wanted to be adopted by her family, which was rich by comparison. Later, the gangster became more powerful, far richer than my mother's family, and one day showed up at my mother's wedding to pay his respects. Here's what she said in part:

"Du Yusong having business like fruit stand. Like off the street kind. He is Du like Du Zong—but not Tsung-ming Island people. The local people call putong, the river east side, he belong to that side local people. That man want to ask Du Zong father take him in like become own family. Du Zong father wasn't look down on him, but didn't take seriously, until that man big like become a mafia. Now important person, very hard to inviting him. Chinese way, came only to show respect, don't stay for dinner. Respect for making big celebration, he shows up. Mean gives lots of respect. Chinese custom. Chinese social life that way. If too important won't have to stay too long. He come to my wedding. I didn't see, I heard it. I gone to boy's side, they have YMCA dinner. Chinese age I was nineteen."

5

You should know that my mother's expressive command of English belies how much she actually understands. She reads the *Forbes* report, listens to *Wall Street Week*, converses daily with her stockbroker, reads all of Shirley MacLaine's books with ease — all kinds of things I can't begin to understand. Yet some of my friends tell me they understand 50 percent of what my mother says. Some say they understand 80 to 90 percent. Some say they understand none of it, as if she were speaking pure Chinese. But to me, my mother's English is perfectly clear, perfectly natural. It's my mother tongue. Her language, as I hear it, is vivid, direct, full of observation and imagery. That was the language that helped shape the way I saw things, expressed things, made sense of the world.

Lately, I've been giving more thought to the kind of English my mother speaks. Like others, I have described it to people as "broken" or "fractured" English. But I wince when I say that. It has always bothered me that I can think of no way to describe it other than "broken," as if it were damaged and needed to be fixed, as if it lacked a certain wholeness and soundness. I've heard other terms used, "limited English," for example. But they seem just as bad, as if everything is limited, including people's perceptions of the limited English speaker.

I know this for a fact, because when I was growing up, my mother's "limited" English limited *my* perception of her. I was ashamed of her English. I believed that her English reflected the quality of what she had to say. That is, because she expressed them imperfectly her thoughts were imperfect. And I had plenty of empirical evidence to support me: the fact that people in department stores, at banks, and at restaurants did not take her seriously, did not give her good service, pretended not to understand her, or even acted as if they did not hear her.

My mother has long realized the limitations of her English as well. When I was fifteen, she used to have me call people on the phone to pretend I was she. In this guise, I was forced to ask for information or even to complain and yell at people who had been rude to her. One time it was a call to her stockbroker in New York. She had cashed out her small portfolio and it just so happened we were going to go to New York the next week, our very first trip outside California. I had to get on the phone and say in an adolescent voice that was not very convincing, "This is Mrs. Tan."

And my mother was standing in the back whispering loudly, "Why he don't send me check, already two weeks late. So mad he lie to me, losing me money."

And then I said in perfect English, "Yes, I'm getting rather concerned. You had agreed to send the check two weeks ago, but it hasn't arrived."

Then she began to talk more loudly. "What he want, I come to New York tell him front of his boss, you cheating me?" And I was trying to calm her down, make her be quiet, while telling the stockbroker, "I can't tolerate any more excuses. If I don't receive the check immediately, I am going to have to speak to your manager when I'm in New York next week." And sure enough, the following week there we were in front of this astonished stockbroker, and I was sitting there red-faced and quiet, and my mother, the real Mrs. Tan, was shouting at his boss in her impeccable broken English.

We used a similar routine just five days ago, for a situation that was far less humorous. My mother had gone to the hospital for an appointment, to find out about a benign brain tumor a CAT scan had revealed a month ago. She said she had spoken very good English, her best English, no mistakes. Still, she said, the hospital did not apologize when they said they had lost the CAT scan and she had come for nothing. She said they did not seem to have any sympathy when she told them she was anxious to know the exact diagnosis, since her husband and son had both died of brain tumors. She said they would not give her any more information until the next time and she would have to make another appointment for that. So she said she would not leave until the doctor called her daughter. She wouldn't budge. And when the doctor finally called her daughter, me, who spoke in perfect English—lo and behold—we had assurances the CAT scan would be found, promises that a conference call on Monday would be held, and apologies for any suffering my mother had gone through for a most regrettable mistake.

I think my mother's English almost had an effect on limiting my possibilities in life as well. Sociologists and linguists probably will tell you that a person's developing language skills are more influenced by peers. But I do think that the language spoken in the family, especially in immigrant families which are more insular, plays a large role in shaping the language of the child. And I believe that it affected my results on achievement tests, IQ tests, and the SAT. While my English skills were never judged as poor, compared to math, English could not be considered my strong suit. In grade school I did moderately well, getting perhaps B's, sometimes B-pluses, in English and scoring perhaps in the sixtieth or seventieth percentile on achievement tests. But those scores were not good enough to override the opinion that my true abilities lay in math and science, because in those areas I achieved A's and scored in the ninetieth percentile or higher.

This was understandable. Math is precise; there is only one correct answer. Whereas, for me at least, the answers on English tests were always a judgment call, a matter of opinion and personal experience. Those tests were constructed around items like fill-in-the-blank sentence completion, such as "Even though Tom was _____, Mary thought he was _____." And the correct answer always seemed to be the most bland combinations of thoughts, for example, "Even though Tom was shy, Mary thought he was charming," with the grammatical structure "even though" limiting the correct answer to some sort of

15

semantic opposites, so you wouldn't get answers like, "Even though Tom was foolish, Mary thought he was ridiculous." Well, according to my mother, there were very few limitations as to what Tom could have been and what Mary might have thought of him. So I never did well on tests like that.

The same was true with word analogies, pairs of words, in which you were supposed to find some sort of logical, semantic relationship — for example, " 'sunset' is to 'nightfall' as _____ is to _____." And here you would be presented with a list of four possible pairs, one of which showed the same kind of relationship: "red" is to "stoplight," "bus" is to "arrival," "chills" is to "fever," "yawn" is to "boring." Well, I could never think that way. I knew what the tests were asking, but I could not block out of my mind the images already created by the first pair, "sunset is to nightfall" — and I would see a burst of colors against a darkening sky, the moon rising, the lowering of a curtain of stars. And all the other pairs of words — red, bus, stoplight, boring — just threw up a mass of confusing images, making it impossible for me to sort out something as logical as saying: "A sunset precedes nightfall" is the same as "a chill precedes a fever." The only way I would have gotten that answer right would have been to imagine an associative situation, for example, my being disobedient and staying out past sunset, catching a chill at night, which turns into feverish pneumonia as punishment, which indeed did happen to me.

I have been thinking about all this lately, about my mother's English, about achievement tests. Because lately I've been asked, as a writer, why there are not more Asian Americans represented in American literature. Why are there few Asian Americans enrolled in creative writing programs? Why do so many Chinese students go into engineering? Well, these are broad sociological questions I can't begin to answer. But I have noticed in surveys — in fact, just last week that Asian students, as a whole, always do significantly better on math achievement tests than in English. And this makes me think that there are other Asian-American students whose English spoken in the home might also be described as "broken" or "limited." And perhaps they also have teachers who are steering them away from writing and into math and science, which is what happened to me.

Fortunately, I happen to be rebellious in nature and enjoy the challenge of disproving assumptions made about me. I became an English major my first year in college, after being enrolled as pre-med. I started writing nonfiction as a freelancer the week after I was told by my former boss that writing was my worst skill and I should hone my talents toward account management.

But it wasn't until 1985 that I finally began to write fiction. And at first I wrote using what I thought to be wittily crafted sentences, sentences that would finally prove I had mastery over the English language.   20

Here's an example from the first draft of a story that later made its way into *The Joy Luck Club*, but without this line: "That was my mental quandary in its nascent state." A terrible line, which I can barely pronounce.

Fortunately, for reasons I won't get into today, I later decided I should envision a reader for the stories I would write. And the reader I decided upon was my mother, because these were stories about mothers. So with this reader in mind — and in fact she did read my early drafts — I began to write stories using all the Englishes I grew up with: the English I spoke to my mother, which for lack of a better term might be described as "simple"; the English she used with me, which for lack of a better term might be described as "broken"; my translation of her Chinese, which could certainly be described as "watered down"; and what I imagined to be her translation of her Chinese if she could speak in perfect English, her internal language, and for that I sought to preserve the essence, but neither an English nor a Chinese structure. I wanted to capture what language ability tests can never reveal: her intent, her passion, her imagery, the rhythms of her speech and the nature of her thoughts.

Apart from what any critic had to say about my writing, I knew I had succeeded where it counted when my mother finished reading my book, and gave me her verdict: "So easy to read."

THINKING CRITICALLY ABOUT THE READING

1. How effectively do the first two paragraphs function as an introduction to this essay? What are your expectations about the essay after Tan reveals her qualifications with language and literature?

2. What specifically are the different Englishes that Tan grew up with? How was each English used?

3. To give readers some idea of what the "family talk" Tan heard while growing up sounded like, Tan quotes her mother's story in paragraph 6. What did you think of Tan's mother after reading this paragraph? Did you understand everything the first time you read it, or did you have to reread portions to make sure you got it?

4. Why do you suppose Tan recounts the story of her mother's stockbroker and her mother's dealings with the hospital in paragraphs 10 through 14?

5. What does Tan mean when she writes, "I think my mother's English almost had an effect on limiting my possibilities in life" (15)?

6. In paragraphs 16 and 17 Tan discusses her difficulties with questions on English tests that called for "fill-in-the-blank sentence completion" and facility with "word analogies." Why do you suppose such questions vexed her? Explain.

LANGUAGE IN ACTION

When we listen to people speak, we readily notice if someone is using nonstandard English. We also recognize conversational or informal standard English. On occasion, we hear people using what might be called hyper- or super-standard English, speech that sounds too formal or proper for everyday conversation. In the following sets of sentences, classify each sentence as being (1) nonstandard English, (2) informal standard English, or (3) super-standard English.

1. a. If I was going to do that, I would start right now.
   b. If I were going to do that, I would start right now.
   c. Were I to do that, I would start right now.
   d. I would start right now, if I was going to do that.

2. a. He's not as smart as she.
   b. He's not so smart as she.
   c. He ain't as smart as her.
   d. He not as smart as her.

Discuss what words or word forms in the sentences that helped you label each one.

WRITING SUGGESTIONS

1. Do you believe that the English spoken at home while you were growing up had any effect on how well you did in school or in your community at large? Using Tan's essay as a model, write an essay exploring the "Englishes" you grew up with and how they affected your performance in and out of school.

2. Write an essay in which you explore the main differences between public language — that is, language used in school, workplace, and government settings — and private language — that is, language used in familial or other intimate relationships.

8

LANGUAGE EVOLUTION: HOW AND WHY DOES LANGUAGE CHANGE?

Anyone interested in language realizes that all languages change over time in vocabulary, grammar, and punctuation. Such changes can be difficult to appreciate in the moment, but over longer periods of time the evidence of language evolution is undeniable. Language evolves when people from different cultures communicate and exchange words, which happens often in our globally connected society. Language change also happens when new technologies, like social media, appear on the scene and encourage us to communicate in different ways. Less noticeably, but no less importantly, language changes in smaller ways every day, through conversations in offices and on street corners, as the meanings of words subtly shift, new words enter the lexicon, established principles of grammar and pronunciation erode, and new codes of linguistic behavior come into play. In this chapter, we examine just a few of the many ways in which language has evolved over the last decade. Taken as a whole, these readings reveal that language is a living construct in which each of us participate every day through interactions both face-to-face and online.

First, in "Words on the Move," John McWhorter makes the positive case for language evolution. He observes that the meanings of words are not fixed and that words gain new meanings in response to new contexts and situations; as he puts it, "a word is a thing on the move." Next, Andy Bodle invites us to take a close look at thirteen specific processes by which words enter a language in his article aptly titled "How New Words Are Born." From derivation to portmanteaus, these categories may help us understand where our words come from and how our language is changing. Meanwhile, in "What Does 'Latinx' Mean?" Yesenia Padilla explores the origin of one specific word that has recently entered the language: *Latinx,* a gender-neutral term for a person of Latin American descent. As she advocates for this new word, Padilla also exposes the larger ongoing debate surrounding gender-neutral language.

The second half of the chapter contains three reading selections about one particular aspect of language evolution: technology's impact on language. Since much of our communication now takes place via texting and social media, it is perhaps no wonder that we have adapted our language accordingly. As Lauren Collister explains in "Textspeak Is Modernizing the Egnlish Language (*English)," textspeak is distinct from traditional spoken language in several important ways. Notably, textspeak is more fluid and streamlined, which Collister argues makes it "perfect for our modern, fast-paced world." In "Smile, You're Speaking Emoji," Adam Sternbergh explores the emoji's explosion in popularity and places the phenomenon in historical context, comparing it with earlier language innovations like the exclamation point. Finally, Deborah Tannen investigates another important aspect of language and technology: metamessages, which "communicate how you mean what you say." In "The (Sometimes Unintentional) Subtext of Digital Conversations," she reveals that our tone and our rate of response often says as much—or more—than the literal meaning of our words. Perhaps it is fitting to say that not only are our words on the move, but that English itself is on the move as a living language.

Words on the Move

John McWhorter

Born in 1965, linguist and writer John McWhorter is an associate professor of English and comparative literature at Columbia University. He grew up in Philadelphia and earned his BA at Rutgers University, his MA from New York University, and his PhD from Stanford University. Formerly, he taught at Cornell University and the University of California, Berkeley. He has written more than fifteen books, including *The Power of Babel: A Natural History of Language* (2001), *Winning the Race: Beyond the Crisis in Black America* (2005), *The Language Hoax: Why the World Looks the Same in Any Language* (2014), and *Talking Back, Talking Black: Truths about America's Lingua Franca* (2017). McWhorter has also written for *The Atlantic, Slate, Time,* and *The New York Daily News,* among many other publications.

As an academic specialist, McWhorter focuses on American linguistic history, especially creole languages, Native American languages, and black English. But he also regularly addresses popular audiences and public debates. "Most academic work is consulted only by the occasional student or professor," he has written. "So I've tossed my hat into the public fray—writing books and newspaper articles for lay readers." That "public fray" includes the popular conversation about the English language. In the following selection, excerpted from his book *Words on the Move: Why English Won't—and Can't—Sit Still (Like, Literally)* (2016), he discusses the fluidity and instability of our language, particularly the way the meanings of words shift over time—despite the efforts of lexicographers and reactionary purists.

WRITING TO DISCOVER: *Is there a word that you use, either in writing or speech, that you could not define if asked? Have you ever used a word that you did not know the meaning of, only to discover its definition later? If so, how did you finally discover the word's meaning?*

IN THE PRESENT: "WHAT'S THE ASK?" OVER "WHAT'S THE REQUEST?"

To understand that words are always moving along also helps us understand things happening in the language today. In America, an interesting novelty especially popular among young corporate types is the use of basic verbs as nouns, as in "What's the ask?" about business transactions, "Is there a solve?" instead of "Is there a solution?," and "Epic fail." The last has spread far beyond the cubicle realm, and "I know that feel" (instead of "I know how that feels" or "I know that feeling") is even associated with "bros" rather than Dilberts.

A linguist's first observation must be that English speakers have been transforming verbs into nouns this way for a good thousand years. English is low on endings that show what part of speech a word is; in French the *-er* in *parler* shows that it is a verb and in Spanish the *-ar* in *hablar* shows the same thing, but in English, nothing about the word *talk* shows that it is a verb. This means that it's easy to use English verbs as nouns—they don't seem as out of place in the role as would a French or Spanish verb, with its verbal ending hanging out inconveniently. Those who assail turning verbs into nouns as inappropriate may not realize that they should also, to be consistent, disapprove of sentences like "She had a funny walk," "He has a scratch next to his eye," and "They simply had too much work." *Walk, scratch,* and *work* all started as verbs.

Yet one might still feel that "What's the ask?" is different, in that the word *request* already exists. Why "Epic fail" when we have *failure,* or "What's the solve?" when we have *solution?* However, today's nouns from verbs are not substitutes for older nouns; they are new words entirely. This is because the older words, as words, have always been drifting in their meanings, and therefore no longer mean exactly what their "vanilla" definition suggests.

Solution, for instance, technically means "a solving." However, the word has, in its journey as a normal word, taken on certain implications. *Solution* brings to mind, for one, math, and overall has an air of the schoolroom about it, as in solutions to science class homework. Those unspoken associations are not what the modern adult in the flinty, competitive atmosphere of a business meeting means. Subconsciously that person reaches for a word that really does mean, in clean fashion, a "solving." What handier way is there to do this than using *solve* itself? But this means that a solve and a solution are subtly different things, in terms of how the words feel in an intimate way to native speakers.

In the same way, a failure and a fail are not the same thing. *Failure* is not, in terms of how it is used in actual speech, simply the act of failing. It once was, but over time it has taken on a whiff of personal condemnation. *Failure* suggests, most readily, a rather large-scale, tragic kind of failing; one thinks of an assessment of a person's entire career, marriage, or life, of a head hung low, and the plays of Arthur Miller. "Epic failure!" then, is a little mean. In modern English, the actual word for simply "a failing," with no ominous hint of therapy sessions or a gun going off offstage, is "a fail." It's certainly handier for people playing video games or rating one another's sales volume.

It's no surprise that men are best known for "I know that feel." *Feeling* has associations with vulnerability, for one. Plus, the word *feeling* is probably most spontaneously associated with the idiom "That hurt my feelings," which is these days, for better or worse, often associated with a certain triviality or tinniness. *Feel* lends a way to use the same *feel* root without the distracting associations. Call it "bro'ly love," also extendable to other younger people wary of excess sentiment (i.e., seeking the "cool"—and note that *cool* and *coolness,* too, have different meanings).

IN THE FUTURE: MAKING PEACE WITH THE EUPHEMISM TREADMILL

When we understand that words inevitably drift in their meanings, then we know why terminology fashioned for euphemistic reasons tends to require constant replacement. What begins as a willfully objective designation is quickly associated in the mind with the phenomenon it refers to, complete with the less savory resonances thereof. As a result, that term comes to have a different meaning than what was intended. In response, a new, faceless term is created—which naturally itself becomes accreted with the same associations and must in time yield to a new term.

It's easy to see some kind of shell game going on, but really, it's just words behaving the way they always have and always will. In a distant day long ago, when a family survived on money from the government, it was popularly called *home relief,* a neutral and benevolent term. However, anyone old enough to have known that term will have to work to imagine *home relief* in its "dictionary" meaning, because quickly *home relief* took on connotations associated with uncomplimentary assumptions about the poor. *Welfare* was thought to be a less pejorative term and became the preferred usage in the 1960s. Again, however, these days it can be sobering to imagine that the word *welfare* refers technically to, simply, being okay. *Welfare* became rusted with so many associations amid the culture wars of the 1980s and '90s that, since then, *cash assistance* has been making new strides into the language as yet another attempt to refer to, well, home relief without setting off alarms.

Note that if you are too young to have known the time when *home relief* was a common term, today it sounds quite handy as a replacement for *welfare.* Perhaps it should be recycled as the next term of art when *cash assistance* takes on abusive tones and becomes dispreferred. We can be quite sure it will—for the same reason that Shakespeare meant "knowledge" by *wit,* and *epic failure* would not mean the same thing as *epic fail.* All these things are of a piece.

In the same way, we must expect that designations for various groups   10 will turn over regularly: the linguist and psychologist Steven Pinker has perfectly titled this "the euphemism treadmill." Long ago, *crippled* was thought a humane way to describe a person—it had the ring, roughly, that *hindered* would today. However, once it became associated with the kind of ridicule tragically common among members of our species, *handicapped* was thought to be a kinder term—less loaded, it sounded like a title rather than a slur. But while words change, people often don't—naturally, after a while, *handicapped* seemed as smudged by realities as *crippled* had. Hence: *disabled,* which is now getting old, as in having taken on many of the same negative associations as *crippled* and *handicapped.* Of late, some prefer *differently abled,* which is fine in itself. Yet all should know that in roughly a generation's time, even that term will carry the very associations it is designed to rise above, just as *special needs* now does. Note the effort now required to imagine how objective and inclusive even *special needs* was fashioned to be.

And here's the rub: since words cannot help drifting in their meanings, we need not worry that people are deliberately keeping us off guard or are given to indecision. The euphemism treadmill must be accepted as an inevitable and unexceptionable result of what a word is: not only a bundle of sounds linked to a meaning, but also one that naturally piles up with implications over time because it is used by human beings living lives. Since words can't sit still, and the implications they attract will sometimes be unpleasant, civility will require changing some of them regularly, like underwear.

BUT THAT ISN'T WHAT IT'S SUPPOSED TO MEAN!

A word is a thing on the move. This means wrapping our heads around something that cannot feel right at first, but that simple logic requires us to accept. To wit, any claim that people in general are using a word "erroneously" is illogical. Of course if the issue is just one person using a word in an unprecedented way, then we might classify it as a mistake. A language is a contract under which there is general, although unconscious, agreement as to where words are moving. To use a word in a fashion that impedes communication with others is therefore a foul. However, mistakes of that kind will usually come from children or foreigners. If a significant proportion of the people speaking a language are using a word in a way that dictionaries tend not to mention, it means that the word is moving—as we would expect, since words always do.

> It's always a safe bet that a word will not be tomorrow what it is today.

A quick example: *Decimate,* it is true, first meant killing one in ten of an army's men as a postvictory punishment. The source was the Latin word for ten, such that the truly original meaning may actually have been "tithe," as in a tax of 10 percent of one's earnings. Either way, *decimate* originally had a very particular meaning, the knowledge of which pleases a person who knows Latin.

This, however, is strictly a historical matter. There are those given to treating it as "wrong" for someone to say, "A virus decimated the ladybug population and after a few years there were none to be found." They complain that the word should not be used to mean general destruction, but only the subtraction of precisely a tenth. That today *destruction* is pretty much the only usage of *decimate* is, according to this complaint, beside the point. Majority does not entail truth, after all: there is a general waywardness afoot, with the flock losing touch with that real meaning of "to subtract by a tenth." H. W. Fowler's doughty old *A Dictionary of Modern English Usage*, cherished over generations as authoritative, intoned that sentences like *A single frosty night decimated the currants by as much as 80 percent* "must be avoided."

Okay — but only if you want to avoid using *merry* to mean "jolly" and will be okay with talking about someone who, after slimming down on a diet, after a while *reduced* back up to his former weight. What's the difference between then and now, except that the older things happened when nobody was complaining? *Decimate* moved — it broadened from meaning "to shave off by a tenth" to referring to more general destruction. Part of the reason, one suspects, is that since ancient times, with their rather barbaric attitudes toward human life, existence offers relatively little need for the concept of reducing something by specifically a tenth: "Oh, sweetie, make sure to *decimate* the cake so that Maude can have her slice before the other nine of us!" 15

So, one answer to the observation "But wasn't it nice to have a way to express that concept?" is: not really, and anyone who wants one anyway has it at the ready. One can say "reduce by a tenth." Hopefully one will do so in comfort with the knowledge that *reduce* once had a different meaning — while *comfort* was once "to make strong," and *strong* once meant "narrow"!

It's always a safe bet that a word will not be tomorrow what it is today. In fact, sometimes words don't just change their meaning — they lose their independence and become parts of brand-new words entirely.

THINKING CRITICALLY ABOUT THE TEXT

1. How are English verbs different than French or Spanish verbs, according to McWhorter? Why is this difference significant?

2. What is McWhorter's thesis? How would you state it in your own words?

3. McWhorter cites a phrase coined by the linguist and cognitive scientist Steven Pinker: "the euphemism treadmill" (10). What does this expression mean?

4. According to McWhorter, what is the difference between one individual using a word the wrong way and the majority of English speakers and writers using a word the wrong way? Do you agree with him? Why is this idea important for McWhorter's overall argument?

5. What point does McWhorter make in his second-to-last paragraph? How does it support his thesis?

LANGUAGE IN ACTION

McWhorter illustrates how a word's meaning can shift over time. He provides several examples of this process, including the word *decimate*. He also notes that such changes in meaning annoy some people, who view the new meaning as "wrong." Research a word whose meaning has changed over time, or a word that has taken on an added meaning, and investigate how and why this shift occurred. What did the word mean in the past? What does it mean now? Then, in small groups in class, talk about your own opinion of the change. Do you think that people who use the word in the new way are using it incorrectly? Explain. You may find your own word or choose one from the following list:

- awful
- bully
- cute
- enormity

- text
- troll
- truck
- viral

WRITING SUGGESTIONS

1. In the opening paragraphs of this selection, McWhorter points out that "an interesting novelty especially popular among young corporate types is the use of basic verbs as nouns, as in 'What's the ask?' about business transactions [and] 'Is there a solve?' instead of 'Is there a solution?'" The more technical, linguistic terms for this process are *zero derivation* and *conversion*. As McWhorter and others point out, this is not a new phenomenon. But some people find these newer usages grating, pretentious, and unnecessary, especially when words already exist that convey the correct denotation (e.g., *solution* instead of *solve*). How do *you* respond to these examples? Do you use any of these words? Why do you think these particular verbs evolved into nouns? Do they capture shades of meaning that other, existing nouns do not? Write a brief essay answering these questions.

2. McWhorter explains how euphemisms — polite, agreeable expressions used to describe concepts that might otherwise offend — change over time and take on different associations. In particular, he describes how the term *home relief* became *welfare,* which then became *cash assistance* because the word *welfare* developed a negative connotation in the 1980s and '90s. Many current American political debates hinge, at least in part, on questions of terminology (e.g., *illegal aliens* vs. *undocumented immigrants;* see also "The Fight Over the Words of Immigration" by Jeff Gammage on pp. 372–374). Find another example of a current political issue where terminology is debated, and write a brief essay about the debate. What connotations do the different terms have? How does this language reveal the views or goals of each politician, media figure, or other person who uses the terms? In your opinion, is the terminology accurate and honest? Is it misleading? Why or why not?

How New Words Are Born

ANDY BODLE

Andy Bodle was born in 1969 in Swindon, Wiltshire, England and grew up in Leeds, England. He completed both his undergraduate and graduate education at Exeter College at Oxford University. In the years since, he has been a stand-up comedian, television writer, blogger, podcaster, and journalist. He has also worked as an editor at *The Guardian,* where he has frequently written about language. In this essay, which originally appeared in *The Guardian* on February 4, 2016, Bodle looks at new words that are becoming part of the English language and the processes by which such words are created. American English, in particular, has long been known to accept and assimilate terms from other languages, particularly as new words and expressions have arrived with new waves of immigrants. Bodle closely examines thirteen of the mechanisms that make a language grow.

WRITING TO DISCOVER: *Think of a word that you have only recently heard or recently started using (say, over the past year or two). What does the word mean? Where do you think it comes from?*

As dictionary publishers never tire of reminding us, our language is growing. Not content with the million or so words they already have at their disposal, English speakers are adding new ones at the rate of around 1,000 a year. Recent dictionary debutants include blog, grok, crowdfunding, hackathon, airball, e-marketing, sudoku, twerk and Brexit.

But these represent just a sliver of the tip of the iceberg. According to Global Language Monitor, around 5,400 new words are created every year; it's only the 1,000 or so deemed to be in sufficiently widespread use that make it into print. Who invents these words, and how? What rules govern their formation? And what determines whether they catch on?

Shakespeare is often held up as a master neologist, because at least 500 words (including critic, swagger, lonely and hint) first appear in his works—but we have no way of knowing whether he personally invented them or was just transcribing things he'd picked up elsewhere.

It's generally agreed that the most prolific minter of words was John Milton, who gave us 630 coinages, including lovelorn, fragrance, and pandemonium. Geoffrey Chaucer (universe, approach), Ben Jonson (rant, petulant), John Donne (self-preservation, valediction) and Sir Thomas More (atonement, anticipate) lag behind. It should come as no great surprise that writers are behind many of our lexical innovations. But the fact is, we have no idea who to credit for most of our lexicon.

If our knowledge of the who is limited, we have a rather fuller understanding of the how. All new words are created by one of 13 mechanisms: 5

239

1. Derivation

The commonest method of creating a new word is to add a prefix or suffix to an existing one. Hence realisation (1610s), democratise (1798), detonator (1822), preteen (1926), hyperlink (1987) and monogamish (2011).

2. Back Formation

The inverse of the above: the creation of a new root word by the removal of a phantom affix. The noun *sleaze,* for example, was back-formed from "sleazy" in about 1967. A similar process brought about pea, liaise, enthuse, aggress and donate. Some linguists propose a separate category for lexicalisation, the turning of an affix into a word (ism, ology, teen), but it's really just a type of back formation.

3. Compounding

The juxtaposition of two existing words. Typically, compound words begin life as separate entities, then get hitched with a hyphen, and eventually become a single unit. It's mostly nouns that are formed this way (fiddlestick, claptrap, carbon dating, bailout), but words from other classes can be smooshed together too: into (preposition), nobody (pronoun), daydream (verb), awe-inspiring, environmentally friendly (adjectives).

4. Repurposing

Taking a word from one context and applying it to another. Thus the crane, meaning lifting machine, got its name from the long-necked bird, and the computer mouse was named after the long-tailed animal.

5. Conversion

Taking a word from one word class and transplanting it to another. The word *giant* was for a long time just a noun, meaning a creature of enormous size, until the early 15th century, when people began using it as an adjective. Thanks to social media, a similar fate has recently befallen friend, which can now serve as a verb as well as a noun ("Why didn't you friend me?"). 10

6. Eponyms

Words named after a person or place. You may recognise Alzheimer's, atlas, cheddar, alsatian, diesel, sandwich, mentor, svengali, wellington and boycott as eponyms—but did you know that gun, dunce, bigot, bugger, cretin, currant, hooligan, marmalade, maudlin, maverick, panic, silhouette, syphilis, tawdry, doggerel, doily and sideburns are too? (The issue of whether, and for how long, to retain the capital letters on eponyms is a thorny one.)

7. Abbreviations

An increasingly popular method. There are three main subtypes: clippings, acronyms and initialisms. Some words that you might not have known started out longer are pram (perambulator), taxi/cab (both from taximeter cabriolet), mob (mobile vulgus), goodbye (God be with you), berk (Berkshire Hunt), rifle (rifled pistol), canter (Canterbury gallop), curio (curiosity), van (caravan), sport (disport), wig (periwig), laser (light amplification by stimulated emission of radiation), scuba (self-contained underwater breathing apparatus), and trump (triumph. Although it's worth noting that there's another, unrelated sense of trump: to fabricate, as in "trumped-up charge").

8. Loanwords

Foreign speakers often complain that their language is being overrun with borrowings from English. But the fact is, English itself is a voracious word thief; linguist David Crystal reckons it's half-inched words from at least 350 languages. Most words are borrowed from French, Latin and Greek; some of the more exotic provenances are Flemish (hunk), Romany (cushty), Portuguese (fetish), Nahuatl (tomato – via Spanish), Tahitian (tattoo), Russian (mammoth), Mayan (shark), Gaelic (slogan), Japanese (tycoon), West Turkic (horde), Walloon (rabbit) and Polynesian (taboo). Calques (flea market, brainwashing, loan word) are translations of borrowings.

9. Onomatopeia

The creation of a word by imitation of the sound it is supposed to make. Plop, ow, barf, cuckoo, bunch, bump and midge all originated this way.

10. Reduplication

The repetition, or near-repetition, of a word or sound. To this method   15
we owe the likes of flip-flop, goody-goody, boo-boo, helter-skelter, picnic, claptrap, hanky-panky, hurly-burly, lovey-dovey, higgledy-piggledy, tom-tom, hip hop and cray-cray. (Willy-nilly, though, came to us via a contraction of "Will he, nill he.")

11. Nonce Words

Words pulled out of thin air, bearing little relation to any existing form. Confirmed examples are few and far between, but include quark (Murray Gell-Mann), bling (unknown) and fleek (Vine celebrity Kayla Newman).

12. Error

Misspellings, mishearings, mispronunciations and mistranscriptions rarely produce new words in their own right, but often lead to new forms in conjunction with other mechanisms. Scramble, for example, seems to have originated as a variant of scrabble; but over time, the two forms have taken on different meanings, so one word has now become two. Similarly, the words *shit* and *science,* thanks to a long sequence of shifts and errors, are both ultimately derived from the same root. And the now defunct word helpmeet, or helpmate, is the result of a Biblical boo-boo. In the King James version, the Latin *adjutorium simile sibi* was rendered as "an help meet for him"—that is, "a helper suitable for him." Later editors, less familiar with the archaic sense of meet, took the phrase to be a word, and began hyphenating help-meet.

13. Portmanteaus

Compounding with a twist. Take one word, remove an arbitrary portion of it, then put in its place either a whole word, or a similarly clipped one. Thus were born sitcom, paratroops, internet, gazunder and sexting. (Note: some linguists call this process blending and reserve the term portmanteau for a particular subtype of blend.

Is this a bodacious development—or a disastrophe?

But since Lewis Carroll, who devised this sense of portmanteau, specifically defined it as having the broader meaning, I'm going to use the terms willy-nilly.)

Some words came about via a combination of methods: yuppie is the result of initialism ((y)oung and (up)wardly mobile) plus derivation (+ -ie); berk is a clipped eponym (Berkshire hunt); cop, in the sense of police officer, is an abbreviation of a derivation (copper derives from the northern British dialect verb cop, meaning to catch); and snarl-up is a conversion (verb to noun) of a compound (snarl + up).

The popularity of the various methods has waxed and waned through the ages. For long periods (1100–1500 and 1650–1900), borrowings from French were *in vogue*. In the 19th century, loanwords from Indian languages (bangle, bungalow, cot, juggernaut, jungle, loot, shampoo, thug) were the cat's *pyjamas*. There was even a brief *onslaught* from Dutch and Flemish.

In the 20th century, quite a few newbies were generated by derivation, using the -ie (and -y) suffix: talkies, freebie, foodie, hippy, roomie, rookie, roofie, Munchie, Smartie, Crunchie, Furby, scrunchie. Abbreviations, though, were the preferred MO, perhaps because of the necessity in wartime of delivering your message ASAP. The passion for initialisms seems to be wearing off, perhaps because things have got a little confusing; PC, for example, can now mean politically correct, police constable, per cent, personal computer, parsec, post cibum, peace corps, postcard, professional corporation or printed circuit.

20

But today, when it comes to word formation, there's only one player in town: the portmanteau. Is this a bodacious development—or a disastrophe? I'll get the debate rolling tomorrow.

THINKING CRITICALLY ABOUT THE TEXT

1. According to the source Bodle cites in his essay, how many new words are created every year?

2. Of the thirteen mechanisms for creating new words, which one is the most common?

3. What is a *portmanteau?* Who is generally credited with inventing the concept of the portmanteau? Give an example of one of these words.

4. In paragraph 2, Bodle asks three rhetorical questions. How do these questions help shape his essay? Does he answer them all? If not, does this make his essay less effective? Why or why not?

5. Bodle writes, "It should come as no great surprise that writers are behind many of our lexical innovations" (4). Why should that be unsurprising?

LANGUAGE IN ACTION

Each year, Merriam-Webster adds new words to its dictionary. This can be a gradual process. As Merriam-Webster's editors explain, "Every word moves at its own pace; there is no average speed for a word's acceptance into the language, the culture, and the dictionary. The dictionary's job is to report that usage as it enters the general vocabulary." Consider the following list of words, all of which were added to the Merriam-Webster dictionary in 2017 and 2018. (Some words, like *ghost,* already existed but were updated with a new meaning.) Without looking up the words, try to figure out the origin of each word using the classifications in Bodle's essay. Then check your answers against the answer key below. Do the any of the word origins surprise you? Why or why not?

1. adorbs	7. Latinx
2. bingeable	8. mocktail
3. biohacking	9. ping
4. bougie	10. rando
5. ghost	11. timesuck
6. hangry	12. tl;dr

Answers

1. back formation / abbreviation 2. derivation 3. compounding 4. back formation / abbreviation 5. repurposing / conversion 6. portmanteau 7. derivation 8. portmanteau 9. repurposing 10. back formation / abbreviation 11. compounding 12. abbreviation

WRITING SUGGESTIONS

1. Bodle notes that the English language is always growing. New words often enter the language to explain a new phenomenon, object, or situation. As the editors of the Merriam-Webster dictionary put it, "A dictionary is almost like a glossary of life: peek inside and you see descriptions of everything around you." With that in mind, come up with a new word of your own (also known as a *neologism*) that you think describes a new or (to this point) unnamed phenomenon. Write a brief essay explaining why you chose this word and why you think it is useful. You might also want to think about why your new word does not already exist in Standard English.

2. Bodle's essay is, among other things, a classification-and-division essay: it takes an amorphous "whole"—the creation of new words—and breaks it down into thirteen specific categories. Write your own classification-and-division essay that breaks down a larger idea or group into different types or categories. As you work on the essay, try to develop categories that are not obvious. For example, if you choose to write about different types of college students, do not simply divide them into first-year students, sophomores, juniors, and seniors. Make sure to develop your categories as Bodle does, with description, explanation, and examples.

What Does "Latinx" Mean? A Look at the Term That's Challenging Gender Norms

Yesenia Padilla

Poet and activist Yesenia Padilla was born to immigrant parents and raised in San Francisco. She earned her BA at the University of California, San Diego, and now writes about politics, social justice issues, and Latinx culture. She self-identifies as *Xicanx*, a term that embraces Mexican American heritage while seeking to be inclusive of feminism and gender nonconformity. Her work has appeared in many online publications, including *Complex*, *Queen Mob's Teahouse*, and *Thought Catalog*. Padilla is a co-founder and poetry editor at *Lumen Magazine*, an online literary journal created for and by women and non-binary people. She also co-curates "Now That's What I Call Poetry," a monthly experimental poetry night in San Diego.

Labels such as *Hispanic, Latino, Chicano,* and *Mestizo* have long been contested. Often, their definitions have depended on context, connotations, and subtle shades of meaning. For example, *Hispanic* emphasizes a shared language and could, potentially, apply to any person anywhere who speaks Spanish. In contrast, *Latino* connotes an identity tied to origins in South and Central America. In the following essay, however, Padilla argues that all of these terms are inextricably tied to Latin America's colonial history. In her view, the newer term *Latinx* may not be perfect, but it suggests real progress. This essay originally appeared in the online magazine *NTRSCTN* on April 18, 2016.

WRITING TO DISCOVER: *How is your sense of identity shaped by your own or your family's origins in a particular nation, region, culture, race, ethnicity, religion, or other heritage? What labels might be used to identify you? Do you prefer some more than others? Why?*

If you've been online at all in the past year, you've probably seen the word "Latinx" and thought: What does it mean?

Latinx (pronounced "La-TEEN-ex") is a gender-inclusive way of referring to people of Latin American descent. Used by activists and some academics, the term is gaining traction among the general public, after having been featured in publications from NPR to *Latina*. But where did Latinx originate, and is everybody on board with using it?

UNGENDERING THE SPANISH LANGUAGE

Spanish is a gendered language, which means that every noun has a gender (in general, nouns that end in "a" tend to be feminine, and nouns that end in "o" tend to be masculine). While some nouns keep their gender when they become plural, others change based on the gender composition of a given group of people.

This approach, however, always defers to the masculine as the dominant gender. For example, if you had a room full of girlfriends, it'd be full of *amigas*, with the "a" denoting everyone's gender as female. But the entire group's gender changes as soon as one guy enters the room, making it full of *amigos;* the "o" denotes the presence of at least one man—no matter how many women are in the room. Some members of Latin American communities claim this gendered language reinforces patriarchal and heterosexist norms, so "Latin@" was later introduced as a way to push back against it.

Using "@" as a suffix became a way to represent male and female   5
genders. Instead of *amigas* or *amigos*, it was *amig@s*. But the term, which was adopted by left-leaning activists and even used in academic texts, didn't include genderqueer and gender-nonconforming people. Consequently, Latin@ began to hit its limit, as those who didn't conform to the male–female gender binary gained more visibility.

THE RISE OF LATINX

According to Google Trends data, Latinx began emerging as early as 2004, but really started popping up in online searches sometime in late 2014. During this period, the term had mostly been used in left-leaning and queer communities as a way to promote inclusivity in language. But thanks to social media users on sites like Tumblr and Twitter, Latinx gained a foothold by mid-2015, and its use began spreading beyond LGBTQIA communities.

They say moving towards non-gendered language is a way to escape the ghost of colonialism that still haunts Latin American culture.

"Once the term 'Latinx' was made more visible, it certainly aligned with what I had been learning about gender non-conformity," Filiberto Nolasco Gomez, founder of Latin American culture blog *El Huateque,* told *NTRSCTN*.[1] "It seemed like the right direction for my website to embrace 'Latinx' as a political statement and a dismantling of binaries."

By dismantling some of the gendering within Spanish, Latinx helped modernize the idea of a pan-Latin American experience—or *Latinidad*—one that reflects what it means to be of Latin American descent in today's world. The term also better reflects Latin America's diversity, which is more in line with intersectionality, the study of the ways that different forms of oppression (e.g. sexism, racism, classism, and heterosexism) intersect.

---

1. *NTRSCTN* (pronounced "Intersection"), an affiliate of Complex Media, was the online magazine in which this article was originally published.

"The use of the 'x' is really important to me," Chicanx performance artist Artemisa Clark told *NTRSCTN*. "The 'x' shows a development of broader Latinx movements, one more actively concerned with issues of gender and queerness."

RESISTANCE IN PROGRESS

In their takedown of an article that says "Latinx" denotes "a lack of respect for the sovereignty of Spanish," professors María R. Scharrón-del Río and Alan A. Aja defend the term, arguing that it should replace "Latino" when referring to people of Latin American descent.

They say moving towards non-gendered language is a way to escape the ghost of colonialism that still haunts Latin American culture. "Latinx" actually represents the people the term is supposed to represent, so it's "a concerted attempt at inclusivity" that "fosters solidarity with all of our Latinx community," Scharrón-del Río and Aja write.

Still, even with the gender inclusivity of a term like "Latinx," there are still issues that arise when grouping a very diverse population—like that of Latin America—under one umbrella term.

"I think there has been a lot of communication and travel between communities and countries within the Americas for centuries, and Latinx kind of gives that some coherence," Ken Eby-Gomez, a San Francisco-based activist and graduate student, told *NTRSCTN*. "But . . . it would be a mistake to essentialize any meaning or characteristics of Latinx."

In other words, creating a single Latin American identity can be problematic because it may lead to the erasure of marginalized identities (e.g., indigenous people), while highlighting lighter-skinned *mestizos* (i.e., people of mixed Spanish and indigenous ancestry).

LIFE AFTER LATINX

In a piece published late last year, writer Monse Arce argues that the identifier "Latino" erases indigenous history and culture from Latin America. Indeed, using a term like "Latino/@/x" emphasizes the privileges of *mestizos*, reinforcing colorism amongst Latin American people. "'Latino/@/x' also implies a uniformity of experience, when in reality, people of Latin American descent have wildly different lives and narratives," she adds.

"The root of [Latinx] bothers me in that it's colonial, and my heart rages against [it]," Eusebio Ricardo Lopez-Aguilar, a Salvadoran activist and census worker based in Winnipeg, Canada, told *NTRSCTN*. "I haven't used it to describe myself, but I also haven't found a word that works."

Many young people of Latin American descent are exploring their complex indigenous roots, and forging new, more personal identities. While some resist using "Latinx," others recognize it as the most inclusive option available, for now. "I guess first-level identification is 'Chicanx' (a political and cultural identifier for Mexican Americans) and second-level is 'Latinx'," said performance artist Clark.

"Latinx" is not the perfect identifying term, so it shouldn't be treated as the answer in the ongoing quest to develop a cohesive postcolonial identity. Given Latin America's turbulent history and the continued disapora of its people, the process of figuring out one's identity is both deeply personal and political. Still, using "Latinx" is a positive step towards recognizing all of *nuestro gente*—our people—and will hopefully challenge every Latin American to think about what it truly means to be part of this complex culture.

THINKING CRITICALLY ABOUT THE TEXT

1. What are some of the benefits of the term *Latinx,* according to Padilla?

2. Padilla discusses the gender-neutral practice of using the @ suffix, as when the gendered terms *amigos* or *amigas* were replaced with amig@s. What is the problem with this usage, according to her?

3. What does the word *intersectionality* mean? How does this word fit into Padilla's overall argument about language?

4. How do the rhetorical questions function in paragraphs 1 and 2? What is their relationship to the rest of the essay?

5. Who do you think is the audience for Padilla's argument? Do you think she is trying to persuade skeptics and people who disagree with her, or do you think she is mostly addressing a like-minded audience? How can you tell?

LANGUAGE IN ACTION

As Padilla acknowledges, not everyone who identifies as Latino or Hispanic embraces the word *Latinx*. In fact, the word originated in the United States and is not widely used in Latin America. In a 2015 op-ed in *The Phoenix*—the student newspaper at Swarthmore College—Latino students Gilbert Guerra and Gilbert Orbea argue that the word *Latinx* is actually disrespectful to the Spanish language:

> The term "Latinx" is used almost exclusively within the United States. According to Google trend data, "Latinx" came into popular use in October of 2014 and has since been widely popularized by American blogs and American institutions of higher education. The term is virtually nonexistent in any Spanish-speaking country. This is problematic for many reasons. It serves as a prime example of how English speakers can't seem to stop imposing their social norms on other cultures. [...] The vast majority of people in Latin America, from personal experience, would likely be confused and even offended by this attempt to dictate for them how their language is to be structured and how they ought to manage their social constructs.

Do you agree with Guerra and Orbea's argument? Why or why not? How do you think Padilla would respond? Discuss with a small group of two or three classmates.

WRITING SUGGESTIONS

1. Padilla repeatedly uses the word *queer*, which, historically, has had negative or even offensive associations. What does that word mean in the context of her essay? What connotations does it have? How has its meaning and connotation changed over time? Is *queer* a word that you use, in any context? Why or why not? Do some research on the word (its history, meaning, usage, etc.) and then write an essay that addresses these questions.

2. Padilla argues that the term *Latinx* should be used instead of *Latino* or *Latina* because, in her view, *Latinx* suggests progress toward a postcolonial, gender-neutral, and inclusive language. Can you think of another word or label that, in your opinion, should be replaced with a better term? What replacement term would you use, and how would you make the case for this new term? Structure a brief essay using a simple template: *We should stop using the word (or phrase) _____ because _____. Instead, we should use the word (or phrase) _____ because _____.* Follow Padilla's lead in giving explanations and evidence to support your argument.

Textspeak Is Modernizing the Egnlish Language (*English)

Lauren Collister

Librarian, linguist, and scholar Lauren Collister, born in 1983, is the Director of the Office of Scholarly Communication and Publishing at the University of Pittsburgh. After growing up in Ohio, she earned her BA at Ohio State University and her MA and PhD at the University of Pittsburgh. Collister's work has appeared in *The Washington Post, The New Republic, Salon, Business Insider,* and other publications. As a scholar, in her words, she strives to "further the scholarly understanding of digital societies by researching how language is used as a social tool in online environments."

In the following essay, which appeared in *The New Republic* in 2015, Collister considers how the language of our digital lives has influenced the ways that we write and speak when we are in *offline* environments, as well. She provides perceptive historical context, too, including the centuries-long tradition of people claiming that language is in decline. She argues that "textspeak" is not harmful to our language, as so many complain, but is instead a source of renewal and vitality.

WRITING TO DISCOVER: *Do you write differently in emails, text messages, and online posts than you do when you write academic essays—or even when you answer a writing prompt for class, like this one? If so, what do you think accounts for the change in your writing style?*

txt msgs r running language
*ruining
^lol, jk!! :)

In many casual discussions of language and the internet, it's not uncommon to hear about how such "textspeak ruins language"—how technology has made everybody lazy with their speech and writing. Major media outlets such as the *Los Angeles Times,* the *BBC,* and the *Daily Mail* have all bemoaned the ways in which people communicate through technology.

Of course, language does change when it's used to text or write messages on the internet. It's even become the focus of the field of linguistics known as Computer-Mediated Communication (CMC). Although it specifies computers in its name, CMC refers to the study of interaction facilitated by technology like computers, mobile phones, and tablets.

And contrary to the idea that these innovations are corrupting language, they actually demonstrate a creative repurposing of symbols and marks to a new age of technology. These evolutions of language are swift, clever, and context-specific, illustrating the flexibility of the language to communicate nonverbal meaning in a nuanced, efficient manner.

CHANGE DOESN'T MEAN DECAY

It turns out that people have been complaining about language being "ruined" for as long as they've been writing and speaking.

In a TED Talk, linguist John McWhorter shared stories of people complaining about language change through the ages. For example, in 63 AD a Roman scholar groused that students of Latin were writing in an "artificial language"—a language that would become French!

And an 1871 quote from Charles Eliot, the president of Harvard University, might sound familiar:

> Bad spelling, incorrectness, as well as inelegance of expression in writing, ignorance of the simplest rules of punctuation . . . are far from rare among young men otherwise well-prepared for college studies.

Young Theodore Roosevelt—a student at Harvard in the 1870s—was possibly among those young men being described. As historian Kathleen Dalton observed in her biography of Roosevelt, the future president would eventually support the revision of American English spelling rules, many of which we still use today, like changing -re endings to -er in words like *center* and changing -our to -or in words like *color.*

THE EMOTICON: MORE THAN A FACE

Today, people are able to communicate rapidly through a range of mediums—and perhaps no linguistic development better indicates changes in the ways we communicate than the ubiquitous emoticon.

The emoticon :)—a colon followed by a parenthesis—is a visual representation of a smiley face turned sideways. Although an emoticon may *look* like a smile, a frown or any number of facial expressions, it doesn't represent a face, as many internet users assume. It's actually intended to convey a feeling ("I'm happy," or "just joking").

This meaning is evident even in the first emoticon, credited to Scott Fahlman at Carnegie Mellon University. In a 1982 e-mail, Fahlman suggested :-) as a "joke marker" to indicate wisecracks or sarcasm in text communication. In this legendary e-mail, he also used the first instance of the frown emoticon :-(.

Words that represent these feelings are what linguists call *discourse particles,* or little pieces of language that convey information about the tone of the statement. Folklorist Lee-Ellen Marvin called them the "paralanguage of the internet, the winks which signal the playfulness of a statement over the seriousness it might denote."

In a study of instant messaging, scholar Shao-Kang Lo describes emoticons as "quasi-nonverbal cues"—something that looks like a word, but performs the functions of a nonverbal cue, like a hand gesture or nod.

In fact, the variations in how you construct this emoticon can imply something about your identity, just like whether you use a soda, pop or Coke can suggest what part of the United States you come from. For example, as linguist and data scientist Tyler Schnoebelen pointed out in a 2012 study, people who put a "nose" in their emoticons tend to be older than non-nose emoticon users.

Though emoticons have been the subject of numerous studies, individual symbols—which serve a different purpose than emoticons—can add meaning to a message or express meaning all on their own.

FLUID CONVERSATION AND CLARIFIED MEANING

Have you ever seen someone fix a typo in a message with an asteriks? (*asterisk)

The asterisk signals a repair of an error in language. Conversational   15 repair, or the act of correcting ourselves or others in spoken language, has been discussed for decades by conversation analysts in spoken language. Saying "sorry, I meant to say" or "er, I mean" can be awkward and interrupt the dynamics of a spoken conversation.

And contrary to the idea that these innovations are corrupting language, they actually demonstrate a creative repurposing of symbols and marks to a new age of technology.

This conversational move has made its way into online written language, where that awkwardness is reduced to a single symbol. Instead of saying "oops, I mispelled 'asterisk' in my previous sentence," people can avoid a conversational detour by simply typing an asterisk before the word: *asterisk.

That's not the only use of the asterisk. A pair of them around a word or phrase can indicate emphasis. This style has gradually given way to words in all caps and repeated letters to show intensity and emphasis, as linguist Deborah Tannen and communication scholar Erika Darics have noted. Tannen provides an example of a text message that uses multiple styles to convey an intensely apologetic, sincere tone:

> JACKIE I AM SO SO SO SORRY! I thought you were behind us in the cab and then I saw you weren't!!!!! I feel soooooooo bad! Catch another cab and ill pay for it for youuuuu

Meanwhile, punctuation marks like hyphens and periods suggest a change in voice and tempo. One example is the ubiquitous ellipses. Traditionally, this mark has been used in text to denote deleted text. Now, it can also indicate a tone of voice that's trailing off or hesitating, such as the following example from a conversation in the popular online role-playing game *World of Warcraft*:

> So…since we live in the same city, do you wanna like…meet up sometime…?

This use of the ellipses adds that extra meaning to the text and it can also do the work of denoting someone else's turn in the conversation.

It's even been incorporated into user interfaces. In instant messaging and chat programs like Skype, an ellipsis is used to show that the other party is typing.

A SINGLE SYMBOL CONVEYS A COMPLEX MESSAGE

A single symbol can also be an entire message on its own. In her contribution to the book *Discourse 2.0: Language and New Media*, Susan Herring describes how a single question mark can be an entire message that indicates that the user is "confused or does not know what to say."

In other words, a question mark does the job of asking for clarification   20
in a single keystroke. Similarly, a single exclamation point as a message can illustrate surprise and excitement. You can repeat either of these symbols as a superlative to show a greater level of surprise. Consider this exchange in which B uses nothing but symbols to express reactions to A's statements:

A: So I have some good news.

B: ?

A: I got a raise today

B: !

A: And it came with a promotion

B: !!!

These two aren't the only punctuation that can stand on their own as a message. In my 2012 study of *World of Warcraft* players, I found that in this community, and others, the carat (^) can stand alone as an entire message that indicates agreement with another person. Meanwhile, an arrow-shaped symbol (<–) signaled volunteering for a task, like raising a hand in the classroom. Here's a hypothetical interaction:

A: I am so ready for vacation.

B: ^

A: Who wants to go to Florida with me?

B: <–

Far from crippling language, these examples indicate how people can now communicate complex feelings in a streamlined manner—perfect for our modern, fast-paced world.

THINKING CRITICALLY ABOUT THE READING

1. When was the first emoticon used, and who invented it?

2. According to Collister, "smiley" emoticons do not actually represent faces. What does she think they "convey" (8)?

3. What is a "discourse particle" (10)?

4. What is the purpose of Collister's first paragraph? Why is it important to both her purpose and her argument?

5. Collister claims that people have been complaining about the decline of language for a long time. What evidence does she use to support this claim? Do you think that language is in decline?

LANGUAGE IN ACTION

Collister performs a rigorous and revealing analysis of different elements of textspeak, such as emoticons, asterisks, question marks, and exclamation points. Indeed, she looks at shades of meaning and tone in much the way a literary critic might analyze a poem. Do you think your own text messages or other electronic communications would reveal a similar complexity? Pull up a recent text conversation between yourself and a friend, family member, or significant other. In these text messages, try to identify the following elements that Collister describes: "discourse particles," "conversational repair," and "quasi-nonverbal cues." Are there other patterns or elements that you notice in your text conversation? In groups of three, share your analyses with your classmates.

WRITING SUGGESTIONS

1. In paragraph 12, Collister writes, "In fact, the variations in how you construct this emoticon can imply something about your identity, just like whether you use a soda, pop, or Coke can suggest what part of the United States you come from." Does your use of language include any markers that suggest where you are from? Do you use any terms, phrases, or expressions that mark your regional identity? Choose a specific characteristic of your language—a particular word, for example—and explain how it reflects your origins or time in a specific place. You might also explore your relationship with the language of your region. For instance, if you have a recognizable accent, do you *like* it? Do you avoid using regional expressions? Do you embrace them? You may find it helpful to read Richard Lederer's essay "All-American Dialects" (pp. 187–192) before starting to write.

2. Collister believes that the influence of "textspeak" is ultimately positive. In her conclusion, she claims that this language allows us to "express complex feelings in a streamlined manner—perfect for our modern, fast-paced world." But she concedes that others disagree. While Collister does not

address counterarguments from specific writers, she alludes to anti-textspeak articles in publications such as the *Daily Mail* and the *Los Angeles Times*. Academic researchers have studied the effects of texting, too. In a 2012 article in the academic journal *New Media & Society*, communications theorists Drew P. Singel and S. Shyam Sundar found a "general negative relationship between the use of techspeak in text messages and scores on a grammar assessment." What do *you* think? Has textspeak influenced your writing, for better or worse? Do you agree with Collister that textspeak is a good thing, or do you agree with critics who argue that it is harmful to grammar, uses too many abbreviations, or fosters lazy writing habits? Write a brief essay in which you take a stand on this issue. Feel free to draw on both your personal experience and outside sources.

Smile, You're Speaking Emoji

ADAM STERNBERGH

Journalist and novelist Adam Sternbergh was born and raised in Toronto. He is a long-time contributing editor to *New York Magazine* and the former culture editor of *The New York Times Magazine*. His nonfiction has appeared in *The New York Times, GQ, Bloomberg Business Week, The Independent on Sunday,* and other publications. His novels are *Shovel Ready* (2014), *Near Enemy* (2015), and *The Blinds* (2017). Known for its distinctive literary style, much of his fiction combines elements of the science fiction, noir, and thriller genres.

By his own account, Sternbergh has always found language fascinating. "As a kid, I was always intrigued by the power of words—especially two words placed in juxtaposition," he once noted in an interview. "The shortest Bible verse, famously, is 'Jesus wept,' which is a really enviable model of literary economy. In the modern world, I absolutely love Twitter and the brevity it forces on you." In the essay that follows, which is excerpted from an article that originally appeared in *New York Magazine* in 2014, Sternbergh analyzes an even more condensed and economic mode of expression: the emoji. While some find emoji silly or annoying, he views them as a whole vocabulary to themselves, one that is well-suited to complex, contemporary communication.

WRITING TO DISCOVER: *How and when do you use emoji in your communications? Are there specific ones that you use more often than others? What are they good at communicating? What, if anything, do you find difficult or impossible to say with emoji alone?*

Consider the exclamation point. For much of its history, the exclamation point had a fairly simple usage: to straightforwardly and sincerely indicate excitement or, if included in a quotation, vehemence or volume. ("Get off my lawn!" as opposed to "Get off my lawn.") Yet for a long time, circa the mid-1990s, it seemed linguistically and socially impossible to use an exclamation point unironically. I'll anchor this observation to Peter Bagge's landmark grunge-culture comic *Hate!*, which debuted in 1990, simply titled *Hate,* but which added the telltale exclamation point to its name at issue No. 16 in 1994. I'll also add, from personal recollection, that if you included an exclamatory phrase such as "I'm so excited!" or "See you tonight!" in any written electronic correspondence up to, say, 1999, you could reliably assume it would be read as the punctuational equivalent of a smirk.

That was how my generation came to use the exclamation point, anyway. More recently, with the advent of new forms such as tweets and text messaging, the exclamation point has reverted to something closer to its original meaning. In fact, it's more or less switched places with the period, so that "I'm excited to see you!" now conveys sincere excitement to see you, while "I'm excited to see you." seems, on a screen at least, to imply the opposite. The exclamation point, once so sprightly and forceful, has come, according to Ben Yagoda in a piece in the *New York Times*, to signify "minimally acceptable enthusiasm."

All this fluidity means that it's very hard to keep up—it's what the writer Emily Gould described to a friend as the "arms race of communication styling that led me to feel that sometimes only one exclamation point seems unenthusiastic or even downright sarcastic." She was, in part, explaining her attraction to emoji—which, she wrote, "make it easier to talk about anything, I think!"

Her friend Phoebe Connelly had texted her about engagement rings—a fraught subject. Connelly often addressed her engagement using emoji: the Heart ♥, the Diamond ♦, the Diamond Ring 💍, the Wedding Cake 🎂, the Party Starters 🎉. (Weirdly, though, not the Bride With Veil 👰, the most obviously wedding-related emoji, which she avoided for reasons she can't quite explain, even to herself.) "Emoji," Connelly wrote in an article for the *Womanzine* special emoji issue, "allow me an ironic space within the dreaded cheery sincerity of being engaged. I can emoji diamond rings; therefore, it is ok that yes, I have a diamond ring. I default to emoji, a safe argot, as a means of discussing a marriage I'm emotionally ready for, but still lack the language to describe."

When I first encountered emoji, I assumed they were used only ironi- 5 cally—perhaps because, as a member of Generation X, I am accustomed to irony as a default communicative mode. And it's certainly true that emoji have proved popular, unsurprisingly, with early adopters and techno-fetishists and people with trend-sensitive antennae—the kinds of people who might, for example, download a Japanese app to "force" their iPhone to reveal a hidden emoji keyboard. But emoji have also proved to be popular with the least techno-literate and ironic among us, i.e., our parents. Many people I spoke to relayed that their moms were the most enthusiastic adopters of emoji they knew. One woman said that her near-daily text-message-based interaction with her mother consists almost entirely of strings of emoji hearts. Another woman, with a septuagenarian mother, revealed to me that her mom had recently sent a text relaying regret, followed by a crying-face emoji—and that this was possibly the most straightforwardly emotional sentiment her mother had ever expressed to her.

And now we're getting to the heart of what emoji do well—what perhaps they do better even than language itself, at least in the rough-and-tumble world online. Aside from the widespread difficulty of expressing yourself in real time with your clumsy thumbs, while hunched over a lit screen, and probably distracted by 50 other things, there's the fact that the internet is mean. The widespread anonymity of the web has marked its nascent years with a kind of insidious incivility that we all now accept with resignation. Comment sections are a write-off. "Troll" is a new and unwelcome subspecies of person. Twitter's a hashtag-strewn battlefield.

But emoji are not, it turns out, well designed to convey meanness. They are cartoons, first of all. And the emoji that exist — while very useful for conveying excitement, happiness, bemusement, befuddlement, and even love — are not very good at conveying anger, derision, or hate. If we can take as a given that millennials, as a generation, were raised in a digital environment — navigating, for the first time, digital relationships as an equally legitimate and in some ways dominant form of interpersonal interaction — it stands to reason they might be drawn to a communicative tool that serves as an antidote to ambient incivility. They might be especially receptive to, and even excited about, a tool that counteracts the harshness of life in the online world. They might be taken with emoji.

> **Emoji's default implication isn't irony; its default is sincerity, but sincerity that's self-aware.**

The word that came up multiple times, in many conversations, with many people about emoji was *soften*.

"The thing it does is soften things," says Tyler Schnoebelen, the linguistics expert.

"I use emoji in personal emails all the time, because I feel like I'm softening the email," says Vulture's Lindsey Weber, who co-curated the "Emoji" art show.   10

Alice Robb, who is in her 20s, wrote in *The New Republic* about saying good-bye to a friend who was moving across the country via text message. "I texted her an emoji of a crying face. She replied with an image of a chick with its arms outstretched. This exchange might have been heartfelt. It could have been ironic. I'm still not really sure. It's possible that this friend and I are particularly emotionally stunted, but I put at least part of the blame on emoji: They allowed us to communicate without saying anything, saving us from spelling out any actual sentiments." And yet what's striking is that her whole story is full of actual sentiment — she is no doubt sad that her friend is leaving, and her friend is no doubt sad to be leaving. Adding an emoji to a message doesn't undercut those sentiments (as irony would) but rather says, "I mean this, but it's hard to say it, and I know it's hard, but that makes it no less true." Emoji's default implication isn't irony; its default is sincerity, but sincerity that's self-aware. If the ironic exclamation point was the signature punctuational flourish of Generation X, the emoji — that attempt to bridge the difficult gap between what we feel and what we intend and what we say and what we text — is the signature punctuational flourish of the millennials.

"There really are no negative or mean emoji," says Weber. "There's no violent or aggressive emoji. Even the angry faces are hilarious or silly." Sure, there's a pistol emoji. But imagine sending a death threat using Pistol and Angry Face 😡 🔫. If it's possible to "soften" a death threat, emoji would do it.

It's frankly pretty strange that, in an online climate that is constantly being called out for excessive aggression and maliciousness, emoji have no in-built linguistic capacity for meanness. There are angry faces and frowning faces and thumbs down and even the so-called Face With No Good Gesture, which, in the Apple set, is a woman with her arms crossed in an X. But, seriously, look at her: 🙅. The Face With No Good Gesture has never actually hurt someone's feelings. One of the many new official emoji being added as part of Unicode 7 is a raised middle finger — like all the new emoji, it's simply being added because it's part of the Wingdings font. At first glance, it seems pretty surly, especially for an emoji. But as an expression of aggression, it's harmless. If the worst that online trolls could do was send you an endless string of raised-middle-finger emoji, I think we'd all agree that we'd be living in a better world.

Consider the Smiling Face With Smiling Eyes 😊. Right now, on Twitter, Smile is being used 157,439,872 times. Popularity-wise, that ranks it as No. 8. Here are a few other popular ones: Face Savoring Delicious Food 😋. Disappointed but Relieved 😥. Man and Woman Holding Hands 👫. Baby 👶. Face Throwing a Kiss 😘. Person Raising Both Hands in Celebration 🙌. Okay Hand Sign 👌. Thumbs Up 👍.

In 1974, the American Institute of Graphic Arts, in conjunction with the U.S. Department of Transportation, designed a new system of symbols to be used in airports around the world in response to the increase in global travel. The 34 symbols it came up with include such undeniably resilient icons as Man Hailing Taxi, Diapered Baby, and the Suitcase symbol, which still direct people to taxi stands, changing tables, and luggage carousels around the world. But the design committee also made the following deduction: "We are convinced that the effectiveness of symbols is strictly limited." Symbols, they found, could only augment language, not replace it.

It's improbable that the Smiling Face With Smiling Eyes is a permanent addition to our language; a cartoon smiling face is just about the crudest method possible to convey to someone "I'm happy." And yet here we are. As Mimi Ito, a cultural anthropologist at UC Irvine, explains, "when people are given the capacity to communicate in these ways, they're picking them up and developing whole new forms of literacy."

For now, emoji does the job. We are more connected than ever — what Ito terms a state of "ambient pervasive communication" — and we need to know that our connections are not being misunderstood. We need to let people know, even people very far away, staring at a screen, that we're happy. Or confused. Or joking. Or missing them. Despite the popularity of the "joy" symbol, emoji are not solely being used to convey joy. My friend (the one with the crying-emoji-sending mother) sent me a combo she's fond of: Grinning Face With Smiling Eyes with Pistol pointed to its head 😁 🔫. (Taken together, they read as "stress," which is particularly useful in New York.) One of my favorite emoji usages was when I asked online whether anyone could give me an emoji-only review of the VMAs on MTV and someone tweeted, simply, a Hammer emoji poised over a TV Set emoji. This was the most succinct and astute review of the show

15

that I could find anywhere, which suggests that emoji are coming into their own as a useful linguistic tool.

Fred Benenson, who works at Kickstarter, is even more optimistic about the future of emoji. He should be: He's the guy who, partly as an art project, partly to see if he could, spearheaded the translation of the whole of Moby-Dick into emoji. He also worked with Lawrence Lessig, the Harvard academic who's written extensively on the ways in which apparently apolitical computer coding can influence our laws and even our human rights. So Benenson recognizes that emoji, for all their supposed transience, are an important addition to language, especially now that we do so much communicating online. "The fact that emoji is available in software legitimizes it as a form of human expression," he says. "And especially now—we're so intimate with these devices and we're saying some of our most compelling things to each other in the form of text messages and social media."

In other words, we've stumbled on whole new confusing ways to communicate with each other, so we've been given a whole new vocabulary to say "I'm laughing," or "joy," or "Well done." This new way will not replace all the old ways, but it can augment them and help us muddle through. In lieu of being able to read each other's faces when we say these things, we've developed these surrogate faces. They're simple. They're silly. They don't yet have a taco. But they work, at least a little, at least right now. We blow each other kisses. We smile with hearts in our eyes. We cry tears of joy. We say "I love you," but in a million different ways, each one freighted with the particular meaning we hope fervently to convey, then send them out hopefully, like a smiley face in a bottle, waiting to be received by the exact person it was intended for, and opened up, and understood completely.

THINKING CRITICALLY ABOUT THE READING

1. How has the meaning of the exclamation point changed over the last few decades, according to Sternbergh? What factors have contributed to the change?

2. Sternbergh writes that "as a member of Generation X, I am accustomed to irony as a default communicative mode" (5). What is *irony*—and what does it mean in this context? How might irony work as a "communicative mode"? (Glossary: *Irony*)

3. According to many people Sternbergh spoke with for this article, who have been the most enthusiastic adopters of the emoji? Why might that be surprising?

4. What do "emoji do well," in Sternbergh's view (6)? Why is this function so important in the context of the internet and social media? Do you agree with Sternbergh's general characterization of the online world?

5. Paragraph 14 is primarily a list of different emojis. What is the purpose of this paragraph? How does it fit into the essay?

6. Sternbergh cites several different sources, including journalists and academic researchers. Why do you think he does this? How do these specific references support his analysis? Find a specific example and explain how it contributes to the essay.

LANGUAGE IN ACTION

Sternbergh argues that emoji are effective at clarifying our communication in many situations. But how expressive are they as a language? For this activity, which is a variation on the game "Paper Telephone," you will need to partner with two of your classmates. Write down a simple, declarative sentence that uses common words to make a basic statement about yourself. Here are some example sentences that you might use:

- I am looking forward to going out to a party with my friends this Saturday.
- My favorite food is pizza, my favorite drink is iced tea, and my favorite color is blue.
- I feel sad because my girlfriend broke up with me last weekend.
- I am tired because I stayed up too late last night studying for a test.

Now pass the sentence to a classmate. Keep track of who wrote the original sentence and what the text of the sentence said. Your classmate's task is to translate your sentence into emoji as accurately as possible, through a text message or any other medium that uses emoji. Finally, your classmate should text the emoji sentence to *the third classmate in your group,* whose job is to interpret the sentence. Afterward, discuss with your classmates how effective the emoji were in communicating meaning. What things, ideas, and meanings were the emoji best able to capture? What was most difficult to express with emoji?

WRITING SUGGESTIONS

1. Sternbergh refers to many different emoji in the essay, especially in paragraph 14. He also discusses the emoji's function and their effects. What emoji do you use the most, and why and how to you use them? Choose three emoji that you commonly use in your day-to-day communications. What do they mean? Why do you use them? How do they help you express your message, convey tone, or communicate meaning? If you rarely use emojis, or do not use them at all, you may use this prompt to explain why you avoid using them.

2. According to Sternbergh, "the internet is mean." He then elaborates: "The widespread anonymity of the web has marked its nascent years with a kind of insidious incivility that we all now accept with resignation. Comment sections are a write-off. 'Troll' is a new and unwelcome subspecies of person. Twitter's a hashtag-strewn battlefield" (6). Do you agree with this generalization about the internet being "mean"? If so, how do you explain or account for that meanness? Do you think Sternbergh identifies the causes accurately? Are there other factors that he does not mention? Alternatively, do you *disagree* with his broad claim? Do you think claims about the overall meanness of the internet are overstated?

The (Sometimes Unintentional) Subtext of Digital Conversations

DEBORAH TANNEN

Born in 1945, Deborah Tannen is a prolific author, linguist, lecturer, and professor. She has found success not only in her specialized academic field, but also as the writer of popular books on language and interpersonal communication. Tannen was born and raised in Brooklyn, New York. She earned her undergraduate degree at Harpur College (now part of Binghamton University), her first MA at Wayne State University, and her second MA and her PhD at the University of California, Berkeley. Since 1979, Tannen has taught linguistics at Georgetown University.

The focus of her research and writing has been — and remains — the informal ways in which people communicate, whether across a kitchen table or in the workplace. As she has said, "The underlying point that runs through everything I've done is the notion of conversational style." Her books include *Conversational Style: Analyzing Talk among Friends* (1984), *You Just Don't Understand: Women and Men in Conversation* (1990), *Talking from 9 to 5: Women and Men at Work* (1994), and *You're the Only One I Can Tell: Inside the Language of Women's Friendships* (2017). Her essays and articles have regularly appeared in publications such as *The New York Times, The Washington Post, Politico, Time,* and *Newsweek*. In the following essay, which appeared in *The Atlantic* in 2017, Tannen turns her attention to communication styles on newer media platforms, such as text messaging and online social media sites. In her view, a key principle applies whether we are communicating online or offline: *how* we say things is just as important as *what* we say.

WRITING TO DISCOVER: *How do you communicate tone in writing — both online and offline? For example, how do you communicate irony and sarcasm, or sincerity and seriousness?*

The meanings we glean in conversation are often, maybe mostly, not found in the words spoken, but in how they're said, and in the spaces between them. Tone of voice, and cadences created by shifts in speed, volume, and pitch, let listeners know whether "Nice job," is complimentary or sarcastic, or whether "Wow" shows that you're impressed or underwhelmed. The literal meaning of words is their message, and everything about how words are said is the metamessage. Metamessages communicate how you mean what you say.

More and more conversations are taking place on screens — via texting, Facebook, Instagram, Snapchat, Twitter, email, and myriad other platforms. Some of these written conversations make up for the lack of voicing with conventions that mimic speech, like exclamation points, CAPS, and repetition of words or letters. I can be "so happy!!!!!!!" or "sooooo happy" or "SO happy" or "sosososo happy" or even "SOSOSOSOOOOOO happy!!!!!!!!!!!!!!!" Emoticons, emojis, and gifs help, too. But these visual signals are only the tip of the metamessage iceberg.

Human beings are always in the business of making meaning and interpreting meaning. Because there are options to choose from when sending a message, like which platform to use and how to use it, we see meaning in the choice that was made. But because the technologies, and the conventions for using them, are so new and are changing so fast, even close friends and relatives have differing ideas about how they should be used. And because metamessages are implied rather than stated, they can be misinterpreted or missed entirely.

Different generations are particularly apt to perceive different meta-messages in the same words or actions. For example, a Sri Lankan woman living in London told me of hosting her sister and her sister's teenage daughter. When the girl refused to go out after 3:00 p.m., because that's when her friends back home got active on WhatsApp, the sisters perceived the metamessage, "I'm not really here. My head and my heart are else-where." But I suspect the girl's perspective was more like: "I'm here with you — that's a given — but I also want to stay connected to my friends, and I can't bear the thought of being left out."

I heard a great range of viewpoints on social media while interviewing over 80 women (ranging in age from 9 to 97) for a study of friendship. And my students at Georgetown University have helped me understand how they manage, and sometimes are tripped up by, the metamessages communicated over social media — and how habits and assumptions can differ.   5

For instance, when Kate Lucey's sister had not given birth by her due date, she kept family and friends apprised of what was happening with her pregnancy by posting frequently on Facebook. In response, even distant relatives and casual friends posted well wishes and encour-aging thoughts. Kate felt that these postings sent her sister a precious metamessage: Many people love her and care about her pregnancy. The posts strengthened her network of support. Kate was stunned to learn that her roommate perceived a negative metamessage in her sister's use of Facebook. She said she would have been offended to be kept up to date about a pregnancy that way; she would think, "Geez, why didn't you call?" Kate's roommate reasoned that posting on Facebook is so easy that it means nothing. A phone conversation reflects and creates a mean-ingful relationship, whereas Facebook creates a false sense of intimacy, not a real relationship.

The impression that posting on Facebook is insincere because it's too easy sounds a lot like the explanation a friend gave me (over email) for disliking "THAT DRAT 'xoxo,' which means nothing, just keys to hit." This perspective — if something is too easy it's meaningless or insincere — makes sense. Taking time sends a metamessage of caring. Yet I like "xoxo" (or my personal variant, "xxoo"), and use it, though only with friends who use it first. I think xoxo fills a need: It's a more affectionate way to close an email than "Best" but not as fervent as "Love," which, in any case, some people don't feel comfortable using with friends, though some do. Maybe it strikes some as fake because it's a substitution, standing for "love and kisses" but not denoting it. Or maybe it seems too cutesy. Whatever the source of these impressions, deciding how to sign off a message becomes a challenge, since any choice you make will send metamessages that you may not intend or suspect.

I was shocked to realize that my students might be perceiving metamessages opposite from what I intend when I reply to their email requests and queries. One of them pointed out that when he emails professors, he begins with a salutation ("Dear Professor Smith") and a greeting like "I hope you're enjoying the weekend." Only then does he explain his request — in detail — followed by a friendly closing, again about the weekend or the weather, before wrapping up with "Sincerely" or "Yours truly" above his name. (I recognized his description: That's the way most of my students' emails look.) The student then complained that many of his professors' responses omit the salutation, greeting, full explanation, friendly closing, signature, and name. All he receives is a naked reply to his question, and usually a cryptic one at that. I realized that I do this, too — or did, before he, and others in class discussion, opened my eyes. I had assumed that dispensing with those formalities sends a metamessage of casual friendliness, more or less the way I use email with close friends and family. But students regard email as formal, so the omission of those niceties often strikes them as disrespectful, even rude. (Now I go back and add the trimmings before pressing SEND.)

It's not surprising that professors' and students' practices would vary, given the difference in power and age. But even best friends can have very different ideas about appropriate ways to use social media. Noelle Miesfeld and Rachel Jacobson had been close friends since college, and they stayed in close touch after graduation, often having long telephone conversations, catching up. After a number of years, however, they began communicating more through texting. This meant more frequent conversations — often daily or even multiple times a day. So Noelle was surprised when Rachel registered a complaint: She'd been telling Noelle about a problem, and she felt that Noelle's responses seemed too casual and brief to show real concern. Rachel missed her caring, emotionally supportive friend. They traced the trouble to their contrasting assumptions about texting. To Noelle, comforting closeness resided in the frequency of their exchanges. To Rachel, frequency didn't substitute for the expression of feeling and detailed discussion of her situation that they'd shared in the past—the kinds of conversations that Noelle didn't feel could or should take place through texting.

When deciding which platform to use and how to use it, as well as how to interpret communications you receive—or don't receive—you have to know which platforms your friends tend to use and how they use them. Some will answer texts but not emails. Others don't check their phones regularly, so you can't rely on texting to reach them. The proliferation of platforms means more options to exploit but also more opportunities for your messages to be misinterpreted. How quickly does a particular friend usually reply to a text or email? What does the lack of an immediate response mean? So firm is some people's expectation of a quick reply to a text that any lapse carries meaning. A student, telling me about a friend who, in her words, "stopped talking" to her, said, by way of explanation, "She'd text me back two days later." To her, a two-day delay was tantamount to not talking at all. 10

Silence can be a deliberate communication. One woman said of a text she received from a friend, "I was so annoyed, I'm just not responding. I just didn't answer." Yet in other cases, silence doesn't mean anything; it results from circumstances. A young woman thought her boyfriend's delay in responding meant he was angry at her. It turned out his phone battery had run out.

Perceived metamessages of annoyance can snowball, whether or not they were intended. A student recounted in an interview a Facebook message exchange with a friend that, she felt, should have been straightforward but became complicated. She sent a message suggesting they go running later than planned. The friend messaged back, "I guess that's okay. Fine, see you then." That little opener, "I guess," and the unenthusiastic "okay" seemed to imply that she wasn't thrilled with the change of plans. So the student responded, "I'm sorry, I didn't mean to be difficult. I'm more flexible than I made it sound. I can actually just do one o'clock like we planned." That set off a back-and-forth that went four rounds—"No no no let's do the time you wanna do," "No no no let's do the time we said." Hair-tearing exchanges like these are particularly common among girls and women because, as the student pointed out, they often worry about coming across as too demanding and hurting others' feelings.

My student Holly DiClemente explained how her peers make creative use of digital features to avoid hurting friends' feelings. One example is ghost reading—reading a message without opening it, by just reading the preview in the text app, or on your lock screen. If a phone automatically sends "read receipt" notices to let others know their messages have been opened and, presumably, read, ghost reading comes in handy to manage the implied metamessages. If you see from the text notification that a friend is asking if you want to hang out, and you don't want to but you don't want to hurt her feelings, you can open the message later and tell her you're sorry you just got it. The "read receipts" feature can also be used to show you're mad; it lets someone know you've read their message and are intentionally not responding—a visual virtual snub. But there, too, they might think you're mad when you're not. Maybe you saw that the message was long, so you put off replying until you'd have more time to read it, or to write a thoughtful response.

Metamessages—intended or not—can reside in just about any aspect of digital communication, even something as minor and automatic as listing recipients' names when sending email. If you enter the addresses on the "to" or "cc" line, everyone who receives it can see not only who else is getting the message but also what order you put the names in.

Every word we speak is chock-full of metamessages telling others not only how we mean what we say but also who we are.

Two women I interviewed together, Lucy McBride and Annie Finnell, pointed out some of the resulting metamessages: "You feel special when you're the first one on there," Lucy said. Annie agreed: "You do. And you feel not special when you're the last one." Lucy added, "Because if you're dead last, it's like they were thinking, 'Who am I forgetting?'" To avoid offending those whose names come later or last, you can put recipients' email addresses on the "bcc" line. But that sends a metamessage, too. It's what people do when the list of recipients is very long, so "It looks like you're inviting all of Northwest Washington!"

Anytime there are multiple recipients, metamessages can get compli-   15
cated. I was part of a group that used email to confer about a joint project. In one such exchange, a member of our group expressed well wishes to another about a medical condition, after which all the others chimed in, echoing the expressions of concern. I was puzzled. I didn't know whether this flurry of well wishes was related to the ongoing medical challenge I knew this group member had been experiencing, or whether there had been a new and dangerous development I didn't know about. I asked another group member, who said she was not aware of any new developments either, but wanted to express her general support for our ailing friend. I went ahead and sent my own well wishes, cc'ing only the one who first expressed concern. But then I worried that the others would think me callous and uncaring. I rather regretted having foregone the option of allowing—or forcing—everyone to overhear my well wishes.

Every word we speak is chock-full of metamessages telling others not only how we mean what we say but also who we are. It has always been that way; it's the only way language can work to communicate ideas and negotiate relationships. With social media, we have ever more ways to do this—and ever more things to worry about, to make sure the self we're displaying is the one we believe we are—or the one we want to be.

THINKING CRITICALLY ABOUT THE READING

1. What are *metamessages* and why are they so important? How do metamessages function in our communication when we are *not* online, as when we are speaking to another person?

2. What are human beings "always in the business of" (3), according to Tannen?

3. Tannen notes that many people find the act of posting a message to another person on Facebook "insincere" (7) compared to other ways of communicating (e.g., a phone call or a handwritten letter). Why? Do you agree?

4. In paragraph 4, Tannen writes, "Different generations are particularly apt to perceive different metamessages in the same words or actions." Do you think that this is true? For example, do you think people of different ages are more likely to misunderstand each other? Why or why not?

5. What is the main type of specific evidence that Tannen uses in this essay to support her generalizations and assertions? Do you find this approach effective? What are its advantages? What are its possible disadvantages?

LANGUAGE IN ACTION

In paragraphs 7 and 8, Tannen discusses the metamessages communicated by various greetings and closings to emails and other written communications. While they seem like formalities, these openings and closings can convey significant meanings: about the purpose of the message, about the context for the writing, about the relationship of the writer and audience, and other factors. Consider the following greetings and sign-offs. What do they connote? What metamessages do they send? Which ones would you use, and in what circumstances? Which ones would you avoid?

Greetings	*Closings*
Hi,	Thanks,
Hey!	Ciao!
Dear Sir or Madam,	Sincerely,
Dear _____,	Xoxo
WHAT'S UP!?!?!?	Love,
Dearest _____,	Best,
To Whom It May Concern,	Thx

WRITING SUGGESTIONS

1. Tannen writes about the ways in which we misinterpret written communication, especially in the case of "[p]erceived metamessages of annoyance," which can "snowball, whether or not they were intended" (12). Can you think of a time when you misinterpreted a piece of writing (online or offline)

from another person based on its metamessages? Was the problem your mis-reading or the writer's lack of awareness or care in writing? Alternatively, you can write about a time when another person misunderstood *your* writing. What were the causes and consequences?

2. In paragraph 10, Tannen discusses how we "decid[e] which platform to use and how to use it." How do you choose which medium to use to commu-nicate in writing? For what purposes? In what context? To what audience? Consider the following media or "platforms." Then, write a brief essay in which you explain under what circumstances and in what context you would use each form of communication and why.

- a tweet
- an email
- a word-processed letter (hard copy)
- a handwritten letter
- a text message
- a Facebook post

9

LANGUAGE THAT MANIPULATES: POLITICS, ADVERTISING, AND DOUBLESPEAK

Political and advertising language can be deliberately manipulated to mislead, deceive, persuade, or cover up. In the wake of tumultuous events like the 9/11 terrorist attacks, the wars in Iraq and Afghanistan, an ongoing epidemic of school shootings, and the federal investigation into alleged collusion with Russia by President Donald Trump's election campaign—among numerous other scandals—many Americans have grown cynical about their political leaders' promises and programs. As midterm and presidential election campaigns seem to get started earlier and earlier, we are fed a daily diet of political language. Political speech saturates print and electronic media, in an ever-shorter news cycle. Fiery sound bites and seemingly spontaneous one-line zingers are presented as though they contained an entire argument or philosophy. Our politicians are savvy about the time constraints in news and social media, and their speechwriters make sure that every speech has at least a few headline-grabbing quotes that might win them wide, albeit brief, coverage. Advertisers and their ad writers are no different. They use deceptive language to pitch their products to you, whether you need them or not. In the end, we are left wondering what we can believe and who we can trust if our politicians and advertisers don't uphold the promises they make.

In "Language That Manipulates: Politics, Advertising, and Double-speak," we present six essays to help you think critically about the political and advertising language that you hear every day so that you can function as a responsible citizen. In the first essay, "Propaganda: How Not to Be Bamboozled," Donna Woolfolk Cross takes the mystery out of the oft-misunderstood word *propaganda* as she identifies and defines thirteen of the rhetorical devices the propagandist uses to manipulate language for political purposes. Her examples and advice, in turn, will help you to detect those nasty "tricks" and not to be misled by the silver tongues of politicians. In "Selection, Slanting, and Charged Language," Newman and Genevieve Birk give us a crash course on how the language people use subtly shapes perceptions. They introduce us to three simple but powerful concepts—selecting, slanting, and charging—that might change the way you view political speech. In the third essay, "The Case of the Missing Perpetrator," Rebecca Solnit dons her cap as a language detective and closely examines a set of guidelines for drinking alcohol published by the Center for Disease Control in 2016. Her analysis helps us to understand how the Center's use of the passive voice has led to a rash of "mysterious pregnancies" and "disappearing men." In the fourth essay, "Fighting Words," journalist Judith Matloff shows how in the world of war, "words are weapons." She strongly believes that reporters covering conflicts need to be sensitive to manipulative language used by political and military leaders and not fall prey to using such loaded language in their stories.

While "fake news" is not something new, this topic has been in the spotlight since the 2016 US presidential election. In an effort to help us navigate this morass of misinformation, Benjamin Horne explains what fake news is. In "Fake News Starts with the Title," he provides us with several statistically reliable criteria to better differentiate fact from fiction in the daily news. Next, William Lutz examines the world of advertising and challenges the manipulative and deceptive language ad writers use. In "Weasel Words: The Art of Saying Nothing At All," he exposes some of the secret tricks of successful advertising language and what those words and phrases really mean. Finally, in "The Ways of Silencing," Jason Stanley brings the idea of silencing to the forefront. He argues that one of the most insidious and harmful types of propaganda is that which makes counterarguments difficult or impossible to mount. When debate is stifled and trust lost, we are all rendered helpless and faith in our institutions is lost.

Propaganda: How Not to Be Bamboozled

Donna Woolfolk Cross

Donna Woolfolk Cross graduated from the University of Pennsylvania in 1969 and went on to receive her MA from the University of California, Los Angeles. A former professor of English at Onondaga Community College in Syracuse, New York, Cross has written extensively about language that manipulates, including the books *Mediaspeak: How Television Makes Up Your Mind* (1983) and *Word Abuse: How the Words We Use Use Us* (1979), which won an award from the National Council of Teachers of English. She also wrote *Pope Joan: A Novel* (1996). Her early work as a writer of advertising copy influences her teaching and writing. In an interview she remarked, "I was horrified to discover that first-year college students were completely unaware of—and, therefore, unable to defend themselves against—the most obvious ploys of admen and politicians. . . . We tend to think of language as something we use; we are much less often aware of the way we are used by language. The only defense is to become wise to the ways of words." As of this writing, Cross is working on a second novel.

Although most people are against propaganda in principle, few know exactly what it is and how it works. In the following essay, which first appeared in *Speaking of Words: A Language Reader* (1977), Cross takes the mystery out of propaganda. She starts by providing a definition of it, and then she classifies the tricks of the propagandist into thirteen major categories. Cross's essay is chock-full of useful advice on how not to be manipulated by propaganda.

WRITING TO DISCOVER: *What do you think of when you hear the word propaganda? What kinds of people, organizations, or issues do you associate with it? Write about why you think people use propaganda.*

Propaganda. If an opinion poll were taken tomorrow, we can be sure that nearly everyone would be against it because it *sounds* so bad. When we say, "Oh, that's just propaganda," it means, to most people, "That's a pack of lies." But really, propaganda is simply a means of persuasion and so it can be put to work for good causes as well as bad—to persuade people to give to charity, for example, or to love their neighbors, or to stop polluting the environment.

For good or evil, propaganda pervades our daily lives, helping to shape our attitudes on a thousand subjects. Propaganda probably determines the brand of toothpaste you use, the movies you see, the candidates you elect when you get to the polls. Propaganda works by tricking us, by momentarily distracting the eye while the rabbit pops out from beneath the cloth. Propaganda works best with an uncritical audience. Joseph Goebbels, propaganda minister in Nazi Germany, once defined his work as "the conquest of the masses." The masses would not have been conquered, however, if they had known how to challenge and to question, how to make distinctions between propaganda and reasonable argument.

People are bamboozled mainly because they don't recognize propaganda when they see it. They need to be informed about the various devices that can be used to mislead and deceive—about the propagandist's overflowing bag of tricks. The following, then, are some common pitfalls for the unwary.

1. NAME-CALLING

As its title suggests, this device consists of labeling people or ideas with words of bad connotation, literally, "calling them names." Here the propagandist tries to arouse our contempt so we will dismiss the "bad name" person or idea without examining its merits.

Bad names have played a tremendously important role in the history   5
of the world. They have ruined reputations and ended lives, sent people to prison and to war, and just generally made us mad at each other for centuries.

Name-calling can be used against policies, practices, beliefs and ideals, as well as against individuals, groups, races, nations. Name-calling is at work when we hear a candidate for office described as a "foolish idealist" or a "two-faced liar" or when an incumbent's policies are denounced as "reckless," "reactionary," or just plain "stupid." Some of the most effective names a public figure can be called are ones that may not denote anything specific: "Congresswoman Jane Doe is a *bleeding heart*!" (Did she vote for funds to help paraplegics?) or "The senator is a *tool of Washington*!" (Did he happen to agree with the president?) Senator Yakalot uses name-calling when he denounces his opponent's "radical policies" and calls them (and him) "socialist," "pinko," and part of a "heartless plot." He also uses it when he calls cars "puddle-jumpers," "can openers," and "motorized baby buggies."

For good or evil, propaganda pervades our daily lives, helping to shape our attitudes on a thousand subjects.

The point here is that when the propagandist uses name-calling, he doesn't want us to think—merely to react, blindly, unquestioningly. So the best defense against being taken in by name-calling is to stop and ask, "Forgetting the bad name attached to it, what are the merits of the idea itself? What does this name really mean, anyway?"

2. GLITTERING GENERALITIES

Glittering generalities are really name-calling in reverse. Name-calling uses words with bad connotations; glittering generalities are words with good connotations—"virtue words," as the Institute for Propaganda

Analysis has called them. The Institute explains that while name-calling tries to get us to *reject* and *condemn* someone or something without examining the evidence, glittering generalities try to get us to *accept* and *agree* without examining the evidence.

We believe in, fight for, live by "virtue words" which we feel deeply about: "justice," "motherhood," "the American way," "our Constitutional rights," "our Christian heritage." These sound good, but when we examine them closely, they turn out to have no specific, definable meaning. They just make us feel good. Senator Yakalot uses glittering generalities when he says, "I stand for all that is good in America, for our American way and our American birthright." But what exactly *is* "good for America"? How can we define our "American birthright"? Just what parts of the American society and culture does "our American way" refer to?

We often make the mistake of assuming we are personally unaffected   10
by glittering generalities. The next time you find yourself assuming that, listen to a political candidate's speech on TV and see how often the use of glittering generalities elicits cheers and applause. That's the danger of propaganda; it *works*. Once again, our defense against it is to ask questions: Forgetting the virtue words attached to it, what are the merits of the idea itself? What does "Americanism" (or "freedom" or "truth") really *mean* here? . . .

Both name-calling and glittering generalities work by stirring our emotions in the hope that this will cloud our thinking. Another approach that propaganda uses is to create a distraction, a "red herring," that will make people forget or ignore the real issues. There are several different kinds of "red herrings" that can be used to distract attention.

3. PLAIN-FOLKS APPEAL

"Plain folks" is the device by which a speaker tries to win our confidence and support by appearing to be a person like ourselves — "just one of the plain folks." The plain-folks appeal is at work when candidates go around shaking hands with factory workers, kissing babies in supermarkets, and sampling pasta with Italians, fried chicken with Southerners, bagels and blintzes with Jews. "Now I'm a businessman like yourselves" is a plain-folks appeal, as is "I've been a farm boy all my life." Senator Yakalot tries the plain-folks appeal when he says, "I'm just a small-town boy like you fine people." The use of such expressions once prompted Lyndon Johnson to quip, "Whenever I hear someone say, 'I'm just an old country lawyer,' the first thing I reach for is my wallet to make sure it's still there."

The irrelevancy of the plain-folks appeal is obvious: even if the man *is* "one of us" (which may not be true at all), that doesn't mean that his ideas and programs are sound — or even that he honestly has our best interests at heart. As with glittering generalities, the danger here is that we may mistakenly assume we are immune to this appeal. But propagandists wouldn't use it unless it had been proved to work. You can protect yourself by asking, "Aside from his 'nice guy next door' image, what does this man stand for? Are his ideas and his past record really supportive of my best interests?"

4. ARGUMENTUM AD POPULUM (STROKING)

Argumentum ad populum means "argument to the people" or "telling the people what they want to hear." The colloquial term from the Watergate era is "stroking," which conjures up pictures of small animals or children being stroked or soothed with compliments until they come to like the person doing the complimenting—and, by extension, his or her ideas.

We all like to hear nice things about ourselves and the group we   15
belong to—we like to be liked—so it stands to reason that we will respond warmly to a person who tells us we are "hard-working taxpayers" or "the most generous, free-spirited nation in the world." Politicians tell farmers they are the "backbone of the American economy" and college students that they are the "leaders and policy makers of tomorrow." Commercial advertisers use stroking more insidiously by asking a question which invites a flattering answer: "What kind of a man reads *Playboy?*" (Does he really drive a Porsche and own $10,000 worth of sound equipment?) Senator Yakalot is stroking his audience when he calls them the "decent law-abiding citizens that are the great pulsing heart and the life blood of this, our beloved country," and when he repeatedly refers to them as "you fine people," "you wonderful folks."

Obviously, the intent here is to sidetrack us from thinking critically about the man and his ideas. Our own good qualities have nothing to do with the issue at hand. Ask yourself, "Apart from the nice things he has to say about me (and my church, my nation, my ethnic group, my neighbors), what does the candidate stand for? Are his or her ideas in my best interests?"

5. ARGUMENTUM AD HOMINEM

Argumentum ad hominem means "argument to the man" and that's exactly what it is. When a propagandist uses *argumentum ad hominem*, he wants to distract our attention from the issue under consideration with personal attacks on the people involved. For example, when Lincoln issued the Emancipation Proclamation, some people responded by calling him the "baboon." But Lincoln's long arms and awkward carriage had nothing to do with the merits of the Proclamation or the question of whether or not slavery should be abolished.

Today *argumentum ad hominem* is still widely used and very effective. You may or may not support the Equal Rights Amendment, but you should be sure your judgment is based on the merits of the idea itself, and not the result of someone's denunciation of the people who support the ERA as "fanatics" or "lesbians" or "frustrated old maids." Senator Yakalot is using *argumentum ad hominem* when he dismisses the idea of using smaller automobiles with a reference to the personal appearance of one of its supporters, Congresswoman Doris Schlepp. Refuse to be waylaid by *argumentum ad hominem* and ask, "Do the personal qualities of the person being discussed have anything to do with the issue at hand? Leaving him or her aside, how good is the idea itself?"

6. TRANSFER (GUILT OR GLORY BY ASSOCIATION)

In *argumentum ad hominem,* an attempt is made to associate negative aspects of a person's character or personal appearance with an issue or idea he supports. The transfer device uses this same process of association to make us accept or condemn a given person or idea.

A better name for the transfer device is guilt (or glory) by association.   20
In glory by association, the propagandist tries to transfer the positive feelings of something we love and respect to the group or idea he wants us to accept. "This bill for a new dam is in the best tradition of this country, the land of Lincoln, Jefferson, and Washington," is glory by association at work. Lincoln, Jefferson, and Washington were great leaders that most of us revere and respect, but they have no logical connection to the proposal under consideration—the bill to build a new dam. Senator Yakalot uses glory by association when he says full-sized cars "have always been as American as Mom's apple pie or a Sunday drive in the country."

The process works equally well in reverse, when guilt by association is used to transfer our dislike or disapproval of one idea or group to some other idea or group that the propagandist wants us to reject and condemn. "John Doe says we need to make some changes in the way our government operates; well, that's exactly what the Ku Klux Klan has said, so there's a meeting of great minds!" That's guilt by association for you; there's no logical connection between John Doe and the Ku Klux Klan apart from the one the propagandist is trying to create in our minds. He wants to distract our attention from John Doe and get us thinking (and worrying) about the Ku Klux Klan and its politics of violence. (Of course, there are sometimes legitimate associations between the two things; if John Doe had been a *member* of the Ku Klux Klan, it would be reasonable and fair to draw a connection between the man and his group.) Senator Yakalot tries to trick his audience with guilt by association when he remarks that "the words 'community' and 'communism' look an awful lot alike!" He does it again when he mentions that Mr. Stu Pott "sports a Fidel Castro beard."

How can we learn to spot the transfer device and distinguish between fair and unfair associations? We can teach ourselves to *suspend judgment* until we have answered these questions: "Is there any legitimate connection between the idea under discussion and the thing it is associated with? Leaving the transfer device out of the picture, what are the merits of the idea by itself?"

7. BANDWAGON

Ever hear of the small, ratlike animal called the lemming? Lemmings are arctic rodents with a very odd habit: periodically, for reasons no one entirely knows, they mass together in a large herd and commit suicide by rushing into deep water and drowning themselves. They all run in together, blindly, and not one of them ever seems to stop and ask, "*Why* am I doing this? Is this really what I want to do?" and thus save itself from destruction. Obviously, lemmings are driven to perform their strange mass suicide rites by common instinct. People choose to "follow the herd" for more complex reasons, yet we are still all too often the unwitting victims of the bandwagon appeal.

Essentially, the bandwagon urges us to support an action or an opinion because it is popular — because "everyone else is doing it." This call to "get on the bandwagon" appeals to the strong desire in most of us to be one of the crowd, not to be left out or alone. Advertising makes extensive use of the bandwagon appeal ("join the Pepsi people"), but so do politicians ("Let us join together in this great cause"). Senator Yakalot uses the bandwagon appeal when he says that "More and more citizens are rallying to my cause every day," and asks his audience to "join them — and me — in our fight for America."

One of the ways we can see the bandwagon appeal at work is in the overwhelming success of various fashions and trends which capture the interest (and the money) of thousands of people for a short time, then disappear suddenly and completely. For a year or two in the fifties, every child in North America wanted a coonskin cap so they could be like Davy Crockett; no one wanted to be left out. After that there was the hula-hoop craze that helped to dislocate the hips of thousands of Americans. [In the 1970s], what made millions of people rush out to buy their very own "pet rocks"? 25

The problem here is obvious: just because everyone's doing it doesn't mean that *we* should too. Group approval does not prove that something is true or is worth doing. Large numbers of people have supported actions we now condemn. [Within the last century], Hitler and Mussolini rose to absolute and catastrophically repressive rule in two of the most sophisticated and cultured countries of Europe. When they came into power they were welled up by massive popular support from millions of people who didn't want to be "left out" at a great historical moment.

Once the mass begins to move—on the bandwagon—it becomes harder and harder to perceive the leader *riding* the bandwagon. So don't be a lemming, rushing blindly on to destruction because "everyone else is doing it." Stop and ask, "Where is this bandwagon headed? Never mind about everybody else, is this what is best for *me*?" . . .

As we have seen, propaganda can appeal to us by arousing our emotions or distracting our attention from the real issues at hand. But there's a third way that propaganda can be put to work against us—by the use of faulty logic. This approach is really more insidious than the others because it gives the appearance of reasonable, fair argument. It is only when we look more closely that the holes in the logical fiber show up. The following are some of the devices that make use of faulty logic to distort and mislead.

8. FAULTY CAUSE AND EFFECT

As the name suggests, this device sets up a cause-and-effect relationship that may not be true. The Latin name for this logical fallacy is *post hoc ergo propter hoc,* which means "after this, therefore because of this." But just because one thing happened after another doesn't mean that one *caused* the other.

An example of false cause-and-effect reasoning is offered by the story 30 (probably invented) of the woman aboard the ship *Titanic.* She woke up from a nap and, feeling seasick, looked around for a call button to summon the steward to bring her some medication. She finally located a small button on one of the walls of her cabin and pushed it. A split second later, the *Titanic* grazed an iceberg in the terrible crash that was to send the entire ship to its destruction. The woman screamed and said, "Oh, God, what have I done? What have I done?" The humor of that anecdote comes from the absurdity of the woman's assumption that pushing the small red button resulted in the destruction of a ship weighing several hundred tons: "It happened after I pushed it, therefore it must be *because* I pushed it"—*post hoc ergo propter hoc* reasoning. There is, of course, no cause-and-effect relationship there.

The false cause-and-effect fallacy is used very often by political candidates. "After I came to office, the rate of inflation dropped to 6 percent." But did the person do anything to cause the lower rate of inflation or was it the result of other conditions? Would the rate of inflation have dropped anyway, even if he hadn't come to office? Senator Yakalot uses false cause and effect when he says "our forefathers who made this country great never had free hot meal handouts! And look what they did for our country!" He does it again when he concludes that "driving full-sized cars means a better car safety record on our American roads today."

False cause-and-effect reasoning is terribly persuasive because it seems so logical. Its appeal is apparently to experience. We swallowed X product—and the headache went away. We elected Y official and unemployment went down. Many people think, "There *must* be a connection." But causality is an immensely complex phenomenon; you need a good deal of evidence to prove that an event that follows another in time was "therefore" caused by the first event.

Don't be taken in by false cause and effect; be sure to ask, "Is there enough evidence to prove that this cause led to that effect? Could there have been any *other* causes?"

9. FALSE ANALOGY

An analogy is a comparison between two ideas, events, or things. But comparisons can be fairly made only when the things being compared are alike in significant ways. When they are not, false analogy is the result.

A famous example of this is the old proverb "Don't change horses in 35 the middle of a stream," often used as an analogy to convince voters not to change administrations in the middle of a war or other crisis. But the analogy is misleading because there are so many differences between the things compared. In what ways is a war or political crisis like a stream? Is the president or head of state really very much like a horse? And is a nation of millions of people comparable to a man trying to get across a stream? Analogy is false and unfair when it compares two things that have little in common and assumes that they are identical. Senator Yakalot tries to hoodwink his listeners with false analogy when he says, "Trying to take Americans out of the kind of cars they love is as undemocratic as trying to deprive them of the right to vote."

Of course, analogies can be drawn that are reasonable and fair. It would be reasonable, for example, to compare the results of busing in one small Southern city with the possible results in another, *if* the towns have the same kind of history, population, and school policy. We can decide for ourselves whether an analogy is false or fair by asking, "Are the things being compared truly alike in significant ways? Do the differences between them affect the comparison?"

10. BEGGING THE QUESTION

Actually, the name of this device is rather misleading, because it does not appear in the form of a question. Begging the question occurs when, in discussing a questionable or debatable point, a person assumes as already established the very point that he is trying to prove. For example,

"No thinking citizen could approve such a completely unacceptable policy as this one." But isn't the question of whether or not the policy *is* acceptable the very point to be established? Senator Yakalot begs the question when he announces that his opponent's plan won't work "because it is unworkable."

We can protect ourselves against this kind of faulty logic by asking, "What is assumed in this statement? Is the assumption reasonable, or does it need more proof?"

11. THE TWO-EXTREMES FALLACY (FALSE DILEMMA)

Linguists have long noted that the English language tends to view reality in sets of two extremes or polar opposites. In English, things are either black or white, tall or short, up or down, front or back, left or right, good or bad, guilty or not guilty. We can ask for a "straightforward yes-or-no answer" to a question, the understanding being that we will not accept or consider anything in between. In fact, reality cannot always be dissected along such strict lines. There may be (usually are) *more* than just two possibilities or extremes to consider. We are often told to "listen to both sides of the argument." But who's to say that every argument has only two sides? Can't there be a third—even a fourth or fifth—point of view?

The two-extremes fallacy is at work in this statement by Lenin, 40 the great Marxist leader: "You cannot eliminate *one* basic assumption, one substantial part of this philosophy of Marxism (it is as if it were a block of steel), without abandoning truth, without falling into the arms of bourgeois-reactionary falsehood." In other words, if we don't agree 100 percent with every premise of Marxism, we must be placed at the opposite end of the political-economic spectrum—for Lenin, "bourgeois-reactionary falsehood." If we are not entirely *with* him, we must be against him; those are the only two possibilities open to us. Of course, this is a logical fallacy; in real life there are any number of political positions one can maintain *between* the two extremes of Marxism and capitalism. Senator Yakalot uses the two-extremes fallacy in the same way as Lenin when he tells his audience that "in this world a man's either for private enterprise or he's for socialism."

One of the most famous examples of the two-extremes fallacy in recent history is the slogan, "America: Love it or leave it," with its implicit suggestion that we either accept everything just as it is in America today without complaint—or get out. Again, it should be obvious that there is a whole range of action and belief between those two extremes.

Don't be duped; stop and ask, "Are those really the only two options I can choose from? Are there other alternatives not mentioned that deserve consideration?"

12. CARD STACKING

Some questions are so multifaceted and complex that no one can make an intelligent decision about them without considering a wide variety of evidence. One selection of facts could make us feel one way and another selection could make us feel just the opposite. Card stacking is a device of propaganda which selects only the facts that support the propagandist's point of view, and ignores all the others. For example, a candidate could be made to look like a legislative dynamo if you say, "Representative McNerd introduced more new bills than any other member of the Congress," and neglect to mention that most of them were so preposterous that they were laughed off the floor.

Senator Yakalot engages in card stacking when he talks about the proposal to use smaller cars. He talks only about jobs without mentioning the cost to the taxpayers or the very real—though still denied—threat of depletion of resources. He says he wants to help his countrymen keep their jobs, but doesn't mention that the corporations that offer the jobs will also make large profits. He praises the "American chrome industry," overlooking the fact that most chrome is imported. And so on.

The best protection against card stacking is to take the "Yes, but . . ."   45
attitude. This device of propaganda is not untrue, but then again it is not the *whole* truth. So ask yourself, "Is this person leaving something out that I should know about? Is there some other information that should be brought to bear on this question?" . . .

So far, we have considered approaches that the propagandist can use to influence our thinking: appealing to our emotions, distracting our attention, and misleading us with logic that may appear to be reasonable but is in fact faulty and deceiving. But there is another approach that is probably the most common propaganda trick of them all.

13. TESTIMONIAL

The testimonial device consists in having some loved or respected person give a statement of support (testimonial) for a given product or idea. The problem is that the person being quoted may *not* be an expert in the field; in fact, he may know nothing at all about it. Using the name of a man who is skilled and famous in one field to give a testimonial for something in another field is unfair and unreasonable.

Senator Yakalot tries to mislead his audience with testimonial when he tells them that "full-sized cars have been praised by great Americans like John Wayne and Jack Jones, as well as by leading experts on car safety and comfort."

Testimonial is used extensively in TV ads, where it often appears in such bizarre forms as Joe Namath's endorsement of a pantyhose brand.

Here, of course, the "authority" giving the testimonial not only is no expert about pantyhose, but obviously stands to gain something (money!) by making the testimonial.

When celebrities endorse a political candidate, they may not be making 50 money by doing so, but we should still question whether they are in any better position to judge than we ourselves. Too often we are willing to let others we like or respect make our decisions *for us,* while we follow along acquiescently. And this is the purpose of testimonial — to get us to agree and accept *without* stopping to think. Be sure to ask, "Is there any reason to believe that this person (or organization or publication or whatever) has any more knowledge or information than I do on this subject? What does the idea amount to on its own merits, without the benefit of testimonial?"

The cornerstone of democratic society is reliance upon an informed and educated electorate. To be fully effective citizens we need to be able to challenge and to question wisely. A dangerous feeling of indifference toward our political processes exists today. We often abandon our right, our duty, to criticize and evaluate by dismissing *all* politicians as "crooked," *all* new bills and proposals as "just more government bureaucracy." But there are important distinctions to be made, and this kind of apathy can be fatal to democracy.

If we are to be led, let us not be led blindly, but critically, intelligently, with our eyes open. If we are to continue to be a government "by the people," let us become informed about the methods and purposes of propaganda, so we can be the masters, not the slaves of our destiny.

THINKING CRITICALLY ABOUT THE READING

1. According to Cross, what is propaganda? Who uses propaganda? Why is it used? (Glossary: *Propaganda*)

2. Why does Cross believe that it is necessary for people in a democratic society to become informed about the methods and practices of propaganda? What is her advice for dealing with propaganda?

3. What is a "red herring," and why do people use this technique? What is "begging the question"? (Glossary: *Logical Fallacies*)

4. What, according to Cross, is the most common propaganda trick? Provide some examples of it from your own experience.

5. How does Cross use examples in her essay? (Glossary: *Examples*) What do you think of the examples from Senator Yakalot? What, if anything, does this hypothetical senator add to the essay? Which other examples do you find most effective? Least effective? Explain why.

6. In her discussion of the bandwagon appeal (23–28), Cross uses the analogy of the lemmings. How does the analogy work? Why is it not a false analogy? (Glossary: *Analogy*) How do analogies help you, as a writer, explain your subject to readers?

LANGUAGE IN ACTION

At the beginning of her essay, Cross claims that propaganda "can be put to work for good causes as well as bad." Consider the following advertisements for the U.S. Postal Service's breast-cancer-stamp campaign and for the University of Vermont's Direct Service Programs. How would you characterize the appeal of each? What propaganda techniques does each use? Do you ever find appeals such as these objectionable? Why or why not? In what situations do you think it would be acceptable for you to use propaganda devices in your own writing?

Women Helping Battered Women

Summer or Fall Semester

Internships

Join the fight against domestic violence! You will work in a friendly, supportive environment. You will do challenging work for a worthwhile cause. You will have lots of learning opportunities. We need reliable people who are committed to social justice. You will need good communication skills, an open mind, and the ability to work somewhat independently.

We are now accepting applications.

Internships will be offered in the following programs:

Shelter Services
Hotline Program
Children's Shelter Services
Children's Playgroup Program
Development and Fundraising

Work Study Positions available in all the above programs as well as in the financial and administrative programs.

All interns in Direct Service Programs have to complete the full Volunteer Training. The next trainings will be in May and September. Call now for more information: 658-3131.

WRITING SUGGESTIONS

1. Cross acknowledges in paragraph 1 that propaganda is "simply a means of persuasion," but she quickly cautions that people need to recognize propaganda and be alert to its potential to mislead or deceive. Write an essay for your campus newspaper arguing for a "short course" on propaganda recognition at your school. You might want to consider the following questions in your essay: How do propaganda and argumentation differ? Do both always have the same intended effect? What could happen to people who don't recognize or understand propaganda when they encounter it?

2. Using Cross's list of propaganda devices, write an essay analyzing several newspaper editorials, political speeches, public-service advertising campaigns, or comparable examples of contemporary prose. What did you learn about the people or organizations as a result of your analysis? How were their positions on issues or their purposes expressed? Which propaganda devices did they use? After reading Cross's essay, did you find yourself "buying" the propaganda or recognizing and questioning it? Submit the original editorials, speeches, or advertisements with your essay.

Selection, Slanting, and Charged Language

Newman P. Birk and Genevieve B. Birk

The more we learn about language and how it works, the more abundantly clear it becomes that our language shapes our perceptions of the world. Because most people have eyes to see, ears to hear, noses to smell, tongues to taste, and skin to feel, it seems as though our perceptions of reality should be pretty similar. We know, however, that this is not the case, and language, it seems, makes a big difference in how we perceive our world. In effect, language acts as a filter, heightening certain perceptions, dimming others, and totally voiding still others.

In the following selection from their book *Understanding and Using Language* (1972), Newman and Genevieve Birk discuss how we use words, especially the tremendous powers that slanted and charged language wields. As a writer, you will be particularly interested to learn just how important your choice of words is. After reading what the Birks have to say, you'll never read another editorial, watch another commercial, or listen to another politician in quite the same way.

WRITING TO DISCOVER: *Choose three different people and write a description of a person, an object, or an event from each of their perspectives. Consider how each would relate to the subject you chose, what details each would focus on, and the attitude each would have toward that subject.*

A. THE PRINCIPLE OF SELECTION

Before it is expressed in words, our knowledge, both inside and outside, is influenced by the principle of selection. What we know or observe depends on what we notice; that is, what we select, consciously or unconsciously, as worthy of notice or attention. As we observe, the principle of selection determines which facts we take in.

Suppose, for example, that three people, a lumberjack, an artist, and a tree surgeon, are examining a large tree in the forest. Since the tree itself is a complicated object, the number of particulars or facts about it that one could observe would be very great indeed. Which of these facts a particular observer will notice will be a matter of selection, a selection that is determined by his interests and purposes. A lumberjack might be interested in the best way to cut the tree down, cut it up and transport it to the lumber mill. His interest would then determine his principle of selection in observing and thinking about the tree. The artist might consider painting a picture of the tree, and his purpose would furnish his principle of selection. The tree surgeon's professional interest in the physical health of the tree might establish a principle of selection for him. If each man were now required to write an exhaustive, detailed report on everything he observed about the tree, the

285

facts supplied by each would differ, for each would report those facts that his particular principle of selection led him to notice.[1]

The principle of selection holds not only for the specific facts that people observe but also for the facts they remember. A student suddenly embarrassed may remember nothing of the next ten minutes of class discussion but may have a vivid recollection of the sensation of the blood mounting, as he blushed, up his face and into his ears. In both noticing and remembering, the principle of selection applies, and it is influenced not only by our special interest and point of view but by our whole mental state of the moment.

The principle of selection then serves as a kind of sieve or screen through which our knowledge passes before it becomes our knowledge. Since we can't notice everything about a complicated object or situation or action or state of our own consciousness, what we do notice is determined by whatever principle of selection is operating for us at the time we gain the knowledge.

It is important to remember that what is true of the way the principle   5
of selection works for us is true also for the way it works for others. Even before we or other people put knowledge into words to express meaning, that knowledge has been screened or selected. Before an historian or an economist writes a book, or before a reporter writes a news article, the facts that each is to present have been sifted through the screen of a principle of selection. Before one person passes on knowledge to another, that knowledge has already been selected and shaped, intentionally or unintentionally, by the mind of the communicator.

B. THE PRINCIPLE OF SLANTING

When we put our knowledge into words, a second process of selection, the process of slanting, takes place. Just as there is something, a rather mysterious principle of selection, which chooses for us what we will notice, and what will then become our knowledge, there is also a principle which operates, with or without our awareness, to select certain facts and feelings from our store of knowledge, and to choose the words and emphasis that we shall use to communicate our meaning.[2] Slanting may be defined as the process of selecting (1) knowledge—factual and attitudinal; (2) words; and (3) emphasis, to achieve the intention of the

---

1. Of course, all three observers would probably report a good many facts in common—the height of the tree, for example, and the size of the trunk. The point we wish to make is that each observer would give us a different impression of the tree because of the different principle of selection that guided his observation.

2. Notice that the "principle of selection" is at work as *we take in* knowledge, and that slanting occurs *as we express* our knowledge in words.

communicator. Slanting is present in some degree in all communication: one may *slant for* (favorable slanting), *slant against* (unfavorable slanting), or *slant both ways* (balanced slanting). . . .

C. SLANTING BY USE OF EMPHASIS

Slanting by use of the devices of emphasis is unavoidable,[3] for emphasis is simply the giving of stress to subject matter, and so indicating what is important and what is less important. In speech, for example, if we say that Socrates was *a wise old man,* we can give several slightly different meanings, one by stressing *wise,* another by stressing *old,* another by giving equal stress to *wise* and *old,* and still another by giving chief stress to *man.* Each different stress gives a different slant (favorable or unfavorable or balanced) to the statement because it conveys a different attitude toward Socrates or a different judgment of him. Connectives and word order also slant by the emphasis they give: consider the difference in slanting or emphasis produced by *old but wise, old and wise, wise but old.* In writing, we cannot indicate subtle stresses on words as clearly as in speech, but we can achieve our emphasis and so can slant by the use of more complex patterns of word order, by choice of connectives, by underlining heavily stressed words, and by marks of punctuation that indicate short or long pauses and so give light or heavy emphasis. Question marks, quotation marks, and exclamation points can also contribute to slanting.[4] It is impossible either in speech or in writing to put two facts together without giving some slight emphasis or slant. For example, if we have in mind only two facts about a man, his awkwardness and his strength, we subtly slant those facts favorably or unfavorably in whatever way we may choose to join them.

More Favorable Slanting	*Less Favorable Slanting*
He is awkward and strong.	He is strong and awkward.
He is awkward but strong.	He is strong but awkward.
Although he is somewhat awkward, he is very strong.	He may be strong, but he's very awkward.

With more facts and in longer passages it is possible to maintain a delicate balance by alternating favorable emphasis and so producing a balanced effect.

---

3. When emphasis is present—and we can think of no instance in the use of language in which it is not—it necessarily influences the meaning by playing a part in the favorable, unfavorable, or balanced slant of the communicator. We are likely to emphasize by voice stress, even when we answer *yes* or *no* to simple questions.

4. Consider the slanting achieved by punctuation in the following sentences: He called the Senator an honest man? *He* called the Senator an honest man? He called the Senator an honest man! He said one more such "honest" senator would corrupt the state.

All communication, then, is in some degree slanted by the *emphasis* of the communicator.

D. SLANTING BY SELECTION OF FACTS

To illustrate the technique of slanting by selection of facts, we shall examine three passages of informative writing which achieve different effects simply by the selection and emphasis of material. Each passage is made up of true statements or facts about a dog, yet the reader is given three different impressions. The first passage is an example of objective writing or balanced slanting, the second is slanted unfavorably, and the third is slanted favorably.

1. Balanced Presentation

Our dog, Toddy, sold to us as a cocker, produces various reactions in various people. Those who come to the back door she usually growls and barks at (a milkman has said that he is afraid of her); those who come to the front door, she whines at and paws; also she tries to lick people's faces unless we have forestalled her by putting a newspaper in her mouth. (Some of our friends encourage these actions; others discourage them. Mrs. Firmly, one friend, slaps the dog with a newspaper and says, "I know how hard dogs are to train.") Toddy knows and responds to a number of words and phrases, and guests sometimes remark that she is a "very intelligent dog." She has fleas in the summer, and she sheds, at times copiously, the year round. Her blonde hairs are conspicuous when they are on people's clothing or on rugs or furniture. Her color and her large brown eyes frequently produce favorable comment. An expert on cockers would say that her ears are too short and set too high and that she is at least six pounds too heavy.

The passage above is made up of facts, verifiable facts,[5] deliberately 10 selected and emphasized to produce a *balanced* impression. Of course not all the facts about the dog have been given — to supply *all* the facts on any subject, even such a comparatively simple one, would be an almost impossible task. Both favorable and unfavorable facts are used, however, and an effort has been made to alternate favorable and unfavorable details so that neither will receive greater emphasis by position, proportion, or grammatical structure.

---

5. *Verifiable facts* are facts that can be checked and agreed upon and proved to be true by people who wish to verify them. That a particular theme received a failing grade is a verifiable fact; one needs merely to see the theme with the grade on it. That the instructor should have failed the theme is not, strictly speaking, a verifiable fact, but a matter of opinion. That women on the average live longer than men is a verifiable fact; that they live better is a matter of opinion, *a value judgment.*

2. Facts Slanted Against

That dog put her paws on my white dress as soon as I came in the door, and she made so much noise that it was two minutes before she had quieted down enough for us to talk and hear each other. Then the gas man came and she did a great deal of barking. And her hairs are on the rug and on the furniture. If you wear a dark dress they stick to it like lint. When Mrs. Firmly came in, she actually hit the dog with a newspaper to make it stay down, and she made some remark about training dogs. I wish the Birks would take the hint or get rid of that noisy, short-eared, overweight "cocker" of theirs.

This unfavorably slanted version is based on the same facts, but now these facts have been selected and given a new emphasis. The speaker, using her selected facts to give her impression of the dog, is quite possibly unaware of her negative slanting.

Now for a favorably slanted version:

3. Facts Slanted For

What a lively and responsible dog! When I walked in the door, there she was with a newspaper in her mouth, whining and standing on her hind legs and wagging her tail all at the same time. And what an intelligent dog. If you suggest going for a walk, she will get her collar from the kitchen and hand it to you, and she brings Mrs. Birk's slippers whenever Mrs. Birk says she is "tired" or mentions slippers. At a command she catches balls, rolls over, "speaks," or stands on her hind feet and twirls around. She sits up and balances a piece of bread on her nose until she is told to take it; then she tosses it up and catches it. If you are eating something, she sits up in front of you and "begs" with those big dark brown eyes set in that light, buff-colored face of hers. When I got up to go and told her I was leaving, she rolled her eyes at me and sat up like a squirrel. She certainly is a lively and intelligent dog.

Speaker 3, like Speaker 2, is selecting from the "facts" summarized in balanced version 1, and is emphasizing his facts to communicate his impression.

All three passages are examples of *reporting* (i.e., consist only of verifiable facts), yet they give three very different impressions of the same dog because of the different ways the speakers slanted the facts. Some people say that figures don't lie, and many people believe that if they have the "facts," they have the "truth." Yet if we carefully examine the ways of thought and language, we see that any knowledge that comes to us through words has been subjected to the double screening of the principle of selection and the slanting of language. . . .

Wise listeners and readers realize that the double screening that is 15 produced by the principle of selection and by slanting takes place even when people honestly try to report the facts as they know them. (Speakers 2 and 3, for instance, probably thought of themselves as simply giving information about a dog and were not deliberately trying to mislead.) Wise listeners and readers know too that deliberate manipulators of language, by mere selection and emphasis, can make their slanted facts appear to support almost any cause.

In arriving at opinions and values we cannot always be sure that the facts that sift into our minds through language are representative and relevant and true. We need to remember that much of our information about politics, governmental activities, business conditions, and foreign affairs comes to us selected and slanted. More than we realize, our opinions on these matters may depend on what newspaper we read or what news commentator we listen to.

Without charged language, life would be but half life.

Worthwhile opinions call for knowledge of reliable facts and reasonable arguments for and against—and such opinions include beliefs about morality and truth and religion as well as about public affairs. Because complex subjects involve knowing and dealing with many facts on both sides, reliable judgments are at best difficult to arrive at. If we want to be fairminded, we must be willing to subject our opinions to continual testing by new knowledge, and must realize that after all they *are* opinions, more or less trustworthy. Their trustworthiness will depend on the representativeness of our facts, on the quality of our reasoning, and on the standard of values that we choose to apply.

We shall not give here a passage illustrating the unscrupulous slanting of facts. Such a passage would also include irrelevant facts and false statements presented as facts, along with various subtle distortions of fact. Yet to the uninformed reader the passage would be indistinguishable from a passage intended to give a fair account. If two passages (2 and 3) of casual and unintentional slanting of facts about a dog can give such contradictory impressions of a simple subject, the reader can imagine what a skilled and designing manipulation of facts and statistics could do to mislead an uninformed reader about a really complex subject. An example of such manipulation might be the account of the United States that Soviet propaganda has supplied to the average Russian. Such propaganda, however, would go beyond the mere slanting of the facts: it would clothe the selected facts in charged words and would make use of the many other devices of slanting that appear in charged language.

E. SLANTING BY USE OF CHARGED WORDS

In the passages describing the dog Toddy, we were illustrating the technique of slanting by the selection and emphasis of facts. Though the facts selected had to be expressed in words, the words chosen were as factual as possible, and it was the selection and emphasis of facts and not of words that was mainly responsible for the two distinctly different impressions of the dog. In the passages below we are demonstrating another way of slanting—by the use of charged words. This time the accounts are very similar in the facts they contain; the different impressions of the subject, Corlyn, are produced not by different facts but by the subtle selection of charged words.

The passages were written by a clever student who was told to choose as his subject a person in action, and to write two descriptions, each using the "same facts." The instructions required that one description be slanted positively and the other negatively, so that the first would make the reader favorably inclined toward the person and the action, and the second would make him unfavorably inclined.

Here is the favorably charged description. Read it carefully and   20 form your opinion of the person before you go on to read the second description.

Corlyn

Corlyn paused at the entrance to the room and glanced about. A well-cut black dress draped subtly about her slender form. Her long blonde hair gave her chiseled features the simple frame they required. She smiled an engaging smile as she accepted a cigarette from her escort. As he lit it for her she looked over the flame and into his eyes. Corlyn had that rare talent of making every male feel that he was the only man in the world.

She took his arm and they descended the steps into the room. She walked with an effortless grace and spoke with equal ease. They each took a cup of coffee and joined a group of friends near the fire. The flickering light danced across her face and lent an ethereal quality to her beauty. The good conversation, the crackling logs, and the stimulating coffee gave her a feeling of internal warmth. Her eyes danced with each leap of the flames.

Taken by itself this passage might seem just a description of an attractive girl. The favorable slanting by use of charged words has been done so skillfully that it is inconspicuous. Now we turn to the unfavorable slanted description of the "same" girl in the "same" actions:

Corlyn

Corlyn halted at the entrance to the room and looked around. A plain black dress hung on her thin frame. Her stringy bleached hair accentuated her harsh features. She smiled an inane smile as she took a cigarette from her escort. As he lit it for her she stared over the lighter and into his eyes. Corlyn had a habit of making every male feel that he was the last man on earth.

She grasped his arm and they walked down the steps and into the room. Her pace was fast and ungainly, as was her speed. They each reached for some coffee and broke into a group of acquaintances near the fire. The flickering light played across her face and revealed every flaw. The loud talk, the fire, and the coffee she had gulped down made her feel hot. Her eyes grew more red with each leap of the flames.

When the reader compares these two descriptions, he can see how charged words influence the reader's attitude. One needs to read the two descriptions several times to appreciate all the subtle differences between them. Words, some rather heavily charged, others innocent-looking but lightly charged, work together to carry to the reader a judgment of a person and a situation. If the reader had seen only the first description of Corlyn, he might well have thought that he had formed his "own judgment on the basis of the facts." And the examples just given only begin to suggest the techniques that may be used in heavily charged language. For one thing, the two descriptions of Corlyn contain no really good example of the use of charged abstractions; for another, the writer was obliged by the assignment to use the same set of facts and so could not slant by selecting his material.

F. SLANTING AND CHARGED LANGUAGE

. . . When slanting of facts, or words, or emphasis, or any combination of the three *significantly influences* feelings toward, or judgments about, a subject, the language used is charged language. . . .

Of course communications vary in the amount of charge they carry and in their effect on different people; what is very favorably charged for one person may have little or no charge, or may even be adversely charged, for others. It is sometimes hard to distinguish between charged and uncharged expression. But it is safe to say that whenever we wish to convey any kind of inner knowledge—feelings, attitudes, judgments, values—we are obliged to convey that attitudinal meaning through the medium of charged language; and when we wish to understand the inside knowledge of others, we have to interpret the charged language that they choose, or are obliged to use. Charged language, then, is the natural and necessary medium for the communication of charged or attitudinal meaning. At times we have difficulty in living with it, but we should have even greater difficulty in living without it.

Some of the difficulties in living with charged language are caused 25 by its use in dishonest propaganda, in some editorials, in many political speeches, in most advertising, in certain kinds of effusive salesmanship, and in blatantly insincere, or exaggerated, or sentimental expressions of emotion. Other difficulties are caused by the misunderstandings and misinterpretations that charged language produces. A charged phrase mis-interpreted in a love letter; a charged word spoken in haste or in anger; an acrimonious argument about religion or politics or athletics or fraternities; the frustrating uncertainty produced by the effort to understand the complex attitudinal meaning in a poem or play or a short story—these troubles, all growing out of the use of charged language, may give us the feeling that Robert Louis Stevenson expressed when he said, "The battle goes sore against us to the going down of the sun."

But however charged language is abused and whatever misunder-standings it may cause, we still have to live with it—and even by it. It shapes our attitudes and values even without our conscious knowledge; it gives purpose to, and guides, our actions; through it we establish and maintain relations with other people and by means of it we exert our greatest influence on them. Without charged language, life would be but half life. The relatively uncharged language of bare factual statement, though it serves its informative purpose well and is much less open to abuse and to misunderstanding, can describe only the bare land of factual knowledge; to communicate knowledge of the turbulencies and the calms and the deep currents of the sea of inner experience we must use charged language.

THINKING CRITICALLY ABOUT THE READING

1. What is the Birks' purpose in this essay? (Glossary: *Purpose*) Do they seem more intent on explaining or on arguing their position? Point to specific lan-guage they use that led you to your conclusion. (Glossary: *Diction*)

2. How do the Birks organize their essay? (Glossary: *Organization*) Do you think the organizational pattern is appropriate given their subject matter and purpose? Explain.

3. According to the Birks, how is slanting different from the principle of selec-tion? What devices can a speaker or writer use to slant knowledge? When is it appropriate, if at all, to slant language?

4. Do you find the examples about Toddy the dog and Corlyn particularly help-ful? (Glossary: *Examples*) Why or why not? What would have been lost, if anything, had the examples not been included?

5. Why is it important for writers and others to be aware of charged words? What can happen if you use charged language unknowingly? What are some of the difficulties in living in a world with charged language?

6. The Birks wrote this essay in 1972, when people were not as sensitive to sexist language as they are today. (Glossary: *Sexist Language*) Reread several pages of their essay, paying particular attention to the Birks' use of pronouns and to the gender of the people in their examples. Suggest ways in which the Birks' diction could be changed so as to eliminate any sexist language.

LANGUAGE IN ACTION

According to the editors of *Newsweek*, the March 8, 1999, "Voices of the Century: Americans at War" issue "generated more than two hundred passionate responses from civilians and veterans." The following five letters are representative of those the editors received and published in the issue of March 29, 1999. Carefully read each letter, looking for slanting and charged language. Point out the verifiable facts you find. How do you know these facts are verifiable?

Kudos for your March 8 issue, "Voices of the Century: Americans at War." This issue surely ranks among the best magazines ever published. As a military historian, I gained a better perspective of this turbulent century from this single issue than from many other sources combined. The first-person accounts are the genius of the issue. And your selection of storytellers was truly inspired. The "Voices of the Century" is so powerful that I will urge all of my friends to read it, buying copies for those who are not subscribers. Many persons today, especially those born after WWII, do not comprehend or appreciate the defining events of this century. How can we be more confident that they will be aware of our vital past when making important social and political decisions during the next century? I have great confidence in the American spirit and will, but this missing perspective is my principal concern as I leave this nation to the ministry of my daughters, my grandchildren, and their generation. Why not publish "Voices of the Century" as a booklet and make it readily available to all young people? Why not urge every school system to make it required reading prior to graduation from high school?

—ALAN R. MCKIE, Springfield, VA

Your March 8 war issue was a powerfully illustrated essay of the men and women who have served our country and the people of other lands in so many capacities. But it was the photos that touched my soul and made me cry all over again for the human loss, *my* loss. As I stared at the pictures of the injured, dead, dying, and crying, I felt as though I were intruding on their private hell. God bless all of them, and my sincere thanks for a free America.

—DEBORAH AMES, Sparks, NV

I arrived in this country at 15 as a Jewish refugee from Nazism. I became an American soldier at 19 and a U.S. Foreign Service officer at 29. As a witness to much of the history covered in your special issue, I wanted to congratulate *Newsweek* on a superb job. In your excellent introduction, I found only one word with which I take issue: that "after the war Rosie and her cohort *happily* went back to the joys of motherhood and built the baby boom." Rosie and her cohort were forced back into their traditional gender roles, and it took the women's movement another generation or two to win back the gains achieved during the war.

—LUCIAN HEICHLER, Frederick, MD

Editor's note: The word "happily" was carefully chosen. Contemporary surveys indicated that most of the American women who joined the work force because of World War II were glad to get back to family life when it was over.

On the cover of your "Americans at War" issue, you have the accompanying text "From WWI to Vietnam: The Grunts and the Great Men—In Their Own Words." In each of these wars, the grunts *were* the great men.

—PAULA S. MCGUIRE, Charlotte, NC

Your March 8 issue was painful for me and other members of my family as a result of the photograph you included on page 62 showing a wounded soldier being dragged from the line of fire during the Tet Offensive. My family had previously confirmed with the photographer that the soldier was my youngest brother, Marine Cpl. Robert Mack Harrelson. His bullet-riddled body fought hard to survive and, with the assistance of many excellent, caring members of our U.S. Military Medical Staff, he was able to regain some degree of normalcy after his return. But the injuries he received were too great to overcome, resulting in the military funeral he had requested. The rekindled grief brought on by your photo is keenly felt throughout our large family, and especially so by our dear 85-year-old mother, who still speaks of Bob as though he might reappear at any time. In spite of the photo, I sincerely congratulate your fine publication for reminding the world of the tragedy of war.

—LOWELL L. HARRELSON, Bay Minette, AL

WRITING SUGGESTIONS

1. When used only positively or only negatively, charged words can alienate the reader and bring the author's reliability into question. Consider the Birks' two examples of Corlyn. In the first example Corlyn can do no wrong, and in the second she can do nothing right. Using these two examples as a guide, write your own multiparagraph description of a person you know well. Decide on the overall impression you want to convey to your readers, and use charged words—both positive and negative—to create that impression.

2. Find a newspaper or magazine editorial on a subject that you have strong opinions about. Analyze the writer's selection of facts and use of charged language. How well does the writer present different viewpoints? Is the editorial convincing? Why or why not? After researching the topic further in your library or on the internet, write a letter to the editor in response to the editorial. In your letter, use information from your research to make a point about the subject. Also comment on any charged or slanted language the editor used. Mail your letter to the editor.

The Case of the Missing Perpetrator

REBECCA SOLNIT

An activist, historian, and award-winning journalist with a wide range of interests as a writer, Rebecca Solnit was born in Connecticut in 1961 and grew up in the San Francisco Bay area. A high school dropout, Solnit earned her GED at 16 and enrolled at the College of Marin, just north of San Francisco. She eventually earned her BA at San Francisco State University and her MA from the University of California, Berkeley. Her many books include *Wanderlust: A History of Walking* (2001), *As Eve Said to the Serpent: On Landscape, Gender, and Art* (2003), and *A Paradise Built in Hell: The Extraordinary Communities That Arise in Disaster* (2010). More recently, she has become known for her 2014 book *Men Explain Things to Me,* which contributed to the popularity of the word *mansplaining* (although Solnit did not invent the word). Her work has appeared in many publications, including *The New Yorker,* the *London Review of Books,* and *The Guardian.* Currently, she is a contributing editor at *Harper's,* where she writes the magazine's "Easy Chair" column. Solnit has won several honors and awards, including a Guggenheim Fellowship, the National Book Critics Circle Award in criticism, and the Lannan Literary Award.

As even the titles of her books suggest, Solnit roams as a writer to where her enthusiasms — and her political commitments — take her: from the history of indigenous people to walking, traveling, disasters, social change, rebellion, and feminism. She has a keen ear for language and its power to frame, clarify, or obscure: as she puts it, "Change the language and you've begun to change the reality or at least to open the status quo to question." That theme can be traced in the following selection, which first appeared on the website *Literary Hub* on February 11, 2016. In her essay, Solnit looks at how abstract, vague, and dishonest language frames our discussions of women, sexual reproduction, and sexual assault, particularly in the context of male agency and responsibility.

WRITING TO DISCOVER: *How easy is it for you to talk about matters of sex and reproduction? Do you tend to use blunt, straightforward words, or do you use euphemisms or mild, indirect words and expressions? Why do you think you speak about these topics in this way?*

In a detective novel, you begin in a state of ignorance and advance toward knowledge, clue by clue. The little indicators add up at last to a revelation that sets the world to right and sees that justice is done, or at least provides the satisfaction of a world made clear in the end. If detective fiction is the literature of disillusion, then there's a much more common literature of illusion that aspires to deceive and distract rather than clarify.

296

   A perfect recent example is the Center for Disease Control's new and widely mocked guidelines to drinking. They are like a detective novel run backward — if you read them with conviction, you'd become muddled about what a woman is and how violence and pregnancy happen and who is involved in those things. On the other hand, if you read more carefully, you might know why the passive voice is so often a cover-up and that the missing subject in a circumlocutionary sentence is often the guilty party.

   What is a woman? According to the CDC, all women are in danger of becoming pregnant. "Drinking too much can have many risks for women," their chart tells us, and itemizes them for "any woman." "Injuries/violence" top the list and "unintended pregnancy" brings up the rear. "Drinking too much can have risks for women including . . . any alcohol use for women who are pregnant or might be pregnant." Medical professionals should "advise a woman to stop drinking if she is trying to get pregnant or not using birth control with sex." This in a few deft, simple strokes reduces all women to fertile females in their breeding years who have what you might call *exposure* to fertile men. It denies the existence of many other kinds of women and the equal responsibility of at least one kind of man. Maybe it denies the existence of men, since women seem to get pregnant here as a consequence of consorting with booze, not boys.

   Women is a category covering a great variety of us who fall outside the CDC criteria. Quite a lot of us are past the age of knock-up-ability and all the uncertainty that goes along with it. Even if we do laps with handsome sommeliers in the great barrels of pinot noir ripening in the Napa Valley, we will not accidentally become pregnant. Many younger women are not fertile at all for some reason or other, from longterm birth-control implants and tubal ligations to consequences of medical conditions and treatments and genetic lotteries. Not even with fountains of mojitos spouting up from the ground like geysers will they become pregnant, no matter what. Thirdly, a meaningful population of women are lesbians and/or, when they drink, keep company with other women and not with men or not with men who have sex with women or who have unprotected sex with women. No river of whiskey will have any impact on whether they get pregnant either. Finally, trans women generally don't get pregnant even in the presence of a Niagara falls of prosecco, though some trans men have borne children intentionally, but that's another story and a kind of nice one, much nicer than the one we have to investigate here.

   Because here's the really wild thing: how do (fertile cis-) women get pregnant? Get on back to sex ed, sixth grade style: remember that bit about the union of the sperm and the egg? Because what struck a lot of us when we read about the new CDC guidelines is that it avoids reference to how women get pregnant. Pregnancy results when particular subsets of men and women get together in particular ways. No man, no pregnancy.   5

If that language is too strong for you, then just say that women become pregnant when a bit of male genetic material is introduced by a male organ (no one becomes unintentionally pregnant by the other methods of introducing sperm or fertilized eggs to uteruses). Oh, and I should mention that the male organ is pretty much always attached to a male person.

A woman can be fertile as the Tigris Valley in the time of Abraham and she's not going to get pregnant absent consort with a seed-bearing man. But if you listened to the way it's often framed, you might believe that women get pregnant on their own. Conservatives assert this when they excoriate women for having "fatherless" children or having sex for pleasure. The anti-abortion narrative is often about depraved women having sex for the hell of it and devil take the consequences; the fact that they cannot be having this risk-of-pregnancy type sex in the absence of men is the freaky part of it, a freakiness that is covered up by its familiarity.

A few election cycles ago politician Todd Akin claimed that women did not get pregnant from "legitimate rape." He was the one who said that women's bodies had ways of "shutting that thing down" as though a uterus has some sort of remote-controlled door on it. Sometimes overlooked in all the attention to the *craziness* of his idea was that his comment was in the service of denying rape victims abortion rights. In the current extremes of anti-abortion advocacy and enforcement (like the cases of women prosecuted for trying to produce miscarriages), women have no value in relation to the fetuses in their wombs, though about half of those fetuses will turn into women who will, in turn, be assessed as having no value in relation to the next potential generation of fetuses. Women may be worthless containers of containers of containers of things of value, namely men. Embryonic men. Or perhaps children have value until they turn out to be women. I don't know. It's a mystery to me how these people think.

Meanwhile, the mechanisms of pregnancy are assiduously avoided in this mystification of reproduction story. First there is what we could call the mystery of the missing man: it absents guys from reproduction and absolves fathers from what is called fatherlessness, as though their absence from the life of a child was somehow something that had nothing to do with them. (And yeah, there are bad women who shut out nice men from contact with their kids, though from personal experience I know more cases of dads missing in action and moms on the run from violent creeps.) Seriously, we know why men are absented from these narratives: it absolves them from responsibility for pregnancies, including the unfortunate and accidental variety, and then it absolves them from producing that thing for which so many poor women have been excoriated for so long: fatherless children. The fathers of the fatherless are legion.

You can imagine a parallel universe of non-misogyny in which men are told that they carry around this dangerous stuff that can blow a woman up into nine months of pregnancy and then the production of other human beings and that they are irresponsible, immoral, and lacking in something or other—what is it that women are lacking?—when they go around putting that stuff in pregnable people without consent, planning, or care for longterm consequences. There is not much scolding along those lines, outside of warnings about women entrapping men with pregnancy, which is often a way of describing male withdrawal of responsibility but not of sperm.

As others have mentioned, recommendations for women around the   10
Zika virus have been similar to these alcohol guidelines for women: the responsibility for preventing pregnancy in the presence of a disease that causes birth defects has been portrayed as entirely up to women, even in countries like El Salvador where abortion is illegal in all circumstances, birth control is not readily accessible, and (like pretty much everywhere else) women do not always have a safe and easy time saying no to sex. Seventeen women accused of having abortions (which is sometimes how a miscarriage is interpreted there) are in prison for homicide in El Salvador. It's arguable who their bodies are thought to belong to but clear their bodies are not regarded as belonging to them. Brazil did get around to telling men to use condoms during sex with pregnant women (but not with women at risk of being impregnated).

This mystification of reproduction is full of missing men and missing access to resources. The CDC's highlighting of unintended pregnancy in the United States raises the questions of how maybe better access to reproductive rights and education and healthcare might have more to do with reducing unintended pregnancies than asserting that all reproductive-age women not on birth control should not drink alcohol (a mandate that ignores how many women get pregnant unintentionally while actually on birth control).

I wish all this telling women alcohol is dangerous was a manifestation of a country that loves babies so much it's all over lead contamination from New Orleans to Baltimore to Flint and the lousy nitrate-contaminated water of Iowa and carcinogenic pesticides and the links between sugary junk food and a host of health conditions and the need for universal access to healthcare and daycare and good and adequate food. You know it's not. It's just about hating on women. Hating on women requires narratives that make men vanish and make women magicians producing babies out of thin air and dissolute habits. This is an interesting narrative for the power it affords women, but I would rather have an accurate one. And maybe a broader one talking about all the ecological and economic factors that impact the well-being of children. But then the guilty party becomes us, not them.

Language matters. We just had a big struggle around the language about rape so that people would stop blaming victims. The epithet that put it concisely is: rapists cause rape. Not what women wear, consume, where they go and the rest, because when you regard women as at fault you enter into another one of our anti-detective novels or another chapter of the mystery of the missing protagonist. Rape is a willful act; the actor is a rapist. And yet you'd think that young women on campuses in particular were raping themselves, so absent have young men on campuses been from the mystificational narratives. Men are abstracted into a sort of weather, an ambient natural force, an inevitability that cannot be governed or held accountable. Individual men disappear in this narrative and rape, assault, pregnancy just become weather conditions to which women have to adapt. If those things happen to them, the failure is theirs. This training begins early. Girls in middle and high school even now, even in supposedly progressive places like New York and San Francisco, are told their forms and garments cause male behavior. Who is responsible for the behavior of boys in these narratives about spaghetti straps and leggings? Girls.

We have a lot of stories like this in this country, stories that, if you believe them, make you stupid. Stories that are not expositions but cover-ups on things like the causes of poverty. Stories that unhitch cause from effect and shunt meaning aside. The CDC extends the absence of perpetrators from crimes by telling women, in their simple orange and green chart, about why they shouldn't drink, that drinking too much carries the risks of "injuries/ violence." Now, falling over and breaking something is a risk of being drunk, but since "injuries" here is coupled with "violence," and tripping over a chair is not commonly regarded as violence, it's clear that what's meant is: someone might hurt and injure you. In sane worlds and grammatically coherent narratives, violence has a cause, and that cause has agency and consciousness: it has to be another living entity. Alcohol cannot be that entity, since alcohol doesn't have agency and consciousness. A tree that falls on you is not violent, though a landlord might be responsible if your ill-maintained house collapses on you.

But people get hurt in part because we don't want to talk about who does the hurting.

You drink, you get injured, but who injures you must not be mentioned, so that it's as though there's only women and alcohol in the room. Even when that someone is the person being addressed; the CDC guidelines telling men that they too should watch their drinking notes that "Excessive alcohol use is commonly involved in sexual assault." It's as though there's a person named "excessive alcohol use, or rather Excessive Alcohol Use whose shirts or maybe hip flasks would be monogrammed EAU. We have all met EAU. He is often involved in sexual assault. But here's the point: he never acts alone. Because the CDC is twisting itself into baroque knots to avoid saying "you" or "men" or "drunk guys" or "perpetrators." They seem less worried that someone might get beat up or raped than that someone's feelings might get hurt. But people get hurt in part because we don't want to talk about who does the hurting.

15

Excessive Alcohol Use has a brother named Excessive Alcohol Consumption on this list, and he's trouble too: "Excessive alcohol consumption increases aggression and, as a result, can increase the risk of physically assaulting another person." EAC apparently acts alone in this narrative, which is a sentence in search of a subject. Whose aggression? Who will assault? Maybe the CDC should cut to the chase and issue warnings about men. After all men are the main source of violence against women (and for that matter the main source of violence against men). Imagine the language! Use of a man may result in pregnancy or injury; men should be used with caution. Assess each man carefully for potential risks. Be careful about using men with alcohol. Maybe they should come with warning labels? But that too would exonerate men from responsibility for their acts, and I think a world in which we don't perform that exoneration so often would be a better one. Seriously, domestic violence is the leading cause of injury to women ages 15-44 in the United States.

In the wildlife sanctuaries of literature, we study the species of speech, the flight patterns of individual words, the herd behavior of words together, and we learn what language does and why it matters. This is excellent training for going out into the world and looking at all the unhallowed speech of political statements and news headlines and CDC instructions and seeing how it makes the world or in this case makes a mess of it. It is the truest, highest purpose of language to make things clear and help us see; when words are used to do the opposite you know you're in trouble and that maybe there's a coverup.

Detective work and the habits of perception it generates can save us from believing lies and sometimes show us who's being protected when a lie is also an alibi. The CDC is right to warn about the dangers of misusing alcohol, if not in how it did so. I am myself trying to warn about the misuses of language. We are all language detectives, and if we pay enough attention we can figure out what things mean even when they don't mean to tell us, and we can even tell when stories are lying to us. So many of them do.

THINKING CRITICALLY ABOUT THE READING

1. Why are the Center for Disease Control's guidelines for drinking alcohol like a "detective novel run backward" (2), in Solnit's view?

2. Who or what causes rape, according to Solnit?

3. Why are men often "absented" from the "narrative" of fatherless children, according to Solnit (8)? What purpose does this "absenting" serve?

4. What metaphor for men does Solnit use in paragraph 13? Why does she choose this metaphor? What point does it make? Is it effective?

5. In paragraphs 6 and 7, Solnit discusses the views of political conservatives with regard to gender, sexual assault, and abortion rights. At the end of paragraph 7, she writes, "It's a mystery to me how these people think." Do you think she is being sincere in this statement? Ironic? Both?

LANGUAGE IN ACTION

In an article titled "Public Doublespeak" in the journal *College English,* scholar Terence Moran presents the following list of recommended language, which school administrators in Brooklyn gave their elementary school teachers to use when talking about student behavior with parents. Read the list and then briefly write down your reactions to the expressions. Why do you suppose the school administrators made up this list? What purpose does such language serve? Do you believe the "acceptable" language serves a useful purpose, or does it only confuse, mislead, or obscure? How do you think Solnit would react to this list of expressions?

For Parent Interviews and Report Cards

Harsh Expression (Avoid)	Acceptable Expression (Use)
Does all right if pushed	Accomplishes tasks when interest is stimulated.
Too free with fists	Resorts to physical means of winning his point or attracting attention.
Lies (Dishonest)	Shows difficulty in distinguishing between imaginary and factual material.
Cheats	Needs help in learning to adhere to rules and standards of fair play.
Steals	Needs help in learning to respect the property rights of others.
Noisy	Needs to develop quieter habits of communication.
Lazy	Needs ample supervision in order to work well.
Is a bully	Has qualities of leadership but needs help in learning to use them democratically.
Associates with "gangs"	Seems to feel secure only in group situations; needs to develop sense of independence.
Disliked by other children	Needs help in learning to form lasting friendships.

WRITING SUGGESTIONS

1. According to Solnit, a double standard exists with regard to men, women, sexuality, and the responsibility for pregnancy: "There is not much scolding [for men] along those lines, outside of warnings about women entrapping men with pregnancy, which is often a way of describing male withdrawal of responsibility but not of sperm" (9). Do you agree that women are judged

more harshly in this context and assigned more responsibility than men? Do you disagree? Respond to her claim with a position of your own. If possible, cite some of the specific language that you have noticed used in these discussions.

2. Solnit argues that "it is the truest, highest purpose of language to make things clear and help us see; when words are used to do the opposite you know you're in trouble and that maybe there's a coverup" (17). Now reflect on how we can use language to "make things clear." Can you come up with some rules or principles to help writers reach that goal? Write an essay that enumerates four or five guidelines to achieve honesty and clarity in writing. Use specific examples, either that you cite or that you create yourself, to support your points.

Fighting Words

JUDITH MATLOFF

Judith Matloff, born in New York City in 1958, is an author, award-winning journalist, and professor who teaches conflict reporting at the Columbia Journalism School. She is also a consultant and expert on safety training for journalists reporting in war zones and other dangerous places. She received her BA from Harvard University and then worked as a global correspondent for Reuters and as the Africa and Moscow bureau chief for *The Christian Science Monitor*. Her writing and reporting has been published in *The Economist, Newsweek, The New York Times Magazine,* and many other publications. She is the author of the non-fiction books *Fragments of a Forgotten War* (1997), *Home Girl: Building a Dream House on a Lawless Block* (2008), and *The War Is in the Mountains: Violence in the World's High Places* (2017).

No one knows for sure who said it first, but the statement is often accurate: "When war is declared, Truth is the first casualty." Certainly, wars often involve large-scale lies and misleading propaganda, but they also invite more subtle, even unintentional forms of deception. In the following essay, published in the *Columbia Journalism Review* (CJR) in 2012, Matloff considers how the language of war can frame, inflame, and obscure. In the process, even supposedly neutral journalists can become "propagandists who unwittingly help normalize violence."

WRITING TO DISCOVER: *Matloff opens her essay with a personal story about a time when she was unintentionally careless and inaccurate with her language. Her words "provoked a fierce outburst." Reflect on a time when you were careless with your words, or spoke (or wrote) without thinking clearly about the right language or expression for your purpose. What were the consequences? What did you learn from the experience?*

Last year, I visited Bogotá, Colombia, to teach a seminar on conflict reporting. Afterward, a soldier missing two legs and most of one arm rolled up in a wheelchair. As we spoke about land mines and their evils, I asked where his "accident" had occurred. My choice of words provoked a fierce outburst from the soldier, whose voice sounded strangled as he asserted that he had been maimed not by a random mishap, but by a premeditated attack.

"Landmines aren't placed by chance," he explained as if I were a small child—which was how I felt at that moment. "Someone sought to kill me."

The woman pushing his wheelchair added, "You really should mind your language."

She was right. For that is what we journalists covering armed confrontations must remember to do. Words are weapons, as much as any gun or bomb, and you'd better believe that governments treat the language they use to describe a war as seriously as they take the war itself. A phrase can create an image of righteous strength to replace fear and trauma, as we saw with "Operation Freedom." Similarly, clashes can be described in neutered terms that normalize violence and blunt the impact of war. From the tame "regime change," with its implications of order instead of violent overthrow, to the false "victory" in Iraq claimed by George W. Bush, words embed themselves in the national psyche and affect public perception of conflict and its consequences.

This isn't a new problem. Almost 70 years ago, in his essay "Politics   5 and the English Language," George Orwell observed how governments manipulated public opinion by describing violent, inhumane policies in imprecise, euphemistic terms. "Defenseless villages are bombarded from the air, the inhabitants driven out into the countryside, the cattle machine-gunned, the huts set on fire with incendiary bullets: this is called *pacification*," wrote Orwell. "Such phraseology is needed if one wants to name things without calling up mental pictures of them."

In 2007, CJR devoted an entire issue to the uses and abuses of political and martial rhetoric. Almost five years later, the topic bears revisiting. Conflict reportage ought to give an accurate picture of war and its costs, to counteract official euphemisms with clarity and precision. But too often, reporters veil the stark, uncomfortable truths of combat in opaque language and terminology. As we prepare to leave Afghanistan, possibly enter Iran, and intervene in myriad other conflicts, and as political rhetoric surrounding these conflicts amps up in the final days of the American presidential campaign, editors and reporters must do their best to reclaim vocabulary from those who would use it to obscure and mislead.

Spend any time in a combat zone or triage ward and you'll realize that, at its most basic level, war is carnage. Yet the words that officials use to describe conflict are chosen to minimize this fact, either by portraying the violence in bland, neutral terms, or with language designed to stoke feelings of anger and revenge.

> **Conflict reportage ought to give an accurate picture of war and its costs, to counteract official euphemisms with clarity and precision.**

It's no surprise that governments and political interests want to frame conflicts in ways that are most favorable to their own goals and objectives. Covering conflict often entails hanging around political and military officials—at briefings, at press conferences, during embeds—and reporters can absorb the jargon without even realizing it. These sterile euphemisms are familiar to any news consumer. The sanitized and manipulative "collateral damage" refers to an unintended killing of civilians; one has to look beyond the words to photographs of massacred wedding parties to fully understand what actually happened. The phrase "smart bomb" conveys intelligence instead of carnage. My 11-year-old son was astounded to hear that "friendly fire" was not friendly at all. "You've got to be kidding," he nearly spat when he learned the definition: killing fellow troops by accident. "I thought it meant you shot at but didn't hurt someone. Why don't they just say it's like a home goal?"

Other times, officials want to inflame rhetoric rather than defuse it. In 2008, a US government memo counseled personnel to avoid using words that have a positive association for many Muslims, such as "mujahidin," "salafi," "ummah," and "jihadi." It prescribes instead such English phrases as "terrorists," "extremists," and "totalitarians." During the 50 years of Basque separatist uprising, the Spanish government tried to convince journalists not to describe the violence as a "conflict." To deploy that word would legitimize the ETA guerrillas, whom Madrid generally prefers to call "criminals." Similarly, during Angola's 27-year civil war, the government often described UNITA rebels as "bandits," a trivializing expression for a formidable force that was amply armed by the US and South Africa.

The more obvious propaganda often escapes us purely because we're   10
so immersed in it. It took an Iraqi acquaintance to make me realize that, early in the Iraq war, *The New York Times* and other papers misused the word "insurgents" for people who attacked US troops. The term lent our side more legitimacy than it legally deserved. If Webster's is to be believed, insurgents rise up against a recognized authority, and not against an occupying force that defied international law by invading.

Reuters, which prides itself on being the only true internationalist news organization, made a point of banning the word "terrorist" in reference to the September 11 attacks, with the argument that one man's murderous extremist is another's freedom fighter. The news agency aims to avoid emotive labels so that customers can come to their own conclusions based on facts. Reuters' decision highlights what is, perhaps, an obvious point: The way conflict stories are written can substantially affect the public debate around those conflicts. Words matter.

Vocabulary twists apply to other types of violence, too. In Mexico, a "drug war"—an inherently debatable term itself—being waged between rival gangs and against authorities and the public has killed more than 47,000 people over six years. Officials usually avoid the phrase "drug cartels," and instead refer to the syndicates as "organized crime." The phrase doesn't adequately convey the grisly methods of the drug gangs. One thinks of money laundering and numbers-running, not vicious groups that hang mutilated bodies from bridges and leave severed heads on streets.

Yet the media are beginning to consider their de facto role as propagandists who unwittingly help normalize violence. Last year, many of Mexico's biggest media outlets signed a voluntary agreement to refrain from adopting the "language and terminology used by criminals" in order to avoid becoming "unwilling spokesmen" for the drug gangsters.

The pact left it to individual newsrooms to decide for themselves which words and phrases to shun. During a gathering earlier this year in Ciudad Juarez, the border town that has long been the epicenter of drug-related homicides, reporters debated the appropriate verb for "kidnap." Until now, common usage was the passive and tame construction *se levantó*, or "lifted."

"That implies no one was responsible," one senior reporter argued. "We should use more direct language like *secuestró*—abducted." The assembled journalists nodded, and then quickly requested anonymity so as to avoid reprisals.   15

Likewise, they discussed the prefix *narco*, which Mexicans place in front of anything relating to drug lords. It often has an allure for impoverished youths impressed by the glitzy lifestyle. Reporters at the meeting weighed the glamorous associations of terms like *narco Polo* (fancy dude who wears designer labels), *narc-architectura* (mansions), and *narco zoos* (kingpins have a predilection for exotic pets).

"Maybe we should just ban *narco*," someone mused.

It's a start. Yet just avoiding words is not enough. Conflict journalists need to be aware of words: where language comes from, what it means, who benefits by its use, and what it obscures. We especially need to consider these issues as we cover the heated rhetoric over Iran's nuclear program. For example, many in the media confuse preemptive and preventive wars, although the two are quite different. A preventive war is initiated to destroy the potential threat of an attack by an enemy. This entails suspicion of an eventual assault, rather than one that is actually proven to be planned or imminent. By contrast, a preemptive war is launched in anticipation of immediate aggression, amid clear signs that the other side is going to attack.

The launch of conflict when no attack has occurred is a violation of international law, unless authorized by the UN Security Council. A preemptive strike is seen as justifiable, however, which is why the Bush administration strained to describe the 2003 invasion of Iraq as such. In the case of Iran, we lack indisputable evidence that an attack on Israel or anyone else is "imminent." It is simply a fear—a well-founded one, perhaps, but nothing as solid as the proof of troop mobilization on the border when Israel struck against Egypt in the Six Day War in 1967.

We, as well as the public, must understand how and why language gets twisted by those who would market war. Those in favor of attacking Iran would like to sell any potential assault as a preemptive war. But unless it fits the criteria, journalists should remain wary.   20

Let's not forget that war can be an abstraction to politicians, but not to those who fight and live through it. To soldiers and conflict-zone residents, war is bloody and devastating, and it's hard for news consumers to realize this when the stories they read are stuffed with bloodless clichés.

Conflict reporters often are the only neutral parties on hand during a skirmish; if they don't accurately report an event, it might never be reported at all. If a society wants to support a war, so be it. But, as journalists, let's do our best to report these conflicts with precision and clarity, so that people know exactly what they're supporting.

THINKING CRITICALLY ABOUT THE TEXT

1. According to Matloff, what is war "at its most basic level" (7)?

2. In Matloff's view, political and military leaders use manipulative language for two main purposes. One purpose is to minimize the horrors of war and violence by framing it in "bland, neutral terms" (7). What is the other purpose?

3. Matloff notes that reporters covering war end up spending a lot of time talking to military and political officials. As a result, these reporters "absorb the [military and political] jargon without even realizing it" (8). What does the word *jargon* mean, both in this context and in general? Is jargon always a bad thing? Why or why not?

4. What is the purpose of paragraph 8? What general claim does this paragraph support, and how does Matloff back up the claim?

5. Matloff concludes that war journalists should report on "conflicts with precision and clarity" (21). Why would this be hard to do? Why would it be easier to use language that is imprecise and vague instead of language that is precise and clear? Do you find that this is true in your own writing and speaking?

LANGUAGE IN ACTION

As Matloff writes, many of these "sterile euphemisms are familiar" (8) to regular news consumers who follow military conflicts in contemporary newspapers and other media. She cites examples such as *collateral damage* (the unintended killing of civilians) and *smart bomb* (a radio-controlled or laser-guided bomb, aimed at a specific target). Arguably, she deploys euphemistic jargon herself when she uses the word *embeds* in paragraph 8: this word refers to journalists who attach themselves to military units during combat. Look at the following list of words and phrases associated with military operations and national security issues. In what ways are the terms imprecise? What do they conceal? Are such words and phrases necessary and valuable? You may define and discuss the terms as a class, or work on them in small groups.

- air campaign
- boots on the ground
- drawdown
- enhanced interrogation techniques
- extraordinary rendition
- improvised explosive device
- kinetic military action
- military intervention
- overseas contingency operations
- surgical strike

WRITING SUGGESTIONS

1. In paragraph 11, Matloff writes about Reuters, a large and influential news agency: "Reuters, which prides itself on being the only true internationalist news organization, made a point of banning the word 'terrorist' in reference to the September 11 attacks, with the argument that one man's murderous extremist is another's freedom fighter. The news agency aims to avoid emotive labels so that customers can come to their own conclusions based on facts." In other words, Reuters aims for a value-neutral or objective approach to language: it does not use the word *terrorist*. This editorial policy has been controversial: in one case, a newspaper editor who ran Reuters stories in a Canadian publication inserted the word *terrorist* into Reuters articles. How do you respond to Reuters' policy? Do you think reporting should avoid "emotive labels" or moral evaluations? Why or why not?

2. As an expert in reporting in war zones, Matloff has a keen ear for the jargon and euphemisms of military action. But jargon and euphemisms are present in nearly all spheres of life, professional and otherwise. For example, education at all levels has expressions that soften, inflate, obscure, and perhaps even mislead (see, for example, the list of expressions in the Language in Action activity on p. 302). Consider also terms and phrases such as *charter schools, underperforming students, quantitative assessments of student progress, twenty-first century learning skills.* You probably encounter this type of language regularly. Identify an example of a euphemism or jargon term that you notice in your classrooms, in your instructor's teaching materials, on your campus, or in any other context. Write a brief essay about the word or phrase. What is its purpose? Where did it come from? Is it precise and clear, or is it vague?

Fake News Starts with the Title

BENJAMIN HORNE

Benjamin D. Horne is a PhD student in computer science at Rensselaer Polytechnic Institute in New York. Born in 1991 in Santa Cruz, California, and raised in Walden, Colorado, he completed his undergraduate education at Union University in Tennessee. He has worked at the US Army Research Laboratory and at the National Science Foundation, among other research and teaching positions. His current research focuses on algorithms that evaluate the credibility of news articles, as well as on sports analytics and science education. In this essay, which originally appeared as a blog post on *Medium* on March 28, 2017, Horne addresses the problem of "fake news": false stories or news items with no basis in fact that are presented as truthful and accurate.

The issue of fake news became more prominent—and contested—after the 2016 US presidential election, during which social media sites like Facebook were implicated in spreading false information designed to manipulate American voters. But instead of writing a political polemic or an argument about bias, Horne addresses the problem by looking at systemic stylistic and structural differences between fake news stories and real news stories in the context of the human tendency to use *heuristics,* or cognitive shortcuts. The good news? If news consumers are careful and pay attention to style, they can detect and avoid fake stories.

WRITING TO DISCOVER: *Have you ever heard, read, or repeated a false urban legend or "fake" story, while believing it was real? Have you ever seen and believed a story on social media that turned out to be false? Have you ever spread or reposted such a story? What was the experience like? Why did you initially believe that the story was true, and how did you later learn that it was untrue?*

This may be the hundredth article you have read on the topic of fake news since the 2016 US Presidential Election. While misinformation and malicious fake news are certainly not new, everyone has become aware of their existence. This increased awareness is well and good—the first step in solving a problem is realizing there is one, right?—but this overload has caused the lines between fake and real to become blurred for many. While it is very hard to say, computationally, what is true, I hope to offer you some new scientific evidence that fake and real news can be differentiated.

In a recent study, being published at NECO 2017, Sibel Adali and I ask the question: Is there any systematic stylistic difference between fake and real news?

To approach this problem, we look at three different types of articles: real, fake, and satire. Real news stories are stories that are known to be true and from "well trusted" news sources. Fake news stories are stories that are from well-known "fake news" sources that are intentionally trying to spread misinformation. Satirical news stories are stories that are from news sources that explicitly state they are satirical and do not intentionally spread misinformation.

Now here is where it gets tricky. It is fairly difficult to get solid ground truth about fake and real news. So, to determine the ground truth of these articles, we take a "strict source" approach. For example, if we are to think about the news as a spectrum from "generally very reliable" to "purposefully fake, never reliable," we want to capture the extreme ends of this spectrum. To find these extreme ends of the spectrum, we use Zimdar's crowdsourced list of fake news and *Business Insider*'s most trusted news list. For satirical news, we simply collect news sites that state they are satirical on the front page.

With this ground-truth approach in mind, we analyze three independent data sets: Craig Silverman's data set from his BuzzFeed article entitled "This Analysis Shows How Viral Fake Election News Stories Outperformed Real News On Facebook," a data set from Burfoot and Baldwin's 2009 study on satire news, and a brand new data set of political fake, real, and satire news collected by ourselves.   5

TITLES ARE A STRONG DIFFERENTIATING FACTOR BETWEEN FAKE AND REAL NEWS.

By far the biggest difference between fake and real news sources is the title. Specifically, we find, across both the BuzzFeed data set and ours, that fake news titles are longer than real news titles and contain words that are simpler in both length and technicality. Fake titles also used more all capitalized words, significantly more proper nouns, but fewer nouns overall, and fewer stop-words (examples: *the, and, a, an*). In addition, we find that in the BuzzFeed data set, fake titles use significantly more analytical words, and in our data set, fake titles use significantly more verb phrases and significantly more past tense words.

Looking at a few random examples from our data will solidify these results:

Example 1

FAKE TITLE: BREAKING BOMBSHELL: NYPD Blows Whistle on New Hillary Emails: Money Laundering, Sex Crimes with Children, Child Exploitation, Pay to Play, Perjury

REAL TITLE: Preexisting Conditions and Republican Plans to Replace Obamacare

Example 2

FAKE TITLE: URGENT: The Mainstream Media Was Hiding One HUGE Fact About Trump Win!

REAL TITLE: Obama Designates Atlantic, Arctic Areas Off-Limits to Offshore Drilling

As you can see, the writers of fake news are attempting to squeeze as much substance into the titles as possible by skipping stop-words and nouns to increase the use of proper nouns and verb phrases. In other words, the fake titles use many verb phrases and named entities to get many points across, while the real titles opt for a brief and general summary statement (*many claims* vs. *few claims*).

THE CONTENT OF FAKE AND REAL NEWS ARTICLES IS ALSO SUBSTANTIALLY DIFFERENT.

Not only is the headline of an article a differentiating factor, but the content structure is actually quite different as well. In particular, we find that real articles are significantly longer than fake articles and that fake articles use fewer technical words, smaller words, fewer punctuation, fewer quotes, and more lexical redundancy. Further, fake news articles are easier to read, use fewer analytic words, have significantly more personal pronouns, and use fewer nouns and more adverbs.

These many differences may seem abstract, so here is the takeaway point: Fake news has very little information or substance in the article content, but packs a ton of disinformation into the titles.

FAKE CONTENT IS MORE CLOSELY RELATED TO SATIRE THAN TO REAL NEWS.

Up to this point we have only looked at the categories of fake news   10
and real news, but including the category of satire may give us more insight. When adding satirical articles to the analysis, we find that the majority of our feature distributions are common between satire and fake news. Specifically, both satirical content and fake content use smaller words, fewer technical words, fewer analytic words, and significantly more lexical redundancy, as well as fewer quotes, fewer punctuation, more adverbs, and fewer nouns than real articles.

This finding is interesting and useful for several reasons. First, much of the journalistic coverage of fake news has assumed that fake news is inherently persuasive and meant to look like real news, but this is actually not the case. The high similarity between satire and fake content demonstrates that fake news is written in a less investigative way, satirical news is written to be absurd and does not have sound arguments. This has some important implications you may not realize. People are still fooled by fake news—just look at the 2016 US Presidential election—but fake news has very little logical or argumentative substance. The field of communications may provide us with some insight.

REAL NEWS PERSUADES THROUGH ARGUMENTS, WHILE FAKE NEWS PERSUADES THROUGH SHORTCUTS.

To better explain our findings, we look to the well-studied Elaboration Likelihood Model (ELM) of persuasion. According to the ELM, people are persuaded through two different avenues: the central route and the peripheral route. The central route of persuasion results from the attentive examination of the arguments and message characteristics presented. This route involves a high amount of energy and cognition. In opposition, the peripheral route of persuasion results from associating ideas or making conjectures that are unrelated to the logic and quality of the information presented. This route can also be called a heuristic route or a short-cut that takes very little energy and cognition.

Humans are prone to these shortcuts, including relying on trust for a friend on Facebook (my friends are smart, they would never share fake news!), skimming an article for content, or simply believing what the title of a news story states (the title makes sense to me and I don't have time to check it out if it's legit). The damage from these shortcuts can be amplified

People are still fooled by fake news . . . but fake news has very little logical or argumentative substance.

by the homophily (the "birds of a feather flock together" effect) of social networks or the algorithms that sort by our estimated interests.

So what does this mean for our results? We found that fake news articles pack a lot of substance into their titles. In spite of this, we also found that the body content of fake articles has very little substance, including high lexical redundancy (fake news articles repeat themselves a lot), a lack of analytical words, and a lack of direct quotations. Moreover, we found that much of fake news' content structure is similar to the content structure of satire. Since humans are prone to taking shortcuts in trust decisions, users may feel very little need to open an article to find out more after they see a loaded, misleading title. Fake news titles often present claims about people and entities in complete sentences and associate these people with actions. Therefore, titles serve as the main mechanism to quickly make claims which are easy to assess. This notion is further supported by what we already know about information in social networks: many of the links shared or commented on are never clicked, and thus, only the titles of the articles are ever read. (One study that discusses this is Wang, Ramachandran, and Chaintreau 2016.)

This finding is concerning, since it means that people believe fake news simply out of having low energy or mental overload, not due to a lack of education or a lack of care. Unfortunately, misleading claims in the titles of fake news articles can activate established beliefs, which can be hard to change through reasoned arguments. One possible remedy is for

15

articles that aim to counter fake claims to pack counterclaims into their titles, taking advantage of human shortcuts in persuasion.

Overall, our work points out that we can detect fake news to some extent, but it is still our responsibility to take the time to read an article's arguments and assess the veracity of our biases before sharing information.

THINKING CRITICALLY ABOUT THE READING

1. What is Horne's purpose in writing this article? What does he hope to achieve?

2. According to Horne, how are the titles of fake news stories different from the titles of real stories? Identify two or three specific differences.

3. Horne describes the mechanics, syntax, and parts of speech used in fake news stories. What is the key "takeaway" (9) from this stylistic analysis?

4. According to Horne, humans are prone to using "heuristics routes" (or cognitive shortcuts) when analyzing information. Have you ever engaged in any of the heuristics that he describes? Can you think of any other specific kinds of heuristics that Horne does not mention? If so, what are they?

5. How do you respond to this essay, particularly the last two paragraphs? Do they make you optimistic or pessimistic? Do you think Horne proposes helpful solutions? Do you think the spread and influence of fake news can be limited or stopped altogether? Why or why not?

LANGUAGE IN ACTION

Horne describes the key differences between titles of real news articles and titles of fake news articles in detail. Consider the list of news articles below. Without looking them up online, try to determine from the titles alone which of these articles are "fake news" and which ones are real. Then check your answers against the answer key below. Did you get any wrong? If so, why do you think you misidentified them?

1. "NFL Lawyer Who Claimed Super Bowl Is 'Rigged' Is Found Dead"
2. "Crocodile Breaks Loose on Australian Flight"
3. "Japanese Fans Say Godzilla Is Too Fat"
4. "Florida Sherriff's Office Will Not Escort Miami Dolphins Until They Stand for the National Anthem"
5. "Trump: 'The Fake News Is Creating Violence'"
6. "Trump Orders Execution of Obama-Pardoned Turkeys"
7. "Pluto Has Been Officially Reclassified as a Planet!"
8. "Flood of Caramel Unleashed by Brazilian Sugar Fire"

1. fake 2. real 3. real 4. fake 5. real 6. fake 7. fake 8. real

Answers

WRITING SUGGESTIONS

1. Horne provides a stylistic analysis of fake news stories. Using the elements and characteristics that he identifies, find an example of a fake news story online and evaluate it in a brief essay. What features does the story share with Horne's examples? Are any features of the story different from what he describes in his article? For example, what is the story's title and how does it function? In what ways might the content play into a reader's tendency to use mental shortcuts?

2. In his introductory paragraph, Horne writes, "While misinformation and malicious fake news are certainly not new, everyone has become aware of their existence." What forms did fake news ("malicious" or otherwise) take in the past, especially before online social media? Who created these earlier forms of fake news? How did it spread? What purposes did it serve? What were its consequences? Identify and research an example of "fake news" from the pre-internet era, and address these questions in a brief essay. You might also examine the similarities and differences between pre-internet fake news and fake news in its current form. If you choose the latter approach, be sure to find and compare specific examples.

Weasel Words: The Art of Saying Nothing at All

WILLIAM LUTZ

William Lutz was born in 1940 in Racine, Wisconsin. An emeritus professor of English at Rutgers University at Camden, Lutz holds a PhD in Victorian literature, linguistics and rhetoric, and a law degree from the Rutgers School of Law. Lutz is the author or coauthor of numerous books having to do with language, including *Webster's New World Thesaurus* (1985) and *The Cambridge Thesaurus of American English* (1994). Considered an expert on language, Lutz has worked with many corporations and government agencies to promote clear, "plain" English. A member of the Pennsylvania bar, he was awarded the Pennsylvania Bar Association Clarity Award for the Promotion of Plain English in Legal Writing in 2001.

Lutz is best known for his series of books on "doublespeak": *Doublespeak: From Revenue Enhancement to Terminal Living* (1989), *The New Doublespeak: Why No One Knows What Anyone's Saying Anymore* (1996), and *Doublespeak Defined: Cut Through the Bull**** and Get to the Point* (1999). Lutz edited the *Quarterly Review of Doublespeak* from 1980 to 1994.

The term *doublespeak* comes from the Newspeak vocabulary of George Orwell's novel *1984.* It refers to speech or writing that presents two or more contradictory ideas in such a way that an unsuspecting audience is not consciously aware of the contradiction and is likely to be deceived. As chair of the National Council of Teachers of English's Committee on Public Doublespeak, Lutz has been a watchdog of public officials and business leaders who use language to "mislead, distort, deceive, inflate, circumvent, and obfuscate." Each year the committee presents the Orwell Awards, recognizing the most outrageous uses of public doublespeak in government and business.

In the following excerpt from his book *Doublespeak,* Lutz reveals some of the ways that advertisers use language to imply great things about products and services without promising anything at all. With considerable skill, advertisers can produce ads that make us believe a certain product is better than it is without actually lying about it. Lutz's word-by-word analysis of advertising claims reveals how misleading — and ridiculous — these slogans and claims can be.

WRITING TO DISCOVER: *Imagine what it would be like if you were suddenly transported to a world in which there were no advertisements and no one trying to sell you a product. Write about how you would decide what to buy. How would you learn about new products? Would you prefer to live in such a world? Why or why not?*

WEASEL WORDS

One problem advertisers have when they try to convince you that the product they are pushing is really different from other, similar products is that their claims are subject to some laws. Not a lot of laws, but there are some designed to prevent fraudulent or untruthful claims in advertising. Even during the happy years of nonregulation under President Ronald Reagan, the FTC did crack down on the more blatant abuses in advertising claims. Generally speaking, advertisers have to be careful in what they say in their ads, in the claims they make for the products they advertise. Parity claims are safe because they are legal and supported by a number of court decisions. But beyond parity claims there are weasel words.

Advertisers use weasel words to appear to be making a claim for a product when in fact they are making no claim at all. Weasel words get their name from the way weasels eat the eggs they find in the nests of other animals. A weasel will make a small hole in the egg, suck out the insides, then place the egg back in the nest. Only when the egg is examined closely is it found to be hollow. That's the way it is with weasel words in advertising: Examine weasel words closely and you'll find that they're as hollow as any egg sucked by a weasel. Weasel words appear to say one thing when in fact they say the opposite, or nothing at all.

"Help"—The Number One Weasel Word

The biggest weasel word used in advertising doublespeak is "help." Now "help" only means to aid or assist, nothing more. It does not mean to conquer, stop, eliminate, end, solve, heal, cure, or anything else. But once the ad says "help," it can say just about anything after that because "help" qualifies everything coming after it. The trick is that the claim that comes after the weasel word is usually so strong and so dramatic that you forget the word "help" and concentrate only on the dramatic claim. You read into the ad a message that the ad does not contain. More importantly, the advertiser is not responsible for the claim that you read into the ad, even though the advertiser wrote the ad so you would read that claim into it.

The next time you see an ad for a cold medicine that promises that it "helps relieve cold symptoms fast," don't rush out to buy it. Ask yourself what this claim is really saying. Remember, "help" means only that the medicine will aid or assist. What will it aid or assist in doing? Why, "relieve" your cold "symptoms." "Relieve" only means to ease, alleviate, or mitigate, not to stop, end, or cure. Nor does the claim say how much relieving this medicine will do. Nowhere does this ad claim it will cure anything. In fact, the ad doesn't even claim it will *do* anything at all. The ad only claims that it will aid in relieving (not curing) your cold symptoms, which are probably a runny nose, watery eyes, and a headache. In other words, this medicine probably contains a standard decongestant and some aspirin. By the way, what does "fast" mean? Ten minutes, one hour, one day? What is fast to one person can be very slow to another. Fast is another weasel word.

Ad claims using "help" are among the most popular ads. One says, "Helps keep you young looking," but then a lot of things will help keep you young looking, including exercise, rest, good nutrition, and a facelift. More importantly, this ad doesn't say the product will keep you young, only "young *looking*." Someone may look young to one person and old to another. 5

A toothpaste ad says, "Helps prevent cavities," but it doesn't say it will actually prevent cavities. Brushing your teeth regularly, avoiding sugars in food, and flossing daily will also help prevent cavities. A liquid cleaner ad says, "Helps keep your home germ free," but it doesn't say it actually kills germs, nor does it even specify which germs it might kill.

"Help" is such a useful weasel word that it is often combined with other action-verb weasel words such as "fight" and "control." Consider the claim, "Helps control dandruff symptoms with regular use." What does it really say? It will assist in controlling (not eliminating, stopping, ending, or curing) the *symptoms* of dandruff, not the cause of dandruff nor the dandruff itself. What are the symptoms of dandruff? The ad deliberately leaves that undefined, but assume that the symptoms referred to in the ad are the flaking and itching commonly associated with dandruff. But just shampooing with *any* shampoo will temporarily eliminate these symptoms, so this shampoo isn't any different from any other. Finally, in order to benefit from this product, you must use it regularly. What is "regular use"—daily, weekly, hourly? Using another shampoo "regularly" will have the same effect. Nowhere does this advertising claim say this particular shampoo stops, eliminates, or cures dandruff. In fact, this claim says nothing at all, thanks to all the weasel words.

Look at ads in magazines and newspapers, listen to ads on radio and television, and you'll find the word "help" in ads for all kinds of products. How often do you read or hear such phrases as "helps stop . . . ," "helps overcome . . . ," "helps eliminate . . . ," "helps you feel . . . ," or "helps you look . . . "? If you start looking for this weasel word in advertising, you'll be amazed at how often it occurs. Analyze the claims in the ads using "help," and you will discover that these ads are really saying nothing.

There are plenty of other weasel words used in advertising. In fact, there are so many that to list them all would fill the rest of this book. But, in order to identify the doublespeak of advertising and understand the real meaning of an ad, you have to be aware of the most popular weasel words in advertising today.

Virtually Spotless

One of the most powerful weasel words is "virtually," a word so innocent that most people don't pay any attention to it when it is used in an advertising claim. But watch out. "Virtually" is used in advertising 10 claims that appear to make specific, definite promises when there is no promise. After all, what does "virtually" mean? It means "in essence or effect, although not in fact." Look at that definition again. "Virtually" means *not in fact*. It does *not* mean "almost" or "just about the same as," or anything else. And before you dismiss all this concern over such a small word, remember that small words can have big consequences.

In 1971 a federal court rendered its decision on a case brought by a woman who became pregnant while taking birth control pills. She sued the manufacturer, Eli Lilly and Company, for breach of warranty. The woman lost her case. Basing its ruling on a statement in the pamphlet accompanying the pills, which stated that, "When taken as directed, the tablets offer virtually 100 percent protection," the court ruled that there was no warranty, expressed or implied, that the pills were absolutely effective. In its ruling, the court pointed out that, according to *Webster's Third New International Dictionary,* "virtually" means "almost entirely" and clearly does not mean "absolute" (*Whittington* v. *Eli Lilly and Company,* 333 F. Supp. 98). In other words, the Eli Lilly company was really saying that its birth control pill, even when taken as directed, *did not in fact* provide 100 percent protection against pregnancy. But Eli Lilly didn't want to put it that way because then many women might not have bought Lilly's birth control pills.

The next time you see the ad that says that this dishwasher detergent "leaves dishes virtually spotless," just remember how advertisers twist the meaning of the weasel word "virtually." You can have lots of spots on your dishes after using this detergent and the ad claim will still be true, because what this claim really means is that this detergent does not *in fact* leave your dishes spotless. Whenever you see or hear an ad claim that uses the word "virtually," just translate that claim into its real meaning. So the television set that is "virtually trouble free" becomes the television set that is not in fact trouble free, the "virtually foolproof operation" of any appliance becomes an operation that is in fact not foolproof, and the product that "virtually never needs service" becomes the product that is not in fact service free.

New and Improved

If "new" is the most frequently used word on a product package, "improved" is the second most frequent. In fact, the two words are almost always used together. It seems just about everything sold these days is "new and improved." The next time you're in the supermarket, try counting the number of times you see these words on products. But you'd better do it while you're walking down just one aisle, otherwise you'll need a calculator to keep track of your counting.

Just what do these words mean? The use of the word "new" is restricted by regulations, so an advertiser can't just use the word on a product or in an ad without meeting certain requirements. For example, a product is considered new for about six months during a national advertising campaign. If the product is being advertised only in a limited test market area, the word can be used longer, and in some instances has been used for as long as two years.

What makes a product "new"? Some products have been around for a long time, yet every once in a while you discover that they are being advertised as "new." Well, an advertiser can call a product new if there has been "a material functional change" in the product. What is "a material functional change," you ask? Good question. In fact it's such a good question it's being asked all the time. It's up to the manufacturer to prove that the product has undergone such a change. And if the manufacturer isn't challenged on the claim, then there's no one to stop it. Moreover, the change does not have to be an improvement in the product. One manufacturer added an artificial lemon scent to a cleaning product and called it "new and improved," even though the product did not clean any better than without the lemon scent. The manufacturer defended the use of the word "new" on the grounds that the artificial scent changed the chemical formula of the product and therefore constituted "a material functional change." 15

Which brings up the word "improved." When used in advertising, "improved" does not mean "made better." It only means "changed" or "different from before." So, if the detergent maker puts a plastic pour spout on the box of detergent, the product has been "improved," and away we go with a whole new advertising campaign. Or, if the cereal maker adds more fruit or a different kind of fruit to the cereal, there's an improved product. Now you know why manufacturers are constantly making little changes in their products. Whole new advertising campaigns, designed to convince you that the product has been changed for the better, are based on small changes in superficial aspects of a product. The next time you see an ad for an "improved" product, ask yourself what was wrong with the old one. Ask yourself just how "improved" the product is. Finally, you might check to see whether the "improved" version costs more than the unimproved one. After all, someone has to pay for the millions of dollars spent advertising the improved product.

Of course, advertisers really like to run ads that claim a product is "new and improved." While what constitutes a "new" product may be subject to some regulation, "improved" is a subjective judgment. A manufacturer changes the shape of its stick deodorant, but the shape doesn't improve the function of the deodorant. That is, changing the shape doesn't affect the deodorizing ability of the deodorant, so the manufacturer calls it "improved." Another manufacturer adds ammonia to its liquid cleaner and calls it "new and improved." Since adding ammonia does affect the cleaning ability of the product, there has been a "material functional change" in the product, and the manufacturer can now call its cleaner "new," and "improved" as well. Now the weasel words "new and improved" are plastered all over the package and are the basis for a multimillion-dollar ad campaign. But after six months the word "new" will have to go, until someone can dream up another change in the product. Perhaps it will be adding color to the liquid, or changing the shape of the package, or maybe adding a new dripless pour spout, or perhaps a___. The "improvements" are endless, and so are the new advertising claims and campaigns.

"New" is just too useful and powerful a word in advertising for advertisers to pass it up easily. So they use weasel words that say "new" without really saying it. One of their favorites is "introducing," as in, "Introducing improved Tide," or "Introducing the stain remover." The first is simply saying, here's our improved soap; the second, here's our new advertising campaign for our detergent. Another favorite is "now," as in, "Now there's Sinex," which simply means that Sinex is available. Then there are phrases like "Today's Chevrolet," "Presenting Dristan," and "A fresh way to start the day." The list is really endless because advertisers are always finding new ways to say "new" without really saying it. If there is a second edition of [my] book, I'll just call it the "new and improved" edition. Wouldn't you really rather have a "new and improved" edition of [my] book rather than a "second" edition?

Acts Fast

"Acts" and "works" are two popular weasel words in advertising because they bring action to the product and to the advertising claim. When you see the ad for the cough syrup that "Acts on the cough control center," ask yourself what this cough syrup is claiming to do. Well, it's just claiming to "act," to do something, to perform an action. What is it that the cough syrup does? The ad doesn't say. It only claims to perform an action or do something on your "cough control center." By the way, what and where is your "cough control center"? I don't remember learning about that part of the body in human biology class.

Ads that use such phrases as "acts fast," "acts against," "acts to prevent," and the like are saying essentially nothing, because "act" is a word empty of any specific meaning. The ads are always careful not to specify exactly what "act" the product performs. Just because a brand of aspirin claims to "act fast" for headache relief doesn't mean this aspirin is any better than any other aspirin. What is the "act" that this aspirin performs? You're never told. Maybe it just dissolves quickly. Since aspirin is a parity product, all aspirin is the same and therefore functions the same.

20

Works Like Anything Else

If you don't find the word "acts" in an ad, you will probably find the weasel word "works." In fact, the two words are almost interchangeable in advertising. Watch out for ads that say a product "works against," "works like," "works for," or "works longer." As with "acts," "works" is the same meaningless verb used to make you think that this product really does something, and maybe even something special or unique. But "works," like "acts," is basically a word empty of any specific meaning.

Like Magic

Whenever advertisers want you to stop thinking about the product and to start thinking about something bigger, better, or more attractive than the product, they use that very popular weasel word "like." The word "like" is the advertiser's equivalent of a magician's use of misdirection. "Like" gets you to ignore the product and concentrate on the claim the advertiser is making about it. "For skin like peaches and cream" claims the ad for a skin cream. What is this ad really claiming? It doesn't say this cream will give you peaches-and-cream skin. There is no verb in this claim, so it doesn't even mention using the product. How is skin ever like "peaches and cream"? Remember, ads must be read literally and exactly, according to the dictionary definition of words. (Remember "virtually" in the Eli Lilly case.) The ad is making absolutely no promise or claim whatsoever for this skin cream. If you think this cream will give you soft, smooth, youthful-looking skin, you are the one who has read that meaning into the ad.

The wine that claims "It's like taking a trip to France" wants you to think about a romantic evening in Paris as you walk along the boulevard after a wonderful meal in an intimate little bistro. Of course, you don't really believe that a wine can take you to France, but the goal of the ad is to get you to think pleasant, romantic thoughts about France and not about how the wine tastes or how expensive it may be. That little word "like" has taken you away from crushed grapes into a world of your own imaginative making. Who knows, maybe the next time you buy wine, you'll think those pleasant thoughts when you see this brand of wine, and you'll buy it. Or, maybe you weren't even thinking about buying wine at all, but now you just might pick up a bottle the next time you're shopping. Ah, the power of "like" in advertising.

> **The word "like" is the advertiser's equivalent of a magician's use of misdirection.**

How about the most famous "like" claim of all, "Winston tastes good like a cigarette should"? Ignoring the grammatical error here, you might want to know what this claim is saying. Whether a cigarette tastes good or bad is a subjective judgment because what tastes good to one person may well taste horrible to another. Not everyone likes fried snails, even if they are called escargot. (*De gustibus non est disputandum*, which was probably the Roman rule for advertising as well as for defending the games in the Colosseum.) There are many people who say all cigarettes taste terrible, other people who say only some cigarettes taste all right, and still others who say all cigarettes taste good. Who's right? Everyone, because taste is a matter of personal judgment.

Moreover, note the use of the conditional, "should." The complete claim is, "Winston tastes good like a cigarette should taste." But should cigarettes taste good? Again, this is a matter of personal judgment and probably depends most on one's experiences with smoking. So, 25 the Winston ad is simply saying that Winston cigarettes are just like any other cigarette: Some people like them and some people don't. On that statement R. J. Reynolds conducted a very successful multimillion-dollar advertising campaign that helped keep Winston the number-two-selling cigarette in the United States, close behind number one, Marlboro.

CAN IT BE UP TO THE CLAIM?

Analyzing ads for doublespeak requires that you pay attention to every word in the ad and determine what each word really means. Advertisers try to wrap their claims in language that sounds concrete, specific, and objective, when in fact the language of advertising is anything but. Your job is to read carefully and listen critically so that when the announcer says that "Crest can be of significant value . . ." you know immediately that this claim says absolutely nothing. Where is the doublespeak in this ad? Start with the second word.

Once again, you have to look at what words really mean, not what you think they mean or what the advertiser wants you to think they mean. The ad for Crest only says that using Crest "can be" of "significant value." What really throws you off in this ad is the brilliant use of "significant." It draws your attention to the word "value" and makes you forget that the ad only claims that Crest "can be." The ad doesn't say that Crest *is* of value, only that it is "able" or "possible" to be of value, because that's all that "can" means.

It's so easy to miss the importance of those little words, "can be." Almost as easy as missing the importance of the words "up to" in an ad. These words are very popular in sale ads. You know, the ones that say, "Up to 50% Off!" Now, what does that claim mean? Not much, because the store or manufacturer has to reduce the price of only a few items by 50 percent. Everything else can be reduced a lot less, or not even reduced. Moreover, don't you want to know 50 percent off of what? Is it 50 percent off the "manufacturer's suggested list price," which is the highest possible price? Was the price artificially inflated and then reduced? In other ads, "up to" expresses an ideal situation. The medicine that works "up to ten times faster," the battery that lasts "up to twice as long," and the soap that gets you "up to twice as clean" all are based on ideal situations for using those products, situations in which you can be sure you will never find yourself.

UNFINISHED WORDS

Unfinished words are a kind of "up to" claim in advertising. The claim that a battery lasts "up to twice as long" usually doesn't finish the comparison — twice as long as what? A birthday candle? A tank of gas? A cheap battery made in a country not noted for its technological achievements? The implication is that the battery lasts twice as long as batteries made by other battery makers, or twice as long as earlier model batteries made by the advertiser, but the ad doesn't really make these claims. You read these claims into the ad, aided by the visual images the advertiser so carefully provides.

Unfinished words depend on you to finish them, to provide the words   30
the advertisers so thoughtfully left out of the ad. Pall Mall cigarettes were once advertised as "A longer finer and milder smoke." The question is, longer, finer, and milder than what? The aspirin that claims it contains "Twice as much of the pain reliever doctors recommend most" doesn't tell you what pain reliever it contains twice as much of. (By the way, it's aspirin. That's right; it just contains twice the amount of aspirin. And how much is twice the amount? Twice of what amount?) Panadol boasts that "nobody reduces fever faster," but, since Panadol is a parity product, this claim simply means that Panadol isn't any better than any other product in its parity class. "You can be sure if it's Westinghouse," you're told, but just exactly what it is you can be sure of is never mentioned. "Magnavox gives you more" doesn't tell you what you get more of. More value? More television? More than they gave you before? It sounds nice, but it means nothing, until you fill in the claim with your own words, the words the advertiser didn't use. Since each of us fills in the claim differently, the ad and the product can become all things to all people, and not promise a single thing.

Unfinished words abound in advertising because they appear to promise so much. More importantly, they can be joined with powerful visual images on television to appear to be making significant promises about a product's effectiveness without really making any promises. In a television ad, the aspirin product that claims fast relief can show a person with a headache taking the product and then, in what appears to be a matter of minutes, claiming complete relief. This visual image is far more powerful than any claim made in unfinished words. Indeed, the visual image completes the unfinished words for you, filling in with pictures what the words leave out. And you thought that ads didn't affect you. What brand of aspirin do you use?

Some years ago, Ford's advertisements proclaimed "Ford LTD—700 percent quieter." Now, what do you think Ford was claiming with these unfinished words? What was the Ford LTD quieter than? A Cadillac? A Mercedes Benz? A BMW? Well, when the FTC asked Ford to substantiate this unfinished claim, Ford replied that it meant that the inside of the LTD was 700 percent quieter than the outside. How did you finish those unfinished words when you first read them? Did you even come close to Ford's meaning?

COMBINING WEASEL WORDS

A lot of ads don't fall neatly into one category or another because they use a variety of different devices and words. Different weasel words are often combined to make an ad claim. The claim,

"Coffee-Mate gives coffee more body, more flavor," uses unfinished words ("more" than what?) and also uses words that have no specific meaning ("body" and "flavor"). Along with "taste" (remember the Winston ad and its claim to taste good), "body" and "flavor" mean nothing because their meaning is entirely subjective. To you, "body" in coffee might mean thick, black, almost bitter coffee, while I might take it to mean a light brown, delicate coffee. Now, if you think you understood that last sentence, read it again, because it said nothing of objective value; it was filled with weasel words of no specific meaning: "thick," "black," "bitter," "light brown," and "delicate." Each of those words has no specific, objective meaning, because each of us can interpret them differently.

Try this slogan: "Looks, smells, tastes like ground-roast coffee." So, are you now going to buy Taster's Choice instant coffee because of this ad? "Looks," "smells," and "tastes" are all words with no specific meaning and depend on your interpretation of them for any meaning. Then there's that great weasel word "like," which simply suggests a comparison but does not make the actual connection between the product and the quality. Besides, do you know what "ground-roast" coffee is? I don't, but it sure sounds good. So, out of seven words in this ad, four are definite weasel words, two are quite meaningless, and only one has clear meaning.

Remember the Anacin ad—"Twice as much of the pain reliever doctors recommend most"? There's a whole lot of weaseling going on in this ad. First, what's the pain reliever they're talking about in this ad? Aspirin, of course. In fact, any time you see or hear an ad using those words "pain reliever," you can automatically substitute the word "aspirin" for them. (Makers of acetaminophen and ibuprofen pain relievers are careful in their advertising to identify their products as nonaspirin products.) So, now we know that Anacin has aspirin in it. Moreover, we know that Anacin has twice as much aspirin in it, but we don't know twice as much as what. Does it have twice as much aspirin as an ordinary aspirin tablet? If so, what is an ordinary aspirin tablet, and how much aspirin does it contain? Twice as much as Excedrin or Bufferin? Twice as much as a chocolate chip cookie? Remember those unfinished words and how they lead you on without saying anything.

Finally, what about those doctors who are doing all that recommending? Who are they? How many of them are there? What kind of doctors are they? What are their qualifications? Who asked them about recommending pain relievers? What other pain relievers did they recommend? And there are a whole lot more questions about this "poll" of doctors to which I'd like to know the answers, but you get the point. Sometimes, when I call my doctor, she tells me to take two aspirin and call her office in the morning. Is that where Anacin got this ad?

35

THINKING CRITICALLY ABOUT THE READING

1. What are weasel words? How, according to Lutz, did they get their name?

2. Lutz is careful to illustrate each of the various kinds of weasel words with examples of actual usage. (Glossary: *Examples*) What do these examples add to his essay? Which ones do you find most effective? Explain.

3. According to Lutz, why is "help" the biggest weasel word used by advertisers (3–8)? In what ways does it help them present their products without having to make promises about actual performance?

4. Why is "virtually" a particularly effective weasel word (10–12)? Why can advertisers get away with using words that literally mean the opposite of what they want to convey?

5. When advertisers use the word "like," they often create a simile — "Ajax cleans *like* a white tornado." (Glossary: *Figures of Speech*) What, according to Lutz, is the power of similes in advertising (22–24)? Explain by citing several examples of your own.

6. What kinds of claims fit into Lutz's "unfinished words" category (29–32)? Why are they weasels? What makes them so difficult to detect?

LANGUAGE IN ACTION

Select one eye-catching advertisement from a website or magazine. Jot down any words that Lutz would describe as weasels. How does recognizing such language affect your impression of the product being advertised? What would happen to the text of the ad if the weasels were eliminated? Share your analysis with others in your class.

WRITING SUGGESTIONS

1. Choose something that you own and like — a mountain bike, a CD or DVD collection, luggage, a comfortable sofa, a stereo, or anything else that you are glad you bought. Imagine that you need to sell it to raise some money for a special weekend, and to do so you need to advertise on radio. Write copy for a 30-second advertising spot in which you try to sell your item. Include a slogan or make up a product name and use it in the ad. Then write a short essay about your ad in which you discuss the features of the item you chose to highlight, the language you used to make it sound as appealing as possible, and how your slogan or name makes the advertisement more memorable.

2. Pay attention to the ads for companies that offer rival products or services (for example, Apple and Samsung, Coca-Cola and Pepsi-Cola, Burger King and McDonald's, and AT&T and T-Mobile). Focusing on a single pair of ads, analyze the different appeals that companies make when comparing their products or services to those of the competition. To what audience does each ad appeal? How many weasel words can you detect? Based on your analysis, write an essay about the advertising strategies companies use when in head-to-head competition with the products of other companies.

The Ways of Silencing

Jason Stanley

Jason Stanley is a philosopher who specializes in the philosophy of language and linguistics, as well as questions involving cognition, context-dependence, and fallibilism, or the philosophical principle that we could be wrong about our beliefs. Stanley was born in Syracuse, New York, in 1969 and earned his BA in philosophy and linguistics at the State University of New York at Stony Brook in 1990 and his PhD at the Massachusetts Institute of Technology in 1995. Stanley has taught at a number of colleges and universities, including Rutgers University from 2004 to 2013, and is currently professor of philosophy at Yale University. He has written five books: *Knowledge and Practical Interests* (2005), *Language in Context: Selected Essays* (2007), *Know How* (2011), *How Propaganda Works* (2015), and *How Fascism Works: The Politics of Us and Them* (2018).

In "The Ways of Silencing," first published in *The New York Times* on June 25, 2011, Stanley examines the ways in which language may be supposed to further discussion or shed light on issues but is gradually manipulated and snuffs out the trust necessary for its very existence.

WRITING TO DISCOVER: *Do you think that most news outlets report the news objectively without any biases, or do you think they either give intentionally or unintentionally biased reports? On what evidence do you base your views? Cite examples where possible.*

We might wish politicians and pundits from opposing parties to engage in reasoned debate about the truth, but as we know, this is not the reality of our political discourse.

Instead we often encounter bizarre and improbable claims about public figures. Words are misappropriated and meanings twisted. I believe that these tactics are not really about making substantive claims, but rather play the role of silencing. They are, if you will, linguistic strategies for stealing the voices of others. These strategies have always been part of the arsenal of politics. But since they are so widely used today, it is worth examining their underlying mechanisms, to make apparent their special dangers.

The feminist scholar Catharine MacKinnon famously declared, "Pornography silences women." In the 1990s, the philosophers of language Jennifer Hornsby and Rae Langton developed an account of the mechanisms of silencing that could substantiate MacKinnon's claim. But their basic ideas extend beyond the examples they chose, and can inform us about silencing in our political discourse today.

In her 1993 paper, "Speech Acts and Pornography," Hornsby used an example, credited to Langton: Suppose that men are led to believe that when women refuse a sexual advance they don't mean it. Women, then, will not be understood to be refusing, even when they are. If certain kinds of pornography lead men to think that women are not sincere when they utter the word "no," and women are aware that men think this, those kinds of pornography would rob women of the ability to refuse. Using "no" to refuse a sexual advance is what is known as a speech act—a way of doing something by using words. Hornsby and Langton's work raises the possibility that a medium may undermine the ability of a person or group—in this case, women—to employ a speech act by representing that person or group as insincere in their use of it.

It is possible to silence people by denying them access to the vocabulary to express their claims.

Silencing extends to politics when   5
outlandish claims are made about public figures. Suppose that President Obama really was a secret Islamist agent, or born in Kenya. In that case, he would be grossly insincere. We would have no reason to believe what he said in any situation. The function of disseminating such claims about the president is not to object to his specific arguments or agenda. It is to undermine the public's trust in him, so that nothing he says can be taken at face value.

There are multiple purposes to political speech, only one of which is to assert truths. Nevertheless, we expect a core of sincerity from our leaders. We do not expect a Muammar el-Qaddafi. It is belief in this core of sincerity that bizarre claims about the president are intended to undermine.

Silencing in the sense described by Hornsby and Langton robs others of the ability to engage in speech acts, such as assertion. But there is another kind of silencing familiar in the political domain, not discussed by these authors. It is possible to silence people by denying them access to the vocabulary to express their claims.

One of the best investigations of propaganda was presented by Victor Klemperer, in his book *The Language of the Third Reich*. The data for Klemperer's claims was the language used by the Third Reich. But the points he makes are applicable to propaganda in the service of much more mundane endeavors, be it to pass health care reform or to increase or decrease taxes. The use of propaganda is not limited to a single political affiliation or intent.

As Klemperer writes in *The Language of the Third Reich*, propaganda "changes the value of words and the frequency of their occurrence . . . it commandeers for the party that which was previously common property and in the process steeps words and groups of words and sentence structures in its poison." When writing these words, Klemperer was thinking of the incessant use of the term "heroisch" ("heroic") to justify the military adventures of the National Socialist state. Obviously, the mechanism described by Klemperer is not used for such odious purposes today. Nevertheless, there has been a similar appropriation of the term "freedom" in American political discourse.

Most would agree that heroism and freedom are fundamentally good   10
things. But the terms "heroisch" and "freedom" have been appropriated
for purposes that do not have much connection with the virtues of their
original meanings. Whatever one thinks of the wisdom of the 2003 invasion of Iraq, it is difficult to have a reasoned debate about its costs and
benefits when the invasion itself is called "Operation Iraqi Freedom."
Similarly, whatever one thinks of tax cuts, or the estate tax, it is difficult
to engage in reasoned debate when they have been respectively relabeled
"tax relief" and "the death tax." It is difficult to have a reasoned debate
about the costs and benefits of a policy when one side has seized control
of the linguistic means to express all the positive claims. It is easy to say
"a tax cut is not always good policy," but considerably more difficult to
say "tax relief is not always good policy," even though "tax relief" is just a
phrase invented to mean the same as "tax cut."

Silencing is by no means limited to its target. The Fox channel
engages in silencing when it describes itself as "fair and balanced" to an
audience that is perfectly aware that it is neither. The effect is to suggest
that there is no such thing as fair and balanced—that there is no possibility of balanced news, only propaganda. The result is the silencing of every
news organ, by suggesting a generalized gross insincerity.

The effects of a belief in general gross insincerity are apparent in
societies in which the state media delivers only propaganda. Citizens who
grow up in a state in which the authorities deliver propaganda have no
experience with trust. So even if the members of that society have access
to reliable news, say via the Internet, they do not trust it. They are trained
to be suspicious of any organ marketing itself as news.

Silencing is only one kind of propaganda. In silencing, one removes
the ability of a target person or group to communicate. As a philosopher
of language I am less qualified to make a judgment about the wisdom of
Plato, Machiavelli, and Leo Strauss than I am to comment about their
favored political tool. However, I do think that given our current environment—of oppression, revolution, intervention, war, pseudo-war and
ever-present human power relations—it is worthwhile bearing in mind
the dangers of the manipulation of language. What may begin as a temporary method to circumvent reasoned discussion and debate for the sake of
a prized political goal may very well end up permanently undermining the
trust required for its existence.

THINKING CRITICALLY ABOUT THE READING

1. What is silencing? In your own terms, why does Stanley consider silencing
   propaganda?

2. Stanley quotes Catharine MacKinnon's statement: "Pornography silences
   women." What do you think MacKinnon meant by her statement?

3. Does Stanley himself engage in silencing? Explain.

4. Is Stanley an unbiased commentator on the question of silencing?

5. If silencing comes from the right as Stanley seems to believe, can you think of any examples of silencing that have come from the left?

LANGUAGE IN ACTION

After Jason Stanley's article appeared in *The New York Times,* the *Times* published several reader comments in response to Stanley ("Media and Mistrust: A Response," *New York Times,* July 18, 2011). Reprinted below is one reader's comments. In a small group with two or three classmates, evaluate the merits of this reader's argument. Do you agree or disagree with the reader? Why or why not?

> So we should not trust Fox News, but we should trust Rutgers University philosophy professors? Why, exactly? We know every news writer/broadcaster has his/her own biases that influence their work, and that every news consumer has his own biases that filter what we [sic] read/hear. In the end, it generally balances out.
>
> MORGAN, **Philadelphia**

WRITING SUGGESTIONS

1. Stanley makes some interesting references in his article to other scholars (e.g., Jennifer Hornsby, Rae Langton, and Victor Klemperer) who have addressed the importance of silencing as a propaganda strategy. Write an essay on silencing based on ideas and examples that you draw from their writings. Be careful to develop an effective thesis, to focus your work, and to include examples of your own in your essay, wherever possible.

2. Some of Stanley's readers have argued that he is guilty in his essay of the same kind of silencing to which he is opposed. Does he write with a political bias? If so, how? Do you find any problems with his examples? Do you also believe that the times we live in are more treacherous than times past, as he argues in paragraph 13? A larger question: Isn't all argumentative writing biased to an extent, even if the writer takes into account opponents' arguments as a way of countering them? Is it possible to write in a totally unbiased manner? Address some of these questions, and others that arise from these questions, in writing an essay on these important issues. You may want to reference comments made by Stanley's readers as well as the comments he has made in response at opinionator.blogs.nytimes.com/2011/07/18/media-and-mistrust-a-response/.

10

The Language of Discrimination: Hate, Prejudice, and Stereotypes

No single issue has absorbed our national consciousness more than prejudice and discrimination. That we are defined by and define others is an inevitability of our human condition, but the manner in which we relate to each other is a measure of our progress as a multiracial, multiethnic, and multicultural society. In a larger sense, it is a measure of our growth as a civilization. Not even the most optimistic observers of our society believe that equality is within sight, or perhaps even ultimately possible, but implicit in all views of the subject is the notion that we can and must improve our appreciation of each other if we are to better our lives.

Our purpose in this chapter is to introduce you to some ideas on the sources of prejudice and to illustrate the role that language plays in the origin and perpetuation of prejudice and discrimination. We begin with Andrew Sullivan's "What's So Bad about Hate?," an in-depth inquiry into the nature of hatred and its relationship to prejudice, bias, bigotry, malice, anger, and all the emotions in between. Next we present Gordon Allport's classic essay "The Language of Prejudice," acknowledged by scholars for the past fifty years as the definitive word on the subject. Allport's concepts of "nouns that cut slices" and "verbal realism and symbol phobia" demonstrate not only how language encodes prejudice but also how we can use language to escape bias and bigotry. In "The 'F Word'" Firoozeh Dumas uses her wit and good sense of humor to recount what life was like growing up in America as an Iranian immigrant. "All of us immigrants knew that moving to America would be fraught with challenges," she confesses, "but none of us thought that our names would be such an obstacle." How can one's name be seen as an obstacle for an immigrant? Dumas uses examples from her own experience to show how her "identifiably 'ethnic' name" left her vulnerable to taunts and name-calling incidents as a child and clear acts of prejudice and discrimination as an adult.

Next, in "The Racist Trope That Won't Die," Brent Staples examines one of the oldest and most pernicious terms of racial abuse that persists in American culture, in the context of a 2017 tweet by comic actor Roseanne Barr. In "The Fight over the Words of Immigration," Jeff Gammage discusses the various labels applied to people who are in the United States illegally. Whatever the labels people choose to use, their critics accuse them of being either too soft or too harsh, making the debate over the language we use almost as important as the immigration debate itself. Finally, in "Nobody Mean More to Me Than You," June Jordan recounts a memorable teaching experience and reveals how the concepts of "Standard English" and "Black English" expose prejudiced attitudes in American society.

What's So Bad about Hate?

ANDREW SULLIVAN

Andrew Sullivan was born in 1963 in South Godstone, Surrey, England, to Irish parents. He earned his B.A. in modern history at Magdalene College, Oxford, and his MA and PhD in government at Harvard University. Sullivan began his career in journalism at *The New Republic,* later wrote for *The New York Times Magazine,* and held an editorial post at *The Atlantic.* A gay, Catholic, conservative, and often controversial commentator, Sullivan is perhaps best known for his blog *The Daily Dish,* which ran from 2000 until 2015 and won the 2008 Weblog Award for Best Blog, and for his pioneering and outspoken advocacy for gay marriage. He has written several books: *Virtually Normal: An Argument about Homosexuality* (1995); *Love Undetectable: Notes on Friendship, Sex and Survival* (1998); and *The Conservative Soul: How We Lost It, How to Get It Back* (2006).

In "What's So Bad about Hate?," first published in *The New York Times Magazine* on September 26, 1999, Sullivan reveals how little we actually know about the emotion that lies at the base of prejudice. As he writes, "For all its emotional punch, 'hate' is far less nuanced an idea than prejudice, or bigotry, or bias, or anger, or even aversion to others."

WRITING TO DISCOVER: *Have you ever been so upset by someone that you could say you hated the person? If so, what prompted your reaction? How would you characterize the nature of the hatred you felt? Do you think it was an uncontrollable response or a conscious one? Do you think you had your reasons and would react the same way again in similar circumstances?*

I.

I wonder what was going on in John William King's head [in 1997] when he tied James Byrd Jr.'s feet to the back of a pickup truck and dragged him three miles down a road in rural Texas. King and two friends had picked up Byrd, who was black, when he was walking home, half-drunk, from a party. As part of a bonding ritual in their fledgling white supremacist group, the three men took Byrd to a remote part of town, beat him and chained his legs together before attaching them to the truck. Pathologists at King's trial testified that Byrd was probably alive and conscious until his body finally hit a culvert and split in two. When King was offered a chance to say something to Byrd's family at the trial, he smirked and uttered an obscenity.

We know all these details now, many months later. We know quite a large amount about what happened before and after. But I am still drawn, again and again, to the flash of ignition, the moment when fear and loathing became hate, the instant of transformation when King became hunter and Byrd became prey.

What was that? And what was it when Buford Furrow Jr., long-time member of the Aryan Nations, calmly walked up to a Filipino-American mailman he happened to spot, asked him to mail a letter and then shot him at point-blank range? Or when Russell Henderson beat Matthew Shepard, a young gay man, to a pulp, removed his shoes and then, with the help of a friend, tied him to a post like a dead coyote to warn off others?

For all our documentation of these crimes and others, our political and moral disgust at them, our morbid fascination with them, our sensitivity to their social meaning, we seem at times to have no better idea now than we ever had of what exactly they were about. About what that moment means when, for some reason or other, one human being asserts absolute, immutable superiority over another. About not the violence, but what the violence expresses. About what — exactly — hate is. And what our own part in it may be.

I find myself wondering what hate actually is in part because we have created an entirely new offense in American criminal law — a "hate crime" — to combat it. And barely a day goes by without someone somewhere declaring war against it. Last month President Clinton called for an expansion of hate-crime laws as "what America needs in our battle against hate." A couple of weeks later, Senator John McCain used a campaign speech to denounce the "hate" he said poisoned the land. New York's mayor, Rudolph Giuliani, recently tried to stop the Million Youth March in Harlem on the grounds that the event was organized by people "involved in hate marches and hate rhetoric."

For all our zeal to attack hate, we still have a remarkably vague idea of what it actually is.

The media concurs in its emphasis. In 1985, there were 11 mentions of "hate crimes" in the national media database Nexis. By 1990, there were more than a thousand. In the first six months of 1999, there were 7,000. "Sexy fun is one thing," wrote a *New York Times* reporter about sexual assaults in Woodstock '99's mosh pit. "But this was an orgy of lewdness tinged with hate." And when Benjamin Smith marked the Fourth of July this year by targeting blacks, Asians, and Jews for murder in Indiana and Illinois, the story wasn't merely about a twisted young man who had emerged on the scene. As the *Times* put it, "Hate arrived in the neighborhoods of Indiana University, in Bloomington, in the early-morning darkness."

But what exactly was this thing that arrived in the early-morning darkness? For all our zeal to attack hate, we still have a remarkably vague idea of what it actually is. A single word, after all, tells us less, not more. For all its emotional punch, "hate" is far less nuanced an idea than prejudice, or bigotry, or bias, or anger, or even mere aversion to others. Is it to stand in for all these varieties of human experience — and everything in between? If so, then the war against it will be so vast as to be quixotic. Or is "hate" to stand for a very specific idea or belief, or set of beliefs, with a very specific object or group of objects? Then waging war against it is almost certainly unconstitutional. Perhaps these kinds of questions are of no concern to those waging war on hate. Perhaps it is enough for them that they share a sentiment that there is too much hate and never enough vigilance in combating it. But sentiment is a poor basis for law, and a dangerous tool in politics. It is better to leave some unwinnable wars unfought.

II.

Hate is everywhere. Human beings generalize all the time, ahead of time, about everyone and everything. A large part of it may even be hard-wired. At some point in our evolution, being able to know beforehand who was friend or foe was not merely a matter of philosophical reflection. It was a matter of survival. And even today it seems impossible to feel a loyalty without also feeling a disloyalty, a sense of belonging without an equal sense of unbelonging. We're social beings. We associate. Therefore we disassociate. And although it would be comforting to think that the one could happen without the other, we know in reality that it doesn't. How many patriots are there who have never felt a twinge of xenophobia?

Of course, by hate we mean something graver and darker than this kind of lazy prejudice. But the closer you look at this distinction, the fuzzier it gets. Much of the time, we harbor little or no malice toward people of other backgrounds or places or ethnicities or ways of life. But then a car cuts you off at an intersection and you find yourself noticing immediately that the driver is a woman, or black, or old, or fat, or white, or male. Or you are walking down a city street at night and hear footsteps quickening behind you. You look around and see that it is a white woman and not a black man, and you are instantly relieved. These impulses are so spontaneous they are almost involuntary. But where did they come from? The mindless need to be mad at someone — anyone — or the unconscious eruption of a darker prejudice festering within?

In 1993, in San Jose, Calif., two neighbors — one heterosexual, one homosexual — were engaged in a protracted squabble over grass clippings. (The full case is recounted in *Hate Crimes,* by James B. Jacobs and Kimberly Potter.) The gay man regularly mowed his lawn without a grass catcher, which prompted his neighbor to complain on many occasions that grass clippings spilled over onto his driveway. Tensions grew until one day, the gay man mowed his front yard, spilling clippings onto his neighbor's driveway, prompting the straight man to yell an obscene and common anti-gay insult. The wrangling escalated. At one point, the gay man agreed to collect the clippings from his neighbor's driveway but then later found them dumped on his own porch. A fracas ensued with the gay man spraying the straight man's son with a garden hose, and the son hitting and kicking the gay man several times, yelling anti-gay slurs. The police were called, and the son was eventually convicted of a hate-motivated assault, a felony. But what was the nature of the hate: anti-gay bias, or suburban property-owner madness?

Or take the Labor Day parade last year in Broad Channel, a small island in Jamaica Bay, Queens. Almost everyone there is white, and in recent years a group of local volunteer firefighters has taken to decorating a pickup truck for the parade in order to win the prize for "funniest float." Their themes have tended toward the outrageously provocative. Beginning in 1995, they won prizes for floats depicting "Hasidic Park," "Gooks of Hazzard" and "Happy Gays." Last year, they called their float "Black to the Future, Broad Channel 2098." They imagined their community a century hence as a largely black enclave, with every stereotype imaginable: watermelons, basketballs and so on. At one point during the parade, one of them mimicked the dragging death of James Byrd. It was caught on videotape, and before long the entire community was depicted as a caldron of hate.

It's an interesting case, because the float was indisputably in bad taste and the improvisation on the Byrd killing was grotesque. But was it hate? The men on the float were local heroes for their volunteer work; they had no record of bigoted activity, and were not members of any racist organizations. In previous years, they had made fun of many other groups and saw themselves more as provocateurs than bigots. When they were described as racists, it came as a shock to them. They apologized for poor taste but refused to confess to bigotry. "The people involved aren't horrible people," protested a local woman. "Was it a racist act? I don't know. Are they racists? I don't think so."

If hate is a self-conscious activity, she has a point. The men were primarily motivated by the desire to shock and to reflect what they thought was their community's culture. Their display was not aimed at any particular black people, or at any blacks who lived in Broad Channel—almost none do. But if hate is primarily an unconscious activity, then the matter is obviously murkier. And by taking the horrific lynching of a black man as a spontaneous object of humor, the men were clearly advocating indifference to it. Was this an aberrant excess? Or the real truth about the men's feelings toward African-Americans? Hate or tastelessness? And how on earth is anyone, even perhaps the firefighters themselves, going to know for sure?

Or recall H. L. Mencken. He shared in the anti-Semitism of his time with more alacrity than most and was an indefatigable racist. "It is impossible," he wrote in his diary, "to talk anything resembling discretion or judgment into a colored woman. They are all essentially childlike, and even hard experience does not teach them anything." He wrote at another time of the "psychological stigmata" of the "Afro-American race." But it is also true that, during much of his life, day to day, Mencken conducted himself with no regard to race, and supported a politics that was clearly integrationist. As the editor of his diary has pointed out, Mencken published many black authors in his magazine, *The Mercury,* and lobbied on their behalf with his publisher, Alfred A. Knopf. The last thing Mencken ever wrote was a diatribe against racial segregation in Baltimore's public parks. He was good friends with leading black writers and journalists, including James Weldon Johnson, Walter White, and George S. Schuyler, and played an underappreciated role in promoting the Harlem Renaissance.

What would our modern view of hate do with Mencken? Probably   15
ignore him, or change the subject. But, with regard to hate, I know lots of people like Mencken. He reminds me of conservative friends who oppose almost every measure for homosexual equality yet genuinely delight in the company of their gay friends. It would be easier for me to think of them as haters, and on paper, perhaps, there is a good case that they are. But in real life, I know they are not. Some of them clearly harbor no real malice toward me or other homosexuals whatsoever.

They are as hard to figure out as those liberal friends who support every gay rights measure they have ever heard of but do anything to avoid going into a gay bar with me. I have to ask myself in the same, frustrating kind of way: are they liberal bigots or bigoted liberals? Or are they neither bigots nor liberals, but merely people?

III.

Hate used to be easier to understand. When Sartre described anti-Semitism in his 1946 essay "Anti-Semite and Jew," he meant a very specific array of firmly held prejudices, with a history, an ideology and even a pseudoscience to back them up. He meant a systematic attempt to demonize and eradicate an entire race. If you go to the Web site of the World Church of the Creator, the organization that inspired young Benjamin Smith to murder in Illinois earlier this year, you will find a similarly bizarre, pseudorational ideology. The kind of literature read by Buford Furrow before he rained terror on a Jewish kindergarten last month and then killed a mailman because of his color is full of the same paranoid loopiness. And when we talk about hate, we often mean this kind of phenomenon.

But this brand of hatred is mercifully rare in the United States. These professional maniacs are to hate what serial killers are to murder. They should certainly not be ignored; but they represent what Harold Meyerson, writing in *Salon*, called "niche haters": cold blooded, somewhat deranged, often poorly socialized psychopaths. In a free society with relatively easy access to guns, they will always pose a menace.

But their menace is a limited one, and their hatred is hardly typical of anything very widespread. Take Buford Furrow. He famously issued a "wake-up call" to "kill Jews" in Los Angeles, before he peppered a Jewish community center with gunfire. He did this in a state with two Jewish female senators, in a city with a large, prosperous Jewish population, in a country where out of several million Jewish Americans, a total of 66 were reported by the F.B.I. as the targets of hate-crime assaults in 1997. However despicable Furrow's actions were, it would require a very large stretch to describe them as representative of anything but the deranged fringe of an American subculture.

Most hate is more common and more complicated, with as many   20
varieties as there are varieties of love. Just as there is possessive love and needy love; family love and friendship; romantic love and unrequited love; passion and respect, affection and obsession, so hatred has its shadings. There is hate that fears, and hate that merely feels contempt; there is hate that expresses power, and hate that comes from powerlessness; there is revenge, and there is hate that comes from envy. There is hate that was love, and hate that is a curious expression of love. There is hate of the other, and hate of something that reminds us too much of ourselves. There is the oppressor's hate, and the victim's hate. There is hate that burns slowly, and hate that fades. And there is hate that explodes, and hate that never catches fire.

The modern words that we have created to describe the varieties of hate — "sexism," "racism," "anti-Semitism," "homophobia" — tell us very little about any of this. They tell us merely the identities of the victims; they don't reveal the identities of the perpetrators, or what they think, or how they feel. They don't even tell us how the victims feel. And this simplicity is no accident. Coming from the theories of Marxist and post-Marxist academics, these "isms" are far better at alleging structures of power than at delineating the workings of the individual heart or mind. In fact, these "isms" can exist without mentioning individuals at all.

We speak of institutional racism, for example, as if an institution can feel anything. We talk of "hate" as an impersonal noun, with no hater specified. But when these abstractions are actually incarnated, when someone feels something as a result of them, when a hater actually interacts with a victim, the picture changes. We find that hates are often very different phenomena one from another, that they have very different psychological dynamics, that they might even be better understood by not seeing them as varieties of the same thing at all.

There is, for example, the now unfashionable distinction between reasonable hate and unreasonable hate. In recent years, we have become accustomed to talking about hates as if they were all equally indefensible, as if it could never be the case that some hates might be legitimate, even necessary. But when some 800,000 Tutsis are murdered under the auspices of a Hutu regime in Rwanda, and when a few thousand Hutus are killed in revenge, the hates are not commensurate. Genocide is not an event like a hurricane, in which damage is random and universal; it is a planned and often merciless attack of one group upon another. The hate of the perpetrators is a monstrosity. The hate of the victims, and their survivors, is justified. What else, one wonders, were surviving Jews supposed to feel toward Germans after the Holocaust? Or, to a different degree, South African blacks after apartheid? If the victims overcome this hate, it is a supreme moral achievement. But if they don't, the victims are not as culpable as the perpetrators. So the hatred of Serbs for Kosovars today can never be equated with the hatred of Kosovars for Serbs.

Hate, like much of human feeling, is not rational, but it usually has its reasons. And it cannot be understood, let alone condemned, without knowing them. Similarly, the hate that comes from knowledge is always different from the hate that comes from ignorance. It is one of the most foolish clichés of our time that prejudice is always rooted in ignorance, and can usually be overcome by familiarity with the objects of our loathing. The racism of many Southern whites under segregation was not appeased by familiarity with Southern blacks; the virulent loathing of Tutsis by many Hutus was not undermined by living next door to them for centuries. Theirs was a hatred that sprang, for whatever reasons, from experience. It cannot easily be compared with, for example, the resilience of anti-Semitism in Japan, or hostility to immigration in areas where immigrants are unknown, or fear of homosexuals by people who have never knowingly met one.

The same familiarity is an integral part of what has become known   25
as "sexism." Sexism isn't, properly speaking, a prejudice at all. Few men live without knowledge or constant awareness of women. Every single sexist man was born of a woman, and is likely to be sexually attracted to women. His hostility is going to be very different than that of, say, a reclusive member of the Aryan Nations toward Jews he has never met.

In her book *The Anatomy of Prejudices,* the psychotherapist Elisabeth Young-Bruehl proposes a typology of three distinct kinds of hate: obsessive, hysterical, and narcissistic. It's not an exhaustive analysis, but it's a beginning in any serious attempt to understand hate rather than merely declaring war on it. The obsessives, for Young-Bruehl, are those, like the Nazis or Hutus, who fantasize a threat from a minority, and obsessively try to rid themselves of it. For them, the very existence of the hated group is threatening. They often describe their loathing in almost physical terms: they experience what Patrick Buchanan, in reference to homosexuals, once described as a "visceral recoil" from the objects of their detestation. They often describe those they hate as diseased or sick, in need of a cure. Or they talk of "cleansing" them, as the Hutus talked of the Tutsis, or call them "cockroaches," as Yitzhak Shamir called the Palestinians.* If you read material from the Family Research Council, it is clear that the group regards homosexuals as similar contaminants. A recent posting on its Web site about syphilis among gay men was headlined, "Unclean."

Hysterical haters have a more complicated relationship with the objects of their aversion. In Young-Bruehl's words, hysterical prejudice is a prejudice that "a person uses unconsciously to appoint a group to act out in the world forbidden sexual and sexually aggressive desires that the person has repressed." Certain kinds of racists fit this pattern. White loathing of blacks is, for some people, at least partly about sexual and physical envy. A certain kind of white racist sees in black America all those impulses he wishes most to express himself but cannot. He idealizes in "blackness" a sexual freedom, a physical power, a Dionysian release that he detests but also longs for. His fantasy may not have any basis in reality, but it is powerful nonetheless. It is a form of love-hate, and it is impossible to understand the nuances of racism in, say, the American South, or in British Imperial India, without it.

Unlike the obsessives, the hysterical haters do not want to eradicate the objects of their loathing; rather they want to keep them in some kind of permanent and safe subjugation in order to indulge the attraction of their repulsion. A recent study, for example, found that the men most likely to be opposed to equal rights for homosexuals were those most likely to be aroused by homoerotic imagery. This makes little rational sense, but it has a certain psychological plausibility. If homosexuals were granted equality, then the hysterical gay-hater might panic that his repressed passions would run out of control, overwhelming him and the world he inhabits.

A narcissistic hate, according to Young-Bruehl's definition, is sexism. In its most common form, it is rooted in many men's inability even to imagine what it is to be a woman, a failing rarely challenged by men's control of our most powerful public social institutions. Women are not so much hated by most men as simply ignored in non-sexual contexts, or never conceived of as true equals. The implicit condescension is

---

* Sullivan has since written that the correct translation of Israeli Prime Minister Yitzhak Shamir's word was *grasshoppers,* not *cockroaches* as he originally wrote here. However, Sullivan stands by his original meaning, saying that the comparison was to insects that were to be crushed.

mixed, in many cases, with repressed and sublimated erotic desire. So the unawareness of women is sometimes commingled with a deep longing or contempt for them.

Each hate, of course, is more complicated than this, and in any one person hate can assume a uniquely configured combination of these types. So there are hysterical sexists who hate women because they need them so much, and narcissistic sexists who hardly notice that women exist, and sexists who oscillate between one of these positions and another. And there are gay-bashers who are threatened by masculine gay men and gay-haters who feel repulsed by effeminate ones. The soldier who beat his fellow soldier Barry Winchell to death with a baseball bat in July had earlier lost a fight to him. It was the image of a macho gay man—and the shame of being bested by him—that the vengeful soldier had to obliterate, even if he needed a gang of accomplices and a weapon to do so. But the murderers of Matthew Shepard seem to have had a different impulse: a visceral disgust at the thought of any sexual contact with an effeminate homosexual. Their anger was mixed with mockery, as the cruel spectacle at the side of the road suggested.

In the same way, the pathological anti-Semitism of Nazi Germany was obsessive, inasmuch as it tried to cleanse the world of Jews; but also, as Daniel Jonah Goldhagen shows in his book, *Hitler's Willing Executioners,* hysterical. The Germans were mysteriously compelled as well as repelled by Jews, devising elaborate ways, like death camps and death marches, to keep them alive even as they killed them. And the early Nazi phobia of interracial sex suggests as well a lingering erotic quality to the relationship, partaking of exactly the kind of sexual panic that persists among some homosexual-haters and antimiscegenation racists. So the concept of "homophobia," like that of "sexism" and "racism," is often a crude one. All three are essentially cookie-cutter formulas that try to understand human impulses merely through the one-dimensional identity of the victims, rather than through the thoughts and feelings of the haters and hated.

This is deliberate. The theorists behind these "isms" want to ascribe all blame to one group in society—the "oppressors"—and render specific others—the "victims"—completely blameless. And they want to do this in order, in part, to side unequivocally with the underdog. But it doesn't take a genius to see how this approach, too, can generate its own form of bias. It can justify blanket condemnations of whole groups of people—white straight males, for example—purely because of the color of their skin or the nature of their sexual orientation. And it can condescendingly ascribe innocence to whole groups of others. It does exactly what hate does: it hammers the uniqueness of each individual into the anvil of group identity. And it postures morally over the result.

In reality, human beings and human acts are far more complex, which is why these isms and the laws they have fomented are continually coming under strain and challenge. Once again, hate wriggles free of its definers. It knows no monolithic groups of haters and hated. Like a river, it has many eddies, backwaters, and rapids. So there are anti-Semites who actually admire what they think of as Jewish power, and there are gay-haters who look up to homosexuals and some who want to sleep with them. And there are black racists, racist Jews, sexist women, and anti-Semitic homosexuals. Of course there are.

IV.

Once you start thinking of these phenomena less as the "isms" of sexism/racism and "homophobia," once you think of them as independent psychological responses, it's also possible to see how they can work in a bewildering variety of ways in a bewildering number of people. To take one obvious and sad oddity: people who are demeaned and objectified in society may develop an aversion to their tormentors that is more hateful in its expression than the prejudice they have been subjected to. The F.B.I. statistics on hate crimes throws up an interesting point. In America in the 1990s, blacks were up to three times as likely as whites to commit a hate crime, to express their hate by physically attacking their targets or their property. Just as sexual abusers have often been victims of sexual abuse, and wife-beaters often grew up in violent households, so hate criminals may often be members of hated groups.

Even the Columbine murderers were in some sense victims of hate 35 before they were purveyors of it. Their classmates later admitted that Dylan Klebold and Eric Harris were regularly called "faggots" in the corridors and classrooms of Columbine High and that nothing was done to prevent or stop the harassment. This climate of hostility doesn't excuse the actions of Klebold and Harris, but it does provide a more plausible context. If they had been black, had routinely been called "nigger" in the school and had then exploded into a shooting spree against white students, the response to the matter might well have been different. But the hate would have been the same. In other words, hate-victims are often hate-victimizers as well. This doesn't mean that all hates are equivalent, or that some are not more justified than others. It means merely that hate goes both ways; and if you try to regulate it among some, you will find yourself forced to regulate it among others.

It is no secret, for example, that some of the most vicious anti-Semites in America are black, and that some of the most virulent anti-Catholic bigots in America are gay. At what point, we are increasingly forced to ask, do these phenomena become as indefensible as white racism or religious toleration of anti-gay bigotry? That question becomes all the more difficult when we notice that it is often minorities who commit some of the most hate-filled offenses against what they see as their oppressors. It was the mainly gay AIDS activist group Act Up that perpetrated the hateful act of desecrating Communion hosts at a Mass at St. Patrick's Cathedral in New York. And here is the playwright Tony Kushner, who is gay, responding to the Matthew Shepard beating in *The Nation* magazine: "Pope John Paul II endorses murder. He, too, knows the price of discrimination, having declared anti-Semitism a sin. . . . He knows that discrimination kills. But when the Pope heard the news about Matthew Shepard, he, too, worried about spin. And so, on the subject of gay-bashing, the Pope and his cardinals and his bishops and priests maintain their cynical political silence. . . . To remain silent is to endorse murder." Kushner went on to describe the Pope as a "homicidal liar."

Maybe the passion behind these words is justified. But it seems clear enough to me that Kushner is expressing hate toward the institution of the Catholic Church, and all those who perpetuate its doctrines. How else to interpret the way in which he accuses the Pope of cynicism, lying, and murder? And how else either to understand the brutal parody of religious vocations expressed by the Sisters of Perpetual Indulgence, a group of gay men who dress in drag as nuns and engage in sexually explicit performances in public? Or T-shirts with the words "Recovering Catholic" on them, hot items among some gay and lesbian activists? The implication that someone's religious faith is a mental illness is clearly an expression of contempt. If that isn't covered under the definition of hate speech, what is?

Or take the following sentence: "The act male homosexuals commit is ugly and repugnant and afterwards they are disgusted with themselves. They drink and take drugs to palliate this, but they are disgusted with the act and they are always changing partners and cannot be really happy." The thoughts of Pat Robertson or Patrick Buchanan? Actually that sentence was written by Gertrude Stein, one of the century's most notable lesbians. Or take the following, about how beating up "black boys like that made us feel good inside. . . . Every time I drove my foot into his [expletive], I felt better." It was written to describe the brutal assault of an innocent bystander for the sole reason of his race. By the end of the attack, the victim had blood gushing from his mouth as his attackers stomped on his genitals. Are we less appalled when we learn that the actual sentence was how beating up "white boys like that made us feel good inside. . . . Every time I drove my foot into his [expletive], I felt better?" It was written by Nathan McCall, an African-American who later in life became a successful journalist at *The Washington Post* and published his memoir of this "hate crime" to much acclaim.

In fact, one of the stranger aspects of hate is that the prejudice expressed by a group in power may often be milder in expression than the prejudice felt by the marginalized. After all, if you already enjoy privilege, you may not feel the anger that turns bias into hate. You may not need to.

For this reason, most white racism may be more influential in society than most black racism—but also more calmly expressed.

So may other forms of minority loathing—especially hatred within 40 minorities. I'm sure that black conservatives like Clarence Thomas or Thomas Sowell have experienced their fair share of white racism. But I wonder whether it has ever reached the level of intensity of the hatred directed toward them by other blacks? In several years of being an openly gay writer and editor, I have experienced the gamut of responses to my sexual orientation. But I have only directly experienced articulated, passionate hate from other homosexuals. I have been accused over the years by other homosexuals of being a sellout, a hypocrite, a traitor, a sexist, a racist, a narcissist, a snob. I've been called selfish, callous, hateful, self-hating, and malevolent. At a reading, a group of lesbian activists portrayed my face on a poster within the crossfires of a gun. Nothing from the religious right has come close to such vehemence.

I am not complaining. No harm has ever come to me or my property, and much of the criticism is rooted in the legitimate expression of political differences. But the visceral tone and style of the gay criticism can only be described as hateful. It is designed to wound personally, and it often does. But its intensity comes in part, one senses, from the pain of being excluded for so long, of anger long restrained bubbling up and directing itself more aggressively toward an alleged traitor than an alleged enemy. It is the hate of the hated. And it can be the most hateful hate of all. For this reason, hate-crime laws may themselves be an oddly biased category—biased against the victims of hate. Racism is everywhere, but the already victimized might be more desperate, more willing to express it violently. And so more prone to come under the suspicious eye of the law.

V.

And why is hate for a group worse than hate for a person? In Laramie, Wyoming, the now-famous epicenter of "homophobia," where Matthew Shepard was brutally beaten to death, vicious murders are not unknown. In the previous 12 months, a 15-year-old pregnant girl was found east of the town with 17 stab wounds. Her 38-year-old boyfriend was apparently angry that she had refused an abortion and left her in the Wyoming foothills to bleed to death. In the summer of 1998, an 8-year-old Laramie girl was abducted, raped and murdered by a pedophile, who disposed of her young body in a garbage dump. Neither of these killings was deemed a hate crime, and neither would be designated as such under any existing hate-crime law. Perhaps because of this, one crime is an international legend; the other two are virtually unheard of.

But which crime was more filled with hate? Once you ask the question, you realize how difficult it is to answer. Is it more hateful to kill a stranger or a lover? Is it more hateful to kill a child than an adult? Is it more hateful to kill your own child than another's? Under the law before the invention of hate crimes, these decisions didn't have to be taken. But under the law after hate crimes, a decision is essential. A decade ago, a murder was a murder. Now, in the era when group hate has emerged as our cardinal social sin, it all depends.

The supporters of laws against hate crimes argue that such crimes should be disproportionately punished because they victimize more than the victim. Such crimes, these advocates argue, spread fear, hatred and panic among whole populations, and therefore merit more concern. But, of course, all crimes victimize more than the victim, and spread alarm in the society at large. Just think of the terrifying church shooting in Texas only two weeks ago. In fact, a purely random murder may be even more terrifying than a targeted one, since the entire community, and not just a part of it, feels threatened. High rates of murder, robbery, assault, and burglary victimize everyone, by spreading fear, suspicion, and distress everywhere. Which crime was more frightening to more people this summer: the mentally ill Buford Furrow's crazed attacks in Los Angeles, killing one, or Mark Barton's murder of his own family and several random day-traders in Atlanta, killing 12? Almost certainly the latter. But only Furrow was guilty of "hate."

One response to this objection is that certain groups feel fear more 45 intensely than others because of a history of persecution or intimidation. But doesn't this smack of a certain condescension toward minorities? Why, after all, should it be assumed that gay men or black women or Jews, for example, are as a group more easily intimidated than others? Surely in any of these communities there will be a vast range of responses, from panic to concern to complete indifference. The assumption otherwise is the kind of crude generalization the law is supposed to uproot in the first place. And among these groups, there are also likely to be vast differences. To equate a population once subjected to slavery with a population of Mexican immigrants or third-generation Holocaust survivors is to equate the unequatable. In fact, it is to set up a contest of vulnerability in which one group vies with another to establish its particular variety of suffering, a contest that can have no dignified solution.

Rape, for example, is not classified as a "hate crime" under most existing laws, pitting feminists against ethnic groups in a battle for recognition. If, as a solution to this problem, everyone, except the white straight able-bodied male, is regarded as a possible victim of a hate crime, then we have simply created a two-tier system of justice in which racial profiling is reversed, and white straight men are presumed guilty before being proven innocent, and members of minorities are free to hate them as gleefully as they like. But if we include the white straight male in the litany of potential victims, then we have effectively abolished the notion of a hate crime altogether. For if every crime is possibly a hate crime, then it is simply another name for crime. All we will have done is widened the search for possible bigotry, ratcheted up the sentences for everyone and filled the jails up even further.

Hate-crime-law advocates counter that extra penalties should be imposed on hate crimes because our society is experiencing an "epidemic" of such crimes. Mercifully, there is no hard evidence to support this notion. The Federal Government has only been recording the incidence of hate crimes in this decade, and the statistics tell a simple story. In 1992, there were 6,623 hate-crime incidents reported to the F.B.I., by a total of 6,181 agencies, covering 51 percent of the population. In 1996, there were 8,734 incidents reported by 11,355 agencies, covering 84 percent of the population. That number dropped to 8,049 in 1997. These numbers are, of course, hazardous. They probably underreport the incidence of such crimes, but they are the only reliable figures we have. Yet even if they are faulty as an absolute number, they do not show an epidemic of "hate crimes" in the 1990s.

Is there evidence that the crimes themselves are becoming more vicious? None. More than 60 percent of recorded hate crimes in America involve no violent, physical assault against another human being at all, and, again, according to the F.B.I., that proportion has not budged much in the 1990s. These impersonal attacks are crimes against property or crimes of "intimidation." Murder, which dominates media coverage of hate crimes, is a tiny proportion of the total. Of the 8,049 hate crimes reported to the F.B.I. in 1997, a total of eight were murders. Eight. The number of hate crimes that were aggravated assaults (generally involving a weapon) in 1997 is less than 15 percent of the total. That's 1,237 assaults too many, of course, but to put it in perspective, compare it with a reported 1,022,492 "equal opportunity" aggravated assaults in America in the same year. The number of hate crimes that were physical assaults is half the total. That's 4,000 assaults too many, of course, but to put it in perspective, it compares with around 3.8 million "equal opportunity" assaults in America annually.

The truth is, the distinction between a crime filled with personal hate and a crime filled with group hate is an essentially arbitrary one. It tells us nothing interesting about the psychological contours of the specific actor or his specific victim. It is a function primarily of politics, of special interest groups carving out particular protections for themselves, rather than a serious response to a serious criminal concern. In such an endeavor, hate-crime-law advocates cram an entire world of human motivations into an immutable, tiny box called hate, and hope to have solved a problem. But nothing has been solved; and some harm may even have been done.

In an attempt to repudiate a past that treated people differently 50 because of the color of their skin, or their sex, or religion or sexual orientation, we may merely create a future that permanently treats people differently because of the color of their skin, or their sex, religion, or sexual orientation. This notion of a hate crime, and the concept of hate that lies behind it, takes a psychological mystery and turns it into a facile political artifact. Rather than compounding this error and extending even further, we should seriously consider repealing the concept altogether.

To put it another way: violence can and should be stopped by the government. In a free society, hate can't and shouldn't be. The boundaries between hate and prejudice and between prejudice and opinion and between opinion and truth are so complicated and blurred that any attempt to construct legal and political fire walls is a doomed and illiberal venture. We know by now that hate will never disappear from human consciousness; in fact, it is probably, at some level, definitive of it. We know after decades of education measures that hate is not caused merely by ignorance; and after decades of legislation, that it isn't caused entirely by law.

To be sure, we have made much progress. Anyone who argues that America is as inhospitable to minorities and to women today as it has been in the past has not read much history. And we should, of course, be vigilant that our most powerful institutions, most notably the government, do not actively or formally propagate hatred; and insure that the violent expression of hate is curtailed by the same rules that punish all violent expression.

But after that, in an increasingly diverse culture, it is crazy to expect that hate, in all its variety, can be eradicated. A free country will always mean a hateful country. This may not be fair, or perfect, or admirable, but it is reality, and while we need not endorse it, we should not delude ourselves into thinking we can prevent it. That is surely the distinction between toleration and tolerance. Tolerance is the eradication of hate; toleration is co-existence despite it. We might do better as a culture and as a polity if we concentrated more on achieving the latter rather than the former. We would certainly be less frustrated.

And by aiming lower, we might actually reach higher. In some ways, some expression of prejudice serves a useful social purpose. It lets off steam; it allows natural tensions to express themselves incrementally; it can siphon off conflict through words, rather than actions. Anyone who has lived in the ethnic shouting match that is New York City knows exactly what I mean. If New Yorkers disliked each other less, they wouldn't be able to get on so well. We may not all be able to pull off a Mencken — bigoted in words, egalitarian in action — but we might achieve a lesser form of virtue: a human acceptance of our need for differentiation, without a total capitulation to it.

Do we not owe something more to the victims of hate? Perhaps we   55 do. But it is also true that there is nothing that government can do for the hated that the hated cannot better do for themselves. After all, most bigots are not foiled when they are punished specifically for their beliefs. In fact, many of the worst haters crave such attention and find vindication in such rebukes. Indeed, our media's obsession with "hate," our elevation of it above other social misdemeanors and crimes, may even play into the hands of the pathetic and the evil, may breathe air into the smoldering embers of their paranoid loathing. Sure, we can help create a climate in which such hate is disapproved of—and we should. But there is a danger that if we go too far, if we punish it too much, if we try to abolish it altogether, we may merely increase its mystique, and entrench the very categories of human difference that we are trying to erase.

For hate is only foiled not when the haters are punished but when the hated are immune to the bigot's power. A hater cannot psychologically wound if a victim cannot psychologically be wounded. And that immunity to hurt can never be given; it can merely be achieved. The racial epithet only strikes at someone's core if he lets it, if he allows the bigot's definition of him to be the final description of his life and his person—if somewhere in his heart of hearts, he believes the hateful slur to be true. The only final answer to this form of racism, then, is not majority persecution of it, but minority indifference to it. The only permanent rebuke to homophobia is not the enforcement of tolerance, but gay equanimity in the face of prejudice. The only effective answer to sexism is not a morass of legal proscriptions, but the simple fact of female success. In this, as in so many other things, there is no solution to the problem. There is only a transcendence of it. For all our rhetoric, hate will never be destroyed. Hate, as our predecessors knew better, can merely be overcome.

THINKING CRITICALLY ABOUT THE READING

1. What does Sullivan mean when he writes in paragraph 8, "A large part of [hate] may even be hard-wired"? If he is correct, what might one conclude about attempts to legislate against hate crimes?

2. In paragraph 21, Sullivan writes that the "modern words that we have created to describe the varieties of hate—'sexism,' 'racism,' 'anti-Semitism,' 'homophobia'—tell us very little" about the different kinds of hate he delineates in the paragraph above. What does he mean by this?

3. Some argue that hatred is a result of ignorance. How does Sullivan respond to this argument?

4. What does Sullivan see as the difference between the hatred of the perpetrator and the hatred of the victim in return (24)?

5. Sullivan cites Elisabeth Young-Bruehl's typology of hate in paragraph 26. What three kinds of hate does she identify, and what characterizes each type? How helpful do you find her classification in understanding hate? (Glossary: *Classification*)

6. What problems does Sullivan see with respect to hate-crime legislation (42–56)? What arguments does he present in favor of repealing hate-crime legislation? Do you agree or disagree with his reasons?

7. What does Sullivan find interesting about the hate that has been directed at him by other gay people? How does he explain it?

LANGUAGE IN ACTION

Sullivan builds a philosophical argument around a single word: hate. Regardless of mainstream dictionary definitions, "hate" is very difficult to define for legal purposes. Without consulting any outside source, work in small groups to come up with a functional, legal definition of hate. Establish criteria that would make an otherwise "ordinary" crime a "hate crime," then provide a list of things that would meet your criteria. Avoid generalizations. For example, if an element of your criteria is a bias against a particular group, what would constitute proof that the offender did in fact have a bias against that group? And what sort of evidence could be provided to prove that the crime itself was motivated, in whole or in part, by that bias?

Once you are able to reach some consensus, join with another group and see in what ways your definitions are alike and in what ways they are different. Where there are differences, try to reach some compromise: try to come up with language that everyone can agree upon.

WRITING SUGGESTIONS

1. Write an essay in which you examine the various terms for hate that Sullivan uses in his essay. How might an examination of these terms help us to understand both the dynamics of prejudice and how we, as individuals and as a society, respond to these dynamics?

2. In paragraph 56, Sullivan writes: "For hate is only foiled not when the haters are punished but when the hated are immune to the bigot's power. A hater cannot psychologically wound if a victim cannot psychologically be wounded. And that immunity to hurt can never be given; it can merely be achieved." Write an essay in which you explore the implications of Sullivan's comments. Consider in particular how what Sullivan writes here relates to the establishment of hate-crime laws.

The Language of Prejudice

GORDON ALLPORT

Gordon Allport was born in Montezuma, Indiana, in 1897. He attended Harvard College and graduated Phi Beta Kappa in 1919 with majors in philosophy and economics. During his undergraduate years, he also became interested in psychology, and a meeting with Sigmund Freud in Vienna in 1920 — during which the founder of psychoanalysis failed to impress him — had a profound influence on him. After studying and teaching abroad, Allport returned to Harvard to teach social ethics and to pursue his PhD, which he received in 1922. He went on to become a full professor at Harvard in 1942, served as chairman of the psychology department, and received the Gold Medal Award of the American Psychological Foundation in 1963. He died in 1967.

Allport became known for his outspoken stance regarding racial prejudice, and he was hopeful about efforts being made to eradicate it. His book *The Nature of Prejudice* (1954) is still regarded as one of the most important and influential texts on the subject. The following selection from that book analyzes the connections between language and prejudice, and explains some of the specific ways in which language can induce and shape prejudice.

WRITING TO DISCOVER: *While in high school and college, many students are associated with groups that bring together people of disparate racial and religious backgrounds. Labels for these groups often carry many positive or negative associations. You may have made such associations yourself without thinking twice about it, as in "He's just a jock," or "She's with the popular crowd — she'll never go out with me." To what group, if any, did you belong in high school? Briefly write about the effects cliques in your school had on you and your classmates. How did labels associated with the different groups influence how you thought about the individual members of each group?*

Without words we should scarcely be able to form categories at all. A dog perhaps forms rudimentary generalizations, such as small-boys-are-to-be-avoided — but this concept runs its course on the conditioned reflex level, and does not become the object of thought as such. In order to hold a generalization in mind for reflection and recall, for identification and for action, we need to fix it in words. Without words our world would be, as William James said, an "empirical sand-heap."

NOUNS THAT CUT SLICES

In the empirical world of human beings there are some two and a half billion grains of sand corresponding to our category "the human race." We cannot possibly deal with so many separate entities in our thought, nor can we individualize even among the hundreds whom we encounter in our daily round. We must group them, form clusters. We welcome, therefore, the names that help us to perform the clustering.

The most important property of a noun is that it brings many grains of sand into a single pail, disregarding the fact that the same grains might have fitted just as appropriately into another pail. To state the matter technically, a noun *abstracts* from a concrete reality some one feature and assembles different concrete realities only with respect to this one feature. The very act of classifying forces us to overlook all other features, many of which might offer a sounder basis than the rubric we select. Irving Lee gives the following example:

> I knew a man who had lost the use of both eyes. He was called a "blind man." He could also be called an expert typist, a conscientious worker, a good student, a careful listener, a man who wanted a job. But he couldn't get a job in the department store order room where employees sat and typed orders which came over the telephone. The personnel man was impatient to get the interview over. "But you're a blind man," he kept saying, and one could almost feel his silent assumption that somehow the incapacity in one aspect made the man incapable in every other. So blinded by the label was the interviewer that he could not be persuaded to look beyond it.

Some labels, such as "blind man," are exceedingly salient and powerful. They tend to prevent alternative classification, or even cross-classification. Ethnic labels are often of this type, particularly if they refer to some highly visible feature, e.g., Negro, Oriental. They resemble the labels that point to some outstanding incapacity — *feeble-minded, cripple, blind man*. Let us call such symbols "labels of primary potency." These symbols act like shrieking sirens, deafening us to all finer discriminations that we might otherwise perceive. Even though the blindness of one man and the darkness of pigmentation of another may be defining attributes for some purposes, they are irrelevant and "noisy" for others.

Most people are unaware of this basic law of language — that every label applied to a given person refers properly only to one aspect of his nature. You may correctly say that a certain man is *human, a philanthropist, a Chinese, a physician, an athlete*. A given person may be all of these; but the chances are that Chinese stands out in your mind as the symbol of primary potency. Yet neither this nor any other classificatory label can refer to the whole of a man's nature. (Only his proper name can do so.)

Thus each label we use, especially those of primary potency, distracts our attention from concrete reality. The living, breathing, complex individual — the ultimate unit of human nature — is lost to sight. As in the figure, the label magnifies one attribute out of all proportion to its true significance, and masks other important attributes of the individual. . . .

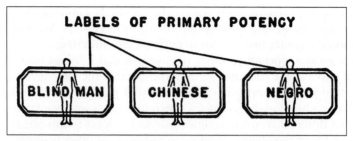

Source: Republished with permission of Perseus Books Group, a division of Hachette Book Group from *The Language of Prejudice* by Gordon W. Allport; originally from *The Nature of Prejudice* by Gordon W. Allport (Perseus Books/Basic Books, 1979), pp. 178–187; permission conveyed through Copyright Clearance Center, Inc.

A category, once formed with the aid of a symbol of primary potency, tends to attract more attributes than it should. The category labeled *Chinese* comes to signify not only ethnic membership but also reticence, impassivity, poverty, treachery. To be sure, . . . there may be genuine ethnic-linked traits, making for a certain *probability* that the member of an ethnic stock may have these attributes. But our cognitive process is not cautious. The labeled category, as we have seen, includes indiscriminately the defining attribute, probable attributes, and wholly fanciful, nonexistent attributes.

> **Most people are unaware of this basic law of language—that every label applied to a given person refers properly only to one aspect of his nature.**

Even proper names—which ought to invite us to look at the individual person—may act like symbols of primary potency, especially if they arouse ethnic associations. Mr. Greenberg is a person, but since his name is Jewish, it activates in the hearer his entire category of Jews-as-a-whole. An ingenious experiment performed by psychologist Gregory Razran shows this point clearly, and at the same time demonstrates how a proper name, acting like an ethnic symbol, may bring with it an avalanche of stereotypes.

> Thirty photographs of college girls were shown on a screen to 150 students. The subjects rated the girls on a scale from one to five for *beauty, intelligence, character, ambition, general likability.* Two months later the same subjects were asked to rate the same photographs (and fifteen additional ones introduced to complicate the memory factory). This time five of the original photographs were given Jewish surnames (Cohen, Kantor, etc.), five Italian (Valenti, etc.), and five Irish (O'Brien, etc.); and the remaining girls were given names chosen from the signers of the Declaration of Independence and from the Social Register (Davis, Adams, Clark, etc.).
>
> When Jewish names were attached to photographs there occurred the following changes in ratings:

decrease in liking
decrease in character
decrease in beauty
increase in intelligence
increase in ambition

For those photographs given Italian names there occurred:

decrease in liking
decrease in character
decrease in beauty
decrease in intelligence

Thus a mere proper name leads to prejudgments of personal attributes. The individual is fitted to the prejudiced ethnic category, and not judged in his own right.

While the Irish names also brought about depreciated judgment, the depreciation was not as great as in the case of the Jews and Italians. The falling of likability of the "Jewish girls" was twice as great as for "Italians" and five times as great as for "Irish." We note, however, that the "Jewish" photographs caused higher ratings in *intelligence* and in *ambition*. Not all stereotypes of out-groups are unfavorable. 10

The anthropologist Margaret Mead has suggested that labels of primary potency lose some of their force when they are changed from nouns into adjectives. To speak of a Negro soldier, a Catholic teacher, or a Jewish artist calls attention to the fact that some other group classifications are just as legitimate as the racial or religious. If George Johnson is spoken of not only as a Negro but also as a *soldier,* we have at least two attributes to know him by, and two are more accurate than one. To depict him truly as an individual, of course, we should have to name many more attributes. It is a useful suggestion that we designate ethnic and religious membership where possible with *adjectives* rather than *nouns.*

EMOTIONALLY TONED LABELS

Many categories have two kinds of labels — one less emotional and one more emotional. Ask yourself how you feel, and what thoughts you have, when you read the words *school teacher,* and then *school marm.* Certainly the second phrase calls up something more strict, more ridiculous, more disagreeable than the former. Here are four innocent letters: m-a-r-m. But they make us shudder a bit, laugh a bit, and scorn a bit. They call up an image of a spare, humorless, irritable old maid. They do not tell us that she is an individual human being with sorrows and troubles of her own. They force her instantly into a rejective category.

In the ethnic sphere even plain labels such as Negro, Italian, Jew, Catholic, Irish-American, French-Canadian may have emotional tone for a reason that we shall soon explain. But they all have their higher key equivalents: nigger, wop, kike, papist, harp, canuck. When these labels are employed we can be almost certain that the speaker *intends* not only to characterize the person's membership, but also to disparage and reject him.

Quite apart from the insulting intent that lies behind the use of certain labels, there is also an inherent ("physiognomic") handicap in many terms designating ethnic membership. For example, the proper names characteristic of certain ethnic memberships strike us as absurd. (We compare them, of course, with what is familiar and therefore "right.") Chinese names are short and silly; Polish names intrinsically difficult and outlandish. Unfamiliar dialects strike us as ludicrous. Foreign dress (which, of course, is a visual ethnic symbol) seems unnecessarily queer.

But of all of these "physiognomic" handicaps the reference to color, clearly implied in certain symbols, is the greatest. The word Negro comes from the Latin *niger* meaning black. In point of fact, no Negro has a black complexion, but by comparison with other blonder stocks, he has come to be known as a "black man." Unfortunately *black* in the English language is a word having a preponderance of sinister connotations: the outlook is black, blackball, blackguard, black-hearted, black death, blacklist, blackmail, Black Hand. In his novel *Moby Dick,* Herman Melville considers at length the remarkably morbid connotations of black and the remarkably virtuous connotations of white.

Nor is the ominous flavor of black confined to the English language. A cross-cultural study reveals that the semantic significance of black is more or less universally the same. Among certain Siberian tribes, members of a privileged clan call themselves "white bones," and refer to all others as "black bones." Even among Uganda Negroes there is some evidence for a white god at the apex of the theocratic hierarchy; certain it is that a white cloth, signifying purity, is used to ward off evil spirits and disease.

There is thus an implied value-judgment in the very concept of *white race* and *black race.* One might also study the numerous unpleasant connotations of *yellow,* and their possible bearing on our conception of the people of the Orient.

Such reasoning should not be carried too far, since there are undoubtedly, in various contexts, pleasant associations with both black and yellow. Black velvet is agreeable, so too are chocolate and coffee. Yellow tulips are well liked; the sun and moon are radiantly yellow. Yet it is true that "color" words are used with chauvinistic overtones more than most people realize. There is certainly condescension indicated in many familiar phrases: dark as a nigger's pocket, darktown strutters, white hope (a term originated when a white contender was fought against the Negro heavyweight champion, Jack Johnson), the white man's burden, the yellow

15

peril, black boy. Scores of everyday phrases are stamped with the flavor of prejudice, whether the user knows it or not.

We spoke of the fact that even the most proper and sedate labels for minority groups sometimes seem to exude a negative flavor. In many contexts and situations the very terms *French-Canadian, Mexican,* or *Jew,* correct and nonmalicious though they are, sound a bit opprobrious. The reason is that they are labels of social deviants. Especially in a culture where uniformity is prized, the name of *any* deviant carries with it *ipso facto* a negative value-judgment. Words like *insane, alcoholic, pervert* are presumably neutral designations of a human condition, but they are more: they are finger-pointing at a deviance. Minority groups are deviants, and for this reason, from the very outset, the most innocent labels in many situations imply a shading of disrepute. When we wish to highlight the deviance and denigrate it still further we use words of a higher emotional key: crackpot, soak, pansy, greaser, Okie, nigger, harp, kike.

Members of minority groups are often understandably sensitive to 20 names given them. Not only do they object to deliberately insulting epithets, but sometimes see evil intent where none exists. Often the word Negro is spelled with a small *n*, occasionally as a studied insult, more often from ignorance. (The term is not cognate with white, which is not capitalized, but rather with Caucasian, which is.) Terms like "mulatto" or "octoroon" cause hard feeling because of the condescension with which they have often been used in the past. Sex differentiations are objectionable, since they seem doubly to emphasize ethnic difference: why speak of Jewess and not of Protestantess, or of Negress and not of whitess? Similar overemphasis is implied in the terms like Chinaman or Scotchman; why not American man? Grounds for misunderstanding lie in the fact that minority group members are sensitive to such shadings, while majority members may employ them unthinkingly.

THE COMMUNIST LABEL

Until we label an out-group it does not clearly exist in our minds. Take the curiously vague situation that we often meet when a person wishes to locate responsibility on the shoulders of some out-group whose nature he cannot specify. In such a case he usually employs the pronoun "they" without an antecedent. "Why don't they make these sidewalks wider?" "I hear they are going to build a factory in this town and hire a lot of foreigners." "I won't pay this tax bill; they can just whistle for their money." If asked "who?" the speaker is likely to grow confused and embarrassed. The common use of the orphaned pronoun *they* teaches us that people often want and need to designate out-groups (usually for the purpose of venting hostility) even when they have no clear conception of the out-group in question. And so long as the target of wrath remains vague and ill-defined specific prejudice cannot crystallize around it. To have enemies we need labels.

Until relatively recently [late 1940s]—strange as it may seem—there was no agreed-upon symbol for *communist*. The word, of course, existed but it had no special emotional connotation, and did not designate a public enemy. Even when, after World War I, there was a growing feeling of economic and social menace in this country, there was no agreement as to the actual source of the menace.

A content analysis of the Boston *Herald* for the year 1920 turned up the following list of labels. Each was used in a context implying some threat. Hysteria had overspread the country, as it did after World War II. Someone must be responsible for the postwar malaise, rising prices, uncertainty. There must be a villain. But in 1920 the villain was impartially designated by reporters and editorial writers with the following symbols:

> alien, agitator, anarchist, apostle of bomb and torch, Bolshevik, communist, communist laborite, conspirator, emissary of false promise, extremist, foreigner, hyphenated-American, incendiary, IWW, parlor anarchist, parlor pink, parlor socialist, plotter, radical, red, revolutionary, Russian agitator, socialist, Soviet, syndicalist, traitor, undesirable.

From this excited array we note that the *need* for an enemy (someone to serve as a focus for discontent and jitters) was considerably more apparent than the precise *identity* of the enemy. At any rate, there was no clearly agreed upon label. Perhaps partly for this reason the hysteria abated. Since no clear category of "communism" existed there was no true focus for the hostility.

But following World War II this collection of vaguely interchangeable labels became fewer in number and more commonly agreed upon. The out-group menace came to be designated almost always as *communist* or *red*. In 1920 the threat, lacking a clear label, was vague; after 1945 both symbol and thing became more definite. Not that people knew precisely what they meant when they said "communist," but with the aid of the term they were at least able to point consistently to *something* that inspired fear. The term developed the power of signifying menace and led to various repressive measures against anyone to whom the label was rightly or wrongly attached.

Logically, the label should apply to specifiable defining attributes, such as members of the Communist Party, or people whose allegiance is with the Russian system, or followers, historically, of Karl Marx. But the label came in for far more extensive use.

What seems to have happened is approximately as follows. Having suffered through a period of war and being acutely aware of devastating revolutions abroad, it is natural that most people should be upset,

25

dreading to lose their possessions, annoyed by high taxes, seeing custom-ary moral and religious values threatened, and dreading worse disasters to come. Seeking an explanation for this unrest, a single identifiable enemy is wanted. It is not enough to designate "Russia" or some other distant land. Nor is it satisfactory to fix blame on "changing social conditions." What is needed is a human agent near at hand: someone in Washington, someone in our schools, in our factories, in our neighborhood. If we *feel* an immediate threat, we reason, there must be a near-lying danger. It is, we conclude, communism, not only in Russia but also in America, at our doorstep, in our government, in our churches, in our colleges, in our neighborhood.

Are we saying that hostility toward communism is prejudice? Not necessarily. There are certainly phases of the dispute wherein realistic social conflict is involved. American values (e.g., respect for the person) and totalitarian values as represented in Soviet practice are intrinsically at odds. A realistic opposition in some form will occur. Prejudice enters only when the defining attributes of *communist* grow imprecise, when anyone who favors any form of social change is called a communist. People who fear social change are the ones most likely to affix the label to any persons or practices that seem to them threatening.

For them the category is undifferentiated. It includes books, movies, preachers, teachers who utter what for them are uncongenial thoughts. If evil befalls — perhaps forest fires or a factory explosion — it is due to com-munist saboteurs. The category becomes monopolistic, covering almost anything that is uncongenial. On the floor of the House of Representa-tives in 1946, Representative Rankin called James Roosevelt a communist. Congressman Outland replied with psychological acumen, "Apparently everyone who disagrees with Mr. Rankin is a communist."

When differentiated thinking is at a low ebb — as it is in times of social crises — there is a magnification of two-valued logic. Things are per-ceived as either inside or outside a moral order. What is outside is likely to be called communist. Correspondingly — and here is where damage is done — whatever is called communist (however erroneously) is immedi-ately cast outside the moral order. 30

This associative mechanism places enormous power in the hands of a demagogue. For several years Senator McCarthy managed to discredit many citizens who thought differently from himself by the simple device of calling them communist. Few people were able to see through this trick and many reputations were ruined. But the famous senator has no monopoly on the device. As reported in the Boston *Herald:* on Novem-ber 1, 1946, Representative Joseph Martin, Republican leader in the House, ended his election campaign against his Democratic opponent by saying, "The people will vote tomorrow between chaos, confusion, bankruptcy, state socialism or communism, and the preservation of our American life, with all its freedom and its opportunities." Such an array of emotional labels placed his opponent outside the accepted moral order. Martin was re-elected. . . .

Not everyone, of course, is taken in. Demagogy, when it goes too far, meets with ridicule. Elizabeth Dilling's book, *The Red Network,* was so exaggerated in its two-valued logic that it was shrugged off by many people with a smile. One reader remarked, "Apparently if you step off the sidewalk with your left foot you're a communist." But it is not easy in times of social strain and hysteria to keep one's balance, and to resist the tendency of a verbal symbol to manufacture large and fanciful categories of prejudiced thinking.

VERBAL REALISM AND SYMBOL PHOBIA

Most individuals rebel at being labeled, especially if the label is uncomplimentary. Very few are willing to be called *fascistic, socialistic,* or *anti-Semitic.* Unsavory labels may apply to others; but not to us.

An illustration of the craving that people have to attach favorable symbols to themselves is seen in the community where white people banded together to force out a Negro family that had moved in. They called themselves "Neighborly Endeavor" and chose as their motto the Golden Rule. One of the first acts of this symbol-sanctified band was to sue the man who sold property to Negroes. They then flooded the house which another Negro couple planned to occupy. Such were the acts performed under the banner of the Golden Rule.

Studies made by Stagner and Hartmann show that a person's political 35 attitudes may in fact entitle him to be called a fascist or a socialist, and yet he will emphatically repudiate the unsavory label, and fail to endorse any movement or candidate that overtly accepts them. In short, there is a *symbol phobia* that corresponds to *symbol realism.* We are more inclined to the former when we ourselves are concerned, though we are much less critical when epithets of "fascist," "communist," "blind man," "school marm" are applied to others.

When symbols provoke strong emotions they are sometimes regarded no longer as symbols, but as actual things. The expressions "son of a bitch" and "liar" are in our culture frequently regarded as "fighting words." Softer and more subtle expressions of contempt may be accepted. But in these particular cases, the epithet itself must be "taken back." We certainly do not change our opponent's attitude by making him take back a word, but it seems somehow important that the word itself be eradicated.

Such verbal realism may reach extreme length.

The City Council of Cambridge, Massachusetts, unanimously passed a resolution (December, 1939) making it illegal "to possess, harbor, sequester, introduce or transport, within the city limits, any book, map, magazine, newspaper, pamphlet, handbill, or circular containing the words Lenin or Leningrad."

Such naiveté in confusing language with reality is hard to comprehend unless we recall that word-magic plays an appreciable part in human thinking. The following examples, like the one preceding, are taken from Hayakawa.

> The Malagasy soldier must eschew kidneys, because in the Malagasy language the word for kidney is the same as that for "shot"; so shot he would certainly be if he ate a kidney.
>   In May, 1937, a state senator of New York bitterly opposed a bill for the control of syphilis because "the innocence of children might be corrupted by a widespread use of the term. . . . This particular word creates a shudder in every decent woman and decent man."

This tendency to reify words underscores the close cohesion that exists between category and symbol. Just the mention of "communist," "Negro," "Jew," "England," "Democrats," will send some people into a panic of fear or a frenzy of anger. Who can say whether it is the word or the thing that annoys them? The label is an intrinsic part of any monopolistic category. Hence to liberate a person from ethnic or political prejudice it is necessary at the same time to liberate him from *word fetishism*. This fact is well known to students of general semantics who tell us that prejudice is due in large part to verbal realism and to symbol phobia. Therefore any program for the reduction of prejudice must include a large measure of semantic therapy.

THINKING CRITICALLY ABOUT THE READING

1. What is Allport's thesis, and where is it stated? (Glossary: *Thesis*)
2. In paragraph 2, why do you think Allport uses a metaphorical image—grains of sand—to represent people? (Glossary: *Figurative Language*) How does this metaphor help him present his point?
3. In paragraph 3, Allport uses Irving Lee's story of a blind man who was unable to get a job as an example of how powerful certain labels can be. (Glossary: *Examples*) What other quotations does he use as examples? What is the purpose of each one? Do you think they are effective? Why or why not?
4. Nouns, or names, provide an essential service in making categorization possible. Yet according to Allport, nouns are also words that "cut slices." What does he mean by that term? What is inherently unfair about nouns?
5. What are "labels of primary potency" (4)? Why does Allport equate them with "shrieking sirens"? Why are such labels important to his essay?
6. What does the experiment with the unlabeled and labeled photos demonstrate? How do labels affect the way the mind perceives reality?

7. What does Allport mean by the "orphaned pronoun *they*" (21)? Why is it used so often in conversation?

8. What does Allport mean by *symbol phobia* (35)? How does this concept illustrate the unfairness of labeling others?

9. Allport wrote "The Language of Prejudice" in the early 1950s. Does this help explain why he devotes many paragraphs to the evolution of the label *communist*? What are the connotations of the word *communist* today? (Glossary: *Connotation/Denotation*)

LANGUAGE IN ACTION

Many people and organizations try to promote tolerance and tone down prejudice by suggesting that certain words and phrases be substituted for less respectful or insensitive ones. Consider the following examples that have been put forth in recent years.

Insensitive Words and Phrases	Respectful Alternatives
handicap	physical disability
fireman, policeman, postman	firefighter, police officer, mail carrier
illegal alien	undocumented immigrant
unemployed	nonwaged
Indian	Native American or First Nations
uneducated	lacking formal education
an autistic person	a person who is on the spectrum
half-breed	multi-ethnic
blacklisted	banned
stewardess	flight attendant
old people, elderly	seniors
gifted children	advanced learners
wheelchair-bound	a person who uses a wheelchair
BC, AD	BCE, CE
deaf	hearing impaired
mental retardation	intellectual disability
ethnic minority	people of color
underdeveloped country	developing country

In each case, what kind of intolerance or prejudice do you think the language switch is attempting to eliminate or at least minimize? Do you think it's possible to change people's attitudes by simply requiring language changes like the ones suggested above? Discuss why or why not.

WRITING SUGGESTIONS

1. Make an extensive list of the labels that have been or could be applied to you at this time. Write an essay in which you discuss the labels that you find "truly offensive," those you can "live with," and those that you "like to be associated with." Explain your reasons for putting particular labels in each of these categories.

2. Allport states, "Especially in a culture where uniformity is prized, the name of *any* deviant carries with it *ipso facto* a negative value-judgment" (19). This was written in the 1950s. Since then, the turbulent 1960s, the political correctness movement of the 1980s and 1990s and the years since the millennium, and the mainstreaming of "alternative" cultures have all attempted to persuade people to accept differences and be more tolerant. Write an essay in which you consider Allport's statement today. Which labels that identify someone as different still carry a negative association? Have the social movements of the past decades changed how we think about others in a fundamental way? Do you think there is more acceptance of nonconformity today, or is a nonconformist or member of a minority still subjected to just as much negative, though perhaps more subtle, labeling as in the 1950s? Support your conclusions with examples from your own experience and from the depiction of current events in the popular media.

3. Allport wrote *The Nature of Prejudice* before the civil rights movement began in earnest, though he did live to see it grow and reach its climax at the famous 1963 March on Washington. Obviously, part of the civil rights movement was concerned with language, and its leaders often used impressive rhetoric to confront the language of prejudice. Write an essay in which you analyze how the kinds of labels and symbols identified by Allport were used in speeches and documents both to justify the continuation of segregation and prejudice and to decry it. How did the leaders of the civil rights movement use language to their advantage? To what emotions or ideas did the language of the opposition appeal? The internet and your library have vast amounts of information about the movement's genesis and history, so it may be difficult at first to decide on a specific area of research. Start by looking at how language was used by both sides in the battle over civil rights.

The "F Word"

FIROOZEH DUMAS

Firoozeh Dumas was born in Abadan, Iran, in 1965. When she was seven, she and her family moved to Whittier, California. Two years later, they moved back to Iran, living this time in Ahvaz and Tehran, only to return to Southern California after several years. Dumas studied at the University of California, Berkeley, where she met and, after graduation, married François Dumas, who is French. In 2001, she started writing her memoir about life in Iran and the United States as a way of preserving this family history and culture for her children. *Funny in Farsi: A Memoir of Growing Up Iranian in America* was published in 2003. She built on her first book in *Laughing Without an Accent: Adventures of an Iranian American at Home and Abroad* (2008), a collection of tender and humorous vignettes about the melding of cultures and the struggles of immigrants living in the United States. In 2016 she published *It Ain't So Awful, Falafel*, a work of fiction intended for middle-school students.

In "The 'F Word,'" a chapter from *Funny in Farsi*, Dumas talks about the troubles she and her Iranian family and friends have had with their "identifiably 'ethnic' name[s]." She witnessed the prejudice toward immigrants that came about as a result of the Iranian hostage crisis (1979–1981) and writes about the difficulties she had getting a job interview as a college graduate with an Iranian name.

WRITING TO DISCOVER: *Do you or any of your friends have names that are identifiably ethnic? For example, are the names clearly Hispanic, Jewish, Arabic, Asian, German, Italian, Greek, or some other ethnicity? How do people react to you when they hear your family name? Describe.*

My cousin's name, Farbod, means "Greatness." When he moved to America, all the kids called him "Farthead." My brother Farshid ("He Who Enlightens") became "Fartshit." The name of my friend Neggar means "Beloved," although it can be more accurately translated as "She Whose Name Almost Incites Riots." Her brother Arash ("Giver") initially couldn't understand why every time he'd say his name, people would laugh and ask him if it itched.

All of us immigrants knew that moving to America would be fraught with challenges, but none of us thought that our names would be such an obstacle. How could our parents have ever imagined that someday we would end up in a country where monosyllabic names reign supreme, a land where "William" is shortened to "Bill," where "Susan" becomes "Sue," and "Richard" somehow evolves into "Dick"? America is a great country, but nobody without a mask and a cape has a z in his name. And have Americans ever realized the great scope of the guttural sounds they're missing? Okay, so it has to do with linguistic roots, but I do believe this would be a richer country if all Americans could do a little tongue aerobics and learn to pronounce "kh," a sound more commonly associated in this culture with phlegm, or "gh," the sound usually made by actors in the final moments of a choking scene. It's like adding a few new spices to the kitchen pantry. Move over, cinnamon and nutmeg, make way for cardamom and sumac.

Exotic analogies aside, having a foreign name in this land of Joes and Marys is a pain in the spice cabinet. When I was twelve, I decided to simplify my life by adding an American middle name. This decision serves as proof that sometimes simplifying one's life in the short run only complicates it in the long run.

My name, Firoozeh, chosen by my mother, means "Turquoise" in Farsi. In America, it means "Unpronounceable" or "I'm Not Going to Talk to You Because I Cannot Possibly Learn Your Name and I Just Don't Want to Have to Ask You Again and Again Because You'll Think I'm Dumb or You Might Get Upset or Something." My father, incidentally, had wanted to name me Sara. I do wish he had won that argument.

To strengthen my decision to add an American name, I had just 5
finished fifth grade in Whittier, where all the kids incessantly called me "Ferocious." That summer, my family moved to Newport Beach, where I looked forward to starting a new life. I wanted to be a kid with a name that didn't draw so much attention, a name that didn't come with a built-in inquisition as to when and why I had moved to America and how was it that I spoke English without an accent and was I planning on going back and what did I think of America?

My last name didn't help any. I can't mention my maiden name, because:

"Dad, I'm writing a memoir."

"Great! Just don't mention our name."

Suffice it to say that, with eight letters, including a *z*, and four syllables, my last name is as difficult and foreign as my first. My first and last name together generally served the same purpose as a high brick wall. There was one exception to this rule. In Berkeley, and only in Berkeley, my name drew people like flies to baklava. These were usually people named Amaryllis or Chrysanthemum, types who vacationed in Costa Rica and to whom lentils described a type of burger. These folks were probably not the pride of Poughkeepsie, but they were refreshingly nonjudgmental.

When I announced to my family that I wanted to add an American 10
name, they reacted with their usual laughter. Never one to let mockery or good judgment stand in my way, I proceeded to ask for suggestions. My father suggested "Fifi." Had I had a special affinity for French poodles or been considering a career in prostitution, I would've gone with that one. My mom suggested "Farah," a name easier than "Firoozeh" yet still Iranian. Her reasoning made sense, except that Farrah Fawcett was at the

height of her popularity and I didn't want to be associated with somebody whose poster hung in every postpubescent boy's bedroom. We couldn't think of any American names beginning with *F*, so we moved on to *J*, the first letter of our last name. I don't know why we limited ourselves to names beginning with my initials, but it made sense at that moment, perhaps by the logic employed moments before bungee jumping. I finally chose the name "Julie" mainly for its simplicity. My brothers, Farid and Farshid, thought that adding an American name was totally stupid. They later became Fred and Sean.

That same afternoon, our doorbell rang. It was our new next-door neighbor, a friendly girl my age named Julie. She asked me my name and after a moment of hesitation, I introduced myself as Julie. "What a coincidence!" she said. I didn't mention that I had been Julie for only half an hour.

Thus I started sixth grade with my new, easy name and life became infinitely simpler. People actually remembered my name, which was an entirely refreshing new sensation. All was well until the Iranian Revolution, when I found myself with a new set of problems. Because I spoke English without an accent and was known as Julie, people assumed I was American. This meant that I was often privy to their real feelings about those "damn I-raynians." It was like having those X-ray glasses that let you see people undressed, except that what I was seeing was far uglier than people's underwear. It dawned on me that these people would have probably never invited me to their house had they known me as Firoozeh. I felt like a fake.

> **All of us immigrants knew that moving to America would be fraught with challenges, but none of us thought that our names would be such an obstacle.**

When I went to college, I eventually went back to using my real name. All was well until I graduated and started looking for a job. Even though I had graduated with honors from UC–Berkeley, I couldn't get a single interview. I was guilty of being a humanities major, but I began to suspect that there was more to my problems. After three months of rejections, I added "Julie" to my résumé. Call it coincidence, but the job offers started coming in. Perhaps it's the same kind of coincidence that keeps African Americans from getting cabs in New York.

Once I got married, my name became Julie Dumas. I went from having an identifiably "ethnic" name to having ancestors who wore clogs. My family and non-American friends continued calling me Firoozeh, while my coworkers and American friends called me Julie. My life became one big knot, especially when friends who knew me as Julie met friends who knew me as Firoozeh. I felt like those characters in soap operas who have an evil twin. The two, of course, can never be in the same room, since they're played by the same person, a struggling actress who wears a wig to play one of the twins and dreams of moving on to bigger and better roles. I couldn't blame my mess on a screenwriter; it was my own doing.

I decided to untangle the knot once and for all by going back to my   15
real name. By then, I was a stay-at-home mom, so I really didn't care
whether people remembered my name or gave me job interviews. Besides,
most of the people I dealt with were in diapers and were in no position to
judge. I was also living in Silicon Valley, an area filled with people named
Rajeev, Avishai, and Insook.

Every once in a while, though, somebody comes up with a new
permutation and I am once again reminded that I am an immigrant with a
foreign name. I recently went to have blood drawn for a physical exam. The
waiting room for blood work at our local medical clinic is in the basement of
the building, and no matter how early one arrives for an appointment, forty
coughing, wheezing people have gotten there first. Apart from reading *Golf
Digest* and *Popular Mechanics*, there isn't much to do except guess the number of contagious diseases represented in the windowless room. Every ten
minutes, a name is called and everyone looks to see which cough matches
that name. As I waited patiently, the receptionist called out, "Fritzy, Fritzy!"
Everyone looked around, but no one stood up. Usually, if I'm waiting to be
called by someone who doesn't know me, I will respond to just about any
name starting with an *F*. Having been called Froozy, Frizzy, Fiorucci, and
Frooz and just plain "Uhhhh . . . ," I am highly accommodating. I did not,
however, respond to "Fritzy" because there is, as far as I know, no *t* in my
name. The receptionist tried again, "Fritzy, Fritzy DumbAss." As I stood
up to this most linguistically original version of my name, I could feel all
eyes upon me. The room was momentarily silent as all of these sick people
sat united in a moment of gratitude for their own names.

Despite a few exceptions, I have found that Americans are now far
more willing to learn new names, just as they're far more willing to try
new ethnic foods. Of course, some people just don't like to learn. One
mom at my children's school adamantly refused to learn my "impossible" name and instead settled on calling me "F Word." She was recently
transferred to New York where, from what I've heard, she might meet
an immigrant or two and, who knows, she just might have to make some
room in her spice cabinet.

THINKING CRITICALLY ABOUT THE READING

1. Dumas confesses that "All of us immigrants knew that moving to America
   would be fraught with challenges, but none of us thought that our names
   would be such an obstacle" (2). What did she and her friends discover was
   the problem with Iranian names like Farbod, Farshid, Neggar, Arash, and
   Firoozeh?

2. How did Firoozeh reinvent herself when she and her family moved from
   Whittier to Newport Beach, California? How did she happen upon her new
   "American name" (10)?

3. Why do you think that Firoozeh couldn't mention her maiden name? What does she tell you about her last name? What would her last name reveal about her? In what ways did Dumas's "first and last name together generally [serve] the same purpose as a high brick wall" (9)?

4. During the Iranian Revolution, Firoozeh witnessed firsthand the expression of some pretty ugly anti-Iranian feelings. Why wasn't she the target of these anti-Iranian sentiments?

5. Why do you think Firoozeh had trouble getting a job interview after graduating from the University of California, Berkeley? What is the problem with "having an identifiably 'ethnic' name" (14)? Explain.

6. Dumas writes about an extremely sensitive subject—personal names and prejudice—with humor. Did you find her humor appropriate for this subject and her audience? Cite several examples where she uses humor effectively.

LANGUAGE IN ACTION

Have you ever thought about changing your name? If so, why? Interestingly, show-business people often change their names to further their careers. Here are the professional names and the original names of a number of celebrities, past and present. Discuss with your classmates any significant associations that the original names might have and the reasons these names might have been changed.

Original Names	Professional Names
Demetria Guynes	Demi Moore
Michael Philip	Mick Jagger
Norma Jean Baker	Marilyn Monroe
Madonna Louise Ciccone	Madonna
Eleanor Gow	Elle MacPherson
Caryn Johnson	Whoopi Goldberg
Robert Zimmerman	Bob Dylan
Doris von Kappelhoff	Doris Day
Frederick Austerlitz	Fred Astaire
Marion Michael Morrison	John Wayne
Cassius Marcellus Clay Jr.	Muhammad Ali
Annemaria Italiano	Anne Bancroft
Maurice J. Micklewhite	Michael Caine
Thomas Mapother IV	Tom Cruise
Carlos Ray	Chuck Norris
Leonard Sly	Roy Rogers
Benjamin Kubelsky	Jack Benny

How do you think Firoozeh Dumas might react to some of these name changes? What celebrity name changes can you add to this list?

WRITING SUGGESTIONS

1. Is your surname very common in American society, very rare, or somewhere in between? Do others have difficulty pronouncing or spelling it? What does your surname reveal about your background or family history? Write an essay in which you reflect on the way your surname has affected your life and the way people react to you. Be sure to give examples of the role your name plays in day-to-day life.

2. Survey the names of the people in your dormitory or in one of your social groups. Analyze the names in light of Dumas's essay. In your opinion, are any of the names unusual? Why? Do they sound strange to you or others? Do they represent a culture different from your own? Do they remind you of another word that you find humorous? How do people feel about their names? What insights, if any, do these names give you into the state of cultural diversity on your campus? Write an essay in which you discuss your findings. Make sure that you do not simply describe the names you found. Instead, build a context for your essay and provide a thesis for your comments. (Glossary: *Thesis*)

3. Write an essay in which you compare and contrast the experiences that Henry Louis Gates Jr. ("What's in a Name?," pp. 17–20) and Dumas had with names. How did each of them feel when others named and thus defined them? What insights into oppression — namely racial, religious, or ethnic — do their experiences give you?

The Racist Trope That Won't Die

BRENT STAPLES

Born in 1951 in Chester, Pennsylvania, Brent Staples is the oldest son of nine children from a working-class family. Though he was not expected to go to college, scholarship opportunities pulled him from the world of industrial Philadelphia where he had grown up into the world of academia. Staples was accepted to Widener University in 1969, where he completed his BA. He earned his MA and PhD in Psychology at the University of Chicago in 1976 and 1982, respectively.

In 1990, Staples joined *The New York Times* editorial board. Since then, he has served as an editor for *The New York Times Book Review* and as an assistant editor for metropolitan news. He is the author of the memoir *Parallel Time: Growing Up in Black and White* (1994) and *American Love Story* (1999), both of which explore themes of family, blackness, and racism in America. Although a black author, Staples says that he "despises" the term "black experience." In a 1994 interview, he said, "black people's lives in this country are too varied to be reduced to a single term." In the following essay, originally published in *The New York Times* on June 17, 2018, Staples examines one particular racist stereotype that has persisted throughout American history and has impacted the portrayal of African Americans in the media and popular culture.

WRITING TO DISCOVER: *Think of a time when you, a friend, or a family member were affected by a negative stereotype. What was the stereotype? How did the experience make you feel?*

The comedian Roseanne Barr resurrected one of the oldest and most profoundly racist slanders in American history when she referred to Valerie Jarrett, an African-American woman who served as an adviser to President Barack Obama, as the offspring of an ape.

This depiction—promoted by slave traders, historians and practitioners of "scientific" racism—was used to justify slavery, lynching and the creation of the Jim Crow state. It made the leap to the silver screen in deeply noxious films like *The Birth of a Nation* and haunted American popular culture well into the 20th century.

The toxically racist ape characterization has been pushed to the margins of the public square. Nevertheless, a growing body of research shows that it has maintained a pernicious grip on the American imagination. It is especially problematic in the criminal justice system, where subhuman treatment of African-Americans remains strikingly visible.

That message comes through powerfully in research by several social scientists, but particularly in the work of the Stanford University psychologist Jennifer Eberhardt and Phillip Atiba Goff, president of the Center for Policing Equity at John Jay College in New York. In six studies published with collaborators a decade ago, Mr. Goff and Ms. Eberhardt found that even younger study participants who were born since the civil rights revolution and claimed to know nothing of the ape caricature of blackness were swayed by it when making judgments about black people. In one study, white male undergraduates who were subliminally exposed to words associated with apes — for example, "chimp" or "gorilla" — were more likely to condone the beating of those in police custody when they thought that the suspect was black.

In another study, the authors analyzed death penalty cases covered   5 in *The Philadelphia Inquirer* between 1979 and 1999. They found that black defendants convicted of capital crimes were four times more likely than whites convicted of capital crimes to be described with labels associated with apes, such as "savage," "brute" or "beast." The researchers also discovered that defendants who were implicitly portrayed as more apelike in the newspaper were more likely to be executed by the state.

This process of dehumanization often leads Americans to view African-American men as larger and more fearsome than they are. This pattern of misperception is troubling. Police officers are often exonerated for killing civilians on the premise that they fired their weapons out of fear for their lives. This issue famously came up in the 2014 killing of Dontre Hamilton, an unarmed black man in Milwaukee who was shot 14 times by Officer Christopher Manney. Officer Manney later portrayed Mr. Hamilton as hulking and muscular, saying he feared being "overpowered." An autopsy showed that Mr. Hamilton was actually of modest build — 5 feet, 7 inches tall and 169 pounds.

The tragedy of 12-year-old Tamir Rice, who was killed by a Cleveland police officer in 2014 while playing with a toy gun, fits this pattern. An officer at the scene described him as being 20 years old. Black children are often seen as significantly older and more menacing than they actually are. And, research suggests, the automatic presumption of threat provoked by a black face applies even the when the face belongs to a 5-year-old child.

Mr. Goff and his colleagues published a striking set of studies the year Tamir was killed. They found that when a group of mainly white college students were shown photographs of white, black, and Latino boys, they overestimated the ages of black boys ages 10 to 17 by an average of 4.5 years. In other words, they perceived 13-year-old boys as adult men — and viewed black children as more culpable for crimes.

> **The process of dehumanization often leads Americans to view African-American men as larger and more fearsome than they are.**

The ape caricature plays a role here, too. The more participants associated black people with apes, the authors showed, the greater the discrepancy between their guesses of the ages of black children and their actual ages—and the more severely the participants judged the children's culpability. A related analysis of police personnel records determined that officers who associated blacks with apes were more likely to have used force against a black child in custody.

These findings have much to say about disparate treatment in the criminal justice system, especially given the recent spate of episodes in which black people were confronted by law enforcement and, sometimes, hauled off to jail for living their lives at Starbucks, among other places.   10

The backlash that forced ABC to cancel Ms. Barr's television series reflects a distaste for passé, plainly stated racism in a society that likes to see itself as having put bigotry behind it. Nevertheless, centuries of institutional racism—and the dehumanization of black people upon which it relied—have left an indelible imprint on how Americans process blackness.

The notion that the country might somehow move past this deeply complex, historically layered issue by assuming an attitude of "color blindness" is naïve. The only real hope of doing that is to openly confront and talk about the powerful, but submerged, forms of discrimination that have long since supplanted the undisguised version.

THINKING CRITICALLY ABOUT THE READING

1. What is a "trope," and what central "racist trope" does Staples identify and discuss?

2. What specific "racist slander" (1) does Staples mention at the beginning of his essay?

3. What terms are used to describe African Americans, according to Staples? In his view, how do these terms affect the way African Americans are perceived by others?

4. In Staples's view, what is the connection between the "dehumanization" (6) of African Americans and police officers' actions toward them?

5. What does Staples mean by "institutional racism" (11)?

6. What does Staples mean when he refers to the attitude of racial "color blindness" (12)? Why does he view the attitude of color blindness as "naïve"?

LANGUAGE IN ACTION

Staples begins this essay by mentioning Roseanne Barr, an actor and comedian who "referred to Valerie Jarrett, an African American woman who served as an adviser to President Obama, as the offspring of an ape." Staples is alluding to a Twitter post from Barr on May 29, 2018. Below is the original text of Barr's tweet, which she subsequently deleted:

muslim brotherhood & planet of the apes had a baby=vj

Shortly after Barr sent this tweet, television network ABC fired her from her leading role in the 2018 revival of acclaimed comedy show *Roseanne*. With her career in jeopardy, Barr deleted the tweet and offered a public apology on Twitter: "I apologize to Valerie Jarrett and to all Americans. I am truly sorry for making a bad joke about her politics and her looks. I should have known better. Forgive me - my joke was in bad taste."

In light of her original tweet's phrasing and the racist history that Staples discusses in his essay, how would you characterize Barr's tweet and her subsequent apology? Do you think that her apology was sincere? If so, do you think that a sincere apology would be enough to warrant forgiveness and reinstatement on her show? Why or why not? Discuss in a small group with one or two classmates.

WRITING SUGGESTIONS

1. Besides the examples that Staples mentions, can you think of any other instances of "racist tropes" relating to African Americans in the media or popular culture? Write a brief essay about one or more examples of racist tropes that you have encountered. Where and in what context did you encounter the trope or tropes? In what ways were the tropes harmful, damaging, or problematic? Before starting to write, you may find it helpful to read Henry Louis Gates Jr.'s essay "What's in a Name?" (pp. 17–20).

2. Consider the idea of "color blindness," which Staples introduces in his final paragraph. Do you think that color blindness is something to which we should aspire? Or do you agree with Staples that the attitude of color blindness is "naïve"? Write a brief essay in which you take a position on this issue. In your essay, be sure to include a definition of "color blindness" and explain what the term means to you.

The Fight Over the Words of Immigration

Jeff Gammage

Jeff Gammage is a staff writer for the *Philadelphia Inquirer*. In 2012, he was part of the five-reporter team that won the Pulitzer Prize for Public Service for their seven-part article series "Assault on Learning," which revealed that violence in Philadelphia public schools was widespread and underreported. Much of Gammage's other writing for the *Inquirer* shows similar concern for underrepresented populations. A 1982 graduate of James Madison University, his notable career in journalism earned him the school's Ronald E. Carrier Distinguished Alumni Achievement Award in 2012. He lives in Elkins Park, Pennsylvania, with his wife and their two adopted daughters.

Gammage is also the author of *China Ghosts: My Daughter's Journey to America, My Passage to Fatherhood* (2007), and he has written about adoption for a number of publications, including *The New York Times*. In *China Ghosts*—a tender, intimate portrait of becoming a family— Gammage draws on his own experiences to chronicle the long, complex process of international adoption. As a father to two children who have migrated to the United States, Gammage is undoubtedly sensitive to the treatment of immigrants and the language used to define them. In the following article, originally published in the *Inquirer* on November 3, 2017, he looks at the many different words and phrases used to refer to immigrants and immigration in the United States.

WRITING TO DISCOVER: *Before you read, consider the words you have heard used to describe immigrants. Make a brief list of these words. Which ones seem positive? Negative? Neutral? Why?*

During a court hearing over Philadelphia's conduct as a sanctuary city, Justice Department lawyer Arjun Garg rarely veered from applying a two-word label to the people at the heart of the case—"illegal aliens."

Philadelphia City Solicitor Sozi Tulante, standing six feet away in the same federal courtroom, never uttered those words.

"If you're here without documents, you hear all that comes with it," he said. "We're very intentional about how we refer to people."

Tulante leads the city's fight against the Trump administration's effort to withhold law-enforcement grant money from sanctuary cities. In court, he spoke of "residents" and "citizens" who might not have the necessary papers to be in this country.

These days, the terminology around immigrants—undocumented, illegal, unauthorized, unlawful, alien—has become as divisive as immigration itself. There's little consensus on what to call a populace estimated at more than 11 million. Different people and groups use different terms, 5 and accuse each other of deliberately choosing words that are too soft or too harsh.

"The language itself becomes part of the argument, part of the battle," said David Spener, author of *Clandestine Crossings: Migrants and Coyotes on the Texas-Mexico Border*, and chair of the sociology and anthropology department at Trinity University in San Antonio, Texas.

Spener prefers "migrants" because it implies long-term travel in different directions, including circles, as opposed to the straight, one-way trip indicated by "immigrants."

He has considered "autonomous migrants," people who move without government permission because they're focused on their families' needs, and "unprotected migrants," since the lack of official approval can put them at the mercy of traffickers.

> These days, the terminology around immigrants — undocumented, illegal, unauthorized, unlawful, alien — has become as divisive as immigration itself.

The debate has sharpened during the last two years, largely driven by Donald Trump, who as a candidate and as president has described border-crossers as "illegals" and "illegal aliens" who foment "illegal immigration" to the United States.

"You know the illegals," Trump told a conference of police chiefs in February. "You know them by their first name. You know them by their nicknames. You're in the neighborhoods. You know the bad ones, you know the good ones. I want you to turn in the bad ones."

The city sued Attorney General Jeff Sessions in August over the administration's plan to withhold money from sanctuary cities, which limit their cooperation with federal immigration authorities.

Last week, outside U.S. District Court in Center City where the case was being heard, Justice Department attorney Garg declined to say why he chose "illegal aliens" as the correct term. But some conservative thinkers argue that phrase is exactly accurate, used in legal opinions and in reports by the Department of Homeland Security. 10

"The correct term is 'illegal alien,' " Hans von Spakovsky wrote in the conservative magazine *National Review.* "The politically correct term 'undocumented immigrant' . . . is a made-up term used by progressive groups and media sources to extinguish the line between legal immigrants and illegal aliens."

For others, the phrase provokes a visceral reaction.

"I'm a human being," said Maria Sotomayor, who immigrated from Ecuador and is now deputy director of the Pennsylvania Immigration and Citizenship Coalition, an advocacy group. "A human being is not a crime."

Nobel Peace Prize winner Elie Wiesel famously said that no human can be illegal. Pope Francis refers to "migrants" and "refugees" as "our brothers and sisters." And last year, the Library of Congress dropped "illegal alien" from its subject headings — angering conservative lawmakers who claimed the library had bowed to liberal pressure.

There's been a push to uncouple "illegal" from immigration by   15
groups like Race Forward, which runs a campaign called "Drop the
I-Word." They argue that "illegal" is never applied to white immigrants,
that it encourages hate crimes, and lacks legal and journalistic accuracy.

"It's dehumanizing," said Jasmine Rivera, a Philadelphia activist and
the daughter of Mexican immigrants. "Folks are always afraid of 'the
other,' and by using language to place a name on who is 'the other,' you
stop looking at people as human beings."

Being in the United States without authorization is a civil violation,
not a criminal offense.

Kevin Fandl, a former counsel to U.S. Immigration and Customs
Enforcement, known as ICE, points out that drug dealers and other criminals are never identified as "illegals."

The Temple University legal-studies scholar prefers "unlawful immigrants," to mean people who are present without legal authority. The
word "undocumented" is imperfect, Fandl said, because many people
have documents, just not the correct ones.

The Associated Press eliminated "illegal immigrant" from its reports   20
in 2013, saying "illegal" should describe an action, not a person. The
Inquirer stylebook says no to the use of "aliens" and strongly discourages
the term "illegal immigrant."

Never, the stylebook warns reporters and editors, use "unauthorized
immigrant"—the phrase chosen as accurate by the Pew Research Center
in a revealing 2017 study on immigration. The center estimated the U.S.
is home to 11.3 million undocumented immigrants, about half of them
Mexican.

"Words are laden always with connotations," said Spener, the Trinity
University sociologist. "To be an 'illegal immigrant' or 'illegal alien' is
not about having committed an illegal act—it's a status. . . . You cross the
border, but the border envelops you even in U.S. territory."

THINKING CRITICALLY ABOUT THE READING

1. Why is there a "fight" over the language of immigration? Who are the various
stakeholders in this fight?

2. Gammage notes that Philadelphia City Solicitor Sozi Tulante intentionally
never uses the term *illegal aliens.* Why do you think Tulante makes the choice
not to use this term? What connotation does *illegal alien* have?

3. What role does Gammage suggest President Donald Trump and his administration have played in the fight over immigration language?

4. What does the term *sanctuary city* mean (1, 4, and 9)? What does the term
connote? Why do you think this term has gained popularity in recent years?

5. Why do you think Gammage quotes Holocaust survivor Elie Wiesel and
Pope Francis in paragraph 14? What words do these figures use to describe
immigration and why?

LANGUAGE IN ACTION

Below is a list of headlines from different news organizations about a group of Central American migrants who, in late 2018, reached the southern border of the United States, seeking asylum and to enter the country. With one or two of your classmates, evaluate these headlines. What does the language in each headline imply about the migrants? For example, do some of the headlines portray the migrants in a more positive or more negative light? What, if anything, can you surmise about each author's opinion about the migrants, based on the headline they've written?

- "Caravan Migrants Cross US Border" (BBC)
- "Ragged, Growing Caravan of Migrants Resumes March Toward US" (The Associated Press)
- "Daunted by U.S. Border, Some Caravan Migrants Seek Asylum in Mexico" (*The Washington Post*)
- "Central American 'Caravan' Women and Children Enter US, Defying Trump" (Reuters)
- "DOJ Cracks Down on Illegal Caravan with Federal Charges" (Townhall.com)
- "Asylum Seekers Don't Think They Can Survive for Months in Mexico. Trump Wants to Force Them To." (Vox.com)
- "Media Admit Caravan Migrants Looking for Jobs, Not Asylum" (Breitbart.com)

WRITING SUGGESTIONS

1. Make a list of all the words used to describe immigrants and immigration that Gammage uses or mentions in his article. Then choose one of these terms and write a brief essay arguing why, in your opinion, the term is either acceptable or unacceptable. To support your argument for or against the term, you may use evidence from Gammage's article or from other articles on this topic.

2. Readers can often identify a writer's position by examining an author's word choice, even if that position is not explicitly stated in the text. In what ways does Gammage's word choice and other rhetorical strategies suggest his own position in the debate over the language of immigration? What is his position? Write a brief essay in which you answer this question. Support your argument with specific language from Gammage's article that indicates his opinion.

Nobody Mean More to Me Than You

JUNE JORDAN

Born to Jamaican immigrant parents in Harlem, New York, June Jordan (1936–2002) was an acclaimed African American poet, playwright, and essayist. Regarded as a key figure among mid-century African American writers, Jordan taught at prestigious universities across the country, including Yale University, the State University of New York at Stony Brook, and the University of California, Berkeley. At Berkeley, she founded Poetry for the People (P4P), an arts and activism organization with the goal of connecting the university with the wider Bay Area community. Jordan also earned fellowships from the National Endowment for the Arts, the Massachusetts Council on the Arts, and the New York Foundation for the Arts.

Jordan was known for her fierce commitment to social justice, including fighting injustices tied to language. As she explains in her anthology *Civil Wars* (1981), "for a long while during childhood I was relatively small, short, and, in some other ways, a target for bully abuse. In fact, my father was the first regular bully in my life." Although she goes on to speak lovingly about her family, these early experiences undoubtedly shaped her view of injustice and inequality. Her other notable works include *Some Changes* (1971), *Things That I Do in the Dark: Selected Poems* (1977), *Living Room: New Poems* (1985), and *Kissing God Goodbye: Poems 1991–1997* (1997), among many others. In the following essay, originally published in the *Harvard Educational Review* in August 1988, Jordan examines the concepts of "Standard English" and "Black English" and explores how these concepts operate in the United States.

WRITING TO DISCOVER: *Before you read, consider your own language. What speech habits (slang, colloquialisms, jargon, etc.) do you use that strays from what is widely regarded as "Standard English"? Do you think these habits of speech affect the way other people perceive you?*

Black English is not exactly a linguistic buffalo; as children, most of the thirty-five million Afro-Americans living here depend on this language for our discovery of the world. But then we approach our maturity inside a larger social body that will not support our efforts to become anything other than the clones of those who are neither our mothers nor our fathers. We begin to grow up in a house where every true mirror shows us the face of somebody who does not belong there, whose walk and whose talk will never look or sound "right," because that house was meant to shelter a family that is alien and hostile to us. As we learn our way around this environment, either we hide our original word habits, or we completely surrender our own voice, hoping to please those who will never respect anyone different from themselves: Black English is not exactly a linguistic buffalo, but we should understand its status as an endangered species, as a perishing, irreplaceable system of community intelligence, or we should expect its extinction, and, along with that, the extinguishing of much that constitutes our own proud, and singular, identity.

What we casually call "English," less and less defers to England and its "gentlemen." "English" is no longer a specific matter of geography or an element of class privilege; more than thirty-three countries use this tool as a means of "intranational communication."[1] Countries as disparate as Zimbabwe and Malaysia, or Israel and Uganda, use it as their non-native currency of convenience. Obviously, this tool, this "English," cannot function inside thirty-three discrete societies on the basis of rules and values absolutely determined somewhere else, in a thirty-fourth other country, for example.

> **White standards of English persist, supreme and unquestioned, in the United States.**

In addition to that staggering congeries of non-native users of English, there are five countries, or 333,746,000 people, for whom this thing called "English" serves as a native tongue.[2] Approximately 10 percent of these native speakers of "English" are Afro-American citizens of the U.S.A. I cite these numbers and varieties of human beings dependent on "English" in order, quickly, to suggest how strange and how tenuous is any concept of "Standard English." Obviously, numerous forms of English now operate inside a natural, an uncontrollable, continuum of development. I would suppose "the standard" for English in Malaysia is not the same as "the standard" in Zimbabwe. I know that standard forms of English for Black people in this country do not copy that of Whites. And, in fact, the structural differences between these two kinds of English have intensified, becoming more Black, or less White, despite the expected homogenizing effects of television[3] and other mass media.

Nonetheless, White standards of English persist, supreme and unquestioned, in these United States. Despite our multi-lingual population, and despite the deepening Black and White cleavage within that conglomerate, White standards control our official and popular judgments of verbal proficiency and correct, or incorrect, language skills, including speech. In contrast to India, where at least fourteen languages co-exist as legitimate Indian languages, in contrast to Nicaragua, where all citizens are legally entitled to formal school instruction in their regional or tribal languages,

---

1. *English Is Spreading, But What Is English.* A presentation by Professor S. N. Sridhar, Department of Linguistics, S.U.N.Y., Stony Brook, April 9, 1985: Dean's Convocation Among the Disciplines.

2. *English Is Spreading.*

3. *New York Times,* March 15, 1985, Section One, p. 14: Report on Study by Linguists at the University of Pennsylvania.

compulsory education in America compels accommodation to exclusively White forms of "English." White English, in America, is "Standard English."

This story begins two years ago. I was teaching a new course,   5
"In Search of the Invisible Black Woman," and my rather large class seemed evenly divided among young Black women and men. Five or six White students also sat in attendance. With unexpected speed and enthusiasm we had moved through historical narratives of the 19th century to literature by and about Black women, in the 20th. I had assigned the first forty pages of Alice Walker's *The Color Purple,* and I came, eagerly, to class that morning:

"So!" I exclaimed, aloud. "What did you think? How did you like it?"

The students studied their hands, or the floor. There was no response. The tense, resistant feeling in the room fairly astounded me.

At last, one student, a young woman still not meeting my eyes, muttered something in my direction:

"What did you say?" I prompted her.

"Why she have them talk so funny. It don't sound right."   10

"You mean the language?"

Another student lifted his head: "It don't look right, neither. I couldn't hardly read it."

At this, several students dumped on the book. Just about unanimously, their criticisms targeted the language. I listened to what they wanted to say and silently marvelled at the similarities between their casual speech patterns and Alice Walker's written version of Black English.

But I decided against pointing to these identical traits of syntax; I wanted not to make them self-conscious about their own spoken language—not while they clearly felt it was "wrong." Instead I decided to swallow my astonishment. Here was a negative Black reaction to a prize-winning accomplishment of Black literature that White readers across the country had selected as best seller. Black rejection was aimed at the one irreducibly Black element of Walker's work: the language—Celie's Black English. I wrote the opening lines of *The Color Purple* on the blackboard and asked the students to help me translate these sentences into Standard English:

You better not never tell nobody but God. It'd kill your mammy.

Dear God,

I am fourteen years old. I have always been a good girl. Maybe you can give me a sign letting me know what is happening to me.

Last spring after Little Lucious come I heard them fussing. He was pulling on her arm. She say it too soon, Fonso. I aint well. Finally he leave her alone. A week go by, he pulling on her arm again. She say, Naw, I ain't gonna. Can't you see I'm already half dead, an all of the children.[4]

---

4. Alice Walker, *The Color Purple* (New York: Harcourt Brace Jovanovich, 1982), p. 11.

Our process of translation exploded with hilarity and even hysterical, shocked laughter: The Black writer, Alice Walker, knew what she was doing! If rudimentary criteria for good fiction include the manipulation of language so that the syntax and diction of sentences will tell you the identity of speakers, the probable age and sex and class of speakers, and even the locale — urban/rural/southern/western — then Walker had written, perfectly. This is the translation into Standard English that our class produced:

> *Absolutely, one should never confide in anybody besides God. Your secrets could prove devastating to your mother.*
>
> Dear God,
>
> I am fourteen years old. I have always been good. But now, could you help me to understand what is happening to me?
>
> Last spring, after my little brother, Lucious, was born, I heard my parents fighting. My father kept pulling at my mother's arm. But she told him, "It's too soon for sex, Alfonso. I am still not feeling well." Finally, my father left her alone. A week went by, and then he began bothering my mother, again: Pulling her arm. She told him, "No, I won't! Can't you see I'm already exhausted from all of these children?"

(Our favourite line was "It's too soon for sex, Alfonso.")   15

Once we could stop laughing, once we could stop our exponentially wild improvisations on the theme of Translated Black English, the students pushed to explain their own negative first reactions to their spoken language on the printed page. I thought it was probably akin to the shock of seeing yourself in a photograph for the first time. Most of the students had never before seen a written facsimile of the way they talk. None of the students had ever learned how to read and write their own verbal system of communication: Black English. Alternatively, this fact began to baffle or else bemuse and then infuriate my students. Why not? Was it too late? Could they learn how to do it, now? And, ultimately, the final test question, the one testing my sincerity: Could I teach them? Because I had never taught anyone Black English and, as far as I knew, no one, anywhere in the United States, had ever offered such a course, the best I could say was "I'll try."

THINKING CRITICALLY ABOUT THE READING

1. In paragraph 1, what metaphor does Jordan use to describe Black English? Why do you suppose she makes the choice she does?

2. What does Jordan mean when she says that English "less and less defers to England and its 'gentlemen'" (2)? How does this statement support her larger argument about Black English and Standard English?

3. Why is the term *Standard English* a "misnomer," according to Jordan?

4. Why do Jordan's students first reject Alice Walker's *The Color Purple*? Why does Jordan initially meet their rejection with "astonishment" (13)?

5. Why does Jordan ask her students to translate a passage from Walker's novel into Standard English? What do her students learn from the translation process?

LANGUAGE IN ACTION

Many of Jordan's poems themselves are not written in Standard English. Visit the Poetry Foundation website (www.poetryfoundation.org) and search for one or two of her poems — for example, "A Poem about Intelligence for My Brothers and Sisters" or "On the Loss of Energy (and Other Things)." Choose a poem and, on your own, try to "translate" one stanza from Jordan's original poetic language into Standard English. What is lost when you translate her language in this way? How does your translation highlight the importance of Jordan's original word choices and other rhetorical techniques?

WRITING SUGGESTIONS

1. Jordan describes the concept of Standard English as "strange" and "tenuous" (3). Do you agree with her? Do you think that there *should* be a Standard English, with rules that all English speakers across the world should follow? Why or why not? Write a brief essay explaining your answer. You may support your argument using evidence from Jordan's article or from other sources.

2. In paragraph 14, Jordan suggests that the "rudimentary criteria for good fiction include the manipulation of language so that the syntax and diction of sentences will tell you the identity of speakers, the probable age and sex and class of speakers, and even the locale — urban/rural/southern/western." Do you agree that manipulating language in this way in order to indicate characters' identities, including their age, sex, and socioeconomic class, is "rudimentary" — that is, essential or fundamental — to "good" fiction? Why or why not? Write a brief essay in which you explain your response. You might want to include examples of writing by some of your favorite fiction authors to support your argument.

11

LANGUAGE AND GENDER: POWER, ABUSE, EQUALITY

When one considers the range of topics and the variety of approaches taken by scholars in the general field of gender studies, there is an astounding body of work that one can access and analyze, and perhaps research even further. When one adds to the mix the scholarly efforts occurring in the study of language, the conjoined field of language and gender offers one of the most vibrant and revealing areas of intellectual pursuit available today. From the various definitions of gender itself to questions of usage, stylistics, ethnography, race, power, education, sociology, folklore, communication, pragmatics, literature, queer culture, and sexuality—to name just a few areas of research in play—the intersecting studies of language and gender have offered some amazing insights into who we are and how we communicate with each other.

The essays in this chapter are but a small sampling of the ways gender and language interact. In the opening selection, "We're All Mad Here: Weinstein, Women, and the Language of Lunacy," Laurie Penny begins the conversation by exploring the societal changes wrought by the #MeToo movement starting in 2017. The language of madness, Penny discovers, has been society's way of dealing with the reality of male abusers and predators—and that social order has been turned on its head now that women are speaking up and speaking out about the powerful and influential men who have abused them. Roxane Gay's piece "The Careless Language of Sexual Violence" continues this conversation by questioning the language that popular culture and the media use to talk and write about rape, and exploring the ramifications of the language we choose to use.

Next, the novelist Chimamanda Ngozi Adichie talks about calling herself a "Happy Feminist" and confronts and explores people's discomfort with the term. In "The Social Harms of 'Bitch,'" Sherryl Kleinman, Matthew B. Ezzell, and A. Corey Frost examine how "bitch" is used as a term of abuse and examine whether it can be reclaimed. Next, Michael Kimmel examines the "Guy Code" that he claims prescribes what it means to be a man in our society and how language aids and abets in the formation and preservation of that strange cultural phenomenon. Finally, Michelle Tea writes about her marriage to her "totally masculine" female partner in "How to Refer to My Husband-Wife." With a good dash of humor, she runs through all the possible labels or gendered pronouns she could use—none of which quite fits the situation—before solving her dilemma in a totally unexpected way.

We're All Mad Here: Weinstein, Women, and the Language of Lunacy

Laurie Penny

Born in London in 1986, Laurie Penny is a writer, feminist, activist, and speaker. She received her undergraduate degree from Wadham College at the University of Oxford in the United Kingdom. Penny's work has appeared in *The Guardian, The Baffler, The New York Times Magazine,* and many other publications. She is currently a contributing editor and columnist for the *New Statesman,* a London-based political and cultural magazine. A prolific author, she has also written several books, including *Meat Market: Female Flesh Under Capitalism* (2011), *Unspeakable Things: Sex, Lies, and Revolution* (2014), and *Bitch Doctrine: Essays for Dissenting Adults* (2017).

Penny sees no contradiction between her work as a journalist and her strong political views, which pervade her work. As she has written, "I hold no truck with the notion of 'objective' reporting . . . To my mind the best one can ever do as a writer is be honest about your background and partialities and try to understand how they affect your outlook." Many of her readers appreciate the fierceness of her prose style, and that voice is evident in the following selection, which appeared in the online journal *Longreads* in October 2017. In the essay, Penny writes about what has been called the "#MeToo Moment": a period in our culture beginning in 2017, during which powerful men (and their enablers) began to face a powerful and destabilizing reckoning over what she refers to as "rape culture."

WRITING TO DISCOVER: *Penny writes about how the backlash against a culture of pervasive male chauvinism, harassment, and assault is now having far-reaching consequences and implications. Where do you see these effects? How has this cultural moment affected you? Have you seen—or felt—the #MeToo backlash, either directly or indirectly? How do you respond to it, regardless of your gender identification?*

We're through the looking glass now. As women all over the world come forward to talk about their experiences of sexual violence, all our old certainties about what was and was not normal are peeling away like dead skin.

It's not just Hollywood and it's not just Silicon Valley. It's not just the White House or Fox News.

It's everywhere.

It's happening in the art world and in mainstream political parties. It's happening in the London radical left and in the Bay Area burner community. It's happening in academia and in the media and in the legal profession. I recently heard that it was happening in the goddamn Lindy Hop dance scene, which I didn't even know was a thing. Men with influence and status who have spent years or decades treating their community like an all-you-can-grope sexual-harassment buffet are suddenly being presented with the bill. Names are being named. A lot of women have realized that they were never crazy, that even if they were crazy they were also right all along, and — how shall I put this? — they (we) are pissed.

"It's like finding out aliens exist," said a friend of mine last night.   5
He was two gins in and trying to process why he never spoke up, over a twenty-year period, about a mutual friend who is facing public allegations of sexual violence. "Back in the day we'd all heard stories about it, but . . . well, the people telling them were all a bit crazy. You know, messed up. So nobody believed them."

I took a sip of tea to calm down, and suggested that perhaps the reason these people were messed up — if they were messed up — was because they had been, you know, sexually assaulted. I reminded him that some of us had always known. I knew. But then, what did I know? I'm just some crazy girl.

The process we are going through in our friendship group and in our culture as a whole is something akin to first contact. Abusers, like little green men in flying saucers, have a habit of revealing their true selves to people nobody's going to find credible — to women who are vulnerable, or women who are marginalized, or who are just, you know, women. But abusers don't come from any planet but this. We grew up with them. We've worked with them. Admired them. Loved them. Trusted them. And now we have to deal with the fact that our reality is not what it seemed.

So who's the crazy one now? To be the victim of sexual assault is to fall down a rabbit hole into a reality shaped by collective delusion: specifically, the delusion that powerful or popular or ordinary-seeming men who do good work in the world cannot also be abusers or predators. To suggest otherwise is to appear insane. You question yourself. Even before anyone calls you a liar — which they will — you're wondering if you've overreacted. Surely he couldn't be like that. Not him. Anyway, it would be insanity to go against someone with so much clout. The girls who do that are sick in the head. At least, that was what we used to think.

Something important has changed. Suddenly women are speaking up and speaking out in numbers too big to shove aside. The public narrative around abuse and sexual entitlement and the common consensus around who is to be believed are changing so fast you can see the seams between one paradigm and the next, the hasty stitching where one version of reality becomes another. Now, instead of victims and survivors of rape and assault being written off as mentally ill, it's the abusers who need help.

"I'm hanging on in there," said Harvey Weinstein, in the wake of   10
revelations about a pattern of abuse that has upended the entertainment industry, tipping all its secrets out. "I'm not doing OK, but I'm
trying. I've got to get help. You know what—we all make mistakes."
Days earlier, Weinstein emailed other Hollywood higher-ups frantic not
to be fired, asking for their assistance convincing The Weinstein Company
board to keep him, begging to be sent to therapy as an alternative. The
same pleas for mercy on the grounds of mental illness have been issued
on behalf of powerful predators in the tech industry. Here's 500 Startups'
statement on the actions of its founder, Dave McClure: "He recognizes
he has made mistakes and has been going through counseling to work on
addressing changes in his previous unacceptable behavior."

The social definition of sanity is the capacity to accept the consensus
of how the world ought to work, including between men and women.
Anyone who questions or challenges that consensus is by definition
unhinged. It is only when the abuse becomes impossible to deny, when
patterns emerge, when photographs and videos are available and are
enough to lead to conviction—then we start hearing the pleas for mercy.
*It was just twenty minutes of action. He's got such a bright future. Think of
his mother. Think of his wife. He couldn't help himself.*

These excuses are never just about the abuser and his reputation.
They are desperate attempts to bargain with a rapidly changing reality.
They are justifications for continuing, collectively, to deny systemic abuse.
Suddenly, it's Weinstein, not the women calling him a rapist and a pig,
who gets to be the one with "demons." He needs to see a therapist, not a
judge. He's a very unhappy and very sick man. And so is Bill Cosby. And
so is Woody Allen. And so was Cyril Smith. And so is that guy in your
industry everyone respects so much, the one with the big smile and all
those crazy ex-girlfriends.

What's the word for what happens when a lot of people are very sick
all at the same time? It's an epidemic. I'm not sure what started this one,
but there's a lot of bullshit in the water.

The language of mental illness is also a shorthand for the articulation
of truths that are outside the realm of political consensus. Anyone who
challenges that consensus is deemed mad by default, including women
who dare to suggest that predators in positions of power might have to be
accountable for their actions.

There's a long, grim history behind the idea that women lie about   15
systemic sexual abuse because they're mentally unwell. Freud was one of
the first to look for a psychiatric explanation for the number of women
patients he saw who told him they had been molested or raped. To report
that such things were going on in polite society would have outraged
Freud's well-heeled and intellectual social circles. So in the course of
his later writings, the father of modern psychoanalysis found alternative
explanations: perhaps some of these girls were unconsciously obsessed

with the erotic idea of the father figure, as opposed to an actual father figure who might have committed actual abuse. Or perhaps they were just hysterical. Either way, no reason to ruffle whiskers in the gentlemen's club by giving too much credence to unhappy young women.

A century later, in absolutely every situation like this that I have ever encountered, the same rhetoric applies. Women are over-emotional. They cannot be trusted, because they are crazy, which is a word patriarchy uses to describe a woman who doesn't know when to shut her pretty mouth. They are not to be believed, because they are unwell, which is a word patriarchy uses to describe women who are angry.

Well, of course they're angry. Of course they are hurt. They have been traumatized, first by the abuse and then by their community's response. They are not able to express righteous rage without consequence, because they are not men. If you had been assaulted, forcibly penetrated, treated like so much human meat; if you had sought justice or even just comfort and found instead rank upon rank of friends and colleagues closing together to call you a liar and a hysteric, telling you you'd better shut up — how would you feel? You'd be angry, but you'd better not show it. Angry women are not to be trusted, which suits abusers and their enablers just fine.

This is what we're talking about when we talk about rape culture — not just the actions of lone sociopaths, but the social architecture that lets them get away with it, a routine of silencing, gaslighting, and selective ignorance that keeps the world at large from having to face realities they'd rather rationalize away. If everyone around you gets together to dismiss the inconvenient truth of your experience, it's tempting to believe them, especially if you are very young.

Ten years ago, when I was raped and spoke out about it, I was told I was toxic, difficult, a compulsive liar. I was told that so consistently that eventually I came to accept it, and I moved away to heal in private while the man who had hurt me went on to hurt other people. In the intervening decade, every time women I know have spoken out about sexual abuse, they have been dismissed as mentally ill. And yes, some of them were mentally ill — at least one in four human beings will experience mental health problems in their lifetime, after all, and violence and trauma are contributing factors. More to the point, predators seek out victims who look vulnerable. Women and girls with raw sparking wires who nobody will believe because they're already crazy.

The thing that is happening now is exactly the thing that the sanity and safety of unnamed thousands of women was once sacrificed to avoid: a giant flaming fuss. It is amazing what people will do to avoid a fuss. They will ostracize victims, gaslight survivors, and provide cover for predators; they will hire lawyers and hand out hundreds of thousands of dollars under the table and, if pressed, rearrange entire social paradigms to make it seem like anyone asking for basic justice is a screeching hysteric.

In decades gone by, women who made a scene, who made the mistake of confronting abusers or even just closing the door on them, were carted off to rot in the sort of hospitals that featured fewer rehabilitation spas and more hosing down with ice water to get you to stop screaming. Now it's the abusers who are seeking asylum. Asking to be treated as sufferers of illness, rather than criminals.

The language of lunacy is the last resort when society at large cannot deny the evidence of structural violence. We hear the same thing in the wake of a mass shooting or a white supremacist terror attack. He was always such a nice boy. Something broke. We couldn't have seen him coming. He was depressed and frustrated. We can't pretend it didn't happen, so instead we pretend that there's no pattern here, just individual maladaption. A chemical imbalance in the brain, not a systemic injustice baked into our culture. Harvey Weinstein is not a rapist, he's a "very sick guy" — at least according to Woody Allen (who may or may not have special insight, being famously interested in both psychoanalysis and recreational sexual harassment).

Woody Allen feels at least as sorry for Weinstein as he does for the forty-plus women and girls who, at the time of writing, have come forward to claim they were assaulted or raped by the movie mogul. We're now supposed to feel pity for rapists because they're messed up. Well, join the queue. All of us are messed up, and having low self-esteem and a dark obsession with sexually intimidating the women around you aren't excuses for abuse. At best, they are explanations; at worst, they are attempts to derail the discussion just as we've started talking about women's feelings as if they matter. In fact, according to researchers like Lundy Bancroft, who has spent decades working with abusive men, abusers are no more or less likely to be mentally ill than anyone else. "Abusiveness has little to do with psychological problems and everything to do with values and beliefs," says Bancroft. "Abusers have a distorted sense of right and wrong. Their value system is unhealthy, not their psychology."

At the end of the day, we're now encouraged to ask, aren't these men the real victims — victims of their own demons? Come off it. We've all got demons, and baggage, and all of the other euphemisms we use to talk about the existential omnishambles of modern life. The moment I meet someone who has arrived at something like adulthood psychologically unscathed by the nightmare fun-house of white supremacist capitalist patriarchy, I assume they're hiding something, or on enough tranquilizers to fell a small elephant, or both. We've all got broken hearts and complicated childhoods, and survivors have spent too long being quietly directed to seek therapy rather than justice.

The abusers who are now being excused as mentally ill are not monsters, or aberrations. They were acting entirely within the unhealthy value system of a society which esteems the reputation and status of men above   25 the safety of women. Many abusers, on some level, do not know that what they are doing is wrong. They believe that they are basically decent. Most men who prey on women have had that belief confirmed over the course of years or decades of abuse. They believe they're basically decent, and a whole lot of other people believe they're basically decent, too. They're nice guys who just have a problem with women, or booze, or their mothers, or all three.

Pleas for mercy on the grounds of emotional distress are surprisingly effective when it's men doing the pleading. Right now, all around me, I see women working to support men, as well as each other, through this dif-

> **We've been raised to believe that men's emotions are our responsibility. Even the men who hurt us.**

ficult time. It's not just because we're nice and it's not just because we're suckers, although it's probably a little bit of both.

It's because we know how much this is going to hurt.

We should. We've carried it all for so long in private. We know how deep the damage goes, how much there is still unsaid. Even as we come together to demand an end to sexual violence, we worry that men are too weak to cope with the consequences of what they've done and allowed to be done to us.

I have for the past three months been nursing intermittent jags of panic at the knowledge of what was about to be revealed (and has now been revealed) about a person I once cared for deeply and, because I am a soft-hearted fool, still care about very much. A person who, it turns out, has hurt more women than any of us guessed when we started joining the puncture wounds in our pasts to make a picture. Panic because none of us want him to hurt himself. Panic because we worry that he might. We want him to be safe, even though none of us have been. Isn't that just delicious? As more stories of private pain come out, it is still the men we're supposed to worry about.

The threat of extreme self-harm is a classic last-resort tactic for abusers who suspect that they're losing control, that their partner is about to leave them or tell someone, or both. It's effective because it's almost always plausible, and who wants to be the person who put their own free-dom and safety ahead of another person's life? Not a great many women, certainly, given the bone-deep knowledge drilled into us from birth that we were put on this earth to protect men from, among other things, the consequences of their actions. We've been raised to believe that men's emotions are our responsibility. Even the men who hurt us.

As the list of names grows longer, the plea for mercy on the grounds of mental illness is being deployed in exactly the same way. These guys are suffering, too. If you carry on calling for them to come clean and change their behavior, well, that might just push them over the edge. And you wouldn't want that, would you? You're a nice girl, aren't you?

I've been told several times by controlling partners that if I left them, they might break down or even kill themselves. Each time, I stayed longer than I should have because I loved them and wanted them alive, and every time, when it finally became unbearable, they were absolutely fine. Not one of them made an attempt to carry out their threat. That doesn't mean they didn't mean it at the time. But the demand that even as we attempt to free ourselves from structural or specific violence, women prioritize the wellbeing of men over and above our own, is a tried-and-true way of keeping a rein on females who might just be about to stand up for ourselves. We are expected to show a level of concern for our abusers that it would never occur to them to show to us—if they'd been at all concerned about our well-being in the first place, we wouldn't be where we are. And where we are is extremely dark, and very difficult, and it'll get darker and more difficult before we're done.

I'm worried about a lot of people right now. I'm worried about the several men I know who have hurt women in the past and who are now facing the consequences. I'm worried about the men who are analyzing their own behavior in horror, who stood aside and let it happen, and who are suddenly realizing their own complicity—and struggling to cope with the guilt, the shame of that knowledge. That's allowed. Empathy is not being rationed here, and we can worry about whoever we like—as long as we worry about the survivors first. We were not liars, or hysterical. We were telling the truth. And if the men are a mess today because they finally have to reckon with that truth, we must not let that stop us from building a world where love and sexuality and gender hurt less, a world where this does not have to happen again as it has happened, in silence, for so many generations.

Reframing serial abuse as a mental health disorder stashes it conveniently on the high shelf marked "not a political issue." The trouble is that sickness does not obviate social responsibility. It never has. Sickness might give a person the overwhelming urge to act in repulsive ways but sickness does not cover for them during business meetings or pay off their lawyers or make sure they get women dropped from films: it takes a village to protect a rapist.

I am perfectly willing to accept that toxic masculinity leaves a lot of 35 broken men in its maw. That culture conspires to prevent men and boys from being able to handle their sexuality, their aggression, and their fear of rejection and loss of status in any adult way; that it is unbearable at times to exist inside a male body without constant validation. But very few men—very few people, period—grow up with wholly healthy attitudes towards their own gender. Not everyone with fucked-up ideas about women goes on to do fucked-up things to women. Toxic masculinity, as Bancroft observes, is a social illness before it is a psychological one.

So what about the rest of us? People say that they are shocked, and perhaps they are. But shock is very different from surprise. When was the last time you were really, truly surprised to hear a story like this? The truth is that a great many of those surrounding Weinstein did know. Just as the friends and associates of most sexual predators probably know — not everything, but enough to guess, if they cared to. The reason they didn't say or do anything is simple and painful. The reason is that nobody had enough of a problem with what was going on to make a fuss. They thought that what was going on was morally acceptable. Polite society or whatever passed for it in their industry told them that this was all normal and par for the course, even if your heart told you otherwise. Polite society hates a fuss. Polite society can be a very dangerous place for a young girl to walk alone, and on this issue, most of us have been. Until now.

It is easier to cope with the idea of sick men than it is to face the reality of a sick society; we've waited far too long to deal with our symptoms because we didn't want to hear the diagnosis. The prognosis is good, but the treatment is brutal. The people finally facing the consequences of having treated women and girls like faceless pieces of property may well be extremely unhappy about it. That's understandable. I'm sure it's not a lot of fun to be Harvey Weinstein right now, but sadly for the producer and those like him, the world is changing, and for once, cosseting the feelings of powerful men is not and cannot be our number-one priority. For once, the safety and sanity of survivors is not about to be sacrificed so that a few more unreconstructed bastards can sleep at night.

THINKING CRITICALLY ABOUT THE READING

1. In paragraphs 5 and 7, what analogy does Penny use to describe the "process" that our culture is going through right now?

2. What is our "collective delusion," in Penny's view?

3. At one point, Penny refers to herself as "just some crazy girl" (6). Is she being serious? Why does she use this term here?

4. What point does paragraph 16 help illustrate? How does it relate to Penny's overall argument?

5. Penny withholds the revelation that she was raped until paragraph 19. Why do you think she does this? Do you think the essay would be more powerful if she shared this information earlier? Why or why not?

6. How would you describe the tone of this essay and Penny's voice as a writer? Point to specific choices or aspects of her style that create her tone. How do you respond to it?

LANGUAGE IN ACTION

Penny is a careful reader of narrative, rhetoric, and language. For example, she is particularly focused on the term *crazy*, which she describes as a "word patriarchy uses to describe a woman who doesn't know when to shut her pretty mouth" (16). Implicitly, then, the word means something different when it is applied to women than when it is applied to men: it has different connotations in the context of gender. What biases, assumptions, and stereotypes are inherent in certain words as they are used to describe men and women, respectively? Consider the following list of words. Which ones seem mainly applicable to one gender? Which ones have different connotations, depending on whether they refer to a man or a woman? What are those connotations? Do they suggest gender biases and stereotypes?

- Aggressive
- Shrill
- Strident
- Abrasive
- Feisty
- Successful
- Helpful
- Hysterical

- Emotional
- Catty
- Ditzy
- Sassy
- Hard-working
- Blunt
- Demanding
- Tough

WRITING SUGGESTIONS

1. In paragraph 35, Penny writes: "I am perfectly willing to accept that toxic masculinity leaves a lot of broken men in its maw." Are you familiar with the term *toxic masculinity*, which she characterizes as a "social illness"? Do some research on the term, including sources that view "toxic masculinity" as a problem and others that view it as a misguided attack on *all* masculinity. What does the term mean? How do *you* interpret it? What are some examples? Do you think our culture encourages toxic masculinity? How do you distinguish *toxic* masculinity from the concept of masculinity or *manliness*, itself? Write an essay that addresses these questions.

2. Writing about the case of producer Harvey Weinstein, who harassed and assaulted women for decades, Penny claims, "The truth is that a great many of those surrounding Weinstein did know [what he was doing]. Just as the friends and associates of most sexual predators probably know—not everything, but enough to guess, if they cared to. The reason they didn't say or do anything is simple and painful. The reason is that nobody had enough of a problem with what was going on to make a fuss" (36). Have you ever been in a situation where you could have—or should have—raised a "fuss"? Have you ever witnessed bad or unacceptable behavior and intervened to stop it? Have you ever witnessed these things and *avoided* intervening, or ignored the situation? Were there any consequences in either case? Write a personal narrative that recounts a situation like this and reflects on what you learned from the experience, in retrospect.

The Careless Language of Sexual Violence

Roxane Gay

Born in 1974 in Omaha, Nebraska, Roxane Gay is an associate professor in the Department of English at Purdue University in West Lafayette, Indiana. Gay attended the prestigious Phillips Exeter Academy in New Hampshire and has a doctorate degree in rhetoric and technical communication from Michigan Technological University. Gay's work has appeared in *Best American Mystery Stories* (2014), *Best American Short Stories* (2012), *Best Sex Writing* (2012), *A Public Space, McSweeney's, Tin House, Oxford American, American Short Fiction, West Branch, Virginia Quarterly Review, NOON, The New York Times Book Review, Bookforum, Time,* the *Los Angeles Times, The Nation, The Rumpus, Salon,* and many others. She is the co-editor of *PANK Magazine.* She is also the author of the books *Ayiti* (2011), *An Untamed State* (2014), *Bad Feminist (2014), Hunger: A Memoir of (My) Body* (2016), and *Difficult Women* (2017). Gay has said that in her work, she wants to get at deeper issues about society and feminism while still "admitting to our humanity and enjoying sometimes inappropriate things."

In the following essay, which appeared on the website *The Rumpus* on March 10, 2011, Gay uses the media story of a gang rape in Cleveland, Texas, as the starting point for an honest discussion about rape. She examines how the horror of rape can be lessened with the use of language. Gay calls for the use of the language that brings to the reader the visceral, physical, brutal impact of rape instead of hiding behind vague language such as "sexual assault."

WRITING TO DISCOVER: *The language used to describe rape is often couched in easier-to-handle terms, such as "sexual assault" and "sexual violence." How is language connected to perceptions of reality? In what sense does a phrase create an acceptance of what is unacceptable? What other phrases are used to ease the reality of a particularly bad situation, such as death, murder, illness, or injury?*

There are crimes and then there are crimes and then there are atrocities. These are, I suppose, matters of scale. I read an article in the *New York Times* about an eleven-year-old girl who was gang raped by eighteen men in Cleveland, Texas.[1] The levels of horror to this story are many, from the victim's age to what is known about what happened to her, to the number of attackers, to the public response in that town, to

---

1. James McKinley, "Vicious Assault Shakes Texas Town," *New York Times* (New York: NY), March 8, 2011. http://www.nytimes.com/2011/03/09/us/09assault.html?_r=2

how it is being reported. There is video of the attack too, because this is the future. The unspeakable will be televised.

The *Times* article was entitled, "Vicious Assault Shakes Texas Town," as if the victim in question was the town itself. James McKinley Jr., the article's author, focused on how the men's lives would be changed forever, how the town was being ripped apart, how those poor boys might never be able to return to school. There was discussion of how the eleven-year-old girl, the child, dressed like a twenty-year-old, implying that there is a realm of possibility where a woman can "ask for it" and that it's somehow understandable that eighteen men would rape a child. There were even questions about the whereabouts of the mother, given, as we all know, that a mother must be with her child at all times or whatever ill may befall the child is clearly the mother's fault. Strangely, there were no questions about the whereabouts of the father while this rape was taking place.

The overall tone of the article was what a shame it all was, how so many lives were affected by this one terrible event. Little addressed the girl, the child. It was an eleven-year-old girl whose body was ripped apart, not a town. It was an eleven-year-old girl whose life was ripped apart, not the lives of the men who raped her. It is difficult for me to make sense of how anyone could lose sight of that and yet it isn't.

We live in a culture that is very permissive where rape is concerned. While there are certainly many people who understand rape and the damage of rape, we also live in a time that necessitates the phrase "rape culture." This phrase denotes a culture where we are inundated, in different ways, by the idea that male aggression and violence toward women is acceptable and often inevitable. As Lynn Higgins and Brenda Silver ask in their book *Rape and Representation*, "How is it that in spite (or perhaps because) of their erasure, rape and sexual violence have been so ingrained and so rationalized through their representations as to appear 'natural' and inevitable, to women as men?" It is such an important question, trying to understand how we have come to this. We have also, perhaps, become immune to the horror of rape because we see it so often and discuss it so often, many times without acknowledging or considering the gravity of rape and its effects. We jokingly say things like, "I just took a rape shower," or "My boss totally just raped me over my request for a raise." We have appropriated the language of rape for all manner of violations, great and small. It is not a stretch to imagine why James McKinley Jr. is more concerned about the eighteen men than one girl.

We live in a culture that is very permissive where rape is concerned.

The casual way in which we deal with rape may begin and end with television and movies where we are inundated with images of sexual and domestic violence. Can you think of a dramatic television series that has not incorporated some kind of rape storyline? There was a time when these storylines had a certain educational element to them, *ala A Very Special Episode.* I remember, for example, the episode of *Beverly Hills 90210* where Kelly Taylor discussed being date raped at a slumber party, surrounded, tearfully, by her closest friends. For many young women that episode created a space where they could have a conversation about rape as something that did not only happen with strangers. Later in the series, when the show was on its last legs, Kelly would be raped again, this time by a stranger. We watched the familiar trajectory of violation, trauma, disillusion, and finally vindication, seemingly forgetting we had sort of seen this story before.

Every other movie aired on Lifetime or Lifetime Movie Network features some kind of violence against women. The violence is graphic and gratuitous while still being strangely antiseptic where more is implied about the actual act than shown. We consume these representations of violence and do so eagerly. There is a comfort, I suppose, to consuming violence contained in 90-minute segments and muted by commercials for household goods and communicated to us by former television stars with feathered bangs.

While once rape as entertainment fodder may have also included an element of the didactic, such is no longer the case. Rape, these days, is good for ratings. *Private Practice,* on ABC, recently aired a story arc where Charlotte King, the iron-willed, independent, and sexually adventurous doctor was brutally raped. This happened, of course, just as February sweeps were beginning. The depiction of the assault was as graphic as you might expect from prime time network television. For several episodes we saw the attack and its aftermath, how the once vibrant Charlotte became a shell of herself, how she became sexually frigid, how her body bore witness to the physical damage of rape. Another character on the show, Violet, bravely confessed she too had been raped. The show was widely applauded for its sensitive treatment of a difficult subject.

The soap opera *General Hospital* is currently airing a rape storyline, and the height of that story arc occurred, yes, during sweeps. *General Hospital,* like most soap operas, incorporates a rape storyline every five years or so when they need an uptick in viewers. Before the current storyline, Emily Quartermaine was raped and before Emily, Elizabeth Webber was raped, and long before Elizabeth Webber, Laura of Luke and Laura was raped by Luke but that rape was okay because Laura ended up marrying Luke so her rape doesn't really count. Every woman, *General Hospital* wanted us to believe, loves her rapist. The current rape storyline has a twist. This time the victim is a man, Michael Corinthos Jr., son of Port Charles mob boss Sonny Corinthos, himself no stranger to violence against women. While it is commendable to see the show's producers trying to address the issue of male rape and prison rape, the subject matter is still handled carelessly, is still a source of titillation, and is still packaged neatly between commercials for cleaning products and baby diapers.

Of course, if we are going to talk about rape and how we are inundated by representations of rape and how, perhaps, we've become numb to rape, we have to discuss *Law & Order: SVU*, which deals, primarily, in all manner of sexual assault against women, children, and once in a great while, men. Each week the violation is more elaborate, more lurid, more unspeakable. When the show first aired, Rosie O'Donnell, I believe, objected quite vocally when one of the stars appeared on her show. O'Donnell said she didn't understand why such a show was needed. People dismissed her objections and the incident was quickly forgotten. The series is in its 12th season and shows no signs of ending anytime soon. When O'Donnell objected to *SVU*'s premise, when she dared to suggest that perhaps a show dealing so explicitly with sexual assault was unnecessary, was too much, people treated her like she was the crazy one, the prude censor. I watch *SVU* religiously, have actually seen every single episode. I am not sure what that says about me.

I am trying to connect my ideas here. Bear with me.   10

It is rather ironic that only a couple weeks ago, the *Times* ran an editorial about the War on Women.[2] This topic is, obviously, one that matters to me. I recently wrote an essay about how, as a writer who is also a woman, I increasingly feel that to write is a political act whether I intend it to be or not because we live in a culture where McKinley's article is permissible and publishable.[3] I am troubled by how we have allowed intellectual distance between violence and the representation of violence. We talk about rape but we don't talk about rape, not carefully.

We live in a strange and terrible time for women. There are days, like today, where I think it has always been a strange and terrible time to be a woman. It is nothing less than horrifying to realize we live in a culture where the "paper of record" can write an article that comes off as sympathetic to eighteen rapists while encouraging victim blaming. Have we forgotten who an eleven-year-old is? An eleven-year-old is very, very young, and somehow, that amplifies the atrocity, at least for me. I also think, perhaps, people do not understand the trauma of gang rape. While there's no benefit to creating a hierarchy of rape where one kind of rape is worse than another because rape is, at the end of day, rape, there is something particularly insidious about gang rape, about the idea that a pack of men feed on each other's frenzy and both individually and collectively believe it is their right to violate a woman's body in such an unspeakable manner.

---

2. "The War on Women" *New York Times* (New York: NY), February 25, 2011.
3. Roxane Gay, "To Write As a Woman Is Political," *HTML GIANT*, February 23, 2011, http://htmlgiant.com/random/to-write-as-a-woman-is-political/

Gang rape is a difficult experience to survive physically and emotionally. There is the exposure to unwanted pregnancy and sexually transmitted diseases, vaginal and anal tearing, fistula and vaginal scar tissue. The reproductive system is often irreparably damaged. Victims of gang rape, in particular, have a higher chance of miscarrying a pregnancy. Psychologically, there are any number of effects including PTSD, anxiety, fear, coping with the social stigma, and coping with shame, and on and on. The actual rape ends but the aftermath can be very far reaching and even more devastating than the rape itself. We rarely discuss these things, though. Instead, we are careless. We allow ourselves [to believe] that rape can be washed away as neatly as it is on TV and in the movies where the trajectory of victimhood is neatly defined.

I cannot speak universally but given what I know about gang rape, the experience is wholly consuming and a never-ending nightmare. There is little point in pretending otherwise. Perhaps McKinley Jr. is, like so many people today, anesthetized or somehow willfully distanced from such brutal realities. Perhaps it is that despite this inundation of rape imagery, where we are immersed in a rape culture, that not enough victims of gang rape speak out about the toll the experience exacts. Perhaps the right stories are not being told or we're not writing enough about the topic of rape. Perhaps we are writing too many stories about rape. It is hard to know how such things come to pass.

I am approaching this topic somewhat selfishly. I write about sexual   15 violence a great deal in my fiction. The why of this writerly obsession doesn't matter but I often wonder why I come back to the same stories over and over. Perhaps it is simply that writing is cheaper than therapy or drugs. When I read articles such as McKinley's, I start to wonder about my responsibility as a writer. I'm finishing my novel right now. It's the story of a brutal kidnapping in Haiti and part of the story involves gang rape. Having to write that kind of story requires going to a dark place. At times, I have made myself nauseous with what I'm writing and what I am capable of writing and imagining, my ability to *go there*.

As I write any of these stories, I wonder if I am being gratuitous. I want to *get it right*. How do you get this sort of thing right? How do you write violence authentically without making it exploitative? There are times when I worry I am contributing to the kind of cultural numbness that would allow an article like the one in the *Times* to be written and published, that allows rape to be such rich fodder for popular culture and entertainment. We cannot separate violence in fiction from violence in the world no matter how hard we try. As Laura Tanner notes in her book *Intimate Violence*, "the act of reading a representation of violence is defined by the reader's suspension between the semiotic and the real, between a representation and the material dynamics of violence which it evokes, reflects, or transforms." She also goes on to say that, "The distance and detachment of a reader who must leave his or her body behind in order to enter imaginatively into the scene of violence make it possible for representations of violence to obscure the material dynamics of bodily violation, erasing not only the victim's body but his or her pain." The way we currently represent rape, in books, in newspapers, on television, on the silver screen, often allows us to ignore the material realities of rape, the impact of rape, the meaning of rape.

While I have these concerns, I also feel committed to telling the truth, to saying these violences happen even if bearing such witness contributes to a spectacle of sexual violence. When we're talking about race or religion or politics, it is often said we need to speak carefully. These are difficult topics where we need to be vigilant not only in what we say but how we express ourselves. That same care, I would suggest, has to be extended to how we write about violence, and sexual violence in particular.

In the *Times* article, the phrase "sexual assault" is used, as is the phrase "the girl had been forced to have sex with several men." The word "rape" is only used twice and not really in connection with the victim. That is not the careful use of language. Language, in this instance, and far more often than makes sense, is used to buffer our sensibilities from the brutality of rape, from the extraordinary nature of such a crime. Feminist scholars have long called for a rereading of rape. Higgins and Silver note that "the act of rereading rape involves more than listening to silences; it requires restoring rape to the literal, to the body: restoring, that is, the violence—the physical, sexual violation." I would suggest we need to find new ways, whether in fiction or creative nonfiction or journalism, for not only rereading rape but rewriting rape as well, ways of rewriting that restore the actual violence to these crimes and that make it impossible for men to be excused for committing atrocities and that make it impossible for articles like McKinley's to be written, to be published, to be considered acceptable.

An eleven-year-old girl was raped by eighteen men. The suspects ranged in age from middle-schoolers to a 27-year-old. There are pictures and videos. Her life will never be the same. The *New York Times,* however, would like you to worry about those boys, who will have to live with this for the rest of their lives. That is not simply the careless language of violence. It is the criminal language of violence.

THINKING CRITICALLY ABOUT THE READING

1. Gay opens with the line, "There are crimes and then there are crimes and then there are atrocities" (1). What does she mean by this? Where do you think she would draw the line between a crime and an atrocity?

2. Gay says, "We live in a culture that is very permissive where rape is concerned" (4). What causes her to make that claim? Do you agree with her statement? Why or why not?

3. In paragraph 4, Gay writes, we "have also, perhaps, become immune to the horror of rape because we see it so often and discuss it so often. . . . We have appropriated the language of rape for all manner of violations, great and small." Why do you think Gay focuses on the seemingly joking uses of words like "rape"? How is such usage different from using a word like "kill" or "murder" as hyperbole?

4. Gay mentions a number of television shows in which rape is depicted (*Beverly Hills 90210, Private Practice, General Hospital*). In your opinion, what responsibilities, if any, does television have in the representation of rape? Consider that the audience for television can be much bigger than for many other types of media. Who is affected by television portrayals of rape, and how? What ideas do viewers take away from such portrayals?

5. Gay brings up the term "rape culture," which she defines as "a culture where we are inundated, in different ways, by the idea that male aggression and violence toward women is acceptable and often inevitable" (4). Where do you see examples of rape culture? How do small instances of aggression (sometimes called micro-aggressions) connect to physical and sexual violence?

6. In paragraph 16, Gay writes, "How do you write violence authentically without making it exploitative?" What is the connection between the two? Is it possible to use language to describe violence without exploitation? What is the writer's responsibility to the victims of such violence?

LANGUAGE IN ACTION

Graphic design student Emma Sulkowicz spent the last months of her senior year at Columbia University carrying a mattress everywhere she went on campus (see p. 398). She did so as a performance art piece titled "Carry That Weight," and as a public protest against the university's lack of attention to her reported rape, promising she would carry it until her alleged rapist was expelled. She even carried it at graduation, though Columbia administrators made it clear they wanted her to leave it out of the ceremonies.

If you were to put Sulkowicz's protest into words, what might those words be? Why do you think she choose a visual, physical protest, and what statements do the details of her protest make? Why a mattress? Why *carry* it, and for so many months? Sulkowicz urged other women to do the same, and many on campuses across the country took her up on the challenge. Why do you think others were convinced to join her? What points from Gay's article shed light on Sulkowicz's action, and how does Sulkowicz reinforce Gay's argument?

Source: Andrew Burton/Getty Images

WRITING SUGGESTIONS

1. Gay points out that we often gloss over the lasting effects of rape, saying "We allow ourselves [to believe] that rape can be washed away as neatly as it is on TV and in the movies where the trajectory of victimhood is neatly defined" (13). What other experiences are given too neat a trajectory in typical media portrayals? Where else do we shy away from the complicated and long-lasting effects of trauma? Write an essay about a specific movie or television portrayal of a traumatic experience (rape, war, terrorist attack, serious injury, etc.) and analyze the portrayal of the victim. To what extent is the person's "trajectory of victimhood" made too neat? Which experiences are emphasized, and which are minimized? Why?

2. Write an essay in which you examine the use of euphemism to cover the unpleasant physical realities of violence in all its forms, including rape, assault, and murder. Investigate how language is created or manipulated to convey a desired impression. What terms do we rely on when describing violence? What do we shy away from discussing explicitly, and why? Are there ever good reasons for using such euphemisms?

Happy Feminist

CHIMAMANDA NGOZI ADICHIE

Chimamanda Ngozi Adichie was born in 1977 in Nigeria, where she was raised in the house formerly occupied by famous Nigerian writer Chinua Achebe. Her father, the country's first professor of statistics, taught at the University of Nigeria, and her mother was the first female registrar at the university. Adichie excelled in her studies of medicine and pharmacy while also editing the *Compass*, a student magazine. She eventually studied at Drexel University in Philadelphia, transferring later to Eastern Connecticut University. After her graduation, she earned a master's degree in Creative Writing from Johns Hopkins University. As an undergraduate, she began working on her first novel, *Purple Hibiscus*, which was released late in 2003 to great critical acclaim, winning the Commonwealth Writer's Prize for Best First Book in 2005. She has also written *Half of a Yellow Sun* (2006), *The Thing Around Your Neck* (2009), *Americanah* (2013), and *We Should All Be Feminists* (2014). She has received numerous awards and recognitions, including a MacArthur Foundation "Genius" grant in 2008. Her writing displays a sense of humor and strength, and she has said, "I didn't choose writing, writing chose me." She is a popular writer, educator, and speaker. For Adichie, writing fiction is a way "to turn fact into truth."

In the following selection from *We Should All Be Feminists*, Adichie speaks about the negative connotations surrounding the word "feminist." She speaks of the importance of confronting directly the oppression of women and the role that gender plays in society. She does so with her typical humor and charm, but she also makes a strong case that "culture is not people, people are culture" and that we must do more to improve the position of women in our culture.

WRITING TO DISCOVER: *Think of important women you have known in your life. They could include your mother, sister, friend, teacher, partner, or any other woman. Which of those women would you describe as feminists? Why or why not? Be specific in your response. Are your associations with the word "feminist" positive or negative? What do you think is behind those associations?*

In 2003, I wrote a novel called *Purple Hibiscus*, about a man who, among other things, beats his wife, and whose story doesn't end too well. While I was promoting the novel in Nigeria, a journalist, a nice, well-meaning man, told me he wanted to advise me. (Nigerians, as you might know, are very quick to give unsolicited advice.) He told me that people were saying my novel was feminist, and his advice to me—he was shaking his head sadly as he spoke—was that I should never call myself a feminist, since feminists are women who are unhappy because they cannot find husbands.

So I decided to call myself a Happy Feminist.

Then an academic, a Nigerian woman, told me that feminism was not our culture, that feminism was un-African and I was only calling myself a feminist because I had been influenced by western books. (Which amused me, because much of my early reading was decidedly unfeminist: I must have read every single Mills & Boon romance published before I was 16. And each time I try to read those books called "classic feminist texts," I get bored, and I struggle to finish them.)

Anyway, since feminism was un-African, I decided I would now call myself a Happy African Feminist. Then a dear friend told me that calling myself a feminist meant that I hated men. So I decided I would now be a Happy African Feminist Who Does Not Hate Men. At some point I was a Happy African Feminist Who Does Not Hate Men And Who Likes To Wear Lip Gloss And High Heels For Herself And Not For Men.

Gender matters everywhere in the world. But it is time we should   5
begin to dream about and plan for a different world. A fairer world. A world of happier men and happier women who are truer to themselves.

Gender is not an easy conversation to have. It makes people uncomfortable, sometimes even irritable. Both men and women are resistant to talk about gender, or are quick to dismiss the problems of gender. Because thinking of changing the status quo is always uncomfortable.

Some people ask, "Why the word *feminist*? Why not just say you are a believer in human rights, or something like that?" Because that would be dishonest. Feminism is, of course, part of human rights in general — but to choose to use the vague expression *human rights* is to deny the specific and particular problem of gender. It would be a way of pretending that it was not women who have, for centuries, been excluded. It would be a way of denying that the problem of gender targets women. That the problem was not about being human, but specifically about being a female human. For centuries, the world divided human beings into two groups and then proceeded to exclude and oppress one group. It is only fair that the solution to the problem should acknowledge that.

> **But it is time we should begin to dream about and plan for a different world. A fairer world. A world of happier men and women who are truer to themselves.**

Some men feel threatened by the idea of feminism. This comes, I think, from the insecurity triggered by how boys are brought up, how their sense of self-worth is diminished if they are not "naturally" in charge as men.

Other men might respond by saying, "Okay, this is interesting, but I don't think like that. I don't even think about gender."

Maybe not.   10

And that is part of the problem. That many men do not *actively* think about gender or notice gender. That many men say that things might have been bad in the past but everything is fine now. And that many men do nothing to change it. If you are a man and you walk into a restaurant and the waiter greets just you, does it occur to you to ask the waiter, "Why have you not greeted her?" Men need to speak out in all of these ostensibly small situations.

Because gender can be uncomfortable, there are easy ways to close this conversation. Some people will bring up evolutionary biology and apes, how female apes bow to male apes — that sort of thing. But the point is this: we are not apes. Apes also live in trees and eat earthworms. We do not. Some people will say, "Well, poor men also have a hard time." And they do.

But that is not what this conversation is about. Gender and class are different. Poor men still have the privileges of being men, even if they do not have the privileges of being wealthy. I learned a lot about systems of oppression and how they can be blind to one another by talking to black men. I was once talking about gender and a man said to me, "Why does it have to be you as a woman? Why not you as a human being?" This type of question is a way of silencing a person's specific experiences. Of course I am a human being, but there are particular things that happen to me in the world because I am a woman. This same man, by the way, would often talk about his experience as a black man. (To which I should probably have responded, "Why not your experiences as a man or as a human being? Why a black man?")

So, no, this conversation is about gender. Some people will say, "Oh, but women have the real power: bottom power." (This is a Nigerian expression for a woman who uses her sexuality to get things from men.) But bottom power is not power at all, because the woman with bottom power is actually not powerful; she just has a good route to tap another person's power. And then what happens if the man is in a bad mood or sick or temporarily impotent?

Some people will say a woman is subordinate to men because it's our culture. But culture is constantly changing. I have beautiful twin nieces who are 15. If they had been born a hundred years ago, they would have been taken away and killed. Because a hundred years ago, Igbo culture considered the birth of twins to be an evil omen. Today that practice is unimaginable to all Igbo people.

What is the point of culture? Culture functions ultimately to ensure the preservation and continuity of a people. In my family, I am the child who is most interested in the story of who we are, in ancestral lands, in our tradition. My brothers are not as interested as I am. But I cannot participate, because Igbo culture privileges men, and only the male members of the extended family can attend the meetings where major family decisions are taken. So although I am the one who is most interested in these things, I cannot attend the meeting. I cannot have a formal say. Because I am female.

Culture does not make people. People make culture. If it is true that the full humanity of women is not our culture, then we can and must make it our culture.

My great-grandmother, from stories I've heard, was a feminist. She ran away from the house of the man she did not want to marry and married the man of her choice. She refused, protested, spoke up whenever she felt she was being deprived of land and access because she was female. She did not know that word *feminist*. But it doesn't mean she wasn't one. More of us should reclaim that word. My own definition of a feminist is a man or a woman who says, "Yes, there's a problem with gender as it is today and we must fix it, we must do better."

All of us, women and men, must do better.

THINKING CRITICALLY ABOUT THE READING

1. Adichie opens her speech with a story about a man who advises her not to identify herself as a feminist. What does he see as the danger behind the word "feminist"?

2. What is the point of Adichie calling herself a "Happy Feminist" (2)? Why does she proceed to refer to herself as a "Happy African Feminist Who Does Not Hate Men and Who Likes to Wear Lip Gloss and High Heels for Herself and Not for Men" (4)? What point is she making overall about her identity as a feminist? About others' expectations of her as a woman and as a feminist?

3. What is the importance of the distinction that Adichie makes between "human rights" (7) and women's rights specifically?

4. Adichie says that many men "feel threatened by the idea of feminism" (8). Why is this so? Note that she uses the word "idea." How is the actual reality of feminism different than what many might imagine? Be specific in your response.

5. Adichie talks about the "blindness" of systems of oppression (13). What does she mean by this? In what ways does oppression by gender follow the same processes as other types of oppression, such as that based on race or class? In what ways might they be different?

6. Adichie states, "Culture does not make people. People make culture" (17). Do you agree with her? Why or why not?

7. How does the use of humor help Adichie to advance her points? In particular, how does Adichie's tone in this essay refute some of the ideas she encounters about feminists? Point to specific lines when possible.

LANGUAGE IN ACTION

In 2014, actor Emma Watson spoke at the United Nations about her HeForShe gender equality campaign. She explained how her identification with the word "feminist" developed and the pushback she experienced as she decided to adopt it for herself. Consider the excerpt below. (You can find her full speech online.)

> I am from Britain and think it is right that as a woman I am paid the same as my male counterparts. I think it is right that I should be able to make decisions about my own body. I think it is right that women be involved on my behalf in the policies and decision-making of my country. I think it is right that socially I am afforded the same respect as men. But sadly I can say that there is no one country in the world where all women can expect to receive these rights.
>
> No country in the world can yet say they have achieved gender equality.
>
> These rights I consider to be human rights, but I am one of the lucky ones. My life is a sheer privilege because my parents didn't love me less because I was born a daughter. My school did not limit me because I was a girl. My mentors didn't assume I would go less far because I might give birth to a child one day. These influencers were the gender equality ambassadors that made me who I am today. They may not know it, but they are the inadvertent feminists who are changing the world today. And we need more of those.

What does Watson's story have in common with Adichie's experience? Why do you think there is so much opposition to the term "feminist"? Do you think you might be what Watson calls an "inadvertent feminist," or do you know anyone who is? Is the term important, if it's possible to advocate for women without connecting one's actions or identity to the word specifically? Why or why not?

WRITING SUGGESTIONS

1. Write an essay in which you examine how language has been used to manipulate attitudes toward women. For instance, describe how slanted or biased language promotes or argues against measures that ensure equality for women, or against the goals of feminists. Be sure to include specific examples.

2. A key idea in Adichie's essay is that not only will women benefit from feminism, but men will, too. Consider the points she makes within her speech about gender roles that men are forced to conform to, and how feminism will free men as well as women from stereotypical gendered expectations. Write an essay in which you show how men will or will not benefit from feminism. You may wish to watch Adichie's entire speech online, called "We Should All Be Feminists," on TED Talks to get a fuller understanding of her argument.

The Social Harms of "Bitch"

SHERRYL KLEINMAN, MATTHEW B. EZZELL, AND A. COREY FROST

Sherryl Kleinman is a professor of sociology at the University of North Carolina at Chapel Hill, where she has been teaching since 1980. Her research focuses on gender and identity and often takes a feminist approach. In addition to scholarly articles, Kleinman has published personal essays and creative nonfiction. Matthew B. Ezzell graduated from the University of North Carolina at Chapel Hill with an undergraduate degree in women's studies. After working as a rape crisis counselor and community educator, he returned to UNC for his PhD in sociology. He is currently an associate professor at James Madison University, where he does research on masculinity and teaches courses on the sociology of race, ethnicity, and gender. A. Corey Frost received his BA in sociology at the University of North Carolina at Chapel Hill in 2008. He studied with Sherryl Kleinman and served as an undergraduate teaching assistant in her "Sex and Gender in Society" course. Frost worked as a public health researcher for several years before earning his JD from the University of North Carolina School of Law. He is now an attorney in private practice.

The reading below comes from a longer article Kleinman, Ezzell, and Frost co-authored and published in 2009 in the journal *Sociological Analysis*. In this excerpt, the authors discuss how the epithet "bitch" is used to express dominance over a person or object. They analyze how some have recently attempted to "reclaim" the term in popular culture and question whether it is possible to endow a sexist term with a positive connotation.

WRITING TO DISCOVER: *Make a list of words you use that you associate with feminine characteristics. Then make a list of words you use that you associate with masculine characteristics. Which group of words do you think conveys more positive impressions? Why?*

We used to believe that feminists found the term "bitch" unacceptable. . . . Unlike "you guys," "bitch" is a slur; and there's no doubt that the word has a female referent, and a non-human one at that. Feminists knew that women could act in mean-spirited ways, but we also knew that using "bitch" to describe them reinforced sexism. If women liked the feel of "bitch" in their mouths more than "jerk," feminists analyzed that preference as internalized oppression, whereby members of an oppressed group learn to enjoy using the dominant group's term for them. And the pleasure of saying "bitch" keeps women from building solidarity, dividing them, as so many other words do, into good women and bad women. Yet, in the last several years, we've heard "bitch" used increasingly among college students, including women who affectionately greet one another with "Hey, bitches, how're you doing?" And this includes women who call themselves feminists. . . .

Despite anyone's intentions, putting "bitches" into the atmosphere, over and again, sends the message that it is acceptable for men to use the term. After all, members of the oppressed group are using it to describe themselves! Even in the case of "nigger," a word considered so vile that jobs have been lost by white people who use it among themselves, there are some whites who have used it among black people (especially black men) after hearing blacks use it with each other in a friendly way (Kennedy 2002). Most white people know better than to do so, or at least fear the consequences of using it, especially if they are white men interacting with black men. Men calling each other on racist terms has the real threat of violence. "Bitch" is much more widely accepted—who uses euphemisms like the "B-word" or the "B-bomb"? And unlike the N-word, men don't worry that women who get upset with them for using "bitches" will react violently, so there is less incentive for men to drop it. By and large, women accept men's use of the term "bitch." A woman who is the target of "bitch" by a man might reject the application of the word to her, but not to other women. The rare woman who sarcastically says "thank you" in response to a man who calls her a bitch, still makes the word acceptable. She might say instead, "No, I'm a feminist."

We're convinced that women feel good when they say "Hey, bitches!" to their friends, just as women accept saying "you guys" and "freshman." But experiencing what we say or do as pleasurable does not make it harmless. The pleasure they derive from using the term, whether as a female generic or as the old-fashioned putdown ("She's a bitch!"), is an instance of false power (Kleinman et al. 2006). The person in the subordinate group may feel good about adopting an oppressive practice, but that feeling does not challenge an oppressive system. The pleasure, after all, is about enjoying the feel of dominance, something that systematically belongs to the privileged group.

"Bitch" is everywhere, so people have become desensitized to its harms, some even enjoying its use. Our point is not that these words are offensive (though they may offend some), but that they unintentionally hurt women as a group. That most people aren't bothered by them is disturbing, indicating that sexism is the water we swim in, and we are the fish who cannot see it. How can people be motivated to make change if nothing seems to be the matter? As one of us wrote (Kleinman 2000: 7), "If we [women] aren't even deserving of our place in humanity in language, why should we expect to be treated as human beings otherwise?"

False power can provide feelings of empowerment among members of   5
the oppressed group (in this case, women), the same feelings that make it difficult for oppressed people to see their lack of empowerment in society.

"Bitch," when uttered by women and girls, masks inequality, deflects attention from its harm, or provides meager compensation for sexism. And if a woman believes that "some" sexism exists, false power allows her to believe that other women might be dupes of sexism, but not her. After all, she can say "bitches" in a friendly way, or spit out "Bitch!" as well as a man. Sexist language, then, reinforces individual "solutions" (e.g., "sexy bitch") to social problems, which ultimately do not threaten the status quo.

The normalizing of "bitch" indicates the lack of imagination that results from living under conditions of entrenched inequalities. Why is "bitch" a preferred tool of women's empowerment? That women would rather call themselves or other women bitches—rather than feminists—suggests that domination and subordination have become the only legitimate options in U.S. society. Even if women who proclaim themselves "bitches" could be taken seriously, that would hardly be a feminist solution; we'd have women divided into the categories of "bitches" (honorary men) and "doormats" (all other women). Sound familiar?

> **"Bitch," when uttered by women and girls, masks inequality, deflects attention from its harm, or provides meager compensation for sexism.**

A woman who enjoys the honorary status of man by using "bitch" may have fun with "the girls" or win temporary acceptance from "the guys." But this individual gain ultimately is part of a collective loss for women. That women use "bitch" reinforces the idea that women are essentially different from men, and in a negative way: men may act like jerks, but women are "bitches." And only men who act "like women" (members of the subordinate category) will be accused of "bitching." Women using men's pejoratives for women is flattering to men; at the same time, those terms legitimate sexist ideas about women.

We envision feminism as a movement in which women and male allies work together to end patriarchy. Our goal would be to replace it with a humane society in which "bitch"—and other terms that reproduce sexism, and every other inequality—would become relics of our patriarchal past.

REFERENCES

Kennedy, Randall. 2002. *Nigger: The Strange Career of a Troublesome Word*. New York: Vintage.

Kleinman, Sherryl. 2000. "Why Sexist Language Matters," The Center Line, a Newsletter of the Orange County Rape Crisis Center, September edition, 6–7.

_____, Martha Copp, and Kent Sandstrom. 2006. "Making Sexism Visible: Birdcages, Martians, and Pregnant Men," *Teaching Sociology* 34: 126–142.

THINKING CRITICALLY ABOUT READING

1. Kleinman, Ezzell, and Frost suggest that a woman who is called a "bitch" by a man might respond by saying, "No, I'm a feminist" (2). Do you think this is an appropriate response? Are the terms "bitch" and "feminist" opposites?

2. The authors mention the "false power" that some women feel when they reclaim the term "bitch" (5). Why is this power "false"? Do you agree with the authors that this power is illusory?

3. In paragraph 2, the authors contrast the gendered epithet "bitch" with the racial epithet "nigger." Is this is an apt contrast? How are the terms similar, and how are they different?

4. The authors are disturbed that "bitch" is not considered universally offensive, arguing that "sexism is the water we swim in, and we are the fish who cannot see it" (4). What metaphor is being used here? Is it successful?

5. In the original article, Kleinman, Ezzell, and Frost discuss the roots of the epithet "bitch." ("Bitch" is the English word for a female dog, and it was used as early as the 1400s to insult a woman as sexually promiscuous.) Do the origins of the word matter when considering how it is used today? Why or why not?

LANGUAGE IN ACTION

Have you ever heard female friends or female family members use the word *bitch* without intending a negative meaning? If so, how did you react to their use of the word in this way? Do you agree with Kleinman, Ezzell, and Frost that *bitch* should be avoided in conversation, even when no negative connotation is intended? Or do you believe that *bitch* is acceptable in certain contexts? If so, in what contexts do you think the word is acceptable? Discuss in a small group with one or two classmates.

WRITING SUGGESTIONS

1. Write an essay in which you investigate how language is used in the depiction of both prominent male and female figures. You might look at popular news sources, talk shows, or political blogs and news feeds. What words are used to show approval of men? What words are used to show disapproval? What words show approval of women? What words show disapproval of women? What can you conclude from your research?

2. In the final paragraph, the authors conclude, "We envision feminism as a movement in which women and male allies work together to end patriarchy." Has this always been the approach of the feminist movement? Write an essay in which you research the history of feminism, and in particular, the role that "male allies" have played in advancing women's rights and equality.

"Bros Before Hos": The Guy Code

MICHAEL KIMMEL

Michael Kimmel has an international reputation as a researcher, lecturer, and writer on men and masculinity. Born in 1951, he earned his BA with distinction from Vassar College in 1972, his MA from Brown University in 1974, and his PhD from the University of California, Berkeley, in 1981. Among his many published works are *Men Confront Pornography* (1991), *Manhood in America: A Cultural History* (1996), *The History of Men: Essays on American and British Masculinities* (2005), *The Guy's Guide to Feminism* (2011), *The Gendered Society* (6th ed., 2016), and *Angry White Men: American Masculinity at the End of an Era* (revised ed., 2017). Kimmel has taught at Bryant University, New York University, Rutgers University, the University of Oslo, and Stony Brook University. At Stony Brook, he is presently Distinguished Professor of Sociology and, in 2013, founded the Center for the Study of Men and Masculinities.

In "'Bros Before Hos': The Guy Code," taken from his book *Guyland: The Perilous World Where Boys Become Men* (2008), Kimmel defines the term "Guy Code" as a "collection of attitudes, values, and traits that together composes what it means to be a man" in American society today. Notice how language is skillfully utilized to encourage compliance with the code by its members and to discourage wandering from its demands by any independent thinkers.

WRITING TO DISCOVER: *Think about the groups that you belong to and how language has been used to unify its members and to characterize those who either do not belong or fail to conform to its requirements.*

Whenever I ask young women what they think it means to be a woman, they look at me puzzled, and say, basically, "Whatever I want." "It doesn't mean anything at all to me," says Nicole, a junior at Colby College in Maine. "I can be Mia Hamm, I can be Britney Spears, I can be Madame Curie or Madonna. Nobody can tell me what it means to be a woman anymore."

For men, the question is still meaningful—and powerful. In countless workshops on college campuses and in high-school assemblies, I've asked young men what it means to be a man. I've asked guys from every state in the nation, as well as about fifteen other countries, what sorts of phrases and words come to mind when they hear someone say, "Be a man!"

The responses are rather predictable. The first thing someone usually says is "Don't cry," then other similar phrases and ideas—never show your feelings, never ask for directions, never give up, never give in, be strong, be aggressive, show no fear, show no mercy, get rich, get even, get laid, win—follow easily after that.

Here's what guys say, summarized into a set of current epigrams. Think of it as a "Real Guy's Top Ten List."

1. "Boys Don't Cry"
2. "It's Better to Be Mad than Sad"
3. "Don't Get Mad—Get Even"
4. "Take It Like a Man"
5. "He Who Has the Most Toys When He Dies, Wins"
6. "Just Do It," or "Ride or Die"
7. "Size Matters"
8. "I Don't Stop to Ask for Directions"
9. "Nice Guys Finish Last"
10. "It's All Good"

The unifying emotional subtext of all these aphorisms involves never   5
showing emotions or admitting to weakness. The face you must show
to the world insists that everything is going just fine, that everything is
under control, that there's nothing to be concerned about (a contemporary version of Alfred E. Neuman of *MAD* Magazine's "What, me
worry?"). Winning is crucial, especially when the victory is over other
men who have less amazing or smaller toys. Kindness is not an option,
nor is compassion. Those sentiments are taboo.

This is "The Guy Code," the collection of attitudes, values, and traits
that together composes what it means to be a man. These are the rules
that govern behavior in Guyland, the criteria that will be used to evaluate whether any particular guy measures up. The Guy Code revisits what
psychologist William Pollack called "the boy code" in his bestselling book
Real Boys—just a couple of years older and with a lot more at stake. And
just as Pollack and others have explored the dynamics of boyhood so well,
we now need to extend the reach of that analysis to include late adolescence and young adulthood.

In 1976, social psychologist Robert Brannon summarized the four
basic rules of masculinity:

1. "No Sissy Stuff!" Being a man means not being a sissy, not being
   perceived as weak, effeminate, or gay. Masculinity is the relentless
   repudiation of the feminine.
2. "Be a Big Wheel." This rule refers to the centrality of success and
   power in the definition of masculinity. Masculinity is measured more
   by wealth, power, and status than by any particular body part.
3. "Be a Sturdy Oak." What makes a man is that he is reliable in a crisis.
   And what makes him so reliable in a crisis is not that he is able to
   respond fully and appropriately to the situation at hand, but rather that
   he resembles an inanimate object. A rock, a pillar, a species of tree.
4. "Give 'em Hell." Exude an aura of daring and aggression. Live life
   out on the edge. Take risks. Go for it. Pay no attention to what
   others think.

Amazingly, these four rules have changed very little among successive generations of high-school and college-age men. James O'Neil, a developmental psychologist at the University of Connecticut, and Joseph Pleck, a social psychologist at the University of Illinois, have each been conducting studies of this normative definition of masculinity for decades. "One of the most surprising findings," O'Neil told me, "is how little these rules have changed."

BEING A MAN AMONG MEN

Where do young men get these ideas? "Oh, definitely, my dad," says Mike, a 20-year-old sophomore at Wake Forest. "He was always riding my ass, telling me I had to be tough and strong to make it in this world."

"My older brothers were always on my case," says Drew, a 24-year-old University of Massachusetts grad. "They were like, always ragging on me, calling me a pussy, if I didn't want to play football or wrestle. If I just wanted to hang out and like play my Xbox, they were constantly in my face."   10

"It was subtle, sometimes," says Warren, a 21-year-old at Towson, "and other times really out front. In school, it was the male teachers, saying stuff about how explorers or scientists were so courageous and braving the elements and all that. Then, other times, it was phys-ed class, and everyone was all over everyone else talking about 'He's so gay' and 'He's a wuss.'"

"The first thing I think of is my coach," says Don, a 26-year-old former football player at Lehigh. "Any fatigue, any weakness, any sign that being hit actually hurt and he was like 'Waah! [fake crying] Widdle Donny got a boo boo. Should we kiss it guys?' He'd completely humiliate us for showing anything but complete toughness. I'm sure he thought he was building up our strength and ability to play, but it wore me out trying to pretend all the time, to suck it up and just take it."

The response was consistent: Guys hear the voices of the men in their lives—fathers, coaches, brothers, grandfathers, uncles, priests—to inform their ideas of masculinity.

This is no longer surprising to me. One of the more startling things I found when I researched the history of the idea of masculinity in America for a previous book was that men subscribe to these ideals not because they want to impress women, let alone any inner drive or desire to test themselves against some abstract standards. They do it because they want to be positively evaluated by other men. American men want to be a "man among men," an Arnold Schwarzenegger-like "man's man," not a Fabio-like "ladies' man." Masculinity is largely a "homosocial" experience: performed for, and judged by, other men.

Noted playwright David Mamet explains why women don't even   15
enter the mix. "Women have, in men's minds, such a low place on the
social ladder of this country that it's useless to define yourself in terms
of a woman. What men need is men's approval." While women often
become a kind of currency by which men negotiate their status with other
men, women are for possessing, not for emulating.

THE GENDER POLICE

Other guys constantly watch how well we perform. Our peers are a
kind of "gender police," always waiting for us to screw up so they can give
us a ticket for crossing the well-drawn boundaries of manhood. As young
men, we become relentless cowboys, rid-
ing the fences, checking the boundary   **Every mannerism, every**
line between masculinity and femininity,   **movement contains a coded**
making sure that nothing slips over. The   **gender language.**
possibilities of being unmasked are
everywhere. Even the most seemingly insignificant misstep can pose a
threat or activate that haunting terror that we will be found out.

On the day the students in my class "Sociology of Masculinity" were
scheduled to discuss homophobia, one student provided an honest and
revealing anecdote. Noting that it was a beautiful day, the first day of
spring after a particularly brutal Northeast winter, he decided to wear
shorts to class. "I had this really nice pair of new Madras shorts," he
recounted. "But then I thought to myself, these shorts have lavender and
pink in them. Today's class topic is homophobia. Maybe today is not the
best day to wear these shorts." Nods all around.

Our efforts to maintain a manly front cover everything we do. What
we wear. How we talk. How we walk. What we eat (like the recent flap
over "manwiches"—those artery-clogging massive burgers, dripping
with extras). Every mannerism, every movement contains a coded gender
language. What happens if you refuse or resist? What happens if you step
outside the definition of masculinity? Consider the words that would be
used to describe you. In workshops it generally takes less than a minute to
get a list of about twenty terms that are at the tip of everyone's tongues:
wimp, faggot, dork, pussy, loser, wuss, nerd, queer, homo, girl, gay, skirt,
Mama's boy, pussy-whipped. This list is so effortlessly generated, so consistent, that it composes a national well from which to draw epithets and
put-downs.

Ask any teenager in America what is the most common put-down
in middle school or high school? The answer: "That's so gay." It's said
about anything and everything—their clothes, their books, the music or
TV shows they like, the sports figures they admire. "That's so gay" has

become a free-floating put-down, meaning bad, dumb, stupid, wrong. It's the generic bad thing.

Listen to one of America's most observant analysts of masculinity, 20 Eminem. Asked in an MTV interview in 2001 why he constantly used "faggot" in every one of his raps to put down other guys, Eminem told the interviewer, Kurt Loder,

> The lowest degrading thing you can say to a man when you're battling him is to call him a faggot and try to take away his manhood. Call him a sissy, call him a punk. "Faggot" to me doesn't necessarily mean gay people. "Faggot" to me just means taking away your manhood.

But does it mean homosexuality? Does it really suggest that you suspect the object of the epithet might actually be attracted to another guy? Think, for example, of how you would answer this question: If you see a man walking down the street, or meet him at a party, how do you "know" if he is homosexual? (Assume that he is not wearing a T-shirt with a big pink triangle on it, and that he's not already holding hands with another man.)

When I ask this question in classes or workshops, respondents invariably provide a standard list of stereotypically effeminate behaviors. He walks a certain way, talks a certain way, acts a certain way. He's well dressed, sensitive, and emotionally expressive. He has certain tastes in art and music—indeed, he has *any* taste in art and music! Men tend to focus on the physical attributes, women on the emotional. Women say they "suspect" a man might be gay if he's interested in what she's talking about, knows something about what she's talking about, or is sensitive and a good listener. One recently said, "I suspect he might be gay if he's looking at my eyes, and not down my blouse." Another said she suspects he might be gay if he shows no sexual interest in her, if he doesn't immediately come on to her.

Once I've established what makes a guy "suspect," I ask the men in the room if any of them would want to be thought of as gay. Rarely does a hand go up—despite the fact that this list of attributes is actually far preferable to the restrictive one that stands in the "Be a Man" box. So, what do straight men do to make sure that no one gets the wrong idea about them?

Everything that is perceived as gay goes into what we might call the Negative Playbook of Guyland. Avoid everything in it and you'll be all right. Just make sure that you walk, talk, and act in a different way from the gay stereotype; dress terribly; show no taste in art or music; show no emotions at all. Never listen to a thing a woman is saying, but express immediate and unquenchable sexual interest. Presto, you're a real man, back in the "Be a Man" box. Homophobia—the fear that people might *misperceive* you as gay—is the animating fear of American guys' masculinity. It's what lies underneath the crazy risk-taking behaviors practiced by boys of all ages, what drives the fear that other guys will see you as weak, unmanly, frightened. The single cardinal rule of manhood, the one from which all the other characteristics—wealth, power, status, strength, physicality—are derived is to offer constant proof that you are not gay.

Homophobia is even deeper than this. It's the fear *of* other men—that   25 other men will perceive you as a failure, as a fraud. It's a fear that others will see you as weak, unmanly, frightened. This is how John Steinbeck put it in his novel *Of Mice and Men*:

> "Funny thing," [Curley's wife] said. "If I catch any one man, and he's alone, I get along fine with him. But just let two of the guys get together an' you won't talk. Jus' nothin' but mad." She dropped her fingers and put her hands on her hips. "You're all scared of each other, that's what. Ever'one of you's scared the rest is goin' to get something on you."

In that sense, homosexuality becomes a kind of shorthand for "unmanliness"—and the homophobia that defines and animates the daily conversations of Guyland is at least as much about masculinity as it is about sexuality.

But what would happen to a young man if he were to refuse such limiting parameters on who he is and how he's permitted to act? "It's not like I want to stay in that box," says Jeff, a first-year Cornell student at my workshop. "But as soon as you step outside it, even for a second, all the other guys are like, 'What are you, dude, a fag?' It's not very safe out there on your own. I suppose as I get older, I'll get more secure, and feel like I couldn't care less what other guys say. But now, in my fraternity, on this campus, man, I'd lose everything."

The consistency of responses is as arresting as the list is disturbing: "I would lose my friends." "Get beat up." "I'd be ostracized." "Lose my self-esteem." Some say they'd take drugs or drink. Become withdrawn, sullen, a loner, depressed. "Kill myself," says one guy. "Kill them," responds another. Everyone laughs, nervously. Some say they'd get mad. And some say they'd get even. "I dunno," replied Mike, a sophomore at Portland State University. "I'd probably pull a Columbine. I'd show them that they couldn't get away with calling me that shit."

Guys know that they risk everything—their friendships, their sense of self, maybe even their lives—if they fail to conform. Since the stakes are so enormous, young men take huge chances to prove their manhood, exposing themselves to health risks, workplace hazards, and stress-related illnesses. Here's a revealing factoid. Men ages 19 to 29 are three times less likely to wear seat belts than women the same age. Before they turn nineteen though, young men are actually *more* likely to wear seat belts. It's as if they suddenly get the idea that as long as they're driving the car, they're completely in control, and therefore safe. Ninety percent of all driving offenses, excluding parking violations, are committed by men, and 93 percent of road ragers are male. Safety is emasculating! So they drink too much, drive too fast, and play chicken in a multitude of dangerous venues.

The comments above provide a telling riposte to all those theories of 30
biology that claim that this definition of masculinity is "hard-wired," the
result of millennia of evolutionary adaptation or the behavioral response
to waves of aggression-producing testosterone, and therefore inevitable. What these theories fail to account for is the way that masculinity
is coerced and policed relentlessly by other guys. If it were biological, it
would be as natural as breathing or blinking. In truth, the Guy Code fits
as comfortably as a straightjacket.

THINKING CRITICALLY ABOUT THE READING

1. In your own words, what is the "Guy Code"? Do you believe it actually
   exists? Explain.
2. According to Kimmel, how is language used to support the Guy Code and
   ward off threats to it?
3. If you are a man, what are the consequences of violating the Guy Code, as
   Kimmel describes them?
4. According to Kimmel, is the Guy Code hard-wired into us biologically or do
   we create it ourselves? Why is the question and how we answer it important?
5. What does Kimmel mean when he writes in paragraph 26, "In that sense,
   homosexuality becomes a kind of shorthand for 'unmanliness'—and the
   homophobia that defines and animates the daily conversations of Guyland is
   at least as much about masculinity as it is about sexuality"?

LANGUAGE IN ACTION

For decades, feminists have argued that people should stop referring to
groups of two or more women as "guys." For example, in a 2012 interview published on the feminist website Makers.com, acclaimed novelist
Alice Walker said this about the expression:

> It's like erasing yourself daily, minute-by-minute. You're just not
> going to be female; you're going to be a guy. The programming of
> erasing what is feminine, what is female, is very strong—and women
> have not gathered themselves together to really fight it.

What relationship, if any, do you see between how Kimmel has characterized "Guyland" and its inhabitants and what Walker finds so wrong
with referring to groups of women as "guys"? Has your opinion about
the use of the word *guys* in this context changed as a result of your reading Kimmel's essay and Walker's statement above? If so, how?

WRITING SUGGESTIONS

1. Write an essay in which you describe your own experiences in growing into manhood (if you are male) or growing up around men. Has Kimmel opened your eyes to what you are experiencing or observing but perhaps not realizing? Do the examples he uses to support his argument sound familiar? What examples and insights of your own can you add? Of course, even more interesting is a thesis to the contrary, one in which you paint an entirely different, perhaps more benign, picture of what it means to be a man. Most important is the role language plays in either approach to manhood. Be sure to use examples of the kind of language involved in the process, examples that shed light because they are both authentic and revealing.

2. In 2018, Bethany Coston—a former PhD student at Stony Brook University who worked with Michael Kimmel—publicly accused Kimmel of engaging in troubling behavior toward female students. Among other accusations, she claims that Kimmel made frequent offensive comments toward female students, gave female students fewer professional opportunities than equally qualified male students, and routinely disrespected transgender students. At this time, Kimmel has denied Coston's allegations, and the situation remains unresolved. On your own, read more about Coston's allegations against Kimmel. Do the allegations change your opinion of Kimmel's credibility on topics related to gender, like those that he explores in his essay? Why or why not? Write a brief essay in which you answer this question.

How to Refer to My Husband-Wife

MICHELLE TEA

Michelle Tea is an award-winning poet, author, essayist, teacher, and self-described literary activist who often writes about feminism, social justice, race, class, and queer culture. Born in Chelsea, Massachusetts, in 1971, she grew up in a working-class family, an economic context that often grounds her writing. After dropping out of college, Tea moved to San Francisco where she helped co-found Sister Spit, a lesbian and feminist spoken-word performance group that toured throughout the United States and Canada. She has written several memoirs, including *The Passionate Mistakes and Intricate Corruption of One Girl in America* (1998), *The Chelsea Whistle* (2002), and *How to Grow Up* (2015). Tea has also written novels such as *Mermaid in Chelsea Creek* (2013) and *Black Wave* (2015), a hybrid work of dystopian fiction and autobiography. As an editor, she has published anthologies like *Without a Net: The Female Experience of Growing Up Working Class* (2003) and *Baby, Remember My Name: An Anthology of New Queer Girl's Writing* (2006). Her writing has appeared in many publications, including *The Believer, Harper's,* and *Cosmopolitan.*

In the following essay, which originally appeared in the online journal *The Bold Italic* on February 16, 2014 (and was later published in Tea's 2018 book *Against Memoir: Complaints, Confessions & Criticisms*), she writes about her marriage to her female partner Dashiell Lippman. Her focus is on the language of weddings, marriage, and domestic life. The result is, among other things, a meditation on the question: What if conventional words and labels do not fit your particular identity or experience?

WRITING TO DISCOVER: *Have you ever been labeled in ways that you dislike or that you find inaccurate or misleading? Has anyone ever made assumptions about your identity based on stereotypes? How much control do you think you have over how others label you?*

For our wedding, my person and I decided to ask a good friend to marry us. There were a few reasons for the selection; our friend was famously grumpy, and marriage—gay marriage in particular—really got her grump rumpled. She wished homos would put their efforts toward less bourgeois activity, and was bitter about her own failed gay marriage. She was also a poet, prone to sentimental weeping, with a humorous presence reminiscent of Fozzie Bear. I told her that working-class queers were going to be getting hitched every bit as much as the upwardly mobile, and begged her to become a minister online so she could tie our knot.

Being a good friend, she acquiesced, penning a stunning speech about the history of queer liberation and eking out a few of those sentimental tears we'd hoped for. She stood behind us, beneath the sagging chuppah, her eyes moist as my beloved and I spoke our vows, promising to be super extra excellent to one another for the rest of our lives. We kissed shyly before our friends and family, then looked to

Like so many people whose bodies, minds, and aesthetics exist in between our two-party gender system, her current options suck.

our reluctant officiant for the final words. "I now pronounce you . . ." The phrase hung in the air, truncated, and we all waited to see what my love and I were about to become.

The question of what to call my totally masculine female partner (partner—ech!) had begun surfacing a month before our wedding. My sister had inquired about what her children, my fiancée's future niece and nephew, should call Dashiell after we were hitched. I was "Auntie Michelle" and my sister did her best to enforce the formality, having sweet memories of our own aunties. I knew Dashiell wouldn't be an auntie. Her hair is military-short and blocky men's eyeglasses sit on her angular face. She leaves for work each morning in a button-down, sometimes a tie, sometimes not. Always men's pants, and wingtips, a cardigan. She looks like a guy—like a superhot male model, and I often accompany her into the ladies' room, ready to put out any "man in the ladies room!" fires that her presence might spark. Female titles feel so wrong with Dashiell, and pronouns are confusing—I often find myself calling her "he" without meaning to. She doesn't mind. It doesn't fit her perfectly, but neither does "she." Like so many people whose bodies, minds, and aesthetics exist in between our two-party gender system, her current options suck. While there is a real effort among genderqueers to institute the unisex pronouns *ze* and *hir,* they sound a little too sci-fi for us. Other androgynes opt for the gender-neutral "they," which does the trick but also suggests multiple personalities. When I write about Dashiell and when I speak to her or about her, I slip in and out of masculine and feminine pronouns, and that's pretty much fine.

It took months to come around to it, but Dashiell decided that she'd simply like the kids to call her "Dashiell." Great. Next came the question from our officiant: "What do you want to be pronounced as? You know, in place of husband and wife? Or, do you *want* husband and wife?" The question was a good one. And a tough one, one that Dashiell and I had both seen coming and had been casually avoiding. It wasn't just a matter of what would be said at our wedding, it was a question of what we would call one another once the rings were on our fingers.

"Can you say, 'I now pronounce you each other's person forever?'" I asked, knowing as I said it that it sounded totally weird and awkward, maybe what a beloved pet would call their gentle master. I did like referring to Dashiell as my person, and she did the same; many nights, snuggled on the couch, one of us would spontaneously turn to the other and proclaim, "You're my person!" delighting in the way we belonged to one another. But "person" sounded both too intimate and too cutesy. Still, as the wedding drew near, neither of us had come up with anything better.

As excited as we were to actually get married, part of me felt reluctant   5
to leave this period of engagement, for purely semantic reasons. "Fiancée" had been blissfully gender-neutral. To strangers I could refer to Dashiell as my fiancée, and if they then jumped to "he" or "husband" I could say, "Oh, my fiancée is female but she's more like a boy than a girl" — but then I would miss the simplicity of using just fiancée.

"I now pronounce you . . ." Dashiell and I looked up at our friend, all of us with sweet-weepy faces. "Married!" Our guests all cheered. Good one! And so we were. "You're not my wife," I said to Dashiell, later. I scrunched my face and shook my head. "*I'm* the wife." Thinking of us as one another's wives made me think of those cheesy gown-wearing twinsie bridal cake-toppers on a lezzie wedding cake. Even though I know there are women out there marrying one another in matching dresses, that completely misses the mark for Dashiell and me, making her gender — and hence, her self — invisible, and making my queer, femme desire invisible as well.

Dashiell *did* feel like my husband, but the word had too much manly baggage for her to be comfortable with it. There was "spouse," a word from government forms that reminded me of the tiny plastic pegs in the Game of Life board game. "Partner" had been so absorbed by hetero liberals that saying it suggested I was married to a stay-at-home dad who campaigned for Green Party candidates and had a feminist blog. Plus, the roots of "partner" are in the bullshit domestic partner option homophobe politicians once pushed for in lieu of actual marriage. *Plus*, its neutrality sounded neutered to me — blah, bland, redolent of linty, sexless marriages.

I hit on our somewhat goofy, imperfectly perfect word accidentally on the phone with the lab at our hospital. I got my thyroid levels checked earlier that day but had forgotten to bring my insurance card, so called back later to provide my info. I recited the numbers and spelled out Dashiell's name, the primary insured person. "Relationship?" the receptionist asked.

"Huh?"

"What is your relationship to the card holder?"   10

"Oh, uh, husband-wife," I said. "We're married."

Husband-wife? Husband-wife! The receptionist didn't miss a beat and I hung up the phone laughing. I started calling her husband-wife as a joke, making fun of my telephone flub, but it's become my go-to word when introducing the topic of my significant other to folks I don't know. Any confusion is swiftly cleared up with "She's female but she's more like a guy." Boom.

As we gear up for another round of in vitro fertilization, the question of what our future baby will call Dashiell is likely to come up again. "Mom" doesn't work, and like "husband," "Dad" is just a little too manly for her to connect with. We've been scouring the Internet, looking for names other cultures have had for the father role in parenting duos; so far in the lead is Baba, which has been used by lots of different people to refer to both male and female family members.

THINKING CRITICALLY ABOUT THE READING

1. Why does Tea often use the masculine pronoun *he* to refer to her female partner?

2. While Tea was excited to get married, why was she "reluctant to leave [her] period of engagement"?

3. In paragraph 6, Tea writes that she did not want to refer to Dashiell as her "wife." Why? What is the problem with this term, in her view, as it applies to their relationship?

4. In her essay, Tea repeatedly uses words that could be interpreted as slurs, including "homos" (1), "queers" (1), and "lezzie" (6). Does she mean these words as insults? How do you respond to their use here? What do they contribute to the tone of her essay?

5. While this essay has an ending, does it have a clear and satisfying *conclusion*: a statement that reframes the writer's main points, leaves the reader with a thought to consider, or accomplishes other goals that conclusions often achieve?

LANGUAGE IN ACTION

Tea discusses the problem of personal pronouns and binary gender labels, which force her to move between referring to her "husband-wife" as both "he" and "she." As she writes, "While there is a real effort among genderqueers to institute the unisex pronouns *ze* and *hir*, they sound a little too sci-fi for us. Other androgynes opt for the gender-neutral 'they,' which does the trick but also suggests multiple personalities" (2). Over the last several years, the use of more inclusive, non-binary language around gender identity has become more common. For example, the *Associated Press Stylebook* now allows the plural pronouns *they, their,* and *them* to refer to individuals in a gender-neutral way. Other less widely used gender-neutral pronouns include *ey/em/eirs* and *co.*

How do you respond to the development of these gender-neutral pronouns? As a general rule, do you think that individuals have the right to be addressed and identified by the pronouns that they choose? Do you think that such labels are important? Why or why not? Are there any complications or problems that might arise from this practice?

WRITING SUGGESTIONS

1. After reading Tea's essay, consider the three essays in the casebook "The Great Gender-Neutral Pronoun Debate" (pp. 553–565). Each of these three authors describes an aspect of the controversy surrounding gender-neutral pronouns. How do you think Tea would respond to each of their arguments? For example, do you think she would agree with Stephanie Golden (pp. 554–556) that the singular *they* is a good solution to ambiguous or confusing situations involving gender?

2. Same-sex marriage has been a controversial political and cultural issue for many years, which Tea refers to in her analysis of the word "partner." She writes that the "roots" of that term "are in the bullshit domestic partner option homophobe politicians once pushed for in lieu of actual marriage" (7). Conduct some research on the topic of same-sex marriage, particularly with regard to the language surrounding it. Then write an essay that addresses the following questions: How and why has language, particularly the word "marriage," been so central to the debate over same-sex marriage? Is Tea historically accurate in her discussion of the term "partner"? In what ways are "domestic partnerships" and "domestic unions" different than "marriages? Keep in mind that Tea's essay was originally published in 2014. Has our language changed at all since then to account for societal changes with regard to gay marriage?

12

THE LANGUAGE OF LYING:
ETHICS, WHITE LIES, AND FRAUD

When one considers the trouble lying causes, it is difficult to fathom why we do it. We are all too familiar with the practice nonetheless. Richard Gunderman tells us in "Is Lying Bad for Us?" that "it has been estimated that the average American tells 11 lies per week." If so many of us are lying so often, might we consider lying normal rather than aberrant behavior? And what's wrong with lying anyhow? Plenty. From the little white lies we tell as children, and more often as adults, to the perjury we commit before a court of law, lies inflict pain and emotional distress, not just on those we deceive but on ourselves as well. Perhaps Fyodor Dostoyevsky in his classic novel *The Brothers Karamazov* put it best: "Above all, don't lie to yourself. The man who lies to himself and listens to his own lie comes to a point that he cannot distinguish the truth within him, or around him, and so loses all respect for himself and for others. And having no respect he ceases to love." We lie to get ourselves out of trouble, to cope, to avoid punishment, and for about as many reasons as the human condition presents us.

In "The Truth about Lying," the first article we present in this chapter, Judith Viorst classifies, describes, and gives examples of the various kinds of lies we commit. Her classification establishes a solid foundation for the discussions that follow. Next, James Pennebaker in "Lying Words" shines a spotlight on a few of the most common verbal markers that indicate a person is lying. Po Bronson, author of "Learning to Lie," examines why kids lie and how they grow out of lies, or sadly double down as they grow older. Richard Gunderman in "Is Lying Bad for Us?" writes clearly, succinctly, and cogently on why lying is unethical. Chana Joffe-Walt and Alix Spiegel in "Psychology of Fraud: Why Good People Do Bad Things" offer a causal analysis of how ethical and business decisions can be divorced from one another with disastrous consequences. Finally, in "Everybody Lies," Seth Stephens-Davidowitz reflects on lying and the dark truths that he gleaned from his research utilizing Google Trends, a service which "tells users how frequently any word or phrase has been searched in different locations and times." Overall, the authors in this chapter offer tangible evidence of Sir Walter Scott's famous warning: "Oh, what a tangled web we weave,/When first we practice to deceive!"

The Truth about Lying

Judith Viorst

Judith Viorst, poet, journalist, author of children's books, and novelist, was born in New Jersey in 1931. She has chronicled her life in such books as It's Hard to Be Hip over Thirty and Other Tragedies of Married Life (1968), How Did I Get to Be Forty and Other Atrocities (1976), and When Did I Stop Being Twenty and Other Injustices: Selected Prose from Single to Mid-Life (1987). In 1981, she went back to school, taking courses at the Washington Psychoanalytic Institute. This study, along with her personal experience of psychoanalysis, helped to inspire Necessary Losses (1986), a popular and critical success. She wrote the very popular children's book, Alexander and the Horrible, No Good, Very Bad Day (1972). Her stories about Alexander, which also include Alexander, Who Used to Be Rich Last Sunday (1987) and Alexander, Who's Not (Do You Hear Me? I Mean It!) Going to Move (1995), deal with the general nature of emotions. Combining theory, poetry, interviews, and anecdotes, Viorst approaches personal growth as a shedding of illusions. Her recent work includes I'm Too Young to Be Seventy: And Other Delusions (2005), and Unexpectedly Eighty: And Other Adaptations (2010).

In the following essay, first published in the March 1981 issue of Redbook magazine, the author approaches lying with delicacy and candor as she carefully classifies the different types of lies we all encounter.

WRITING TO DISCOVER: *What is your attitude toward lying? Do you allow yourself "little white lies" or no lies at all, or a lot of lies in order to get you out of awkward situations? What have been the consequences of lying in your life?*

I've been wanting to write on a subject that intrigues and challenges me: the subject of lying. I've found it very difficult to do. Everyone I've talked to has a quite intense and personal but often rather intolerant point of view about what we can—and can never *never*—tell lies about. I've finally reached the conclusion that I can't present any ultimate conclusions, for too many people would promptly disagree. Instead, I'd like to present a series of moral puzzles, all concerned with lying. I'll tell you what I think about them. Do you agree?

SOCIAL LIES

Most of the people I've talked with say that they find social lying acceptable and necessary. They think it's the civilized way for folks to behave. Without these little white lies, they say, our relationships would be short and brutish and nasty. It's arrogant, they say, to insist on being so incorruptible and so brave that you cause other people unnecessary embarrassment or pain by compulsively assailing them with your honesty. I basically agree. What about you?

Will you say to people, when it simply isn't true, "I like your new hairdo," "You're looking much better," "It's so nice to see you," "I had a wonderful time"?

Will you praise hideous presents and homely kids?

Will you decline invitations with "We're busy that night—so sorry   5 we can't come," when the truth is you'd rather stay home than dine with the So-and-sos?

And even though, as I do, you may prefer the polite evasion of "You really cooked up a storm" instead of "The soup"—which tastes like warmed-over coffee—"is wonderful," will you, if you must, proclaim it wonderful?

There's one man I know who absolutely refuses to tell social lies. "I can't play that game," he says; "I'm simply not made that way." And his answer to the argument that saying nice things to someone doesn't cost anything is, "Yes, it does—it destroys your credibility." Now, he won't, unsolicited, offer his views on the painting you just bought, but you don't ask his frank opinion unless you want *frank*, and his silence at those moments when the rest of us liars are muttering, "Isn't it lovely?" is, for the most part, eloquent enough. My friend does not indulge in what he calls "flattery, false praise, and mellifluous comments." When others tell fibs he will not go along. He says that social lying is lying, that little white lies are still lies. And he feels that telling lies is morally wrong. What about you?

PEACE-KEEPING LIES

Many people tell peace-keeping lies; lies designed to avoid irritation or argument; lies designed to shelter the liar from possible blame or pain; lies (or so it is rationalized) designed to keep trouble at bay without hurting anyone.

I tell these lies at times, and yet I always feel they're wrong. I understand why we tell them, but still they feel wrong. And whenever I lie so that someone won't disapprove of me or think less of me or holler at me, I feel I'm a bit of a coward, I feel I'm dodging responsibility, I feel . . . guilty. What about you?

Do you, when you're late for a date because you overslept, say that   10 you're late because you got caught in a traffic jam?

Do you, when you forget to call a friend, say that you called several times but the line was busy?

Do you, when you didn't remember that it was your father's birthday, say that his present must be delayed in the mail?

And when you're planning a weekend in New York City and you're not in the mood to visit your mother, who lives there, do you conceal—with a lie, if you must—the fact that you'll be in New York? Or do you have the courage—or is it the cruelty?—to say, "I'll be in New York, but sorry—I don't plan on seeing you"?

(Dave and his wife Elaine have two quite different points of view on this very subject. He calls her a coward. She says she's being wise. He says she must assert her right to visit New York sometimes and not see her mother. To which she always patiently replies: "Why should we have useless fights? My mother's too old to change. We get along much better when I lie to her.")

> **And we never can be sure, once we start to juggle lies, just where they'll land, exactly where they'll roll.**

Finally, do you keep the peace by telling your husband lies on the subject of money? Do you reduce what you really paid for your shoes? And in general do you find yourself ready, willing and able to lie to him when you make absurd mistakes or lose or break things? 15

"I used to have a romantic idea that part of intimacy was confessing every dumb thing that you did to your husband. But after a couple of years of that," says Laura, "have I changed my mind!"

And having changed her mind, she finds herself telling peace-keeping lies. And yes, I tell them, too. What about you?

PROTECTIVE LIES

Protective lies are lies folks tell—often quite serious lies—because they're convinced that the truth would be too damaging. They lie because they feel there are certain human values that supersede the wrong of having lied. They lie, not for personal gain, but because they believe it's for the good of the person they're lying to. They lie to those they love, to those who trust them most of all, on the grounds that breaking this trust is justified.

They may lie to their children on money or marital matters.

They may lie to the dying about the state of their health. 20

They may lie about adultery, and not—or so they insist—to save their own hide, but to save the heart and the pride of the men they are married to.

They may lie to their closest friend because the truth about her talents or son or psyche would be—or so they insist—utterly devastating.

I sometimes tell such lies, but I'm aware that it's quite presumptuous to claim I know what's best for others to know. That's called playing God. That's called manipulation and control. And we never can be sure, once we start to juggle lies, just where they'll land, exactly where they'll roll.

And furthermore, we may find ourselves lying in order to back up the lies that are backing up the lie we initially told.

And furthermore—let's be honest—if conditions were reversed, we   25 certainly wouldn't want anyone lying to us.

Yet, having said all that, I still believe that there are times when protective lies must nonetheless be told. What about you?

If your Dad had a very bad heart and you had to tell him some bad family news, which would you choose: to tell him the truth or lie?

If your former husband failed to send his monthly child-support check and in other ways behaved like a total rat, would you allow your children—who believed he was simply wonderful—to continue to believe that he was wonderful?

If your dearly beloved brother selected a wife whom you deeply disliked, would you reveal your feelings or would you fake it?

And if you were asked, after making love, "And how was that for   30 you?" would you reply, if it wasn't too good, "Not too good"?

Now, some would call a sex lie unimportant, little more than social lying, a simple act of courtesy that makes all human intercourse run smoothly. And some would say all sex lies are bad news and unacceptably protective. Because, says Ruth, "a man with an ego that fragile doesn't need your lies—he needs a psychiatrist." Still others feel that sex lies are indeed protective lies, more serious than simple social lying, and yet at times they tell them on the grounds that when it comes to matters sexual, everybody's ego is somewhat fragile.

"If most of the time things go well in sex," says Sue, "I think you're allowed to dissemble when they don't. I can't believe it's good to say, 'Last night was four stars, darling, but tonight's performance rates only a half.' "

I'm inclined to agree with Sue. What about you?

TRUST-KEEPING LIES

Another group of lies are trust-keeping lies, lies that involve triangulation, with A (that's you) telling lies to B on behalf of C (whose trust you'd promised to keep). Most people concede that once you've agreed not to betray a friend's confidence, you can't betray it, even if you must lie. But I've talked with people who don't want you telling them anything that they might be called on to lie about.

"I don't tell lies for myself," says Fran, "and I don't want to have   35 to tell them for other people." Which means, she agrees, that if her best friend is having an affair, she absolutely doesn't want to know about it.

"Are you saying," her best friend asks, "that if I went off with a lover and I asked you to tell my husband I'd been with you, that you wouldn't lie for me, that you'd betray me?"

Fran is very pained but very adamant. "I wouldn't want to betray you, so . . . don't ask me."

Fran's best friend is shocked. What about you?

Do you believe you can have close friends if you're not prepared to receive their deepest secrets?

Do you believe you must always lie for your friends?   40

Do you believe, if your friend tells a secret that turns out to be quite immoral or illegal, that once you've promised to keep it, you must keep it?

And what if your friend were your boss — if you were perhaps one of the President's men — would you betray or lie for him over, say, Watergate?

As you can see, these issues get terribly sticky.

It's my belief that once we've promised to keep a trust, we must tell lies to keep it. I also believe that we can't tell Watergate lies. And if these two statements strike you as quite contradictory, you're right — they're quite contradictory. But for now they're the best I can do. What about you?

Some say that truth will out and thus you might as well tell the truth.   45
Some say you can't regain the trust that lies lose. Some say that even though the truth may never be revealed, our lies pervert and damage our relationships. Some say . . . well, here's what some of them have to say.

"I'm a coward," says Grace, "about telling close people important, difficult truths. I find that I'm unable to carry it off. And so if something is bothering me, it keeps building up inside till I end up just not seeing them anymore."

"I lie to my husband on sexual things, but I'm furious," says Joyce, "that he's too insensitive to know I'm lying."

"I suffer most from the misconception that children can't take the truth," says Emily. "But I'm starting to see that what's harder and more damaging for them is being told lies, is not being told the truth."

"I'm afraid," says Joan, "that we often wind up feeling a bit of contempt for the people we lie to."

And then there are those who have no talent for lying.   50

"I'm willing to lie. But just as a last resort — the truth's always better."

"Over the years, I tried to lie," a friend of mine explained, "but I always got found out and I always got punished. I guess I gave myself away because I feel guilty about any kind of lying. It looks as if I'm stuck with telling the truth."

For those of us, however, who are good at telling lies, for those of us who lie and don't get caught, the question of whether or not to lie can be a hard and serious moral problem. I liked the remark of a friend of mine who said, "I'm willing to lie. But just as a last resort — the truth's always better."

"Because," he explained, "though others may completely accept the lie I'm telling, I don't."

I tend to feel that way, too.   55

What about you?

THINKING CRITICALLY ABOUT THE READING

1. Viorst divides lying into a series of categories. Do you find her categories convincing, or do you think she has overlooked other types of lying? Why or why not?

2. Viorst talks about different kinds of lies: social lies, peace-keeping lies, protective lies, and trust-keeping lies. Which lies is she most in favor of? Why? Do you agree with her assessments? Why or why not?

3. Of the categories of lies that Viorst writes about in this essay, which sort are you most likely to commit? Why?

4. What is the difference between yourself accepting a lie that you tell, and others accepting it? Is the difference between the two significant? Explain.

5. Some lies may be considered relatively inconsequential (e.g., "No, honey, that dress does not make you look fat.") while others are more significant (e.g., being cheated on by a lover). What attitude does Viorst reveal towards these differences, and do you agree with her? Why or why not?

LANGUAGE IN ACTION

In a small group with one or two classmates, try to list at least one real-life example of each of the four types of lies that Viorst describes in her essay. Your examples can be lies that you personally told or that someone you know told. Can you think of any white lies or polite lies from your personal experience that do *not* fit into any of Viorst's four categories? If so, what are they, and how would you categorize them?

WRITING SUGGESTIONS

1. Viorst believes that the types of lies she describes in this article are sometimes acceptable, and indeed may be necessary in order for a society to function. Do you agree with her? Or do you agree with the person she describes in paragraph 7, who "says that social lying is lying, that little white lies are still lies"? Write a brief essay in which you take a position on this issue. Be sure to respond to at least one of the specific scenarios that Viorst describes and explain why you think the lie in that scenario is or is not acceptable. You may also support your position with additional examples drawn from your personal experience.

2. Recall a time when someone lied to you with good intentions—for example, to prevent your feelings from being hurt, or to prevent an argument from breaking out—and then you found out about the lie. How did the experience make you feel? After you found out about the lie, did you agree with the other person's initial decision to lie? Why or why not? Write a brief narrative essay in which you describe the experience and address these questions.

Lying Words

JAMES PENNEBAKER

James W. Pennebaker is the Regents Centennial Professor of Liberal Arts and Professor of Psychology at the University of Texas at Austin. Born in Midland, Texas, in 1950, he received his BA from Eckerd College and his PhD from the University of Texas at Austin. In the course of his career as a teacher, researcher, and writer, Pennebaker's work has encompassed linguistics, communications, medicine, and computer science, along with both clinical and cognitive psychology. His books include *Opening Up: The Healing Power of Confiding in Others* (1990), *Writing to Heal: A Guided Journal for Recovering from Trauma and Emotional Upheaval* (2004), and *The Secret Life of Pronouns: What Our Words Say About Us* (2011). He is also the author of hundreds of scholarly articles. While he is a pioneer in the field of writing therapy, Pennebaker's more recent research has focused on computerized text analysis, which links our use of words in over 80 linguistic categories to various psychological states and personality types. He and his colleagues have used this approach to gain insight into the language use of a variety of figures, from Al Qaeda leader Osama bin Laden to American politicians.

In the following selection from *The Secret Life of Pronouns*, Pennebaker examines how people's everyday language can reveal whether or not they are lying. He is not so much interested in the morality or motives of liars; instead he drills down into the rhetoric, syntax, and grammar of dishonesty. As he writes, we are "constant victims of deception," and we all regularly tell lies ourselves.

WRITING TO DISCOVER: *Can you usually tell when someone is not being honest with you? If so, how can you tell? Are there specific verbal or nonverbal cues (e.g., body language, eye contact or lack thereof) that you find to be reliable indicators that someone is lying?*

SELF-REFERENCES: THE I-WORDS

In deception research, the word *I* (including *I'm, I'll, I'd, I've,* and related contractions) is the best single marker of a person's being honest.

The use of I-words has tremendous social and psychological significance. By definition, it is an identity statement. Using *I* in conversation is announcing to your speaking companion that you are aware of yourself, that you are paying attention to yourself. There is a certain degree of vulnerability in doing this—especially if there is a chance that your companion is judging you or seeking to harm you in some way. I've often thought of the use of *I* as a subtle submissive gesture—much like the lower-status dog rolling over and baring his belly to the bigger, more dangerous dog. "Hey, I'm not a problem. I'm at your service. I'm not a threat."

There have been several studies that suggest that when people are forced to pay attention to themselves, they become more humble and honest. Robert Wicklund, who is now at the University of Bergen in Norway, pioneered a theory of self-awareness in the 1970s. He and his colleagues devised dozens of imaginative studies where people would have to do some kind of task in one of two conditions—in front of a mirror or away from a mirror. If they completed a questionnaire in front of a mirror, they reported having lower self-esteem and generally less positive moods. More intriguing, their answers to questions tended to be more honest—their reports of their weight, grades, and behaviors tended to match objective measures of their true weight, grades, and behaviors. Also, completing questionnaires in front of a mirror caused people to use the word *I* more.

Why does self-attention make people more honest? Wicklund posited that paying attention to the self made people briefly ponder who they ideally wanted to be. Perhaps their lifelong dreams were to be strong, honest, beautiful, brave, and compassionate. Looking in the mirror made them realize that they had not attained these ideals. Ultimately, then, people would see the gulf between their ideal and real selves, which made them feel bad about themselves but, at the same time, motivated them to try to be better people. Self-awareness, in Wicklund's view, drives us all to be the people we always wanted to be.

Indeed, most of us usually want to be honest with others and with ourselves. Self-attention provokes honesty. I-words simply reflect self-attention. Across the multiple studies, when we see the use of I-words increase, it is likely that self-attention is higher. And, with self-attention, people tend to be more honest.   5

COGNITIVE COMPLEXITY

The stories that people generate when telling the truth are generally more complex than false stories. Not only do people say more when telling the truth but each sentence they put together is longer and more complex. Their words are bigger, suggesting that their statements are more precise and nuanced. The statements of truth-tellers also come across as more thoughtful, using insight words such as *realize, understand, think,* and the like.

One reason truth-tellers have longer sentences is that they are linking multiple phrases with conjunctions. Conjunctions include words such as *and, or, but, because,* etc. Many of these conjunctions are exclusive words such as *but, or, except, without, excluding.* As described in previous chapters, exclusive words are used when people are making distinctions. They are distinguishing what did happen versus what did not, what they

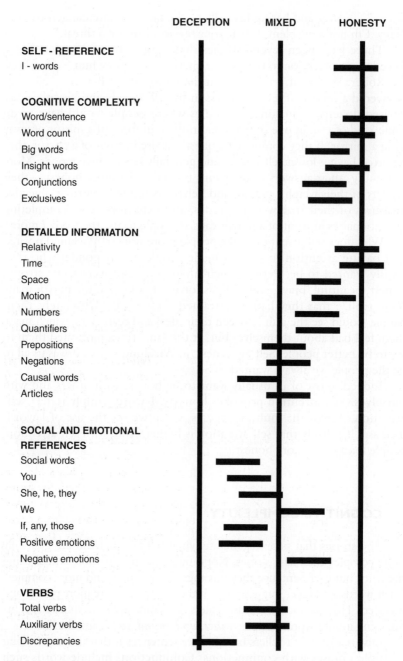

Note that words with bars on the left side of the table are reliably associated with deception. The farther to the left, the less trustworthy. Those on the right side are markers of honesty. Those words with bars close to the center line are not reliably associated with either truth or deception.

Source: © *The Secret Life of Pronouns: What Our Words Say About Us* by James Pennebaker, copyright 2013, Bloomsbury Publishing Inc.

were thinking and what they were not thinking about, what was in the category and what was not in the category.

The ability to talk about what you did not do, did not see, or did not think about is a remarkably difficult task when you are lying. If you are telling a completely fabricated story, everything you are saying is something you didn't experience. In making up a false story, you can quickly get a headache trying to add what you didn't not do. Most lies, then, are made up of simple and straightforward statements about what the person presumably did or saw. Relatively few specific comments are about what they did not do.

DETAILED INFORMATION

When conveying a true incident, we have access to a rich group of memories about the event and exactly where we were as it unfolded. More specifically, we have knowledge of precisely where our bodies were at the time. Our bodies and the relevant events existed in three-dimensional space that unfolded in real time. It is not surprising, then, that when we describe an event that really happened, we naturally include information about time, space, and motion. Together, these dimensions are captured by relativity words. As can be seen in the table, truth-tellers are far more likely to include words that invoke time (e.g., *before, ten o'clock, morning*), space (e.g., *above, next, around*), and movements (e.g., *went, put, leap*). Along the same dimensions, truth-tellers are more specific in using numbers and quantifiers, which include words like *more, less, few, larger.*

The use of words signifying greater cognitive complexity and detailed   10 information fits nicely with recent research on statements found in the questioning of witnesses. Aldert Vrij, one of the world's experts on the analysis of interviews of people suspected of crimes, points out that the detection of lying depends on the ways people are asked questions. A policeman, parent, or friend who is accusatory in their interview will likely just get brief statements full of denials—which can be extremely difficult to evaluate. Instead, Vrij and his colleagues recommend that interrogations or interviews should be more open-ended, less judgmental, and aimed at information gathering. The more that a suspect is allowed to say, the more likely that their stories will exonerate or convict them.

Although Vrij and other law enforcement researchers have only recently started to use computer-based methods, they have independently discovered that truth-tellers make statements that are more complex and more detailed.

SOCIAL AND EMOTIONAL DIMENSIONS

Many forms of deception are associated with optimism and overconfidence. The person trying to sell you a new rug, a new religion, or a new war often brims with the certainty of truth. Part of the effective salesperson's approach is convincing you that once you buy the product *there is absolutely no doubt that* you too will be as happy and confident as the salesperson.

Counter to common sense, people who are deceptive make more references to other people and rely on more positive emotion words. The stereotype of the liar is the lonely, furtive, shifty, self-loathing, treacherous, and nervous person who is desperately avoiding capture. There may be a few such liars around but I would urge you to hang on to your wallet more tightly when you happen upon the bubbly, enthusiastic, outgoing, warm, and self-assured person who has a great deal just for you.

Social words, by the way, are a mix of words that indicate a social relationship — including nouns like *friend*, *pal*, and *mother* as well as actions such as talking, calling, and listening. In reading over many of the deception transcripts, it is impressive how frequently people bring up other individuals to try to validate their own statements or to shift the blame to someone else.

VERBS AND ACTIONS

Verbs are complicated. Hang around a language expert such as Steven   15
Pinker for a few hours and your head will soon be swimming with an ocean of verb types. Regular verbs generally express a particular action and can distinguish between past tense and present (but not future). Auxiliary verbs, sometimes called helping verbs, are really only a handful of verbs such as *to be*, *to have*, and *to do*. Auxiliary verbs are associated with a passive voice and are frowned on in American English classes but celebrated in British English classes. Another type, called discrepancy verbs (or modal verbs), includes words like *should*, *could*, *ought*, *must*, and *would*. Discrepancy verbs are used when people suggest some kind of subtle discrepancy between how the world is and how it could, should, or ought to be.

As you can see in the chart, people who use verbs at high rates tend to be more deceptive than people who use fewer verbs. This pattern is particularly strong for auxiliary verbs and discrepancies. Let's say that you are a grade school teacher and three of your students give practically the same excuse:

1. I finished my homework but the dog ate it.
2. I had finished the homework but the dog must have eaten it.
3. The homework was finished but must have been eaten by the dog.

The first excuse is far more likely to be true. It includes two past-tense verbs that indicate that the actions were specific and were completely finished. The second excuse relies on five verbs that hint that the actions were not completed and, with the word *must*, may not have even happened. And the third person's excuse is the most scurrilous lie of the three—six verbs, past tense, and not a single I-word.

In English, verbs provide a remarkable amount of information about actions. They hint at whether an action is ongoing, partly completed, or completely finished. Some verbs, such as discrepancies, subtly assert that an action may have occurred—but possibly didn't. Saying that dog *could* or *must* have eaten the homework strongly implies something about the dog's behavior but, at the same time, distances the speaker from asserting that the behavior actually occurred.

OTHER COMMON DECEPTION MARKERS

The use of discrepancy verbs points to one of several ways we all try to mislead others while, at the same time, not technically lying. Some of my favorites:

Passive constructions: "Mistakes were made." In a delightful book on misinformation, *Mistakes Were Made (But Not By Me)*, Carol Tavris and Elliot Aronson examine how people frequently avoid responsibility through ingenious linguistic maneuvers. For example, historians are in general agreement that Secretary of State Henry Kissinger frequently deceived the American people about the direction and scope of the Vietnam War during the 1970s. Years later, in an interview, Tavris and Aronson quote Kissinger as saying, "Mistakes were quite possibly made by the administrations in which I served." Note his wording. Obviously, Kissinger didn't make any mistakes. Rather, someone probably did.

Avoiding answering a question. In the mock-crime experiment where students were asked to "steal" a dollar, we asked each person point-blank: "Did you steal the dollar that was in the book?" People who actually did take the money said things such as:

> I don't believe in stealing. I have a problem with it. I did it once a long time ago; I was . . . younger. I really didn't like the feeling of knowing they're going to catch me. I just, you know, especially you said for a dollar? I wouldn't have taken it.

> Why would I? I would never even think to look in the book to look for a dollar. I was just writing in my journal for my freshman seminar.

> It really offends me that you would accuse me of something like that. I would never do something like that.

The most common response of people who were telling the truth 20 was "No, I didn't take your dollar." Unlike the liars, the truth-tellers answered the question directly without any embellishment. As these examples attest, when someone doesn't directly answer your question, there is a good chance they are hiding something no matter how earnest they may sound.

Let me be clear about that: performatives. Linguists and philosophers have long been intrigued by a language device called a performative. Performatives are statements about statements. In the statement "I promise you that I did not steal the money," the phrase "I promise you" is a performative. It is simply claiming "I say to you" or "I am uttering the following words to you." What is interesting about performative statements is that they cannot be assessed on their truthfulness. In the sentence starting with "I promise you," the claim "I did not steal the money" is not directly asserted. The truth of the phrase is that the speaker is merely saying that he or she promises that they didn't steal the money. It's fine distinction but one used surprisingly frequently.

Toward the end of his term, President Bill Clinton was being hounded by the press concerning rumors of sexual misconduct with a White House aide, Monica Lewinsky. In a January 26, 1998, press 9 conference, Clinton announced:

> I'm going to say this again: I did not have sexual relations with that woman, Miss Lewinsky.

We are constant victims of deception from friends, politicians, advertisers, and just about everyone else.

A naïve human being would think that the president did not have sex with Lewinsky. Actually, the statement he said is true: "I'm going to say this again . . ." In fact, it is technically correct. He was saying it again. OK, so he later admitted that he had had sexual relations with "that woman" but in the press conference, he was not officially lying.

One of the great baseball pitchers of all time, Roger Clemens, was accused by former teammates of taking performance-enhancing drugs during his baseball career. In a press conference several months before later admitting that he had, in fact, taken drugs, Clemens said:

> I want to state clearly and without qualification: I did not take steroids, human growth hormone or any other banned substances at any time in my baseball career or, in fact, my entire life . . .

There again, you can see that Mr. Clemens was technically honest. He did, in fact, state clearly and without qualification. What he stated was a lie but it was truthfully a statement.

WE ALL TELL lies to ourselves, to our friends, and to the world at large. Most of these are innocent lies intended to avoid hurting others' feelings or to try to make ourselves look a bit better than we should. In the same way, we are constant victims of deception from friends, politicians, advertisers, and just about everyone else. Lies, of course, are not entirely bad. They make our lives more interesting. As the writer, director, and star of the movie *The Invention of Lying*, Ricky Gervais, claims, without lies we would have no fiction, no good stories. In other words, without lies and deception, there would be very little need for art, literature, philosophy, and psychology.

One of the primary vehicles for the art of deceiving others is lan- 25 guage. Not surprisingly, the language of lies is generally seen in the function words we use. As noted in other chapters, function words are essentially social. They tell us about our relationships with objects, events, and most importantly other people. As we've seen, lies ultimately reflect a subtle shift in the relationship between the speaker and the listener. At the moment of deception, the human relationship changes, which is reflected in the function words being used.

THINKING CRITICALLY ABOUT THE READING

1. According to Pennebaker, what happens when people speaking "are forced to pay attention to themselves" (3)? What effect does it have on their claims?

2. How are the stories that people tell when they are being truthful different than the stories they tell when they are lying? What are some of the specific differences?

3. The writer discusses a common stereotype of liars. In what ways is this stereotype misleading? When should you, in his words, "hang on to your wallet more tightly"? (13).

4. Pennebaker discusses several different linguistic or rhetorical "deception markers" that may suggest a person is lying. What are some of them? Have you ever noticed any of them and doubted someone's honesty because of them? Are there any other rhetorical moves (words or phrases, for example) that put you on your guard or make you suspicious of a person's claims?

5. As the writer points out, English teachers and professors usually discourage the use of the passive voice in writing. Does Pennebaker's discussion of the passive voice give you insight into *why* that is the case? In this context, how might writing *style* be related to the validity of the writing's content or substance?

LANGUAGE IN ACTION

In his discussion of lying, Pennebaker identifies several indicators of possible deception, including passive constructions ("Mistakes were made") and performatives ("Let me be clear about that"). He provides specific examples, including misleading or false statements from Secretary of State Henry Kissinger and President Bill Clinton. Now, get together with one or two of your classmates and find an example of a dishonest statement online. It can be from a politician or other public figure (past or present), or from some other source. Analyze the quotation using the "deception markers" from Pennebaker's article. Are any of the markers he describes present in the dishonest statement? How would you characterize the lie (is it a "blatant falsehood," an "exaggeration," a "lie of omission," a "white lie")?

WRITING SUGGESTIONS

1. According to Pennebaker, we all lie—and are lied to—on a regular basis. Have you ever told a lie (or acted dishonestly in a way) that had serious consequences, or that you simply remember for some reason? Why did you lie? What did you hope to gain (or avoid) by lying? How did you feel about it? What was the experience like, at the time? How do you reflect on it differently now? Write a personal narrative essay that addresses these questions.

2. The writer Stephanie Ericsson argues that even a so-called white lie is problematic: ". . . [I]n effect, it is the liar deciding what is best for the lied to. Ultimately, it is a vote of no confidence. It is an act of subtle arrogance for anyone to decide what is best for someone else." Do you agree with Ericsson's statement? Do you disagree? Write an essay in which you take a position on this issue. If you agree with Ericsson, explain why. If you disagree with her, write an essay in which you distinguish between acceptable (or "innocent") lies and unacceptable lies. Include specific examples, either real or hypothetical.

Learning to Lie

PO BRONSON

Born in 1964 in Seattle, Washington, and educated at Stanford University and San Francisco State University, Po Bronson has a long career as a professional writer of both fiction and nonfiction. He has written six books, a combination of fiction and nonfiction. *Bombardiers* (1995), his first novel, became an international best-seller. His next novel, *The First $20 Million Is Always the Hardest* (1997) spoofs the cutthroat culture of tech startup companies in Silicon Valley. His subsequent books also met with success: for example, his nonfiction book *What Should I Do With My Life?* (2002) made the *New York Times* best-seller list. His articles have been published extensively in outlets from NPR to the *Wall Street Journal* to *Time* magazine. In regard to writing as a career, Bronson states, "Most writers, rather unglamorously, are really just people who find some solace in expression. Combined with some tenacity, or refusal to give up, we spend years learning the skills of writing. One day we get published and expression becomes our profession. We continue to seek an elusive mastery of our art. What makes us good writers is our constant devotion to this craft, a willingness to keep learning. More tenacity."

In this article, published in *New York Magazine* on February 10, 2008, Bronson writes about how children, even from the very young ages of three or four, learn to lie. Rather than growing out of lying, as many parents hope—and parenting guidebooks assure them—children in fact become better liars. By the time they reach their young teenage years, many have become quite proficient at lying, often as a means of social coping.

WRITING TO DISCOVER: *How important is lying as a means of getting along in society? Think of different kinds of lies: lying to your grandmother about how much you like her present when you actually don't like it; lying about how you spent your time when you were supposed to be studying for a test; lying about the quality of a meal someone special cooked for you. Is it really possible to get along with others without the occasional lie?*

In the last few years, a handful of intrepid scholars have decided it's time to try to understand why kids lie. For a study to assess the extent of teenage dissembling, Dr. Nancy Darling, then at Penn State University, recruited a special research team of a dozen undergraduate students, all under the age of 21. Using gift certificates for free CDs as bait, Darling's Mod Squad persuaded high-school students to spend a few hours with them in the local pizzeria.

Each student was handed a deck of 36 cards, and each card in this deck listed a topic teens sometimes lie about to their parents. Over a slice and a Coke, the teen and two researchers worked through the deck, learning what things the kid was lying to his parents about, and why.

"They began the interviews saying that parents give you everything and yes, you should tell them everything," Darling observes. By the end of the interview, the kids saw for the first time how much they were lying and how many of the family's rules they had broken. Darling says 98 percent of the teens reported lying to their parents.

Out of the 36 topics, the average teen was lying to his parents about twelve of them. The teens lied about what they spent their allowances on, and whether they'd started dating, and what clothes they put on away from the house. They lied about what movie they went to, and whom they went with. They lied about alcohol and drug use, and they lied about whether they were hanging out with friends their parents disapproved of. They lied about how they spent their afternoons while their parents were at work. They lied about whether chaperones were in attendance at a party or whether they rode in cars driven by drunken teens.

Being an honors student didn't change these numbers by much; nor   5 did being an overscheduled kid. No kid, apparently, was too busy to break a few rules. And lest you wonder if these numbers apply only to teens in State College, Pennsylvania, the teens in Darling's sample were compared to national averages on a bevy of statistics, from academics to extracurriculars. "We had a very normal, representative sample," Darling says.

For two decades, parents have rated "honesty" as the trait they most wanted in their children. Other traits, such as confidence or good judgment, don't even come close. On paper, the kids are getting this message. In surveys, 98 percent said that trust and honesty were essential in a personal relationship. Depending on their ages, 96 to 98 percent said lying is morally wrong.

So when do the 98 percent who think lying is wrong become the 98 percent who lie?

It starts very young. Indeed, bright kids—those who do better on other academic indicators—are able to start lying at 2 or 3. "Lying is related to intelligence," explains Dr. Victoria Talwar, an assistant professor at Montreal's McGill University and a leading expert on children's lying behavior.

Although we think of truthfulness as a young child's paramount virtue, it turns out that lying is the more advanced skill. A child who is going to lie must recognize the truth, intellectually conceive of an alternate reality, and be able to convincingly sell that new reality to someone else. Therefore, lying demands both advanced cognitive development and social skills that honesty simply doesn't require. "It's a developmental milestone," Talwar has concluded.

This puts parents in the position of being either damned or blessed,   10 depending on how they choose to look at it. If your 4-year-old is a good liar, it's a strong sign she's got brains. And it's the smart, savvy kid who's most at risk of becoming a habitual liar.

By their 4th birthday, almost all kids will start experimenting with lying in order to avoid punishment. Because of that, they lie indiscriminately—whenever punishment seems to be a possibility. A 3-year-old will say, "I didn't hit my sister," even if a parent witnessed the child's hitting her sibling.

Most parents hear their child lie and assume he's too young to understand what lies are or that lying's wrong. They presume their child will stop when he gets older and learns those distinctions. Talwar has found the opposite to be true—kids who grasp early the nuances between lies and truth use this knowledge to their advantage, making them more prone to lie when given the chance.

Many parenting websites and books advise parents to just let lies go—they'll grow out of it. The truth, according to Talwar, is that kids grow into it. In studies where children are observed in their natural environment, a 4-year-old will lie once every two hours, while a 6-year-old will lie about once every hour and a half. Few kids are exceptions.

By the time a child reaches school age, the reasons for lying become more complex. Avoiding punishment is still a primary catalyst for lying, but lying also becomes a way to increase a child's power and sense of control—by manipulating friends with teasing, by bragging to assert status, and by learning he can fool his parents.

Thrown into elementary school, many kids begin lying to their peers 15 as a coping mechanism, as a way to vent frustration or get attention. Any sudden spate of lying, or dramatic increase in lying, is a danger sign: Something has changed in that child's life, in a way that troubles him. "Lying is a symptom—often of a bigger problem behavior," explains Talwar. "It's a strategy to keep themselves afloat."

In longitudinal studies, a majority of 6-year-olds who frequently lie have it socialized out of them by age 7. But if lying has become a successful strategy for handling difficult social situations, a child will stick with it. About half of all kids do—and if they're still lying a lot at 7, then it seems likely to continue for the rest of childhood. They're hooked.

"My son doesn't lie," insisted Steve, a slightly frazzled father in his mid-thirties, as he watched Nick, his eager 6-year-old, enthralled in a game of marbles with a student researcher in Talwar's Montreal lab. Steve was quite proud of his son, describing him as easygoing and very social. He had Nick bark out an impressive series of addition problems the boy had memorized, as if that was somehow proof of Nick's sincerity.

Steve then took his assertion down a notch. "Well, I've never heard him lie." Perhaps that, too, was a little strong. "I'm sure he must lie some, but when I hear it, I'll still be surprised." He had brought his son to the lab after seeing an advertisement in a Montreal parenting magazine that asked, "Can Your Child Tell the Difference Between the Truth and a Lie?"

Steve was curious to find out if Nick would lie, but he wasn't sure he wanted to know the answer. The idea of his son's being dishonest with him was profoundly troubling.

But I knew for a fact his son did lie. Nick cheated, then he lied, and   20
then he lied again. He did so unhesitatingly, without a single glimmer of
remorse.

Nick thought he'd spent the hour playing a series of games with a
couple of nice women. He had won two prizes, a cool toy car and a bag
of plastic dinosaurs, and everyone said he did very well. What the first-
grader didn't know was that those games were really a battery of psychological tests, and the women were Talwar's trained researchers working
toward doctorates in child psychology.

One of Talwar's experiments, a variation on a classic experiment
called the temptation-resistance paradigm, is known in the lab as "the
Peeking Game." Through a hidden camera, I'd watched Nick play it with
another one of Talwar's students, Cindy Arruda. She told Nick they were
going to play a guessing game. Nick was to sit facing the wall and try to
guess the identity of a toy Arruda brought out, based on the sound it
made. If he was right three times, he'd win a prize.

The first two were easy: a police car and a crying baby doll. Nick
bounced in his chair with excitement when he got the answers right.
Then Arruda brought out a soft, stuffed soccer ball and placed it on top
of a greeting card that played music. She cracked the card, triggering it
to play a music-box jingle of Beethoven's *Für Elise*. Nick, of course, was
stumped.

Arruda suddenly said she had to leave the room for a bit, promising
to be right back. She admonished Nick not to peek at the toy while she
was gone. Nick struggled not to, but at thirteen seconds, he gave in and
looked.

When Arruda returned, she could barely come through the door   25
before Nick—facing the wall again—triumphantly announced, "A soccer
ball!" Arruda told Nick to wait for her to get seated. Suddenly realizing he
should sound unsure of his answer, he hesitantly asked, "A soccer ball?"

Arruda said Nick was right, and when he turned to face her, he acted
very pleased. Arruda asked Nick if he had peeked. "No," he said quickly.
Then a big smile spread across his face.

Without challenging him, or even a note of suspicion in her voice,
Arruda asked Nick how he'd figured out the sound came from a soccer
ball.

Nick cupped his chin in his hands, then said, "The music had sounded
like a ball." Then: "The ball sounded black and white." Nick added that
the music sounded like the soccer balls he played with at school: They
squeaked. And the music sounded like the squeak he heard when he
kicked a ball. To emphasize this, his winning point, he brushed his hand
against the side of the toy ball.

This experiment was not just a test to see if children cheat and lie
under temptation. It was also designed to test a child's ability to extend
a lie, offering plausible explanations and avoiding what the scientists call

"leakage"—inconsistencies that reveal the lie for what it is. Nick's whiffs at covering up his lie would be scored later by coders who watched the videotape. So Arruda accepted without question the fact that soccer balls play Beethoven when they're kicked and gave Nick his prize. He was thrilled.

Seventy-six percent of kids Nick's age take the chance to peek during the game, and when asked if they peeked, 95 percent lie about it.   30

But sometimes the researcher will read the child a short storybook before she asks about the peeking. One story read aloud is "The Boy Who Cried Wolf"—the version in which both the boy and the sheep get eaten because of his repeated lies. Alternatively, they read "George Washington and the Cherry Tree," in which young George confesses to his father that he chopped down the prized tree with his new hatchet. The story ends with his father's reply: "George, I'm glad that you cut down the tree after all. Hearing you tell the truth instead of a lie is better than if I had a thousand cherry trees."

Now, which story do you think reduced lying more? When we surveyed 1,300 people, 75 percent thought "The Boy Who Cried Wolf" would work better. However, this famous fable actually did not cut down lying at all in Talwar's experiments. In fact, after hearing the story, kids lied even a little more than normal. Meanwhile, hearing "George Washington and the Cherry Tree"—even when Washington was replaced with a nondescript character, eliminating the potential that his iconic celebrity might influence older kids—reduced lying a sizable 43 percent in kids. Although most kids lied in the control situation, the majority hearing George Washington told the truth.

The shepherd boy ends up suffering the ultimate punishment, but the fact that lies get punished is not news to children. Increasing the threat of punishment for lying only makes children hyperaware of the potential personal cost. It distracts children from learning how their lies affect others. In studies, scholars find that kids who live in threat of consistent punishment don't lie less. Instead, they become better liars, at an earlier age—learning to get caught less often.

Ultimately, it's not fairy tales that stop kids from lying—it's the process of socialization. But the wisdom in "The Cherry Tree" applies: According to Talwar, parents need to teach kids the worth of honesty, just like George Washington's father did, as much as they need to say that lying is wrong.

The most disturbing reason children lie is that parents teach them to.   35 According to Talwar, they learn it from us. "We don't explicitly tell them to lie, but they see us do it. They see us tell the telemarketer, 'I'm just a guest here.' They see us boast and lie to smooth social relationships."

Consider how we expect a child to act when he opens a gift he doesn't like. We instruct him to swallow all his honest reactions and put on a polite smile. Talwar runs an experiment where children play games to win a present, but when they finally receive the present, it's a lousy bar of soap. After giving the kids a moment to overcome the shock, a researcher asks them how they like it. About a quarter of preschoolers can lie that they like the gift—by elementary school, about half. Telling this lie makes them extremely uncomfortable, especially when pressed to offer a few reasons *why* they like the bar of soap. Kids who shouted with glee when they won the Peeking Game suddenly mumble quietly and fidget.

Meanwhile, the child's parent usually cheers when the child comes up with the white lie. "Often, the parents are proud that their kids are 'polite'—they don't see it as lying," Talwar remarks. She's regularly amazed at parents' seeming inability to recognize that white lies are still lies.

When adults are asked to keep diaries of their own lies, they admit to about one lie per every five social interactions, which works out to one per day, on average. The vast majority of these lies are white lies, lies to protect yourself or others, like telling the guy at work who brought in his wife's muffins that they taste great or saying, "Of course this is my natural hair color."

Encouraged to tell so many white lies and hearing so many others, children gradually get comfortable with being disingenuous. Insincerity becomes, literally, a daily occurrence. They learn that honesty only creates conflict, and dishonesty is an easy way to avoid conflict. And while they don't confuse white-lie situations with lying to cover their misdeeds, they bring this emotional groundwork from one circumstance to the other. It becomes easier, psychologically, to lie to a parent. So if the parent says, "Where did you get these Pokémon cards?! I told you, you're not allowed to waste your allowance on Pokémon cards!" this may feel to the child very much like a white-lie scenario—he can make his father *feel better* by telling him the cards were extras from a friend.

Now, compare this with the way children are taught not to tattle.   40 What grown-ups really mean by "Don't tell" is that we want children to learn to work it out with one another first. But tattling has received some scientific interest, and researchers have spent hours observing kids at play. They've learned that nine out of ten times, when a kid runs up to a parent to tell, that kid is being completely honest. And while it might seem to a parent that tattling is incessant, to a child that's not the case—because for every time a child seeks a parent for help, there are fourteen instances when he was wronged but did not run to the parent for aid. So when the frustrated child finally comes to tell the parent the truth, he hears, in effect, "Stop bringing me your problems!"

By the middle years of elementary school, a *tattler* is about the worst thing a kid can be called on the playground. So a child considering reporting a problem to an adult not only faces peer condemnation as a traitor but also recalls the reprimand "Work it out on your own." Each year, the problems they deal with grow exponentially. They watch other kids cut class, vandalize walls, and shoplift. To tattle is to act like a little kid. Keeping their mouth shut is easy; they've been encouraged to do so since they were little.

The era of holding back information from parents has begun.

By withholding details about their lives, adolescents carve out a social domain and identity that are theirs alone, independent from their parents or other adult authority figures. To seek out a parent for help is, from a teen's perspective, a tacit admission that he's not mature enough to handle it alone. Having to tell parents about it can be psychologically emasculating, whether the confession is forced out of him or he volunteers it on his own. It's essential for some things to be "none of your business."

The big surprise in the research is when this need for autonomy is strongest. It's not mild at 12, moderate at 15, and most powerful at 18. Darling's scholarship shows that the objection to parental authority peaks around ages 14 to 15. In fact, this resistance is slightly stronger at age 11 than at 18. In popular culture, we think of high school as the risk years, but the psychological forces driving deception surge earlier than that.

Many books advise parents to just let lies go—they'll grow out of it.   45
The truth is, kids grow into it.

In her study of teenage students, Darling also mailed survey questionnaires to the parents of the teenagers interviewed, and it was interesting how the two sets of data reflected on each other. First, she was struck by parents' vivid fear of pushing their teens into outright hostile rebellion. "Many parents today believe the best way to get teens to disclose is to be more permissive and not set rules," Darling says. Parents imagine a trade-off between being informed and being strict. Better to hear the truth and be able to help than be kept in the dark.

Darling found that permissive parents don't actually learn more about their children's lives. "Kids who go wild and get in trouble mostly have parents who don't set rules or standards. Their parents are loving and accepting no matter what the kids do. But the kids take the lack of rules as a sign their parents don't care—that their parent doesn't really want this job of being the parent."

Pushing a teen into rebellion by having too many rules was a sort of statistical myth. "That actually doesn't happen," remarks Darling. She found that most rules-heavy parents don't actually enforce them. "It's too much work," says Darling. "It's a lot harder to enforce three rules than to set twenty rules."

> **Many books advise parents to just let lies go—they'll grow out of it. The truth is, kids grow into it.**

A few parents managed to live up to the stereotype of the oppressive parent, with lots of psychological intrusion, but those teens weren't rebelling. They were obedient. And depressed.

"Ironically, the type of parents who are actually most consistent in   50
enforcing rules are the same parents who are most warm and have the most conversations with their kids," Darling observes. They've set a few

rules over certain key spheres of influence, and they've explained why the rules are there. They expect the child to obey them. Over life's other spheres, they supported the child's autonomy, allowing them freedom to make their own decisions.

The kids of these parents lied the least. Rather than hiding twelve areas from their parents, they might be hiding as few as five.

In the thesaurus, the antonym of *honesty* is *lying,* and the opposite of *arguing* is *agreeing.* But in the minds of teenagers, that's not how it works. Really, to an adolescent, arguing is the opposite of lying.

When Nancy Darling's researchers interviewed the teenagers from Pennsylvania, they also asked the teens when and why they told the truth to their parents about things they knew their parents disapproved of. Occasionally they told the truth because they knew a lie wouldn't fly — they'd be caught. Sometimes they told the truth because they just felt obligated, saying, "They're my parents, I'm supposed to tell them." But one important motivation that emerged was that many teens told their parents the truth when they were planning on doing something that was against the rules — in hopes their parents might give in and say it was okay. Usually, this meant an argument ensued, but it was worth it if a parent might budge.

The average Pennsylvania teen was 244 percent more likely to lie than to protest a rule. In the families where there was less deception, however, there was a much higher ratio of arguing and complaining. The argument enabled the child to speak honestly. Certain types of fighting, despite the acrimony, were ultimately signs of respect — not of disrespect.

But most parents don't make this distinction in how they perceive arguments with their children. Dr. Tabitha Holmes of SUNY–New Paltz conducted extensive interviews asking mothers and adolescents, separately, to describe their arguments and how they felt about them. And there was a big difference. 55

Forty-six percent of the mothers rated their arguments as being destructive to their relationships with their teens. Being challenged was stressful, chaotic, and (in their perception) disrespectful. The more frequently they fought, and the more intense the fights were, the more the mother rated the fighting as harmful. But only 23 percent of the adolescents felt that their arguments were destructive. Far more believed that fighting *strengthened* their relationship with their mothers. "Their perception of the fighting was really sophisticated, far more than we anticipated for teenagers," notes Holmes. "They saw fighting as a way to see their parents in a new way, as a result of hearing their mother's point of view be articulated."

What most surprised Holmes was learning that for the teens, fighting often, or having big fights, did not cause them to rate the fighting as harmful and destructive. Statistically, it made no difference at all. Certainly, there is a point in families where there is too much conflict, Holmes notes. "But we didn't have anybody in our study with an extreme amount of conflict." Instead, the variable that seemed to really matter was how the arguments were resolved.

It will be many years before my own children become teenagers, but having lying on my radar screen has changed the way things work around the Bronson household. No matter how small, lies no longer go unnoticed. The moments slow down, and I have a better sense of how to handle them.

Just the other day, my 6-year-old son, Luke, came home from school having learned a new phrase and a new attitude—quipping "I don't care" snidely, and shrugging his shoulders to everything. He repeated "I don't care" so many times I finally got frustrated and demanded to know if someone at school had taught him this dismissive phrase.

He froze. And I could suddenly intuit the debate running through his head—should he lie to his dad, or rat out his friend? Recognizing the conflict, I told him that if he learned the phrase at school, he did not have to tell me who taught him the phrase. Telling me the truth was not going to get his friends in trouble.

"Okay," he said, relieved. "I learned it at school." Then he told me he did care, and he gave me a hug. I haven't heard it again.

Does how we deal with a child's lies really matter down the road in life? The irony of lying is that it's both normal and abnormal behavior at the same time. It's to be expected, and yet it can't be disregarded.

Dr. Bella DePaulo of the University of California, Santa Barbara, has devoted much of her career to adult lying. In one study, she had both college students and community members enter a private room equipped with an audiotape recorder. Promising them complete confidentiality, DePaulo's team instructed the subjects to recall the worst lie they ever told—with all the scintillating details.

"I was fully expecting serious lies," DePaulo remarks. "Stories of affairs kept from spouses, stories of squandering money, or being a salesperson and screwing money out of car buyers." And she did hear those kinds of whoppers, including theft and even one murder. But to her surprise, a lot of the stories told were about when the subject was a mere child—and they were not, at first glance, lies of any great consequence. "One told of eating the icing off a cake, then telling her parents the cake came that way. Another told of stealing some coins from a sibling." As these stories first started trickling in, DePaulo scoffed, thinking, "C'mon, that's the worst lie you've ever told?" But the stories of childhood kept coming, and DePaulo had to create a category in her analysis just for them. "I had to reframe my understanding to consider what it must have been like as a child to have told this lie," she recalls. "For young kids, their lie challenged their self-concept that they were a good child, and that they did the right thing."

Many subjects commented on how that momentous lie early in life 65 established a pattern that affected them thereafter. "We had some who

60

said, 'I told this lie, I got caught, and I felt so badly, I vowed to never do it again.' Others said, 'Wow, I never realized I'd be so good at deceiving my father, I can do this all the time.' The lies they tell early on are meaningful. The way parents react can really affect lying."

Talwar says parents often entrap their kids, putting them in positions to lie and testing their honesty unnecessarily. Last week, I put my 3½-year-old daughter in that exact situation. I noticed she had scribbled on the dining table with a washable marker. Disapprovingly, I asked, "Did you draw on the table, Thia?" In the past, she would have just answered honestly, but my tone gave away that she'd done something wrong. Immediately, I wished I could retract the question. I should have just reminded her not to write on the table, slipped newspaper under her coloring book, and washed the ink away. Instead, I had done just as Talwar had warned against.

"No, I didn't," my daughter said, lying to me for the first time.

For that stain, I had only myself to blame.

THINKING CRITICALLY ABOUT THE READING

1. The article begins with a discussion of a study done at Penn State University with college-age students under the age of twenty-one who then recruited high school students to get involved in a study about honesty and lying. Why do you think the professors themselves did not perform the study directly with the high-schoolers? Do you believe proximity in age ensured more honesty among the participants? Why or why not?

2. Bronson quotes Dr. Victoria Talwar as saying, "Lying is related to intelligence" (8). How is this so? Were you surprised by these findings? Why or why not?

3. How does lying give a child a sense of control or power? In what circumstances would this sense of power be useful to a child? Does this mean that children learn to see honesty as a losing strategy? Why or why not?

4. Beginning with paragraph 17, Bronson tells the story of Steve and his six-year-old son Nick. Steve doesn't believe his son lies, but Nick tells quite the whopper: that a soccer ball being kicked makes the sound of a Beethoven musical composition. Nick does this to get a prize. To an adult, of course, Nick's lie is absurd, but in what ways might adults lie in order to get something they value? Make a list of lies you've seen or heard of adults telling in order to get ahead (perhaps some you've told yourself). What does this say about the difference between adult lying and the lies children tell?

5. Talwar notes that parents unwittingly teach children to lie. Parents serve as role models, and children see their own parents lie, perhaps to avoid annoyances like a telemarketer or to "smooth social relationships" (35). What are the consequences of this learning? Is there any realistic way around this problem? Should there be?

LANGUAGE IN ACTION

Think back to your own childhood and adolescence. Is there a particular lie that you remember telling—for instance, in elementary school or middle school—that still stands out in your mind? Why do you think the experience of telling that particular lie has stuck in your memory? After reflecting, compare your memory with a few of your classmates' memories. Can you identify any common features between your own early experience with lying and your classmates' early experiences?

WRITING SUGGESTIONS

1. According to Bronson, children of "permissive" parents are actually *more* likely to engage in widespread lying than children of parents who establish robust rules and boundaries (47). Does this claim surprise you? Is it consistent with your own experience? Write a brief narrative essay in which you reflect on how your parents' approach affected the way that you did or did not engage in lying or other acts of rebellion during adolescence.

2. Bronson ends his essay with a discussion of parents and the choices they face about rules and restrictions. When is a parent too strict or too permissive? Do further research on the relationship between parent-imposed rules and the behavioral responses of children. Consider how rules and restrictions lead (or don't lead) to lying, obedience, rebellion, aggression, passivity, depression, or self-confidence. Then write an essay in which you present your findings.

Is Lying Bad for Us?

RICHARD GUNDERMAN

Richard Gunderman, born in 1961, teaches many courses at Indiana University, from radiology to philosophy to medical humanities. He earned his AB from Wabash College, his MD and PhD with honors from the University of Chicago, and his MPH from Indiana University. He has written over 700 articles and twelve books, including *Leadership in Healthcare* (2009), *Achieving Excellence in Medical Education* (second ed., 2011), *Essential Radiology* (third ed., 2014), and *We Come to Life with Those We Serve* (2017). On the importance of writing, Gunderman says, "Writing is thinking, and thinking is living. By learning to write better we can think better, and by learning to think better we can live better. And what could be more important than leading the best lives of which we are capable?"

He is also a contributing writer for *The Atlantic*. In the following article, published in *The Atlantic* on February 13, 2013, Gunderman examines the problem of lying. Not only does the average American lie, Americans lie on average more than once a day. Gunderman examines the causes and the consequences of this tendency in terms of both social interaction and physical health. Ultimately, he argues that when we lie, not only are we deceiving others, but we are also deceiving ourselves.

WRITING TO DISCOVER: *How often do you lie? What sorts of lies do you tell: little white lies you hope harm no one? Bigger lies that you hope will get some advantage? Big lies that, if exposed, might ruin personal relationships or cost you your job?*

It has been estimated that the average American tells 11 lies per week. Is this bad for us? Suppose we knew that a lie would never be detected, nor would we be punished. Suppose we had some means of ensuring that the lie would never cause us any physical or psychological harm through loss of sleep or the like. Suppose even that telling the lie would actually redound to our benefit, at least in the sense that it would secure us the pleasure, status, wealth, or power that those fudging the truth commonly seek. Under these circumstances, would it still make sense to tell the truth? Or would lying becoming the prudent course of action?

In his 2005 runaway philosophy best-seller, *On Bullshit*, Princeton University's Harry Frankfurt distinguishes between lying and what he called "bullshit." Though liars do not tell the truth, they care about it, while the bullshitter does not even care about the truth and seeks merely to impress. Liars tell deliberate untruths, while bullshitters merely do not admit when they do not know something. This is a particularly pervasive form of untruth in my own orbits, medicine and academia, where people wish others to believe that we know more than we do. So instead of saying, "I don't know," we make things up, merely giving the appearance of knowledge while actually saying nothing.

We live in a culture where it is increasingly common to encourage lying, and even to suppose that there is nothing problematic about doing so. In his new book, *Heads in Beds,* former hospitality industry employee Jacob Tomsky encourages hotel guests to bend the truth to their own advantage. For example, he states that guests need never pay for in-room movies. Here is how: "Watch and enjoy any movie. Call down and say you accidentally clicked on it. Or it froze near the end. Or it never even started. If the desk attendant offers to restart the movie, say you are about to go to bed or leave, and ask them instead just to remove the charges." Voila!

This bit of advice has been presented under the rubric, "Things every guest must know." It is only one of many points at which Tomsky shows guests how, by saying things that are not true, it is possible to avoid all manner of hotel charges. Ever pay for using items in a minibar? "These are the most often disputed charges on any hotel bill." After enjoying your snack or beverage, just say, "I never used these items." Worried about a same-day cancellation penalty? Call the property and tell the front desk you've had a personal emergency and won't arrive till next week. They will change the reservation. Then call back later and cancel next week's reservation at no penalty.

The implicit message? Honesty is for the unsophisticated.   5

One recent study laid the groundwork of a case for honesty by suggesting that liars are less healthy. Researchers at the University of Notre Dame followed 110 people over a period of ten weeks. Half of the participants were asked to stop lying over this period of time, and the other half were not. Both groups took weekly polygraph tests to determine how many times they had lied in the previous week. Those who were able to reduce by three the number of lies they told had four fewer mental health complaints (such as feeling tense) and three fewer physical health complaints (such as headaches) than those who did not.

Why might this be? A number of explanations might be invoked. One would be that it takes more work to lie, because liars need to think through everything they say to a much greater degree in order to avoid detection. Another might be that it is more stressful to lie. This is likely to be particularly true when lies are exposed, resulting in shame, embarrassment, and other unpleasantries. But even if the lying is never detected, the piling up of lies tends to make relationships with colleagues, friends, and family members shallower and less meaningful. And it could be that living with the guilt of lying is toxic in itself, especially in extreme cases where we are "living a lie." Could we lower our blood pressure, narrow our waistline, reduce our dependence on antidepressants, and perhaps even prolong our lives merely by exaggerating less about our accomplishments and making up fewer excuses when we are late or fail to complete tasks? Suppose the answer to this question is yes. Suppose that those who reduce their weekly lies by one-half lose on average ten pounds, report feeling more confident and content, and end up living on average an additional three years, compared to those who continue lying at the same rate. Would this reduce the level of mendacity in America?

I suspect the answer is a resounding yes. Many of us would tell fewer lies if we thought doing so would make us healthier. Of course, it would not be good news for some sectors of the health care industry, which have a vested interest in collecting revenue from efforts to improve health. What if the sales of antidepressants, the number psychologist and psychiatrist office visits, and the number of heart surgeries all declined? On the other hand, perhaps pharmaceuticals could be developed that would reduce the impulse to tell falsehoods, and mental health professionals and hospitals could offer tuition-generating courses on how to stop lying.

Whether the health care industry can monetize honesty or not, however, a more fundamental problem remains. Do we want to live in families, communities, or societies where truth telling needs to be incentivized? Do we want our spouses and children, our friends and neighbors, and our colleagues and associates to be asking themselves on a regular basis, "Really, why shouldn't I lie?" Surely most of us wish to live in a community where people can be relied on to tell the truth, regardless its effects on waistlines, pocketbooks, social standing, career prospects, and even our general level of happiness. Isn't there something inherently wrong with lying?

Perhaps the most powerful moral argument for honesty has to do with   10 what the French philosopher Jean-Paul Sartre called "bad faith." Liars deceive others, but in a sense, liars also deceive themselves. When we lie we tend to distort our own view of reality, and the more often we lie, the more habitual this distortion becomes. Over time, the habit of lying divorces us further and further from reality, so we see less and less clearly the choices before us and what is at stake in them. Eventually, we may find ourselves unable to see what we are really doing and how it is affecting others and ourselves. We end up leading inauthentic and irresponsible lives.

Do we want to live in families, communities, or societies where truth telling needs to be incentivized?

To tell the truth is to live authentically and responsibly, to really live. At times we may make honest mistakes, misperceiving what is really happening, failing to see things in appropriate context, or even operating unknowingly on deliberate untruths. Whenever possible, however, we should be honest with others and ourselves. When we are honest, we ground ourselves most completely in the world we actually inhabit, being as real as we can with others, and reducing as much as possible the distance between the way things seem to be and the way they really are. In the final analysis, honesty means avoiding illusion and unreality, instead keeping life as real as we possibly can.

THINKING CRITICALLY ABOUT THE READING

1. In paragraph 3, Gunderman says, "We live in a culture where it is increasingly common to encourage lying." Do you agree with this statement? Why or why not?

2. Gunderman concludes, based on the advice given by Jacob Tomksy on how to cheat a hotel out of money, that the lesson is "Honesty is for the unsophisticated" (5). How does this go against basic moral values held in our society? Or, has this society changed to the point where only suckers—"the unsophisticated"—are honest?

3. What is Gunderman's argument about the relationship between honesty and physical health? Did you find his argument convincing? Why or why not? What would make it more persuasive?

4. In paragraph 7, Gunderman states that "the piling up of lies tends to make relationships with colleagues, friends, and family members shallower and less meaningful." Why is this so? If this is true, why then do people continue to lie? Is our ability to manage people's impressions of us more important than the depth of our relationships with them?

5. There is a certain cynicism in Gunderman's comment about the ability of the healthcare industry to "monetize honesty" (9), but his observation gets at the larger question of why people need an extra incentive (e.g., financial, medical) to be honest. Why, beyond securing more money and good health, should we tell the truth? Why do we feel as though telling the truth is an act worthy of special reward? What does that say about our expectations of ourselves and others?

6. In paragraph 11, Gunderman concludes by saying that telling the truth is "to live authentically and responsibly, to really live." What does that last phrase mean, "to really live"? Can a frequent liar not claim that he or she "really lives"? How does Gunderman's conclusion relate to his question in the headnote preceding his essay: "And what could be more important than leading the best lives of which we are capable?"

LANGUAGE IN ACTION

Can you think of a time when you or someone you know told a lie that led to a positive outcome? On the other hand, can you recall a time when you or someone you know told the truth, instead of telling a white lie, and this decision led to a *negative* outcome? Get together with a small group of one or two classmates and compare your answers. Has everyone in your group experienced situations where lying was actually beneficial and truth-telling was harmful? Does thinking about these scenarios change your view about lying or about Gunderman's opinion on the topic?

WRITING SUGGESTIONS

1. In paragraph 9, Gunderman asks, "Isn't there something inherently wrong with lying?" Write an essay in which you shape an argument in response to this question. You may support your argument using examples from Gunderman's essay or from any of the other essays in this chapter. If you believe that lying is inherently "wrong," be sure to specify what exactly you think is wrong with it, and why. If you do *not* believe that lying is inherently wrong, explain why. Be sure to address counterarguments that could disprove your claims.

2. Gunderman explores the idea of "incentives" for truth-telling: "Do we want to live in families, communities, or societies where truth telling needs to be incentivized?" (9). Write an essay in which you explore and analyze Gunderman's concept of "incentives." In your experience, what kinds of incentives exist for telling the truth? What incentives exist for lying? Which incentives do you find more compelling, and why?

Psychology of Fraud:
Why Good People Do Bad Things

CHANA JOFFE-WALT AND ALIX SPIEGEL

Chana Joffe-Walt is a reporter for *This American Life* on National Public Radio (NPR), and she previously worked as a reporter for Seattle-based radio station KPLU. While working on Planet Money, NPR's podcast about economic issues, she developed a style of reporting that she calls the "idea story"—stories about a big theme rather than about individual people. She brings her experience in this style to the following selection, which uses the personal story of Toby Groves to explore the larger question of why people commit fraud.

Alix Spiegel grew up in Baltimore, Maryland, and graduated from Oberlin College in Ohio. Spiegel currently works at NPR's Science Desk, with a focus on psychology and human behavior. Previously, she was one of the founding producers of the NPR podcast *This American Life*. Spiegel's many accolades include a George Foster Peabody Award, a Livingston Award, an Alfred I. duPont–Columbia University Award, a Scripps Howard National Journalism Award, and a Robert F. Kennedy Journalism Award.

The following article was initially broadcast as a segment on NPR's *All Things Considered* and then posted as a web story on May 1, 2012. The authors examine the psychology of fraud, questioning the assumption that those who commit fraud are always conscious of wrongdoing. The work focuses primarily on the story of Toby Groves, who—despite a promise to his father—committed fraud some twenty years after his older brother had done the exact same thing. His story serves as a challenge to the belief that those committing fraud are simply thieves.

WRITING TO DISCOVER: *What is your relationship with fraud? Have you had direct experience with being defrauded by someone, or is your experience confined to reading or hearing about it on the news? In your opinion, what is at the root of most fraud? Greed? Incompetence? Desperation?*

Source: Illustrations by Adam Cole/NPR

Enron, Worldcom, Bernie Madoff, the subprime mortgage crisis.

Over the past decade or so, news stories about unethical behavior have been a regular feature on TV, a long, discouraging parade of misdeeds marching across our screens. And in the face of these scandals, psychologists and economists have been slowly reworking how they think about the cause of unethical behavior.

In general, when we think about bad behavior, we think about it being tied to character: Bad people do bad things. But that model, researchers say, is profoundly inadequate.

Which brings us to the story of Toby Groves.

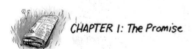

CHAPTER 1: The Promise

Toby grew up on a farm in Ohio. As a kid, the idea that he was a   5
person of strong moral character was very important to him. Then one
Sunday in 1986, when Toby was around 20, he went home for a visit
with his family, and he had an experience that made the need to be good
dramatically more pressing.

Twenty-two years after Toby made that promise to his father, he found himself standing in front of the *exact same judge* who had sentenced his brother, being sentenced for the *exact same crime*: fraud.

And not just any fraud—a massive bank fraud involving millions of dollars that drove several companies out of business and resulted in the loss of about a hundred jobs.

In 2008, Toby went to prison, where he says he spent two years staring at a ceiling, trying to understand what had happened.

Was he a bad character? Was it genetic? "Those were things that haunted me every second of every day," Toby says. "I just couldn't grasp it."

This very basic question—what causes unethical behavior?—has been getting a fair amount of attention from researchers recently, particularly those interested in how our brains process information when we make decisions.   10

And what these researchers have concluded is that most of us are capable of behaving in profoundly unethical ways. And not only are we capable of it—without realizing it, we do it all the time.

CHAPTER 2: The First Lie

Consider the case of Toby Groves.

In the early 1990s, a couple of years after graduating from college, Toby decided to start his own mortgage loan company—and that promise to his father was on his mind.

So Toby decided to lie.

He told the bank that he was making $350,000, when in reality he was making nowhere near that.   15

This is the first lie Toby told—the unethical act that opened the door to all the other unethical acts. So, what was going on in his head at the time?

"There wasn't much of a thought process," he says. "I felt like, at that point, that was a small price to pay and almost like a cost of doing business. You know, things are going to happen, and I just needed to do whatever I needed to do to fix that. It wasn't like . . . I didn't think that I was going to be losing money forever or anything like that."

Consider that for a moment.

Here is a man who stood with his heartbroken father and pledged to behave ethically. Anyone involved in the mortgage business knows that it is both unethical and illegal to lie on a mortgage application.

 ## CHAPTER 3: Why We Don't See The Ethical Big Picture

How could that promise be so easily broken?   20

To understand, says Ann Tenbrunsel, a researcher at Notre Dame who studies unethical behavior, you have to consider what this looks like from Toby's perspective.

There is, she says, a common misperception that at moments like this, when people face an ethical decision, they clearly understand the choice that they are making.

"We assume that they can see the ethics and are consciously choosing not to behave ethically," Tenbrunsel says.

This, generally speaking, is the basis of our disapproval: They knew. They *chose* to do wrong.

But Tenbrunsel says that we are frequently blind to the ethics of a   25 situation.

Over the past couple of decades, psychologists have documented many different ways that our minds fail to see what is directly in front of us. They've come up with a concept called "bounded ethicality": That's the notion that cognitively, our ability to behave ethically is seriously limited, because we don't always see the ethical big picture.

One small example: the way a decision is framed. "The way that a decision is presented to me," says Tenbrunsel, "very much changes the way in which I view that decision, and then eventually, the decision it is that I reach."

Essentially, Tenbrunsel argues, certain cognitive frames make us blind to the fact that we are confronting an ethical problem at all.

Tenbrunsel told us about a recent experiment that illustrates the problem. She got together two groups of people and told one to think about a business decision. The other group was instructed to think about an ethical decision. Those asked to consider a business decision generated one mental checklist; those asked to think of an ethical decision generated a different mental checklist.

Tenbrunsel next had her subjects do an unrelated task to distract   30
them. Then she presented them with an opportunity to cheat.

Those cognitively primed to think about business behaved radically different from those who were not—no matter who they were, or what their moral upbringing had been.

"If you're thinking about a business decision, you are significantly more likely to lie than if you were thinking from an ethical frame," Tenbrunsel says.

According to Tenbrunsel, the business frame cognitively activates one set of goals—to be competent, to be successful; the ethics frame triggers other goals. And once you're in, say, a business frame, you become really focused on meeting those goals, and other goals can completely fade from view.

Tenbrunsel listened to Toby's story, and she argues that one way to understand Toby's initial choice to lie on his loan application is to consider the cognitive frame he was using.

"His sole focus was on making the best business decision," she says,   35
which made him blind to the ethics.

Obviously we'll never know what was actually going through Toby's mind, and the point of raising this possibility is not to excuse Toby's bad behavior, but simply to demonstrate in a small way the very uncomfortable argument that these researchers are making:

That people can be genuinely unaware that they're making a profoundly unethical decision.

It's not that they're evil—it's that they *don't see.*

And if we want to attack fraud, we have to understand that *a lot of fraud is unintentional.*

CHAPTER 4: Fraud Spreads

Tenbrunsel's argument that we are often blind to the ethical dimen- 40
sions of a situation might explain part of Toby's story, his first unethical
act. But a bigger puzzle remains: How did Toby's fraud spread? How did
a lie on a mortgage application balloon into a $7 million fraud?

According to Toby, in the weeks after his initial lie, he discovered
more losses at his company—huge losses. Toby had already mortgaged
his house. He didn't have any more money, but he needed to save his
business.

The easiest way for him to cover the mounting losses, he reasoned,
was to get more loans. So Toby decided to do something that is much
harder to understand than lying on a mortgage application: He took out
a series of entirely false loans—loans on houses that didn't exist.

Creating false loans is not an easy process. You have to manufacture
from thin air borrowers and homes and the paperwork to go with them.

Toby was CEO of his company, but this was outside of his skill set.
He needed help—people on his staff who knew how loan documents
should look and how to fake them.

And so, one by one, Toby says, he pulled employees into a room.   45

"Maybe that was the most shocking thing," Toby says. "Everyone
said, 'OK, we're in trouble, we need to solve this. I'll help you. You know,
I'll try to have that for you tomorrow.'"

According to Toby, no one said no.

Most of the people who helped Toby would not talk to us because
they didn't want to expose themselves to legal repercussions.

Of the four people at his company Toby told us about, we were
able to speak about the fraud with only one—a woman on staff named
Monique McDowell. She was involved in fabricating documents, and her
description of what happened and how it happened completely conforms
to Toby's description.

If you accept what they're saying as true, then that raises a troubling 50 scenario, because we expect people to protest when they're asked to do wrong. But Toby's employees didn't. What's even more troubling is that according to Toby, it wasn't just his employees: "I mean, we had to have assistance from other companies to pull this off," he says.

To make it look like a real person closed on a real house, Toby needed a title company to sign off on the fake documents his staff had generated. And so after he got his staff onboard, Toby says he made some calls and basically made the same pitch he'd given his employees.

Human beings commit fraud because human beings *like* each other.

"It was, 'Here is what happened. Here is the only way I know to fix it, and if you help me, great. If you won't, I understand.' Nobody said, 'Maybe we'll think about this. . . .' Within a few minutes [it was], 'Yes, I'll help you.' "

So here we have people outside his company, agreeing to do things completely illegal and wrong.

Again, we contacted several of the title companies. No one would speak to us, but it's clear from the legal cases that title companies were involved. One title company president ended up in jail because of his dealings with Toby; another agreed to a legal resolution.

So how could it be that easy? 55

CHAPTER 5: We Lie Because We Care

Typically when we hear about large frauds, we assume the perpetrators were driven by financial incentives. But psychologists and economists say financial incentives don't fully explain it. They're interested in another possible explanation: Human beings commit fraud because human beings *like* each other.

We like to help each other, especially people we identify with. And when we are helping people, we really don't see what we are doing as unethical.

Lamar Pierce, an associate professor at Washington University in St. Louis, points to the case of emissions testers. Emissions testers are supposed to test whether or not your car is too polluting to stay on the road. If it is, they're supposed to fail you. But in many cases, emissions testers lie.

"Somewhere between 20 percent and 50 percent of cars that should fail are passed—are *illicitly* passed," Pierce says.

Financial incentives can explain some of that cheating. But Pierce and 60 psychologist Francesca Gino of Harvard Business School say that doesn't fully capture it.

They collected hundreds of thousands of records and were actually able to track the patterns of individual inspectors, carefully monitoring those they approved and those they denied. And here is what they found:

If you pull up in a fancy car—say, a BMW or Ferrari—and your car is polluting the air, you are likely to fail. But pull up in a Honda Civic, and you have a much better chance of passing.

Why?

"We know from a lot of research that when we feel empathy towards others, we want to help them out," says Gino.

Emissions testers—who make a modest salary—see a Civic and iden-   65
tify, they feel empathetic.

Essentially, Gino and Pierce are arguing that these testers commit fraud not because they are greedy, but because they are *nice*.

"And most people don't see the harm in this," says Pierce. "That is the problem."

Pierce argues that cognitively, emissions testers can't appreciate the consequences of their fraud, the costs of the decision that they are making in the moment. The cost is abstract: the global environment. They are literally being asked to weigh the costs to the global environment against the benefits of passing someone who is right there who needs help. We are not cognitively designed to do that.

"I've never talked to a mortgage broker who thought, 'When I help someone get into a loan by falsifying their income, I deeply consider whether or not I would destabilize the world economy,'" says Pierce. "You are helping someone who is real."

Gino and Pierce argue that Toby's staff was faced with the same kind   70
of decision: future abstract consequences, or help out the very real person in front of them.

And so without focusing on the ethics of what they were doing, they helped out a person who was not focusing on the ethics, either. And together they perpetrated a $7 million fraud.

CHAPTER 6: Searching for Resolution

As for Toby, he says that maintaining the giant lie he'd created was exhausting day in and day out.

So in 2006, when two FBI agents showed up at his office, he quickly confessed everything. He says he was relieved.

Two years later, he was standing in front of the same judge who had sentenced his brother. A short time after that, he was in jail, grateful that his father wasn't alive to see him, wondering how he ended up where he did.

"The last thing in the world that I wanted to do in my life would be to break that promise to my father," he says. "It haunts me."   75

Now if these psychologists and economists are right, if we are all capable of behaving profoundly unethically without realizing it, then our workplaces and regulations are poorly organized. They're not designed to take into account the cognitively flawed human beings that we are. They don't attempt to structure things around our weaknesses.

Some concrete proposals to do that are on the table. For example, we know that auditors develop relationships with clients after years of working together, and we know that those relationships can corrupt their audits without them even realizing it. So there is a proposal to force businesses to switch auditors every couple of years to address that problem.

Another suggestion: A sentence should be placed at the beginning of every business contract that explicitly says that lying on this contract is unethical and illegal, because that kind of statement would get people into the proper cognitive frame.

And there are other proposals, of course.

Or, we could just keep saying what we've always said — that right is right, and wrong is wrong, and people should know the difference.   80

THINKING CRITICALLY ABOUT THE READING

1. The article begins with a list of frauds that have all made the front page of national newspapers and the lead in television news programs: "Enron, Worldcom, Bernie Madoff, the subprime mortgage crisis." Why list famous frauds to start the article? Do the authors expect their readers (and listeners) to have been personally affected or morally outraged by at least one of these frauds? If not, what is the advantage of leading with this list?

2. In recounting the story of Toby Groves, the authors begin by letting the reader (or listener) know the conclusion: that Groves committed fraud just like this older brother. What is the advantage of giving away the ending at the beginning? How does this better set up the reader to understand the details about Toby's fraud?

3. In the case of Toby Groves, one fraud (overstating his income on a loan application) led to additional frauds. Why do you suppose Groves didn't stop? What drove his decision to keep going — and his decision to confess when confronted by the FBI?

4. One surprising element to the story is how much help Groves received in continuing to commit fraud, not just from his own employees but from people in other companies and other parts of the mortgage business. Why would they agree to go along with his scheme even as they were putting themselves

in legal jeopardy? What was it about Groves that made them want to help him? To what extent did Groves tell them the truth?

5. Professor Lamar Pierce of Washington University contributes the example of the emissions testers who pass sub-performing vehicles. According to Pierce, why does this ethical lapse occur? Have you ever witnessed—or perhaps benefited from—such an occurrence yourself? Pierce makes the point that people tend to base ethical decisions on what they see in front of them (e.g., a modestly paid worker with a polluting car) rather than larger abstractions (e.g., the global environment). Where might similarly skewed ethical decisions happen in other industries with even larger implications?

LANGUAGE IN ACTION

This article, which was originally posted on National Public Radio's website, uses both text and images to tell Toby Groves's story. Do you find that the images enhance the story? Do you think the story—and the authors' argument about concepts of right and wrong in our society—would be less effective if this was a purely text article, without images? In other words, does the visual "language" of the images convey any information that the text does not? Discuss in a small group with one or two classmates.

WRITING SUGGESTIONS

1. According to Joffe-Walt and Spiegel, we tend to believe that "Bad people do bad things. But that model [...] is profoundly inadequate" (3). As the authors suggest, Toby Groves's story indicates that our concepts of "good" and "bad" might need revision. What do *you* think? Write an essay in which you criticize or defend Joffe-Walt's and Spiegel's statement about the complexity of human criminal behavior. Do you agree that our ideas about good and bad, right and wrong, need to be changed—or do you take the view, given at the end of the essay, that "right is right, and wrong is wrong, and people should know the difference" (80)? You may support your position with examples from the story of Toby Groves or from other stories of wrongdoing—for example, in the news or in your personal experience.

2. Research an instance of large-scale fraud—corporate, political, personal, artistic, or whatever interests you. Write an essay in which you examine how the fraud began, what the motivation was for the fraud, how it grew, how it was discovered, and what the results were. What kinds of lies served as the foundation for the fraud?

Everybody Lies

SETH STEPHENS-DAVIDOWITZ

New Jersey native Seth Stephens-Davidowitz earned his BA in Philosophy, Phi Beta Kappa, at Stanford University and his PhD in Economics from Harvard University in 2013. He has also been a visiting lecturer at the Wharton School of the University of Pennsylvania and is currently a contributing op-ed writer for *The New York Times*. He is also a former quantitative analyst at Google, a job that inspired his interest in using internet searches to measure controversial topics such as racism, child abuse, and self-induced abortion, on which he has written columns for the *Times*.

In 2017 he published *Everybody Lies*, which became a *New York Times* bestseller and was also named as one of the *Economist*'s Books of the Year. In the book, Stephens-Davidowitz examines data from internet searches, particularly Google searches, in an attempt to gain insights about the human psyche. As he explains in the following excerpt from the introduction to *Everybody Lies*, people are remarkably honest when presented with an online search box, treating the box as a sort of confessional that highlights the degree to which we all lie. In other words, according to Stephens-Davidowitz, our searches reveal what we really think, what we really want, and what we really do in ways that face-to-face interactions cannot.

WRITING TO DISCOVER: *Look through your internet search history for the last week. What might your search history reveal about you to an observer?*

I am an internet data expert. Every day, I track the digital trails that people leave as they make their way across the web. From the buttons or keys we click or tap, I try to understand what we really want, what we will really do, and who we really are. Let me explain how I got started on this unusual path.

The story begins—and this seems like ages ago—with the 2008 presidential election and a long-debated question in social science: How significant is racial prejudice in America?

Barack Obama was running as the first African-American presidential nominee of a major party. He won—rather easily. And the polls suggested that race was not a factor in how Americans voted. Gallup, for example, conducted numerous polls before and after Obama's first election. Their conclusion? American voters largely did not care that Barack Obama was black. Shortly after the election, two well-known professors at the University of California, Berkeley pored through other survey-based data, using more sophisticated data-mining techniques. They reached a similar conclusion.

And so, during Obama's presidency, this became the conventional wisdom in many parts of the media and in large swaths of the academy. The sources that the media and social scientists have used for eighty-plus years to understand the world told us that the overwhelming majority of Americans did not care that Obama was black when judging whether he should be their president.

This country, long soiled by slavery and Jim Crow laws, seemed   5
finally to have stopped judging people by the color of their skin. This seemed to suggest that racism was on its last legs in America. In fact, some pundits even declared that we lived in a post-racial society.

In 2012, I was a graduate student in economics, lost in life, burnt-out in my field, and confident, even cocky, that I had a pretty good understanding of how the world worked, of what people thought and cared about in the twenty-first century. And when it came to this issue of prejudice, I allowed myself to believe, based on everything I had read in psychology and political science, that explicit racism was limited to a small percentage of Americans—the majority of them conservative Republicans, most of them living in the deep South.

Then, I found Google Trends.

Google Trends, a tool that was released with little fanfare in 2009, tells users how frequently any word or phrase has been searched in different locations at different times. It was advertised as a fun tool—perhaps enabling friends to discuss which celebrity was most popular or what fashion was suddenly hot. The earliest versions included a playful admonishment that people "wouldn't want to write your PhD dissertation" with the data, which immediately motivated me to write my dissertation with it.*

At the time, Google search data didn't seem to be a proper source of information for "serious" academic research. Unlike surveys, Google search data wasn't created as a way to help us understand the human psyche. Google was invented so that people could learn about the world, not so researchers could learn about people. But it turns out the trails we   10
leave as we seek knowledge on the internet are tremendously revealing.

In other words, people's search for information is, in itself, information. When and where they search for facts, quotes, jokes, places, persons,

---

* Google Trends has been a source of much of my data. However, since it only allows you to compare the relative frequency of different searches but does not report the absolute number of any particular search, I have usually supplemented it with Google AdWords, which reports exactly how frequently every search is made. In most cases I have also been able to sharpen the picture with the help of my own Trends-based algorithm, which I describe in my dissertation, "Essays Using Google Data," and in my *Journal of Public Economics* paper, "The Cost of Racial Animus on a Black Candidate: Evidence Using Google Search Data." The dissertation, a link to the paper, and a complete explanation of the data and code used in all the original research presented in this book are available on my website, sethsd.com.

things, or help, it turns out, can tell us a lot more about what they really think, really desire, real fear, and really do than anyone might have guessed. This is especially true since people sometimes don't so much query Google as confide in it: "I hate my boss." "I am drunk." "My dad hit me."

The everyday act of typing a word or phrase into a compact, rectangular white box leaves a small trace of truth that, when multiplied by millions, eventually reveals profound realities. The first word I typed in Google Trends was "God." I learned that the states that make the most Google searches mentioning "God" were Alabama, Mississippi, and Arkansas—the Bible Belt. And those searches are most frequently on Sundays. None of which was surprising, but it was intriguing that search data could reveal such a clear pattern. I tried "Knicks," which it turns out is Googled most in New York City. Another no-brainer. Then I typed in my name. "We're sorry," Google Trends informed me. "There is not enough search volume" to show these results. Google Trends, I learned, will provide data only when lots of people make the same search.

But the power of Google searches is not that they can tell us that God is popular down South, the Knicks are popular in New York City, or that I'm not popular anywhere. Any survey could tell you that. The power in Google data is that people tell the giant search engine things they might not tell anyone else.

Take, for example, sex (a subject I will investigate in much greater detail later in this book). Surveys cannot be trusted to tell us the truth about our sex lives. I analyzed data from the General Social Survey, which is considered one of the most influential and authoritative sources for information on Americans' behaviors. According to that survey, when it comes to heterosexual sex, women say they have sex, on average, fifty-five times per year, using a condom 16 percent of the time. This adds up to about 1.1 billion condoms used per year. But heterosexual men say they use 1.6 billion condoms every year. Those numbers, by definition, would have to be the same. So who is telling the truth, men or women?

This is especially true since people sometimes don't so much query Google as confide in it.

Neither, it turns out. According to Nielsen, the global information and measurement company that tracks consumer behavior, fewer than 600 million condoms are sold every year. So everyone is lying; the only difference is by how much.

The lying is in fact widespread. Men who have never been married claim to use on average twenty-nine condoms per year. This would add up to more than the total number of condoms sold in the United States to married and single people combined. Married people probably exaggerate how much sex they have, too. On average, married men under sixty-five tell surveys they have sex once a week. Only 1 percent say they have gone the past year without sex. Married women report having a little less sex but not much less.

Google searches give a far less lively — and, I argue, far more accurate — picture of sex during marriage. On Google, the top complaint about a marriage is not having sex. Searches for "sexless marriage" are three and a half times more common than "unhappy marriage" and eight times more common than "loveless marriage." Even unmarried couples complain somewhat frequently about not having sex. Google searches for "sexless relationship" are second only to searches for "abusive relationship." (This data, I should emphasize, is all presented anonymously. Google, of course, does not report data about any particular individual's searches.)

And Google searches presented a picture of America that was strikingly different from that post-racial utopia sketched out by the surveys. I remember when I first typed "nigger" into Google Trends. Call me naïve. But given how toxic the word is, I fully expected this to be a low-volume search. Boy, was I wrong. In the United States, the word "nigger" — or its plural, "niggers" — was included in roughly the same number of searches as the word "migraine(s)," "economist," and "Lakers." I wondered if searches for rap lyrics were skewing the results? Nope. The word used in rap songs is almost always "nigga(s)." So what was the motivation of Americans searching for "nigger"? Frequently, they were looking for jokes mocking African-Americans. In fact, 20 percent of searches with the word "nigger" also included the word "jokes." Other common searches included "stupid niggers" and "I hate niggers."

There were millions of these searches every year. A large number of Americans were, in the privacy of their own homes, making shockingly racist inquiries. The more I researched, the more disturbing the information got.

On Obama's first election night, when most of the commentary focused on praise of Obama and acknowledgment of the historic nature of his election, roughly one in every hundred Google searches that included the word "Obama" also included "kkk" or "nigger(s)." Maybe that doesn't sound so high, but think of the thousands of nonracist reasons to Google this young outsider with a charming family about to take over the world's most powerful job. On election night, searches and signups for Stormfront, a white nationalist site with surprisingly high popularity in the United States, were more than ten times higher than normal. In some states, there were more searches for "nigger president" than "first black president."

There was a darkness and hatred that was hidden from the traditional 20 sources but was quite apparent in the searches that people made.

Those searches are hard to reconcile with a society in which racism is a small factor. In 2012 I knew of Donald J. Trump mostly as a businessman and reality show performer. I had no more idea than anyone else that he would, four years later, be a serious presidential candidate. But those ugly searches are not hard to reconcile with the success of a candidate who—in his attacks on immigrants, in his angers and resentments—often played to people's worst inclinations.

The Google searches also told us that much of what we thought about the location of racism was wrong. Surveys and conventional wisdom placed modern racism predominantly in the South and mostly among Republicans. But the places with the highest racist search rates included upstate New York, western Pennsylvania, eastern Ohio, industrial Michigan, and rural Illinois along with West Virginia, southern Louisiana, and Mississippi. The true divide, Google search data suggested, was not South versus North; it was East versus West. You don't get this sort of thing much west of the Mississippi. And racism was not limited to Republicans. In fact, racist searches were no higher in places with a high percentage of Republicans than in places with a high percentage of Democrats. Google searches, in other words, helped draw a new map of racism in the United States—and this map looked very different from what you may have guessed. Republicans in the South may be more likely to admit to racism. But plenty of Democrats in the North have similar attitudes.

Four years later, this map would prove quite significant in explaining the political success of Trump.

In 2012, I was using this map of racism I had developed using Google searches to reevaluate exactly the role that Obama's race played. The data was clear. In parts of the country with a high number of racist searches, Obama did substantially worse than John Kerry, the white Democratic presidential candidate, had four years earlier. The relationship was not explained by any other factor about these areas, including education levels, age, church attendance, or gun ownership. Racist searches did not predict poor performance for any other Democratic candidate. Only for Obama.

And the results implied a large effect. Obama lost roughly 4 percentage points nationwide just from explicit racism. This was far higher than might have been expected based on any surveys. Barack Obama, of course, was elected and reelected president, helped by some very favorable conditions for Democrats, but he had to overcome quite a bit more than anyone who was relying on traditional data sources—and that was just about everyone—had realized. There were enough racists to help win a primary or tip a general election in a year not so favorable to Democrats.

My study was initially rejected by five academic journals. Many of the peer reviewers, if you will forgive a little disgruntlement, said that it was impossible to believe that so many Americans harbored such vicious racism. This simply did not fit what people had been saying. Besides, Google searches seemed like such a bizarre dataset.

Now that we have witnessed the inauguration of President Donald J. Trump, my finding seems more plausible.

THINKING CRITICALLY ABOUT THE READING

1. What does the term "post-racial society" (5) mean? What 2008 event convinced some pundits that the United States had become a post-racial society?
2. According to Stephens-Davidowitz, in what way do Americans commonly lie about their sex lives?
3. What did Stephens-Davidowitz find when he ran a Google search for the racial slur "nigger" (17)? How are these search results important to his larger argument?
4. What did Stephens-Davidowitz's Google research reveal about the geographic location of racist searches in the United States?
5. Based on his research, what conclusion does Stephens-Davidowitz draw about the role of racism in the 2008 and 2016 US presidential elections? What correlation did he find between search terms and voting in those elections?
6. At the end of his essay, Stephens-Davidowitz reveals that his work was rejected from five academic journals because Google searches seemed like a "bizarre dataset." Why do you think academics were reluctant to embrace Google search terms as data?

LANGUAGE IN ACTION

In a small group in class, conduct a search of your own in Google Trends. For example, recalling ideas discussed in June Jordan's essay "Nobody Mean More to Me Than You" (pp. 376–379), you might search for "Black English" and see which states and which regions of the United States most frequently search for that term.

Alternatively, you might search for the word *Latinx* (see "What Does Latinx Mean?" by Yesenia Padilla, pp. 245–248)—or for one of the terms used to describe immigrants in Jeff Gammage's article "The Fight Over the Words of Immigration" (pp. 372–374).

Of course, feel free to search for any other term that you are interested in. What insights, if any, does your search yield about the word or phrase? What other trending search terms does Google Trends highlight in relation to your inquiry?

WRITING SUGGESTIONS

1. Think about the conclusions that Stephens-Davidowitz draws about racism in the United States based on his Google research. In particular, consider his findings about the geographic locations of racist searches and his

conclusions about the impact of racism on the US presidential elections of 2008 and 2016. Do his conclusions surprise you? Do you find his arguments convincing? Why or why not? Write a brief essay in which you evaluate his arguments. You may use external sources to support your position.

2. As the title of Stephens-Davidowitz's essay asserts, "everybody lies." Yet, from another perspective, his data suggests ways in which technology provides a space for confessing the truth. Have you ever found that you were more honest when interacting remotely via text message or chat? Or have you ever deliberately avoided conversations in person so that you could have them later via text because you thought it might be easier? Write a brief reflective essay in which you discuss one experience in your life when you found that you were more honest online than in person.

13

THE LANGUAGE OF CONFLICT RESOLUTION: DIGNITY, APOLOGY, DE-ESCALATION

The American poet Carl Sandburg in his poem "Primer Lesson" cautioned:

Look out how you use proud words.

When you let proud words go, it is not easy to call them back.

They wear long boots, hard boots; they walk off proud; they can't hear you calling—

Look out how you use proud words.

His words ring as true for us today as they did for his post-World War I audience one hundred years ago. Sandburg had witnessed firsthand the power of words to both start conflicts and to enflame them.

Language often plays a powerful role in the conflict's inception and impacts the trajectory of all conflicts. The way people talk about the problematic group or individual—whether using name-calling or stereotypes— exacerbates conflicts of all kinds. Many conflicts can be positively addressed by examining how we articulate the problem and solution. Inevitably, changing the conflict will require changing the language we use to talk about it. For example, Germany is now called an "ally" and "friend," not an "enemy." Words change as conflicts shift or end.

But once started, conflicts seem to have a life of their own, and at the heart of every conflict one can usually find an argument, disagreement, or misunderstanding that centers on how the parties are using or interpreting language. Hardly a day goes by that social media and the news networks do not call out some celebrity, politician, diplomat, organization, or country for starting a fight or escalating one with their sloppy or insensitive use of language. Even on a personal level, we can find ourselves enmeshed in arguments because we express ourselves via social media before we think something out, and end up using language indiscriminately.

By analyzing conflicts that have happened in the past or those that are currently unfolding, we can come to better understand how our words affect others and their words us. During the summer of 2015, demonstrations broke out in Ferguson, Missouri, after white police officer Darren

Wilson fatally shot Michael Brown, an unarmed black man, after an altercation. Immediately the finger pointing began and the pent-up anger raged. Dr. Martin Luther King Jr. once observed, "Riots are the language of the unheard." The crowds of protesters taunted the Ferguson Police Department with cries of "racists," "murderers," and "pigs," while the supporters of the police and Officer Wilson retaliated by calling the victim Michael Brown a "thug" and the demonstrators "looters," "rioters," and "a plague of black violence." Such language served one purpose — to drive the two sides further apart in spite of attempts at intervention. Simply changing the words may have an impact, but real change requires deeper shifts. Using politically correct terms may simply disguise deeper beliefs. Looking at language in conflict also requires an examination of who gets to speak and who remains excluded from the conversation. Achieving societal transformation rather than simple change requires deep shifts in how we talk about and listen to one another.

Most people will agree that it seems easier to get into a conflict than it is to get out of one, resolve one, or even find some common ground on which to stand. The acts of apology and forgiving and the concept of dignity — and the language we use to convey an apology, and a forgiving, and to create or nurture dignity — are all important ingredients in any effort to resolve a conflict or achieve a sense of justice restored.

Our purpose in this chapter is to help you think critically about and be sensitive to the language used in ongoing conflicts as well as the language being used to seek resolution so that you can function as a responsible citizen. In the opening selection, "Resolve Current and Future Conflicts with Dignity," Donna Hicks provides readers with a model for resolving conflicts. Her model is constructed on the foundation of human dignity. She strongly believes that "normalizing ways to address conflict is at the core of maintaining a safe culture for everyone to speak up, be recognized, and take responsibility for hurtful behavior." Next, in "Language and Conflict," Karol Janicki examines the role that language and communication play in creating and escalating conflicts as well as ultimately in establishing peace. First and foremost, he believes "language matters," and that people need to become more aware of how language works. Such knowledge, he thinks, can help prevent conflicts and disputes between nations as well as between individuals. In the third selection, "Sorry, Regrets, and More," Edwin L. Battistella analyzes a number of interesting historical examples of public "apologies" to show how important people have used the words *sorry* and *regrets* to avoid giving a sincere apology. By showing readers what is really being said, we can all better understand why the underlying conflict is not really resolved.

In "Further Adventures of Flex Cop," Cincinnati police officer Michael Gardner tells how he and his partner developed strategies to use when called to respond to domestic disputes. After a while they volunteered to take all the domestic violence calls so that they could refine their strategies for de-escalating hostile situations. Gardner and his partner learned how the creative use of language and an ability to be spontaneous and untraditional in critical situations often resulted in magical solutions to dangerous disputes. For Gary Noesner, the former chief of the FBI's Crisis Negotiation Unit, self-control and active listening are the keys to defusing potentially explosive confrontations. In "Stalling for Time," he explains the role of the language of negotiation in domestic violence situations and in the infamous Branch Davidian hostage standoff in Waco, Texas, in 1993. In the final selection, "Letting Go," Amy Westervelt uses the example of herself and her friend Leah to explore the nature and value of forgiveness. In the process she discovers that even though we know how good it is for us to forgive both ourselves and others, forgiveness requires a degree of selflessness as well as practice and hard work. Her advice is to "feel the feelings you need to feel, express them, then leave them in the past where they can no longer have power over you."

Resolve Current and Future Conflicts with Dignity

DONNA HICKS

Donna Hicks is an associate at the Weatherhead Center for International Affairs at Harvard University and has taught courses at Harvard, Clark, and Columbia universities. Hicks earned her BA in educational psychology (1983) and her MS (1987), MSW (1988), and PhD (1991) from the University of Wisconsin before completing a post-doctoral fellowship at Harvard University with Herbert Kelman, director of the Program on International Conflict Analysis, which largely shaped her career in international conflict resolution. Hicks has more than twenty years of experience as a facilitator during international conflicts in the Middle East, Sri Lanka, Colombia, Cuba, Northern Ireland, and the United States. As her personal website explains, "her unique focus on dignity, and the essential role it plays in resolving conflict, has transformed work environments for the world's most prominent companies, non-profits, and governmental agencies," and past clients have included the World Bank, United Nations, and the US Navy.

She is the author of *Dignity: The Essential Role It Plays in Resolving Conflict* (2011), a bestselling book that was also the New England Book Festival's 2011 runner-up for best nonfiction title. Hicks and the subjects she discusses in *Dignity* have been featured on the BBC, *Fox News*, NPR, and radio stations across the country, as well as in *Psychology Today* and *Newsday*. The essay here, taken from her second book *Leading with Dignity: How to Create a Culture That Brings Out the Best in People* (2018), provides readers with some practical advice about resolving conflicts. Hicks believes that conflicts need to be addressed within the healthy framework of dignity.

WRITING TO DISCOVER: *What does the word dignity mean to you? What does it mean to treat others with dignity? How, in your estimation, does dignity differ from related concepts like empathy and respect?*

Conflict is the signal that there is something about the relationship that needs to change.

One of the most useful tools that I have shared with organizations is how to address conflicts between groups. Conflict is a normal occurrence in the workplace—it is hard to avoid. Having a process to help parties through their difficulties opens up opportunities for growth in the relationship. As the opening quotation suggests, conflict is an indication that there is something in the relationship that needs to change. Knowing how to address conflict with a dignity framework is key to maintaining a healthy culture in which people feel safe to speak up when they run into problems with their colleagues.

Knowing how to manage conflicts is a leadership challenge that doesn't come naturally. As with all matters related to dignity, knowing how to address the concerns that so often are at the core of conflicts requires learning.

DEFENDING DIGNITY

Most of us find it difficult to speak up to others—especially those who have power over us—when they have violated our dignity. We come up with excuses not to speak up, such as "It's not worth the energy," "She doesn't mean that much to me," or "The situation might get worse if I do confront him." Remember that one of the ten temptations is to avoid conflict, for fear of getting hurt again. No wonder it feels so hard to confront others when they have violated our dignity—our biology wants us to protect ourselves at all costs.

But healthy relationships do not handle conflicts by avoiding them. We need to be able to discuss the hurtful behavior with those who have violated our dignity. Here are some helpful steps to implement before speaking up:

- *Acknowledge to yourself that speaking up is difficult* but not impossible, and that it may require practice to get used to the idea.
- *Practice role-playing* with a friend or colleague. When you feel ready, the following are the steps to defending your dignity.

HOW TO DEFEND YOUR DIGNITY

Step 1: Acknowledge to Yourself that your Dignity has Taken a Hit

- Recognize that your "Me" has been injured and that it wants to lash back and get even, or to withdraw from the relationship.
- Remember the ninety-second rule, and give the stress hormones that are coursing through your body a chance to clear out. Push the pause button and let your anger run its course.
- Get to the metaphorical balcony—recognize that your "I" needs to take charge so that you don't respond by taking the bait and returning the violation.

Step 2: Switch the Default Reaction from Revenge to Self-Reflection

- Ask yourself: "Is there anything I might have done to contribute to this failed interaction? Is there any possibility that I might have unknowingly violated his or her dignity?" (Note that even if you did do something to the other person, you still may have suffered a dignity violation.)

5

Step 3: Respond to the Violator

- If you think you might have contributed to the conflict, take responsibility: "I realize that I might have offended you when I said _____. I am sorry for that." (Do not say "but" and then proceed to describing your own violation. Saying "but" deletes all the benefit of the apology taken on your part.) Pause and let the person respond.
- Next, address the hurt you experienced: "Maybe you are not aware of it, but what you said in the meeting about me was hurtful (explain the incident). My relationship with you is important to me, and I'm concerned that if I let the hurtful remarks pass without talking to you about how I feel, it might jeopardize our relationship. I want to give you the benefit of the doubt that you weren't aware of the impact of your comments."

My experience is that when you approach a violator in this way, saying that the relationship is important to you, and that you want to give the offender the benefit of the doubt that she was unaware of how hurtful the violation was, she will feel disarmed and at least somewhat open to this feedback. She was almost certainly not expecting to hear that you care about your relationship or that you want to give her the benefit of the doubt—instead she's probably been bracing herself for an unpleasant encounter in which you return the harm. Nor is she prepared for your taking responsibility for possibly violating her dignity. Your deeply humanizing response, which I call a "surprise attack," is just what is needed when dignity violations put us on a fast track to disconnecting not only from the suffering relationship, but also from the offender's human vulnerability.

> **We need to be able to discuss the hurtful behavior with those who have violated our dignity.**

It goes without saying that it is nearly impossible to do this when your "Me" is in charge of your behavior and the stress hormone is still preparing you for a fight or a flight. A few trips up to the balcony help a lot, along with practicing the encounter with a friend or colleague.

ADDRESSING INTERGROUP CONFLICT: DIGNITY DIALOGUES

A manager asked me to help him with an ongoing conflict that he was trying to resolve between two factions in his team. One group worked on the technical (IT) aspects of his department, and the other group handled the interface with customers. The manager told me that he had found it challenging to build a bridge between the two groups because they had such diverse talents and there was little overlap between them. He had heard about the dignity work I was doing in other departments and asked whether I would work with him to try to address the issues that divided the team. He thought that underlying dignity violations were fueling the conflict.

I have developed what I call dignity dialogues to help groups find a   10
way out of their conflicts. My methodology was inspired by the work of my mentor at Harvard, Herbert Kelman.[1] As a social psychologist specializing in the social psychological dimensions of international conflict, he developed the Interactive Problem-Solving Approach that he used to bring Israelis and Palestinians together for dialogue. The approach focuses on the underlying, unmet psychological human needs that contribute to conflict. My adaptation of the method focuses on the unaddressed dignity violations that fuel the inability of parties to end their conflicts.

Dignity dialogues are an educational approach to addressing conflict. When I work with groups who are unable to get along, I quickly discover that they typically know next to nothing about dignity, except that they all agree that it is important to them.

The first step of a dignity dialogue, then, is to learn the basic building blocks of the Dignity Model, which I have described in detail earlier in the book. These building blocks include the definition of dignity, Mandela consciousness, the ten elements of dignity, the three Cs, the ten temptations to violate dignity, and self-knowledge of the "I" and the "Me." What is most powerful about this first step is that groups of participants *learn about dignity together.* I tell them that during the first step of the process, they will all be sharing the identity "students of dignity." I ask them to briefly suspend other aspects of their identity (such as members of the IT team or the customer service team) until they have learned together the basics of the Dignity Model.

This step also includes experiential exercises that involve reenactments of dignity violations, which I have described earlier in the book. I ask for volunteers to describe a time, early in their lives, when their dignity was violated. I ask about their childhood experiences because they are powerful and tend to create a lasting effect on one's sense of worth. These exercises that focus on childhood violations also take participants out of the present, which is filled with current violations that are harder to empathize with when both sides feel like adversaries.

One of the goals of the reenactments is to try to restore the natural capacity for empathy that we typically feel for one another.[2] One of the first things to go with groups in conflict is empathy. The disconnection brings out what my colleague at Harvard Law School, Dan Shapiro, calls the "tribes effect" that creates an "us versus them," adversarial mentality.[3]

Observing others reenact painful injuries to their dignity can ignite   15
our mirror neurons and make us feel the heartbreaking effects of their violations.[4] It can also restore the empathy that was lost in the conflict, turning adversaries back into fellow human beings.

Seeing the suffering of others can trigger something deep in us. Yes, we might feel their pain, but does observing the suffering cause us also to reach further into our shared human experience? Do we experience a moment of recognition of a tragic aspect of what it means to be human—that we have yet to wake up to the reality that we are all so fragile, yet we are treating one another as if we weren't? Most of the time we can live our lives in denial of all the indignities that are happening around us. But when we are face to face with someone's real-life experience of being treated badly, it is hard to look away.

One of the most compelling examples of the power of face-to-face interactions is a video entitled *Look Beyond Borders,* made by Amnesty International.[5] It demonstrates how just four uninterrupted minutes of eye contact between people can create a deep human connection. I urge you to take a look at this powerful demonstration of what we humans are capable of, if we take the time to look at and listen to what is happening inside the lived experience of others.

The combination of the shared learning and the recognition of the shared pain and suffering brought on by hurtful violations to dignity sets the stage for the dialogue to begin. It goes without saying that the facilitator of these dialogues needs to be trained in basic facilitation skills. Here is a typical agenda for a dignity dialogue after the participants learn the building blocks of the model.

Session I: Introducing the Dignity Dialogue

In this session, I explain to the participants that the purpose of the dialogue is to strengthen the relationship between the two groups. I remind them that we will be using a dignity framework to guide our work together, drawing on the learning that we gained as "students of dignity."

Establish the ground rules for discussion. The first ground rule is *con-* 20 *fidentiality.* No attributions of who said what are to be made outside of the sessions, unless everyone agrees that doing so is okay. Second, I tell them to *listen to understand and speak to be understood.* I ask them to ask themselves: *Are you listening or waiting to speak?* I then always ask the participants if there are other ground rules they would like to add.

Defining the shared dignity purpose. After the ground rules are agreed on, we begin our first working session. The goal is to *define the "dignity purpose" of the participants' work together as a team.* The discussion uses the ten elements of dignity to guide their framing of the purpose. We start by defining the general purpose of the team (for example, to provide a technically efficient way for customers to gain access to the company's services). The next step is to articulate how promoting dignity could contribute to a successful outcome of their teamwork.

Session 2: Identifying Dignity Issues, by Group

The goal of this session is to clarify and identify the problems in the relationship between the two groups. One of the most common mistakes people make when trying to resolve conflict is to rush to find a solution to the problem before having a clear sense of what caused the breakdown in the relationship. The felt need to "fix" what is wrong is compelling, but without an accurate assessment of what is creating and fueling the problem, the solution will not lead to an enduring end to the conflict. With a dignity-based approach, the next step is instead to identify and discuss the violations that both sides have experienced.

At the beginning of the session, the members of one of the groups are asked to talk about the dignity violations they have experienced in their interactions at work. Each person has an opportunity to tell his or her story. I ask them not to name names but still to describe in detail the kinds of violations they have experienced. The other group is instructed to sit quietly and listen to the stories, asking questions only for clarification. It is a time not to debate the issues, but to listen and gain a deeper understanding of what the other side has experienced.

When Group 1 feels that they have finished telling their stories, someone from Group 2 is asked to go to the board and write down what the group heard from Group 1—the dignity violations they felt they had experienced in the relationship. While members of Group 2 are writing down what they heard, the members of Group 1 are not allowed to speak or otherwise correct them. When they have finished writing the list of what they heard, Group 1's members are given the opportunity to amend the list.

Next it is Group 2's turn to tell their stories about ways in which they 25 felt their dignity has been violated in the relationship. All the steps (telling their stories, repeating back by the other side, and editing the list) are repeated for Group 2.

Session 3: Responding to Stories

Up to this point, the facilitator has not allowed the groups to discuss or respond to the issues that were raised during the previous session. This session is an opportunity for them to react to what they heard and to gain a deeper understanding of the issues, but *it is not the time to come up with solutions.* The goal of this session is to open the space for *acknowledgment and/or apology* by both parties of the dignity violations they heard the other side describe. It is an opportunity for them to switch their default setting from blaming the other side for a wrongdoing to taking responsibility for the harm they themselves have done.

Session 4: Finding Solutions and New Steps

This session begins with the question "What can our side do to avoid violating the dignity of the other side and to improve the working relationship?" The goal of this session is to find solutions to the issues that were raised. Now that the groups have a deeper understanding of the violations they have both endured, steps that they take to repair the relationship will be framed in terms of protecting and promoting a culture of dignity. For example, if one of the concerns had to do with a failure to include each other in important decisions that affect the whole team and its purpose, they would commit to erring on the side of inclusion in the future. The groups establish new "rules of engagement" that are based on the ten elements of dignity.

Session 5: Reflecting On The Original Dignity Purpose and the Dignity Dialogue Experience

In the final session, both groups are asked to look again at the dignity purpose they developed in the beginning of the workshop to see whether there is anything they'd like to change. Then the groups are asked to reflect on what they learned about themselves and the other group after going through the dignity dialogue. The last question I ask them to answer is "What happened in the workshop that had the greatest effect on you?" Each person answers the question while the others listen. They are also invited to say anything else about what it was like for them in the workshop.

If the organization hasn't already conducted a system-wide dignity education program, these dialogue workshops typically take two days— one for the initial dignity education component and one for the dialogue itself.

I am reminded of a quotation from Winston Churchill: "Criticism ³⁰ may not be agreeable, but it is necessary. It fulfills the same function as pain in the human body. It calls attention to an unhealthy state of things." Establishing a process and a methodology to address conflicts and allow for constructive criticism in the workplace is one of the essential elements of a healthy, dignity-honoring culture.

When an organization commits to institutionalizing a way to address conflicts as they arise, the process is normalized. In contrast, if conflict is avoided and allowed to fester, it creates a toxic work environment where people do not feel safe to speak and they do not feel that their concerns have been recognized and addressed. Without a way to be listened to and heard, people who have been violated often resort to gossiping about the perpetrators, polluting the workplace environment with negativity. Matthew Feinberg, Joey Cheng, and Robb Willer sum it up beautifully,

"Gossip represents a widespread, efficient and low-cost form of punishment."[6] Robert Sapolsky, author of *Behave: The Biology of Humans at Our Best and Worst* says: "Gossip (with the goal of shaming) is a weapon of the weak against the powerful."[7] And as Daniel Kahneman asks, "Why should we be concerned with gossip? Because it is much easier, as well as far more enjoyable, to identify and label the mistakes of others than to recognize our own."[8] If a mechanism is in place whereby people feel their concerns can be acknowledged and addressed, the temptation to talk disparagingly about those who have committed dignity violations could be eliminated.

Normalizing ways to address conflict is at the core of maintaining a safe culture for everyone to speak up, be recognized, and take responsibility for hurtful behavior. Most important, it gives people an opportunity to learn something about themselves that only others can see. Because we all have blind spots, we need the perspective of others in order to continue to develop into more dignity-conscious human beings. Without conflict and a healthy way to address it, we remain in an arrested state of development. If we want to grow and flourish, we should welcome having a mirror held up to us in a way that can expand our ability to preserve our dignity and the dignity of those around us.

NOTES

1. Kelman, Herbert C. "Informal Mediation by the Scholar/Practitioner," pp. 64–96 in J. Bercovitch and J. Z. Rubin, eds., *Mediation in International Relations: Multiple Approaches to Conflict Management.* New York: St. Martin's, 1992.

2. de Waal, Franz. *The Age of Empathy: Nature's Lessons for a Kinder Society.* New York: Harmony Books, 2009.

3. Shapiro, Daniel. *Negotiating the Nonnegotiable: How to Resolve Your Most Emotionally Charged Conflicts.* New York: Viking, 2016.

4. Iacoboni, Marco. *Mirroring People: The New Science of How We Connect with Others.* New York: Farrar, Straus, and Giroux, 2008.

5. Amnesty International, "Look Refugees in the Eye: Powerful Video Experiment Breaks Down Barriers," May 24, 2016, at https://www.amnesty.org/en/latest/news/2016/05/look-refugees-in-the-eye/.

6. Feinberg, Matthew, Joey Cheng, and Robb Willer. "Gossip as an Effective and Low-Cost Form of Punishment." *Behavioral and Brain Sciences* 35, 1 (February 2012).

7. Sapolsky, Robert M. *Behave: The Biology of Humans at Our Best and Worst.* New York: Penguin, 2017.

8. Kahneman, Daniel. *Thinking, Fast and Slow.* New York: Farrar, Straus, and Giroux, 2011.

THINKING CRITICALLY ABOUT THE READING

1. In the first paragraph, Hicks uses the phrase *dignity framework*. What does she mean by this phrase? How does she use this concept throughout the essay?

2. What distinction does Hicks draw between the "Me" and the "I"? What qualities does she ascribe to each, and why?

3. In paragraph 4 and again in paragraph 8, Hicks uses "the balcony" as a metaphor. How does this metaphor serve her larger points about dignity? Why do you think she chooses the term *balcony*?

4. Why does Hicks use language associated with physical ailments—"suffering" (5, 7, 16, 17), "injury" (4, 15), and "pain" (15, 16, 17, 30)—to describe experiences of indignities? What other words does she use to characterize those who injure and those who are injured?

5. What are the five sessions of the dignity model, as Hicks outlines them? Why does she choose the word *session*?

LANGUAGE IN ACTION

In small groups or pairs, roleplay one or more of the following conflict scenarios. What different types of language would you use in each scenario? See if you and your partner(s) can find ways to resolve each scenario while preserving each other's dignity. After roleplaying one or more of these scenarios, share your most successful scenario with the class.

- You believe a professor has made a mistake while grading your exam.
- Your manager blames you for your coworker's error.
- You and your roommate are having a disagreement about who is responsible for cleaning which parts of the apartment.

WRITING SUGGESTIONS

1. Write about a time when you violated another person's dignity or about a time when you felt that your own dignity was violated. How did you handle the incident? In hindsight, and in light of Hicks's work on dignity, would you have handled the situation differently? Write a reflective personal essay addressing these questions. In your reflection, be sure to draw on specific ideas from Hicks's essay about dignity.

2. In paragraph 30, Hicks quotes Winston Churchill, who once said, "Criticism may not be agreeable, but it is necessary. [...] It calls attention to an unhealthy state of things." Choose one of Hicks's "sessions" and examine it with a critical eye. Think of a recent conflict you've had—at home, in class, in the workplace, or anywhere else. Do you think Hicks's sessions would have helped you resolve the conflict? Why or why not? Write an essay in which you explain your answer to this question. In your essay, be sure to include a brief discussion of the benefits and/or shortcomings of one or more of Hicks's sessions.

Language and Conflict

KAROL JANICKI

Karol Janicki has taught in the Department of Foreign Languages at the University of Bergen in Norway since 1994. Before that, he taught in the Department of English at the University of Poznan in Poland, where he also received his PhD. He is the author of ten books about social linguistics, most of which center on the relationship between language and conflict, including *The Foreigner's Language: A Sociolinguistic Perspective* (1982), *Language Misconceived: Arguing for Applied Cognitive Sociolinguistics* (2006), and *Confusing Discourse* (2009). He has been a guest lecturer at The American University, the University of Tromsø, the University of Rostock, and the University of Hamburg.

The following essay is drawn from Janicki's most recent book, aptly titled *Language and Conflict: Selected Issues* (2017). Using real-life examples, he looks at how language can be used to both create and resolve conflict.

WRITING TO DISCOVER: *Think of a recent time in your life when you or someone you know used language to start or escalate an argument or conflict. What language was used? Why did that particular language ignite a conflict?*

When World War I was coming to an end, Alfred Korzybski, the founder of the discipline called General Semantics, was appalled when he contemplated the enormous material destruction, human loss and suffering he had witnessed. He started to wonder why people can be ingenious enough to invent complicated machines such as the locomotive and build huge bridges that do not collapse, and at the same time be so utterly unable to prevent war and large-scale human suffering. Shortly after, he came to the conclusion that one of the main reasons for this dismal state of affairs is the human being's lack of awareness and understanding of some of the fundamentals of language. Korzybski expressed his views in detail in his seminal book entitled *Science and Sanity* (1933). His work has been revered and promulgated by a number of followers (for instance, Hayakawa 1939/1992; Lee 1941/1994; Kodish and Kodish 2001; Kodish 2011).

Other people also realized decades ago that language is a serious matter. One of these was the writer Aldous Huxley, who said: 'Words and the meanings of words are not matters merely for the academic amusement of linguists and logisticians, or for the aesthetic delight of poets; they are matters of the profoundest ethical significance to every human being' (Huxley 1940: 28).

As some researchers claim (for instance, Hamelink 2011), conflict is built into human relations and we cannot eliminate it. According to

Hamelink, it can be seen not only as to a large degree unavoidable, it 'can sometimes even be positive and desirable' (2011: 2). Other authors have pointed to positive evaluations of conflict in some cultures and contexts (for instance, Kakavá 2001). Whether we agree with these views (especially the former) depends on our definition of 'conflict'. If we define it as 'opposing positions' or 'dispute', we may assume that indeed conflict cannot be avoided. We are all individuals and we all have our idiosyncratic views, ideas, goals, values and so on. We will always see things somewhat differently (though often in ways similar to others) and if we call this state of affairs 'conflict', it may be seen as an integral part of life. If, however, we operate with a different definition of conflict—for instance, as a verbal or physical fight aiming at the destruction of the opponent—conflict seems to be avoidable and for most people will be a phenomenon we will gladly dispense with. In the present book, I use the notion of conflict in the latter sense (that is, as a verbal or physical fight aiming at the destruction of the opponent—as a phenomenon that we can and should try to avoid) and propose some ideas relating to language that may contribute to alleviating conflicts of various kinds.

What causes conflict? Researchers have discussed this question and related ones for a long time (for thorough treatments of conflict, see Wright 1942; Schellenberg 1982; Rapoport 1995; Barash and Webel 2002). I do not intend to elaborate on this discussion. Here, I make the assumption that one of the main reasons for conflict is human ignorance, lack of knowledge, or what one might want to see as lack of awareness. This may be true about ignorance in all walks of life. Needless to say, however, my concern here will be limited to questions of ignorance in the area of language, in how language works.

On 29 May 2012, the President of the United States, Barack Obama, posthumously honoured Polish World War II hero Jan Karski, a courier for the Polish Resistance. He handed the Presidential Medal of Freedom to a high Polish official and delivered a speech extolling Karski's heroic deeds. In this speech, Obama mentioned Karski's attempts to get first-hand information about the atrocities committed by the Nazis. In this context, he referred to a 'Polish death camp' into which Karski was smuggled by the Polish Resistance to see for himself what was actually happening in the camp. The phrase 'Polish death camps' (to mean Nazi/Hitler/German death camps in the occupied territory of Poland) had been used before by various non-Polish journalists, and Polish government officials had vehemently protested against this unfortunate, highly inappropriate and unjustly incriminating formulation. This time, however, the phrase was used by one of the world's leading politicians, and it immediately caused an outrage in Poland and in the Polish community in the US. The incident was widely reported in the international press and numerous people posted angry comments on the incident to electronic newspapers and in blogs. The White House spokesperson, Caitlin Hayden, said at a press conference that the president misspoke and that the administration regretted the misstatement.[1]

For many people, including some Polish politicians, regretting the misstatement was not sufficient. In an atmosphere of growing conflict, many Poles expected an official apology from Obama. As such an apology did not arrive by the end of the second day after the incident, many people became very angry, as did some Americans who understood the gravity of the president's mistake and the deeply hurt feelings of most Poles. In numerous comments, more or less official, allegations against the American administration were raised, and facts from the distant and more recent past brought back to widespread attention. It was not until a few days later that Obama finally wrote a letter to Polish President Bronisław Komorowski expressing regret for his unfortunate formulation.

We have here a salient example of language (using the ambiguous 'Polish death camps' rather than the much clearer 'Nazi death camps *in* Poland') with the potential to lead to conflict. Whether it was an unfortunate formulation or not, the words Obama uttered shocked and angered many people. In this case, a conflict about words died out quickly and never turned into a conflict in deeds. Sometimes it does, though. Language matters.

I recently ran into a highly educated native speaker of British English, who had just returned from the US and who complained about the Americans there (native speakers of American English) not being able to speak 'English properly'. She told me she could not understand the phrase 'they plotted against him' (the 't' in 'plotted' being pronounced as voiced, which sounds like the mid consonant in 'ladder'), which annoyed her. She also complained about someone in the US pronouncing 'humanities' by dropping the initial 'h' sound. She talked to me about her language 'problems' in the US with a significant measure of superiority, implying that British English is superior and proper compared to American English, which is inferior and improper. When I tried to explain that American English is simply different, that British English is not any better in any absolute sense, that languages change and that there is variation—all these being platitudes for linguists—the person in question did not accept my argument, got very irritated, started ridiculing my own American English pronunciation, and we parted in an atmosphere of mild conflict. Language matters.

A few days later, I came across an article in a Polish newspaper in which reference was made to the secretary of a recently deceased Polish Nobel Prize winner in literature (Szostkiewicz 2012). The man is reported to have said that he does not reply to emails starting with the salutation *witam* (roughly, 'I greet you'). He finds the heading so disgusting that he refuses to have anything to do with anyone who uses it. This salutation is a recent form, one of many surfacing in Polish. The form does not invite any widely recognized negative associations. It is simply new in the context of email messages. Someone who rejects the *witam* form does not seem to know or rejects the fact that new forms appear in all languages all the time, whether one likes them or not. Rejecting someone only because you do not like a language form that the other person uses may be seen as belittling and denigrating, and may lead to conflict. Language matters.

We often do not to seem to realize how language works. As the three examples indicate, it is not commonly known that language ambiguity is rampant, that languages change all the time, or that variation is one of the basic characteristics of any language. Our lack of awareness of these facts may lead to unintended conflicts. Moreover, there seems to be little understanding of how we use language, how we get manipulated through language, how we use metaphors, how we address other people, how we handle a telephone conversation linguistically, how words may mean different things to different people and so on. What is worse is that many people who do not know how language works seem to believe that they do:

On the other hand, and fortunately, language may foster conciliation, social stability, and peace.

> . . . people are generally very interested in language and linguistics. Unfortunately, our institutions are very good at producing citizens who truly believe that they understand the inner workings of language and that their understanding is enough to justify not only vociferous opinions but also to act on those opinions in ways that sometimes will be detrimental and even destructive to others. (Lippi-Green 2012: xx)

I believe that we can endorse the following two statements with a fair amount of certainty:

> . . . language is often taken for granted—more or less in the same way as the air we breathe is taken for granted. (Bolívar 2012: 592)

> . . . most people act about as conscious of their linguistic environment as fish appear conscious of the water in which they swim. (Bourland 1974: 89)

Does this matter? Very much so, as many of us do not seem to be aware of the social consequences to which language use may lead. Consider the following:

> What does it take for the citizens of one society to hate the citizens of another society to the degree that they want to segregate them, torment them, even kill them? It requires a 'hostile imagination', a psychological construction embedded deeply in their minds by propaganda that transforms those others into 'The Enemy' . . . It is all done with *words and images*. (Zimbardo 2007: 11; italics added)

> It has sometimes been said that words can cut deeper than daggers. This wise observation acquires dramatic new meanings in the context of war

in Yugoslav lands, which actually started as a war of words—waged most ruthlessly in the media . . . (Bugarski 2001: 75–76)

Language use may be dangerous, detrimental; it may lead to conflicts in the family, among friends, to arguments at work, major international friction and war. The role language plays in warmongering has been widely confirmed:

> Humans never engage in war without the mediating force of discourse. From the rhetorical saber rattling that precedes conflict through the diplomatic overtures that sue for peace, discourse plays an integral role in the outbreak, conduct, and disputation of armed political conflict around the world. (Hodges 2013a: 3)

On the other hand, and fortunately, language use may foster conciliation, social stability and peace. The social consequences depend to a significant degree on what we know about language and how we use it in communication.

NOTE

1. http://thecaucus.blogs.nytimes.com/2012/05/30/white-house-says president-misspoke-on-polish-death-camp/ (accessed 1 October 2014).

THINKING CRITICALLY ABOUT THE READING

1. How does Janicki define *conflict* in paragraph 3? How does his definition differ from other frequently used definitions of this word?

2. Why did President Barack Obama's phrase "Polish death camp" cause controversy in 2012? What phrase does Janicki suggest Obama should have used instead, and why?

3. What potential consequences of language use does Janicki identify in paragraph 10?

4. In paragraph 8, why does Janicki recount his experience with a native speaker of British English who spoke about language "problems" in American English? How does this anecdote relate to Janicki's larger argument about language and conflict?

5. In paragraph 10, Janicki "endorses" two truths about how we treat language. The first is that "language is often taken for granted," and the second is that "most people act about as conscious of their linguistic environment as fish appear conscious of the water in which they swim." Why do you think Janicki endorses these particular statements "with a fair amount of certainty"? Do these statements ring true to you? In what ways do the examples throughout his essay support these two truths?

LANGUAGE IN ACTION

In a small group with one or two classmates, discuss a recent conflict that you experienced. The conflict can be either major (for example, a breakup with a romantic partner) or minor (for example, a debate with a friend over which party to attend on Saturday). As much as you can, try to recall the specific language that participants in the conflict used. With your classmates, analyze how the language changed as the conflict evolved. For example, with what words or phrases did the conflict begin? If the conflict escalated, how did the language change? Can you identify any point at which, in hindsight, you could have de-escalated the conflict—and, if so, what language might you have used to de-escalate? What language was used to resolve the conflict if the conflict was, indeed, resolved?

WRITING SUGGESTIONS

1. In paragraph 10, Janicki writes that "many people who do not know how language works seem to believe that they do." Think of an encounter you have had with someone who thought they understood how language works, but actually didn't. Write a brief narrative essay in which you describe the encounter and explain why this person was misguided in their understanding of language. Include at least one specific reference to Janicki's essay to support your explanation.

2. In paragraph 8, Janicki describes a conflict he had with a speaker of British English, who "ridiculed" Janicki's American English. Write a brief argument essay in which you try to convince this speaker of British English that British English is not, in fact, any "better" or "worse" than American English. Before you write, be sure to review the arguments that Janicki tried (as he explains in paragraph 8) and consider how you might expand on or alter these arguments in your own essay.

Sorry, Regrets, and More

Edwin L. Battistella

Edwin L. Battistella is a professor of English and writing at Southern Oregon University in Ashland, Oregon, where he has also served as Dean of the School of Arts and Letters and as the interim provost. Battistella studied linguistics at the City University of New York and received his PhD in 1981. Prior to teaching in Oregon, he held academic positions at the University of Alabama in Birmingham, the Thomas J. Watson Research Center, and Wayne State College. From 1995 to 2001 Battistella served as the book review editor for *Language*, the journal of the Linguistic Society of America, and in 2014 began a term on the society's Executive Committee.

Battistella is the author of six books on varying aspects of linguistics, including three books on linguistic markedness, two on nineteenth- and twentieth-century language attitudes, one about word-making theory, and a book on public apologies. *Sorry About That: The Language of Public Apology* (2014) examines the public apologies offered by politicians, entertainers, and others, to analyze how certain language is perceived as creating sincere or insincere apologies. The essay here, excerpted from *Sorry About That*, focuses on the grammar and reception of notorious public apologies.

WRITING TO DISCOVER: *Have you apologized recently? To whom? Why? Spend a few minutes trying to recall your apology. What language did you use? How did you convey your sincerity? Could your language or tone have been misconstrued as insincere? Why or why not?*

"I'M VERY SORRY FOR THAT"

When he became president in 1993, Bill Clinton quickly set up the Task Force on National Health Care Reform. Headed by first lady Hillary Clinton, the task force was intended to make good on Clinton's campaign promise to enact universal health care. The effort failed, as had previous efforts beginning with Theodore Roosevelt, and health-care reform became a major factor in Democratic losses in the 1994 midterm elections. Opponents personalized the failure by portraying the task force as an intrusive bureaucracy being imposed by the first lady. They called it HillaryCare.

After the 1994 midterm losses, Bill Clinton began to adjust his priorities and adapt his approach. Hillary Clinton also began to think about her role, at one point organizing an off-the-record lunch with a group of columnists and journalists that included syndicated columnist

Ann Landers, Cindy Adams and Louis Romano of the *New York Post,* Marian Burros of *The New York Times,* and others. At the lunch, Clinton described how she believed her health-care efforts had been twisted by opponents and how she herself had been portrayed. She told the journalists, "I regret very much that the efforts on health care were badly misunderstood, taken out of context and used politically against the Administration. I take responsibility for that, and I'm very sorry for that." What Clinton was saying was that the fault lay with others who were distorting her efforts on health care and that she should have better understood the political machinations.

Was Clinton apologizing? She regrets three grammatically passive actions—efforts on health care being misunderstood by the public, efforts being taken out of context, and efforts being used by political opponents—and she says she is sorry. However, her sorry refers to the actions of others who misunderstood or misrepresented health-care reform. Sorry indicates regret for a situation, not regret for an offense. Taken alone, her sorry is more like the usage in "I'm sorry that I missed your call" than "I'm sorry that I lost your book."

Clinton confused matters somewhat by also saying "I take responsibility for that." With that phrasing she also asserted responsibility for the public's misunderstandings and her opponents' misrepresentations. She treated what happened as something she might have prevented with different actions—in other words she treated it as a transgression. Her "I'm very sorry for that" was thus ambiguous, carrying both the sense of reporting on a regrettable situation and that of taking the blame for that situation. The conversational logic of her statement was unresolved.

When Clinton's comments came out, she was criticized for apologizing. The *Chicago Sun Times* headline was "Hillary 'Sorry' About Health Care," and the article led with the statement that "over a plate of heart-healthy American cuisine, Hillary Rodham Clinton took full responsibility for the failure of the health-care program she helped design . . . and said she was 'sorry.'" The *Arkansas Democrat-Gazette* wrote "First Lady Says She's Sorry, But Insists She Won't Hide For Next 2 Years" and *The New York Times*—which broke the story—wrote that "Mrs. Clinton put most of the fault on herself."

As the story developed, others commented on the first lady's words and whether or not saying sorry was a stereotypical feature of women's speech. One state legislator said, "When [Clinton] says she is responsible for the failure of health care, that is the woman trying to take all the burdens on herself. She could have been Mother Teresa and that health care bill still would have failed." Linguist Deborah Tannen even discussed the incident and its relationship to gender in a *New York Times Magazine* article, quoting an unnamed political scientist saying, "To apologize for substantive things you've done raises the white flag. There's a school of thought in politics that you never say you're sorry."

Ironically, Clinton had noted, "I can only guess that people are getting perceptions about me from things I am saying or doing in ways that don't correspond with things I am trying to get across." Were her words treated as an apology because she was woman? Let's start by taking a closer look at the grammar of *sorry* and how it differs from *apologize*.

THE GRAMMAR OF *SORRY*

Saying "I'm sorry" is different from saying "I apologize." The former reports on an internal state of the speaker but does not literally perform an apology. Instead, speakers and hearers use the conversational maxims of quality, quantity, relation, and manner to imply or infer an apology. By itself, the minimal report "I'm sorry" (or, the simple "Sorry" used for minor transgressions) doesn't tell us much. Much of the meaning-making comes from the complements that follow *sorry*.

Like *apologize, sorry* can occur with a gerund complement or a conditional (*if*) complement—I can be sorry for speaking out of turn or I can be sorry if I have offended you. Unlike *apologize, sorry* can occur with an infinitive complement. If the following infinitive is *to be, sorry* is understood as an apology ("I'm sorry to be such a bother"), while if the verb is one of perception it is often understood as report of empathy ("I'm sorry to hear about your loss").

Sorry differs from *apologize* in that it frequently occurs with a noun ⟨10⟩ clause. Noun clauses, you'll recall, are tricky because the choice of the subject of the clause can affect the meaning: I can be sorry that I was so inconsiderate or I can be sorry that you were offended. When the subjects of both clauses are the first person *I* (or *we*), the speaker is sorry for something he or she has done. But when the subordinate clause subject does not match the first-person subject of the main clause, then the speaker is sorry for something that happened. So "I'm sorry that it's raining" expresses disappointment but not apology. *Sorry* also differs from *apologize* in not allowing an expressed indirect object. That means that the grammar of *sorry* does not indicate to whom the apology is addressed. An apology using *sorry* must either rely on context (by uttering the expression face to face or in a person-to-person communication like a letter or email) or on making the recipient of the apology clear by mentioning it elsewhere.

Sorry provides somewhat more grammatical flexibility than *apologize* and somewhat more semantic flexibility. When a speaker says "I'm sorry," he or she may be implying an apology or making a report. Thus, when businesswoman Martha Stewart was convicted of several charges related to insider stock trading in March 2004, she said she was sorry. In court she told the judge:

Today is a shameful day. It is shameful for me, for my family, and for my beloved company and all of its employees and partners. What was a small personal matter became over the last two and a half years an almost fatal circus event of unprecedented proportions spreading like oil over a vast landscape, even around the world. I have been choked and almost suffocated to death.

She ended by saying "I'm very sorry it has come to this." Was Stewart apologizing? Perhaps she intended it to be taken that way. But her ambiguous language can also be understood as meaning that she regrets the unfortunate situation she is in. And both the abstractness of the shame ("Today is a shameful day") and the vague passiveness of the language ("a small personal matter . . . has become," "I have been choked . . ." ". . . it has come to this") suggest that she is not performing an apology but merely reporting her feelings.

The distinction between performing an apology by saying "I apologize" and reporting a mental state by saying "I'm sorry" provides insight into another aspect of apologetic discourse—apologies sometimes combine the two expressions. Thus when England's Prince Harry apologized for dressing in a Nazi uniform for a 2005 costume party, he said this: "I am very sorry if I caused any offense or embarrassment to anyone. It was a poor choice of costume and I apologize." The use of "I apologize" extends and supplements the conditional "I am very sorry if" in the first sentence. There is also a bit of a verbal trick in the positioning of the word *apologize*. The prince is apologizing for an abstraction—a poor choice of costume—not for offensive behavior or the values implied in dressing as a Nazi. Putting the apology last allows the speaker to shape the transgression in a more innocuous way. A similar verbal trick arises with the positioning of *sorry* in our next example, from the 2004 presidential election.

RATHER SORRY

Shortly before the 2004 presidential election, CBS broadcast a *Sixty Minutes* segment calling into doubt President George W. Bush's National Guard record. The September 8 report by Dan Rather aired on *Sixty Minutes Wednesday* and showed four documents that appeared to have been written by Bush's commanding officer. The documents created the impression that Bush had disobeyed orders to report for a physical, had been grounded from flying, and had used political influence to receive more positive evaluations than he deserved. The presumed author of the memos, Lieutenant Colonel Jerry Killian, had died in 1984, and the memos were provided to a CBS producer by another retired National Guard lieutenant colonel, Bill Burkett, who claimed to have burned the originals after faxing them to CBS. Prior to airing the segment, CBS producers consulted with several document experts and interpreted the results in the most positive light for the potential news story, but failed to contact a crucial typography expert.

Immediately after the story aired, bloggers and then the print news media began to question the authenticity of the documents. For a time, CBS and Rather defended the segment, but soon they had to disavow it. On the September 20 *CBS Evening News,* Rather explained that in light of additional research on the authenticity and source of the documents: 15

> I no longer have the confidence in these documents that would allow us to continue vouching for them journalistically. I find we have been misled on the key question of how our source for the documents came into possession of these papers. That, combined with some of the questions that have been raised in public and in the press, leads me to a point where—if I knew then what I know now—I would not have gone ahead with the story as it was aired, and I certainly would not have used the documents in question.
>
> But we did use the documents. We made a mistake in judgment, and for that I am sorry.

Dan Rather first explains the situation and concludes that he would have acted differently if he had more information. At the end, he names the offense—a mistake in judgment—and he explains that he is sorry, inviting viewers to infer an apology. Because an apology was in order, *sorry* was indeed understood as implying an apology instead of simply regrets that something happened. Conversational logic suggests that Rather would not be saying CBS made a mistake and that he was sorry if he did not intend an apology.

I hope you noticed how Rather used the plural *we* in the last two sentences cited above, switching from an earlier *I*. He switches from "I no longer have confidence," "I find we have been misled," and "I would not have gone ahead," to "we did use" and "we made a mistake." He depersonalizes the naming of the offense then switches back to *I* at the end to personalize his regret. Rather uses pronouns to ever so slightly separate himself from the offense.

Following the incident, CBS commissioned an independent review panel whose report led to several executive- and producer-level firings. The panel's report noted that Rather still felt the documents were accurate and that he had merely "delivered the apology" in support of the corporate decision to back off the story. Two months after the panel report was issued, Rather left the CBS anchor position, a year ahead of his planned retirement, and sued the network. In the lawsuit, Rather argued that he was forced to apologize by CBS, that he was not responsible for the errors in the reporting, and that he was being made a scapegoat. The seventy-million-dollar suit was unsuccessful.

Soon after the original story aired, CBS also issued a separate statement saying, "Based on what we now know, CBS News cannot prove that the documents are authentic, which is the only acceptable journalistic standard to justify using them in the report. We should not have used them. That was a mistake, which we deeply regret." Here CBS makes its apology with *regret* rather than *sorry*. But how does *regret* differ from *sorry*?

REGRETS

The sorries expressed by Hillary Clinton and Dan Rather illustrate self-reports of speakers' attitudes about their actions or inactions. Just as common is the verb *regret,* which also reports on a speaker's internal state. The grammar of *regret* largely

Like *sorry*, *regret* is ambiguous.   parallels that of *sorry*. *Regret* does not allow indirect objects, but it does take direct object nouns and pronouns, conditionals, noun clauses, gerunds, and infinitives as complements. I can regret my actions, regret it if anyone was offended, regret that I behaved so poorly, regret calling him mean, or regret to have to tell you bad news. Again, a gerund can provide an especially strong grammatical foundation for an implied apology: "I regret calling him mean" aligns the subject of the main clause with the understood subject of the gerund. A noun clause can similarly invite interpretation as an apology when the subjects match, as in "I regret that I behaved so poorly." Both gerunds and noun clauses, however, can complement *regret* in ways that merely report on situations without assuming agency for them: "I regret your being inconvenienced" and "We regret that they feel that way." Here, the speaker regrets a situation but does not assume responsibility for it.

Regret also occurs with noun phrases, as we have seen: "I sincerely 20 regret the unfortunate choice of language" (Harry Truman), "I . . . profoundly regret my horrific relapse" (Mel Gibson), and "I deeply regret any offense my remark in the *New York Observer* might have caused anyone" (Joe Biden). And *regret* of course may be a noun, which provides a further option for apologies: "I always put the victim first but here I didn't follow my principle and that is my greatest regret" (said by Scotland Yard assistant commissioner John Yates on his decision not to reopen an investigation into *News International* in 2009) or "I'm very disappointed and want to express my regret to The Open fans" (Tiger Woods commenting on his performance at the 2011 British Open). Having or expressing regrets makes the attitude more abstract—it is more a thing than a mental action—and distances the regretter from the regret.

Like *sorry*, *regret* is ambiguous. Literally, *regret* refers to one's attitudes toward an event or action. It can be used to indicate an apologetic stance toward one's own actions but can also merely comment on a disagreeable state of affairs. Often the difference is clear. When a Soviet court sentenced captured pilot Francis Gary Powers to a ten-year sentence in 1960, President Dwight Eisenhower's press secretary released a statement that Eisenhower "deplored the Soviet propaganda activity associated with the episode beginning last May and regrets the severity of the sentence." Eisenhower was not apologizing. He was expressing disapproval. When President John F. Kennedy sent troops to oversee the integration of the University of Mississippi, he noted that it was his responsibility to enforce the court decision even though the government had not been a part of the court case. Kennedy said: "I deeply regret the fact that any action by the executive branch was necessary in this case, but all other avenues and alternatives, including persuasion and conciliation, had been tried and exhausted." Kennedy was explaining and regretting that circumstances made federal action necessary. But he was not apologizing.

Sometimes in partisan politics there is public debate about whether an expression of regret implies apology. This was the case when secretary of state William Jennings Bryan presented a treaty to the Senate expressing "sincere regret" to the nation of Colombia. Was this an apology? We will get to this controversy in just a moment. First, one last question.

Does "I regret" mean the same thing as "I'm sorry"? There is overlap of course, but as we have seen, *sorry* reports on internal emotional states and de-emphasizes the calculus of acts and consequences. *Regret,* on the other hand, places more weight on situations and on the analysis of acts and consequences. Thus, *sorry* is typically used for mild transgressions (jostles and spills) and *regret* for more formal, serious, and detached situations. Of course, as speakers of English, we use and understand the nuances intuitively. The overlap and distinction between regretting and being sorry are evident in fixed expressions like "I regret to inform you that we selected another applicant" as opposed to "I'm sorry for your loss." *Sorry* is too personal for some professional and business exchanges, while *regret* is usually too impersonal and detached for condolences.

DID THE WILSON ADMINISTRATION APOLOGIZE TO COLOMBIA?

In the early part of the twentieth century, US relations with Colombia deteriorated because of the Panama Canal conflict. The geographically strategic state of Panama had been a part of Colombia since 1821. Panamanian secession efforts had repeatedly failed, most notably during the Thousand Days War of 1899 to 1902. At the same time, the United States was negotiating with the Colombian government to gain rights to a five-hundred-square-mile area for a canal.

Events turned when the Colombian Senate rejected the Hay-Herrán 25 Treaty, which would have given the United States rights to the canal zone in perpetuity in return for a $10 million initial payment and annual payments of $250,000. Determined to have the canal, the Roosevelt administration threw its support behind the Panamanian independence movement. American ships, ordered to the area by President Roosevelt, blockaded Colombian forces. In November 1903, Panama proclaimed its independence and was immediately recognized by the United States. American troops landed with the stated role of keeping order and protecting American lives and property, but also to interfere with and intimidate Colombian forces. Five days after independence was declared, the treaty the United States had sought was signed, and in 1904, work began on the five-hundred-mile-long canal.

The Colombians, and many Americans as well, insisted that the separation of Panama was an immoral and illegal action instigated by American commercial interests and abetted by Roosevelt. Later in the Roosevelt administration and through the Taft years, efforts were made to repair the rift. Diplomatic contacts continued, and when Woodrow Wilson became president, one of his priorities was to improve relations with the strategic region of Central and Latin America. By 1914, a treaty had been negotiated to ensure full recognition of Panama. The Thomson-Urrutia Treaty proposed to pay Colombia twenty-five million dollars and to grant special canal privileges in return for Colombia's recognition of Panama's independence and sovereignty. The treaty also included this sentence:

> The government of the United States of America, wishing to put at rest all controversies and differences with the Republic of Colombia arising out of which the present situation on the Isthmus of Panama have resulted on its own part and in the name of the people of the United States expresses sincere regret that anything should have occurred to interrupt or to mar the relations of cordial friendship that had so long subsisted between the two nations.

When the treaty was presented in April of 1914, it met with strong opposition from Roosevelt's supporters in the Senate. Roosevelt himself lobbied against it, calling the payment "blackmail." And some senators objected to the words *sincere regret* as an apology to Colombia. California senator George Perkins, for example, said, "I do not believe that the United States Senate will ever ratify this treaty, which implies an apology to Colombia and payment of $25,000,000 in reparations. Colombia should apologize to the United States." *The New York Times* added its opinion that "a formal apology is uncalled for," since the Colombians were trying to prevent construction of the canal.

James Du Bois, the minister to Colombia under William Howard Taft, argued that the treaty was not an apology at all but rather a "simple expression of regret." Du Bois reported telling the Colombian negotiators that the United States "would never apologize for a political act" and noted that neither he nor the Colombian negotiators viewed the statement as an apology. The apology claim was, he said, "only the cry of the Roosevelt people to defeat the treaty." Woodrow Wilson too denied that the treaty had an apology, describing that view as "pure guff." Nebraska senator Gilbert Hitchcock elaborated: "The language of the treaty falls very far short of an apology, and an apology in this case is not called for."

The wording of the treaty supports the view that there was no apology. Look back at the phrase "expresses sincere regret that anything should have occurred to interrupt or to mar the relations of cordial friendship." The noun clause following *regret* is nonspecific. Expressing regret for "anything that might have occurred" does not name any particular transgression. An apology might be inferred, but the implication is weak given the vagueness in the sentence and in the context. Nevertheless, those who argued against the treaty carried the day through the Wilson administration. The treaty would not have included the word *regret*, they argued, unless apology was implied. By 1915, it was clear that the treaty would not be ratified with the expression of regret included. Wilson was soon occupied by other issues and never returned to the treaty. But in 1921, two years after Theodore Roosevelt had died, the new Harding administration succeeded in passing the treaty, with the expression of regret omitted.

SHORTCUTS

The expressions "I was wrong" and "Forgive me" are also sometimes taken to imply apologies. "I was wrong" concedes error. "Forgive me" asks for reconciliation. To conversationally cooperative listeners, either can imply the full apology process. Recall our earlier modeling of the apology process as made up of a call to apologize, a two-part expressed apology (a naming and a regretting), and a response. When we shortcut a full apology by merely saying "I was wrong," we are relying on the naming of the offense to perform the work of the apology without the sorry-saying. And when we shortcut a full apology with "Forgive me," we are jumping directly to the response step of the process.

Sometimes such shortcuts are sufficient, especially if the person apolo- 30 gizing is sufficiently contrite or if the audience is particularly receptive. Consider this terse public admission by Senator John McCain: "It was the wrong thing to do, and I have no excuse for it." McCain was referring to a joke he had made about Chelsea Clinton's appearance and parentage, which he characterized as a "very unfortunate and insensitive remark." Saying he was wrong suggests regret, and saying he had no excuse condemns the behavior. The statement thus contains two key elements of an apology: regret and condemnation of one's behavior. McCain was not literally apologizing here, but his statement uses conversational logic to invite the inference.

Shortcutting the apology process is understandable. John McCain had apologized privately to the Clinton family, so he perhaps felt no need to apologize expansively in public. But for a serious offense, a shortcut apology often seems like a verbal trick to gain the social benefits of apologizing without having to say you are sorry. Thus, McCain seems to be not quite apologizing. And the converse is true as well. Admitting a mistake can be treated as an apology, even when no apology is intended.

For very minor offenses, of course, a shortcut is often exactly what is called for. For the stepped-on foot or jostled elbow, a linguistically elaborate process is overkill. For small social offenses, we may skip the call to apologize and the naming of the offense, Both are apparent from the immediate situation, so we move right to a quickly spoken "Sorry," "'Scuse me," "Pardon," or "My fault" which may or may not be followed by a response from the person harmed. The French-derived counterparts of "Forgive me," "Excuse me," and "Pardon me" are especially common for very minor transgressions. And they are conventionally used to pre-apologize for an imposition. We say "Pardon me, do you have the time?," or "Excuse me, can I ask you a question?"

Just as we take a shortcut by saying "I was wrong," we can also imply an apology with the simple possessive phrase *my fault*. Even shorter is the phrase *my bad*, used as a tic of adolescent speech in the 1995 movie *Clueless*. Lexicographers have traced the origin of the phrase to basketball. Ben Zimmer, who for a time wrote the On Language column at the *New York Times*, favors the view that *my bad* originated on playgrounds in the 1970s and 1980s. He cites *Oxford English Dictionary* examples from the 1980s as proof, including a 1986 guide which gives this definition: "My bad, an expression of contrition uttered after making a bad pass or missing an opponent." Today, *my bad* lends itself to any quick expressions of apology where the call to apologize is apparent and no response is expected.

THINKING CRITICALLY ABOUT THE READING

1. How does Battistella analyze Hillary Clinton's 1994 apology? What grammatical voice does Clinton use? How is the text of the apology different than the way it is received?

2. What role may Clinton's gender have played in how her words were received? Why? Why might women, stereotypically, apologize more in our society?

3. How does "I'm sorry" differ from "I apologize," according to Battistella? Which focuses on one's own feelings or "mental state"? Which focuses on the feelings of the other and performs an act showing regret? Why and how do these words work? Why is their difference important?

4. In what ways can "I'm sorry" be manipulated or changed in meaning? Can the phrase actually convey the opposite of its proposed meaning? If so, how?

5. How does regret differ from "I'm sorry" and "I apologize" in public apologies? What are the limitations of "regret"?

LANGUAGE IN ACTION

Though the percentage varies depending on circumstance, some social scientists estimate that nonverbal communication makes up as much as 93 percent of our communication. This means that our body language—the way we carry ourselves, our facial expressions, our gestures, etc.—constitutes the vast majority of what we actually "say." With that in mind, why does Battistella say so very little about body language in the context of public apologies?

To decide whether you think body language should have bearing on how apologies are perceived, search for video of famous public apologies. Compare what you notice about body language to Battistella's written analysis. Does what you see affect how you interpret the words said, and should Battistella have accounted for visual cues? Based on what you see versus what you read, what percentage of communication is nonverbal? Does 93 percent seem like an accurate number?

WRITING SUGGESTIONS

1. Battistella usefully diagrams the difference between "I'm sorry," "I apologize," and "I regret" in speeches perceived as public apologies, and he models a pattern for analyzing these words and their effect in the public forum. Choose a public figure's recent "apology" to closely analyze as Battistella does. Although you do not need to focus, as the linguist does, on parsing and identifying the parts of speech in operation, his approach should help you identify the "quirks" within the apology you choose to analyze. What words of apology does the speech use? Does the apology focus on an action or on the speaker's feelings? What words seem to limit the apology? Does the speaker deflect blame in any way? Write an essay analyzing how these aspects of the apology affect denotative meaning (the meaning of the words as used in the sentence) and connotative meaning (the meaning implied by the context of the speech and what readers infer about it). Be sure to weigh in on whether or not the speaker has actually apologized.

2. Choose a public "apology" that appears insincere or evasive, and rewrite it to convey an actual apology. Read and compare the original version with your own and write a reflective essay. What are the differences between the actual apology and your version? Why do those differences matter? What do you think the consequences would have been if your version had been the one used publicly—both for the perpetrator and the victims of the offense?

Further Adventures of Flex Cop

MICHAEL GARDNER

Michael Gardner is a veteran sergeant of the Cincinnati Police Department, where he served as the department's legal liaison, expert witness
for use of force issues, and academy instructor. He and his wife, Debbie,
met at the police academy in 1973, where they were both students,
but it was an incident the following year that would alter their careers.
In 1974, Debbie, despite all her physical and martial arts training, was
assaulted with a gun and froze. It was this "dramatic failure," as the
couple calls it on their website, that led them to rethink their traditional
police training and refocus on "visual and verbal persuasion." This tactic, which they felt was most crucial to their survival as officers, was also
the most under-emphasized in the police academy, which focused on
physical preparedness and weaponry. The assault compelled Debbie to
found the Survive Institute — an organization dedicated to promoting
mental and verbal self-defense — in 1981. Mike continued working in the
police force to conduct real-life research into innovative visual and verbal
tactics that focused on self-control and de-escalation. His tactics worked.
As Gardner explains in the essay included here, "during my thirty-year
police career, I never fired my gun." In fact, he reports that he only had
to use mace — once.

In 1990 Gardner's approach was formally recognized when he was
named Officer of the Year by the Cincinnati Police Department. His
ideas about crisis control were not only deployed in Cincinnati's police
academy but have been featured in newspapers all over the United States.
After serving as the commander of the police academy and retiring from
the Warren County Sheriff's Office, he and Debbie co-authored *Raising
Kids Who Can Protect Themselves* (2004). Gardner continues to work
with the Survive Institute and serve as a professional consultant for a
number of law enforcement agencies.

WRITING TO DISCOVER: *Have you ever been so profoundly persuaded by
language that you changed your belief or position? If so, why and how did this
language affect you? What made it extraordinarily convincing? Do you think
it would have been equally effective if you had been in mental or emotional
distress?*

Everyone in the field knows that the most dangerous part of police
work is handling domestic disputes. Roughly one-third of the police officer assaults and killings in this country occur during domestic disputes.
A cop may go in to arrest the attacker and suddenly the spouse turns on
him with the frying pan when she sees he's making an arrest. There's no

telling who may be a problem, and people are much more likely to fight to defend their homes against intruders.

A lot of the calls we got on night shift were domestic violence runs. Cops hate making domestic runs because they're so dangerous, but for research purposes my partner and I asked other cops, "Do you mind if we start taking over your domestic runs so we can experiment with defusing hostile situations?" Of course we got no objections.

Traditionally, police officers are limited to only four choices for controlling situations—visual and verbal persuasion, chemical irritant, impact weapon, and deadly force. In training, most emphasis was on weaponry defense, without nearly enough on visual and verbal defense. My partner and I saw the need to stretch our flexibility to hundreds of choices in this uncharted territory.

The traditional approach in police work for a domestic run was to show up at an apartment and bang on the door using a raid-type knock with the police night stick, BAM BAM BAM BAM! I even hate it when the UPS or mail carrier bangs on my door to give me something I *want*, so I tried to imagine how someone already in emotional distress would be angered even more with a raid-type bang on their door. To be less intrusive and confrontational we started showing up and doing the "shave and haircut" knock, a very light "Rap ta-ta tap tap, tap tap." Even if the people inside didn't catch on to the jingle, it was a less invasive knock, and its association with a harmless advertisement was more to relax *us* than the people inside. It kept us at a condition orange—alert, but not the red of alarmed. We would even joke sometimes going into an apartment, "Hey let's be condition purple." What we were really saying was, "Hey let's not get red, because if we go in there red, we're going to have a fight."

The usual question police were trained to ask when entering a home   5
was, "What's the problem here?" Well, if you enter after a loud raid-type knock and ask them, "What's the problem here?" They'll give you a problem, usually several. They may tell you their problems from twenty years ago.

Instead we'd ask something like, "What have you decided to do between the time you called us and the time we got here?" That put them in solution mode. Other times we'd ask people to step out into the hallway so they wouldn't feel the need to defend their turf. We also purposely wore our hats when we approached, so when we did enter their house or apartment we could take them off as a sign of respect.

My partner and I became known to our fellow officers as the Dork Police, because no one knew what crazy thing we were going to do next. They were equally amazed at our success in non-violent control of tense situations. We experimented daily with ways of startling subjects into confusion in order to interrupt their dangerous mental patterns and provide a space for something more positive.

For example, we would sometimes approach potentially dangerous domestic disputes with our jackets purposely buttoned improperly, or with our caps pulled down so our ears stuck out. Other times we'd say "no" while nodding our heads up and down. Unless the combatants were too intoxicated or high to observe this odd behavior, they stopped, at least temporarily. They couldn't help responding to what they saw. Then it was hard for them to pick up their fight where they had left off.

Sometimes we'd walk into a shouting match between a couple, and we'd just run over and switch the channel on the TV set. If one of them said, "Hey, what the hell are you doing?" We'd say cheerfully, "Hey, you're not going to listen to us anyway, so we're going to watch some TV."

All we were trying to do was get them to refocus out of their anger and   10
onto something else. We would do anything to create a change. Once that was accomplished, we'd offer suggestions for where couples could go for longer-term help.

Using humor was particularly useful when performing routine, uncomfortable tasks like patting down or frisking a suspect. While maintaining physical control, we would like to say, "You don't have any hand grenades, swords, or bazookas hidden on you, do you?" Subjects generally laughed it off. Now and then, one would disclose that he had a knife or razor.

When couples were screaming at each other we'd start sniffing and shouting out. "Oh, do you smell gas? Where's your stove? There must be a burner on!" While the fight was temporarily stopped, my partner and I would go to the kitchen and pretend to check the stove for gas leaks. After a few minutes of sniffing the stove and kitchen area, we would advise the people that everything was OK, then ask "What else can we help you with?" The response was amazing. Often they said, "Nothing, officer . . . " If the argument did begin again, all my partner and I had to do was to sniff with a concerned look on our faces. With this pattern interruption, the subjects' personal fighting became secondary to the threat of a gas explosion in their home. They may even start getting an unconscious connection of, *Every time I start getting nasty there's danger, maybe I should try something else.*

> **All we were trying to do was get them to refocus out of their anger and onto something else.**

Other times, we would enter a residence and be greeted by someone standing in a fighting position and shouting, "You two think you can take me? Come on!" We would mirror his stance, but hold our palms up instead of making fists, saying, "No way. We heard how tough you are. We can't beat you, we'd have to call ten more guys in here." If that statement had any effect, we would follow up with, "Why don't we talk first, then you can kick our butts." On several occasions the potentially violent subject changed his mind. And if he didn't respond to our initial statement, that signaled us to try something else. Initially it was hard for us to give this kind of "pull" statement when a violent subject "pushed" us verbally. We instinctively wanted to "push" back with an "attack" statement. Yet the patience of our "pull" statement always minimized the force of our arrest.

One time we had a husband and wife close to killing each other. They were shouting countless obscenities at each other, and their hand gestures were disjointed and out of sync with the tone and tempo of their verbal language. I remembered the metaphor of an orchestra conductor—when people talk in rhythm with their gestures it tends to be good venting; letting their anger come out verbally rather than physically. But when their gestures are short, choppy, stab-like motions, disconnected from their language, it is likely that they're about to explode physically. This couple was actually making verbal threats like, "I'm going to kill you, you son of a bitch!" "You're dead, motherfucker!"

In a flash I said, "In all my years of police work, I've never seen some- 15 body able to express their anger like you can! I appreciate that, because sometimes things really piss me off and I wish I could express my anger like you are!" I was empathizing with them to bring their attention to me and to the importance of what they were feeling, and away from a fight.

Another time we came into an argument with the woman yelling and screaming at her husband. I said to her, "I bet you don't talk to the mailman this way, do you?"

"What? Of course not!"

"And I bet you don't talk to your car mechanic that way, do you?"

"No, of course not!"

"Well the reason you talk to your husband like that is obviously 20 because you care a whole lot more about what he says than what the mailman or the mechanic says."

"Yeah, well I guess so."

My questions first took her attention away from her emotions and what she was mad about. Then I offered her a new meaning for her outburst—it was because she *cared* about her husband. After about 15–20 minutes of me telling them how frustrated I was at not being able to express my feelings the way they could, they started counseling me. Soon it was apparent by the way they were sitting next to each other and looking at each other that they were eager to be left alone. I think we reframed their anger toward each other to such an extent that they wanted us gone so they could make up!

Once we came into a heated dispute and I said to the man, "Hey, you don't work for the city, do you?"

"NO!"

"That car out there with the lights on, that's not your car, is it?"   25

"NO!"

"You don't want us here, do you?"

"NO!"

"You'll be happy when we leave here, won't you?"

"Fuck yeah!"   30

This way I matched him and let him express himself. He was in the mood to disagree, so I started with questions all of which let him say "No." Then I shifted to a "Yes" question, leading him to a more positive place and getting his explicit agreement that when we left he'd be happy. It might sound like a small thing, but it made a huge difference. Now we were on the same page and he was more relaxed—no longer disagreeing with everything we said.

We'd also do a thing I called "word salad." I never did it in a disrespectful way, but when people get violent they're behaving worse than childish. Sometimes I'd say, "What you're saying here sounds like a phonological ambiguity to me, so rather than jeopardize any other litigation circumstances why don't you just take a walk and let things cool off?"

They got so confused by the first part of my sentence, they would jump on the first thing that made sense, usually responding. "I'll just take a walk and cool off a bit."

I'd say, "Great, I appreciate that."

Often we would use many of these different tactics one after the   35
other, until we found what worked. By systematically attempting to stop violence by using our appearance or words, we put ourselves in a position where we would be much more justified—both emotionally and legally—if we ended up having to resort to a higher degree of force. Yet in all these experiments on permanent night shift, and during my thirty-year police career, I never fired my gun. I had to use mace on a person only once, simply because the man was so intoxicated I couldn't communicate with him. We had tried many things, but he just wasn't there because of the alcohol. He had a little paring knife that he wouldn't drop. Technically I could have shot him, but I had been relaxed and aware enough to keep a table between us, so I was able to subdue him with the mace. As amazing as these techniques were for defusing violence in the moment, our biggest success was that we stopped getting return calls from the places we visited. Before we started using these techniques, it was common to get calls from the same location two or three times a night. Sometimes my partner and I would spend 15 or 30 minutes out on a call, and we'd get in trouble from our supervisor because he wanted us in and out. If they didn't straighten up right away he wanted us to simply arrest them. But we knew we could save time in the long run by coming to a peaceful resolution.

Probably our most interesting encounter came in June of 1984. My partner and I were patrolling our beat on a Saturday afternoon, when the dispatcher's voice crackled over our radio:

"Car 405, Car 405, respond to 755 East McMillan Street, reference a man with a gun. The only description we have is he's male, black, and his last name is Large. He threatened to kill a person and stated he would kill the police. Car 405.''

We replied, "Car 405, OK.''

Our sergeant came on the air with, "Car 422, advise Car 405 to wait for my arrival before they approach the address. I'll respond with a taser gun.''

Unfortunately for us, my partner and I happened to be on the one-way McMillan Street heading for that very address when the dispatch came out. Other police units were coming over the air advising that they would also respond. Since we were so close already, we parked near the location and advised our dispatcher that we were on the scene. Needless to say, our adrenaline was pumping. We often got calls where the details sounded frightening, but this one was different. We were afraid. As we approached an alley between two buildings, we observed a man in an army coat arguing with a woman. Without thinking, I blurted out, "Anyone here order a *large* pizza?''

The male subject turned and looked at me with a puzzled expression. Even my partner was looking at me funny. I could see the man's hands were empty. He said, "My name is Large...''

With that we knew who he was. We quickly handcuffed him and put him in the back seat of our car. Fortunately, he did not have a gun—something we did not know until after we had him under control. It turned out that he was a walk-away mental patient from the Veteran's Hospital Psychiatric Unit. He had been walking around threatening to kill people, hoping to force the police to kill him. Who knows what might have happened if Mr. Large hadn't been caught off guard. I sincerely believe that on this particular day the flexibility that I'd learned saved the life of a mentally disturbed veteran—and perhaps my life as well.

My partner, himself a Vietnam veteran, was able to chat with Mr. Large on the way to the Veteran's Hospital. Upon our arrival, the hospital staff was shocked that we didn't have to struggle with Mr. Large. I can't thank the people enough who taught me how to use these skills. Even though we may have been justified legally with some tactical force, we could never have lived with ourselves if we had hurt Mr. Large.

Unfortunately, it's very difficult to measure what *doesn't* happen, but I can say confidently that I was involved in hundreds of peaceful resolutions that would have ended up in arrests or fights had we used traditional police procedure. Ever since my eyes were opened to what is possible, I've been studying and researching how police officers everywhere can increase their choices by using visual and verbal persuasion to prevent, or at least minimize, their use of force in violent situations. Believe me, police officers all over this country need new tools for accomplishing their duties. They are hungry for positive education that will enhance their control over themselves and others. No group of professionals needs flexibility more than police officers.

THINKING CRITICALLY ABOUT THE READING

1. From the beginning of the essay, Gardner's focus is on changing his inter-actions as a police officer from more intrusive to more inquisitive. What are some of the verbal and non-verbal tactics Gardner and his partner change? What do they use instead? Why does the method require "flexibility," as Gardner concludes?

2. What do Gardner's colleagues call him and his partner? Is it a flattering mon-iker? Despite such a handle, do their tactics work? How successful are they?

3. How do Gardner's tactics rely on "visual and verbal" persuasion (3)? How do some of the visual tactics Gardner describes compare with our typical idea of how a police officer looks or moves?

4. What is a "word salad," and how does it work (32)? Why do you think it's successful? Do you think it could have ever been seen as disrespectful?

5. In what ways does Gardner suggest the pattern of one's language use is con-nected to or predictive of behavior? How did he and his partner work with the sound or rhythm of language to defuse tense situations?

6. What does Gardner's experience suggest about the power of language, obser-vation, and flexibility in police work?

LANGUAGE IN ACTION

In another essay entitled "Flex Cop," Gardner briefly narrates the follow-ing story of how he and his partner responded to a domestic dispute call:

> My buddy and I were on night shift when the police dispatcher asked us to respond to a domestic call. We came in and here was this guy who had just torn up the apartment. He was standing there in a fighting stance as we came in. Of course it's absurd that an unarmed guy would really want to take on two armed cops with sticks and mace and guns, but it looked like he might do it anyway. I looked at my partner and he nodded, so we immediately started rearranging the furniture and stretching our muscles like we were preparing for an athletic contest. The man just looked at us and said, "What the fuck are you doing?!"
>
> "Hey, look," I answered, "You just tore this apartment up. You've been fighting for the last ten minutes while we've been sitting in our car."
>
> "We're not loosened up," my partner added. "Give us a few min-utes to get ready like you are so this can be fair."
>
> The man looked at us like we were insane, but really our actions only brought to light the ridiculousness of the original situation. His rage was gone; there was no way he was going to try fighting us anymore.

What, if anything, strikes you about the way Gardner and his partner handled the potentially volatile situation? How did they turn a situa-tion that could have been confrontational into one that encouraged communication?

WRITING SUGGESTIONS

1. As a police officer, Gardner observes that "most emphasis was on weaponry defense, without nearly enough on visual and verbal defense" (3), a tool that he and his partner saw as underutilized and misunderstood. In the last several years, police forces across the nation have been under scrutiny for their questionable use of force and inability to verbally defuse situations. According to Gardner, officers "are hungry for positive education that will enhance their control over themselves and others" (44), yet these tactics do not seem to be widespread. Research phrases like "excessive force" and "police brutality," and choose a specific case for further research and discussion. How did the situation go awry? Do you think police training in Gardner's tactics would have helped create a different outcome? If so, how? If not, why not? Write an informative essay discussing how you would use the case you've chosen as a training scenario for future officers using Gardner's tactics. Which tactics might work best? Which might have unintended consequences? How would you get future officers thinking about the power their words might hold in protecting themselves and their suspects in threatening situations?

2. Gardner states, "As amazing as these techniques were for defusing violence in the moment, our biggest success was that we stopped getting return calls from places we visited. . . . [W]e knew we could save time in the long run by coming to a peaceful resolution" (35). Why do you think Gardner's tactics resulted in fewer return calls for domestic disputes? How might couples and families benefit from Gardner's approach even after the police have left? Write an essay in which you explore the ways in which Gardner's tactics might help couples resolve their own problems or keep the situation from escalating again.

Stalling for Time

GARY NOESNER

Gary Noesner worked for thirty years as an investigator, instructor, and hostage negotiator; he spent twenty-three of those years at the Federal Bureau of Investigation (FBI). He was the agency's lead negotiator in many standoffs with armed groups and individuals, including with the religious group known as the Branch Davidians during the infamous 51-day Waco siege in 1993. In that conflict, Noesner successfully negotiated the peaceful release of thirty-five hostages before being placed on another assignment. (The conflict later ended tragically when the Branch Davidians' compound burned to the ground with hostages still inside.)

Noesner was involved in numerous other crisis incidents ranging from prison riots to airplane hijackings, as well more than 120 overseas negotiations involving kidnapped American citizens. He finally retired from the FBI in 2003. He recounts his experiences and the crucial role language plays in negotiation in his book *Stalling for Time: My Life as an FBI Hostage Negotiator* (2010). In this essay, first published online at *The Trace* on August 25, 2016, Noesner highlights the importance of narrative to successful negotiation. He also emphasizes his belief that the language of negotiation is more effective than aggressive tactics in peacefully resolving standoffs.

WRITING TO DISCOVER: *Although few of us are ever likely to face the type of high-stakes scenarios that punctuate Noesner's career, most of us have experienced some type of negotiation. Can you recall a time when you negotiated well or poorly? Think about the negotiation tactics that you used: what was successful? What failed?*

The most damaging thing for a hostage negotiator is losing self-control. If you can't control your own emotions, how can you begin to influence someone else's? If you get angry at what the person has said or done, if you overreact when they don't follow through on what they said, if you overreact to a verbal attack, that's self-defeating and self-destructive.

The first task of a negotiator is to bring down the emotions. We use a diagram in training that looks like a child's teeter-totter. On one side you have "emotions," and on the other side you have "rational thinking." When emotions go up, rational thinking goes down.

Let's say a guy has been fired from a job and he goes back with a gun and holds his employer at gunpoint. He's angry, he feels unappreciated, misunderstood, mistreated, and he may actually have a valid point in some respect.

So he holds a gun to his former employer and threatens to kill him. Now, a negotiator can show up and say, "You know, killing your boss is not going to get you your job back." And most assuredly it won't. But the guy's not thinking clearly right now. He's acting on emotions. Before we can get him to appreciate the logic of that argument, we've got to work through the emotional part of it.

Rather than just say, "We can talk about all this later, put your gun down," you say, "Tell me what happened. I can see you're upset." You're not agreeing with him, you're just saying: I understand how you feel.

Only when the hostage-taker feels heard and understood can you begin to establish a relationship of trust. Then you can start to talk him out of violence. You can say, "You sound like a good man that's been through a bad situation and things have not gone the way you wanted them to. But do you really think becoming violent is going to solve the problem? What impact will that have on your family?"

That's why I titled my book *Stalling for Time*. It takes time to lower those emotions and create that relationship.

There's a common misperception in law enforcement that everyone we face has this carefully drawn out agenda and they know exactly how they want a situation to end. But my experience has been quite the opposite: In all but rare cases, the individuals are acting moment-to-moment. They got into a situation based on an emotional outburst, and they simply don't know how to get out of it.

Domestic violence situations are the most likely to have a violent outcome. The men — usually it's men — are desperate and they're in emotional turmoil. She's left him, she's taken the kids, and she's never coming back. Some individuals get to the point where they say, "Well, there's nothing left to lose, I'm going to jail if I surrender, and I'll never get my kids back now, so I might as well kill everybody and be done with it."

Certainly, the presence of guns can hinder a negotiator's ability — you have to negotiate from a distance. So much of communication is based not only on verbal interpretation, but on body language. So if some guy's holding a gun, the negotiator, as a matter of policy and good common sense, is not going to expose himself or herself to being shot.

Guns raise the whole potential for serious injury or death. You have to be infinitely more cautious. In some cases, you might have to start off using the bullhorn, which isn't very conducive to demonstrating a calm, empathic voice. Or you may have to speak from behind a barricade position in which you have a SWAT guy sitting there protecting you in his heavy armament. All these things can be impediments to relationship-building.

In these cases, we try to conduct negotiations over the phone. We have a somewhat humorous saying: "No negotiator's ever been killed over the phone." That's the kind of approach we like: We like it to be safer and less stressful for both the guy we're talking with and ourselves.

As a police officer, you want to convey the right message: We're not here to make your life worse, but to help you and to get this resolved. Nothing guarantees success all the time, but if you do achieve success, it's likely going to be through that approach.

I always told people that Waco wasn't so much that we didn't know what to do, it was that we, as an organization, had departed from what we had been doing successfully for quite some time: patience and perseverance.

Obviously Waco began in a very horrific shootout between the ATF and the Branch Davidians. There had been loss of life. Those are hard situations to bring back to a non-emotional level.

But I feel as though the first half of the incident, when we secured the safe release of all 35 people who came out, was a significant success.

The key was listening to the Davidians, acknowledging their point of view without agreeing with it, giving them the opportunity to say what was important to them, and treating them with civility. And if left intact, that strategy probably stood a chance of saving many more lives.

After I was replaced at Waco, I flew overseas. The day after I returned, I went into FBI headquarters, and sat in a room similar to what you'd envision with NASA—with cameras and all the top FBI leadership. Then I saw the tear gas go, and saw the fire start.

I don't know that words can adequately describe my frustration and my anger—anger particularly directed at David Koresh for being so willing to throw his followers' lives away. But I was also angry at the FBI for not having stuck with the strategy that we had been successful with when I was still there. It was probably the worst day of my career, and then I had to jump on a plane and fly to Ohio for a prison riot.

We're not here to make your life worse, but to help you and to get this resolved.

I was depressed for a long time after Waco. I wouldn't categorize it as clinical depression where you can't function, but certainly I was down in the dumps.

I'm often asked how to use negotiation skills in daily life. Ultimately, listening is the most powerful tool we have in terms of social influence. Listening is not a passive endeavor. It's asking follow-up questions, it's asking open-ended questions, it's paraphrasing what the person has just told you to demonstrate that you're hearing what they have to say.

It's so important to get away from "zero sum"—whether it's in law enforcement, foreign policy, or certainly our current dysfunctional political state. Your gain is not my loss and vice versa. People need to find a way to compromise when it's possible. And in almost all cases, it is.

THINKING CRITICALLY ABOUT THE READING

1. What simile does Noesner use to describe the relationship between "emotions" and "rational thinking" (2)? How are these two concepts related, according to him?

2. What types of language does Noesner use to address the "emotional part" (4) and calm hostage-takers down? Why does he take that approach?

3. Why does Noesner title his book *Stalling for Time*? What does *stalling* mean? In what way is language central to "stalling" for Noesner?

4. Why does Noesner emphasize "listening" as "the most powerful tool we have in terms of social influence" (21)?

5. In the essay's concluding paragraph, Noesner writes "it's so important to get away from 'zero sum.'" What does the phrase *zero sum* mean in this context?

LANGUAGE IN ACTION

Discuss as a team with one or two classmates how you might negotiate in each of the following scenarios, including specific language that you might use. Then discuss your approach and the reasoning for your language choices with the class.

- An hourly raise at work
- An extension for a homework assignment
- Increased financial aid from your college or university
- A lower price for a car you are preparing to buy

WRITING SUGGESTIONS

1. Noesner has extensive professional experience in high-stakes conflict resolution situations. Do you think that the guidelines he offers are relevant and applicable in the context of the *lower-stakes* personal conflicts that we all experience in our day-to-day lives? Why or why not? Write a brief essay in which you address this question. Be sure to mention specific pieces of advice from Noesner's essay as you explain why, in your view, his advice is or is not helpful to lower-stakes situations. You may also want to support your argument with examples of conflicts from your own life.

2. Most of us have experienced conflicts in personal relationships that we wish we could have avoided or handled better. Recall a memorable conflict in your own life—for example, with a sibling or roommate—and write a brief reflective essay in which you analyze the approach that you took and identify what you did well and what you could have improved. How could you have negotiated the conflict more effectively? In your essay, try to include at least one suggestion from Noesner's article and explain how you could have applied his advice to your own conflict.

Letting Go

Amy Westervelt

Amy Westervelt is a freelance journalist who lives in California with her husband, son, cat, and dog. Westervelt graduated from the University of California, Berkeley, in 2000 and has been involved in regional environmental writing in California. Her research into the prospects and challenges of biofuels, "Algae Arms Race," won a 2007 Folio Award, and in 2015 she won a Rachel Carson Award from the Audubon Society, celebrating "women greening journalism." She is also the co-founder of the Boxwood Bureau, a crowd-funded collective of journalists with a focus on environmental protection. Westervelt is the author of *The Pitch Bitch's Guide to How the Media Works* (2015) and *Forget "Having It All": How America Messed Up Motherhood—and How to Fix It* (2018).

As a contributor to *The Wall Street Journal*, *The Guardian*, *Forbes*, *Slate*, and *Aeon*, where this essay first appeared on January 5, 2015, she has primarily written about technology, the environment, and health issues. The essay included here considers the effect of forgiveness on physical and mental health though a compelling personal narrative about the death of a friend.

WRITING TO DISCOVER: *What, if anything, have you been taught about forgiveness? Where did you learn about forgiveness, and what kind of importance does it hold for you? How have you seen forgiveness portrayed in songs, stories, and films?*

In the cleanest college library I've ever seen, women of various ages and ethnicities were seated around a long wooden table. A few were chatting, but most were nervously shuffling notebooks and pens or staring at the floor. The men—there were five, ranging in age from early 20s to mid-50s—showed up just before class began. I tried to divine, one by one, what horrible tragedy had brought them all there.

This was the Tuesday night forgiveness course at Stanford University. I was there strictly to observe. Formalized forgiveness training—complete with a reading list, lectures, practice sessions, and homework—was for people who had survived genocide, not for me with my garden-variety baggage (even if I had read everything I could about forgiveness training, developing a not-unhealthy obsession with the topic). Professor Frederic Luskin told me I could sit in on his class, but would have to participate so it wouldn't seem weird. No problem. I prepared an almost-true story about a fight with my mother.

Then, his large eyes flashing and greying hair standing on end, Luskin held his hands out in front of him like a zombie, palms down and spaced about a foot apart. "Most of our disappointment in life stems from wanting this," he jabbed at the air with his left hand, the higher of the two, for emphasis, "and getting this," he said, jiggling the lowered right hand. Then he stared at all of us, intently. "OK? And forgiveness is about what you decide to do with this space in the middle. Are you going to adjust what you expect and let the rest go, or are you going to live in this space? Because I'll tell you what, living in there is miserable."

Shit. Now all I could think about was living in that terrible, empty space between his two giant hands. How I'd been stuck there for years, waiting for things to change and then being angry and disappointed when nothing happened.

When we got paired off to share our stories, my fake mom story was running through my head on rapid repeat, but my mouth rebelled, blurting out to the nice man on my left: "My best friend died and now I hate everyone for not being her and I really need to let it go. And actually this is really weird because Leah died here. Not right here in this library, but over there at the university hospital. This is the first time I've been back since."

It was a moment I'd read about—this sudden shift when the need to forgive outweighs the drive for revenge. I felt weightless, nauseous, sad, the prospect of letting go of all those years of anger finally opening up a space for grief. It is this rare freedom for the soul that has made forgiveness a cornerstone of all major world religions for hundreds of years as well as an increasingly popular subject in modern psychology—both the traditional and pop varieties. But while its benefits have been proved, forgiveness remains a thorny subject, bound up in ideas about everything from doctrinal religion to justice.

My research began when I stumbled across a story about Robert Enright, a psychologist at the University of Wisconsin. Enright was raised Catholic, but abandoned religion for academia early in his career. "I became a professor and thought I knew who God was—it was me," he said.

By the time he returned to his faith, Enright had established himself as "the father of forgiveness," creating a therapeutic protocol for how to practice it that was officially sanctioned by the American Psychology Association and the United Nations. He thought the Catholic Church could be doing more to emphasize its deep history in the subject, and spreading the gospel of forgiveness to the masses, and said so in a speech at the Vatican.

As a lapsed Catholic myself, Enright's story resonated with me. Forced to attend church and Catholic school in my youth, I'd rebelled in my teens and twenties, not because I didn't believe in God but because I didn't like the self-righteous way in which most of the religious people I knew behaved. I didn't really miss religion, apart from those moments at the end of Mass where Holy Communion absolved me of my sins and I'd be given a few moments of silence to pray in gratitude. I'd looked forward to those moments—and the peace they brought me—every week.

Few other experiences delivered a similar relief from daily worries, and when I read about Enright and his work I wondered if forgiveness might be the thing.

Each of the Abrahamic faiths—Islam, Judaism, Christianity—include   10
teachings on forgiveness, both the sort that God doles out and the sort that human beings can (and should) bestow on each other. The Torah, the Bible, and the Qur'an are all filled with dictates about forgiveness, and rules about what God can and cannot, or will not, forgive. The non-Abrahamic faiths, meanwhile, have a wellness-focused approach to forgiveness that's not so different from modern, secular treatments of the subject in the context of the positive psychology movement. Buddhism, for example, teaches that people who hold on to the wrongs done to them create an identity around that pain, and it is that identity that continues to be reborn.

But what about the nuts and bolts of forgiveness, about which all the Catholic rituals around penance and confession had taught me nothing? I knew exactly how to ask God for forgiveness, but I had no idea how to forgive, or ask forgiveness from the people in my life. This turns out to be an important distinction: University of Michigan researchers have found that forgiveness between people tends to have more reliably positive physical benefits than any perceived forgiveness from God.

Forgiveness is a relatively new academic research area, studied in earnest only since Enright began publishing on the subject in the 1980s. The first batch of studies were medical in focus. Forgiveness was widely correlated with a range of physical benefits, including better sleep, lower blood pressure, lower risk of heart disease, even increased life expectancy; really, every benefit you'd expect from reduced stress. The late Kathleen Lawler, while working as a researcher in the psychology department at the University of Tennessee in Knoxville, studied the effects of both hostility and forgiveness on the body's systems fairly extensively. "Forgiveness is aptly described as 'a change of heart,'" she wrote, in summarizing a series of studies focused on the impact of forgiveness on heart health. Meanwhile, Duke University researchers found a strong correlation between improved immune system function and forgiveness in HIV-positive patients, and between forgiveness and improved mortality rates across the general population.

More recently, the subject has surged in popularity as everyone from the United Nations to the victims of mass shootings espouses the virtues of forgiveness for everything from mental health to managing war zones. Even Oprah Winfrey has gotten in on the forgiveness game: her favorite life coach, Iyanla Vanzant, frequently spotlighted the subject in her Oprah Winfrey Network show *Iyanla: Fix My Life*, and launched an e-learning class entitled "How to Forgive Everyone for Everything."

In her book, *Forgiveness: 21 Days to Forgive Everyone for Everything*, Vanzant lays out a 21-day program to set readers on the path to forgiveness.

Perhaps unsurprisingly (Winfrey is the queen of self-improvement, after all), the book is focused largely on self-forgiveness. Vanzant is also a proponent of Progressive Energy Field Tapping (Pro EFT)—tapping specific energy points just under the surface of the skin, "releasing emotions trapped in our energy system," according to the official Pro EFT Web site. It's a bit New Age-y for my taste, but hey, it's a process and a lot of people are saying it works.

It's not just Oprah who's promoting the self-improvement side of forgiveness. The rise of popular interest in forgiveness has coincided with a second wave of academic studies, focused on self-forgiveness. After investigating the relationship between forgiveness and health, Jon R. Webb at East Tennessee State University found that "it may be that forgiveness of self is relatively more important to health-related outcomes" than other forms of forgiveness. Sara Pelucchi, at the Catholic University in Milan, claims that it is beneficial to romantic relationships, and Thomas Carpenter at Baylor University found that we have an easier time forgiving ourselves if those we have hurt forgive us first.

> **Feel the feelings you need to feel, express them, then leave them in the past where they can no longer have power over you.**

Enright has also examined self-forgiveness, although he's more measured about it than Vanzant. "The issue of self-forgiveness is much more complicated than forgiveness in general and here's why: when you offend yourself, you are both the victim and the perpetrator," he told me. "The problem is compounded by the fact that we rarely offend ourselves in isolation from offending others."

Enright recommends that people struggling with self-forgiveness learn to forgive others first, before offering that same compassion to themselves. "Otherwise it can be tricky: If you're a compulsive gambler and keep squandering the family's money, for example, you could forgive yourself and keep doing it, but true self-forgiveness requires stopping the behavior that led to the offense in first place."

It's the "learn to forgive" part that's key to making forgiveness stick. According to Luskin, religion might help to motivate or oblige people to forgive, but it's the secular realm that is bringing the idea of forgiveness to the masses. It's also teaching us precisely how to do it.

While researchers have spent the past 20 years proving the physical and mental benefits of forgiveness, it's the step-by-step forgiveness guides they've developed that might turn out to be academia's most important contribution to the subject. Like Vanzant's pop-psych version, the protocols that Enright and Luskin have developed offer specific steps towards forgiveness rooted in decades of research and clinical experience. While the various approaches differ, all include practical guidance and the basics are consistent: feel the feelings you need to feel, express them, then leave them in the past where they can no longer have power over you.

When I first met my friend Leah, it was all off-color jokes and dares.   20
Then she invited me to her ex-boyfriend's funeral and things got real.
I met her mother, who was sweet and funny and cooked us dinner in an
apron, but also smoked around Leah even though it was likely to trigger an asthma attack. Her father, a retired physician, and the sort of stiff
grown-up that people like me (and Leah) loved to get a rise out of, patted
Leah's shoulder and tousled her hair as we got into the car to leave.

Later Leah said that was the most affection he had ever shown her in
public. Then she told me how, when she was about five, her father had
killed her cat because it was annoying him, and had buried it in the carrot
patch. Telling her to go find it there, he had then laughed gleefully when
the horrified child uncovered her dead pet. We traded unpleasant stories
the whole ride home, and after that our friendship was sealed.

Shortly after that outing, I barged into her apartment and found her
on her living-room floor wheezing in and out of a massive steroid inhaler.
She explained that she had cystic fibrosis and that her brother had died
from it, but that she, the beneficiary of various trial drugs, would most
likely be OK.

A couple years later, after we graduated from college, I got Leah a
job at the magazine where I worked. When I had to fire her because she
showed up late every day and spent hours hanging out under my desk,
sipping lattes, I didn't make up excuses or lie. I just called her at the
end of the day and, before she could even say "Hello?" I yelled: "You're
fired!"

She erupted in laughter.

"No, but seriously, you're fired. I mean, come on, I don't think   25
you've made it to the office on time once. Plus you spend most of that
time under my desk. AND you really blew that call the other day."

Our boss had asked her to make some advertising sales calls. Leah's
technique had been to play it cool and say: "I know the last thing you
want to do is advertise, especially in this lousy magazine." She thought
they'd find it refreshing and humorous, but our boss, overhearing her,
did not appreciate her creativity.

"Ach. Yeah, OK, I get it. I'm sorry — did I get you into trouble?"

"No, but I think having me fire you is some sort of test."

"Well, tell that egg-shaped douche you passed."

In my first conversation with Enright, he explained that he'd started   30
researching forgiveness in 1985, "when no one in the social sciences would
even touch the topic. It was either totally off their radar or just too scary
because it is really rooted in the monotheistic traditions. I thought that
was folly. Forgiveness might be important to the human condition and
scientists have the obligation to go where the ideas lead, no matter what."

That conversation led to other scholars who had waded into forgiveness research, Luskin among them. Like Enright, Luskin had worked with
civil war survivors (in Sierra Leone), various factions within Northern

Ireland, and death row inmates in the United States. When I found him, Luskin had been running forgiveness classes at Stanford for about a decade, and had moved away from what he called the "big, dramatic" forms of forgiveness, to which youth and media attention had drawn him early in his career.

"Even the stuff that forgiveness was supposed to be good for—stuff like murders . . . it's so rare," he told me. "More important is can you forgive your brother-in-law for being annoying? Can you forgive traffic? Those things happen every day. Big things? They happen once in a life-time, maybe twice. It's a waste of forgiveness. That's my perspective. But forgiveness is really important for smoothing over the normal, interpersonal things that rub everyone the wrong way."

Part of what makes the word—and practice—tough for people, in Luskin's view, is that it requires a degree of selflessness. "For me to say, 'Even though you were a shithead, it's not my problem; it's your problem, and I'm not going to stay mad at you, because that's you, not me,' that's a huge renunciation of self," he said. "And I don't know whether it's our [Western] culture or a human thing, but it's hard."

Plus it requires acknowledgement of our fundamental human vulnerability, without getting angry or bitter about it. "A lot of times people start with this idea that 'I shouldn't have been harmed,'" Luskin said. "Why not? We live on a planet where harm happens all the time, where children are murdered and horrible things happen; to think that you should escape that is a mammoth overstatement of your own importance and a lack of sensitivity to everyone else on the planet."

But even for those who might find themselves nodding along with   35 Luskin's sentiments, walking the walk is another story. What all of the researchers and pop-psych proponents of forgiveness agree on is that it takes practice and that it is hard work. Vanzant compares it to pulling out a tooth without Novocaine. Luskin described it as re-training the brain. "You can get upset about anything—you can also get un-upset about anything, it's just a matter of learning how," he said.

In the eight years since Leah died, I've married, had a child and made new friends, yet I still miss her desperately. If I had a bad experience at work, Leah thought I should quit. Screw them. If I argued with a boy-friend, he was an asshole. Period. Even when everyone, including me, knew I was the asshole. It was the kind of backup she craved, too, which is why it's been so hard to shake the feeling that ultimately I failed her.

Toward the end of her life, Leah's doctors said the only way she'd be able to continue living was on a ventilator. Knowing she wouldn't want to live that way, her parents decided to take her off life support. I agreed with their choice, difficult as it would be to lose her. When I went to be with her on that last night, she was alone. Her parents couldn't bear to see Leah suffer the same slow, painful death they'd watched their son endure. I couldn't imagine doing otherwise.

When the nurse took Leah off the machines, she panicked, opened her eyes wide, clenched my hand and mouthed, "Help me." Several hours later, when the nurse came to check on her, she reported with surprise that Leah's blood oxygenation levels were normal. When I asked what that meant, she said, "Well, it means she didn't really need to be on that ventilator." At that point, I asked if we shouldn't reconsider things, but the nurse was quick to squash that idea. "I've probably just had her on too much oxygen," she said. "I'll turn it down."

It is the biggest regret of my life that I didn't make a huge fuss in that moment, and demand to see the doctor. That I did not call Leah's parents and beg them to reconsider. That I did not wait until the nurse left the room, then jack the oxygen back up. That I did precisely nothing but hold my friend's hand while she died.

In the weeks following Luskin's forgiveness seminar, it all clicked. 40 I'd been waiting for a magical moment in which I would forgive myself for failing Leah—and the rest of the world for being around when she wasn't. That moment never came and in the meantime, I had justified a lot of my own bad behavior.

After reading everything from religious scripture to academic studies, I finally realized that's not at all how forgiveness works, and that's what makes it so damn hard. Time does not heal all wounds. This too shall not pass. Letting go of hurt and anger is a grind, and forgiveness only works if you practice it regularly, and are prepared to fail often without giving up. But the pay-off is so huge it just might be worth it.

THINKING CRITICALLY ABOUT THE READING

1. How does Westervelt describe the space, atmosphere, and participants of the forgiveness workshop? How does she describe Professor Luskin? What effect do his words have on her? Why might she begin the story this way?

2. Although the essay links forgiveness with religion, "University of Michigan researchers have found that forgiveness between people tends to have more reliably positive physical benefits than any perceived forgiveness from God" (11). What are the health benefits of forgiveness? What do you make of the idea that forgiveness from others trumps forgiveness from a higher power? Why might that be true?

3. Why does forgiveness require "a degree of selflessness" (33)? Why might this requirement pose problems in our culture?

4. What metaphors have forgiveness researchers used to describe the act of learning to forgive? Why is it important to see forgiveness as a quality we can learn? Do you think we can get better at forgiving?

5. Westervelt discusses her friend Leah and Leah's death in the essay. How does Westervelt link this story to forgiveness? What is the purpose of including a personal story? What kind of language does it allow into the essay, and how does that language affect the reader?

6. In the conclusion of her essay, Westervelt contradicts well-known adages that many accept as truth. She writes: "time does not heal all wounds" and "this too shall not pass." What do these adages mean? How do they overlook the role of forgiveness? How might they keep us from the work of forgiveness?

LANGUAGE IN ACTION

In line with Westervelt's discovery that forgiveness can have positive impacts on health, the Mayo Clinic website — a significant resource for health information maintained by one of the leading research hospitals in the world — includes an article (excerpted below) on the benefits of forgiveness.

FORGIVENESS: LETTING GO OF GRUDGES AND BITTERNESS

When someone you care about hurts you, you can hold on to anger, resentment and thoughts of revenge — or embrace forgiveness and move forward.

BY MAYO CLINIC STAFF

Nearly everyone has been hurt by the actions or words of another. Perhaps your mother criticized your parenting skills, your colleague sabotaged a project or your partner had an affair. These wounds can leave you with lasting feelings of anger, bitterness or even vengeance.

But if you don't practice forgiveness, you might be the one who pays most dearly. By embracing forgiveness, you can also embrace peace, hope, gratitude and joy. Consider how forgiveness can lead you down the path of physical, emotional and spiritual well-being.

What Is Forgiveness?

Generally, forgiveness is a decision to let go of resentment and thoughts of revenge. The act that hurt or offended you might always remain a part of your life, but forgiveness can lessen its grip on you and help you focus on other, more positive parts of your life. Forgiveness can even lead to feelings of understanding, empathy, and compassion for the one who hurt you.

Forgiveness doesn't mean that you deny the other person's responsibility for hurting you, and it doesn't minimize or justify the wrong. You can forgive the person without excusing the act. Forgiveness brings a kind of peace that helps you go on with life.

What Are the Benefits of Forgiving Someone?

Letting go of grudges and bitterness can make way for happiness, health and peace. Forgiveness can lead to:

- Healthier relationships
- Greater spiritual and psychological well-being

- Less anxiety, stress and hostility
- Lower blood pressure
- Fewer symptoms of depression
- Stronger immune system
- Improved heart health
- Higher self-esteem

What does it mean when a hospital website includes information on how and why we ought to forgive? As a society, we generally accept the idea that there is a connection between our emotional and physical health, but do we use that knowledge well? How might an article like this one — or like Westervelt's — make it easier to incorporate that understanding into our lives? In what other places have you seen a similar message?

WRITING SUGGESTIONS

1. We are taught to think of forgiveness as a kind thing to do for someone else, but it also has some benefits for the forgiver. In her essay, Westervelt cites some real physical benefits: "Forgiveness was widely correlated with a range of physical benefits, including better sleep, lower blood pressure, lower risk of heart disease, even increased life expectancy; really, every benefit you'd expect from reduced stress" (12). How do these findings affect our idea of forgiveness? What do you see as the relationship between forgiveness (or lack of it) and stress? Is it more selfish to forgive or to withhold forgiveness? Who suffers, in each case? Write an essay in which you analyze a situation in which you were able to give or felt compelled to withhold forgiveness. What effects did that decision have on you? On the person you did or did not forgive? How did you handle subsequent situations as a result?

2. In addition to briefly addressing religious traditions and teachings about forgiveness, Westervelt discusses a few popular, secular paths to forgiveness: "While the various approaches differ, all include practical guidance and the basics are consistent: feel the feelings you need to feel, express them, then leave them in the past where they can no longer have power over you" (19). Write a process analysis in which you lay out the steps of offering someone forgiveness in a specific situation (say, forgiving a cheating partner or a thieving roommate). Expand on Westervelt's overview here to offer specific and practical advice on the situation you've chosen. What considerations might you add to Westervelt's list of steps?

14

ARGUING ABOUT LANGUAGE: TWO CONTEMPORARY DEBATES

This chapter presents two casebooks, each containing three readings about an aspect of language that has generated heated debate in recent years. In each casebook, the readings and the accompanying questions and activities are designed to first give you a range of perspectives and opinions on each topic, and then to challenge you to take a position of your own.

THE CAMPUS FREE SPEECH CONTROVERSY

Over the last several decades, college campuses across the United States have become a flashpoint in a cultural controversy over the First Amendment right to free speech. Many campuses have enacted policies that allow for "safe spaces," places where students can engage in debate but are not allowed to personally attack each other or to make overtly provocative or offensive comments. Furthermore, some instructors have taken to including "trigger warnings" in syllabi and at the beginning of lectures, warning students about potentially offensive content and, in some cases, offering students the option not to read, watch, or participate in discussion about such content. At the same time, student protests of controversial speakers on campus—especially conservative speakers like Ann Coulter and Milo Yiannopoulos—have garnered significant media attention. Taken together, all of these developments raise the question of whether college campuses have become overly restrictive and, potentially, whether these campus practices constitute a threat to freedom in speech in academic discourse.

Critics argue that policies like safe spaces and trigger warnings damage the quality of the academic conversation by setting certain topics as "off limits" and shielding students from uncomfortable issues. Some critics, moreover, claim that such policies dangerously undermine students' right to free speech by setting unreasonable limits on what they are and are not allowed to say. Meanwhile, on the other side of the debate, defenders of these campus practices argue that safe spaces, trigger warnings, and similar practices actually strengthen academic discourse by providing students with spaces where they can comfortably express their opinions without being unfairly attacked on the basis on their gender, race, ethnicity, religion, or sexual orientation.

In this casebook, you will read three different perspectives to help you decide where you stand in the debate. First, in "The Coddling of the American Mind," Greg Lukianoff and Jonathan Haidt claim that safe spaces and related policies constitute an attack on freedom of speech and also negatively impact students' intellectual development. They claim that these policies fail to prepare students for the wide range of opinions that they will encounter in the real world after they graduate and that, moreover, this "coddling" will have long-term consequences for American society as a whole. Next, John Palfrey takes an opposing position in "Safe Spaces, Brave Spaces," arguing that certain restrictions on speech are acceptable—and, indeed, necessary—to ensure that students of all backgrounds feel welcome on campus. In his view, certain types of speech, particularly hate speech, should be discouraged and sometimes actively suppressed in order to maintain a healthy academic discourse. Finally, in "What Campuses Can and Can't Do," Erwin Chemerinsky and Howard Gillman take a nuanced approach that attempts to reconcile the need to protect students' First Amendment rights with the need to foster "an inclusive environment" in which all students feel comfortable joining the conversation.

The Coddling of the American Mind

Greg Lukianoff and Jonathan Haidt

Greg Lukianoff received his JD from Stanford Law School and was a practicing lawyer in California before he joined the Foundation for Individual Rights in Education (FIRE), a nonprofit organization that focuses on issues surrounding freedom of speech and other civil liberties on college campuses. He is now the president and CEO of FIRE. Lukianoff's work has been published extensively, including in *The Wall Street Journal, The New York Times, Time*, and *Forbes*. He was also an executive producer of *Can We Take a Joke?* (2015), a feature-length documentary that explores the collision between comedy, censorship, and "outrage culture," both on and off college campuses. Given the scope of his work, Lukianoff is frequently a guest on a variety of news programs, including C-SPAN's *Washington Journal* and NBC's *Today Show*.

Jonathan Haidt received his PhD in psychology from the University of Pennsylvania and has taught at the University of Virginia and New York University. He has written a number of books exploring the nature of intellectual discourse, including *The Happiness Hypothesis: Finding Modern Truth in Ancient Wisdom* (2006) and *The Righteous Mind: Why Good People Are Divided by Politics and Religion* (2012). Haidt is currently the Thomas Cooley Professor of Ethical Leadership at NYU's Stern School of Business.

The selection included here is from an article co-written by Lukianoff and Haidt that originally appeared in *The Atlantic* in September 2015. Here the authors explain the dangers they see in language that coddles university students. According to the authors, while such language might help protect the emotional well-being of students on college campuses, it is also directly correlated with a decline in students' freedom of speech, which they view as essential to education.

WRITING TO DISCOVER: *Have you ever felt that your right to free speech was curtailed on campus, either directly (i.e., you were asked to stop) or indirectly (i.e., you didn't feel that your viewpoint was welcome)? If so, describe the circumstances. Have you ever witnessed the free speech of others restricted? Explain.*

Something strange is happening at America's colleges and universities. A movement is arising, undirected and driven largely by students, to scrub campuses clean of words, ideas, and subjects that might cause discomfort or give offense. Last December, Jeannie Suk wrote in an online article for *The New Yorker* about law students asking her fellow professors at Harvard not to teach rape law—or, in one case, even use the word *violate* (as in "that violates the law") lest it cause students distress. In February,

Laura Kipnis, a professor at Northwestern University, wrote an essay in *The Chronicle of Higher Education* describing a new campus politics of sexual paranoia—and was then subjected to a long investigation after students who were offended by the article and by a tweet she'd sent filed Title IX complaints against her. In June, a professor protecting himself with a pseudonym wrote an essay for Vox describing how gingerly he now has to teach. "I'm a Liberal Professor, and My Liberal Students Terrify Me," the headline said. A number of popular comedians, including Chris Rock, have stopped performing on college campuses. Jerry Seinfeld and Bill Maher have publicly condemned the oversensitivity of college students, saying too many of them can't take a joke.

Two terms have risen quickly from obscurity into common campus parlance. *Microaggressions* are small actions or word choices that seem on their face to have no malicious intent but that are thought of as a kind of violence nonetheless. For example, by some campus guidelines, it is a microaggression to ask an Asian American or Latino American "Where were you born?," because this implies that he or she is not a real American. *Trigger warnings* are alerts that professors are expected to issue if something in a course might cause a strong emotional response. For example, some students have called for warnings that Chinua Achebe's *Things Fall Apart* describes racial violence and that F. Scott Fitzgerald's *The Great Gatsby* portrays misogyny and physical abuse, so that students who have been previously victimized by racism or domestic violence can choose to avoid these works, which they believe might "trigger" a recurrence of past trauma.

Some recent campus actions border on the surreal. In April, at Brandeis University, the Asian American student association sought to raise awareness of microaggressions against Asians through an installation on the steps of an academic hall. The installation gave examples of microaggressions such as "Aren't you supposed to be good at math?" and "I'm colorblind! I don't see race." But a backlash arose among other Asian American students, who felt that the display itself was a microaggression. The association removed the installation, and its president wrote an e-mail to the entire student body apologizing to anyone who was "triggered or hurt by the content of the microaggressions."

This new climate is slowly being institutionalized, and is affecting what can be said in the classroom, even as a basis for discussion. During the 2014–15 school year, for instance, the deans and department chairs at the 10 University of California system schools were presented by administrators at faculty leader-training sessions with examples of microaggressions. The list of offensive statements included: "America is the land of opportunity" and "I believe the most qualified person should get the job."

The press has typically described these developments as a resurgence   5 of political correctness. That's partly right, although there are important differences between what's happening now and what happened in the

1980s and '90s. That movement sought to restrict speech (specifically hate speech aimed at marginalized groups), but it also challenged the literary, philosophical, and historical canon, seeking to widen it by including more-diverse perspectives. The current movement is largely about emotional well-being. More than the last, it presumes an extraordinary fragility of the collegiate psyche, and therefore elevates the goal of protecting students from psychological harm. The ultimate aim, it seems, is to turn campuses into "safe spaces" where young adults are shielded from words and ideas that make some uncomfortable. And more than the last, this movement seeks to punish anyone who interferes with that aim, even accidentally. You might call this impulse *vindictive protectiveness*. It is creating a culture in which everyone must think twice before speaking up, lest they face charges of insensitivity, aggression, or worse.

We have been studying this development for a while now, with rising alarm. (Greg Lukianoff is a constitutional lawyer and the president and CEO of the Foundation for Individual Rights in Education, which defends free speech and academic freedom on campus, and has advocated for students and faculty involved in many of the incidents this article describes; Jonathan Haidt is a social psychologist who studies the American culture wars.) The dangers that these trends pose to scholarship and to the quality of American universities are significant; we could write a whole essay detailing them. But in this essay we focus on a different question: What are the effects of this new protectiveness *on the students themselves*? Does it benefit the people it is supposed to help? What exactly are students learning when they spend four years or more in a community that polices unintentional slights, places warning labels on works of classic literature, and in many other ways conveys the sense that words can be forms of violence that require strict control by campus authorities, who are expected to act as both protectors and prosecutors?

There's a saying common in education circles: Don't teach students *what* to think; teach them *how* to think. The idea goes back at least as far as Socrates. Today, what we call the Socratic method is a way of teaching that fosters critical thinking, in part by encouraging students to question their own unexamined beliefs, as well as the received wisdom of those around them. Such questioning sometimes leads to discomfort, and even to anger, on the way to understanding.

But vindictive protectiveness teaches students to think in a very different way. It prepares them poorly for professional life, which often demands intellectual engagement with people and ideas one might find uncongenial or wrong. The harm may be more immediate, too. A campus culture devoted to policing speech and punishing speakers is likely to engender patterns of thought that are surprisingly similar to those long identified by cognitive behavioral therapists as causes of depression and anxiety. The new protectiveness may be teaching students to think pathologically.

HOW DID WE GET HERE?

It's difficult to know exactly why vindictive protectiveness has burst forth so powerfully in the past few years. The phenomenon may be related to recent changes in the interpretation of federal antidiscrimination statutes (about which more later). But the answer probably involves generational shifts as well. Childhood itself has changed greatly during the past generation. Many Baby Boomers and Gen Xers can remember riding their bicycles around their hometowns, unchaperoned by adults, by the time they were 8 or 9 years old. In the hours after school, kids were expected to occupy themselves, getting into minor scrapes and learning from their experiences. But "free range" childhood became less common in the 1980s. The surge in crime from the '60s through the early '90s made Baby Boomer parents more protective than their own parents had been. Stories of abducted children appeared more frequently in the news, and in 1984, images of them began showing up on milk cartons. In response, many parents pulled in the reins and worked harder to keep their children safe.

The flight to safety also happened at school. Dangerous play structures were removed from playgrounds; peanut butter was banned from student lunches. After the 1999 Columbine massacre in Colorado, many schools cracked down on bullying, implementing "zero tolerance" policies. In a variety of ways, children born after 1980 — the Millennials — got a consistent message from adults: life is dangerous, but adults will do everything in their power to protect you from harm, not just from strangers but from one another as well.

These same children grew up in a culture that was (and still is) becoming more politically polarized. Republicans and Democrats have never particularly liked each other, but survey data going back to the 1970s show that on average, their mutual dislike used to be surprisingly mild. Negative feelings have grown steadily stronger, however, particularly since the early 2000s. Political scientists call this process "affective partisan polarization," and it is a very serious problem for any democracy. As each side increasingly demonizes the other, compromise becomes more difficult. A recent study shows that implicit or unconscious biases are now at least as strong across political parties as they are across races.

So it's not hard to imagine why students arriving on campus today might be more desirous of protection and more hostile toward ideological opponents than in generations past. This hostility, and the self-righteousness fueled by strong partisan emotions, can be expected to add force to any moral crusade. A principle of moral psychology is that "morality binds and blinds." Part of what we do when we make moral judgments is express allegiance to a team. But that can interfere with our ability to think critically. Acknowledging that the other side's viewpoint has any merit is risky — your teammates may see you as a traitor.

Social media makes it extraordinarily easy to join crusades, express solidarity and outrage, and shun traitors. Facebook was founded in 2004, and since 2006 it has allowed children as young as 13 to join. This means that the first wave of students who spent all their teen years using Facebook reached college in 2011, and graduated from college only this year.

These first true "social-media natives" may be different from members of previous generations in how they go about sharing their moral judgments and supporting one another in moral campaigns and conflicts. We find much to like about these trends; young people today are engaged with one another, with news stories, and with prosocial endeavors to a greater degree than when the dominant technology was television. But social media has also fundamentally shifted the balance of power in relationships between students and faculty; the latter increasingly fear what students might do to their reputations and careers by stirring up online mobs against them.

We do not mean to imply simple causation, but rates of mental illness in young adults have been rising, both on campus and off, in recent decades. Some portion of the increase is surely due to better diagnosis and greater willingness to seek help, but most experts seem to agree that some portion of the trend is real. Nearly all of the campus mental-health directors surveyed in 2013 by the American College Counseling Association reported that the number of students with severe psychological problems was rising at their schools. The rate of emotional distress reported by students themselves is also high, and rising. In a 2014 survey by the American College Health Association, 54 percent of college students surveyed said that they had "felt overwhelming anxiety" in the past 12 months, up from 49 percent in the same survey just five years earlier. Students seem to be reporting more emotional crises; many seem fragile, and this has surely changed the way university faculty and administrators interact with them. The question is whether some of those changes might be doing more harm than good.

THE THINKING CURE

For millennia, philosophers have understood that we don't see life as it is; we see a version distorted by our hopes, fears, and other attachments. The Buddha said, "Our life is the creation of our mind." Marcus Aurelius said, "Life itself is but what you deem it." The quest for wisdom in many traditions begins with this insight. Early Buddhists and the Stoics, for example, developed practices for reducing attachments, thinking more clearly, and finding release from the emotional torments of normal mental life.

Cognitive behavioral therapy is a modern embodiment of this ancient wisdom. It is the most extensively studied nonpharmaceutical treatment of mental illness, and is used widely to treat depression, anxiety disorders, eating disorders, and addiction. It can even be of help to schizophrenics. No other form of psychotherapy has been shown to work for a broader range of problems. Studies have generally found that it is as effective as antidepressant drugs (such as Prozac) in the treatment of anxiety and depression. The therapy is relatively quick and easy to learn; after a few months of training, many patients can do it on their own. Unlike drugs, cognitive behavioral therapy keeps working long after treatment is stopped, because it teaches thinking skills that people can continue to use.

The goal is to minimize distorted thinking and see the world more accurately. You start by learning the names of the dozen or so most common cognitive distortions (such as overgeneralizing, discounting positives, and emotional reasoning). Each time you notice yourself falling prey to one of them, you name it, describe the facts of the situation, consider alternative interpretations, and then choose an interpretation of events more in line with those facts. Your emotions follow your new interpretation. In time, this process becomes automatic. When people improve their mental hygiene in this way—when they free themselves from the repetitive irrational thoughts that had previously filled so much of their consciousness—they become less depressed, anxious, and angry.

The parallel to formal education is clear: cognitive behavioral therapy teaches good critical-thinking skills, the sort that educators have striven for so long to impart. By almost any definition, critical thinking requires grounding one's beliefs in evidence rather than in emotion or desire, and learning how to search for and evaluate evidence that might contradict one's initial hypothesis. But does campus life today foster critical thinking? Or does it coax students to think in more-distorted ways?

Let's look at recent trends in higher education in light of the distortions that cognitive behavioral therapy identifies. We will draw the names and descriptions of these distortions from David D. Burns's popular book *Feeling Good*, as well as from the second edition of *Treatment Plans and Interventions for Depression and Anxiety Disorders*, by Robert L. Leahy, Stephen J. F. Holland, and Lata K. McGinn.

HIGHER EDUCATION'S EMBRACE OF "EMOTIONAL REASONING"

Burns defines *emotional reasoning* as assuming "that your negative emotions necessarily reflect the way things really are: 'I feel it, therefore it must be true.'" Leahy, Holland, and McGinn define it as letting "your feelings guide your interpretation of reality." But, of course, subjective feelings are not always trustworthy guides; unrestrained, they can cause people to lash out at others who have done nothing wrong. Therapy often involves talking yourself down from the idea that each of your emotional responses represents something true or important.

Emotional reasoning dominates many campus debates and discussions. A claim that someone's words are "offensive" is not just an expression of one's own subjective feeling of offendedness. It is, rather, a public charge that the speaker has done something objectively wrong. It is a demand that the speaker apologize or be punished by some authority for committing an offense.

There have always been some people who believe they have a right not to be offended. Yet throughout American history—from the Victorian era to the free-speech activism of the 1960s and '70s—radicals have pushed boundaries and mocked prevailing sensibilities. Sometime in the 1980s, however, college campuses began to focus on preventing offensive speech, especially speech that might be hurtful to women or minority groups. The sentiment underpinning this goal was laudable, but it quickly produced some absurd results.

Among the most famous early examples was the so-called water-buffalo incident at the University of Pennsylvania. In 1993, the university charged an Israeli-born student with racial harassment after he yelled "Shut up, you water buffalo!" to a crowd of black sorority women that was making noise at night outside his dorm-room window. Many scholars and pundits at the time could not see how the term *water buffalo* (a rough translation of a Hebrew insult for a thoughtless or rowdy person) was a racial slur against African Americans, and as a result, the case became international news.

Claims of a right not to be offended have continued to arise since then, and universities have continued to privilege them. In a particularly egregious 2008 case, for instance, Indiana University–Purdue University at Indianapolis found a white student guilty of racial harassment for reading a book titled *Notre Dame vs. the Klan.* The book honored student opposition to the Ku Klux Klan when it marched on Notre Dame in 1924. Nonetheless, the picture of a Klan rally on the book's cover offended at least one of the student's co-workers (he was a janitor as well as a student), and that was enough for a guilty finding by the university's Affirmative Action Office.

These examples may seem extreme, but the reasoning behind them has become more commonplace on campus in recent years. Last year, at the University of St. Thomas, in Minnesota, an event called Hump Day, which would have allowed people to pet a camel, was abruptly canceled. Students had created a Facebook group where they protested the event for animal cruelty, for being a waste of money, and for being insensitive to people from the Middle East. The inspiration for the camel had almost certainly come from a popular TV commercial in which a camel saunters around an office on a Wednesday, celebrating "hump day"; it was devoid of any reference to Middle Eastern peoples. Nevertheless, the group organizing the event announced on its Facebook page that the event would be canceled because the "program [was] dividing people and would make for an uncomfortable and possibly unsafe environment."

Because there is a broad ban in academic circles on "blaming the victim," it is generally considered unacceptable to question the reasonableness (let alone the sincerity) of someone's emotional state, particularly if those emotions are linked to one's group identity. The thin argument "I'm offended" becomes an unbeatable trump card. This leads to what Jonathan Rauch, a contributing editor at this magazine, calls the "offendedness sweepstakes," in which opposing parties use claims of offense as cudgels. In the process, the bar for what we consider unacceptable speech is lowered further and further.

Since 2013, new pressure from the federal government has reinforced this trend. Federal antidiscrimination statutes regulate on-campus harassment and unequal treatment based on sex, race, religion, and national origin. Until recently, the Department of Education's Office for Civil Rights acknowledged that speech must be "objectively offensive" before it could be deemed actionable as sexual harassment—it would have to pass the "reasonable person" test. To be prohibited, the office wrote in 2003, allegedly harassing speech would have to go "beyond the mere expression of views, words, symbols or thoughts that some person finds offensive."

But in 2013, the Departments of Justice and Education greatly broadened the definition of sexual harassment to include verbal conduct that is simply "unwelcome." Out of fear of federal investigations, universities are now applying that standard—defining unwelcome speech as harassment—not just to sex, but to race, religion, and veteran status as well. Everyone is supposed to rely upon his or her own subjective feelings to decide whether a comment by a professor or a fellow student is unwelcome, and therefore grounds for a harassment claim. Emotional reasoning is now accepted as evidence.

If our universities are teaching students that their emotions can be used effectively as weapons—or at least as evidence in administrative proceedings—then they are teaching students to nurture a kind of hypersensitivity that will lead them into countless drawn-out conflicts in college and beyond. Schools may be training students in thinking styles that will damage their careers and friendships, along with their mental health.

FORTUNE-TELLING AND TRIGGER WARNINGS

Burns defines *fortune-telling* as "anticipat[ing] that things will turn out badly" and feeling "convinced that your prediction is an already-established fact." Leahy, Holland, and McGinn define it as "predict[ing] the future negatively" or seeing potential danger in an everyday situation. The recent spread of demands for trigger warnings on reading assignments with provocative content is an example of fortune-telling.

The idea that words (or smells or any sensory input) can trigger searing memories of past trauma — and intense fear that it may be repeated — has been around at least since World War I, when psychiatrists began treating soldiers for what is now called post-traumatic stress disorder. But explicit trigger warnings are believed to have originated much more recently, on message boards in the early days of the Internet. Trigger warnings became particularly prevalent in self-help and feminist forums, where they allowed readers who had suffered from traumatic events like sexual assault to avoid graphic content that might trigger flashbacks or panic attacks. Search-engine trends indicate that the phrase broke into mainstream use online around 2011, spiked in 2014, and reached an all-time high in 2015. The use of trigger warnings on campus appears to have followed a similar trajectory; seemingly overnight, students at universities across the country have begun demanding that their professors issue warnings before covering material that might evoke a negative emotional response.

In 2013, a task force composed of administrators, students, recent alumni, and one faculty member at Oberlin College, in Ohio, released an online resource guide for faculty (subsequently retracted in the face of faculty pushback) that included a list of topics warranting trigger warnings. These topics included classism and privilege, among many others. The task force recommended that materials that might trigger negative reactions among students be avoided altogether unless they "contribute directly" to course goals, and suggested that works that were "too important to avoid" be made optional.

It's hard to imagine how novels illustrating classism and privilege could provoke or reactivate the kind of terror that is typically implicated in PTSD. Rather, trigger warnings are sometimes demanded for a long list of ideas and attitudes that some students find politically offensive, in the name of preventing other students from being harmed. This is an example of what psychologists call "motivated reasoning" — we spontaneously generate arguments for conclusions we want to support. Once *you* find something hateful, it is easy to argue that exposure to the hateful thing could traumatize some *other* people. You believe that you know how others will react, and that their reaction could be devastating. Preventing that devastation becomes a moral obligation for the whole community. Books for which students have called publicly for trigger warnings within the past couple of years include Virginia Woolf's *Mrs. Dalloway* (at Rutgers, for "suicidal inclinations") and Ovid's *Metamorphoses* (at Columbia, for sexual assault).

Jeannie Suk's *New Yorker* essay described the difficulties of teaching rape law in the age of trigger warnings. Some students, she wrote, have pressured their professors to avoid teaching the subject in order to protect   35 themselves and their classmates from potential distress. Suk compares this to trying to teach "a medical student who is training to be a surgeon but who fears that he'll become distressed if he sees or handles blood."

However, there is a deeper problem with trigger warnings. According to the most-basic tenets of psychology, the very idea of helping people with anxiety disorders avoid the things they fear is misguided. A person who is trapped in an elevator during a power outage may panic and think she is going to die. That frightening experience can change neural connections in her amygdala, leading to an elevator phobia. If you want this woman to retain her fear for life, you should help her avoid elevators.

But if you want to help her return to normalcy, you should take your cues from Ivan Pavlov and guide her through a process known as exposure therapy. You might start by asking the woman to merely look at an elevator from a distance — standing in a building lobby, perhaps — until her apprehension begins to subside. If nothing bad happens while she's standing in the lobby — if the fear is not "reinforced" — then she will begin to learn a new association: elevators are not dangerous. (This reduction in fear during exposure is called habituation.) Then, on subsequent days, you might ask her to get closer, and on later days to push the call button, and eventually to step in and go up one floor. This is how the amygdala can get rewired again to associate a previously feared situation with safety or normalcy.

Students who call for trigger warnings may be correct that some of their peers are harboring memories of trauma that could be reactivated by course readings. But they are wrong to try to prevent such reactivations. Students with PTSD should of course get treatment, but they should not try to avoid normal life, with its many opportunities for habituation. Classroom discussions are safe places to be exposed to incidental reminders of trauma (such as the word *violate*). A discussion of violence is unlikely to be followed by actual violence, so it is a good way to help students change the associations that are causing them discomfort. And they'd better get their habituation done in college, because the world beyond college will be far less willing to accommodate requests for trigger warnings and opt-outs.

> **According to the most-basic tenets of psychology, the very idea of helping people with anxiety disorders avoid the things they fear is misguided.**

The expansive use of trigger warnings may also foster unhealthy mental habits in the vastly larger group of students who do not suffer from PTSD or other anxiety disorders. People acquire their fears not just from their own past experiences, but from social learning as well. If everyone around you acts as though something is dangerous — elevators, certain neighborhoods, novels depicting racism — then you are at risk of acquiring that fear too. The psychiatrist Sarah Roff pointed this out last year in an online article for *The Chronicle of Higher Education*. "One of my biggest concerns about trigger warnings," Roff wrote, "is that they will apply not just to those who have experienced trauma, but to all students, creating an atmosphere in which they are encouraged to believe that there is something dangerous or damaging about discussing difficult aspects of our history."

In an article published last year by *Inside Higher Ed*, seven humanities   40 professors wrote that the trigger-warning movement was "already having a chilling effect on [their] teaching and pedagogy." They reported their colleagues' receiving "phone calls from deans and other administrators investigating student complaints that they have included 'triggering' material in their courses, with or without warnings." A trigger warning, they wrote, "serves as a guarantee that students will not experience unexpected discomfort and implies that if they do, a contract has been broken." When students come to *expect* trigger warnings for any material that makes them uncomfortable, the easiest way for faculty to stay out of trouble is to avoid material that might upset the most sensitive student in the class.

MENTAL FILTERING AND DISINVITATION SEASON

As Burns defines it, *mental filtering* is "pick[ing] out a negative detail in any situation and dwell[ing] on it exclusively, thus perceiving that the whole situation is negative." Leahy, Holland, and McGinn refer to this as "negative filtering," which they define as "focus[ing] almost exclusively on the negatives and seldom notic[ing] the positives." When applied to campus life, mental filtering allows for simpleminded demonization.

Students and faculty members in large numbers modeled this cognitive distortion during 2014's "disinvitation season." That's the time of year—usually early spring—when commencement speakers are announced and when students and professors demand that some of those speakers be disinvited because of things they have said or done. According to data compiled by the Foundation for Individual Rights in Education, since 2000, at least 240 campaigns have been launched at U.S. universities to prevent public figures from appearing at campus events; most of them have occurred since 2009.

Consider two of the most prominent disinvitation targets of 2014: former U.S. Secretary of State Condoleezza Rice and the International Monetary Fund's managing director, Christine Lagarde. Rice was the first black female secretary of state; Lagarde was the first woman to become finance minister of a G8 country and the first female head of the IMF. Both speakers could have been seen as highly successful role models for female students, and Rice for minority students as well. But the critics, in effect, discounted any possibility of something positive coming from those speeches.

Members of an academic community should of course be free to raise questions about Rice's role in the Iraq War or to look skeptically at the IMF's policies. But should dislike of *part* of a person's record disqualify her altogether from sharing her perspectives?

If campus culture conveys the idea that visitors must be pure, with résumés that never offend generally left-leaning campus sensibilities, then higher education will have taken a further step toward intellectual homogeneity and the creation of an environment in which students rarely encounter diverse viewpoints. And universities will have reinforced the belief that it's okay to filter out the positive. If students graduate believing that they can learn nothing from people they dislike or from those with whom they disagree, we will have done them a great intellectual disservice.

WHAT CAN WE DO NOW?

Attempts to shield students from words, ideas, and people that might cause them emotional discomfort are bad for the students. They are bad for the workplace, which will be mired in unending litigation if student expectations of safety are carried forward. And they are bad for American democracy, which is already paralyzed by worsening partisanship. When the ideas, values, and speech of the other side are seen not just as wrong but as willfully aggressive toward innocent victims, it is hard to imagine the kind of mutual respect, negotiation, and compromise that are needed to make politics a positive-sum game.

Rather than trying to protect students from words and ideas that they will inevitably encounter, colleges should do all they can to equip students to thrive in a world full of words and ideas that they cannot control. One of the great truths taught by Buddhism (and Stoicism, Hinduism, and many other traditions) is that you can never achieve happiness by making the world conform to your desires. But you can master your desires and habits of thought. This, of course, is the goal of cognitive behavioral therapy. With this in mind, here are some steps that might help reverse the tide of bad thinking on campus.

The biggest single step in the right direction does not involve faculty or university administrators, but rather the federal government, which should release universities from their fear of unreasonable investigation and sanctions by the Department of Education. Congress should define peer-on-peer harassment according to the Supreme Court's definition in the 1999 case *Davis v. Monroe County Board of Education*. The *Davis* standard holds that a single comment or thoughtless remark by a student does not equal harassment; harassment requires a pattern of objectively offensive behavior by one student that interferes with another student's access to education. Establishing the *Davis* standard would help eliminate universities' impulse to police their students' speech so carefully.

Universities themselves should try to raise consciousness about the need to balance freedom of speech with the need to make all students feel welcome. Talking openly about such conflicting but important values is just the sort of challenging exercise that any diverse but tolerant community must learn to do. Restrictive speech codes should be abandoned.

Universities should also officially and strongly discourage trigger warnings. They should endorse the American Association of University Professors' report on these warnings, which notes, "The presumption that students need to be protected rather than challenged in a classroom is at once infantilizing and anti-intellectual." Professors should be free to use trigger warnings if they choose to do so, but by explicitly discouraging the practice, universities would help fortify the faculty against student requests for such warnings.

Finally, universities should rethink the skills and values they most want to impart to their incoming students. At present, many freshman-orientation programs try to raise student sensitivity to a nearly impossible level. Teaching students to avoid giving unintentional offense is a worthy goal, especially when the students come from many different cultural backgrounds. But students should also be taught how to live in a world full of potential offenses. Why not teach incoming students how to practice cognitive behavioral therapy? Given high and rising rates of mental illness, this simple step would be among the most humane and supportive things a university could do. The cost and time commitment could be kept low: a few group training sessions could be supplemented by Web sites or apps. But the outcome could pay dividends in many ways. For example, a shared vocabulary about reasoning, common distortions, and the appropriate use of evidence to draw conclusions would facilitate critical thinking and real debate. It would also tone down the perpetual state of outrage that seems to engulf some colleges these days, allowing students' minds to open more widely to new ideas and new people. A greater commitment to formal, public debate on campus—and to the assembly of a more politically diverse faculty—would further serve that goal.

Thomas Jefferson, upon founding the University of Virginia, said:

> This institution will be based on the illimitable freedom of the human mind. For here we are not afraid to follow truth wherever it may lead, nor to tolerate any error so long as reason is left free to combat it.

We believe that this is still—and will always be—the best attitude for American universities. Faculty, administrators, students, and the federal government all have a role to play in restoring universities to their historic mission.

THINKING CRITICALLY ABOUT THE READING

1. What do Lukianoff and Haidt mean by the term "coddling"?

2. What do the authors mean by the term "vindictive protectiveness"? How does this term relate to their broader concept of "coddling"?

3. What connection do the authors draw between shifts in speech on campus and an increase in rates of mental illness among adults? Why do they draw this connection, and why is it important to their overall argument?

4. What is "cognitive behavioral therapy" (47)? Why do the authors see this therapy as a remedy to present problems?

5. Explain the term "emotional reasoning" (21). What connection does this term have to the "water buffalo" case the authors describe in paragraph 24?

6. What changes do the authors recommend to resist "coddling" university students? What language do they wish to change or eliminate?

LANGUAGE IN ACTION

With a small group of your classmates, search YouTube for a clip of a controversial campus speaker who has been protested, such as Ann Coulter, Milo Yiannopoulos, or Ben Shapiro. Watch 5 to 10 minutes of one of these presentations and take notes on what the speaker says and how he or she says it. What is the speaker's major argument? Do you find his or her ideas objectionable? Why or why not? Would you welcome the speaker to *your* campus?

WRITING SUGGESTIONS

1. In the last section of their essay, titled "What Can We Do Now?", Lukianoff and Haidt offer several suggestions for ending or reducing the "coddling" that they perceive is occurring on college campuses. Do you agree with their suggestions? Do you think that the suggestions are helpful? Do you think that they are practical? Write a brief essay in which you answer these questions. Be sure to include specific language from Lukianoff and Haidt's essay to support your argument either for or against their proposed recommendations.

2. Lukianoff is the president and CEO of the Foundation for Individual Rights in Education (FIRE), an organization established to "defend and sustain the individual rights of students and faculty members at America's colleges and universities," according to its mission statement. FIRE's website keeps a record of all the cases in which it has been involved. Visit the "Cases" section of FIRE's website (https://www.thefire.org/category/cases/) and find a case that interests you related to free speech. Write a brief essay in which you analyze this particular case. What was FIRE's role in defending "individual rights" to free speech in this case? Do you agree with FIRE's involvement in this case and with the approach the organization took? Why or why not?

Safe Spaces, Brave Spaces

John Palfrey

John Palfrey, a graduate of Harvard University, the University of Cambridge, and Harvard Law School, is the Head of School at Phillips Academy, a private high school in Andover, Massachusetts. His research and teaching focus on new media and learning. He has written extensively on internet law, intellectual property, and the potential of technology to strengthen democracy in the United States and around the world. He is the author or co-author of eight books, including *Safe Spaces, Brave Spaces: Diversity and Free Expression in Education* (2017), from which the following selection is drawn.

In this selection, Palfrey challenges the misconception that diversity and free expression are inherently at odds. He suggests that students thrive in "safe spaces" and that such spaces actually strengthen academic discourse, because they allow students to engage in academic inquiry without feeling marginalized. He argues that free expression on campus is important but that campuses can reasonably restrict speech "more than the First Amendment would allow" in certain specific cases.

WRITING TO DISCOVER: *Have you encountered discussions of "safe spaces" on your campus? If so, what was the context and how did you respond?*

When might it be appropriate for a private school or university to restrict hate speech more than the First Amendment would allow? Recall, again, that the First Amendment allows for a degree of restriction of hate speech—that which falls under the "fighting words" doctrine or that which constitutes gender or racial harassment, for instance. Imagine, though, that the speech involved does not meet the strict requirements of today's Supreme Court doctrine when it comes to hate speech. When could the school or university reasonably intervene in the interest of protecting minorities, or any target of hate speech, in a campus environment?

Suppose, for example, that a group espousing hatred—say, the KKK or a neo-Nazi group—were to begin a march on the grounds of a private college or university campus in the middle of a school day. The same march in the town square two miles away would be frowned on by the locals but it would be hard, if not impossible, for the government to shut it down under the First Amendment. The famous case involving the neo-Nazi group that sought to demonstrate publicly in the town of Skokie, Illinois, established the First Amendment protection for such hateful expression.[1] Would a school administrator be within his or her rights to call campus security to force the marchers to leave the campus?

In my view, the answer is plainly yes, especially if the school had been clear up front about its values and policies, and established that its commitment to a diverse, equitable, and inclusive campus is on a par with its commitment to free expression. In this show of hate speech on the campus green, in front of the students who have freely assembled together in the school community, the neo-Nazi marchers would be acting in a manner inconsistent with the values of the school. The right to free expression of the marchers is not greater than the right of the campus community members to a learning environment free of this sort of hate. The balance points exactly the other way: the intrusion of this hateful speech exceeds the value of permitting this particular form of speech in the campus community.

This example demonstrates the extent to which there is a reasonable limit as to how and when a campus community must practice tolerance. While certain political speech — even obnoxious speech — must be permitted on campuses in order to pursue the truth and to allow free and open debate, there must be a limit to the degree of hatefulness of the speech that the community should allow.

The paradox of tolerance lies at the heart of this example. Must the   5
tolerant always tolerate the intolerant?

* * *

We teach more than just mathematics, science, writing and reading, languages, the arts, and other academic topics in our schools. We also teach character and moral development. Many schools do so explicitly, through the lessons that we choose; all schools do so implicitly, through the personal examples that faculty members, coaches, administrators, and staff set for our students. Whether parents like it or not, there is no way for teachers to avoid teaching character to some extent; after all, our students watch us as they learn.

At the core of this character development, we ought to teach tolerance. But tolerance can be an extremely tricky value to convey when it comes down to it. Never in recent memory has it been trickier than in the wake of the 2016 presidential election.

It is extremely easy to be a tolerant person when everyone around you is tolerant. It is easy to tolerate the tolerant. It is easy to teach the tolerant. If everyone in a learning community commits to this principle, things go well. Schools should aim for a community in which everyone commits to a deep, abiding sense of tolerance. That would make matters much more straightforward — in this respect, anyway.

The problem with tolerance is when it comes to the intolerant. To the extent that some people in society are intolerant of other people — and we know that to be true — there becomes, all of a sudden, a problem with tolerance. The tolerant are called on to tolerate the intolerant. Meanwhile, the intolerant, in turn, are not asked to tolerate anyone.

To some degree, in a democracy, we must tolerate intolerance; that   10
is part of the deal. We do not just give votes to the tolerant. It is also

true that we grow and learn when we tolerate the views of others with whom we disagree. As Lee Bollinger argued in *The Tolerant Society,* a community, and individuals, grow stronger through the extraordinary self-control of tolerating harmful speech.

But the idea of tolerance must also have its limits. The philosopher Karl Popper, writing in 1945, defined this "paradox of tolerance": "Unlimited tolerance must lead to the disappearance of tolerance. If we extend unlimited tolerance even to those who are intolerant, if we are not prepared to defend a tolerant society against the onslaught of the intolerant, then the tolerant will be destroyed, and tolerance with them." In this famous passage, Popper went a great deal further in exploring when intolerant political philosophies should be suppressed:

> In this formulation, I do not imply, for instance, that we should always suppress the utterance of intolerant philosophies; as long as we can counter them by rational argument and keep them in check by public opinion, suppression would certainly be unwise. But we should claim the right to suppress them if necessary even by force; for it may easily turn out that they are not prepared to meet us on the level of rational argument, but begin by denouncing all argument; they may forbid their followers to listen to rational argument, because it is deceptive, and teach them to answer arguments by the use of their fists or pistols. We should therefore claim, in the name of tolerance, the right not to tolerate the intolerant. We should claim that any movement preaching intolerance places itself outside the law, and we should consider incitement to intolerance and persecution as criminal, in the same way as we should consider incitement to murder, or to kidnapping, or to the revival of the slave trade, as criminal.[2]

Popper went too far in this powerful statement, but the essence of his point still rings true today. One need not extend the argument so far as he does — say, to the criminalization of incitement to intolerance (with which I do not agree) — to grasp the rationale for a degree of liberal intolerance. Writing these words in Europe at the end of World War II, Popper had good reason to wish there had been an earlier restriction of intolerance.

There is no reason why a private campus should be required to play host to a group that espouses racial or ethnic hatred that is counter to a core value of the institution. Even if that same speech would be permitted in the city square, an administration that allows it to disrupt an otherwise functional learning environment does more harm than good. It may be that a democracy will come to a point at which it can tolerate all forms of hateful speech in all its educational institutions, but I do not believe that we are at that point today. The disruptive psychological toll of the most extreme, hateful speech is too high a price for members of marginalized groups on campuses to be expected to pay — especially during this period of steady diversification and growing, but incomplete, equity and inclusion on campuses.

Though the law almost certainly says otherwise today, I believe that   15 even public colleges and universities ought to be able to reach the same decision when it comes to keeping the most hateful speech — of the sort embodied, say, in a KKK or neo-Nazi rally — off campus. The value in terms of teaching and learning of this sort of expression in the context of an academic community does not compensate for the distraction and harm caused to students. The fact that the harm and the distraction would fall disproportionately on a subset of students should factor into the analysis by educators. If schools are in fact about ensuring that a diverse group of young people have a place to learn, administrators should be able to choose whether the most hateful forms of speech have a place on campus. A specific statute or a new Supreme Court holding might be required to make such campus rules possible at a state university. While those who believe that free speech is more important than diversity might disagree, a conversation about line drawing at the edges of permissible speech on campus is well worth having.

Even as we all must tolerate views we hate up to a point in a democracy, there must also be a point at which the tolerant are allowed to be intolerant of those who are intolerant. Our study of history points to examples when it was a terrible mistake to tolerate intolerance for too long. This paradox of tolerance is much on our minds today, once again, as we seek a way forward after a wrenching election season in 2016. As schools and as a democracy at large, we need to determine where the line falls between hateful speech that we must tolerate and intolerant speech that we must resist.

The 2016 election has given rise to hard conversations on this point. What made that election so painful for many people was that too much of the rhetoric was about exclusion, not inclusion; it was about hate, not about love; it was about elevating some people above others. The winning presidential candidate, Donald Trump, espoused hatred during his campaign toward Mexicans and Muslims in particular — and as president immediately moved to put restrictive policies in place toward both groups. During the campaign, Trump failed to denounce hate groups that target underrepresented people of color. He mocked the disabled on national television. He demonstrated a misogynist streak that made members of his own party denounce his candidacy in large numbers — and led to one of history's largest demonstration, in dozens of cities, the day after his inauguration. The rhetoric during the campaign, from all sides, emphasized division and supremacy of some over others, not equity and inclusion. It is also a fact that this patently divisive approach to running for president resulted in his victory in the Electoral College, if not in the popular vote. We are a divided nation, separated from one another in some fundamental way. The 2016 election cycle was structured around this divide.

These facts are not presented in a manner meant to be partisan. The problem is not about Democrats and Republicans. It is about the values that we hold as educational institutions and how to honor them as we teach our young people. Many of the views expressed during the 2016 campaign are inconsistent with the kinds of values that many, if not virtually all, of our schools stand for—the kinds of values, including tolerance, that we seek to teach.

In our schools, we value and support all our students and their well-being equally. That must include those who are Muslims and Mexican, and those who come from all faiths and all racial and ethnic backgrounds. That must include conservatives as well as liberals. In our classrooms, those on the right must tolerate those on the left; those on the left must tolerate those on the right. No one should be bullied or otherwise mistreated because of who they are or who they or their parents voted for. Serious political discussion must have a place in our academic communities as well as in society at large. Students need to have equal support when it comes to their learning and growth, no matter their perspective or background. (The expectation of equality and inclusion is not limited to our school environments. Recall that we are expected to value and support all people equally in society at large, too, in the plain language of our Declaration of Independence and our Constitution.)

> **Hateful speech, targeting individuals and groups on our campuses, is not serious political discussion; it should have no place in our schools.**

Hateful speech, targeting individuals and groups on our campuses, is not serious political discussion; it should have no place in our schools. In the hyped-up context of campus and electoral events between 2014 and 2017, we must be vigilant for the way our students interpret political events and their lessons. We must focus on where the line should fall between the political speech that we must tolerate and the hateful speech that we should not.

As an educator, I believe we must do everything we can to focus on building tolerance and respect for one another so we do not find ourselves, as school communities, faced with this paradox repeatedly. As a citizen, I believe the same is true for the United States at large. We ought to make extensive room for the conversations we need to have about politics and difference. But intolerance of one another on our campuses, and in our communities, is something that we ought to find ways to prevent and to resist.

* * *

No speech code or disciplinary handbook—no matter how carefully drafted—can anticipate every controversy, especially of this sort. The approach of educational leaders should be to state clearly the values of the institution; to teach tolerance and limit hateful speech in the first place; to teach about the values of free expression and the free exchange of ideas as a general matter; to be clear with students and adults up front about how disputes will be handled; and to ensure that the ensuing debates are as open and constructive as possible. Despite these best efforts, the most complicated acts of expression by those wishing to push the boundaries will prompt case-by-case analysis. Just as they do in the courts, these cases will always give rise to strong emotions and heated debates.[3]

For a democracy comprised of diverse constituents to work, everyone must be tolerant of others to a very large degree. Both those liberals and those conservatives who espouse tolerance of others' views as a key virtue must be prepared to tolerate a great deal of speech with which they disagree. Serious philosophical disagreement must be able to take place on campuses or the intellectual enterprise is lost.

Our system of governance must also allow for a point at which the tolerant may become intolerant of intolerance. The intolerant should not be able to dominate merely by calling on the tolerant to tolerate their intolerance. The hard problem of hate speech is where that line—between the political speech we must tolerate, no matter how obnoxious, and the hate speech we should not tolerate—is drawn. Educational communities may have to struggle through more hard cases, not fewer, as campuses become more heterogeneous. Some campuses are plainly getting more adept than others at managing this heterogeneity. A full-throated commitment to both diversity and free expression, interdependent and mutually supporting, should preface, and then carry through, each instance of that struggle.

NOTES

1. Stone, Geoffrey. "Remembering the Nazis in Skokie." *Huffington Post,* May 20, 2009, at http://www.huffingtonpost.com/geoffrey-t-stone/remembering-the-nazis-in_b_188739.html. See also *National Socialist Party of America v. Village of Skokie,* 432 U.S. 43 (1977).

2. Popper, Karl R. *The Open Society and Its Enemies.* 5th ed. London: Routledge & Kegan Paul, 1966.

3. For one side of the debate, framing some of the key issues involved, see "Hate Speech on Campus," American Civil Liberties Union (ACLU) website, https://www.aclu.org/other/hate-speech-campus.

THINKING CRITICALLY ABOUT THE READING

1. According to Palfrey, what type of speech can be reasonably restricted "more than the First Amendment would allow" (1) on a private college or university campus?

2. In paragraph 4, Palfrey suggests there is a "reasonable limit" to both "how and when a campus community must practice tolerance." What does he mean by "reasonable limit"? What does it mean to "practice tolerance"?

3. What is the "paradox of tolerance" (5, 11)? Who first defined it and when? According to Palfrey, how is this paradox relevant to the campus free speech controversy?

4. In paragraph 15, what does Palfrey mean when he writes, "The value in terms of teaching and learning this sort of expression [hate speech] in the context of an academic community does not compensate for the distraction and harm caused to students"?

5. In what way does Palfrey see the dynamics of tolerance and intolerance as central to the 2016 US presidential election?

LANGUAGE IN ACTION

With one or two of your classmates, look up and then evaluate policies (or lack thereof) on your own campus relating to "safe spaces." Do you agree with your campus policies on safe spaces? Do you think that Palfrey would support your campus policies? Why or why not?

WRITING SUGGESTIONS

1. In paragraph 20, Palfrey writes clearly and directly, "hateful speech, targeting individuals and groups on our campuses, is not serious political discussion; it should have no place in our schools." Write a letter to Palfrey in response to this claim. Discuss why you agree or disagree with his contention about hateful speech and explain what policies you would choose for your own campus. Support your argument with specific evidence from Palfrey's essay or from other sources, such as the other two essays in this casebook.

2. Palfrey's argument is, in many ways, in opposition to the argument of Greg Lukianoff and Jonathan Haidt in "The Coddling of the American Mind" (pp. 525–537). Palfrey claims that "safe spaces" strengthen academic discourse by allowing students of all backgrounds to feel confident expressing their opinions in the classroom. By contrast, Lukianoff and Haidt argue that safe spaces harm academic discourse and contribute to a larger social problem of students being "coddled." After you read both of these essays, consider whose viewpoint you agree with more, and write a brief essay explaining your position. You might agree with Palfrey, you might agree with Lukianoff and Haidt, or you might fall somewhere in between. Take any position you wish, but be sure to support it with specific examples and evidence from one or both essays.

What Campuses Can and Can't Do

Erwin Chemerinsky and Howard Gillman

Erwin Chemerinsky is the dean of the University of California, Berkeley, School of Law, where he joined the faculty in 2017. Prior to his time at Berkeley Law, he was the founding dean and Distinguished Professor of Law at the University of California, Irvine School of Law. He also has taught at the University of California, Los Angeles School of Law. He is the author of ten books, including *The Case Against the Supreme Court* (2014) and *Closing the Courthouse Doors: How Your Constitutional Rights Became Unenforceable* (2017). He is a prolific author, and his syndicated articles have appeared in many newspapers across the United States, including the *Sacramento Bee*, the *ABA Journal*, and the *Daily Journal*.

Howard Gillman is chancellor of the University of California, Irvine, where he holds faculty appointments in the School of Law, the Department of Political Science, the Department of History, and the Department of Criminology, Law and Society. He is an award-winning scholar and teacher with expertise in the American Constitution and the Supreme Court. He has written nine books, including *The Supreme Court in American Politics* (1999) and *American Constitutionalism: Structures of Government* (2013). He also serves as co-chair of the advisory board of the University of California's National Center for Free Speech and Civic Engagement.

The following selection is drawn from the book *Free Speech on Campus* (2017), which Chemerinsky and Gillman co-wrote. Here they discuss three specific aspects of the campus free speech debate: trigger warnings, safe spaces, and microaggressions. They place each of these concepts within the larger context of the debate. While they advocate for a clear understanding of the role and importance of such terms, they also reject the idea that universities should use such concepts to "protect students from being exposed to disagreeable or offensive ideas."

WRITING TO DISCOVER: *Think about how your own campus supports free speech. Have controversial speakers been welcomed? Have they been turned away? Do you feel welcome to speak freely in your classes?*

TRIGGER WARNINGS

Faculty members may choose to provide students warnings before presenting material that might be offensive or upsetting to them.

Colleges and universities should not impose requirements that faculty provide "trigger warnings" before presenting or assigning material that might be offensive or upsetting to students.

Recently, many campuses have considered requiring faculty members to post warnings on syllabi and course materials if some students might find the course content emotionally disturbing.[1] In February 2014, student leaders at the University of California, Santa Barbara, passed a resolution encouraging professors to include trigger warnings in the syllabi for courses that contain potentially upsetting content. The resolution also urged professors of any such course to "not . . . dock points from a student's overall grade for being absent or leaving class early if the reason for the absence is the triggering content."[2] A guide distributed to professors at Oberlin College instructed them: "Triggers are not only relevant to sexual misconduct, but also to anything that might cause trauma. Be aware of racism, classism, sexism, heterosexism, cissexism, ableism, and other issues of privilege or oppression."[3]

Warning students before exposing them to offensive or upsetting material is nothing new. Before we read our students the racist chant from the fraternity at the University of Oklahoma, we cautioned them that it was racist and deeply offensive. Long before anyone coined the phrase "trigger warnings," we would warn students when we were coming to material that might be offensive, such as in playing for them George Carlin's monologue on the "seven dirty words" when studying the Supreme Court decision about it.[4]

Trigger warnings might be seen as "more speech," since they use   5 speech — the warnings — to prepare students for exposure to offensive material. They also show that the professor is sensitive to the difficulty in dealing with the material.[5] We thus reject the view that all trigger warnings are to be condemned as "coddling of students."[6]

Still, although we do not object such warnings, it is wrong for universities to require them. Professors need to decide how to best educate their students, and for some faculty members, this might include a professional judgment that being exposed to material without a warning makes for more effective instruction. Requiring trigger warnings might cause some professors to change their course assignments and course coverage.[7] It also may force professors to characterize their material in a way that does not reflect their views of the material or the appropriate response to it. Labels warning students that a book's themes are racist or sexist may bias students' reactions in a way that faculty members consider wrong or unfair, and would cast the same pall of censorship that would exist if college librarians were required to add warning labels to the front of selected library books. Although trigger warnings are often desirable, we agree with the Committee on Academic Freedom for the AAUP, which declared, "Institutional requirements or even suggestions that faculty use trigger warnings interfere with faculty academic freedom in the choice of course materials and teaching methods."[8]

SAFE SPACES

Campuses can create "safe spaces" in educational settings that ensure that individuals feel free to express the widest array of viewpoints, and can support student efforts to self-organize in ways that reflect shared interests and experiences.

Campuses can't use the concept of "safe spaces" to censor the expression of ideas considered too offensive for students to hear.

The phrase "safe spaces" has been applied to many different activities on campuses. The concept can be used in ways that enhance free speech and in ways that undermine it.[9] For example, it is appropriate—and even necessary—for campuses and professors to do all they can to make sure that the classroom is a safe space for scholarly exploration, civil debate, reasoned discussion, and making mistakes. The best educational environments remove fears that students may have about asking certain questions or challenging prevailing explanations; the worst environments are those where students feel that they can be punished for expressing views that the professor or other classmates consider heretical. A classroom should be a place where antiracism advocates can ask about the role of race in the choice of course materials, conservatives can question the wisdom or constitutionality of affirmative action, and socialists can criticize the dominant position of the concept of efficiency in economic models. It is a good thing when the idea of a "safe space" refers to a place where one feels safe to *express* an opinion, without punishment, harassing judgment, or bullying condemnation. It is the theme of this book that campuses must be safe spaces in this sense.

The concept is also used to refer to efforts by students to exercise   10
their rights of association and create places on campus where they are with people who are like-minded or who share certain experiences. Campuses have always had student societies, fraternities and sororities, student government groups, chess clubs, band rooms, gatherings of College Republicans and College Democrats, theater groups, Christian clubs, Hillel and Chabad, and countless other associations that allow members of a diverse student body to find their place. It raised no concerns in earlier years and should raise no concerns today when its advocates are underrepresented minority students or the LGBTQ community. In fact, if campuses prevented such ordinary activity they would be limiting the associational rights of students in violation of free speech principles.

However, the concept of space spaces also has been used as a basis for demanding that campuses protect students from being exposed to disagreeable or offensive ideas. This is the "safe space activism" underlying the "no platform" movement among students in the UK,[10] and also underlies much of the rhetoric used by some student groups who demand that American campuses remove all hateful or offensive speech. At Emory University, after Trump supporters chalked "Trump" on sidewalks, one protestor complained, "I'm supposed to feel comfortable and safe [here]. . . . I don't deserve to feel afraid at my school."[11] When Wesleyan University's newspaper, the *Argus*, published an opinion essay that criticized the Black Lives Matter Movement, critics pushed to defund the newspaper on the grounds that publishing such an essay "neglects to provide a safe space for the voices of students of color."[12] When conservative commentator Ben Shapiro spoke at the University of Wisconsin on the topic of "Dismantling Safe Spaces: Facts Don't Care About Your Feelings," protestors declared Shapiro's mere presence on the campus as a threat to the sense of safety and "personal violences" of many students, and interrupted the speech with repeated shouts of "safety!"[13] Campuses cannot and should not accommodate the language of safe spaces when the focus is protecting members of the campus *from* the expression of ideas, rather than creating a safe environment *for* the expression of ideas.

"MICROAGGRESSIONS"

A campus can't prohibit students or faculty from using words that some consider to be examples of "microaggressions."

A campus can sensitize students and faculty to the impact that certain words may have, as part of an effort to create a respectful work and learning environment.

The concept of microaggressions is now much discussed. As one commentator observed: "The term 'microaggression' was used by Columbia professor Derald Sue to refer to 'brief and commonplace daily verbal, behavioral, or environmental indignities, whether intentional or unintentional, that communicate hostile, derogatory, or negative racial slights and insults toward people of color.' Sue borrowed the term from psychiatrist Dr. Chester Pierce who coined the term in the '70s."[14]

In most current debates, the word "microaggression" refers to a very familiar idea: sometimes, even if we do not intend it, our everyday language is disrespectful to others. The language commonly used in society and in the workplace has changed dramatically for the better over the years. The "honeypies" or "darlings" that might have been prevalent in the office during the age of Mad Men are happily less prevalent. It should embarrass all people of goodwill to remember what the dominant culture thought was permissible to say, in polite company, about racial, ethnic, and religious minorities, or what used to be considered funny. At each moment of progress it has also been common to hear people grumble that the complaining groups are too sensitive or are engaging in annoying gestures of political correctness.

To the extent that current debates about microaggressions are an extension of this ordinary social evolution, the topic raises no free speech

15

issues. Campuses should try to sensitize their communities to the kinds of words and statements that might be unintentionally offensive. We should all listen when others tell us they feel insulted and hurt. If the changes in language that campuses occasionally suggest seem unnecessary or too extreme, that can be debated or criticized. Campuses should also take steps—through formal training and other initiatives—to sensitize the community about the insidious effects of implicit bias.

A problem arises only when there are efforts to force campuses to police and punish such expression. Outside the legal limits on harassment and other unprotected activities, campuses are not permitted to do this. This occasional use of a phrase that some people find offensive cannot be the basis for censorship or punishment. There is an enormous difference between advocating norms of civility in expression—which always exist and which we all are taught from a young age—and enforcing these norms by censorship or punishment.

> **We have been very specific about what campuses can and can't do to reconcile free speech, academic freedom, and the need for an inclusive learning environment.**

Microaggressions are an example of how a false dichotomy is often drawn between campuses punishing speech or their doing nothing. There is a middle course of campuses working to educate students as to situations where their words can cause harm, often unknowingly.

AN AGENDA FOR CAMPUSES

We have been very specific about what campuses can and can't do to reconcile free speech, academic freedom, and the need for an inclusive learning environment. Some people feel strongly that the last value requires compromising free expression, but we disagree. Still, our strong free speech views should not distract attention away from a wide range of activities that campuses can (and must) do to protect student well-being and promote an inclusive environment.

NOTES

1. *See* Kim D. Chanbonpin, *Crisis and Trigger Warnings: Reflections on Legal Education and the Social Value of the Law,* 90 Chi.-Kent L. Rev. 615, 623 (2015).

2. *Id.* at 624.

3. *Id.* at 623.

4. *See FCC v. Pacifica Found.,* 438 U.S. 726 (1978).

5. Chanbonpin writes: "Making trigger warnings available on course materials is one way for students to reclaim power. The student-led call for their use creates an opportunity for faculty to thoughtfully curate the classroom as a democratic space 'where students gain a public voice and come to grips with their own power as individuals and social agents.' With content advisories, students can decide for themselves whether to attend class or how to participate in classroom discussion." Chanbonpin, *Crisis and Trigger Warnings*, at 632.

6. *See, e.g.*, Greg Lukianoff and Jonathan Haidt, *The Coddling of the American Mind*, ATLANTIC (Sept. 2015).

7. *See* Erica Goldberg, *Free Speech Consequentialism*, 116 COLUM. L. REV. 687, 750 (2016) (trigger warnings have a chilling effect on course material and professorial free speech).

8. American Association of University Professors, *On Trigger Warnings* (2014), http://www.aaup.org/report/trigger-warnings.

9. Emily Crockett, *Safe Spaces, Explained*, VOX.COM (Aug. 25, 2016), http://www.vox.com/2016/7/5/11949258/safe-spaces-explained, and Sarah Brown and Katherine Mangan, *What "Safe Spaces" Really Look Like on College Campuses*, CHRON. OF HIGHER ED. (Sept. 8, 2016), http://www.chronicle.com/article/What-Safe-Spaces-Really/237720.

10. Rachael Pells, *NUS "No Platform" Policy Goes "Too Far" and Threatens Free Speech, Peter Tatchell Warns*, THE INDEPENDENT. (April 25, 2016), http://www.independent.co.uk/news/uk/nus-no-platform-safe-space-policy-goes-too-far-threatens-free-speech-warns-peter-tatchell-a6999801.html (claim by students that universities should "balance freedom of speech and freedom from harm" in order to accommodate "safer space activism").

11. Nina Burleigh, *The Battle Against "Hate Speech" on College Campuses Gives Rise to a Generation that Hates Speech*, NEWSWEEK (May 26, 2016), http://www.newsweek.com/2016/06/03/college-campus-free-speech-thought-police-463536.html.

12. Katherine Timpf, *Students and Faculty Petition to Defund Campus Newspaper Because It's Not a "Safe Space,"* NATIONAL REVIEW (Sept. 22, 2015), http://www.nationalreview.com/article/424473/students-and-faculty-petition-defund-campus-newspaper-because-its-not-safe-space.

13. Dana Kampa, *Conservative Pundit Ben Shapiro Lectures to Turbulent Crowd on Safe Spaces, Freedom of Speech*, BADGER HERALD (Nov. 17, 2016), https://badgerherald.com/news/2016/11/17/conservative-pundit-ben-shapiro-lectures-to-turbulent-crowd-on-safe-spaces-freedom-of-speech/.

14. Heben Nigatu, *21 Racial Microaggressions that You Hear on a Daily Basis*, BUZZFEED (Dec. 3, 2013) https://www.buzzfeed.com/hnigatu/racial-microaggressions-you-hear-on-a-daily-basis?utm_term=.bi2n3bKvx9#.svrwezpEVy.

THINKING CRITICALLY ABOUT THE READING

1. How do Chemerinsky and Gillman define "trigger warnings"? Do they see this type of content warning as a new development?

2. In paragraph 5, the authors write that "trigger warnings might be seen as 'more speech.'" What do they mean by the phrase "more speech"?

3. According to the authors, what does the term "safe space" mean? In what ways do they argue that the idea of safe spaces be used to "enhance free speech," and in what ways can the idea be used to "undermine" free speech (9)?

4. In paragraph 15, how do the authors define the word "microaggression"?

5. In paragraph 17, the authors write, "There is an enormous difference between advocating norms of civility in expression ... and enforcing these norms by censorship or punishment." What do they mean here? In what way does "advocating" differ from "enforcing"?

LANGUAGE IN ACTION

With a small group of your classmates, scan your syllabus for this course and your syllabi for other courses you are taking this semester. Do any of your syllabi include "trigger warnings"? Do you find any other statements about classroom conduct that pertain to issues of free speech that Chemerinsky and Gillman mention in their essay? If so, what are they?

WRITING SUGGESTIONS

1. Choose one of the three specific topics that Chemerinsky and Gillman discuss in this essay: trigger warnings, safe spaces, or microaggressions. Do you agree with the authors' arguments about what campuses can and can't do on that particular issue? Do you disagree? Write a brief essay in which you explain your position. Support your argument with specific language from Chemerinsky and Gillman's essay, and consider drawing on other sources, such as the two previous readings in this casebook.

2. Chemerinsky and Gillman conclude their essay by re-emphasizing the importance of an "inclusive learning environment." As they put it, "Some people feel strongly that [an inclusive learning environment] requires compromising free expression, but we disagree." In many ways, this sentence cuts to the heart of the campus free speech controversy: some people believe that a campus can have *both* an "inclusive learning environment" and "free expression," while others view these values as mutually opposed. Now that you have read all three essays in this casebook, where do *you* stand on the debate? Consider which arguments you find most persuasive, and then write an essay arguing for your own position. Support your position with evidence from all three readings. You may also draw upon your own personal experience on campus and upon other external sources as support.

THE GREAT GENDER-NEUTRAL PRONOUN DEBATE

As the readings in Chapter 8 reveal, language is constantly evolving as new words appear and existing words take on new meanings in response to cultural and technological shifts. However, some changes to our language are more controversial than others. In this casebook, we examine one particular language development that has garnered significant media attention in recent years: the debate over gender-neutral pronouns. This debate is closely tied to a larger cultural conversation surrounding transgender people, who—along with other members of the LGBTQ community—have led a push for pronouns that include people who choose not to identify with the traditional third-person singular pronouns *he* or *she*.

Gender-neutral pronouns have recently gained popularity. In particular, the word *they* used as a singular pronoun—repurposing the word beyond its traditional role as the third-person plural pronoun—has picked up widespread support. In 2017, both the Associated Press and the *Chicago Manual of Style* revised longstanding guidelines to announce that they now consider the singular *they* acceptable in some, though not all, contexts. Moreover, some states and cities have enshrined "pronoun protections" into law: New York City, for instance, may issue fines up to $250,000 against managers who repeatedly use the wrong pronoun when speaking to an employee.

As gender-neutral pronouns have become increasingly common on college campuses and in corporate offices in the United States, they have also become increasingly controversial. Supporters of gender-neutral pronouns argue that such pronouns serve an important function: protecting transgender and nonbinary individuals' right to free expression. One such advocate is Stephanie Golden, who in her essay "We Need the Singular *They*" argues that the singular, gender-neutral *they* is both morally necessary and also a logical continuation of previous language developments relating to pronouns. On the opposite side of the debate, Abigail Shrier vehemently opposes gender-neutral pronouns, arguing in "The Transgender Language War" that such pronouns are a threat to American values and an "Orwellian" method of controlling people's thoughts. Finally, in "Are Gender-Neutral Pronouns Actually Doomed?", Christen McCurdy explains what she has learned about the history of gender-neutral pronouns and about their likely future from her conversations with several language experts. As you read these three essays, consider where you stand and what you think the best solution is to the great gender-neutral pronoun debate.

We Need the Singular *They*

Stephanie Golden

Stephanie Golden, who lives in Brooklyn, New York, earned her BA. in English at the University of Pennsylvania in 1968. She has worked as a writer, ghostwriter, and editor for more than thirty years. She is the award-winning author or co-author of nine books and a writer of website content, reports, manuals, and other copy for nonprofits and small businesses. Most recently, she is the author of *Mermaid No More: Breaking Women's Culture of Sacrifice* (2016), a book that explores how a "culture of self-sacrifice" often impacts women's identity and development.

In the following essay, originally published online in *Aeon* on February 23, 2018, Golden advocates for the use of *they*—traditionally the third-person plural pronoun—as a singular, gender-neutral pronoun. She puts the growing popularity of the repurposed singular *they* in context alongside earlier language shifts to eliminate the use of sexist pronouns. At the same time, she recognizes the continued challenges to the singular *they* from language purists and from those who are uncomfortable with nonbinary pronouns.

WRITING TO DISCOVER: *Have you ever been corrected in your writing for using they as a singular pronoun? If so, was your use a mistake or an intentional use of the singular they?*

It's been decades since I was a copyeditor, but I haven't given up my long, trusting relationship with the *Chicago Manual of Style*. So when I learned that Chicago, along with the Associated Press (AP) had accepted the use of 'they' as a singular pronoun last year, I was ready to go along. Not everyone was, though. As gender-neutral pronouns gained wider currency, accounts of a 'war over pronouns' struck a weirdly familiar note, and I realised: I've been here before – twice.

In 1968, as a young copyeditor at the *Encyclopaedia Britannica*, I was trained on *Webster's Third New International Dictionary, Unabridged* (1961), which had broken from the dignified, impeccable second edition by jettisoning refined 'literary' language in favour of the colloquial language that people actually spoke. This dictionary's publication had created a sensation, literally evoking prophecies of calamity and the end of the world. Quoting William Shakespeare's *Troilus and Cressida,* the critic Dwight Macdonald wrote in *The New Yorker* in 1962 that *Webster*'s had 'untuned the string' of harmony and order in the universe, and chaos would follow. But I loved the dictionary's dismissal of inflated, pompous language, and happily followed its practice of removing hyphens and lowercasing everything within sight.

A few years later, as a manuscript editor at the New York branch of Oxford University Press, I helped engineer the next contentious usage shift. Feminism was acquiring legitimacy (much like non-binary gender identities today), and feminists pushed for nonsexist language, including alternatives to 'man' and 'he' as generics. In 1974, the McGraw-Hill Book Company—to my knowledge the first publisher to tackle the nuts and bolts of accomplishing this change—created the 11-page document 'Guidelines for Equal Treatment of the Sexes.'

One day, my boss handed me this guide. I was known as 'the feminist,' and I imagine she saw me as a guinea pig to test how it would go over. In any case, I jumped on it. The workarounds that McGraw proposed to avoid *man* and *he*—make the verb plural, 'reword to eliminate unnecessary gender pronouns,' use 'he or she, her or his' (though I rarely had the nerve to put the female pronoun first)—were hedged with cautions to avoid producing 'an awkward or artificial construction.' So I did my utmost to introduce these changes without damaging my authors' prose, but it was a stretch. Even to me, 'he or she' seemed awkward and downright weird. The responses from my recalcitrant (almost entirely male) authors ranged from bursts of fury, to erudite lectures on English usage and the importance of tradition, to kindly pointing out how much more felicitous was their original phrasing. Feminism was weird and outlandish, too, and to most of these academics didn't seem important enough to justify mauling their prose. I was pushing these innovations on my own; there was no policy at Oxford, as at McGraw. I got away with it because despite being young, female and without a PhD, in their eyes I incarnated 500 years of literary authority.

Today, it's hard to remember the degree of resistance that nonsexist language evoked at the time. A long excerpt from the McGraw guide that ran in *The New York Times Magazine* elicited anguished responses: 'A conspiracy is afoot to reform society by purging the language . . . innocent children [are] to be cast adrift from the security of traditional roles' through the machinations of 'Orwellian editors,' warned one letter. The honorific Ms., which had been around since the turn of the century but spread particularly after the launch of *Ms.* magazine in 1971, met with resistance for years. Sonia Jaffe Robbins, a copyeditor, then copy chief, at *The Village Voice* between 1975 and 1986, recalls encountering resistance even at this Leftist publication, for example from a theatre critic who insisted on referring to actresses as 'Miss.'

Now comes 'they,' and I admit it's a tough one. Paula Froke, the *AP Stylebook* lead editor, gives two reasons for embracing 'they': 'recognition that the spoken language uses they as singular' and 'the need for a pronoun for people who don't identify as a he or a she.' The first 'they,' as in 'Everyone can decide which personal pronoun best matches their identity,' is what people have been doing for centuries anyway; most of us already use it without thinking. But the second usage, which raises fundamental questions about identity, society and the nature of reality itself, has met furious resistance.

A sentence like 'Carey makes themself coffee every morning – they hate tea' violates deeply engrained rules of grammar. Saying 'Lisa told me they love gardening' calls into question basic categories of being. For many people, 'they' is the untuned string that portends discord and chaos.

> **Language evolves, and no amount of fulminating, or imposition of rules, can stop it.**

Yet *Webster's* third edition and nonsexist language did not cause the sky to fall. In fact, their innovations became normalised surprisingly soon. Diane Aronson, who began as a copy and production editor at Simon & Schuster in 1989, reports that most authors and editors of the self-help books she worked on there and at other publishers wanted to use nonsexist language. Authors, editors and publishers considered such language 'important to create a welcoming environment for readers,' she explains.

Language evolves, and no amount of fulminating, or imposition of rules, can stop it. But more importantly, justice demands that we make the effort to accept 'they,' 'themself' or any new gender-neutral pronoun that achieve widespread use. A language that collapses male and female into 'man' reflects a society that strips women of their separate being. And a language that collapses the spectrum of gender identities into male and female reflects a society that refuses to acknowledge the identity and very existence of a significant segment of its population. In the *Trans Allyship Workbook* (2017), Davey Shlasko writes:

> The rule against using singular *they* is enforced neither because it preserves some consistent, objective grammatical standard, nor because it serves our communication needs. It is enforced because enforcing language norms is a way of enforcing power structures.

This issue of power is central to all three of these usage shifts. In each case, the shift gave a voice to a marginalised group: the non-educated non-elite; women; and those with non-binary gender identities. 'They' might not be particularly felicitous, but until we find something better, we need it. After years of working with 'he or she,' I don't think it's clunky if used well, but I believe that we must drop it now, simply because it leaves out other gender identities.

Macdonald accused *Webster's* third edition of impoverishing the language, coarsening it, and destroying its beauty. But people still write beautiful prose, and we will get comfortable with singular 'they,' much as, centuries ago, people adapted to singular 'you' as 'thee' fell out of use. Once a copyeditor, always a grammar nerd, and I confess that 'Carey makes themself coffee every morning' makes me wince. But I'm willing to wince for as long as it takes—most likely, not very long.

THINKING CRITICALLY ABOUT THE READING

1. What does Golden mean by the "war over pronouns" (1)? What does this phrase connote?

2. In paragraph 4, Golden recalls the types of "workarounds" that the McGraw-Hill Book Company suggested for eliminating sexist language. What were those workarounds, and why do you think McGraw-Hill suggested them?

3. In paragraph 7, Golden writes "'they' is the untuned string that portends discord and chaos." What type of figurative language does she use in this sentence?

4. In paragraph 7, Golden offers an example of a sentence that "violates deeply engrained rules of grammar." What rules does she claim this sentence "violates"?

5. In what way does Golden see the "issue of power" as "central" to language shifts like the singular *they* (9)?

LANGUAGE IN ACTION

Work in pairs to revise the following sentences to use the singular *they* instead of the gendered pronouns *he* or *she*. After you have rewritten the sentences, discuss the effect of the changes with your partner. Which changes are most noticeable? Which are least noticeable? Which changes most and least affect the meaning of the sentence?

> Everyone wants his or her essay returned quickly.
> He went to the movies.
> What is her name?
> When he arrived at school this morning, he was relieved to find his coat in his locker.
> She made herself flashcards so that she could study for the exam.

WRITING SUGGESTIONS

1. Do you agree with Golden that "We need the singular *they*"? Consider the pros and cons that she outlines in the essay, and then write a brief argument essay in which you take a position advocating for or against this language shift. In your essay, be sure to include specific language from Golden's essay, which you may either use to support your argument or refute with your own counterarguments.

2. Golden writes that "it's hard to remember the degree of resistance that non-sexist language evoked at the time." She is referring to her experiences in the 1970s, advocating for new (at the time) constructions like *he or she*. Consider your own experience with gendered language and think about how such language has changed during your own lifetime. For example, did you learn "mankind" or "humankind," "police officer" or "policeman," "fireman" or "firefighter," "chairman" or "chair"? For any of these words, has the most commonly used term changed during your lifetime? Did any of these terms encounter "resistance," similar to what Golden describes? Do any of the terms *still* meet with resistance? Address these questions in a brief personal narrative about your experience with and perception of gendered language.

The Transgender Language War

ABIGAIL SHRIER

Abigail Shrier is a Los Angeles-based writer and graduate of Columbia University and Yale Law School. Her opinion pieces have appeared in *The Wall Street Journal, The National Review, The Times of Israel, Real Clear Politics*, and *The Federalist*. She has written extensively—and often controversially—about the intersection of politics, race, and the so-called "culture war" in the United States. She is also sharply critical of contemporary feminism, which she believes has grown beyond its original intent and now serves to undermine male identity. With these strong opinions in mind, it is perhaps no surprise that Shrier also views nonbinary language as a "war" against traditional values. In the following essay, published in *The Wall Street Journal's* opinion page on August 29, 2018, she criticizes recent shifts in language that she characterizes as downright "Orwellian."

WRITING TO DISCOVER: *Given the language of Shrier's title, what argument do you expect her to make in her essay? Why?*

If you want to control people's thoughts, begin by commandeering their words. Taking this Orwellian lesson to heart, Virginia's Fairfax County public school system recently stripped the phrase "biological gender" from its family life curriculum, replacing it with "sex assigned at birth."

Without permitting parents to opt out, public schools across the country are teaching children that "gender" is neither binary nor biological. It's closer to a mental state: a question of how girllike or boylike you feel. Students will fall anywhere along a gender spectrum, according to these educators.

So how girllike does any girl feel? The answer might reasonably be expected to vary throughout adolescence, depending on whether a girl was just dumped by a boy or tripped in the hall. Mishaps that once only compromised one's pride now threaten a child's gender identity, the ever-evolving claim to a "girl card." As if adolescence weren't already hard enough.

This is the left's allegedly defensive battle, waged on behalf of an aggrieved microminority even as it sets its sights on broader ideological territory. Consider recent state and local actions punishing those who decline to use an individual's pronouns of choice. California Gov. Jerry Brown signed legislation last year threatening jail time for health-care professionals who "willfully and repeatedly" refuse to use a patient's preferred pronouns. Under guidelines issued in 2015 by New York City's Commission on Human Rights, employers, landlords and business owners

558

who intentionally use the wrong pronoun with transgender workers and tenants face potential fines of as much as $250,000.

Typically, in America, when groups disagree, we leave them to employ   5 the vocabularies that reflect their values. My "affirmative action" is your "racial preferences." One person's "fetus" is another's "baby boy." This is as it should be; an entire worldview is packed into the word "fetus." Another is contained in the reference to one person as "them" or "they." For those with a religious conviction that sex is both biological and binary, God's purposeful creation, denial of this involves sacrilege no less than bowing to idols in the town square. When the state compels such denial among religious people, it clobbers the Constitution's guarantee of free exercise of religion, lending government power to a contemporary variant on forced conversion.

But individuals need not be religious to believe that one person can never be a "they"; compelled speech is no less unconstitutional for those who refuse an utterance based on a different viewpoint, as the Supreme Court held in *West Virginia State Board of Education v. Barnette* (1943). Upholding students' right to refuse to

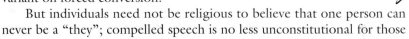
If you want to control people's thoughts, begin by commandeering their words.

salute an American flag even on nonreligious grounds, Justice Robert H. Jackson declared: "If there is any fixed star in our constitutional constell-ation, it is that no official, high or petty, can prescribe what shall be ortho-dox in politics, religion or other matters of opinion or force citizens to confess by word or act their faith therein." This is precisely what forced reference to someone else as "ze," "sie," "hir," "co," "ev," "xe," "thon" or "they" entails. When the state employs coercive power to compel an utterance, what might otherwise be a courtesy quickly becomes a plank walk.

In most contexts, I would have no problem addressing others in any manner they chose. If a therapist wants to be called "doctor," far be it from me to point out that she has a marriage and family therapy license, not a medical degree. But the Constitution's protection of free speech neither begins nor ends with good manners. It extends all the way from rudeness to meekness, protecting those who hurl insults and those who would rather say nothing at all.

To the extent that the transgender movement seeks to promote compassion for those who struggle with their biological sex, we should be grateful for it. To the extent that it seeks to regulate others' perspectives—commanding them to ignore biology and obey the dictates of new, state-mandated perception—we should resist it as an incursion into our most sacred liberties.

"Words in their primary or immediate signification, stand for nothing, but the ideas in the mind of him that uses them," wrote John Locke. Ideas are merely the concatenations of words; if you can compel the use of certain words, you control thought and force those who differ into silence. Often, that seems to be the actual goal of gender-identity enthusiasts, since the minuscule numbers of those afflicted with true dysphoria couldn't otherwise justify the rewriting of all manner of school applications and government forms.

If there is any issue that can rouse conservatives and drive them to the   10
polls, it is this one, with good reason. They perceive that their way of life is at stake. They know that if gender activists prevail, they will be left with a world they neither recognize nor like very much. They will be unable to communicate their displeasure; the words will have been stolen from them.

THINKING CRITICALLY ABOUT THE READING

1. What does Shrier mean by the word "Orwellian" (1)? Where does this word originate?

2. In what way do words influence thoughts, according to Shrier? How does she explain the relationship between changing one's language and changing one's ideas?

3. In paragraph 4, Shrier mentions recent legislation in California and New York City that enshrined protections for transgender individuals who prefer to choose their own pronouns. How are these cases pertinent to Shrier's overall argument?

4. According to Shrier, how do language shifts to accommodate transgender individuals affect religious freedom?

5. Why does Shrier quote seventeenth-century English philosopher John Locke in paragraph 9? What effect does this quotation have on you as the reader?

LANGUAGE IN ACTION

The idea of a "war on language" has become commonplace on both sides of the political spectrum. For example, in contrast to Shrier's conservative perspective, Karen J. Greenberg published an article on the left-leaning news site *Mother Jones* on May 25, 2018, titled "Ignorance Is Strength: The Trump Administration's Creepy War on Language." How do you feel when authors on both sides of the aisle describe language controversies as "war"? Do you think that using such a militaristic term to describe language serves any useful purpose? Why or why not? Discuss in a small group with one or two classmates.

WRITING SUGGESTIONS

1. Throughout her essay, and particularly in her final two paragraphs, Shrier uses strong emotional appeals to make her case. Do you find her appeals to the reader's emotions effective? Do these appeals persuade you? Why or why not? Explain your response in a brief essay, drawing on specific language from Shrier's essay to support your argument.

2. Shrier's argument starkly contrasts with that of Stephanie Golden in "We Need the Singular *They*" (pp. 554–556). Golden praises the singular *they* in large part because it is gender-neutral, and she encourages dropping the *he or she* construction "because it leaves out other gender identities." Shrier, by contrast, would likely characterize the singular *they* as an example of harmful "Orwellian" language. After reading both of these essays, which author's argument do you find more compelling? Why? Write a brief essay in which you answer these questions. Support your argument with specific language from both Shrier and Golden.

Are Gender-Neutral Pronouns Actually Doomed?

CHRISTEN MCCURDY

Although Christen McCurdy earned her BA in English at Oregon State University in 2006, she has written and edited for publication since 1999. Her work has appeared in many publications, including *The Oregonian, Street Roots,* and *Pacific Standard,* among others. She has earned numerous accolades, including awards from the Oregon Society of Professional Journalists, the national Society of Professional Journalists, and the Oregon Newspaper Publishers Association.

McCurdy's work often covers issues of social justice, including reproductive rights and the rights of the LGTBQ population. This context informs her approach in the following essay, which was originally published in *Pacific Standard* on October 8, 2013.

WRITING TO DISCOVER: *Have you ever been asked to identify your preferred pronoun or asked anyone for their preferred pronoun? Have you ever seen a person wear a pin or sticker disclosing their preferred pronouns? Consider your own experience with nonbinary pronouns before reading McCurdy's essay. Where do you stand on their use in public discourse?*

Dennis Baron calls it the word that failed.

Baron, a professor of linguistics at the University of Illinois, has been monitoring the development of epicene — that is, gender-neutral, third-person singular pronouns — since the 1986 publication of his book *Grammar and Gender.* He keeps a list tracking the introduction of new epicene pronouns in English and has counted dozens, with the first documented in 1850 — most of those being proposed by writers who took grammatical issue with, say, the singular "they."

"They were the ones I found from the 19th century, when a rationale was given for them, it was a grammatical one rather than an issue of social equality or social justice," Baron says.

I got in touch with Baron this summer after a heated meltdown with my friend Eric. It was right after "ougate" — a minor flap in which writer s.e. smith, who identifies as genderqueer and prefers the pronoun "ou," was misgendered by Gawker writer Hamilton Nolan; the ensuing correction spurred a minor tizzy after which smith and Nolan both moved on.

Eric's a grad student in linguistics, wrapping up his dissertation on 5 Balkan languages as I write this, and his argument was a little more specific: Prescribing a new pronoun for speakers of a language to adopt is an effort that's not all that likely to succeed. Some languages don't gender personal pronouns, but English does, and has for so long that reversing the trend seems completely impracticable.

562

I grant that as an English speaker, gender is inextricably tied to how I want to talk about people and even animals (why do so many people, by the way, refer to cats as "she"?). For years, I despised the numeric inconsistency of the singular "they" in writing (though I used it all the time in conversation), and usually struck it when editing others' work.

But I'm also deeply skeptical of claims that humans or speakers of a given language will inevitably think about gender in a certain way—or what languages are intrinsically built to do. They strike me nearly the same way as arguments using evolutionary psychology to bolster rigid gender roles—though I wonder if the latter flies because most people don't know enough about primitive humans to argue that primitive men probably didn't use the pre-agricultural equivalent of sports cars and expensive briefcases to lure primitive ladies into their primitive caves. Even non-linguists—say, every high school kid trying to figure out how French nouns are gendered—know there's remarkable diversity in the way living languages handle gender.

And anyway, there's the theoretical notion of how pronouns ought to work in languages, and then there's the practice, which is more a matter of etiquette than argument about what a language will "naturally" do.

Clouds Haberberg, a social worker in the United Kingdom who identifies as gender neutral, came out asking to be referred to as "they," and while most friends were supportive and some merely confused, a few argued that singular "they" is ungrammatical and refused to use it.

"This stings, because my gender identity is not semantic to me," 10 Haberberg writes, adding that they are not out at work, because explaining gender-neutral identity would get too complicated, so they get misgendered all the time. "There's not much I can do about it until non-binary genders gain more recognition in mainstream society—which, I feel confident saying, is not imminent in the U.K. right now—so I am learning to tune it out. It hurts, but what else can I do?"

"I think the bulk of the population is just so locked into gender binarism that they can't get their heads around anything else. It just discombobulates them," says Sally McConnell-Ginet, a professor emerita at Cornell, whose research has focused on the intersection of gender and language. "They're not at all at ease around this."

Baron argues that pronouns are the most conservative part of speech in English, and that speakers are incredibly slow to adopt new ones broadly. The most recent one he counts is "its," which appears in some of Shakespeare's work (though Shakespeare uses other words, including "is," to mean precisely the same thing), but not in the King James Bible.

Baron's essay, "The Epicene Pronoun: The Word That Failed," first appeared in *Grammar and Gender* and appears in a truncated form online, where he also collects news items related to gender-neutral pronouns. If the first attempts at creating an epicene pronoun came from nitpicky writers and grammarians, it's only been fairly recently—say, the 1950s and '60s—that writers started proposing epicene pronouns as an argument for greater inclusiveness. Feminists trying to shift away from the generic "he" were among the first; transgender and genderqueer writers came later. Baron finds broad use of the Spivak pronouns—"e," "eim," and "eir," coined by mathematician Michael Spivak—in transgender forums online, and in science fiction, but hasn't found an instance of a new epicene pronoun gaining traction in English.

The work of Lal Zimman, a visiting linguistics professor at Reed College who focuses on patterns in the speech of LGBT people, differs. Zimman tracks regional variants on the plural "you" (the Southern "y'all," and the Pittsburgher "yin" for instance) as newer pronouns are created to serve a purpose other English words don't—and notes English used to have more pronouns than it currently does. There are even regionally specific instances of gender-neutral pronouns, like in Baltimore, where, at least a few years ago, "yo" was gaining traction.

Zimman agrees that language doesn't really work as a top-down 15 system, with authoritative sources dictating how speakers should use it. But social and political change often does have a major effect on at least formal writing and, more slowly, speech. For instance, Zimman says, the use of the generic "he" wasn't an accident, but the result of an act by the British parliament that ordered that official documents be edited to use it. Prior to that, use of the singular "they" was common in formal writing.

"Their reasoning was explicitly that men are better than women," Zimman says. "Later on, we kind of viewed it as a natural part of the language, but actually it's something where a major change took place."

So, Zimman argues, it may not be fair to say pronouns are intrinsically more conservative. "If pronouns are slow to change, I would attribute that to social processes rather than linguistic ones," he says.

And of course, even binary transgender identities aren't typically handled well in mainstream formal writing: Most media style guides specify that people should be referred to by the name and pronoun with which they publicly identify, but major media outlets balked nonetheless at referring to Chelsea Manning as "she" after her coming-out statement was released—at least until enough people yelled at them on the Internet.

Zimman notes that in the first days after Manning's statement was released, different reporters for the same media outlet referred to Manning differently, sometimes minutes apart within the same newscast, likely because reporters on the military desk simply have less experience reporting on LGBT issues.

But social and political change often does have a major effect on at least formal writing and, more slowly, speech.

Changing one's informal lan- 20 guage can be more challenging, even when the situation is cut and dry: My best friend died in May, and I still catch myself referring to him in present tense, for reasons no more advanced or defensible than habit.

A genderqueer friend who came out this summer admits that they still sometimes slip up when signing emails. And about 10 years ago, my mom was a long-term substitute at a rural Idaho high school that had a lot of Asian exchange students who went by Anglophone names because school administrators had told them Americans would never be able to pronounce those given to them. "We can try," my mom said, and asked how they said their names. The administrators had a point—many Asian languages have sounds native English speakers can't hear or just have a hard time pronouncing—but their rightness mattered less to the kids than mom's kindness, however clumsy. Her students cried when they heard their real names for the first time in months.

Earlier this year, the Swedish national encyclopedia added the gender-neutral "hen," which has been used in various contexts there since the 1990s after being coined by a linguist in the late '60s. McConnell-Ginet says she's not sure how that will play out in terms of broad, informal adoption—and notes Swedish is spoken by a smaller, more homogeneous group of speakers than English, which is spoken by multiple cultures and multiple groups within cultures. McConnell-Ginet and Zimman both point out that other forms of gender-based language planning have been somewhat successful, such as the use of "Ms.," which was scoffed at when it was reintroduced in the 1970s. While it hasn't been adopted across the board, it's still more often than not the default courtesy title given to women (or junk-mail recipients assumed to be women). McConnell-Ginet says that her dissertation is riddled with the generic "he," and example dialogues using male names only.

"I look back and I think, 'Oh my god, how could I have done that?,'" she says. "At the time I would certainly have embraced gender egalitarianism. I didn't see it as connected, that they weren't just these dead examples."

Now McConnell-Ginet has not only dropped the generic "he," but is more likely than not to use the singular "they" in writing. She thinks the singular "they" is the epicene pronoun most likely to take off, since it's already in the language, and it would be easier to stretch its use than try to get a new word to take off.

"It's sort of the default, certainly in speech, and has been for centuries. It's perfectly acceptable. You see it more and more in writing," Baron says. "But now you see it, I think people are a little more lax about it in writing. I use it all the time. I use it fully aware of what I'm doing. It just sounds better." While there are still people who object—including students in a classroom setting—more and more academics have begun to accept the singular "they" in formal writing, he says.

McConnell-Ginet is also optimistic that as trans people become more   25 visible worldwide, speech will become more inclusive, at least in receptive communities: "The increased visibility of trans people is going to change the practice. It just is."

THINKING CRITICALLY ABOUT THE READING

1. What is an "epicene pronoun" (2)? When did they first appear, according to Dennis Baron? What was their initial purpose?

2. In paragraph 8, McCurdy writes: "there's the theoretical notion of how pronouns ought to work in languages, and then there's the practice." What does she mean by this statement?

3. How does Clouds Haberberg explain the relationship between pronouns and identity in paragraph 9? What does the word "semantic" mean in this context?

4. What are the Spivak pronouns, and what is their significance?

5. In paragraph 14, why does Lal Zimman disagree with Baron's notion that pronouns are inherently conservative?

6. In paragraph 23, why does Sally McConnel-Ginet think "the singular 'they' is the epicene pronoun most likely to take off"? Do you agree with her?

LANGUAGE IN ACTION

In paragraph 12, McCurdy cites linguistic professor Dennis Baron, who claims that pronouns are the "most conservative part of speech" (*conservative,* in this context, meaning "slow to change or adapt"). Do you agree with Baron's assertion? In a small group with one or two classmates, try to identify other aspects of language that are slow to adapt in response to technological, social, or cultural developments. Then share your findings with the class.

WRITING SUGGESTIONS

1. The title of McCurdy's article poses a provocative question: "Are gender-neutral pronouns actually doomed?" What do you think the answer is? Write a brief essay in which you give your answer. Support your position with specific examples from McCurdy's article, including the various linguists that she cites.

2. Reflect on all the arguments for and against gender-neutral pronouns that Stephanie Golden, Abigail Shrier, and Christen McCurdy put forth in this casebook. Consider the pros and cons of gender-neutral pronouns that each author describes. Now, with all of their arguments in mind, what do *you* think is the best way forward? For example, you might argue that we should officially adopt a certain gender-neutral pronoun, like the singular *they,* to replace traditional gendered constructions like *he or she.* You might argue that our pronouns are perfectly fine as is, with no need for modification. Or you might take a middle ground — arguing, for instance, that gender-neutral pronouns are useful in some circumstances but not in others. Whatever your position is, write an argument essay in which you advocate for it. Support your position by citing at least two of the authors in the casebook.

Glossary of Rhetorical and Linguistic Terms

Abstract   See *Concrete/Abstract.*

Accent   Characteristics of pronunciation that reflect regional or social identity.

Allusion   A passing reference to a familiar person, place, or thing drawn from history, the Bible, mythology, or literature. An allusion is an economical way for a writer to capture the essence of an idea, atmosphere, emotion, or historical era, as in "The scandal was his Watergate," "He saw himself as a modern Job," or "Everyone there held those truths to be self-evident."

American Sign Language (ASL, Ameslan)   A system of communication used by deaf people in the United States, consisting of hand symbols that vary in the shape of the hands, the direction of their movement, and their position in relation to the body. It is different from finger spelling, in which words are signed in the order in which they are uttered, thus preserving English structure and syntax.

Analogy   A special form of comparison in which the writer explains something complex or unfamiliar by comparing it to something familiar: "A transmission line is simply a pipeline for electricity. In the case of a water pipeline, more water will flow through the pipe as water pressure increases. The same is true of a transmission line for electricity." When a subject is unobservable or abstract, or when readers may have trouble understanding it, analogy is particularly useful.

Argument   A strategy for developing an essay. To argue is to attempt to convince a reader to agree with a point of view, to make a given decision, or to pursue a particular course of action. Logical argument is based on reasonable explanations and appeals to the reader's intelligence. See also *Persuasion, Logical Fallacies, Deduction,* and *Induction.*

Attitude   A writer's opinion of a subject, which may be very positive, very negative, or somewhere between these two extremes. See also *Tone.*

Audience   The intended readership for a piece of writing. For example, the readers of a national weekly newsmagazine come from all walks of life and have diverse opinions, attitudes, and educational experiences. In contrast, the readership for an organic chemistry journal may be comprised of people with similar scientific interests and educational backgrounds. The essays in this book are intended for general readers, intelligent people who may lack specific information about the subjects being discussed.

Beginnings and Endings   A *beginning* is the sentence, group of sentences, or section that introduces an essay. Good beginnings usually identify the thesis or main idea, attempt to interest the reader, and establish a tone. Some effective ways to begin essays include (1) telling an anecdote that illustrates the thesis, (2) providing a controversial statement or opinion that engages the reader's interest, (3) presenting startling statistics or facts, (4) defining a term that is central to the discussion that follows, (5) asking thought-provoking questions, (6) providing a quotation that illustrates the thesis, (7) referring to a current event that helps to establish the thesis, or (8) showing the significance of the subject or stressing its importance to the reader.

An *ending* is the sentence or group of sentences that brings an essay to closure. Good endings are well planned; they are the natural outgrowths of the essays themselves and give readers a sense of finality or completion. Some of the techniques mentioned above for beginnings may be effective for endings as well.

Biased Language   Language that is used by a dominant group within a culture to maintain its supposed superior position and to disempower others. See also *Racist Language* and *Sexist Language*.

Black English   A vernacular variety of English used by some black people; it may be divided into Standard Black English and Black English Vernacular (BEV).

Brainstorming   A discovery technique in which writers list everything they know about a topic, freely associating one idea with another. When writers brainstorm, they also make lists of questions about aspects of the topic for which they need information. See also *Clustering* and *Freewriting*.

Cause and Effect Analysis   A strategy for developing an essay. Cause and effect analysis answers the question *why*. It explains the reasons for an occurrence or the consequences of an action. Whenever a question asks *why,* answering it will require discovering a *cause* or series of causes for a particular *effect;* whenever a question asks *what if,* its answer will point out the effect or effects that can result from a particular cause.

Classification   See *Division and Classification*.

Cliché   An expression that has become ineffective through overuse, such as *quick as a flash, dry as dust, jump for joy,* and *slow as molasses.* Writers normally avoid such trite expressions and seek instead to express themselves in fresh and forceful language. See also *Figures of Speech*.

Clustering   A discovery technique in which a writer puts a topic or keyword in a circle at the center of a blank page and then generates main ideas about that topic, circling each idea and connecting it with a line to the topic in the center circle. Writers often repeat the process in order to add specific examples and details to each main idea. This technique allows writers to generate material and sort it into meaningful clusters at the same time. See also *Brainstorming* and *Freewriting*.

Coherence   A quality of good writing that results when all of the sentences, paragraphs, and longer divisions of an essay are naturally connected. Coherent writing is achieved through (1) a logical sequence of ideas (arranged in chronological order, spatial order, order of importance, or some other appropriate order), (2) the thoughtful repetition of keywords and ideas, (3) a pace suitable for your topic and your reader, and (4) the use of transitional words and expressions. Coherence should not be confused with unity. See also *Unity* and *Transitions*.

Colloquial Expressions   Informal expressions that are typical of a particular language. In English, phrases such as *come up with, be at loose ends,* or *get with the program* are colloquial expressions. Such expressions are acceptable in formal writing only if they are used for a specific purpose.

Comparison and Contrast   A strategy for developing an essay. In comparison and contrast, the writer points out the similarities and differences between two or more subjects in the same class or category. The function of any comparison and contrast is to clarify—to reach some conclusion about the items being compared and contrasted. An effective comparison and contrast does not dwell on obvious similarities or differences; instead, it tells readers something significant that they may not already know.

Conclusions   See *Beginnings and Endings.*

Concrete/Abstract   A *concrete word* names a specific object, person, place, or action that can be directly perceived by the senses: *car, bread, building, book, John F. Kennedy, Chicago,* or *hiking.* An *abstract word,* in contrast, refers to general qualities, conditions, ideas, actions, or relationships that cannot be directly perceived by the senses: *bravery, dedication, excellence, anxiety, friendship, thinking,* or *hatred.*

   Although writers must use both concrete and abstract language, good writers avoid using too many abstract words. Instead, they rely on concrete words to define and illustrate abstractions. Because concrete words appeal to the senses, readers can easily comprehend them.

Connotation/Denotation   Both terms refer to the meanings of words. *Denotation* is the dictionary meaning of a word, its literal meaning. *Connotation,* on the other hand, is a word's implied or suggested meaning. For example, the denotation of *lamb* is a "a young sheep." The connotations of lamb are numerous: *gentle, docile, weak, peaceful, blessed, sacrificial, blood, spring, frisky, pure, innocent,* and so on. Good writers are sensitive to both the denotations and the connotations of words and use these meanings to advantage in their writing.

Deduction   The process of reasoning that moves from stated premises to a conclusion that follows necessarily. This form of reasoning moves from the general to the specific. See also *Induction* and *Syllogism.*

Definition   A strategy for developing an essay. A definition, which states the meaning of a word, may be either brief or extended; it may be part of an essay or an entire essay itself.

Denotation   See *Connotation/Denotation.*

Description   A strategy for developing an essay. Description tells how a person, place, or thing is perceived by the five senses. Objective description reports these sensory qualities factually, whereas subjective description gives the writer's interpretation of them.

Dialect   A variety of language, usually regional or social, that is set off from other varieties of the same language by differences in pronunciation, vocabulary, and grammar.

Diction   A writer's choice and use of words. Good diction is precise and appropriate—the words mean exactly what the writer intends, and the words are well suited to the writer's subject, intended audience, and purpose. The word-conscious writer knows, for example, that there are differences among *aged, old,* and *elderly; blue, navy,* and *azure;* and *disturbed, angry,* and *irritated.* Furthermore, this writer knows when to use each word. See also *Connotation/ Denotation.*

Direct Quotation   A writer's use of the exact words of a source. Direct quotations, which are put in quotation marks, are normally reserved for important ideas stated memorably, for especially clear explanations by authorities, and for proponents' arguments conveyed in their own words. See also *Paraphrase, Summary,* and *Plagiarism.*

Division and Classification   A strategy for developing an essay. *Division* involves breaking down a single large unit into smaller subunits, or separating a group of items into discrete categories. *Classification,* on the other hand, involves arranging or sorting people, places, or things into categories according to their differing characteristics, thus making them more manageable for the writer and more understandable for the reader. Division, then, takes apart, while classification groups together. Although the two processes can operate separately, most often they work hand in hand.

Doublespeak   According to doublespeak expert William Lutz, "Doublespeak is a blanket term for language which pretends to communicate but doesn't, language which makes the bad seem good, the negative appear positive, the unpleasant attractive, or at least tolerable. It is language which avoids, shifts, or denies responsibility."

Endings   See *Beginnings and Endings.*

English-Only Movement   The ongoing attempts, which began in the Senate in 1986, to declare English the official language of the United States. Although these attempts have failed thus far at the federal level, a number of states have passed various forms of English-only legislation.

Essay   A relatively short piece of nonfiction in which the writer attempts to make one or more closely related points. A good essay is purposeful, informative, and well organized.

Ethnocentrism   The belief that one's culture (including language) is at the center of things and that other cultures (and languages) are inferior.

Euphemism   A pleasing, vague, or indirect word or phrase that is substituted for one that is considered harsh or offensive. For example, *pacify* is a euphemism for *bomb, pavement deficiency* for *pothole, downsize* or *release from employment* for *fire.*

Evidence   The data on which a judgment or an argument is based or by which proof or probability is established. Evidence usually takes the form of statistics, facts, names, examples or illustrations, and opinions of authorities.

Examples   Ways of illustrating, developing, or clarifying an idea. Examples enable writers to show and not simply to tell readers what they mean. An example may be anything from a statistic to a story; it may be stated in a few words or go on for several pages. An example should always be *relevant* to the idea or generalization it is meant to illustrate. An example should also be *representative.* In other words, it should be typical of what the writer is trying to show.

Fallacy   See *Logical Fallacies.*

Figurative Language   Language that uses figures of speech, especially metaphor, to convey or emphasize a particular meaning.

Figures of Speech   Brief, imaginative comparisons that highlight the similarities between things that are basically dissimilar. They make writing vivid and interesting and therefore more memorable. Following are the most common figures of speech:

Simile: An implicit comparison introduced by *like* or *as.* "The fighter's hands were like stone."

Metaphor: An implied comparison that uses one thing as the equivalent of another. "All the world's a stage."

Onomatopoeia: The use of words whose sound suggests the meaning, as in *buzz, hiss,* and *meow.*

Personification: A special kind of simile or metaphor in which human traits are assigned to an inanimate object. "The engine coughed and then stopped."

Freewriting   A discovery technique that involves writing for a brief uninterrupted period of time — ten or fifteen minutes — on anything that comes to mind. Writers use freewriting to discover new topics, new strategies, and other new ideas. See also *Brainstorming* and *Clustering.*

Grammar   The system of a language including its parts and the methods for combining them.

Idiom   A word or phrase that is used habitually with a particular meaning in a language. The meaning of an idiom is not always readily apparent to nonnative speakers of that language. For example, *catch cold, hold a job, make up your mind,* and *give them a hand* are all idioms in English.

Induction   A process of reasoning whereby a conclusion about all members of a class is reached by examining only a few members of the class. This form of reasoning moves from a set of specific examples to a general statement or principle. As long as the evidence is accurate, pertinent, complete, and sufficient to represent the assertion, the conclusion of the inductive argument can be regarded as valid; if, however, readers can spot inaccuracies in the evidence or point to contrary evidence, they have good reason to doubt the assertion as it stands. Inductive reasoning is the most common of argumentative structures. See also *Deduction.*

Introductions   See *Beginnings and Endings.*

Irony   The use of words to suggest something different from their literal meaning. A writer can use irony to establish a special relationship with the reader and to add an extra dimension or twist to the meaning.

Jargon   See *Technical Language.*

Language   Words, their pronunciation, and the conventional and systematic methods for combining them as used and understood by a community.

Logical Fallacies   Errors in reasoning that render an argument invalid. Some of the more common logical fallacies are listed here:

Oversimplification: The tendency to provide simple solutions to complex problems. "The reason we have inflation today is that OPEC has unreasonably raised the price of oil."

Non sequitur ("It does not follow"): An inference or a conclusion that does not follow from established premises or evidence. "It was the best movie I saw this year, and it should get an Academy Award."

Post hoc, ergo propter hoc ("After this, therefore because of this"): Confusing chance or coincidence with causation. Because one event comes after another one, it does not necessarily mean that the first event caused the second. "I must have caught a cold at the hockey game, because I certainly didn't have it before I went there."

Begging the question: Assuming in a premise that which needs to be proven. "If American autoworkers built a better product, foreign auto sales would not be so high."

False analogy: Making a misleading analogy between logically unconnected ideas. "He was a brilliant basketball player; therefore, there's no question in my mind that he will be a fine coach."

Either/or thinking: The tendency to see an issue as having only two sides. "Used car salesmen are either honest or crooked."

Logical Reasoning   See *Deduction* and *Induction*.

Metaphor   See *Figures of Speech*.

Narration   A strategy for developing an essay. To narrate is to tell a story, to tell what happened. Although narration is most often used in fiction, it is also important in nonfiction, either by itself or in conjunction with other strategies. A good narrative essay has four essential features. The first is *context:* The writer makes clear when the action happened, where it happened, and to whom. The second is *point of view:* The writer establishes and maintains a consistent relationship to the action, either as a participant or as a reporter simply looking on. The third is *selection of detail:* The writer carefully chooses what to include, focusing on those actions and details that are most important to the story while merely mentioning or actually eliminating others. The fourth is *organization:* The writer organizes the events of the narrative into an appropriate sequence, often a strict chronology with a clear beginning, middle, and end.

Objective/Subjective   *Objective writing* is factual and impersonal, whereas *subjective writing,* sometimes called impressionistic writing, relies heavily on personal interpretation.

Onomatopoeia   See *Figures of Speech*.

Organization   In writing, the thoughtful arrangement and presentation of one's points or ideas. Narration is often organized chronologically, whereas other kinds of essays may be organized point by point or from most familiar to least familiar. Argument may be organized from least important to most important. There is no single correct pattern of organization for a given piece of writing, but good writers are careful to discover an order of presentation suitable for their subject, audience, and purpose.

Paradox   A seemingly contradictory statement that may nonetheless be true. For example, *we little know what we have until we lose it* is a paradox.

Paragraph   A series of closely related sentences and the single most important unit of thought in an essay. The sentences in a paragraph adequately develop its central idea, which is usually stated in a topic sentence. A well-written paragraph has several distinguishing characteristics: a clearly stated or implied topic sentence, adequate development, unity, coherence, and an appropriate organizational pattern.

Parallelism   The arrangement of words, phrases, or sentences in similar grammatical and stylistic form, often to emphasize important ideas.

Paraphrase   A restatement of the information a writer is borrowing. A paraphrase closely parallels the presentation of the ideas in the original, but it does not use the same words or sentence structure. See also *Direct Quotation, Summary,* and *Plagiarism*.

Personification   See *Figures of Speech*.

Persuasion   An attempt to convince readers to agree with a point of view, to make a given decision, or to pursue a particular course of action. See also *Argument, Induction,* and *Deduction*.

Phonetics   The study of speech sounds.

Plagiarism   The use of someone else's ideas in their original form or in an altered form without proper documentation. Writers avoid plagiarism by (1) putting direct quotations within quotation marks and properly citing them and (2) documenting any idea, explanation, or argument that is borrowed and presented in a summary or paraphrase, making it clear where the borrowed material begins and ends. See also *Direct Quotation, Paraphrase,* and *Summary.*

Point of View   The grammatical person of the speaker in an essay. For example, a first-person point of view uses the pronoun *I* and is commonly found in autobiography and the personal essay; a third-person point of view uses the pronouns *he, she,* or *it* and is commonly found in objective writing.

Process Analysis   A strategy for developing an essay. Process analysis answers the question *how* and explains how something works or gives step-by-step directions for doing something.

Propaganda   Ideas, facts, or rumors purposely spread to further one's cause or to damage the cause of an opponent.

Purpose   What a writer wants to accomplish in a particular composition—his or her reason for writing. The three general purposes of writing are *to express* thoughts and feelings and lessons learned from life experiences, *to inform* readers about something about the world around them, or *to persuade* readers to accept some belief or take some action.

Racist Language   A form of biased language that makes distinctions on the basis of race and deliberately or subconsciously suggests that one race is superior to others.

Rhetorical Questions   Questions that are asked but require no answer from the reader. "When will nuclear proliferation end?" is such a question. Writers use rhetorical questions to introduce topics they plan to discuss or to emphasize important points.

Semantics   The study of meanings in a language.

Sexist Language   A form of biased language that makes distinctions on the basis of gender and shows preference for one gender over the other.

Signal Phrase   A phrase alerting the reader that borrowed information is to follow. A signal phrase usually consists of the author's name and a verb (for example, "Keesbury argues") and helps to integrate direct quotations, paraphrases, and summaries into the flow of a paper.

Simile   See *Figures of Speech.*

Slang   The unconventional, very informal language of particular subgroups in a culture. Slang words such as *zonk, split, rap, cop,* and *stoned* are acceptable in formal writing only if they are used for a specific purpose. A writer might use slang, for example, to re-create authentic dialogue in a story.

Specific/General   *General words* name groups or classes of objects, qualities, or actions. *Specific words,* on the other hand, name individual objects, qualities, or actions within a class or group. To some extent the terms *general* and *specific* are relative. For example, *dessert* is a class of things. *Pie,* however, is more specific than *dessert* but more general than *pecan pie* or *chocolate cream pie.* Good writing judiciously balances the general with the specific. Writing with too many general words is likely to be dull and lifeless because general words do not create vivid responses in the reader's mind. On the other hand, writing that relies exclusively on specific words may lack focus and direction, which more general statements provide.

Standard English A variety of English that is used by the government and the media and that is taught in the schools. It is often best expressed in written form.

Style The individual manner of a writer's self-expression. Style is created by the author's particular selection of words, construction of sentences, and arrangement of ideas.

Subjective See *Objective/Subjective*.

Summary A condensed form of the essential idea of a passage, an article, or an entire chapter. A summary is always shorter than the original. See also *Paraphrase, Direct Quotation*, and *Plagiarism*.

Syllogism An argument that utilizes deductive reasoning and consists of a major premise, a minor premise, and a conclusion. For example,
All trees that lose leaves are deciduous. (major premise)
Maple trees lose their leaves. (minor premise)
Therefore, maple trees are deciduous. (conclusion)
See also *Deduction*.

Symbol A person, place, or thing that represents something beyond itself. For example, the eagle is a symbol of America, and the bear is a symbol of Russia.

Syntax The way words are arranged to form phrases, clauses, and sentences. Syntax also refers to the grammatical relationships among the words themselves.

Taboo Language Language that is avoided in a given society. Almost all societies have language taboos.

Technical Language The special vocabulary of a trade or profession. Writers who use technical language do so with an awareness of their audiences. If the audience is a group of peers, technical language may be used freely. If the audience is a more general one, technical language should be used sparingly and carefully so as not to sacrifice clarity. Technical language that is used only to impress, hide the truth, or cover insecurities is termed *jargon* and is not condoned. See also *Diction*.

Thesis A statement of the main idea of an essay, the point the essay is trying to make. A thesis may sometimes be implied rather than stated directly.

Tone The manner in which a writer relates to an audience, the "tone of voice" used to address readers. Tone may be described as friendly, serious, distant, angry, cheerful, bitter, cynical, enthusiastic, morbid, resentful, warm, playful, and so forth. A particular tone results from a writer's diction, sentence structure, purpose, and attitude toward the subject. See also *Attitude*.

Topic Sentence The sentence that states the central idea of a paragraph and thus limits and controls the subject of the paragraph. Although the topic sentence normally appears at the beginning of the paragraph, it may appear at any other point, particularly if the writer is trying to create a special effect. See also *Paragraph*.

Transitions Words or phrases that link the sentences, paragraphs, and larger units of an essay in order to achieve coherence. Transitional devices include parallelism, pronoun references, conjunctions, and the repetition of key ideas, as well as the many transitional expressions such as *moreover, on the other hand, in addition, in contrast*, and *therefore*. See also *Coherence*.

Unity A quality that is achieved in an essay when all the words, sentences, and paragraphs contribute to its thesis. The elements of a unified essay do not distract the reader. Instead, they all harmoniously support a single idea or purpose.

Usage The way in which words and phrases are actually used in a language community.

ACKNOWLEDGEMENTS

CHAPTER 1

Page 5, "Be Specific," from *Writing Down the Bones: Freeing the Writer Within* by Natalie Goldberg. Copyright © 1986 by Natalie Goldberg. Reprinted by arrangement with The Permissions Company, Inc., on behalf of Shambhala Publications Inc., Boston, MA. www.shambhala.com.

Page 17, "'What's in a Name?' Some Meanings of Blackness" by Henry Louis Gates Jr., from *Dissent* 36.4, Fall 1989. Copyright © 1989. Reprinted with permission from University of Pennsylvania Press.

Page 21, "Refusal to Use Name Is the Ultimate Insult" by Eppie Lederer (under the pen name Ann Landers), from "Ask Ann Landers," August 26, 2007. Copyright © 2007. Reprinted with permission of Esther P. Lederer Trust and Creators Syndicate, Inc.

CHAPTER 3

Page 48, "Reading to Write," from *On Writing: A Memoir of the Craft* by Stephen King. Copyright © 2000 by Stephen King. Reprinted with the permission of Scribner, a division of Simon & Schuster, Inc. All rights reserved.

Page 54, Anne Lamott, "Shitty First Drafts," from *Bird by Bird: Some Instructions on Writing and Life* by Anne Lamott. Copyright © 1994 by Anne Lamott. Used by permission of Pantheon Books, an imprint of the Knopf Doubleday Publishing Group, a division of Penguin Random House LLC. All rights reserved.

Page 60, Iman Humaydan, "The First Sentence," originally published in Arabic in the book *Kitabat alkitabah* (*Writers on Writing*), edited by Iman Humaydan (Beirut: ARRAWI Publishing, 2010). Reprinted by permission of the author.

Page 67, Donald Murray, "The Maker's Eye: Revising Your Own Manuscripts." *The Writer*, 1973. Copyright © 1973 by Donald M. Murray. Reprinted by permission of The Rosenberg Group on behalf of the author's estate.

Page 74, Adler, "How to Mark a Book." Originally published in *Saturday Review of Literature*, July 6, 1940. Reprinted by permission.

CHAPTER 4

Page 82, Excerpt from "Women Talk Too Much" by Janet Holmes, originally published in *Language Myths*, edited by Laurie Bauer and Peter Trudgill (Penguin Books, 1998). Copyright © 1998. Reprinted by permission of the author.

CHAPTER 6

Page 133, Jimmy Santiago Baca. "Coming into Language," from PEN America, March 3, 2014, https://pen.org/coming-into-language/. Reprinted by permission.

Page 146, "The Transformation of Silence into Language and Action," from *Sister Outsider: Essays and Speeches* by Audre Lorde, published by Crossing Press. Copyright © 1984, 2007 by Audre Lorde. Used herein by permission of the Charlotte Sheedy Literary Agency.

Page 152, Material drawn from "Stupid Rich Bastards" by Laurel Johnson Black from *This Fine Place So Far From Home: Voices of Academics from the Working Class* edited by C.L. Barney Dews and Carolyn Leste Law. Used by permission of Temple University Press. Copyright © 1995 Temple University. All Rights Reserved.

Page 164, Meredith McCarroll, "On and On: Appalachian Language and Academic Power," from *Southern Cultures* (http://www.southerncultures .org/article/on-and-on-appalachian-accent-and-academic-power/). Reprinted by permission of the author.

Page 169, Reproduced with permission of Curtis Brown Group Ltd, on behalf of Malala Yousafzai. Copyright © Malala Yousafzai, 2013. Malala Yousafzai's Speech to the United Nations.

CHAPTER 7

Page 187, Richard Lederer, "All-American Dialects." Reprinted with the permission of the author.

Page 197, "Sign of the Times" by Sara Nović. Copyright © 2016 by Sara Nović, used by permission of The Wylie Agency LLC.

Page 203, Bharati Mukherjee, "Two Ways of Belong in America." Originally published in the *New York Times*, September 22, 1996. Copyright © 1996 by Bharati Mukherjee. Reprinted by permission of the author.

Page 208, Julie Sedivy, "The Strange Persistence of First Languages," *Nautilus*, November 5, 2015, http://nautil.us/issue/30/identity/the-strange-persistence-of-first-languages. Copyright © 2015. Reprinted by permission of the author.

Page 217, Excerpts from *Little Big Man* by Alex Tizon. Copyright © 2014 by Alex Tizon. Reprinted by permission of Houghton Mifflin Harcourt Publishing Company. All rights reserved.

Page 224, "Mother Tongue," by Amy Tan. First appeared in the *Threepenny Review*. Copyright © 1990 by Amy Tan. Reprinted by permission of the author and the Sandra Dijkstra Literary Agency.

Chapter 8

Page 233, Excerpt from "It's the Implication That Matters: Words on the Move" from the book *Words on the Move: Why English Won't—and Can't—Sit Still (Like, Literally)* by John McWhorter. Copyright © 2016 by John H. McWhorter. Reprinted by permission of Henry Holt and Company. All rights reserved.

Page 239, Bodle, "How New Words Are Born," *The Guardian,* February 4, 2016. Copyright © Guardian News & Media Ltd 2016. Reprinted by permission.

Page 245, Yesenia Padilla, "What Does Latinx Mean? A Look at the Term That's Challenging Gender Norms," originally published in *Complex* online, April 18, 2016. Reprinted by permission of the author.

Page 248, "The argument against the use of the term 'Latinx'" (excerpt) by Gilbert Guerra and Gilbert Orbea, the Swathmore College *Phoenix,* November 19, 2015. Copyright © 2015. Reprinted by permission.

Page 250, Lauren Collister (University of Pittsburgh), "Textspeak Is Modernizing the Egnlish Language (*English)." Originally published under the title "Emoticons and symbols aren't ruining language—they're revolutionizing it" in *The Conversation,* April 6, 2015, https://theconversation.com /emoticons-and-symbols-arent-ruining-language-theyre-revolutionizing -it-38408. Copyright © 2015.

Page 256, Sternbergh, "Smile, You're Speaking Emoji." Originally published in *New York* Magazine, November 17, 2014. Copyright © 2014 Adam Sternbergh/*New York* Magazine. Reprinted by permission.

Page 262, Tannen, "The (Sometimes Unintentional) Subtext of Digital Conversations," *The Atlantic,* April 27, 2017. Copyright © 2017 The Atlantic Media Co., as first published in *The Atlantic* Magazine. All rights reserved. Distributed by Tribune Content Agency, LLC. Reprinted by permission.

Chapter 9

Page 271, Donna Woolfolk Cross, "Propaganda: How Not to Be Bamboozled," from *Speaking of Words: A Language Reader.* Copyright © 1977. Reprinted by permission of the author.

Page 285, "Selection, Slanting, and Charged Language," from Birk/Birk, *Understanding and Using English,* 5th edition. Copyright © 1972. Reprinted by permission of Pearson Education, Inc., New York, New York.

Page 296, Rebecca Solnit, "The Case of the Missing Perpetrator," *Literary Hub,* Februry 11, 2016. Copyright © 2016 by Rebecca Solnit. Reprinted by permission of the author.

Page 304, Judith Matloff, "Fighting Words," originally published in the *Columbia Journalism Review,* September/October 2012. Reprinted by permission of The Joy Harris Literary Agency, Inc.

Page 310, Benjamin D. Horne, "Fake News Starts with the Title," from *Medium.com,* March 28, 2017. Copyright © 2017 by Benjamin D. Horne. Reprinted by permission of the author.

Page 316, "Weasel Words: The Art of Saying Nothing at All," from *Doublespeak* by William Lutz. Copyright © 1989 by William Lutz. Used by permission

Page 404, Sherryl Kleinman, Matthew B. Ezzell, and A. Corey Frost, "The Social Harms of 'Bitch,'" excerpted from "Reclaiming Critical Analysis: The Social Harms of 'Bitch,'" originally published in *UET Sociological Analysis Journal* 3.1 (Spring 2009). Reprinted by permission of the authors.

Page 408, Excerpt (pp. 44–51) from "'Bros Before Hos': The Guy Code," from *Guyland: The Perilous World Where Boys Become Men* by Michael Kimmel. Copyright © 2008 by Michael Kimmel. Reprinted by permission of HarperCollins Publishers.

Page 416, Michelle Tea, "How to Refer to My Husband-Wife," from *Against Memoir: Complaints, Confessions, & Criticisms.* Originally published in *The Bold Italic*, February 16, 2014. Copyright © 2014, 2018 by Michelle Tea. Reprinted by permission of The Permissions Company, Inc., on behalf of The Feminist Press, www.feministpress.org. All rights reserved.

CHAPTER 12

Page 422, Judith Viorst, "The Truth About Lying" Copyright © 1981 by Judith Viorst. Reprinted by permission of Don Congdon Associates, Inc.

Page 428, "Lying Words," from *The Secret Life of Pronouns*, Copyright © 2011 by James W. Pennebaker, Bloomsbury Publishing Inc. Reprinted by permission.

Page 437, Po Bronson, "Learning to Lie." Originally published in *New York* Magazine, February 10, 2008. Copyright © 2008. Reprinted by permission of Curtis Brown, Ltd. All rights reserved.

Page 448, Richard Gunderman, "Is Lying Bad for Us?" *The Atlantic*, February 13, 2013. Copyright © 2013 The Atlantic Media Co., as first published in *The Atlantic* Magazine. All rights reserved. Distributed by Tribune Content Agency, LLC. Reprinted by permission.

Page 453, Copyright © 2012 National Public Radio, Inc. NPR news report titled "Psychology Of Fraud: Why Good People Do Bad Things" by Chana Joffe-Walt and Alix Spiegel was originally published on *NPR.org* on May 1, 2012, and is used with the permission of NPR. Any unauthorized duplication is strictly prohibited.

Page 466, 1–9 from *Everybody Lies* by Seth Stephens-Davidowitz. Copyright © 2017 by Seth Stephens-Davidowitz. Reprinted by permission of HarperCollins Publishers.

CHAPTER 13

Page 476, From *Leading with Dignity: How to Create a Culture That Brings Out the Best in People* by Donna Hicks. Copyright © 2018 by Donna Hicks. Reprinted by permission of Yale University Press.

Page 485, Karol Janicki, "Language and Conflict," from the Introduction to *Language and Conflict: Selected Issues* by Karol Janicki (Red Globe Press, 2015). Copyright © 2015. Reproduced with permission of SNCSC.

Page 491, Sorry, Regrets and More, from *Sorry About That: The Language of Public Apology* by Edwin Battistella (2014) from pp. 56–75. By

CHAPTER 14

INDEX OF AUTHORS
AND TITLES